THE PRACTICE

OF

CHRISTIAN AND RELIGIOUS

PERFECTION.

WRITTEN IN SPANISH,

BY V. F. ALPHONSUS RODRIGUEZ,

Of the Society of Jesus.

IN THREE VOLUMES.

VOL. II.

DUBLIN:

JAMES DUFFY AND SONS,

15 WELLINGTON QUAY,

AND 1 PATERNOSTER ROW, LONDON.

1882.

ISBN 9781737191063

Published by:
St Athanasius Press
133 Slazing Rd
Potosi, WI 53820
1-608-763-4097
http://www.stathanasiuspress.com
Melwaller@gmail.com

Email can be the best way to contact us. Stores and
retail customers can order via our web site or directly.

For as little as $500, you can help bring a Catholic
Classic back into print. Please contact us to assist us
in bringing solid Catholic books back into print.

Check out our other titles on last page of this book!

CONTENTS OF VOL. II.

THE FOURTH TREATISE.
On Temptations.

THE FIFTH TREATISE.
On Disorderly Affections for our relations.

THE SIXTH TREATISE.
On Joy and Sadness.

THE SEVENTH TREATISE.
On the advantages and infinite treasures we possess in Jesus Christ, How we are to meditate upon the mysteries of his passion—what fruit we ought to reap from thence.

ALPHONSUS RODRIGUEZ

TO

THE READER.

———◆———

THOUGH this work is composed principally for religious, yet it is very useful to all Christians; and this second part, in particular, is so disposed, as to be of very great advantage to all secular persons who desire to give themselves entirely to God's service. For their first duty is to subdue their hearts by mortifying their passions, by subjecting their senses, (especially their tongue,) and by humbling themselves before God, in order that those virtues and good works which they have planted in their souls, may spring up and bring forth such fruit as should be expected. It is for this reason that I treat first of mortification, then of modesty and silence, and afterwards of humility; which are the virtues a Christian ought chiefly practise in the beginning of his conversion. And because the Holy Ghost would have those that enter into God's service remain in fear, and prepare themselves for temptation, I therefore speak in the fourth treatise of the profit and advantage of temptations, and point out the means of overcoming them. In the fifth and sixth treatises, I show

the obstacles that occur in the paths of virtue, and of how
great advantage it is to walk always in these paths with
joy and liberty. And because nothing can better produce
this effect than the knowledge of the infinite treasure we
possess in Jesus Christ, I make that the subject of the
seventh treatise; in which I also show how we are to
meditate on the mysteries of the passion, and what fruit
we are to reap from them. Lastly, I conclude this second
part with a treatise on holy communion; in which I show
what we are to do, in order to prepare ourselves for it,
and to render it profitable to us; all which I endeavour to
treat of as methodically as possible, that the practice may
be more easy; which is the chief aim I had in this whole
work. If the Christian reader vouchsafes favourably to
receive it, I hope, by the assistance of God's grace, that it
will help him to subdue his passions, to practise modesty
and moderation in all his words and actions, to overcome
temptations, to make his profit of the immense treasures
with which the passion of Jesus Christ has enriched the
faithful, to receive his body and blood with pious fervour,
and to gather and lay up such fruit as may conduce to his
everlasting happiness and salvation.

THE PRACTICE

OF

CHRISTIAN AND RELIGIOUS PERFECTION.

THE FIRST TREATISE.

ON MORTIFICATION.

CHAPTER I.

That we must join mortification to prayer, to be a help one to the other.

"It is good to join prayer to fasting," (Tob. xii. 8,) said the angel Raphael to Tobias, when he made himself known unto him. The holy fathers, by fasting, commonly understand, whatsoever belongs to penance and mortification of the flesh ; and accordingly they consider mortification and prayer as the two principal means we have to advance in perfection, and which ought to be inseparable companions. St. Bernard, upon the words of the Canticles, " Who is she that ascends by the desert as a little cloud of smoke, composed of the perfumes that proceed from myrrh and incense ?" (Cant. iii. 6,) says, that myrrh and incense, which are the symbols of mortification and prayer, ought always to accompany us—that it is by these two wings we must raise ourselves to the sovereign degree of perfection, and render ourselves a sweet smelling odour or perfume before the throne of God ; and that the one is scarce of any use without the other. For he who only mortifies his flesh, without humbling his mind by prayer, becomes proud, and deserves to have these words of the royal prophet applied to him : " Shall I feed upon the flesh of bulls ? or shall I drink the blood of goats ?" (Ps. xlix. 13.) These sort of sacrifices that contain nothing but flesh and blood are not at all pleasing to God. And on the other hand, he who gives himself to prayer, and neglects to mortify his flesh, ought to be afraid of our Saviour's words in the gospel : " Why do you

call me Lord, Lord, if you do not what I desire of you ?"—
(Luke vi. 45.) And also that of the wise man in the Proverbs,
" If any one turns his ears from hearkening to the law, his
prayer shall be rejected as execrable." (Prov. xxviii. 9.)
Your prayer cannot be pleasing to God if you perform not his
will.

St. Austin says, that as there were two altars in the temple of
Solomon, the one without, where they cut the throats of the
victims to be sacrificed ; and the other within the sanctuary,
upon which they offered incense to God ; so there must also be
two altars in us, the one interior, to offer to him the incense of
prayer. conformably to those words of St. Matthew : " But you,
when you would pray, enter into your closet, and having shut
the door, pray to your father in privnte" (Matt. vi. 6 ;) and the
other exterior, to make a sacrifice of ourselves by corporal mortifications, so that mortification and prayer may go hand in hand
together ; for if mortification be a necessary disposition to prayer,
prayer is also a very useful means of attaining perfect mortification.

As to the first point, that mortification is a necessary disposition to prayer, it is a truth that all the saints and masters of a
spiritual life teach us. They say, that as we cannot write upon
a skin of parchment, if it be not well shaved, and all the flesh
taken off; so if the affections and bad inclinations of the flesh be
not all rooted out of our mind, and if it be not quite disengaged
from them, it has not the disposition it ought to have for our
Lord to write and imprint upon it the characters of his grace
and wisdom. "To whom will he give knowledge ?" says the
prophet Isaias ; " and to whom will he give understanding ? To
such as are weaned from milk, and taken from their mother's
breasts." That is to say, to those who for his love mortify
themselves, and forsake the pleasures of the world, and the
affections and desires of the flesh. God wishes to find the heart
free and disengaged from all things, before he enters into it ; he
wishes to find first a profound peace and tranquillity therein,
before he makes his entry. "His abode is established in
peace." (Ps. lxxv. 3.)

The pagan philosophers acknowledged this truth. They all
agreed that wisdom consisted in a certain peace which the soul
enjoyed when its sensual appetites were entirely repressed.
Then it is that there remain no violent passions, which, by their
irregular motions, trouble the peace of the soul, and obscure the

understanding; as in the case when the passions are in agitation.
For the property of passion is to blind reason, and to diminish in
us the liberty of free will ; as we see every day in a man overcome by passion.   It seems that passion even deprives him of
his judgment, and renders him quite mad and furious.   For if
you ask him afterwards, why did you say this, or why did you
do such and such actions ? he will answer you, because he was
beside himself.   But, when the passions are calm, the understanding has also more pure and clear light to know what is
good, and the will a fuller liberty to embrace it.   But this peace
and tranquillity is what God would always find in our hearts
that he may the better pour down his wisdom, and other gifts
upon us.   The mortification of our passions and irregular appetites is the true means of obtaining this peace ; and it was upon
this account that the prophet Isaias said—" That peace shall be
the work of justice."—(Is. xxxii. 17.)

This is very well explained by St. Austin, writing upon those
words of the royal prophet, "Justice and peace have kissed each
other "—(Ps. lxxxiv. 11 ;) " would you," says he, " that justice
and peace should embrace each other ?   Perform the works of
justice, and you will infallibly have peace.   If you love not
justice, you will never enjoy peace.   For peace and justice are
friends linked together so closely, that if you love not justice,
peace will not love you, and will never come near you.   Peace
is not obtained but by war."   So that if you will not make war
with yourself, by mortifying and constraining your desires, and
by getting the mastery over your passions, you will never obtain
this peace, which is so necessary to be able to apply yourselves
to prayer.   " What is a greater hindrance and trouble unto
you," says Thomas-à-Kempis, " than the unmortified affections of your heart ?"   Those irregular passions and bad inclinations you have, are what trouble you and hinder you from
being devout.   These disquiet you in prayer, and cause such
disturbance in your soul, that the sweet sleep and repose enjoyed
in prayer is continually disturbed and interrupted ; or, to speak
more properly, these hinder your soul from seeking after, or
taking this repose.   It ordinarily happens, that when one has
eaten too much at night, he is not able to sleep, because the
crudity that remains in the stomach, and the gross vapours
which the meat sends continually to the brain, so disquiet him,
that he can do nothing else but turn from one side to another,
without being able to sleep at all.   The same thing happens in

prayer. The irregularity of self-love, the desire we have of satisfying our passions, and of being esteemed, are so great, that do what we can, they so charge and overcome our hearts, excite such vapours in us, and produce such phantoms in our imagination, that we cannot recollect ourselves, nor have our minds united unto God. It is in this sense we are wont to explain these words of our Saviour—"Take care lest your hearts be overcharged with gluttony, drunkenness, or with the cares of this world."—(Luke xxi. 34.) For this passage ought to be understood not only of drunkenness caused by wine, but of that which is occasioned by all other things in the world, according to those words of Isaias : "Hearken, then, poor miserable creature, that art drunk, but not with wine."—(Is. li. 21.) When the heart is not well purified by mortification, there arises from it a thick mist or cloud, that deprives our soul of the presence of God. St. Paul well expresses this, when he says— "that the sensual or carnal man understands not what the spirit of God teaches."—(1 Cor. ii. 14.) For those things are spiritual and he is wholly carnal ; so that to be able to conceive and taste them, he must spiritualize and purify himself by mortification.

From this we obtain the solution of a doubt that is ordinarily proposed. Prayer, it is said, is an entertainment and familiar conversation with God, and consequently an exercise full of joy and sweetness, according to the words of the wise man : "His conversation has no bitterness, nor has his company any tediousness, but brings all joy and satisfaction along with it."—(Wis. viii. 16.) What is the reason then that prayer, which of itself is replenished with so much sweetness, and which on the other hand is so profitable and necessary for us, should oftentimes become so hard, that we go to it with great reluctance and difficulty, and that but few give themselves to this exercise ? "It is with repugnance and much against our will," says St. Bonaventure, "that we assist at spiritual duties; and are present at prayer like dogs chained to a block." The cause of this is what I before touched on. Prayer is not hard of itself, but mortification is, and since mortification is a necessary disposition to prayer, we find prayer hard, because we have not this disposition. The same is easily perceived even in natural things, for the difficulty does not consist in the introducing a form into any matter, but in disposing the matter to receive it. Consider, for example, what happens when we cast green wood upon the fire.

See how active the fire is in drying up its moisture or greenness —see the thick smoke that it sends forth, and the time it takes to dispose it to burn ; but as soon as the wood has all the dispositions that are necessary, it presently takes fire, and is easily consumed. It is the same in the present case. All the difficulty consists in taking from our passions their strength and greenness, in mortifying our irregular appetites, and in entirely withdrawing ourselves from the things of this world. If we can but compass this, the rest will cost us nothing ; our soul will of itself move towards God, and feel great pleasure and delight in conversing with him. Each one takes delight in conversing with one of his own humour and inclination. But he who applies himself to the mortification of his flesh, does thereby spiritualise and render himself in some measure like unto God ; and God reciprocally takes pleasure in communicating himself unto him. " My delight," says he, by the wise man, " is to be, and to converse with the sons of men. (Prov. viii. 31.) But when the heart is filled with all sorts of passions—when not quite free from vain-glory, we have some slight attachments, pleasing ourselves in worldly conversation, loving our own ease and satisfaction—when we are in this disposition, as we are far from resembling God, so we find it hard to converse with him, and we take no pleasure but in earthly things, by reason of the likeness we have unto them : " They are become as abominable," says the holy prophet Osee, " as the things they love." (Osee ix. 10.)

A holy father says very well, that as when the water is troubled, we can neither see ourselves, nor anything else in it ; so when our hearts are not purified from all terrene affections, and are not free from a thousand vain impertinences, we can never see the face of God in prayer—that is, we can never penetrate the depth of his mysteries, and he will never communicate himself unto us. " Blessed are the pure of heart, for they shall see God. (Matt. v. 8.) Prayer is properly a spiritual view of the works and mysteries of God : and as to see well with our corporal eyes, we must have them neat and clean ; so to see the works of God with the eyes of our soul, we must have a pure and clean heart. " Do you desire to see God? " says St. Austin, "take care first to purify your heart, and cast out of it whatsoever is displeasing to him." (Aug. Serm. ii. de Asc. Dom. ; and Serm. clxxv. de Temp. Cass. Coll. ix. cap. 4.)

The abbot Isaac, as Cassian relates, explained this by an

excellent comparison. He said that our soul was like to a feather, that was so very light that the least wind raised it from the ground, and made it fly about in the air, when it was neither wet nor besmeared with pitch, nor glued to anything that held it fast; but if it was wet, or if it was glued to something that hindered it from rising, it was forced to remain upon the ground amongst dirt and filth. So if our soul be pure and free from all things, the least breath or whisper of the Holy Ghost, in time of meditation, will raise it even to God himself; but, if it be tied to earthly things, if it be sullied by its irregular passions, it becomes so heavy, that it cannot elevate itself to heavenly things, nor feel any satisfaction in prayer. Moses, says the abbot Nilus, was forbid to approach the burning bush, till he had pulled off his shoes. And how can you think to approach towards God, or come to conversation with him, till you have cast away your passions, and all the ties you have to the things of the world ?

We have an excellent example in the fourth book of Kings, which shows us how calm our passions ought to be, when we wish to pray and to converse with God. The holy scripture recounts, that Joram king of Israel, Josophat king of Juda, and the king of Edom, marching all three against the king of Moab, they wanted water in the desert, so that their army was heady to perish. In this extremity they consulted the prophet Elias; and the king of Israel, who was an idolater, said to him—" Why has the Lord assembled these three kings here, to deliver them into the hands of Moab ? " What is that to you or me ?" replied the prophet Elias; " go to your father's and mother's prophets. As the God of armies lives, in whose presence I am, were it not for the respect I bear to Josophat king of Juda, I would have had no regard to you at all, nor would have so much as come into your presence. Notwithstanding let there be a musician brought hither." (4 Kings iii. 13—15.) Thus did the prophet, full of zeal and courage, reprehend the king of Israel, and reproached him for his idolatry. Yet, in fine, for the sake of Josophat, who was a holy and just king, he resolved to let them know the favours God designed to do them in that enterprise. But, because the fervour of his zeal had a little moved and disturbed him, that he might put himself into a right disposition to converse with God and receive his answer, they brought him a musician to calm and quiet his mind by the sweetness of music ; and when he found it in a calm and repose, he declared the wonders that God would work in their favour—sending them water in abundance, and giving the victory over their enemies. If it was necessary that a prophet, who was justly and piously moved, should appease this agitation of his mind before he could speak to God, or receive any answer from him, how far more necessary is it for us to calm our irregular passions, thereby to cause him to communicate himself to us in prayer?

As to the second point, that prayer is an efficacious means of mortification, I have sufficiently proved it in the treatise on prayer. There I showed that the mortification of ourselves is properly the fruit we must reap from prayer; and the saints with reason suspect that prayer which is not accompanied with mortification. For, as in order to shape iron, it is not sufficient to heat and soften it in the fire, but it must be beaten with the hammer before it receives the form they desire to give it; so it is not sufficient to mollify our heart by the heat of prayer, but we must also make use of the hammer of mortification to fashion and perfect our soul, to free it from all defects, and to imprint in it all those virtues it stands in need of. That sweetness and calm we feel in the exercise of prayer and divine love, is what ought to soften and render easy the pains we find in mortification. It is this which ought to encourage us to renounce ourselves, and to overcome the malignity of our nature. Wherefore let us pray continually without ceasing, till by the mercy of God we have acquired this perfect mortification of ourselves, so necessary for us, and which the scripture and the saints continually recommend unto us.

St Austin, upon these words of Genesis: "the child began to grow up, and was taken from his mother's breasts, and the day he was weaned, Abraham made a great feast" (Gen. xxi. 8:) "how it came to pass," says he, "that at the birth of Isaac, that infant so longed for, that child of promise, in whom all nations were to be blessed, they showed no signs of joy; no more than they did at his circumcision, which notwithstanding was a ceremony of solemnity; and that when he was weaned, when they forced him to cry and lament his being taken from the breast, that then his father rejoiced with his friends, and made a great feast for them? What is the meaning of this? There must needs be," says St. Austin, "some hidden mystery contained therein. And the Holy Ghost would have us hereby understand, that we must spiritually rejoice when any one grows or increases in virtue, and begins to be more perfect, and to enter into man's estate, and is no longer numbered among those of whom the apostle speaks—

' Being still infants in Jesus Christ I nourish with milk, and not with solid meats.' " (1 Cor. iii. 1.)   Wherefore applying this at present to ourselves, what we are hereby to understand is, that our superiors, who are our spiritual fathers, have great joy and comfort, not when we are born in religion, or first enter into it, nor when they give us a more entire entrance at the end of our noviceship ; but when they find we begin to wean ourselves, and cease to be children, and that forsaking the nourishment and trifles and toys of infants, we begin to nourish ourselves with solid meats, and conduct ourselves like spiritual and mortified men.

But prayer is still more closely allied to mortification.   For it is not only a proper means of attaining mortification, but it is of itself a very great mortification : according to these words of the Holy Ghost—" The watching which we employ in virtuous reflections dries up the body.   And frequent meditation is an affliction of the flesh." (Eccl. xxxi. 1.)   The holy scripture teaches us this truth in the wrestling that happened between Jacob and the Angel; Jacob became blind by it: and we see by experience, that those who are very much given to prayer and meditation are ordinarily exhausted, weak, and infirm.   It is a kind of smooth file that makes no noise, but wears out and weakens the flesh by little and little, and destroys health. Whatever view, therefore, we take of prayer, it always helps very much to mortification.

———o———

CHAPTER II.

In what mortification consists, and how necessary it is.

THE better to examine and penetrate so difficult a matter, it is necessary, in the first place, to presuppose that our soul consists of two principal parts, which by divines are called the superior and inferior ; and which they ordinarily also distinguish by the names of reason and the sensitive appetite.   Before sin came into the world, man was in the happy state of innocence and original justice in which God first created him ; the inferior part was perfectly subject and obedient to the superior, as a less noble is subject to a more noble thing, or as a servant to a master. " God made man just and righteous " (Eccl. vii. 30) says the scripture.   He did not create him so irregular as we now find ourselves to be.   The sensitive appetite obeyed reason, without any pain or repugnance; and man was of himself carried to love and serve his Creator, without any hindrance at all This subjection also of the sensitive appetite to reason was so great, that then it could not excite any irregular motion in man, nor any temptation, unless he chose it himself.   In this state he would not have been subject to choler, envy, gluttony, impurity, or to any other corrupt inclination, unless of ourselves, by a determined will, we wished to give way to it.   But reason having since revolted, and turned rebel against God by sin, the sensitive appetite rebelled also against reason ; so that whether we will or not, and even against our will and consent, there are sometimes excited such motions and affections in our sensitive appetite as we ourselves condemn ; according to these words of the apostle : " I do not that which I would do, but I commit the evil which I would not." (Rom. vii. 19.)   If man, therefore, had not sinned, the body would always have been disposed, without any pain or contradiction, to what the soul desired ; but at present, "the corruption of the body depresses the soul." (Wis. ix. 15.) The body hinders it from doing many things it could and would do.   The body may be called a vicious horse, that is to be rode a long journey ; it is a horse that has no gaits, that starts at everything, that tires soon, that is restive, and even lies down when it is most necessary to hasten forward.   " This punishment was justly due to man," says St. Austin, " for his disobedience to his Creator, that by God's just judgment his flesh should also become disobedient to himself ; and that this rebellion of his appetite should cause in him a continual war." (Aug. lib. 1, contra adv. legis et pro. c. 14.)   Many divines think with venerable Bede, " that by sin man was wholly deprived of the gifts of grace, and also grievously wounded in those of nature."   For he was not only deprived of original justice, and of the supernational gifts united thereto ; but he suffered a very great alteration and prejudice in the pure gifts of nature.   His understanding was obscured, his free will weakened, his inclination to good lessened, and his propensity to evil much increased ; his memory diminished ; his imagination disquieted, and so easily dissipated and distracted, that he is scarce able to make the least prayer with attention.   Now his imagination presently makes him rove and wander up and down in all places, and upon all objects, except those upon which he should fix his mind.   His senses have quite lost what was exquisite in them ; his flesh remains full of corruption and bad inclinations ; and in fine, his whole nature is so changed and spoiled, that what was before very easy to him to perform, is now become in a manner impossible. Before sin, man loved God better than himself; but now he loves himself better than God; or rather he loves himself only. He has no zeal or fervour but to do his own will, to satisfy his irregular appetites, and to let himself be carried away with his passions, how contrary soever they are both to reason and to the law of God.

Moreover, we must take notice, that though baptism has delivered us from original sin, which is the cause of all this disorder, yet it has not freed us from the rebellion of our natural appetite against reason, and even against God, which is called by divines the fuel or incentive to sin. And it is by a just judgment, and by an adorable and special providence, that God would always have this rebellion remain in us to punish and abate our pride; in order that the consideration of this, our misery and baseness, might serve to humble us in his presence. On creating man he heaped honour and dignity upon him, he adorned and embellished him with his gifts and graces: "But man being ignorant of his own worth and excellency, and becoming ungrateful to his Creator, deserved to be deprived of his excellency, and to degenerate so far as to be like unto beasts." (Ps. xlviii.) He became subject to the same desires and inclinations that violently transport them. Wherefore God would hereby humble man, that he might see and enter into himself, and have no more occasion of being puffed up with pride. And in effect, if we thoroughly knew ourselves, we should see that we are so far from having anything to be proud of, that we have every moment innumerable reasons to humble ourselves.

Secondly, we must presuppose another leading truth, which is as necessary as that we last spoke of, namely, that the disorder of our sensitive appetite, and the perverseness of our carnal inclinations, is the greatest obstacle to our advancement in virtue. It is for this reason that ordinarily we say, that our flesh is our greatest enemy; because in effect it is from this that all temptations and all our imperfections proceed. Wherefore, the apostle St. James had reason to say, " Whence proceed those wars and strifes that are in us? It is not from our passions that make war against our flesh?" (James iv. 1.) Sensuality, concupiscence, and the disorder of self-love, are the causes of all our domestic wars, of all sins, of all faults, and even of our imperfections; and consequently the greatest obstacle we meet with in the way of perfection. The ancient philosophers, who were illuminated only by the light of natural reason, knew very well this truth. Aristotle placed all the difficulty we find in virtue, in the moderating of our cares, solicitudes, and pleasures. And Epictetus reduced all philosophy to the short compendium of these two words :—" Suffer and abstain." (In Epictet. man.) In effect, all virtue consists in courageously suffering pains and afflictions, and in prudently abstaining from pleasures. This the experience of every day teaches : for we sin only to avoid some pain or trouble, or to obtain some pleasure or convenience, or not to be deprived of some pleasure. One man sins through a desire of riches, honours, or sensual pleasures ; another through fear of the pain and trouble he feels in observing the commandments of God and of the church, and through the difficulty he has to love his enemies, to fast, and to confess his most hidden and grievous sins. All sins, therefore, flow from these two fountains ; not only the most grievous, but even the lightest sins ; and all the imperfections we fall into in the way of virtue.

All this being presupposed, there is no difficulty in conceiving that mortification helps to repair the disorder of our passions, that is to say, to suppress our bad inclinations, and the irregu-larity of self-love. St. Jerome, explaining those words of Jesus Christ : " If any one will come after me, let him deny himself and take up his cross and follow me," (Luke ix. 23,) says, that he renounces himself and takes up his cross " who, from having been unchaste, becomes chaste—from having being irregular, becomes regular—from having being weak and fearful, becomes strong and courageous." This is truly to renounce himself, and to become quite a different man from what he was before.

But that which makes us most clearly see the necessity of mortification is, as St. Basil takes notice, that our Saviour first bids us renounce ourselves, and then commands us to follow him. That is to say, if you do not first renounce yourself, if you do not entirely cast away your own will, if you do not mortify your bad inclinations, you will meet with a thousand impediments and obstacles that will hinder you from being able to follow Jesus Christ. It is after this manner " we must always carry his mortification about us, to the end that the purity of his life may remain in us."—(2 Cor. iv. 10.) " The life of man is a continual warfare upon earth."—(Job. vii. 1.) " For the flesh," as St. Paul says, " has its desires, contrary to those of the spirit, and the spirit has such as are also contrary to those of the flesh."—

(Gal. v. 17.) Behold whence proceeds that continual warfare we have within ourselves. He who knows best how to overcome his flesh and sensual appetites, will become the best and bravest soldier of Jesus Christ. St. Gregory and St. Ambrose say, that in this the true valour of the servant of God consists. The strength of the body signifies little, and adds nothing unto it ; there is question only of that courage which overcomes the flesh, stifles our passions, contemns the pleasures of this life, and patiently supports the adversities and labours thereof. In effect, it is a greater thing, say they, to command and become masters of ourselves, and passions, than to command others. "A patient man," according to Solomon, " is more to be esteemed than one that is valiant ; and he who is master of his choler and passion, than he who takes cities by assault."—(Prov. xvi. 32.) The reason that St. Ambrose gives for this truth is, " because our own bad inclinations or domestic enemies are far more dangerous than external or foreign enemies." " St. Joseph also," says he, " gained more glory in commanding himself, and in resisting the solicitations of Potiphar's wife, than afterwards in commanding all Egypt." St. Chrysostom is of the same opinion, and says, that " David obtained a greater victory, when he could have revenged himself upon Saul by killing him in his tent, and did not, than he did in overcoming Goliah." The trophies of this first victory were not raised in the terrestrial, but the celestial Jerusalem. And it was upon this account he deserved, that not only the virgins should go before him singing his praises, when he returned conqueror of Goliah, but that all the choirs of angels in heaven should rejoice and admire his virtue and courage, in this great victory over himself.

——o——

CHAPTER III.

That one of the greatest punishments God inflicts upon man, is to give him up to his own desires, and permit him to follow his own passions.

THAT we may the better come to a knowledge of the necessity we are in of overcoming our flesh, and be the more encouraged to take up arms against it, it is of great importance that we should know how great and dangerous an enemy it is. It is so formidable a one, that the saints say, that one of the greatest of God's punishments, and whereby he shows his severest wrath against a sinner, is when he delivers him into the hands of this enemy, and when he abandons him to his sensual desires and appetites, as to so many merciless executioners. They cite for the proof of this many passages in holy Scripture, and amongst others, that of the royal prophet : " My people have not hearkened to my voice ; Israel has not joined itself to me ; wherefore I will abandon them to the desires of their heart, they shall hereafter only follow their own imaginations and ihventions."—(Ps. lxxx. 12 and 13.) St. Paul says, that this was the way that God took to punish the pride of the ancient philosophers—"Who knowing God, did not glorify him as God, and rendered him not the thanks due unto him; but strayed and alienated themselves from him, by vain dissipations ; and for this reason," says he, "God delivered them up to the desires of their hearts, and to impurity; that abandoning themselves thereunto, they themselves might dishonour their own bodies."—(Rom. i. 21, 24.) The chastisement which God inflicted upon them was to deliver them up to their own desires. But we must take notice with St. Ambrose, that when the holy Scripture says that God delivers up a man to his desires, we must not hereby understand that God incites him to evil, or causes any one to fall into sin ; but only that he permits those bad desires we have secretly conceived in our heart to appear exteriorly in action and execution, by the instigation and assistance of the devil.

We may see how grievous and horrible this chastisement is, by what the apostle afterwards adds. He shows us in what manner these proud philosophers were treated by this furious enemy, to whose power God had delivered them up. And it is impossible to express to what an excess of disorder they were carried by him. He drew them into all sorts of vices ; so far as to make them plunge themselves into the most abominable and shameful sins. " God delivered them up," says he, " to infamous passions."—(Rom. i. 26.) Miserable, therefore, are you, if you permit yourself to fall into the hands of so terrible an enemy, into the claws of so cruel and savage a beast ! Do you know how he will treat you. Hear St. Ambrose : " He," says the saint, " who knows not how to command his desires, finds himself presently carried away with them, as by an unruly horse, who, having got the bit between his teeth, runs even to inaccessible places ; and never rests till he falls with his rider into some precipice."—(Amb. l, 3, de vir.) Thus it is, if you do not destroy concupiscence—if you do not tame and bring it under, it will carry you from one disorder to another, from one vice to another, and will not desist till it has precipitated you into most enormous crimes, and even into the abyss of hell itself. "Permit not yourself to be carried away with concupiscence," says Ecclesiastes, "and take care not to follow your own will; if you give up yourself to your desires to do what they command, you will become a laughing-stock and a scorn to your enemies."—(Eccl. xviii. 30, 31.) We cannot give the devils, our enemies, a greater subject of joy, than to deliver up ourselves to our passions. For they treat us after so ill a manner, that all the devils in hell together cannot treat us worse. Wherefore Ecclesiastes earnestly begs of God, that he would hinder this chastisement from falling upon him. "Thou, O Lord, who art my father, and the God of my life, drive away from me all unchaste and impure thoughts, permit me not to be possessed by the desires of the flesh, and give me not over to a shameless and foolish mind."—(Eccl. xxiii. 4, 6.) It is therefore with very good reason the saints affirm that God cannot show a greater mark of his wrath to a sinner, than to leave him to his own will, and to let him have his liberty in following the inclinations and motions of his passions. It is a very bad sign when a physician permits his patient to eat and drink whatsoever he wishes for; it is a mark that he quite despairs of his cure: and that he looks upon him as a dead man. God deals after the same manner with a sinner who has provoked him to anger; he lets him do whatsoever he will: and in so desperate a state, full of those bad inclinations and passions that reign in him, what can he do but that which is quite contrary to his own good, and which will bring him unto death? It is very easy hereby to comprehend in what a miserable condition those are who place all their happiness in doing whatsoever they wish to do.

———o———

CHAPTER IV.

Of the hatred of ourselves, and of the spirit of mortification and penance it produces.

IF we reflect well upon what has been already said, it will be sufficient to give us that holy hatred of ourselves which our Saviour Jesus Christ requires of us; and without which, he says, we cannot be his disciples. For what greater reason can we have to hate our bodies, than to know that it is not only one of the greatest enemies we have, and even the greatest traitor that we have ever seen, but also a mortal enemy, and a malicious traitor, that every moment endeavours to inflict death—eternal death on the soul which supports it and bestows all necessaries upon it; a traitor, that for a moment's pleasure matters not to offend God, and to precipitate itself into an abyss of eternal miseries? If any one should deliver this message to you: know for certain, that one of your domestics, who daily eats and drinks at your table, has traitorously formed a plan to murder you; what apprehension and terror would not this strike into you? But if he should add: know moreover, so deep is his hatred of you, that he cares not to be put himself to death if he can but kill you; for he knows very well that he shall be taken in the fact, and put to a cruel death, but he cares not at all for the loss of his own life, so he can destroy yours; with what terror would you not be seized? would you not imagine every moment that he was coming to give you a mortal stab? And if you could discover or find out the traitor, what a hatred would you conceive against him, and what revenge would you not take upon him? But our own body is this traitor, that both eats and drinks, and lies within us; which knows very well that in hurting our soul he also hurts himself, and that he cannot precipitate her into hell without falling thereinto himself. Notwithstanding, from a desire of doing what he pleases, he tramples all under foot, and values nothing; see then if we have not reason to hate him. How often has this traitor driven you to the brink of hell? How often has he made you offend the goodness of God? How many graces and favours has he made you lose? And how often does he every day expose you to the danger of losing your eternal salvation? What holy indignation ought you not to have against an enemy that has done you so much harm, and deprived you of so much good, and continually exposes you to so great dangers? If we hate the devil, and look upon him as our greatest enemy, by reason of the continual hurt he does us, how much more ought we to hate our flesh, which is a more cruel and dangerous enemy? The devils are so weak that they are not able to hurt us, if our flesh did not combine with them to wage continual war against us.

Behold here what it was that moved the saints to have so great a hatred of themselves; and hence sprung up in them that spirit of mortification and penance, whereby they revenged themselves upon this their enemy, and always kept him in subjection. They took care not to treat their body well, nor to give it any ease or

pleasure, being persuaded that this was to furnish their enemy
with weapons against themselves, and to give him new force and
vigour against them.   "Let us take care," says St. Austin, "not
to permit our body to get strength, lest it use it to make war
against our soul." (Aug. lib. de salut. monit. cap. 35.)   But
let us rather apply ourselves to discipline and mortify it, thereby
hindering it from rebelling against us: " For whosoever educates
a domestic servant too delicately, will find him afterwards become too insolent." (Prov. xxix. 22.)

The ancient anchorets applied themselves with great zeal to this
exercise of mortification of the body; and thought it so necessary
to weaken their bodies, that when they had no other means to do
it, they had recourse to great labours, which they imposed upon
themselves, to extenuate and abate their strength.   Palladius
relates, that a holy anchoret, finding himself extremely tormented
with proud and vain thoughts, which he was not able to drive
away, resolved to take a basket upon his back, and continually to
carry earth in it from one place to another.   And when they
asked him what he did, " I vex him," says he, " that vexes me,
and revenge myself upon my enemy." (Pallad. in vita S. Mac.
Alex.)   The same thing is related of St. Macharius: and it is said
that St. Dorotheus, who practised great penance and austerities,
being one day asked why he so grievously tormented his body :
" It is," says he, "because it torments me."   St. Bernard incensed
with a holy choler against his body, as against his enemy, breaks
forth into these words : " Let God arise," says he, " and let this
armed giant fall at his feet ; yea, let him fall, and let this enemy
of God be crushed in pieces, this self-lover, this friend of the
world, this slave of the devil.   What do you think ? adds the
saint, "certainly you will show yourselves to be just and righteous
judges, and will cry out with me, he is worthy of death, let him be
hanged, let him be crucified." (Bern. Serm. 90. de Div. num. 3,)

It is with such courage as this, and with such arms as these,
that we ought to fight, and subject our bodies, lest they rebel,
and in their revolt, force the mind and reason to take part with
them.   This victory will gain us another ; for having once overcome our flesh, we shall with great ease be able to overcome the
devil.   Since it is by the help of the flesh, whose rebellion he
foments, that he makes war against us, we must therefore wage
war against him also, by mortifying and macerating our flesh,
thereby hindering it from revolting against us.   St. Austin writing
upon these words of the apostle : " For my part I run, not as at
an uncertainty ; I fight, but not as beating the air ; but I chastise

my body, and bring it into subjection" (1 Cor. ix. 26, 27;) takes notice, that this is the true means to triumph over the devil. "Chastise your body," says he, "and you will overcome the devil, for this is the way, the apostle assures us, we must fight against him." When a captain in garrison upon the frontiers of the Moors, hears any alarm given, if he has a slave that is a Moor, he presently puts him in chains into a dungeon, lest he should rebel against him, and take part with his enemies. We must use our body after the same manner; we must mortify it; we must clap it into chains, lest at our enemies' approach he put himself on their side.

———o———

CHAPTER V.

That our advancement in perfection depends upon mortification.

THE knowledge of this truth, now proposed, has caused the masters of a spiritual life to affirm, that our advancement in perfection depends upon mortification. "You will not be able to make any progress in virtue," says St. Jerome, "without using violence to yourself." (Imit. Christ. i. 3, c. 23, Hier. in illud.) And explaining that passage in Job, "Wisdom is not found in the land of those that live at ease and repose" (Job xxviii. 13;) that is to say, of those who live according to their own will—he declares, that as we ordinarily say arable land rests when we let it bear what it will, which is commonly nothing else but thorns and thistles; and, on the contrary, when we make it bear corn, we say that it labours; so when a man lives after his own will and fancy, we say he leads an easy and idle life. But it is not in fallow ground of this sort that wisdom grows. No! it is in land which is highly cultivated—in the land of such as mortify themselves, and renounce their sensual appetites. It is this mortification, this renouncing of ourselves, which the saints look upon as the rule and measure of our spiritual advancement. Would you therefore know what progress you have made in virtue? Examine what you have done to mortify yourself— what victory you have gained over your passions—how you are disposed, in point of patience and humility; whether you have an aversion to things of this world; whether the affections of flesh and blood are mortified and dead in you. It is in this, and not in sweetness and consolation in prayer, that you will see whether you have advanced or not. St. Ignatius was of this sentiment; he made greater account of mortification than of prayer; and it was from their mortification that he framed his judgment of every man's advancement. And St. Francis Borgia, when any one extolled or commended another to him as a saint— "he will be so indeed," says he, "if he be truly mortified." Blosius compares a mortified servant of God to a ripe bunch of grapes, which is sweet and pleasing to the taste ; and he that is not mortified, to a bunch of wild grapes, which is sharp and sour, according to the words of the prophet Isaias : "I expected from my vine that it should yield me good grapes, to make wine, and it has given me only wild grapes." (Is. v. 4.)   The difference there is between the children of God, and the children of the world, is, that these follow the motions of their passions, and think not of mortifying their bodies : but those that are of Jesus Christ, have crucified their flesh, with their vicious desires and inclinations, and are not guided but by the spirit which gives them life." (Galat. v. 24.)

It is true that Christian perfection does not essentially consist in mortification, but in the love of God : and man is not perfect till he is united to God by the bond of love.   But, as a stone which is raised from the ground falls back again to its centre, as soon as that is taken away which hinders it from its natural inclination of falling back ; so, no sooner is our soul, which is a spiritual substance and created for God, freed from the impediment of its passions, and from all other things that miserably fasten it to the earth, but it presently raises itself unto God as to its end and centre, and by the assistance of his grace unites itself unto him by charity.   "All things," says St. Austin, "move according to their bias ; light things move upwards, and heavy things downwards." (Confess. lib. 13, cap. 9.)   But what bias causes in natural bodies, love occasions in reasonable creatures. "My love is my moving principle, and I am carried to that to which it carries me." (St. Aug. ibid.)   And, as natural things move according to the natural principle that moves them, so rational creatures move according to that love and passion that is predominant in them.   So that if the love of earthly things, if the desire of being honoured and esteemed, if the desire of doing our own will, and of enjoying our ease, predominates in us, all our motions and desires will become sensual, and will carry us towards the earth.   But, if by mortification, we free ourselves from sensual things, the love of our Creator will prevail within us, it will be our moving principle ; and then our heart will, with a far swifter motion, elevate itself to God, than a stone falls to its centre. "You have made us for yourself, O God, and our heart can never enjoy any repose but in you."—(Aug. conf. c. 5.) Behold, therefore, the reason why the saints affirm that mortification is the measure of our advancement in Christian perfection. For he who is very much mortified, is also very much touched and inflamed with the love of God, and will consequently become perfect.

St. Austin, upon those words of the Psalmist :—" As the hart pants and seeks after the fountains of water, so does my soul seek after thee, O Lord," (Ps. xli. 2), says, " that the hart tramples under foot and kills all the serpents he meets with, when he seeks after water ; but having killed them, he finds his thirst augmented, and runs so much the swifter to seek water." Still applying the simile, he says, " Would you know why you thirst not very much after your perfection, and after the love of God ? it is because you do not, like the hart, destroy those serpents that stand in your way. Your vices are the serpents— you must destroy those serpents of iniquity ; and then you will run with fervour to the fountain of truth and life." We cannot advance in perfection and the love of God, but in proportion to our advancement in mortification. " The diminution of concu-piscence," says he, in another place, " is the increase of charity, and the greatest perfection consists in having our concupiscence quite extinguished. As gold is purified and refined, according as the bad alloy of other metals is consumed ; so charity and the love of God grows more perfect in us, and is augmented, as the love of the world and of ourselves is diminished. And when this inordinate love shall quite be extinguished and destroyed, then the love of God will be wholly perfected in us."

Cassian relates, " that John, the abbot, being upon his death bed, which was surrounded by his disciples, as by children about the bed of their dying father, they earnestly begged of him to give them the comfort of some short document for their spiritual advancement, to leave behind him as a spiritual legacy, that might help them with greater facility to ascend to the height of perfection. ' I have never,' says he, smiling, ' done my own will, nor ever taught anything to another, that I have not first practised myself.' "—(Lib. 5. de renunt. c. 28.)

CHAPTER VI.

That mortification is peculiarly necessary for religious, but above all for those who are employed in the exercises of charity towards their neighbour.

THE exercise of mortification regards all God's servants in general, and all stand in need of it, to be able continually more and more to conform themselves to the will of God : but it more particularly regards religious persons ; because, in effect, we left the world and entered into religion for no other end than to mortify ourselves. St. Bennet says, that to be religious is to correct our ill habits ; and hence it comes, that at the profession which those of his order make, they say, " I promise the change of my manners."—(In form. votarum.) We also make the same promise to God when we renounce the world, and it is to this we ought to apply ourselves by the help of mortification—"Casting off the old man with his works, and clothing ourselves with the new one."—Coloss. iii. 9, 10.) St. Bernard was wont to say to those he received into religion, "Take notice," says he, " that your mind only is to enter, and that you are to leave your body behind you at the gate." Giving them hereby to understand, that in religion they ought not to think of treating their bodies well, nor as living as they please, but that they ought to take care only of their souls, and of their mind, according to the words of the apostle : " Walk according to the spirit, and fulfil not the works of the flesh."—(Gal. v. 26.) To walk according to the spirit, is to live according to the sentiments of our more noble part, which are those of the mind, and of reason, and not according to the motions and inclinations of our inferior part ; which is our flesh and sensuality. Cassian says, " It was the general opinion of all the ancient fathers, founded upon frequent experience, that it was impossible for any one to persevere in a religious state of life, if he had not learned to overcome his own inclinations."—(Cass. lib. 4, de instit. renunt. c. 8. In effect, what is more contrary to a religious life than those worldly inclinations we bring with us into it ?

But if mortification be so necessary for all religious, it is far more necessary for us, who, according to our institute, are designed to help our neighbour in all sorts of charitable functions. St. Chrysostom going about to prove the particular necessity those have to mortify their passions who are forced to converse with the world, thereby to assist their neighbour, grounds himself upon this, that the occasions are there more frequent, and more dangerous, and our passions, which he calls savage beasts, find there more food to nourish them. A soldier, says he, may keep secret his cowardice, till he has some occasion given him whereby he discovers it. It is the same with a Christian. He who keeps at home and in retirement may hide his defects; but he who goes forth to combat and fight against the world, and is become a public spectacle, being exposed to the view thereof, it is fit he should excel in virtue and mortification. Add to this, that to gain those to God with whom you converse, you must, as much as you can, accommodate yourself to their manners and humour; according to St. Paul's example, who says himself, "I became all to all, that I might gain all unto God, and save the whole world."—(1 Cor. ix. 22.) And how far the spirit of mortification, and renouncing our own will is necessary for this, is apparent enough in itself, and wants no reason to prove it.

Philosophers say that the part of the eye which receives the impression of colours, and wherein the vision is framed, has no colour in itself; and it was necessary it should be without any, that it might be able to receive the impressions of the colours, and see them as they are. For if it had any particular colour, it would not be able to receive any other, according to that common axiom—"What is within hinders what is without from entering." If it were red, all that we saw would appear red, as we find by experience when we look through certain red glasses; and if it were green, all things we looked upon would to us also appear green. It is in the same manner that each one of us, mortifying his passions, and rendering himself master of them, casts away his own particular humour, having properly none at all; that he may, with St. Paul, be able so to accommodate himself to every one, that thereby he may gain all unto God. The spirit of religion does not require that we should sympathize and agree with those only of the same temper with us; or that the choleric should not accommodate themselves, or converse but with the choleric; that such as are melancholy should not be able to suffer those that are not of that humour; and far less that they should have a greater inclination to those of their own than to those of a different nation. Would you not believe it to

be a very great misfortune to have two eyes, that should be able
to see one colour only? But it is far greater to have so narrow
and limited a will, and so ill disposed, that it is bent towards
such only as are of the same humour or of the same country.
Charity equally embraces all, because it loves all for God, and
in God. It makes no distinction or difference between one
nation and another, nor between one person and another; and, as
St. Paul well expresses : "It makes no distinction between Jew
and Gentile, between the circumcised and uncircumcised, between
barbarian and Christian, between a slave and one that is free-
born ; but in all beholds Jesus Christ, who is all in all."—
(Coloss. iii. 11.) It would hide all within its charitable bowels,
because it looks upon all as the children of God, and brethren of
Jesus Christ ; and what is there more proper to make us gain
this universal charity than the mortification of ourselves.

It is also very necessary for us to keep amongst us that spirit
of union and friendly charity which Jesus Christ has so recommended to us ; and which is the character whereby he would
have his disciples known and distinguished from all others. For
nothing does more destroy this union than to seek ourselves in
all things, to love our own ease, to desire to attract or to keep
to ourselves the esteem or reputation of the world. Let each
one examine himself, and he will find, as often as he offends
against charity, that it is always some one of those things that
is the occasion thereof. But the mortification we speak of, frees
us from all these bad attachments to ourselves, and makes the
way of charity become plain and easy. It causes us, "not to
seek our own interest." (1 Cor. xiii. 5.) And it is for this
reason that St. Ambrose says, "If any one desires to please all,
let him not seek what is profitable or pleasing to himself, but
what is so to others, as St. Paul did ; " who would have us,
"not to think upon our own interest, but upon the interest of
our neighbour." (Phil. ii. 4.)

———o———

CHAPTER VII.

Of two sorts of mortification and penance.

St. Austin, speaking of that passage of St. Matthew : "Since
the coming of St. John Baptist, the kingdom of heaven suffers
violence, and the violent take it by force."—(Matt. xi. 12.)
"There are," says he, "two sorts of abstinences and crosses :

the one corporal, the other spiritual."—(Ser. xx. de sanc. and 1 de S. Joan. Bap.) The one afflicts the body, as, for example, to fast, to take a discipline, to wear a hair-cloth, to lie upon the ground, and such like practices that mortify the flesh, and deprive it of its ease and pleasure ; and this is what we call exterior penance.   The other is more meritorious and more sublime ; which is to command our passions, daily to make war on our vices, to become rigorous censors of ourselves, and to be in continual strife against our inward man.   That is, constantly to break our own will, to despoil ourselves of our own judgment, to overcome our choler, to repress and keep under our impatience, and in a word, to command our mouth, our eyes, our tongue, and all our senses, and bad inclinations.   " It is he," says St. Gregory, " who, after this manner, having broken down this rampart of his passions, ascends with violence to the kingdom of heaven."   We must become brave and valiant after this manner, to be able to carry it by assault.   This kind of mortification, therefore, is far more excellent than the former ; because there is far greater merit in curbing our mind, in trampling under foot honour and the esteem of the world, than in afflicting our bodies by fasts, disciplines, and hair cloths.   But as this sort of mortification is better, and more meritorious than the other, so it is also more hard, and costs us a great deal more pain and labour ; because what is more perfect always costs more than what is less perfect.   This very doctrine is what St. Gregory, St. Dorotheus, and many other saints in several places teach us.

Our society embraces and puts in practice these two sorts of penance and mortification.   As to the first, it is true that St. Ignatius has not yet subjected us to any ordinary determined penance of obligation, being desirous, for very good reasons, that the society might lead a life common to all in the exterior.   But yet he has not omitted to take care we should mortify ourselves, as I shall show in its due place.   Many just considerations moved him to than ordain the manner of living in the society should have nothing extraordinary in the exterior; because the means ought always to bear some proportion to the end ; and the end of the society being to labour not only for its own advancement, but also for the advancement and salvation of our neighbour, it was very fit that we might have a more easy access to all sorts of persons, that we should wear no other habit but what was then common to all priests ; because, by this means, it was a religious habit with religious, a priest's habit with priests, and amongst secular persons, it was a habit that rendered us in some sort suitable also to them—it being very little different from the habit of secular priests. Add to this, that the society was instituted in Luther's time, when heretics had so great an aversion to all rêligious that they even hated their habit; wherefore, to give a more free access to them, and to be the better able to dispute against them, thereby to convince them, (which is a function peculiar to our institute,) it was convenient that we should have nothing extraordinary in our habit that might distinguish us from other ecclesiastics ; lest heretics, having a horror and aversion to us before they even began to confer with us, this might be an obstacle to one of the chief ends for which God instituted our society. Moreover, if we should wear an austere habit, it is to be feared that it might frighten sinners too much from us, who commonly desire to be brought to their duty by sweetness, and would otherwise be afraid to come near us from an apprehension that the austerity of our habit might be a mark of that of our miud, and that we would treat them too severely. We have therefore taken such a kind of common habit as is welcome to all persons, whereby we may gain a more free entrance and access to all, in order that no one may have any repugnance to treat with us. Our holy founder, also, would even by our habit have us become all to all, to be the better able to gain all unto God. Imitating in this Jesus Christ, of whom St. Austin and St Thomas say, that the better to accommodate himself to all persons, and for their greater profit, he rather chose such a kind of life as was common in the exterior, than such an austere and penitential life as St. John Baptist led.

As to exterior mortifications, though our rules do not appoint any, yet there is a living rule, which is our superior, who prescribes to every one what he ought to do. And these sorts of mortification may, as St. Ignatius says, be taken two ways; either when, by permission of the superior, we make choice of them ourselves, thereby to make a greater progress in virtue, or when the superior, for the same reason, shall impose them upon us. This great saint thought it more to the purpose to practise them after this manner than to determine them by any rule or constitution. Because a dead rule could not be made just and equal for all, all having not the strength to support the same austerities ; and therefore if he had established in this a general rule for all persons, those who could not observe it would have been troubled, because they could not do what others did. Moreover, as the same regimen or treatment, and the same physic, is not fit for all sorts of sick persons, so the same penances are not fit for all. Some are more proper for young persons, others for old. These are good for the weak and sickly ; those for such as enjoy a perfect health. One sort of penance is proper for those who entered into religion, without having lost their baptismal innocence ; and another sort is fit for those who entered into religion, all covered, with the wounds of sin, and pierced, as I may say, all over, like a sieve. It is for this reason that St. Austin and St. Basil say, we must not wonder if, in religion, they treat not every one after the same manner, and that some use greater austerities than others ; because there would be a very great inequality in an equal treatment. But it is not only in regard of different persons that such a difference and distinction is necessary ; it is also necessary for the same person, according to different times, and according to the want he has of it. Such a penance is good in time of temptation and interior aridity, and another is good in time of peace and fervour. This is proper to preserve the peace of God in our hearts ; and that to regain it when upon any occasion we are deprived of it. It is for these reasons that our founder would not determine the exterior penances to be practised amongst us, which were generally practised by other orders ; but has left it to the discretion of our superior, who is our spiritual physician, to impose greater or lesser penances, according to each one's strength and necessity. It was after this manner prescribed in the rule which the angel brought to Pachomius from Almighty God, and which ordered that the superior should prescribe to each religious what penance he was obliged to perform. So that though there be no ordinary penances in the society that are prescribed by rule, as they usually are in other religious orders, yet it is not because there are no corporal penances in practice amongst us, or that we do not highly esteem those holy constitutions and observances in other religious orders, (the variety of which contribute to the beauty of the church), but it is because our founder judged it more suitable to the end of his constitution, and more conformable to the ancient doctrine of saints, to leave the measure and manner to the prudence and charity of the superior. Yet this is far from causing fewer auterities to be practised amongst us ; but on the contrary, it causes far more to be in use, and to be embraced with greater fervour. At least, hitherto, by the mercy of God, we find that by this means more are performed amongst us than could have been appointed by the rule. God grant that this fervour and spirit of mortification, so praiseworthy, so holy, and so conform-able to the practice of the Church of God, may still go on, in-creasing more and more amongst us, and that, as hitherto we have experienced, there may be more need of a bridle to keep us in, than of a spur to excite us to the practice of penance and mortification.

The second kind of penance, which consists in the mortifying of our passions and self-love, is what the society more strictly embraces ; and it is for this reason that St Ignatius would not establish amongst us any ordinary penances determined by the rule, having a particular desire that we should, above all things, apply ourselves to the interior mortification of our passions and sensual appetites, and that this kind of penance, which is without comparison more meritorious and more excellent than the other, might be our chief employment and occupation. Moreover, he prescribes to us such things in the constitutions as are of very high perfection, and which require a very great interior mortifi-cation, and renouncing of ourselves, to be our chief study ; and that our whole application should be to make a daily progress in all solid virtues and true perfection. He fears, and perhaps not without reason, that if he prescribed ordinary and general pen-ances. we might give ourselves only to fasting, hair-cloths, and disciplines, to which we saw ourselves obliged, and should think we had done all in satisfying this obligation ; whereby we might come to leave off the mortification of our passions, which is of greatest importance, as is the practice also of those virtues that are most essential to our institute. Wherefore he desires we should have no other prop or foundation, than this interior morti-fication ; he would have our manner of life to be common accord-ing to the exterior, in order that we may entirely apply ourselves to this interior perfection, which will render our lives pure, holy, and excellent, till the unction and odour of this interior sanctity comes to discover itself in the exterior, and makes us appear to be true religious. It is this in reality that we stand more in need of than any other religious do. For as to other religious, their habit and manner of living makes and leaves a good impres-sion upon the minds of secular persons; but for us, who have not this exterior distinction of habit, for the reasons before mentioned, it behoves us to supply the want thereof by the interior ; and therefore to be full of humility, modesty, charity, zeal for the sal-vation of souls, and of the unction of the Holy Ghost ; that all that see and treat with us may take us to be truly religious of

the society of Jesus Christ, and may say of us : " These are the
seed which our Lord has blessed."—(Is. lxi. 9.) We must
therefore apply ourselves to the exercise of interior mortification,
and make account that, from the moment we cease to practise it,
we leave off also to live like religious men of the society ; and as
to exterior mortifications, we must make use of them to help us
to the gaining of the interior. This is the lesson that the
apostolical man, the great Xaverius, has left us ; and what St.
Bonaventure taught long before him.

That great sweetness of manner, so much spoken of, and by the
assistance of God's grace every day experienced, which the society
manifests in treating with the neighbour, is the effect of this
interior mortification. For this sweetness does not consist in the
facility of our obligations, nor in the compliance of our superiors
with us in all things we could wish ; (for then there would be no
form of religion, and moreover there are amongst us things very
hard to practise ;) but it consists in this, that all of us are obliged
to practise mortification, and to renounce ourselves ; and in this,
that each one ought to be entirely resigned to whatsoever his superiors think fit to ordain concerning him. This pious disposition of
mind, and this holy indifference, is the cause of that sweetness
which is found in the society, either in the government of superiors, or in the submission of inferiors. For by this means all
religious are in the hands of their superiors as the clay is in the
potter's : for when subjects of themselves desire nothing, the
superior very easily effects whatsoever he thinks proper.   We
may also say, that the care our holy founder had, to oblige us
chiefly to this interior mortification and renouncing of ourselves,
was the effect, not only of an admirable penetration, but also of a
particular inspiration of God. He saw that there were very hard
and difficult things amongst us; but he foresaw at the same time,
that to render them easy to all, and to prevent superiors from
being too backward in commanding, he needed only to establish
and lay a good foundation of mortification and resignation of
ourselves.   And it is for this reason that he would have us entirely resign ourselves into the hands of our superiors, and so to
cast off our will, that they might do with us whatsoever they
pleased—as the potter does with his clay, or as the tailor does
with his stuff. The tailor cuts his stuff where and how he pleases
—and for what use he pleases—one piece for the sleeves, another
for the back, another for the collar, and another for the skirts ;
yet one part of the stuff is as good as another, because it is all

of the same piece. The clay also, of which vessels and pots are
made for the kitchen, is as good as that of which they make
vessels for the table ; " because it is all of the same mass."—
(Rom. ix. 21.) Now let us come to the application—many religious entered at the same time into the society and studied all
together ; yet perhaps he who is designed to teach grammar, is
as good a scholar as he who is taken to teach philosophy or
divinity ; but howsoever it happens, he ought not to complain
any more than the clay or the stuff, or to say, why do you apply
me to this use ? So that the cause of this sweetness of conduct
in the society depends purely upon ourselves, that is to say, on
our having our minds mortified, resigned, and indifferent to all
things ; without contradiction, or any exterior or interior repugnance for anything that our superiors shall require of us. Wherefore cast not the fault upon them, if sometimes you find not all
the facility and sweetness imaginable in those things they shall
command you; but cast the fault upon yourself, that you are not
so well disposed, nor so mortified as you should be.   For as to
your superior, he does his duty; he supposes you to be a true and
good religious man, and that you are indifferent to all things ;
that there is no need of consulting you, or asking your consent,
because you ought always to approve of whatsoever he would
have you do, and be always ready to perform whatsoever he shall
order. The superior, on the contrary, does you an honour to have
so good an opinion of you, and so to treat and command you as if
you were such a one as you ought to be.   When a stone is well
cut, there is nothing more easy than to adjust and put it in its
proper place; it is only to let it fall into its birth; but when it is not
well cut or fitted, what blows of hammers and chisels are required;
what pains are there not taken to make it lie even and well ?

   A thing most worthy of consideration follows also from hence,
which is taken notice of by St. Bonaventure ; it is that though
interior mortification should be far harder than exterior penances,
yet we may more justly and easily dispense with one than the
other.   It may be a true and lawful excuse for any one, that he
has not sufficient strength to fast, to wear hair-cloths, to take disciplines, to suffer the inconvenience of going barefoot, or of rising
at midnight; but no one can say that he has not strength or health
enough to be humble, patient, or to have tractableness, submission, and resignation, so necessary in the society. No! you cannot
excuse yourself by saying, that you have not health or strength
enough for this ; for here there is no dispute about the disposition

of the body, but only of that of the mind. The healthful and the sickly, the strong and the weak, are, by the mercy of God, alike capable of undergoing this mortification if they choose themselves.

This is a great subject of comfort for those who have sometimes the temptation of dejection, imagining that they want those qualities that are necessary for so sublime an end as that of the society of Jesus. We read in the first book of Kings, that Saul having given notice to David, that he desired to give his daughter to him in marriage, David gave this answer to those that brought him the message: "Do you believe then that it is a small matter to be son-in-law to a king? For my part I am neither rich nor powerful enough to receive so great an honour."—(1 Reg. xviii. 23, 25.) They brought back this answer to Saul, who commanded them to return to David, and to tell him, " the king stood not in need of riches, nor of any dowry for his daughter, but only of twenty prepuces of the Philistines, to be revenged of his enemies."— (Ibid.) We may make the same answer to those who, by means of the diffidence they have in themselves, are too timid in the practices of religion. God wants not so great a capacity in you, nor so many talents as you think. Therefore the royal prophet said well, " You are my God, because you stand not in need of my goods."—(Ps. xv. 2.) What he desires of you is, that you would circumcise the Philistine ; that is to say, overcome your passions, and mortify your appetites. The society desires nothing of you but this: wherefore you will render yourself a fit and profitable member thereof if you do it. Be but humble, submissive, and resigned to all they desire of you, and this will suffice. God preserve you from having the least vanity or pride, from loving your ease, from gaping after amusements ; but endeavour to walk uprightly, and to act sincerely with your superiors. If you do this, no religion in the world can be too hard or severe for you; for to him who is humble, who is mortified, who is truly poor in spirit, who is resigned to all things, and has no will of his own, whatsoever is hard in the society will prove sweet and easy.

We ought, therefore, gratefully to acknowledge the extraordinary grace God has bestowed upon us, by rendering those things easy and pleasant which of themselves are so hard and painful : for it is very certain, that what our constitutions oblige us to in this point is a very high perfection, and the exercise thereof so very hard, that all other penances and corporal austerities are nothing in comparison thereof. In proof of this, I ask is not the

giving an account to our superior or spiritual father of all the
faults and imperfections we fall into, very hard ? Yet this obligation the society imposes upon us, and is one of our most essential
constitutions. Nay, is it not a thousand times harder than all the
fasts, hair-cloths, and disciplines in the world ? As to the rule
which requires that to be the better able to make progress in
spiritual things, and particularly to exercise ourselves in humility
and abjection, we must be content that all our faults and negligences should be discovered to our superior by any one that
knows them, out of confession—is there not a very great humility,
and a great submission of mind required to make no complaint
at all :—either because we were not admonished of them beforehand, or because they have made them greater than they were ?
Yet the severity of the rule stops not here, but also requires that
we should be content to be reprehended in public, either with,
or even without any cause given by us; and St. Ignatius requires
of us, that we should always be disposed to receive all the false
accusations that can be made against us, not only without mur-
muring, but also with joy, having given no occasion for them ;
and as those of the world are glad to be honoured and esteemed,
so we should also be no less glad to be exposed to all sorts of
injuries, contempts, and affronts. But is there not a very extraordinary virtue required for all this ? Yet it is moreover exacted
of us to be entirely indifferent to all offices, occupations, or
employments whatsoever, in which obedience shall place us, as
also to any station the society may mark out for us ; and since
there are so many degrees and employments therein, the one
above the other, is it not a mark of no small virtue, and does it
not require a mind truly mortified, to be thus indifferent to the
one or the other, and to be as well contented with the lowest as
with the highest ? We must, moreover, be always content and
ready to go to any part of the world our superiors shall send us,
in order to exercise these functions ; either in another province
or kingdom, in the East or West Indies, in Rome, Germany,
England, Transylvania, or in any other place so far distant that
we can never expect to see our friends or parents any more, all
hopes of this satisfaction being entirely lost and given up. As to
poverty, what the society practises is so strict and rigorous, that
no one can so much as receive any present, nor keep anything in
his chamber, either to eat, or for any other use ; no ! not so much
as a book, upon which also he must make no mark, to show it
belongs to him, nor carry it away with him when he is sent to
another college. Lastly, we must renounce altogether, and be

quite detached from all things ; for as I shall show in the treatise on poverty, it is not permitted us to put a lock upon any box or cover, to keep anything therein, but all things must be open in our chambers, whereby we in a manner signify to our superiors that they may take what they please, there being nothing in our chambers that belongs to us.

It is easy to conceive how these things, and many others like unto them, that are practised by the society, do either advance us to a very great perfection, or expose us to such difficulties as are above all penances and corporal austerities. So that he who, out of a spirit of mortification, desires to do great penance in the society, will find therein sufficient to satisfy his desires ; for though there should be some less faithful and constant in their vocation, who would fain palliate their slothful cowardice by a specious pretence of going to a stricter order to practise greater penances, thereby to gain a higher perfection ; yet, in reality, the cause or subject of this their change and inconstancy comes from the difficulty they find in that perfect interior mortification we make profession of in the society. We have evident proofs of this, even from their own confessions ; and which is still more, from a declaration of the Holy See Apostolic. Pius V. (who had been a religious of the order of St. Dominick) declares this in express terms, in a bull granted to the society against any such apostates, who should either leave it to return to the world or to enter into any other religious order whatsoever, except amongst the Carthusians. In this bull, after he had spoken of the perfection of our institute, and of those difficulties to which we are subject, he comes to that which was the cause or source of the temptation which some have had to leave us, to enter into other religious orders, speaking of them after this manner :—" Some," says he, " let themselves be carried away with such a levity of mind, as moves them to avoid the pains and labours to which the society is continually exposed, for the good and increase of Christian religion ; indiscreetly preferring their particular convenience to the public good and profit of the society, and even of Christianity itself ; yet would notwithstanding make us believe, by false insinuations, that what they do is for nothing else but to embrace a more perfect life, and a more strict observance ; and boast that without their superior's consent they have leave given them to enter into other, even mendicant orders." So that, in effect, it is not the desire of a greater perfection, or of a greater austerity of life that makes them change, but only the fear of

pain and difficulty ; and lastly, because they feel not in themselves so great a fund or stock of virtue as to seek after so high
a perfection, so entire a mortification, such an indifference and
absolute resignation, as is required in the society.   See, therefore, the reason why St. Ignatius insists so much upon this
interior mortification, and will have us apply ourselves seriously
thereunto, making it our chief study.

——o——

CHAPTER VIII.

*That mortification is not a hatred of ourselves, but rather a true
love of our soul, and even of our body also.*

WE have already said, according to the doctrine of the holy fathers,
taken from the gospel, that we must hate ourselves.   But though
this seems hard and repugnant to nature, yet, that no one may
hence take occasion of discouragement, and thereby leave off
mortification, I shall here explain how it is to be understood; and
shall make it appear, that this hatred is so far from doing us any
harm, that it is rather a true love that we have not only for our
souls, but even for our bodies also ; and that, in effect, we cannot
express a greater hatred both of soul and body than by not mortifying ourselves.   St. Austin, speaking of this passage of St. Paul
that " the spirit fights against the flesh : "—" Far be it from me,
dear brethren," says he, " that the spirit should hate the flesh, by
fighting agsinst it; no, it hates only the vices of the flesh, it hates
the prudence of the flesh, it hates the treachery and contradiction
of the flesh, which is capable of procuring the death of the soul."
(Aug. 1. 1, Serm. de Verb. Apost. ; Serm. 6 in illud, Gal. v. 17.)
For as to the flesh, the spirit loves it in effect by mortifying and
contradicting it just as the physician who hates not his sick
patient, but the disease against which he continually fights, and
is so far from hating, that he loves him very much ; for according
to Aristotle, to love any one, is nothing else than to wish him
well ; and to hate one, is indeed nothing else than to wish him
ill.   Now he who is bent upon mortifying his body, who resists
his irregular desires and appetites, wishes and procures for his
body the greatest good he can ; and a greater good cannot be
procured than its eternal happiness; and therefore such a one
truly loves his body ; but he who caresses and flatters it, and
permits it to follow its bad inclinations, procures the greatest
evil that can befall it, which are everlasting pains and sufferings ;

and therefore such a one truly and in effect, hates his body. For as St. Austin moreover affirms with the royal prophet, " he who loves iniquity hates his soul " (Psal. x. 6), because he procures hell for it; so he who loves iniquity hates his own body, because he procures it the like misfortune. Wherefore divines say, that just and virtuous persons love themselves far better than sinners do, not only in regard of their souls, but in regard of their bodies also; because they wish and procure for them what is truly good, which is eternal happiness, of which the body after its manner partakes with the soul. St. Thomas adds, that for this very reason, the just love their bodies not with an ordinary love, but with the love of charity, which is the most sublime and most excellent of all kinds of love.

This is easily perceived by the example of two sick persons. The one eats and drinks whatsoever he fancies, being unwilling either to be let blood or purged : the other governs himself more prudently, and abstains from eating or drinking though his hunger and thirst be ever so great ; he takes what physic is prescribed him, though ever so bitter or distasteful ; he is content to be let blood, or suffer any other pain which the physician thinks will do him good. Is it not certain, that this last loves his body far better than the first; because to procure its health, he is content to mortify himself in his diet, and to take physic ? And will not all people say, the first in a manner killed himself, because he would not overcome himself by suffering a little mortification for the present ? The same thing happens in our regard ; and this was the answer St. Bernard was wont to give to secular persons, who were astonished at the austerities of his religious, and who said, that without doubt they must needs hate their bodies, since they treated them so ill. "You are deceived,"said he, "it is you that in effect hate your bodies, since for a few passing pleasures you expose them to eternal torments ; and these, my religious, truly love their bodies, since they treat them ill only for a short time here, to gain hereby eternal repose and felicity for them hereafter.

This truth is taught us by the Son of God in the gospel ; for after he had said, " Whosoever will come after me, let him deny himself, take up his cross and follow me," he presently adds this reason : " For he who would save his life shall lose it, and whosoever shall lose his life for my sake shall find it." (Matt. xvi. 24, 25.) St. Austin hereupon cries out, " Behold," says he, " a great and wonderful sentence, that the love of a man for his soul should be the occasion of losing it, and the hatred he shows

towards it, should be the cause of its salvation! So it is," says
he, "if thou hast loved it irregularly, in effect thou hast hated
it ; and if thou hast hated it as thou shouldst do, in effect thou
hast loved it ; because thereby thou hast eternally preserved it ;
according to the words of Jesus Christ, 'whosoever preserves
his soul in this world, preserves it for life everlasting' (John
xii. 25.) Thrice happy," adds this saint, "are those who
have hated it by preserving it, for fear of losing it by loving it
too much ; wherefore take care of loving it too much in this
life, for fear of losing it eternally in the next."

St. Austin also alleges another very solid reason to confirm all
I have said. "We cease not," says he, "to love one thing,
though we love another better ; for example, he who permits
his arm or leg to be cut off to save his life, ceases not to love his
arm or his leg, but he still loves his life more than he does them,
and he parts with a lesser to preserve a greater good." It is
also very certain, that a covetous man loves his money, and
that he extremely desires to keep it ; yet he notwithstanding,
parts with it to procure him necessaries to preserve his life,
because he loves his life better than his money ; and therefore
to keep what is dearer to him, he parts with the other. For
the same reason, he that mortifies his flesh ceases not to love it,
but he loves his soul better ; and he mortifies and treats his
body ill, for no other reason than to save his soul. This, then,
is not to hate our body, but it is to love eternal life better than
our body.

——o——

CHAPTER IX.

*That he who mortifies not himself, leads not the life of a
Christian, nor even of a man.*

ST. AUSTIN says, that the life of beasts is of one kind, that of
angels of another, while the life of man differs from both. The
life of beasts is wholly terrene ; the angels lead a heavenly life,
and are occupied solely with God ; the life of man is partly the
one and partly the other, because man partakes of both natures.
If he lives according to the spirit, he renders himself equal to the
angels ; if according to the flesh, he becomes like unto beasts. This
agrees perfectly well with what St. Ambrose says, that " he who
lives according to the desires and appetites of his body, is flesh ;
and he who lives according to the commandments of God, is all
spirit." (Amb. in Ps. cxviii.) And hence he that lives accord-

ing to the desires of the flesh, does not only lead no spiritual life, nor the life of a rational man, but even the brutish life of beasts. This alone ought to suffice to excite us to mortification ; for what can there be more unworthy, and unbecoming the nobility and generosity of man, created according to the image and likeness of God, and for the purpose of enjoying him eternally, than to make himself like unto beasts ; rendering himself a slave to flesh and sensuality ; governing himself only by the dictates of flesh and blood, and permitting himself to be carried away with the impetuosity of a beastly concupiscence ? "It is a great abuse," says St. Bernard, " for the mistress to serve, and the servant to domineer." (Ber. c. v. Med.) It is properly that disorder of which Solomon speaks, when he says, " that he saw slaves ride on horseback, and princes like slaves walk on foot." (Eccl. x. 7.) " Would you not think it a monstrous thing," says Father Avila, "and that it would surprise the whole world, if a beast should lead a man bound after him, and should oblige him to follow wheresoever it should lead him ? Yet, notwithstanding, there are a great many people of all sorts, who let themselves be led by beastly appetites, and the greatness of their number makes them to be less taken notice of, and is the cause why so strange a thing as this is not wondered at—a circumstance no less surprising than the thing itself." It is related of Diogenes, that walking with a lantern and a lighted candle in it at mid-day, in the market-place of Athens, as if he looked for something he had lost, one asked him what he sought for ? "I seek a man," says he. "Do you not see a great many," replied the other ; "the market place is full of them ?" "You are deceived," says he, "they are not men, but irrational creatures; because they live not as men, but as beasts, permitting themselves to be led by their beastly appetites."

St. Austin takes from certain tricks, which rope dancers, or tumblers are wont to play, an example which is adapted to our present subject, and which explains it very well. "He who permits his flesh to domineer over him," says he, "is in God's and the angels' sight, like one who walks upon his hands, or stands upon his head." (Ser. 1, ad. fr. in erem.) Is there anything more contemptible, or of less esteem amongst us, than persons of this description are ? And yet we permit ourselves to fall every day into the like contempt, subjecting our reason to the flesh, and are not at all ashamed of it. Seneca had far more honourable and reasonable thoughts, when he said : "I am born for a more noble end, than to become a slave to my body."

These words deserve to be engraved on the hearts, not only of all Christians, but of all religious persons likewise. Now, if a pagan, iluminated only by the light of nature, thought this a shameful and ignoble thing; what ought a Christian, aided with the light of faith, or a religious man, prevented and favoured with so many extraordinary blessings and graces, to think it? Wherefore, St. Austin had reason to say, whosoever is not sensible of this shame and ignominy, has entirely lost the use of reason ; and is become a monster, that deserves more to be wondered at, than a man who should be changed into a beast, without his perceiving it, or being at all troubled at it.

Galen relates, that when he was very young he one day saw a man run with a key in his hand to open a door ; but when he could not open it, having out of too much haste set the key fast in the lock, he fell into such a fury, that he began to take the key between his teeth, and to break open the door with his feet : afterwards he began to blaspheme, even foaming at the mouth like a madman, his eyes sparkling and inflamed with rage, which seemed as if they would start out of his head. "This sight," says Galen, "gave me such a horror of anger and choler, and so great an apprehension of falling into the like disorder, that since, I do not remember to have been angry upon any account." All this ought to teach us how to live like reasonable creatures, without permitting ourselves to fall into passion. St. Jerome, writing upon these words of Job : " There was a man in the land of Hus, called Job ;" says, "he was truly a man," presently giving the reason why he was so, "because in him the flesh did not command the spirit, but he regulated all his actions according to the command of reason ;" as the Scripture ordains : "your appetite shall be subject to you, and you shall command it." (Gen. iv. 7.)

——o——

CHAPTER X.

That there is less pain and trouble in mortifying than in not mortifying ourselves.

I CLEARLY see, some one will say, of what profit, and how necessary mortification is, however I cannot at the same time but think of the pain and difficulty found therein ; and it is *this* which deters me from it. To this I answer, first, with St. Basil, that if for the health of our body we willingly take bitter medicines ; if we suffer most cruel operations in surgery ; if, to gather together a little riches, men expose themselves to so many dangers, both by sea and land, and overcome all obstacles in their way ; what ought we not to do for the spiritual health of our soul, and to gain everlasting riches ? Is it not just that we should undertake all things possible, and that we should not be afraid of any difficulty ? Notwithstanding, because we are naturally willing and inclined to avoid all pain and labour, and that, in the indispensable necessity we are all in of suffering, we would suffer as little as possible ; I answer in the second place, that there is more pain in avoiding, than embracing mortification. "It is by your order, O Lord," says St. Austin, "that all irregularity of mind should carry its punishment along with it." (Conf. i. 1, c. 12.) This interior irregularity of the appetite in regard of reason, and of reason in regard of God, causes very great pain and uneasiness in man ; and it is the same in all other things of the world. For what is there in nature, which is not in disquiet and disorder, and does not suffer very much, whilst it is not in that state or situation in which the law of nature has ordained and placed it ? What pain does not a bone out of joint occasion ? What violence do not natural bodies suffer when they are out of their element ? Now, since it is so very natural to man to live according to reason, ought not nature to cry out against him ? And ought not his own conscience continually check him, when he leads a life so contrary to the dictates of reason ? "Who is able to resist him," says Job, speaking of God, "and enjoy any peace ?" (Job. ix. 4.) We can never hope to be in peace with ourselves, living in this manner ; and therefore St. John says in the Apocalypse, "that those who adored the beast, enjoyed no peace day or night."— (Apoc. xiv.) Your flesh, your sensuality, is the beast ; if you will be subject to it, you will never enjoy any peace.

Physicians say, that health and a good disposition of body, consists in a due habit, and a just proportion of the humours ; when this habit comes to be altered, the irregularity of the humours causes great pains and diseases ; but when the humours are well tempered, they produce a marvellous health, and cause a cheerfulness and vigour in our bodies. The same happens in the health and good disposition of the soul. It consists in the regularity and moderating of our passions, which are so many humours belonging to it. When they are not tempered and mortified, they occasion spiritual diseases ; but when they are well regulated, the soul enjoys a perfect health ; of which joy and peace are the inseparable companions. The passions in the heart of man are also compared to high winds at sea ; for as the winds agitate and disturb the sea, and trouble its calm, by their impetuous and violent gales, so our passions, by their motions and irregular appetites, raise tempests in our hearts, and disturb our peace. Sometimes anger or choler raises a storm ; sometimes a blast of pride and vain-glory domineers and transports us farther than they should do ; sometimes impatience, sometimes envy does the like ; and therefore the prophet Isaias said very well, " the wicked are like a rough and raging sea, which cannot be calmed or quieted." (Isa. lvii. 20.) But as soon as these winds are appeased, presently a calm follows: "He commanded the winds and the sea," says the gospel, " and a very great calm followed." (Matt. viii. 26.) If you know therefore how to command the winds of your passions and appetites by mortifying them, and subjecting them to reason, you will enjoy a wonderful peace and tranquillity. But so long as you do not apply yourself in this manner to appease them, you will be subject to continual tempests. But still, to let you see more clearly that he who hates and flies mortification, suffers more pain and carries a far heavier cross than he who embraces it, let us descend to particulars, and reflect upon what we daily experience. See what disposition of mind you are in, when it happens that you permit yourself to be so far transported with choler and impatience, as to give ill-language to your brother, or to do something that gives scandal ! What pain, what trouble, what discontent, what uneasiness do you find in yourself ? It is very certain, that the pain you feel hereby is far greater than that you would have felt in mortifying and moderating your passions. Consider, moreover, how great the fears are of a religious person that has not the spirit of mortification, indifference, and resignation to whatsoever obedience shall think fit to impose upon him ; one thing only to which he has a repugnance is sufficient to keep him continually upon the rack, because he has a continual idea thereof before his eyes ; and though superiors, perhaps, think not at all of imposing such an obedience ; yet knowing it to be what they may command, should it come into their minds, and that it is what they sometimes have commanded, and not knowing but they may do so to him, he is in continual alarms and frights about it. And as a man who has the gout in his hands and feet, imagines that all who are about him may come so near as to hurt him, so a religious, who has not the spirit of mortification, is always afraid that superiors are about to order what gives him the greatest pain and difficulty. When, on the other hand, he who is indifferent to all employments, and resigned to all things, is always cheerful, is always content, and has nothing to be afraid of. Take notice also, how much a proud and vain-glorious man suffers when he sees himself forgotten—when he is made no account of, and when he is put in no great or honourable employment. And if some employment be given him, to content his vanity, or if he is ordered to do anything extraordinary in public, what disquiet does he not undergo, lest he should not come off well ; and lest he should get more shame than honour and glory, which he proposed to himself in the performance thereof ? So that his pride torments him every way ; and the same he also suffers in all other things. Your passions are so many executioners, that continually torment you, so long as you do not labour to mortify yourself : whether what they urge you to desire and covet happens or not, yet pain always remains, so long as you obtain not what you desire; " the hopes which are deferred afflict the mind," (Prov. xiii. 14), and even when that is obtained or effected which was desired, this also gives pain and trouble to a religious, as often as he thinks upon it. What ! Have I then performed what I aimed at, and got thereby no merit at all, because I only sought my own will and satisfaction therein ? And thus all the sweetness of the action is presently turned into gall and bitterness.

Add to this the remorse of conscience which always accompanies a person that does not apply himself to mortification, and who does not his duty. For what satisfaction can a religious find, who, having entered into religion to advance in virtue and perfection, labours not at all to make any progress therein ? It is impossible but he must interiorly suffer a great deal of trouble and disquiet of mind. We may say the same of any one who does not his duty in what calling or condition soever he is ; for we always carry about us the worm of conscience, which gnaws our bowels with continual remorse, whilst we do not perform our duty. Father Avila says very well, that should we put in one scale of the balance all the pains required to perform our duties well, and to live with the spirit of fervour and mortification; and in the other scale, all those who suffer by the neglect of our duty, and by our negligence and tepidity therein ; we should find the last a thousand times to outweigh the first. It is a thing very much to be wondered at, that he who serves God with fervour, should find more pleasure and satisfaction in fasting, watching, and praying, and in all other mortifications he meets with, than a loose and tepid religious feels in all his conversations, entertainments, and seeming sweetness of an easy life, and in the full enjoyment of his own will. A tepid religious is outwardly cheerful, whilst he is bitterly afflicted within ; but a just man always feels a holy joy in his heart, even in the midst of all his suffering. " The way of the slothful," says the wise man, " is like a hedge of thorns." (Prov. xv. 19.) That is to say, in all they do, they are always as if they were walking upon thorns ; and it is to such as these to whom God speaks by the prophet Osee, when he says : " behold I have encompassed your way with thorns." (Osee ii. 6.) He wills, that even the pastimes and pleasures that they take in following their own will, should be always mingled with remorse, bitterness, and discontent; and here it is that the tepid and negligent find those thorns which prick them, and even pierce their hearts. " But there is no stumbling-block in the way of the just ; their path is very smooth." (Prov. xv. 19.) What peace, what satisfaction is enjoyed by a good and truly mortified religious, who takes to heart his spiritual advancement, and performs what a true religious person ought to do ? There is no content like unto his. We daily experience, that when we serve God with fervour, we feel such joy and interior satisfaction as cannot be expressed; and when we serve him tepidly and negligently we fall into dejection and disquiet. And, in effect, it is very often the cause of that sadness and bitterness we feel, as I shall afterwards show in its due place. So that sometimes, to evade a little pain, we cause ourselves far greater : according to the words of Job, " he that fears frost, shall be overwhelmed with snow." (Job vi. 16.) You say because you are afraid of trouble, you do not mortify ysurself ; and I say, that if this were your motive ; if you wished to enjoy true peace of soul, and if you derived therefrom no other advantage, you ought to labour to mortify yourself. With how far greater reason then ought you do it, since you will thereby gain many other advantages.

———o———

CHAPTER XI.

In which I begin to treat of the exercise of mortification.

THE chief disposition we must bring on our part, in order to gain this mortification, and to overcome ourselves is, courageously to exercise ourselves in putting down our own wills; in opposing our appetites; in not gratifying our flesh, nor allowing it anything it desires. In this manner we shall overcome nature by little and little; we shall root out our vicious and ill habits; we shall become masters of our passions; and virtue will begin to enter, to take possession, and to fortify itself in our souls. St. Dorotheus, gives a very profitable instruction upon this subject. "When you are tormented by any passion or bad inclination," says he, "if you be so weak as to yield to it and to go wheresoever it would lead you, believe it for a certain truth, that it will take deeper root and become stronger and stronger; and from that time forward it will wage a more violent war against you, and give you greater pain and difficulty. But, if at the first onset, you courageously resist it, it will daily diminish; and it will every day have less strength to set upon you, till at length it will come to have no strength at all, nor will be able any more to disquiet you."

This counsel is very profitable and powerful against temptations, for the same reason, as I shall prove hereafter; and, without doubt, it imports us very much to resist by times, lest the ill habit should grow stronger in us, and make us fall into greater inconveniences. The saints counsel us to behave towards our body as a good horseman does, who being mounted upon a mettlesome steed that is hardmouthed, does not fail however to master him by his skill and vigour; and makes him go where and at what gait he pleases. We must do the same—we must, as he does, always keep a stiff rein, and now and then clap spurs to his sides, and by this means, we shall tame our body, do with it what we please, carry it wherever we choose, and at what pace we think proper. But if we have not skill and vigour to keep him in, and to manage him well, he will become our master, will run away with us, and cast us headlong into some precipice. When a horse is stubborn the mode ordinarily used to correct him, is not to give him his way upon any occasion. We must do the same towards our flesh, to overcome its stubbornness and bad inclinations. We must not suffer it to do any thing it fancies, but contradict it in all things : we must, in the height and heat of its desires and appetites, keep a strong hand upon it, and not gratify it upon any account.

It will be very profitable for us to excite ourselves to this exercise, and always to act from this motive. The outward man, that is our flesh and sensuality, is the greatest enemy we have, and in this quality he continually endeavours to destroy us, by rebelling against the interior spirit, against reason, and even against God himself. One of the chief reasons why the saints say, that the knowledge of ourselves is one of the most efficacious means to overcome all temptations, is, because he who applies himself to this knowledge sees very well his own weakness and misery, and therefore he no sooner discovers any bad thought or desire in himself, but he perceives it to be a temptation of his enemy, who would deceive him, and cast him headlong into a precipice ; and hence, instead of hearkening to it, or believing what it suggests, he carefully stands upon his guard. But he who knows not himself, or studies not to acquire this knowledge, perceives not the temptation when it comes, and does not believe it to be one ; especially if it suits with his inclination. On the contrary, he imagines that what in reality is a temptation, is a reasonable thought ; and that which in effect is sensuality, appears to him a pure necessity, and thus he easily yields. Wherefore, convince yourself well that you have to do with your greatest enemy; that all those bad desires and temptations you feel are the treasons of your flesh and blood, and of your sensuality ; that you have in them a mortal enemy who seeks your destruction ; and by this means it will be far more easy for you to overcome and mortify yourself; for who is so foolish as to confide in his enemy ?

St. Bernard, who makes an excellent reflection upon this matter, says, "that we must treat ourselves, that is, our bodies, as we would treat a sick person committed to our charge; to whom we ought to refuse whatsoever would do him hurt, though he should desire it ever so earnestly ; and oblige him to take, even against his will, what would do him good." If we were fully convinced that we are sick persons, and that our desires and irregular appetites are only such longings after what is hurtful to us as sick persons commonly have, and that they are the temptations of our enemy, who would destroy us ; how easy would it be for us to drive them away, and thereby to overcome him ? But if, instead of believing yourself sick, you believe you are in perfect health; and instead of looking upon yourself as the greatest enemy you have, you think yourself the truest and best friend, you are in great danger. For how can you evade an evil which you do not perceive; or how can you resist one whom you look upon as a friend? And how can you doubt of that which, so far from thinking to be a deception, you firmly believe to be a truth, and far from the least deceit?

St. Dorotheus relates, that having the charge of spiritual things in the monastery where he lived, all the religious came to give him an account of their temptations; and amongst the rest, one came to discover the temptation of gluttony, which very much tormented him. As one disorder commonly causes another, this temptation was so great as to make him steal, in order to get something to eat. The saint having sweetly asked the cause of his theft, he answered, that it was because they gave him not enough at table to satisfy his hunger, which even devoured him. St. Dorotheus counselled him to go and make known his wants to the abbot. But perceiving that he had a great difficulty to do so, and that he was ashamed to speak to his superior thereof, he goes to the abbot himself, and makes known the necessity of this religious. The abbot leaving the whole matter to be managed by the saint as he should judge best, the saint called for the dispenser who gives out meat and drink, and commanded him to give this religious whatsoever he should desire, and as often as he should ask for it. The dispenser obeyed, and the religious having in abundance whatsoever he could desire, passed some days without stealing any thing; but returning by little and little to his former bad habit, he goes all bathed in tears to the saint, discovers his fault to him, and begs a penance for it. For he had still this quality, which was very good in him, that he made known his defects as soon as he had committed them, which is a very proper means soon to overcome them. St. Dorotheus asked him, whether the dispenser had given him what he asked for, and whether he had ever refused him anything? The religious answered, no; but that he was ashamed to go so often as his hunger urged him. "And would you be ashamed or afraid," says the saint, "to come to me, now you know I am not ignorant of your temptation?" He answered, that he should not be ashamed at all; whereupon the saint ordered him to come to him when he wanted anything, and he would supply him, and therefore advised him to steal no more. St. Dorotheus at that time had care of the sick and treated him very well, which hindered him for a little while from stealing. But after some time he returned to his bad habit; and then, full of tears and confusion, he discovered his fault, begged pardon, and desired a penance for it. " But how, dear brother, comes it to pass," says the saint, " since you say you are not ashamed nor afraid of coming to me, and you receive from me what you desire, that you still persist in your ill custom of stealing ? " " I neither can conceive this," replied he, " nor the reason why I steal; it is, without doubt, the bad habit I have got that moves me to it. For I neither want anything, nor do I eat what I steal, but even give it to the horses." And in effect they went to his chamber, and there under his bed they found several things to eat, which he had hidden and left there till they were spoiled, and then not knowing what to do with them, he carried them to the stables, and gave them to the horses. " We may perceive by this," says St. Dorotheus, " the deplorable condition to which a bad habit or passion leads us, and, therefore, how great reason we have to look upon ourselves as sick persons, and as our own greatest enemies." The religious easily perceived he did ill, was afflicted for it, and wept to see himself faulty, and yet could not refrain from falling into the same fault. Wherefore, the abbot Nisqueron said very well, that we become slaves to our passions and bad habits, when we once permit ourselves to be led by them.

————o————

CHAPTER XII.

How the exercise of mortification ought to be put in practice.

SINCE the exercise of mortification is the chief means we can make use of to overcome ourselves, and to master our passions and irregular appetites, it is fit I should explain more particularly what you ought to do, to put this exercise in practice. The general rule given in things of this sort is, to look to what is most necessary, and first of all to endeavour to obtain that. Begin this exercise then, by profiting of those occasions of mortification which are daily offered you by your superiors, your brethren, or by any cause whatsoever. Receive all with a good will, and make your profit of them; because it is what is most necessary for your own peace, as well as for the edification of your neighbour. The advantage we must derive from mortifications ought to make us love them so far as continually to importune our superiors to mortify us in something; to command us those things to which we have the greatest repugnance; to impose penance upon us; and to give us particular reprehensions in public. But if your fervour carries you not thus far, take at least in good part, and bear patiently, the occasions of mortification that present themselves, and which God sends you for your good, and greater advancement in perfection. Many of them offer every day; and if we attended to them, with design to profit by them, we should daily find sufficient matter of mortification. For, first, as to those that may happen to us in the point of obedience; you will oftentimes think that they command you the hardest things, and that the whole burden is put upon you, whilst others ought to bear their part: and does it not frequently happen that something or other in every thing you do gives you some pain and mortification? Reap profit from this—prepare yourself for it, and believe that the difficulty you feel in it is the cross you are to carry after the Son of God. At another time, subject of mortification will arise from your meat, drink, lodging, or clothing; rejoice, as the rule counsels, that the worst things of the house are given to you. Again, it will happen, that a superior will give you a penance, or reprehend you for what you think has not deserved it, or at least that your fault was not so great as he makes it, and that the matter was otherwise represented to him than it happened. Well, then, be glad of what has passed—do not excuse yourself nor make any complaint at all, nor say anything in your own defence to make your ignorance appear. Hence, if we will profit of all these cases of mortification that happen to us from our neighbour or brethren, we shall meet with a sufficient number of all sorts; some will mortify us unintentionally; others through negligence, but without a bad intention; whilst others, in fine, will mortify us either through contempt, or through want of due esteem and concern for us. But if we consider those which God immediately sends us, as sickness, temptations, disquiet of mind, the unequal distribution of his gifts, as well natural as supernatural: we shall find them to be numberless, and that an infinity of these daily present themselves. Behold here the occasions, in which we ought, in the first place, to exercise mortification; and since these occasions happen continually, and depend not at all upon us, we must endeavour to make a virtue of necessity, that being obliged to suffer them, we may reap some fruit from them. But, besides the spiritual profit we shall hereby gain, we shall also spare

ourselves a great deal of labour and pains, if we receive them
well ; because oftentimes it happens that the difficulty we find
in things comes not so much from the things themselves, as from
the contradiction and repugnance of our own wills; and hence,
the great secret of rendering them easy and supportable is to
embrace them with a good and cheerful heart.

There are other mortifications which we must also voluntarily
practise. They are called active, in order to distinguish them
from those mortifications which, because we are not at liberty to
suffer, or not to suffer them, are called passive. But though the
active mortifications are to be received voluntarily, yet they are
necessary ; and, of course, are to be placed in the first rank. Of
these some are necessary in order to our becoming true Christians,
and for the attainment of our salvation ; as is the mortifying
ourselves in whatsoever hinders the observance of God's commandments. Others are necessary in order to our becoming good
religious men, and acquiring perfection ; as the observing our
rules of religion, and the performing well whatever is required
of us by obedience. For it is certain, not only all sins, but also
all negligences and imperfections into which we fall in the way
of virtue, spring only from a want of mortification ; and from
our eagerness to avoid some pain that we find in the exercise of
virtue and perfection, or from our unwillingness to abstain from
some pleasure we experience in bad and vicious courses. But let
us descend to a more particular examen of matter of fact : for
example, when we offend against obedience, against the observance of rules, against temperance, against silence, against modesty, against patience, or, in fine, against any other virtue
whatsoever, we find it always through want of mortification ;
it is because that either we will not undergo the pain annexed
to these virtues, or will not deprive ourselves of the pleasure we
take in committing the vices contrary to them. Now, as in order
to become good Christians, and to save our souls, we must mortify ourselves in all things that are opposite to the law of God,
according to the words of Jesus Christ, "He that desires to follow
me, let him deny himself," (Matt. xvi. 24), and if he does not
deny and mortify himself in this point, he can never be a good
Christian, or save his soul: even so, to become good religious,
and to attain perfection, we must mortify ourselves in all things
that are contrary to the state of perfection. Look, then, upon
all things you do from morning till night ; take notice of what
hinders you from performing your ordinary actions with due

perfection; and endeavour to remove that impediment, and strive to mortify yourself in that, which is the cause why you do not what you ought to do ; and by this means, your actions daily becoming better and more perfect, you yourself will also become better and more perfect. For the whole affair of your spiritual advancement depends upon resolving to do what I have said.

A religious proposing this question—how it could come to pass, that having very good desires, yet he found himself, notwithstanding, very weak in executing them, and fell into many faults, without being able to arrive at perfection—they to whom he proposed it attributed this weakness to a want of attending to himself ; and each one prescribed what means he judged most profitable for him. But they prescribing several, which he found did him no good at all, he at length addressed himself to an ancient father, well versed in spirituality, who told him that this happened not from a want of attending to himself, but rather from a want of courage and resolution. It is this, therefore, which is in effect the cause why we make so little progress in virtue, and why we cannot compass an entire correction of our faults and defects. Take courage, then, and make a firm resolution of mortifying yourself in what I have spoken of, and by this means you will soon become perfect.

———o———

CHAPTER XIII.

Of mortification in lawful and indifferent things, as also in those that are of obligation.

It seems as if nothing could be added to what has already been said, and that the two kinds of mortification before mentioned are sufficient to make us become good and perfect religious, and that nothing remains but to exercise ourselves therein ; but that we may the better effect it, and dispose ourselves thereunto, the masters of a spiritual life establish another exercise of mortification in such things as are lawful for us, either to do or to omit. Good Christians are not content to perform the things only that are purely of obligation, and necessary for salvation, but they also perform others of devotion, which divines call works of supererogation. For they are not content to hear mass upon days of precept only, but upon other days also. They give themselves to particular practices of devotion, and frequently approach the sacraments of confession and communion. A good religious ought not to content himself with the bare observance only of his rule, and with the practice of such mortifications as that prescribes; but must impose others upon himself, by depriving himself of such things as are permitted. St. Dorotheus says, that there is nothing so much helps to our progress in virtue, and the acquiring of peace and tranquillity of mind, as to oppose and resist our own will; and teaches us, at the same time, the means to mortify it in such things as are permitted us to make use of. "You are going somewhere," says he, "and you have a great mind to turn about and look upon something in the way; overcome your curiosity, and do not look at it. You are in conversation, something occurs to your mind that is much to the purpose, and it seems to you, that the saying it would make you pass for a wit; let it alone, say nothing of it. A thought occurs of going to the kitchen to see what is making ready; do not hearken to it. By chance you cast your eyes upon something brought into the house that is new, and you wish to know who brought it; ask not who did so. You see a stranger enter, curiosity urges you to know who he is, whence he comes, whither he goes, and for what business; mortify yourself by making no inquiry after him."

St. Dorotheus says, this exercise helps very much to get a habit of mortifying your will; because if we accustom ourselves to renounce our own will in these small things, we shall the sooner be able to deprive ourselves of greater. As those who design to make themselves soldiers practise, in time of peace, military evolutions, which, though but mock-fights, yet qualify them for real combats; even so a religious must endeavour to mortify himself, and renounce his will in small things that are permitted and lawful for him to do; that he may be the more ready, and better disposed to mortify himself in those which are forbidden. St. Bonaventure teaches the same practice of mortification in things which are indifferent; as in plucking or not plucking a flower when one walks in a garden; "for," says he, "though there is no hurt in plucking it, yet it is very pleasing to God to refrain from it; thereby to mortify and overcome ourselves. Wherefore," he adds, " that a servant of God ought often to say within himself, for the love of you, my God, I will deprive myself of the sight of this, of hearing that; of tasting this or that, or of taking this or that recreation." It is related of St. Borgia, that while in the world, he loved hawking very much, and was wont to fly his hawks at the heron; but the moment the falcon darted on her prey, he looked on the ground, and took, as I may say, the lure from his eyes, depriving them of that pleasure which, with a great deal of pains, they had all the day long sought after. St. Gregory says, that it is peculiar to the servants of God to deprive themselves of those things they may lawfully make use of, that they may be the further from making use of such as are unlawful. The ancient fathers, also, of the desert, brought up their disciples in this exercise, hindering them from doing little things they had a wish to do, in which there was no sin or imperfection ; and making them do such as they had no mind to do, hereby to teach them to mortify themselves in all things; and to render them able to stand the proof even in the very hardest. It is from these fathers that the society has taken that custom or practice which, in the beginning, it observes towards the novices; employing them in various things, and sometimes making them leave off what they had begun; at other times making them undo what they had done, or obliging them to do it over again; and all this to hinder them from any attachment to their own wills and judgments, and to habituate them betimes to divest themselves of them.

The saints advance yet farther in this point. They are not content that we should accustom ourselves to put down our own will in indifferent and innocent things only; but they counsel us to mortify ourselves in such as are absolutely necessary. But it may be said, how can this be done? Must we, to mortify ourselves, dispense with our obligations ? No ! by no means; " we must not do evil, that good may come from it."—(Rom. iii. 8.) What then are we to do? The saints have found out a wonderful secret in this point ; and they have taken it from the doctrine of St. Paul. Take care, say they, to do nothing, to think nothing, to speak nothing purely to please your own will, or to satisfy your sensual appetite. Before meals mortify in yourself your desire of eating; and eat not to satisfy your appetite, but to obey God, who will have you eat to nourish yourself ; and imitate the abbot Isidore, of whom Palladius relates, that he was wont to weep as he went to the refectory, and went there only through obedience. Before you go to study, mortify your desire thereof, and then study, because God commands you to do so, and not because you find any pleasure in your studies. Before you go into the pulpit to preach, or to explain any public lesson, mortify your own desire of doing it ; and then preach or teach, not because you have a desire of it, but because it is what you are commanded to do ; and because it is God's will. Observe the same practice in all other things ; and thus depriving every action of the attachment you have thereunto, perform them all purely for God's sake. For it is not fit that they should lead or draw us after them ; but we must be masters of them, to carry and offer them to God alone, and to do nothing but for his sake ; according to the words of the apostle St. Paul ; "whether you eat or drink, or whatsoever you do, do all to the glory of God." (1 Cor. x. 31.)

This point is without any doubt very considerable, and contains in it a very sublime spirituality ; *i.e.* to do nothing, even of what belongs to our charge or employment, for the pleasure we take in it, but only for God's sake ; to accustom ourselves, in all our actions, not to do our own, but his will ; and to take delight in them, not because they are pleasant in themselves, and because our inclination moves us to perform them ; but because in doing them, we do the will of God. He who shall perform them in this manner, will at the same time accustom himself, not only to mortify his own will, but also to do the will of God in all things— which is an exercise of the love of God, the most sublime, most profitable, and of the highest perfection, as I have elsewhere proved.

And here is opened to us a spacious field indeed ; so that whosoever would apply himself particularly to the mortification of his will, must by little and little raise himself by those degress or steps, which we have marked out in these two chapters. To do this he must in the first place endeavour to mortify himself in those things which, without being sought for, present themselves. In this practice he will for some days find enough to do ; nay, even for many days ; especially if we would bring ourselves not only to bear crosses with patience, but to receive them with joy. This is the third and most perfect degree of mortification, as I shall prove hereafter. Secondly, we must mortify our wills in whatsoever hinders us from doing such things as are necessary to make us good religious, to observe our rules, and to live with edification; and these things can scarce be numbered. In the third place, we must mortify ourselves in some of those things which we may lawfully perform ; that we may the better hereby accustom ourselves to cast off our own wills in other things that are of obligation ; and be the better disposed to do so. And to this effect we may purpose to mortify ourselves so many times in the morning, and so many times in the afternoon ; beginning at first with a small number, and going on every day increasing, according to the progress we make in perfection—imitating certain religious persons of our society whom I knew, who counted their mortifications upon the beads of their rosary, and every day completed the number thereof ; as it appeared very well, by the great progress they made in virtue. In the fourth and last place, we may extend this mortification even to those things that are of obligation ; endeavouring to perform them, not only because they are pleasing to us, but because they are ordained by God ; and this practice is of so great perfection, that we may continue it during our whole lives.

I add, moreover, that always keeping the same order in the points which I have now set down, we may also observe this practice as an exercise of conformity to the will of God ; receiving all things as coming from his hand, and as sent us by him with the tender and compassionate bowels of a father, for our greater good ; imagining that Jesus Christ himself says to us ; son, I would have you to do this, or suffer that at present. For by this means we shall find so great facility and sweetness therein, that it will at length become such an exercise of the love of God, as will render all things easy and pleasant. The thought alone that what we perform is the will of God, and that he desires this of us, is what will prevent our sticking or making any demur at all in the performance, but will absolutely determine us to do it ; which motive is also the most profitable and most perfect that can be imagined.

We read in the life of St. Francis Borgia, that departing one day very late from Valladolid, whilst it froze and snowed very hard, to go to Simanques, wherein was the house of novices, he arrived thither not till it was very late at night, after the novices were all gone to bed. He remained a long time knocking at the gate, the snow all the while falling in great flakes upon him ; and every one being in his first sleep, and the gate being a good distance from that part of the house where they lodged, no one made answer. At length they heard him, and went to open the gate ; and because he perceived the novices were extremely troubled for having made him wait so long at the gate, where all were trembling and stiff with cold, he said to them with a cheerful countenance : " Dear brothers, be not troubled, or in any pain at all. I assure you, God gave me a great deal of comfort whilst I was waiting. For I thought it was he that caused the snow to fall upon me, and made the wind to blow ; that whatsoever he does he performs with an infinite satisfaction ; and consequently, that I ought to rejoice at the satisfaction he took in mortifying me, and make his pleasure become mine ; as we see for the pleasure of some great prince, they often kill and cut lions and bulls in pieces." It is in this manner that we ought to receive all occasions of mortification. by entertaining a holy joy and satisfaction, that the will of God is fulfilled in us.

———o———

CHAPTER XIV.

That we ought to mortify ourselves chiefly in that vice or passion which predominates in us, and causes us to fall into the greatest faults.

It is written in the first book of Kings, that God, by the mouth of Samuel, commanded Saul entirely to destroy the Amalecites ; not to spare sex or age, but to kill all, even their herds of cattle, and domestic creatures. " Saul," notwithstanding, and all the people," says the scripture, " pardoned Agag, and spared the fairest and the best amongst the flocks and spoils, and destroyed all the rest which was of little or no value." (1 Reg. xv. 9.) There are many persons that now-a-days do the same. They mortify themselves in small matters, but spare themselves in great things that are of importance ; and hereby still persist in their ill habits. But it is for such as these, I say, that what is most precious and dear to us, is what we must chiefly take notice of, to mortify ourselves therein, and to make a a sacrifice thereof to God. What then did Samuel do ? He goes and finds out Saul, gives him a short reprehension on God's part, caused Agag king of Amalec to be brought before him ; " and Agag, who was very fat, being brought to him, Samuel cut him in pieces before our Lord." (1 Reg. xv. 32, 33.) Behold what you ought to do ; you must destroy the king of the Amalecites, that is to say, sacrifice to God, by means of mortification, that passion which chiefly reigns in you, that vanity, this pride with which you are puffed up, that desire of glory and reputation, this impatience, this bad and untractable humour wherein you abound.

There are some who labour strenuously thereat, and who make sanctity consist in the exterior—in preserving a meek and edifying manner, and in displaying great moderation in all they do. But as to interior mortification, which is of greatest importance, they think not at all of it ; but, on the contrary, are attached only to their own wills and judgments, and are more jealous of their honour and fame than any one can be. To such as these we may say in some measure, what our Saviour said to the scribes and pharisees : " wo to you, scribes and pharisees, who make clean the outside of your cups and dishes, and yet are full of rapine and impurity within. Blind pharisees, first make clean the inside of the cup and platter, that the outside may also become clean." (Matt. xxiii. 25.) Make clean therefore, and mortify first your interior, if you would have your exterior neat and clean. For if this exterior modesty proceeds not from an interior peace and tranquillity of mind, all this is but deceit and hypocrisy. " You are," says our Saviour, " like painted sepulchres, which appear fair on the outside to the eyes of men, but within are full of dead men's bones, and all kinds of corruption." (Ibid. v. 27.) And what he said a little before in the same chapter, is more to our purpose. " Wo be to you, scribes and pharisees, who pay your tithes of mint, anise, and cummin, and have neglected what is of greater importance in the law, which is judgment, mercy, and faith." (Ibid. v. 23.) This is exactly adapted to our subject ; because there are some who take great care to mortify themselves in small matters, which cost them little or nothing ; but what hurts or touches them to the quick, they take very great care to avoid. This, however, is what we must attack —this passion, this vice, this bad inclination, this ill habit which most of all reigns within us, which leads and governs us, which exposes us to greatest dangers, and causes us to fall into the worst of faults—it is this we ought chiefly to mortify. We see by experience, that there is scarce any one but feels within himself some one thing that makes a more dangerous war against him than all the rest ; and that more strongly opposes his spiritual advancement in perfection. It is to this that every one is particularly to apply himself, to endeavour by mortification to draw it out by the root. It is upon this we ought chiefly to cast our eyes, in our particular examen, and must dwell upon in our prayer ; because it is this which each one has most need to reform in himself.

———o———

CHAPTER XV.

That we must not neglect the mortifying ourselves in small matters, and how pleasing this kind of mortification is unto God, and useful for our advancement in perfection.

WE must so fix our eyes upon great things, as not to neglect those of less importance ; and this admonition is addressed to those who neglect lesser mortifications and make no account of them, looking upon them as trifles, that help not to our spiritual advancement and perfection. This is a very great error, which the Son of God takes notice of, in the reprehension he gives to the scribes and pharisees. For he blames not the care they had taken of small things, but the neglect they had of greater and more essential. " These," says he, " ought to have been done, and the others not to have been left undone." (Matt. xxxiii. 23.) I have already very often repeated how much it imports to make account of little things, and not to neglect them ; and in truth it is a point of so great importance, that it deserves very often to be spoken of, lest through this door laxity and disorder should enter, as happens but too frequently. But I shall now speak only of what regards our present subject, and for this reason shall explain two things ; the one, of what advantage these sorts of mortification are ; the other, how dangerous a thing it is to neglect them. As to the first, how pleasing these kinds of mortifications, though but small, are unto God, and of how great merit they are unto us, may easily be comprehended, if we consider that the chief thing in mortification consists, not in the performance of the austerity, but in the casting off our own will, for that is properly the true mortification and renouncing of ourselves that Jesus Christ requires of us in the gospel. But we may renounce our own wills no less in little than in great things, and sometimes even more, and with greater merit, if they be more contrary to our inclinations. We daily experience that such things as are very small in themselves, give us a great deal more pain than those which are more considerable ; because mortification consists not so much in the things themselves, as in the repugnance our will has to them. So that when we mortify ourselves in anything whatsoever, we offer a sacrifice of our wills unto God, striving with them, and overcoming them for the love of God. And as in this we offer the choicest thing we have, which is our will, so we may say, that in sacrificing that, we make an entire sacrifice of ourselves,

St. Ambrose, upon this account, examines what the scripture says of David, when he was encamped in sight of the Philistines, and his whole army was in great want of water; " Oh," says the king, " that any one would get me some of the water of the fountain of Bethlem !" (1 Paral. xi. 17), which was beyond the enemies' camp. Whereupon, three brave soldiers, hearing him say this, departed presently, twice passed the army of the Philistines, and brought to David the water of this fountain. But the Scripture adds, " that he who would not drink of it, but made a sacrifice of effusion to our Lord, by pouring it forth and offering it unto him." (1 Paral. v. 18.) Is it therefore so great a sacrifice to offer a pot of water to our Lord? " Yes," says St. Ambrose, " it was a great sacrifice, and very pleasing unto God ; and fully to convince us of this truth, it is enough that the Scripture speaks of it as one of David's greatest exploits. But would you know," says St. Ambrose, " in what the greatness of this action consists? He overcame nature by not drinking in extreme thirst, and thereby taught the whole army by his own example how to support the thirst they suffered.—(Apol. de Dav. c. vii.) It was not only the pot of water he offered, but it was his own will ; and therefore in the mortifying ourselves, though in ever so small things, it is the will always that is sacrificed unto God, and consequently it is a sacrifice of great value that we offer unto him, which is always very pleasing to his Divine Majesty.

St. Gregory also relates another example of David, to the same purpose as this, which St. Ambrose mentions. The scripture in the second book of Kings says, that David transported the ark of the covenant unto the city of Sion, with very great solemnity : and it is to be supposed that the people in those times were wont to dance before the ark of God, when they carried it from one place to another, as the Spaniards at present are wont to do, in the processions of the blessed sacrament. David, as great a prince as he was, altogether forgetting what became his gravity, and the greatness and majesty off his rank, cast of his royal robes, " and naked like a common dancer," (2 Kings, vi 20,) (for which Michol reproached him), joining himself to the people, began to dance and play upon the harp. St. Gregory cannot forbear admiring this action of David, and speaking of it : " I know not," says he, " what thoughts others may have of this action ; for my part I stand more in admiration, to behold David dancing before the ark, as one of the common rank of men, than when he tore the lion in pieces, that when he killed Goliah, or when he defeated the Philistines. In all these occasions his glory was only in taming wild beasts, and in overcoming his enemies ; but in dancing before the ark, he became conqueror of himself ;" (L. 27, de Moral.) and there is far greater pain and glory in overcoming ourselves, than in gaining the victory over others.

Wherefore, let us make great account of these sorts of morti-

fication, and take care not to contemn or undervalue them, lest
the same happen to us which did to Michol ; who being so far
displeased at this action as to contemn David, and reproach him
for it to his face, was chastised by God with a perpetual barrenness.   If you disdain to mortify yourself in small matters; if you
be ashamed exactly to subject yourself to little things, pretending they are beneath you, and that such a subjection as this is
only good for children and novices, be afraid lest this become the
cause of your spiritual barrenness or sterility, either in prayer,
or in your conferences with your neighbour ; and be an occasion,
also, that your words make no impression, and produce no fruit
in their hearts ; and that thereby you be for ever deprived of the
comfort of spiritual children.   This is what, above all things, is
to be feared by those who reproach others for their exact performance of all their duties, who treat them as weak persons,
and scoff and jeer at them.   There is scarce anything more
dangerous, or of what we ought to have greater scruple than
this ; because at bottom it goes so far as to discourage and impede
the practice of virtue.   The answer which David gave Michol is
admirable : " I will play before the Lord," says he   " who has
chosen and preferred me to your father, and will render myself
yet more despicable than hitherto I have done, and will humble
myself yet more and more." (2 Kings, vi. 22.)   " An excellent
sport and diversion, indeed," cries out St. Bernard, " which
pleases God and displeases Michol ; which appears a ridiculous
sight before men, and is a very pleasing spectacle to the angels."
(Ep. lxxxvii.)   He who said, " we are become a spectacle to
angels and men," (1 Cor. iv. 9), was accustomed to this sport or
diversion which we ought to render familiar without putting
ourselves in pain at what they will say of us.   " Let us play,"
says St. Bernard, " that we may become the may game of the
world."   For by this means we shall indeed become a spectacle
of contempt to the world, but of admiration to the angels, and of
joy to God.

——o——

CHAPTER XVI.

*That it is very dangerous to neglect or contemn mortification in
small things.*

By this it is very easy to comprehend, how dangerous it is to
contemn or neglect small mortifications.   For it is not only the

thing in which we neglect to mortify ourselves, that we must look upon, but the refusing to overcome our will for the love of God, even in small matters. There is also in this another very great inconvenience, which deserves to be particularly attended to ; it is, that by this means we permit our will to accustom itself to seek its satisfaction in several things, and that it entertains and fortifies itself in this habit in such a manner, that afterwards we cannot master it in any thing. At first we perceive not the hurt we do ourselves in it ; for our own will is in the beginning only a lion's whelp, but in a short time it grows up so cruel and fierce a lion, that it is not to be tamed, and that it will be impossible for us to resist it. Self-love is the cause of all evils and sins, and by consequence of hell itself. "If there were no self-love," says St. Bernard, "there would be no hell." But by these sorts of mortification we have spoken of, we accustom ourselves to overcome our will, and take away from it the liberty of doing what it pleases. Richard of St. Victor says, "that as the devil endeavours to make us commit little faults, that after having gained some small advantages over us, and thereby weakened us, he may gain greater ; just so ought we endeavour to overcome ourselves by frequent mortifications in small things, that it may be impossible for him to overcome us in greater. "And afterwards," he adds, " we must begin with little things, that we may fortify ourselves by this exercise, and that the victory we gain over ourselves in small things, may be the means to overcome ourselves in greater." Cassian gives the same counsel, and makes use of an example to strengthen his advice :—" When you find yourself," says he, " moved to choler, either because your pen is not good, or that your penknife cuts not well, or for some other such like cause ; you must take great care to repress these irregular motions of anger, how little soever the cause of them appears to be ; because this victory gives you new strength to mortify yourself in greater occasions that shall present themselves, and to preserve peace of mind and charity amidst the greatest injuries and contempts.

There is also another advantage in the practice of these voluntary mortifications which is that it renders the assaults of the devil less dangerous, as St. Eusebius teaches, who, as St. Theodoret relates, continually exercised himself in them. One day they asked this saint, why he so applied himself to this practice ? " It is," says he, " because I have the devil, a crafty enemy, to deal with ; and therefore I endeavour to reduce the temptations of anger, impurity, envy, and all other sins that may put my soul in danger, unto small things, in which, if I be overcome, the loss will not be great ; but if I gain the victory, he cannot behold it with double indignation and confusion ; since even in these small things he is not able to overcome me." This deserves to be taken notice of, for it is a truth experienced by the servants of God, that the more you endeavour to mortify yourself in small things, the more the devil will endeavour to turn all his forces that way, and all his temptations will ordinarily be to hinder you from some mortification, and prevent your overcoming yourself, in some other such like thing, in which you cannot lose very much, though it should happen you should some time or other be overcome. But if you leave off this exercise, and neglect to resist and fight the devil and your own flesh in small things, both the one and the other will set upon you with far more dangerous temptations, to which, if you give way, your loss will certainly be very great.

St. Austin relates, that a Catholic being provoked to passion by flies that continually tormented him, was visited by a Manichean, to whom he related the inconvenience he received from them, and the emotions of impatience they caused in him. The Manichean thought he had found a fit occasion to instil his error, which was, that there were two origins or causes of things; the one of invisible things, which was God ; the other of visible, which was the devil. (It is against this error, that in the creed of St. Athanasius, sung by the church at mass, these words are inserted, " of all things, visible and invisible ;" whereby we acknowledge God to be the creator of all things, and not only of those that are spiritual and invisible, but also of those that are corporeal and visible.) The Manichean, therefore, perceiving that so excellent an occasion was offered him, of persuading the Catholic to a belief of his error : " Who, do you believe," says he, " was the creator of these flies ?" The Catholic, who found himself so tormented by them, durst not say that it was God ; but if it was not God, replied the Manichean, who was it that made them ? The other replied, that he thought it was the devil ; the Manichean still pressed the argument more home ; " but if the devil," says he, " made these flies, who made the bees ?" By reason of the small difference he perceived between the one and the other, he answered, that if God had not created the flies, probably he had not also created the bees. The Manichean perceiving this, by little and little, drew him on farther, passing from the bee to the grasshopper, a little bigger than the bee ; from the grasshopper to the lizard, from the lizard to the sheep, thence to an ox, then to an elephant, and last of all to man himself : "and hereby persuaded this poor man," says St. Austin, " that God had not created man." (Aug. Tract. ii. sup. Joan.) See into what an abyss of misieries he fell, because he could not patiently suffer the small inconvenience which was caused by the flies "Birdcatchers," says he, "are wont to make use of little flies to catch certain small birds with ; the devil also made use of flies to catch this unhappy man with." Wherefore, take care that the like happen not to you, when you find the least aversion to ever so small a thing ; when anything angers or troubles you, defy the devil, for it is by such sorts of flies that the devil catches a great many, and, by little and little, draws them into very great disorders.

———o———

CHAPTER XVII.

Three very important admonitions upon this subject.

THERE are three admonitions to be given hereupon, which regard three sorts of persons ; and it is for the consolation of the one, and to disabuse the others, that I shall here set them down. All men are not born with the same dispositions. Some are of a temper which is hard to overcome ; so that finding in themselvs a continual contradiction to all actions they are to perform, they are hereby much afflicted, and think all is lost. It is to such as these to whom I address the first advice I have to give; which is to let them know that there is no sin nor imperfection in the repugnances we feel of this kind, nor in any emotions contrary to reason, but only in following them. Involuntary motions, bad thoughts that happen against purity, against faith, or against any other virtue whatsoever, for which many afflict themselves very much, are not that which cause the sin in these temptations. Wherefore, the saints bid us not to put ourselves at all in pain about them ; it is not the feeling these thoughts, but the consenting to them, which occasions the sin ; for when you are troubled at these temptations, and endeavour to resist them, and do not entertain or take satisfaction in them, they are no sin, but, on the contrary, an occasion of great merit. It is the same of those natural bad inclinations which we feel, some more, some less, whence arise irregular motions in our sensual appetite, and so many repugnances and contradictions to virtue. It is not from hence that we become good or bad, perfect or imperfect ; because this is a thing that is purely natural, which depends not on us, but which we have inherited with sin. Did not St. Paul feel this rebellion within himself, this contradiction of his flesh ! " I feel," says he, " another law in my body, that wars against the law of my mind, and subjects me to the law of sin, which is in my members." (Rom. vii. 23.) St. Austin, explaining these words of the Psalmist : " Be angry and sin not "—" though some motions," says he, " that rise in our sensual appetites, being the punishment of sin, be not in our power, let us, at least, endeavour that our reason and will give no consent to them, but let us in spirit be obedient to the law of God, though in the flesh we are still subject to the law of sin." (Aug. in Ps. iv. 5.) It is taken notice of in the first book of Kings, that the cows that carried the ark of the covenant bellowed as they went along, because they had taken their calves from them ; yet, notwithstanding, they omitted not to go straight on their way, without turning either to the right or to the left. Do you do the same, persist in the straight way of virtue, without permitting yourself to be put out of your way by the bellowing of flesh and blood, and hereby you shall become perfect.

The difference that there is between spiritual persons who labour after perfection, and carnal and sensual persons who think not at all of it, does not consist in feeling or not feeling these motions and contradictions of their flesh, but in permitting or not permitting themselves to follow them. The fish that is alive swims against the stream, but a dead one is carried down with it ; so to know whether the spirit of God be living or dead within us we need only to see whether we go against the current of our passions, or whether we permit ourselves to be carried and driven along by their impetuosity. The spiritual man "hearkens not to the voice of the exactor," (Job. xix. 7,) that is, according to St. Gregory's interpretation, " they do not at all consent to the violent motions of temptation." The whole matter, therefore, consists in not giving ear to temptations, and not consenting to them ; so that we must be so far from being discouraged, by reason of these bad inclinations we find in ourselves, that we must, on the contrary, take courage and excite ourselves to gain a greater crown by overcoming them. This is what St. Austin counsels us in his third sermon on the ascension ; where, having exhorted the faithful to ascend to heaven with Jesus Christ, he proposes their own passions and bad inclinations as means or steps to help themselves with. " Let us ascend after him," says he, " by the help of our vices and passions ; and would you know how this can be done ? It is by casting them under foot, and making them, as it were, a ladder to climb up by." If we raise ourselves above our passions they will raise us above ourselves, and become as so many ladders to raise and elevate us even to heaven itself.

We read in the life of St. Ignatius, that, being naturally choleric, he had so overcome and changed his nature, by the help and assistance of grace, that they thought him to be of a phlegmatic temper. Plutarch relates almost the same thing of Socrates. He says, that " an excellent physiognomist having with attention considered him, could not refrain from telling him that he was a man inclined to lewdness, debauchery, drunkenness, and many other vices;" the disciples and friends of Socrates fell into a very great passion against this man, and were ready to treat him ill, had not Socrates hindered them saying, " the man is in the right, for I should be," says he, " such a one as he points me out, or describes me to be, were I not given to the study of philosophy, and to the practice of virtue." Now, if a philosopher, who had only the assistance of the light of nature, was able in such a manner to overcome his bad inclinations, what may not a Christian, or a religious, be able to do, by the help of divine grace, which is a thousand times more strong and powerful than nature is ?

There is another description of persons, who naturally are well inclined, and are so happy as to have inherited a good temper and disposition. It seems, as Alexander de Hales said to Saint Bonaventure, as if they had not sinned in Adam, they are of a sweet temper, of a nature that is inclined to good, that finds all things easy ; nothing is painful to them ; they find not in their flesh those contradictions and repugnances that others are tormented with ; but, on the contrary, alas !" say they, " people do nothing else but complain of the difficulties they find in religion, and we for our parts find none at all !" It is to these the second admonition belongs, which I promised to give and which they must make use of to undeceive themselves. If you have so good and pious inclinations as you speak of ; if you are of so easy, sweet, and uniform a temper that even the hardest things give you no pain at all, and that you scarce know what a temptation is, be not at all puffed up upon this account ; this is not virtue that you have acquired, but a temper with which you were born ; and the virtue and progress of a Christian consists not in a happy or good complexion, in an agreeble exterior, in a sweet temper; but it consists in our endeavours to overcome ourselves, and in the victory we gain over our passions. This is an infallible rule of any one's advancement in perfection ; and, therefore, one who is naturally choleric, does far more, and merits a greater recompense, when he resists and overcomes this passion, than you who in reality are of a sweeter and milder disposition ; for you are always of the same temper, and have nothing at all to resist or overcome.

Plutarch extolled Alexander the Great above all other kings : " because," says he, " others were born to great kingdoms, but Alexander conquered them by his sword and valour, and purchased them by the many wounds he received in battle." In like manner, such as have rendered themselves masters of their passions by dint of sword, if I may say so, moderating and mortifying themselves in all things, are far more worthy of praise than those who are born with sweet and peaceable tempers, and never have any provocation to fight at all. Wherefore, neither the sweetness of your humour, nor the natural heat or impetuosity that another suffers by his, ought to make you esteem yourself the more, or him the less ; but, on the contrary, you must hereby take more occasion to humble yourself ; acknowledging that what appears to be virtue in you, is not so, but a pure effect of your natural temper ; and that it is a great virtue in others to do the self-same things you perform. For in what you have hitherto done you have made little or no progress at all ; because you have overcome yourself in little or nothing ; but others have made a very great one ; because they have resisted and overcome themselves in many and great things. He who is born with a temper or disposition that is harder to overcome, finds himself thereby obliged to stand more upon his guard, to take greater measures of precaution, and to be more fervent; by which means he daily increases in virtue. But as for you, the confidence you have in the goodness of your nature makes you continually to relent, and causes you to fall into greater negligence and tepidity. For, having no enemies, you neglect your perfection, and permit yourself to lead a kind of easy and idle life. It will be very good also, that sometimes you call to mind what you should have been, had God given you a harder nature and humour to overcome ; and believe that you would have fallen into greater faults than others have done. For, alas ! if you, notwithstanding that good inclinations that God has bestowed upon you, daily fall into many faults, an are so lazy and tepid in your duty; what would you have been, had you been born with bad inclinations, and if you had been continually obliged to fight against yourself? Wherefore, if God suffers you not to be tempted, you must believe it is because he sees you so very weak, that you would not have strength to resist. And you must also persuade yourself, that the having given you so sweet and tractable a nature, is a pure effect of his mercy, and the particular conduct of his providence over you; for if you had more lively passions, you would not perhaps have strength enough to overcome them. By this means you will at the same time, preserve such sentiments of humility, as you ought to have of yourself, and will harbour such thoughts and esteem also of your neighbour, as you are obliged to have of him.

The third admonition I promised, is to disabuse another sort of persons, that experience not in themselves those contradictions and rebellions of the flesh, but, on the contrary, imagine they enjoy a very great peace within themselves. Yet this proceeds not, either from their mortifying themselves, or from their being born with these good inclinations; but happens because they never think of using any violence to themselves, but follow their own inclination in all things; whereby they find themselves exempt from all those repugnances, which others feel in every thing they do. They however flatter themselves that they enjoy a peace, which in reality they have not. "They only speak of peace, but enjoy none at all." (Jerem. vi. 53.) St. Austin writing upon these words of the apostle: "I see in my members another law, which is repugnant to my reason, and subjects me to the law of sin," (Rom. vii. 14), says, that "only those that fight under the standard of virtue, and that make war against vice, experience these combats within themselves." Moreover, if we take notice, when we speak of mortification to secular persons, it is a language they understand not; because they are wont to do such things only as please them, and they follow no other rule or law, than their own inclinations; and because they know not what it is to constrain themselves in any thing; therefore they feel no interior war or contradiction, there being indeed none at all. But those who seek after perfection, who labour to gain the true virtues of a Christian, and endeavour to pluck up by the roots their bad habits and inclinations, are exposed to a continual warfare, and to the contradictions of the flesh. And as a bird that is taken in a net, perceives it not, till it wishes to get out of it; so a man who is engaged in irregularity, never knows truly the strength of his passions, and how hard it is to overcome them, but when he labours to disengage and disentangle himself. It is when we embrace virtue, that vice renders the contradictions of irregular nature very apparent.

We read in the lives of the fathers of the desert, that one day an hermit proposed this question to a holy old man:—How comes it to pass, says he, that I feel not within myself those interior combats and violent temptations, that many others suffer? The holy man made this answer; it is because you are like a house, whose doors stand always wide open; into which all people enter at what hour they please, without the knowledge of the master. The gate of your heart is always open; you keep no guard at all over it; you live with little or no attention to yourself, with no recollection of mind at all; and therefore you must not wonder that you are not disquieted as others are. But if you would keep the door of your heart shut; if you hindered bad thoughts from entering, you would then see, what combats and violence they would use to get in. If therefore you feel not this war within yourself, nor any of these combats of your flesh, it is perhaps because you follow your own will in all things; and because you use no endeavours to contradict your sensual appetites, nor to root out the bad inclinations you have.

———o———

CHAPTER XVIII.

That it is always necessary to exercise ourselves in mortification; how advanced soever we be in virtue.

St. Bernard says, that in the exercise of mortification, we must always carry the hook in our hands; and that there is no person, how mortified soever, who stands not in need of pruning or retrenching something or other. " Believe me," says he, " that which is cut, sprouts out anew; that which is cast away, returns; that which is extinct, takes fire again; and that which apppears asleep, awakes upon a sudden. It is not sufficient therefore," adds the saint, " to have pruned it once, we must cut it often, and even daily if possible; for if you will not deceive yourself, you will always find something to cut, and to retrench within yourself." (Ser. lviii. sup. Cant.)   The hedges which we see in certain gardens furnish us with a very fit comparison for this subject. The myrrh and the box are cut with so much art, that here they represent the figure of a lion, there that of an eagle, and also a variety of other figures. But if the gardener be not very careful to cut off the leaves and little branches, which shoot out every moment, in a very short time, we shall not see the form of an eagle, nor of a lion, nor of anything else; because nature continually, according to its custom, shoots forth new wood and leaves. The same happens here; though you should be a lion or an eagle; though you seem to yourself so strong, as to fear nothing; nevertheless, if you do not daily cut and retrench something by mortification, you will soon become like a monster without shape; because the root of the evil, which is within us, shoots forth new branches every moment; so that there is always something to be mortified within us. "What progress soever you may have made in virtue," says St. Bernard, "you deceive yourself, if you believe you have entirely destroyed all vices within you; for you have only brought them under, and whether you will or not, the Jebusite will always remain with you. It is an enemy you may overcome, but you will never be able to exterminate." "I know," says St. Paul, "that there is nothing good within me, that is to say within my flesh." (Rom. vii. 17.) And the same saint discoursing upon these words, says, that the apostle had said very little, if he had not presently added, that sin made its abode in him; saying, "I do not the good which I would do, but execute the evil I would not. But if I do what I would not, then it is not I that do it, but it is sin that dwells within me." "Wherefore, hereafter," adds the saint, "you must either prefer yourself to the apostle, or acknowledge with him, that you are not exempt from vice." (Ser. lviii. sup. Cant.)

St. Ephraim is of the same opinion, when he says, that "the war which soldiers make is short, but that which a religious man is obliged to, lasts all his life." It is a greater labour to mortify our passions and sensual appetites, than to cut or polish the hardest stone. For, besides that the stone of itself makes no actual resistance to the cutter, it is certain, that when it is once polished, it becomes not rough again or uneven, as it was before. But what opposition do we not find in overcoming our passions? And when we have once got the mastery over them, do they not again rebel every moment against us, and continually re-assume new strength? We must, therefore, always endeavour anew, without any relaxation, to overcome them. St. Jerome, writing upon these words

of the prophet, " Sing a hymn to our Lord upon the harp,"
(Psal. xcvii. 5), says, that as we cannot play any agreeable air
upon a harp, if all the strings be not in tune ; and that one of
them being broken or slackened, causes discord in all the rest;
so one irregular passion is sufficient to discompose the harmony
of our soul, and hinder it from wafting any pleasing music to
God's ears.   When all our passions are equally subdued, it is
then that " we sing his praises upon an instrument of music of
ten strings," (Psal. xxxii. 2) ; but to be able to subdue them
in this manner, it is absolutely necessary we should continually
exercise ourselves in mortification.

It was for this reason, that the ancient fathers continually
tried those, who were already advanced in perfection, by all sorts
of mortifications and contempts.   Because they who seemed to
have entirely gained the virtue of mortification, lost, by little
and little, the spirit of docility, together with the habit they
had got in suffering, when their superiors, looking upon them
already as men of consummate virtue, ceased to make any
farther trial of them.   For as the most fertile land becomes full
of weeds, and produces nothing but thorns and thistles, if we
neglect to cultivate it ; so let a Christian be ever so perfect, if
this perfection be not cultivated by a continual exercise of
penance and mortification, he will soon become like a wild and
fruitless field, full of thorns and rushes ; that is, full of many
bad thoughts, and of a vain and dangerous confidence in himself.
So that all persons stand in need of mortification, not only such
as have any bad or corrupt inclinations, but even those also,
who have very good ones ; not only those who are still imperfect,
and are newly entered into the way of virtue, but those also,
who have made great progress therein ; and lastly, not only
those who have sinned, but those also who have preserved their
baptismal innocence.   Wherefore, generally speaking, all stand
in need of mortification ; some to acquire, others to preserve
virtue.   How good and sure-footed soever a horse may be, it is
always good to keep a stiff rein, and to let him now and then
feel the spur.

" If any one will follow me," says our Saviour, " let him deny
himself, and daily take up his cross." (Luke ix. 23.)   Which is
as much as to say, that we ought to let no day pass, without
mortifying our will in something or other.   If you neglect to do
this, says St. John Climacus, believe you thereby suffer a very
great loss ; and that you lose a day, and that it is a day in which

you could not properly call yourself religious. "Friends," said the Emperor Titus, when he had passed a day without conferring favours, " I have lost this day." And for that day he looked upon himself, as not to have been; and esteemed it also as a day that ought not to be counted in his reign. But, without doubt, it is far more essential for a religious to mortify himself, and renounce his own will, than it is for kings and emperors to bestow their favours. For it is the character of a religious person, to perform whatsoever he had no mind to do, and to do nothing that he has a mind to perform.

St. Francis Borgia in this, as well as in other things, has given us an excellent example to imitate. He said, that he found everything that he eat very bitter, and disagreeable to his palate, upon the day he had not chastised his body by some penance and mortification; and added, that he would be inconsolable, if he knew he should die upon a day, in which he had not mortified his senses, nor performed some penance. He therefore, let no day pass without having mortified himself. Moreover, he begged this grace of Almighty God, that all the pleasures of this life might become a punishment and cross unto him, and that sufferings might be to him instead of pleasure. It is in this that the third and most sublime degree of mortification does consist, and therefore he said that till he had arrived to it, he wished much attention might not be paid to him. He watched continually to make war against his body ; he daily found out means of mortifying and treating it ill; and gave the title of friend to whatsoever helped him to afflict it. When he walked in the sun in summer time, and was scorched and extremely incommoded thereby; our friend, says he, treats us as he should do. He gave the same title to cold, wind, rain, the gout and pain of the heart, to which he was very much subject. Lastly, those that persecuted him, and spoke ill of him, he also called his friends ; because all these helped him to conquer and subdue his body, which he looked upon as his mortal enemy. But he was not content with these occasions of suffering and mortification, which daily presented themselves, but he sought and found out new ways of mortifying himself. Sometimes he put gravel and pebbles into his shoes, that he might feel pain in his feet whilst he walked. He walked very slowly in summer time, in the heat of the sun, to suffer the heat so much the longer ; and did the same in winter, even in the middle of the snow, to suffer more cold. By his drawing the hairs out of his temples, they were become quite bald ; and when he could not give himself the discipline, he found other means of mortifying himself either by pinching it, or inflicting some other punishment upon his body.   In his sickness he sought out new pains, to add to those he suffered ; for when they gave him loathsome physic, he took it at several draughts very slowly, as if it had been some pleasant soup ; when he took any pills, how bitter soever they were, he always chewed them, and kept them a long time in his mouth.   Thus did he apply himself to the mortification of his senses, and the crucifying his flesh.   And it was hereby, he arrived at so high a pitch of sanctity and perfection.

———o———

CHAPTER XIX.

Of two sufficient means to render mortification sweet and easy ; which are the grace of God and his holy love.

I shall now speak of such means, as may help us to render this so necessary a practice of mortification, not only light and easy, but sweet and pleasant also.   The first means is the grace of God, with which all things become easy.   St. Paul supplies us with both an example, and a proof of this truth.   The sting of the flesh, the angel of Satan tormented him ; thrice he begged of God to be delivered from it ; and God made this answer to him : "My grace is sufficient for you." (2 Cor. xii. 9.)   On this he felt himself so fortified, that he said, "I am able to do all things, in him that strengthens me." (Philip. iv. 13.)   And added moreover, in the same place, "yet it is not I that do it, but the grace of God assisting me." (1 Cor. xv. 10.)   We must not believe that God leaves us to our own strength, in time of mortification and suffering.   No! he bears the greatest part of the burden himself ; and for this reason the law is called a yoke, which is to be borne by two.   For Jesus Christ joins himself to us, to help us to support it ; and with his assistance who can be discouraged ?   Wherefore let nothing in the law appear to you too hard, since you will have nothing but the easiest part of it to bear.   It is for this reason also, that he calls it a yoke and a burden ; when he says, "my yoke is easy, and my burden light." (Mat. xi. 30.)   For though, in regard of our nature and weaknesses, it be ever so hard a yoke, and ever so heavy a burden, yet the grace of God renders it very easy and light ; because our Lord himself helps us to bear it according to his promise made us by the prophet Osee, " I will be unto them, as he that takes the yoke from off their heads." (Osee xi. 4.) God says the same in Isaias, " That he will make the yoke rot before the oil." (Isa. x. 27.) For though mortification appears a troublesome and a heavy yoke, yet the grace of God, which is signified by oil, will make it rot, that is to say, will sweeten it in such manner, that so far from its hurting us, we shall scarce feel it.

St. Bernard, in his first Sermon upon the dedication of a church, says, that as in the consecration of a church, the walls are anointed with holy oil, so our Saviour does the same in religious souls, sweetening, by the spiritual unction of his grace, all their crosses, penances, and mortifications. Worldlings are afraid of a religious life, because they see its crosses, but perceive not the unction with which they are covered and made easy. " But you," says the saint speaking to his religious, " know by experience, that our cross is truly full of unction, whereby it is not only light, but all the bitterness and hardship we find in our state, is rendered by the grace of God sweet and pleasant." St. Austin owns, that before he knew the power of grace, he could never comprehend what chastity was, nor believe that any one was able to practise it.   But the grace of God renders all things so very easy, that if we possess it, we may say with St. John, " that the commandments of God are not at all heavy" (1 John v. 3), because the abundance of grace he bestows upon us, whereby to fulfil them, renders them most sweet and easy.   St. Gregory, writing upon these words of the prophet Isaias, " they who hope in God shall change their strength," (Isa. xl. 31), says, there are two sorts of strength ; that of the just, which makes them suffer all mortifications for the love of God; and that of the wicked, which makes them undergo all sorts of pain for the love of the world, for the maintaining of their vanity, for the obtaining riches, and for the satisfying all their irregular appetites.   He adds, that those who confide in the grace of our Lord, shall change the vain strength of worldlings, into that of the servants of God.

The second means, which makes the practice of mortification easy, is the love of God. Love, more than anything else, sweetens pain of every kind.   " He who loves," says St. Austin, " thinks nothing hard; and the least labour is insupportable to those who love not.   There is nothing but love, that is ashamed to find difficulty in anything." (Serm. ix. de Verb. Dom.) It is after this

manner that those who love hunting, make no account of the
labour and pains they take in it, but rather look upon it as a
pleasure. Is it not love that makes the mother find no difficulty
in nursing or bringing up her infant? Is it not love that keeps
the wife day and night at her sick husband's bedside? Is it
not love that causes all sorts of creatures to take so much care
in nourishing their young ones, that they even abstain from
eating, and expose themselves to dangers for their sakes? In
fine, was it not love that made Jacob think his fourteen years'
service for Rachael short and sweet? "His love," says the
scripture, "for her was so great, that he counted so long a time
as nothing." (Gen. xxix. 20.) St. Bernard upon these words of
the spouse, "my beloved is to me a little posy of myrrh,"
(Cant. ii. 12,) "she calls him," says the saint, "a little posy,
by reason that the excess of her love made her look upon all the
pains she could suffer as little or nothing." (Serm. xliii. in
Cant.) Moreover, adds the saint, take notice that she not only
says, "my beloved is a posy of myrrh," which is used for pleasure,
but a little posy of myrrh "to me;" by which last words, she
would explain that it is only a little and pleasant posy to those
that love. Wherefore, if this little posy seems great or unpleasant to you, it is because you love not. For we are to
measure the love we have for God, by the greater or less difficulty which we feel in things. The difficulties in virtue are not
great in themselves, it is the weakness of our love, that makes
them appear so to us. "Wherefore love much, and you will
not only feel no pain, but much pleasure therein." (Serm. lxxxv.
in Cant.) For no sooner does love appear, but all pain vanishes,
and all sweetness accompanies it. A certain holy woman said,
that from her first being touched with the love of God, she knew
not what it was to suffer, either exteriorly or interiorly; neither
from the world, the flesh, nor the devil; nor, in fine, by any
other way or means whatsoever :—because pure love knows not
what pain or torment is. Love, therefore, not only raises the
price of all our actions, and renders them more perfect, but it gives
us strength and courage to support all sorts of mortifications, and
makes us feel great felicity and sweetness, even in the most
bitter and hard things. It was in this manner, that St.
Chrysostom explained these words of the apostle, "love is the
fulfilling of the law" (Rom. xiii. 10); for he does not only say,
as this great saint takes notice, that the law and all the
commandments are included in love, but that it is love which
renders the observance of both most easy.

This is confirmed by these words of the wise man : " love is as strong as death." (Cant. viii. 6.) Amongst many explanations which the saints gave of these words, there are two which serve very well our purpose. The first is St. Gregory's, who says, that as death separates the soul from the body, so the love of God separates the soul from corporeal and sensible things, and as death takes a man away from the commerce of all things of this world, so the love of God, when it is become master of our heart, entirely disengages us from all ties either of the world or the flesh. Love is as strong as death, because as death kills the body, so the love of God kills and extinguishes our affection to all carnal objects, and causes a Christian to die to the world and self-love, and makes him enjoy no other life but what is in Jesus Christ : and therefore he may say with St. Paul, " I live indeed, yet it is not I who live, but Jesus Christ who lives in me." (Gal. ii. 20.) The second explanation is of St. Austin, who says, that the love of God is as strong as death, because nothing can resist death when it comes. No remedy, no knowledge, no riches, nor any greatness is able to withstand it : in like manner, when the love of God has taken full possession of a heart, nothing in the world is able to cast it out. Riches, honours, prosperity, and adversity are very insignificant obstacles, and serve only to increase and so much the more fortify it in a soul. Such as have renounced the world, to follow the narrow path of religion, know very well, that by a spark only of this love, they made a courageous resistance to all things that opposed their design ; so that no consideration of friends, parents, or any thing else in the world, was able to withdraw them from it. On the contrary, they joyfully trod them all under foot, and thought them mere vanity and misery, in comparison of the happy life they embraced. Let us therefore love much, and nothing will be able to stop us in the way of perfection. Then we shall be able to say with the apostle : " Who then shall be able to separate us from the love of Jesus Christ? Shall tribulation, affliction, hunger, nakedness, dangers, persecutions, or even the sword itself be able to do it? For my part, I am certain, that neither death, nor life, nor angels, nor principalities, nor powers, nor any thing that is in heaven above, or in hell beneath, nor lastly any creature whatsoever, shall be able to separate us from the love of God, which is in Jesus Christ our Lord."— (Rom. viii. 35-38.)

———0———

CHAPTER XX.

*Another means to render the exercise of mortification sweet and easy,
which is the hope of future recompense.*

THE third means whereby we may render the exercise of mortification sweet and easy, is the greatness of the recompense we
expect. Job comforted himself hereby, and encouraged himself to
undergo the greatest sufferings, when he said: "who will be so
kind to me, as to write down what I say? who will grant my
request, by engraving it upon a plate of lead, or upon flint?"
(Job xix. 23, &c.) Why do you think he so earnestly desired
that his words might remain and be left to posterity? It was
nothing else but that those that should come after him, might
receive in their afflictions the same comfort he received in his. And
what are these words, that are, he says, so full of comfort. They
are these : "I know that my Redeemer lives, and that at the last
day I shall be raised from dust, and shall be again clothed with
this my skin, and that I shall see God in my flesh ; that I myself
shall see him, and shall behold him with these very eyes. This is
the hope that I preserve in my heart." It is from this endless
treasure of consolation that I continually get comfort in my sufferings. By this hope God encouraged Abraham, when he appeared
to him, and assured him that his recompense was abundantly great.
By this hope, Moses renounced all the riches and grandeurs of
Pharaoh. "Moses," says St. Paul, "being grown up, and having
a lively faith, could pass no longer for the son of Pharaoh's
daughter, choosing rather to be afflicted with God's people than to
enjoy for a short time any happiness that sin could procure him;
believing that the ignominy of Jesus Christ was a far greater
treasure, and more to be esteemed, than whatsoever Egypt could
bestow upon him, because he considered the recompense to come."
(Heb. xi. 24, &c.) By this hope, the royal prophet exercised
himself continually, in the observance of God's law and commandments, as he himself tells us : "I was resolved to persevere in the
observance of your precepts, whilst I beheld the recompense I
thereby expected." (Ps. cxviii. 112.) "You will perhaps object,"
says St. Austin, "that here is a great deal to do. But consider on the other hand the promises made you ; for there is no

pain, though ever so great, which will not become light, when you think upon the recompense annexed thereunto ; for the hope of a recompense is of great comfort in our labours." (Ep. cxliii. ad Vir. Dem.) : as we daily see and experience in merchants, labourers, and soldiers. The merchant is not discouraged by tempests and shipwrecks ; bad weather does not keep the labourer from his work ; neither are the continual labours, wounds, nor even death, though it presents itself every moment, able to affright the soldier; because they all have continually before their eyes the emporal gain which awaits them. How comes it then to pass, that a Christian, whose hopes and inheritance are in heaven, should shudder and be afraid of mortifications and sufferings upon earth, since they are the best means whereby to gain the possession of what he hopes for ? Shall those persons expose themselves to inconveniences and dangers "for a fading corruptible crown; and shall we who expect an immortal one," (1 Cor. ix. 25), stand looking on and do nothing ? Did we but consider the vast reward which will infallibly follow the performance of what is required of us, we should presently be convinced that our labour is trifling, and that to get to heaven at such an easy rate, is to purchase it for nothing. It is not sufficient to know the price, but the true value also of a thing, before we can judge whether it be dear or cheap. For should I ask you, do you think it dear to give a hundred crowns for a thing ? you would answer me, that is according to the value of the thing which is thereby purchased, since perhaps it may not be worth one, and perhaps it may be worth a thousand crowns. For if it be a diamond of an extraordinary size, if it be an estate of very great extent, it is to have it for nothing. Would you therefore know whether God asks much or little of you, take notice what it is you buy of him ; see what he gives you in exchange for the price you give him : "I myself," says he, "will be your recompense." (Gen. xv. 1.) It is nothing less than himself that God gives you. It is therefore a very cheap purchase, and what he asks for it is nothing ; since what he desires of you is only the renouncing your will, and the mortifying your senses. "He will save his servants for nothing," (Psal. lv. 8), says the Psalmist ; and can you purchase any thing at a cheaper rate ? "Make haste therefore, you that have no money, come and buy wine and milk without it, or without giving any thing in exchange for it :" (Is. lv. 1,) run, make haste, and lose not the advantage of so good a market.

St. Basil also most strongly recommends this means unto us ; let your heart," says he, " be continually employed in thinking upon the heavenly promises, that they may encourage you to advance in the way of virtue.   It was by this St. Anthony likewise excited his disciples to persevere continually in the severity of a religious course; and sometimes, astonished at God's liberality, he says, there is a great equality in the traffics that men make in the world, each one gives as much as he receives ; and what is sold, is worth the price given for it ; but as for eternal glory, it is given for a small price, since holy writ tells us, that, " the ordinary course and life of man lasts only for sixty years ; and that even the strongest scarce arrive to four score; and the years above this age abound only in pain and misery." (Psalm lxxxix. 10, 11.)   Wherefore, though we should have served God for fourscore or an hundred years, or more, he does not recompense us only with so many years of glory, but our recompense will have no end ; we shall reign eternally in glory, as long as God shall be God.   " Wherefore my beloved children," says St. Paul, " be not weary in fighting against your enemy, nor let the ambition of vain-glory flatter and deceive you.   For all the sufferings of this life have no proportion with that future glory, that shall be revealed in us.   These short and light afflictions produce in us an inconceivable and eternal weight of glory." (Rom. viii. 18, and 2 Cor. iv. 17.)   St. Bernard makes use of a very fit comparison.   There is no farmer, though ever so stupid, says he, that complains that the seed-time lasts too long ; because he knows for certain, that " the less time he spends in sowing, the less plentiful will be his harvest."   That of a Christian ought to be the same ; the sufferings and mortifications of this life ought not to seem long, because now it is our seed-time, and the more we labour and sow at present, the greater will be our crop hereafter.   And we cannot increase our sowing, though it be ever so little, adds the saint, but it will always produce a greater abundance of grain, when the time of harvest is come.   When the farmer sees that for a bushel of wheat he sowed, he reaps twenty or thirty, he could wish that he had sown a greater quantity.

——o——

CHAPTER XXI.

What has been said in the preceding chapter confirmed by some examples.

WE read that the companions and scholars of one of the ancient fathers, having observed his continual mortifications and rigid austerities, pressed him once to be more moderate in his excessive penances. He answered them, saying : my dearest children, were the condition of the blessed in heaven capable of grief, they would extremely regret their not having suffered more in this world, since they now clearly see the reward they might have had, and how much they might have increased their happiness, and at how easy a rate. St. Bonaventure's sentiment is the very same, who says, "that as much as we spend of idle time here, so much do we diminish our degrees of glory hereafter, which, if we had employed our time well, we might have very much improved."

This is confirmed by what is recorded of St. Mechtilda. Jesus Christ, whom this saint had chosen for her spouse, and to whom she entirely dedicated herself, frequently used to visit her and give her a view of the glory of heaven. One day she heard the happy souls cry out, and say, O thrice happy you, who still live in the world, in whose power it is to augment your glory every moment! Did but man know how much he might increase his merit every day, he would never wake without a cheerful heart replenished with joy, to think he is to begin another day, in which living to God, he may be assisted by his divine grace every moment to advance his honour, and his own merit. This very thought is sufficient to encourage and strengthen us against all difficulties and mortifications, and make us suffer them with satisfaction.

The Spiritual Meadow (approved of in the second council of Nice, and written by John Evirat, though others say St. Sophronius, patriarch of Jerusalem, was its author), tells us that an hermit who went about twelve miles to fetch all the water he used, finding himself once extremely weary, began to complain upon the way, that he was not able any longer to undergo so great labour, and said thus to himself :—what necessity is there of giving myself all this trouble? It is better for me to go and build myself a little cell near the fountain, and live there. The next time he went with his pitcher for water, he began to consider what place would be

most convenient for an hermitage, and in what form he should
build it, and what kind of life he should lead therein.   Immediately he heard the voice of a man, as he supposed, counting
one, two, three, &c. : being surprised to hear one measuring the
way, or casting up accounts in the desert, he turned about, but
saw nobody.   Going on his way, he had no sooner thought of
his new design of building, but he heard the same voice again,
and looking round about him he still saw nothing.   But the
same thing happening a third time, he stopped and saw a lovely
youth, all in glory following him, who bid him take courage; I am,
says he, an angel of God, who have counted every step you have
taken, each of which shall be particularly rewarded. Having said
thus he vanished out of his sight. The hermit reflecting seriously
within himself, cried out, how is it possible, that I should lose my
senses so far as to be willing to renounce so great a blessing, and
deprive myself of so certain a reward ?   From that very moment
he resolved to live still farther from the water than before, in
order to increase his labour, and thereby his merit.

    It is related in the lives of the fathers, that an ancient
anchoret, who lived in the desert of Thebias, used every evening to make an exhortation to a young disciple of his, who lived
with him, and was very much liked by him ; after which they
said some prayers together, and so went to rest.   It happened
one day that some secular persons, invited by the sanctity and
reputation of this good old man, came to visit him, and stayed
with him very late.   He had no sooner dismissed them, but he
began, according to custom, his exhortation, which he made so
long that he fell asleep.   His scholar expected every moment
he should awake to finish their usual devotions, and then retire
to rest.   But the old man continuing to sleep, the scholar grew
somewhat impatient, and found himself moved to go to rest.
This temptation attacked him seven times, but he courageously
resisted and overcame them all.   Being now past midnight the
holy anchoret awoke, and finding his scholar still by him, asked
him why he let him sleep all that while ?   He answered, that he
was afraid to disturb him.   Here they began matins together,
which being ended, the good old man gave his disciple his blessing, and sent him to rest.   The holy hermit had no sooner fallen
to his prayers, but he was in spirit rapt unto paradise, where an
angel shewed him a bright and glorious throne, upon which stood
seven very rich crowns. The saint desired to know for whom these
crowns were designed, and the angel told him they were for his

young disciple, to whom God had allotted the throne as a reward of his holy life, and as for the crowns, he had purchased them that very night. As soon as it was day, the good hermit calls his scholar, and asks him what had happened to him after his falling asleep. To whom he replied : I found myself often moved to impatience ; and the temptation of going to sleep before you awoke, attacked me seven times, but I yielded to none of them. Here the good father understood how his scholar had purchased those seven crowns he had seen. (Pa. iii. fol. 237.)

The brother of St. Francis the seraphic, met him once in the middle of winter, and seeing him almost naked and shivering with cold, scornfully bid one ask him to sell him a drop of his sweat. The saint, putting on a pleasant countenance, answered, tell my brother, that I have already sold it to God, and that at a very dear rate. The same saint was at another time most grievously tormented with such excess of pain, and with such troublesome temptations, that in all human appearance it was impossible for him to suffer them for any considerable time. Notwithstanding, a comfortable voice from heaven bid him rejoice, and told him that his sufferings would procure him a treasure in heaven, to which were the whole earth one solid mass of gold, the stones all turned into pearls and diamonds, and all the waters here below changed into the most precious balm, they would not be comparable, nor ever reach the greatness and value of that reward which was laid up for him there. This assurance so softened and mitigated his pains, that from that time forward he scarcely felt any, and being transported with spiritual joy, he called his religious and acquainted them with the comfort Almighty God had bestowed upon him.

———o———

CHAPTER XXII.

Another help to render the practice of mortification very easy ; which is, the example of our suffering Saviour.

The example of our Lord and master Jesus Christ, is the fourth means, and most powerful encouragement to mortify ourselves. It is what St. Paul proposes to us, and invites us to follow in these words :—" Armed with patience, let us run to the combat proposed unto us, having our eyes constantly fixed on Jesus Christ, the author and finisher of our faith, who contemning ignominy, died with satisfaction upon the cross. Think continually upon those contradictions he suffered from sinners, barely that you should not relent nor be dejected; for as yet, you have not resisted the shedding of your blood, in fighting against sin." (Heb. xii. 1, 2, &c.) Holy writ tells us, that the children of Israel found the waters of Mara so bitter, that they could not drink of them. Upon which Moses fell to his prayers, and Almighty God showed him a sort of wood, which being thrown into the water, rendered it very sweet and pleasant. This was a figure of the wood of the holy cross, which sweetens all our mortifications, though ever so bitter and painful. The memory of Christ's passion, of his whipping at the pillar, of his crown of thorns, of the gall and vinegar given him to drink, is sufficient to make all our sufferings easy and delightful.

We read in the chronicles of St. Francis' order, that a person of great property, and who had been brought up in all the ease and delicacies of the age, became a Franciscan. The devil much concerned at this change, resolving to try his skill, used all his power to divert him from his undertaking. He begins his persecution, by representing to him every moment the austerities of his order, in which instead of a plentiful table, he found nothing but a few beans, very ill dressed; instead of a good suit of clothes, and lodgings richly furnished, nothing but a coarse habit, and a straw bed; in fine, he suggested to him, that instead of all those other conveniences the world afforded him, he met with nothing here but a very great want of all things. This picture was certainly a very gloomy one; but the devil made all things much worse than they were, and continually represented them before his eyes, still soliciting him to quit these hardships and return to the world. This temptation prevailed so far as to make him resolve to leave his order. Being thus resolved, it happened that he passed through the chapter-house, when kneeling down before a crucifix, and fervently recommending himself to God, he fell into an ecstasy.—Christ and his blessed mother appeared to him, and asking him the cause of his departure; he modestly replied, that his nice and tender education in the world, had made him very unfit and even unable to undergo the hardships of religion. At this our Saviour lifting up his right arm, showed him the wound in his side bleeding fresh, and spoke thus unto him:—"Put here your hand; rub it all over with the blood that comes forth, and whenever those painful austerities which you are to suffer come into your mind, refresh and comfort yourself with this blood; and the most severe penances shall unto him :—" Put here your hand ; rub it all over with the blood that comes forth, and whenever those painful austerities which you are to suffer come into your mind, refresh and comfort yourself with this blood, and the most severe penances shall always seem sweet and easy unto you." The novice being come to himself, did all that our Saviour had commanded him, and whenever he was attacked by fastidiousness or impatience, he called to mind the passion of our Saviour ; and all the bitterness of mortification turned into sweetness, How is it possible, that man formed out of dirt, and a mere worm of the earth, should look upon any suffering or mortification as too great, after he has seen his God crowned with thorns, and nailed to a cross for love of him ? And who is there that is not ready to suffer and expiate his own sins, that has seen the God of Majesty, the Lord of heaven and earth, suffer so much for him ?

This means of which I speak has always been very much practised by all holy men. For there is nothing can more encourage us to mortification, than to propose to ourselves the example of Jesus Christ, and endeavour to follow it. Besides, it is an exercise of the highest perfection, and adds a new value to our good works ; because they then spring from an ardent love of God. Hence it happened that St. Ignatius, who at the beginning of his conversion used only to mortify himself whilst he called to mind the sins of his life past, arrived at last to so high a pitch of mortification, that in his greatest austerities he thought more of imitating Jesus Christ than of satisfying for his sins. Holy men reflect that our Saviour has chalked out unto them the way of mortification, and that he loved his cross so well, as to shed his very last drop of blood upon it for our redemption. And, as naturalists say that elephants become furious in battle at the sight of blood ; so holy men took more courage, and burned with a greater desire of martyrdom, when they beheld the sacred blood our Saviour shed so plentifully for their sakes ; but unable to accomplish their wishes, they became their own executioners ; they crucified themselves by their long penances, and by mortifying their will and exterior senses ; and thus in some degree, they appeased their great thirst of suffering, having been gratified at the idea of their having followed, so far as in their power, the example of our Saviour. Thus we ought to do, " carrying always the passion of Jesus Christ in our bodies, that the life of Jesus Christ may appear in us," (2 Cor. iv. 10,) that is, we ought to harass our bodies with suffering and mortification, that they may always represent unto us the life and death of our Saviour. "What a shame it is," says St. Bernard, "to be the delicate member of a head crowned with thorns," Let us therefore afflict and crucify our flesh, that we may be the more like our head, Christ Jesus, whose members we are.

It were easy to set down several other means, since all those that the saints have left us, and the many arguments they have used to exhort and move us to penance, may also serve us at present as so many motives to mortification. St. Bernard, writing upon these words of the apostle :—"The sufferings of this life bear no proportion to the glory that shall hereafter be revealed in us ;" (Rom. viii. 18,) says, " that they not only bear no proportion to the glory of heaven, but none also to the punishment we deserve for the sins we daily commit, or to the benefits we continually receive from God." Each one of which considerations seriously pondered, is a sufficient and most lively encouragement to this practice of mortification.

———o———

CHAPTER XXIII.

Of the three degrees of mortification.

BEFORE I conclude this treatise, I shall briefly explain the three degrees of mortification, established by St. Bernard, and assigned as so many steps to raise us to the highest pitch of perfection. The first degree is taught us by St. Peter, in his first canonical epistle :—" I conjure you," says he, " my dear brethren, to look upon yourselves as strangers and passengers only in this world, and to abstain from all carnal desires which make war against the soul." (1. Pet. ii. 11.) We are no more than strangers here, and banished from heaven, our native country. "We have no fixed abode at present, we are in pursuit of another, and we wander like pilgrims, and are far from God, so long as we carry about us these our mortal bodies." (Heb. xiii. 14.) Let us therefore behave ourselves like travellers who are far distant from home. "A traveller," says St. Bernard, "always keeps the straight road, and endeavours to avoid all turning and winding paths as much as he can. If he chances to see people on the way, either quarrelling or making mirth, he is not at all concerned nor troubled, but prosecutes his journey without stopping ; because these things do not constitute his business. His chief affair is to long after his country, and advance every day towards it; for this reason he contents himself with ordinary clothes and homely fare, and takes nothing along with him that is burthensome, or that may retard his journey." Thus we ought to do in the pilgrimage of this world ; we must look upon ourselves, as really we are, to be on a journey : nothing ought to stop us upon the way, nor must we carry anything along with us which is unnecessary. " Having food and raiment, we ought to be content ;" (1 Tim. vi. 8,) and as for the rest, we must leave behind us every thing that is useless or superfluous; that we may perform our journey so much the better and more speedily. Let us therefore languish after our dear native country, and let us testify our grief at being so far from it, by crying out with the Psalmist :—" Woe is me that my sojourning is prolonged !" (Ps. cxix. 5.) " Happy is the man," says St. Bernard, " that really thinks himself a pilgrim in this world ; he knows, and knowing laments his unhappy exile, in these pathetic words :— ' Be not deaf to my tears, O Lord; I am a stranger and a pilgrim before you, as all my predecessors were ; call me home to live for ever with you.' " (Ps. xxxviii. 13.)

It is certain this degree implies a more than ordinary virtue; and to arrive to it requires no small pains ; but there is another of a more elevated perfection. " For though a traveller," says St. Bernard, " makes no long stay in a country, where he passes; yet it often happens that, curious to know the customs and manners of the inhabitants, he delays for some time; and though this delay does not quite break off his journey, yet it certainly interrupts his return ; and he may also be disposed to take so much pleasure in gratifying his curiosity, that he will not only return late, but perhaps will never arrive in his native country." You will perhaps ask me, who can be more estranged and disengaged from the world than he who lives in it like a traveller ? It is he who lives in it and is dead to it. A traveller is always in want of something or other for his journey, and were there nothing else but the care of providing necessaries, and the carriage of them, it would be a sufficient hindrance. But he that is dead does not feel a want of any thing, not so much as a grave. He is equally indifferent to praise and censure : flattery and detraction sound both alike to him, or to speak more properly, he understands neither the one or the other. This is the second degree of perfection which is far more sublime and perfect than the first, and is thus described by St. Paul : " You are dead, and your life is hidden with God in Christ."—(Col. iii.

3.) Hence you see, that it is not enough to be in the world as a traveller, but you must be truly dead to it. Would you know how to effect this? Look on a man that is dead—"He neither hears, sees, nor speaks—no passion of pride or anger disturbs him" (Lansperg;) nothing at all troubles him, all sense and motion has left him. If then you still have eyes to pry into other people's actions; if you are never at a loss for an answer to excuse yourself, and to do away the obligation of obedience; if you take it ill when your failings are reprehended; and lastly, if you feel proud or angry when you are neglected or despised, be assured that you are so far from being dead to the world that you live and act by a worldly spirit. For one that is dead is altogether unconcerned at any contempt or injury done him. "Happy is the man," says St. Bernard, "that is thus dead. This kind of death is the only true life—it disengages us from the world, even in the midst of it, or rather it separates us from all things in this present life."

"See here," continues the saint, "a very noble degree of mortification, but perhaps we may find one yet more sublime." (Bern. Serm. vii. Quadrages.) Where shall we seek for it, or where shall we find it but in him that was wrapt to the third heaven. For if there be another degree more sovereign than what we have spoken of, it very well deserves the name of a third heaven. For what can we do more than to lay down our lives in imitation of "Jesus Christ, who was obedient even to death." (Philip. ii. 8.) Nothing sure can go beyond this. Yes, there still remains something more, it is the death of the cross, as the apostle adds, and as the holy church sings upon Good Friday, in memory of the passion. To die upon a cross, is more than barely to die; for in those days it was the greatest infamy to die upon a cross. This is the third degree of mortification, far more sublime than the two others, and to which St. Paul was elevated, as well as to the third heaven, when he said, "the world is crucified to me, and I to the world." (Gal. vi. 14.) He was not content to say, that he was dead to the world, but would add that he was crucified to it, and that the world was a cross to him, and he to it. It is the same as if he had said, "pleasures, honours, riches, the esteem and praise of men, and all the world courts and adores, is a sensible cross to me, and an object of hatred and horror; on the contrary, I love and embrace with the greatest tenderness of my heart, all that the world looks upon as infamy and disgrace. It is then that a

Christian is truly crucified to the world, and the world to him, when he perceives that the world is a cross to him, and he to it. This made St. Bernard own that this third degree of mortification was far more perfect than the two others. For though a traveller only passes by, without making any considerable stay, to look upon what offers itself to his sight, yet he still beholds those objects, and in that must needs spend some little time. And as for him that is dead to the world, which is the second degree, he is indeed equally indifferent to adversity and prosperity, to infamy and honour. But still the third degree far surpasses this; and is not satisfied with this holy indifference. He that attains this perfection, thinks it a poor business to look upon the esteem and glory of the world as nothing, and as if he were dead, unless he really thinks them a cross and the greatest punishment which can be inflicted on him. To be insensible to affronts and disgrace is but a very small matter in his sight, who rejoices and glories in them, and says with St. Paul; " far be it from me to glory, unless in the cross of Christ Jesus, by which the world is crucified to me, and I to it." It is the love of Jesus Christ that makes me hate all the world loves, and causes me to place my greatest content and delight in what the world hates. " I am filled with comfort, and I feel a superabundant joy in my afflictions," (2 Cor. vii. 4); and all my satisfaction is in suffering for Jesus Christ.

This is the third degree, which St. Bernard justly terms the third heaven, because it is so sublime. Holy men and masters of a spiritual life are of the same opinion, since the most sovereign perfection of mortification consists in it; and philosophy teaches, that it is a certain sign of having acquired any virtue in perfection when we perform its acts with ease and pleasure. Do you then desire to know if you have arrived at this third and most perfect degree of mortification? Examine yourself, whether you rejoice when your inclinations are thwarted, your petitions denied, and you yourself contemned; on the contrary, when people respect and honour you, does this trouble and afflict you? "Wherefore, let every one of us consider," says St. Bernard, " in what degree we are, and endeavour to make a new progress; for by our advancing from one virtue to another we shall enjoy the beatific vision in the heavenly Zion." This was the sublime state which our Saviour spoke of to St. Francis in these words: " If you desire to enjoy me, make all bitter things sweet, and all sweet things bitter to you."

Cæsarius in his dialogues tells us, that there was a lay-brother in one of the monasteries of the Cistertians, called Rodolphus, a great servant of God, and frequently favoured with divine revelations, who staying one night in the Church after matins, saw our blessed Saviour and fifteen Cistertian monks about him, all hanging upon crosses. Our Saviour's body reflected so great a light, that by the help thereof he easily knew the monks, for they were all still living. On his being much surprised at this sight, our Saviour asked him if he knew those persons who were there crucified with him ? He answered yes, but could not comprehend what the vision meant. "These," says our Saviour, " whom you see, are the only persons that are crucified with me, by a conformity of their lives to my death and passion." (2 Cor. vii. 4.)

THE SECOND TREATISE.

———o———

MODESTY AND SILENCE.

———o———

CHAPTER I.

*How necessary modesty is for the edification and profit of our
neighbour.*

MODESTY, of which we treat at present, consists in this : that our
exterior be so composed, our senses so recollected, our conduct,
our conversation, our very carriage, and all our gestures and
motions, be such as may edify those that shall live and converse
with us. All that regards this kind of modesty, is comprehended in
this short sentence of St. Austin, "Let there be nothing offensive
in your exterior ; take care that everything there be suitable to
your holy profession." (Reg. S. Aug.)   It is not my intention
to point out all the particular cases wherein modesty is violated
or practised.   The general rule laid down by St. Austin, and
followed by the best and most spiritual men, shall suffice at present.   Endeavour that all your actions be so well ordered that
they never give scandal ; but on the contrary, that they edify
every one : and be sure that humility, joined with a grave religious behaviour, shine in your exterior, and then you will keep
all the laws of modesty.   All I pretend at present then, is to
show how far this kind of modesty is necessary for those who, by
their end and institute are obliged not only to labour in procuring
their own, but also their neighbour's salvation.

It is certain that man cannot see but the exterior ; and hence
it is, that what most edifies and wins our neighbour is a prudent
and modest behaviour.   This preaches more forcibly than the
most eloquent orator.   St. Francis one day, calling one of his religious, said to him, "Come, let us go to preach," whereupon they
went abroad, and having taken a turn in the city, returned home.

Being returned, his companion asked him when he would make the sermon he promised? "It is done already," replied the saint, insinuating hereby, that the religious modesty with which they had appeared in the town, had been an admirable sermon to all that saw them. And indeed an humble and mortified exterior excites not only to devotion, but to a contempt of the world. It causes in the beholders sorrow for their sins, and raises their thoughts and hearts towards heaven. In a word, this silent preaching oftener works more upon the minds of men than the most eloquent and sublime discourses from a pulpit.

With respect to ourselves, it is also very certain, that to be composed and modest in the exterior, is of very great advantage for the obtaining of virtue, as you will afterwards see more at large. For so intimate is the union between body and soul, between the outward and the inward man, that all that is in the one appears in the other by a secret communication. When the motions of our mind are composed and regular, those of our body sympathise with them; on the contrary, when these are disturbed, those are disturbed also. Hence it is, that exterior modesty is an argument of interior recollection, and of a Christian's proficiency in virtue; in the same manner, as the hand of a watch is an infallible sign of the exact and regular motion of the wheels.

It is for this reason that our neighbour, as we said in the beginning, esteems it so highly, and is so much edified by exterior modesty and gravity, for he thence infers the good qualities of the interior. St. Jerome says that, "our face is the mirror of our soul, and that our eyes, though silent, discover the secrets of our heart."(Ep. ad. Furi. vid.) The Wise man says in his proverbs, that, "as those who look into the water, see their faces clearly represented, so a prudent man, by looking upon another, easily sees the bottom of his heart." (Prov. xxvii. 19.) No glass represents an object better than the exterior does the interior. "A man is known by his looks," says Ecclesiasticus, "and the lineaments of his face discover his humour. His manner of apparel, his laughter, and his gait, tells us what he is." (Eccl. xix, 26.) And the holy Ghost describes a wicked man to us in these words: "This son of Belial is restless and unprofitable, his steps are fierce and cruel, his eyes continually rolling, and his hands and feet are always employed in antic gestures." (Prov. vi. 12.) St. Gregory Nazianzen, speaking of Julian the apostate, says, "a great many knew not Julian till he made himself known by his infamous actions, and by his abuse of sovereignty ; but for my part," says the saint, " when I first knew him, and lived and conversed with him at Athens, I never could perceive the least mark of goodness in him. He carried his head extremely high, his shoulders as well as his eyes were always in motion, his behaviour was haughty and fierce, his feet never stood still, every moment either anger caused his nostrils to swell, or disdain drew them in : he frequently played the buffoon. His conversation was very scurrilous, his laughter was ungraciously loud. He would freely grant and deny the same thing with the same breath. His discourse was imme-thodical and irrational ; his questions importune, and answers impertinent—but why do I dwell so long in describing his ex-terior by detail ? To conclude then I knew him by these ex-terior marks, before I had heard anything of his impiety, which now confirms my former judgment of him. Those that lived with us then at Athens, were they here present, would testify that having observed his manners, I said, that the Roman Em-pire was bringing up a dangerous and pernicious serpent. This I then said, and the same time I heartily wished I might be mistaken ; and without doubt it had been much better that I had been so, since we then should have not seen those evils which have almost rendered the world desolate." Thus you see that an irregular exterior is a sign of a disordered interior, as well as an exterior modesty is a mark of a composed interior ; which is the reason why men are ordinarily so much moved and edified by it.

It is upon this very account, that we are more strictly bound than others to be observant of religious modesty and decorum. For by our institute we are bound to preach, hear confessions, teach, reconcile enemies, visit prisons and hospitals, and, in fine, to do all the duties which charity requires of us. And it is not to be doubted, but that from a modest, humble, and mortified exterior, those functions make deeper impression, and are ren-dered more efficacious in order to the salvation of souls. By this, preachers gain credit with their auditors, who hereupon, forming a great opinion of the sanctity of those that speak to them, receive their words as oracles coming from heaven, and engrave them in their hearts. Surius tells us, that when Inno-cent II. went to visit the monastery of Clairvaux, he was met by St. Bernard and all his monks, at whose modesty his holi-ness and the cardinals that waited upon him were so edified that

they wept for joy.   Nor were they able sufficiently to admire
the gravity and modesty of those good religious, who, notwithstanding the solemnity of the day, and that extraordinary occasion of receiving his holiness, attended by the sacred college of
cardinals, kept their eyes fixed upon the ground, without once
lifting them up; and though they were viewed by all, yet had
not so much as once the curiosity to look upon any one present.

This modesty we speak of, serves for the edification not only
of persons in the world, but also of our brethren in religion.
For as secular people when they see a religious in the church
very devout and recollected, or modestly walking the streets in
silence, without taking notice of what happens round about him,
conceive a great esteem for him, and feel themselves moved to
devotion; so in a religious house, those that are modest and recollected give extraordinary edification to the whole community.
" Their looks," says St. Jerome, " is an exhortation of silence to
those that break it, their very presence is a lesson of modesty
and recollection to those, whose words and actions are any
ways irregular.   Lastly, those persons keep up religious houses,
by maintaining their esteem abroad, and supporting virtue and
regular observance at home; because their example draws
others to devotion, and creates in them a love of heavenly
things. (In Reg. Mon. c. xxi.)   Hence, it is, that our holy
founder recommends this conduct to us, that by observing and
considering one another's actions, we may all increase in piety,
and thereby eternally praise our blessed Redeemer.

It is said of St. Bernardine, that he had so grave and modest
an air, that his presence alone inspired modesty and recollection
into his companions.   We read also, that Pagans were converted by only looking upon St. Lucien the martyr.   These
were good preachers and true imitators of him, who was, as
the gospel says, "a bright and shining lamp" (John v. 37),
that is to say, in whom the fire of the love of God did not only
burn, but send forth a clear light to guide men through the
paths of salvation, by the example of his own miraculous life.
All this must needs extremely encourage us to an observance
of modesty in all our actions, in order to edify our neighbours
and brethren, and to produce in both the fruit we have spoken
of.   Otherwise what is become of the zeal for God's glory which
we profess?   Where is our care to save souls, if we do not endeavour to effect this one thing so proper for their edification
in this world, and salvation in the next, and which is also so
easy to be performed by us?

CHAPTER II.

How necessary modesty is for our own particular advancement.

IT is the common opinion of holy men that modesty and a guard over our senses, are among the chief means left us to advance in virtue, inasmuch as they highly contribute to interior recollection. For our senses are the gates by which all evil enters into our hearts, and therefore ought to be well guarded, that our hearts may be in greater security. St. Jerome, upon the words of Job, " Are not the gates of death open to you, and have you not seen the doors of darkness?" (Job. xxxviii. 17), says, " that our senses are the gates of death, and that sin, which is the death of the soul, enters by them, as the prophet Jeremias affirms : ' Death ascends by our windows ; ' " (Jerem. ix. 21) and he moreover adds, that they are called the doors of darkness, because they give entrance to the night of sin. St. Gregory is of the same opinion, and this axiom in philosophy, " there is nothing in the understanding which has not first passed through the senses," is frequently quoted by holy men for a proof of this. When the gates of a house are shut and well guarded, all within doors is secure ; but if they are left open and no one appointed to look to them, so that all people may go in and out at pleasure, it is unsafe to be in that house ; at least, no one can be secure or quiet while so many go in and out every moment. Wherefore we see that those who take care to secure the gates of their senses live devoutly, and enjoy the blessings of an interior peace ; but, on the contrary, such as are negligent in this affair, never enjoy true peace and quiet in their souls. Hence the Wise Man advises us, " to use all possible diligence in defending our heart, because it is the fountain of life." (Prov. iv. 23.) St Gregory is of opinion, that a guard upon our senses is the best defence of our heart ; " for," says he, " we must not give leave to our senses to sally out, if we desire to preserve purity of heart." (In Job. lib. ii.) St. Dorotheus bids us " never to accustom our eyes to look here and there upon vain and unprofitable objects, which only serve to divert our thoughts from being better employed, and to render them unprofitable." (Ser. xxii.) If we are not diligent in watching our senses, we shall easily lose all the stock we have spent so much time and pains in treasuring up, and in the end find our hands empty ; as a short negligence destroys both God's grace and our own painful endeavours. "Avoid much speaking," says St. Dorotheus, "as the very bane of pious thoughts and divine inspirations." (Ser. xxx.) "Silence and quiet," says St. Bernard, "do with a very sweet kind of necessity force us to meditate upon heavenly things after we are once freed from the noise and bustle of the busy world." (Ep. 378.) The same saint says in another place, that modest and downcast eyes make the heart look up to God; and we find by daily experience that the more we guard our eyes the more we improve in devotion, and the greater is our interior recollection.

It was for this reason, as Cassian assures us, that the fathers of the desert said, that one should be blind, deaf, and dumb, to acquire true perfection, to keep a pure heart, and to live interiorly recollected; for in this case nothing could be able to sully or defile the soul, which would hereby be disengaged and more free to converse with God. Here you will ask me, how can blindness, deafness, or dumbness suit us, who, being so much engaged in conversing with our neighbour, are consequently obliged to hear and see many more things than we desire? The remedy is, that we are to see them as if we did not see them; and to hear as if we did not hear; nothing that is either heard or seen must be permitted to dwell one moment in our hearts, but must be immediately chased away. On this subject, St. Ephrem relates, that a monk asked an old father what he should do, as his abbot appointed him to go every day to the bake-house to assist the baker, where he met with some young people whose conversation was disedifying and licentious? The old father answered him thus: "Have you not seen a great many boys in a school, and observed the noise they made in getting their lessons by heart, which they were to say to their master? Every one there only minds his own lesson, that being what he is to give an account of, and troubles not himself with another's. Do you the same; do not be in pain for what others do or say, but mind your own duty; since Almighty God will call you to account for that only."

It is said that St. Bernard was so strongly united to God, that he saw without seeing, and heard without hearin . Nay, he seemed even to have lost the use of his senses; since he did not know whether the floor of his cell, in which he had lived the year of his noviceship, was made of boards or of bricks. There were three glass windows in the church, yet he never perceived more than one. He had walked almost a whole day by the side of a lake with some other religious, who speaking to him of it, he asked them what lake they meant, for he had seen none that day? The same is related of Abbot Palladius, who lived twenty years in the same cell, without ever looking up to the roof of it. In the same manner, whilst we converse with the world, in order to procure the neighbour's salvation, we should be blind, deaf, and dumb; and thus whatsoever should offer itself to our eyes or ears, would not in the least hinder our spiritual advancement.

————o————

CHAPTER III.

Of the error of those who make little account of this exterior modesty as not being essential to perfection.

WHAT I am about to say at present is chiefly to disabuse those who make little or no account of what appears in the exterior; under pretence that perfection consists not in modesty and silence, but in the interior, and in the practice of true and solid virtues. Lipomanus relates an excellent example upon this subject, taken from the Spiritual Meadow, which is as follows:— One of the ancient hermits who lived in the deserts of Egypt came one day to Alexandria, to sell some little wicker baskets he had made; and seeing a young hermit go into a tavern, he was extremely disedified, and resolved to wait his coming out. After some little time the old man seeing him come out, called him, and taking him aside, spoke to him in the following manner:—" Do you not consider, dear brother, that you are as yet very young, and that your enemy is continually laying snares to entrap you? Do you not reflect upon the danger to which an hermit exposes himself by entering into cities, where his eyes and ears meet so many dangerous objects? How comes it then to pass that you dare hazard yourself in a place frequented by so much bad company, both of men and women, and where you cannot possibly avoid the hearing and seeing of many improper things? In the name of God, then, do so no more, but hasten back to your solitude in the desert, where, by the assistance of God's grace, you will be secure from danger." The young man replied—" Good father, be not uneasy at what I have done, since perfection does not consist in what you see in the exterior, but in the purity of the heart; for as long as I keep my heart undefiled I shall perform all that God requires of me." At this the old man, lifting up his hands to heaven, cried out, "Lord, be you for ever blessed and praised; for my part, I have spent five-and-fifty years in the desert, and lived with all recollection possible, yet I find not this purity of heart; and this young man, notwithstanding his frequenting scandalous houses, has obtained it." This is the best answer to all those that shall make the same objection. For notwithstanding all agree that the very essence of perfection consists in purity of heart, in charity, and the love of God, yet no man will ever attain these unless he be extremely careful in guarding his senses, and in the observance of exterior modesty.

To prove this point, St. Bonaventure says that interior recollection is acquired an preserved by exterior recollection ; the latter being the chief guard and outwork of the heart. Nature never produces a tree without leaves and bark, or fruit without skin ; but still in all her productions provides both for ornament and preservation. Grace, in like manner, whose acts are conformable to those of nature, though much more perfect, never forms a virtue in the heart, but she gives as companion to it the modest exterior we speak of. This is the bark and skin of devotion, and also of all interior recollection and purity of heart. If you take this off, the rest will quickly decay and corrupt. Every one knows that a good or bad habit of body consists not in outward appearances, or in looking well or ill, but in the due proportion or disproportion of the humours within. Notwithstanding, when we see a man look ill, we presently conclude that he is not well, saying, do you not observe his countenance, his colour, his eyes ? The same parity holds in order to our soul's health, which is easily inferred from outward symptoms.

St. Basil farther explains this doctrine by another apposite comparison, which is frequently made use of by other holy men. " Our senses," says he, " are the windows of our soul, through which it beholds all that passes by." This established, he adds, that there is the same difference between a recollected and dissipated soul as there is between an honest and dishonest woman. The first you will rarely see at her window ; the second is continually either there or at the door, to see who passes by, and to call in some one or other to talk with her. " Observe here," says St. Basil, " the difference between a modest, sober religious, and one that is not so. The modest man seldom looks through the windows of his senses—he lives retired within himself, and is always recollected. The other is always at the window, to see and hear all that is done and said, and spends his time idly with any one that passes by." But to return to our comparison : it is certain that, though to frequent or not frequent a window must be no infallible sign of a woman's honesty or dishonesty. yet, notwithstanding, it betrays too much levity, and will certainly sooner or later be the loss of her honour, if it be not already forfeited. In the same manner it is also certain that Christian perfection is not essentially contained in the recollection of our senses, yet certainly a vain and curious soul, which is delighted in pouring out itself upon all exterior objects it meets with, will never acquire this Christian perfection, nor true purity of heart.

Let us here observe one thing more that is very essential, which is, that as exterior recollection helps to create and preserve a good exterior, so interior recollection infallibly causes a good, edifying exterior. "Where Jesus Christ is, there also is modesty." (Epist. cxxiii.) says St. Gregory Nazianzen. When solid virtue is within, there is always gravity and modesty and a good comportment without; and the modesty which flows from an humble and peaceful interior is what St. Ignatius requires of us. He does not look for that feigned and short-lived one which, on the first occasion proves to be false. No! he requires the modesty which springs from an humble, mortified, and recollected heart, and which produces effects proportionate to its cause.

What I have said will help us easily to discover whether a man be fit for a spiritual life or not, and whether or not he be a proficient in virtue. In the following simile St. Austin shows how we can make this discovery. "We are now," says he, "come to man's estate, and have left off all those little amusements we had when children, which, if any body had then interrupted, we should have been very much offended; but now being men, we can part with them without the least difficulty, since we perceive they are sports fit only for children." The same thing happens in a spiritual course. When a Christian has once tasted the sweetness of heaven and heavenly things, and begins by little to advance in spirit and perfection, he is not troubled at being bereft of those sensual pleasures he was before delighted with, because now these appear to him as fit only for children, and unbecoming one at man's estate. "When I was a child," says St. Paul, "I spoke as a child, I thought as a child, and discoursed as a child; but now being grown a man, I have left off all childish toys." (1 Cor. xiii. 11.) If you desire to know whether you are still a child, look and consider well whether you have left off all childish sports. Do you still please yourself with the little follies and trifles of children? Do you feed your eyes with all the vain objects they meet with? Do you glut your ears with all sort of discourses, and give full scope and liberty to your tongue? Be assured if you do this, that you are still a child, and very imperfect; because such childish sports as these are your only satisfaction. For the spiritual man who daily increases in perfection disdains such foolish trifles, and is far from taking any pleasure in them —being a man, he contemns and laughs at this children's play, and is ashamed to engage himself therein.

————o————

CHAPTER IV.

Of the profit and advantage of silence.

MODERATION in speaking is one of those means which conduce very much to our progress in virtue and perfection; and, on the contrary, intemperence of speech is the greatest hindrance to both. These two great truths are set down by St. James in his canonical epistle, where he says, "If there be any one that offends not with his tongue, he is a perfect man." (James iii. 2.) Again, "If any one thinks himself religious, and bridles not his tongue, but permits it upon all occasions to discover his thoughts, his religion is vain and unprofitable." (James i. 26.) St. Jerome makes use of this passage to recommend silence to us, and says, that the fathers of the desert, resting upon this authority, were extremely careful in the observance of this virtue; and that he himself had met with several of them who for seven years together had not spoken to any one. Denis the Carthusian assures us that this sentence of the apostle caused the rule of silence to be made in all religious orders, and urged superiors to order a public penance to be inflicted upon those who should break it.

Now, let us see the reason why it is so earnestly recommended to us. Can then one idle word be so great a crime? Does it include any other injury than the loss of a moment of time, or is it any more than a venial sin which a little holy water is able to wash away? Yes, certainly, there is more harm in it than the bare loss of a moment, and it must needs be of greater importance than we are aware of; since the holy scripture, which is far from exaggerating our faults, and does not use false weights to make them the heavier, insists so much upon it. The saints and doctors of the church, whom God has favoured with particular lights, for the better understanding of holy mysteries, have taken a great deal of pains to make us sensible of the advantages of holy science, and of the great inconveniences caused by a breach thereof.

St. Basil recommends it to beginners in virtue as a help to speak well, which is a thing very difficult, and requires a great deal of prudence. We employ several years to make ourselves masters of other arts and sciences, and why should we not do the same in the art of speaking, since it is a science we shall never perfect ourselves in without long study and much application? You will answer me, perhaps, that frequent practising of an art is the best way to acquire it, and, consequently, speaking much is the readiest way to speak well. "No," says St. Basil, "if you would learn to speak well first learn to be silent." The reason he gives is this; many circumstances are required to speak well, which, not being accustomed to observe, we speak whatever occurs to us, in the manner we please, and without either rule or method. On the contrary, silence produces two admirable effects, which teaches us how to speak well. The first is, to forget all the language the world had taught us—a circumstance which is as necessary for us, in order to speak well, as it is for one that pretends to be master of any science to abandon the false maxims he had already learned. The second effect is, that long silence gives us time to learn how to speak; it gives us leisure to observe the most accomplished in this science—their manner, their deliberation, their sweetness; and also their gravity and prudence, that we may form ourselves on these models. An apprentice observes how his master works, thereby to inform himself, and to become afterwards master of his trade; so we ought continually to hearken to the best masters in the art of speaking, and endeavour to imitate them as much as we are able. Take notice, therefore, of some one of the more ancient and exemplary religious: observe with how much sweetness and ease he gives ear to all that come to him; and with how much charity he despatches their affairs. See! notwithstanding any other business he has in his hands, he seems as if he had nothing else to do but to attend to the concerns of those that come to him. Nay, what is still more, his temper is ever even—he is ever himself. But how different is his manner from yours, when at any time you are employed in ever so small a

matter.   Are not your answers not only too brisk and peremp-
tory, but sometimes very disobliging ?   Look upon another, and
see with what joy and readiness he submits to his superior's
orders, without alleging any pretended excuses, or desiring that
any one else should supply his place.   Take notice of another,
who is never heard to say what may give the least offence to his
brother, either in or out of time of recreation, either in jest or
earnest, either to his face or behind his back ; so that when,
where, or of whomsoever he speaks, he always shows respect
and esteem for the person he speaks of ;—and learn of all these
to do the like.   Last of all, observe another, who, upon some
harsh and ill language given him, makes no reply, but hand-
somely and charitably dissembles, as if he did not hear it, veri-
fying the royal prophet's words, " I am become like a man that
is deaf." (Ps. xxxvii. 15.)   Observe also how that at the same
time, by thus conquering himself he gains his brother's heart ;
and learn to behave yourself thus also, in the like occasion.
These are happy effects of silence which St. Basil points out.
The same saint farther adds, " As often as we leave off the custom of speaking ill, so often we forget what we ought to be ignorant of ; and at the same time get an opportunity of learning
what we ought to know." (In Reg. xiii.)

St. Ambrose and St. Jerome, writing upon this passage of
Ecclesiastes, " There is a time to be silent and a time to speak,"
(Eccl. iii. 7,) confirm what I have said, and tell us that
Pythagoras ordained five years' silence to his scholars, that they
might in that time forget those errors they had before learned
from others ; and that by hearing only him, their master, they
might make themselves able men, and learn those truths they
were afterwards to discourse of and teach others.   " Let us,
then," concludes St. Jerome, " first learn to hold our tongues,
that hereafter we may never use them but to the purpose.   Let
us, then, keep silence for some time, and hearken with attention
to what our masters teach us; looking upon this as an undoubted
truth, that after a long silence, and having been a long time
scholars, we shall also have our turn, and become masters."
(Hier. in Eccl.)

Though what these great saints have said seems intended only
for beginners, yet, without doubt, it equally concerns all.   For
either you are a long time in religion, or you are not ; or you
desire to behave yourself like a novice, in what relates to your
tongue, or else like a senior—-take which you please.   If you

will govern yourself like a novice, the first lesson they will set you will be to hold your peace, till you shall be able to speak as you should do. If you would act as a senior, you must be a living example to others, and the very model according to which the novices are to be formed, and from whom all young beginners must take their pattern. But I could wish you would rather govern yourself like a senior than like a novice; since in this case your obligation is the stricter. For, having done your noviceship, and for a long time observed the rule of silence, in order to learn to speak, it is not to be doubted, after all this, but that you know the art of speaking, and are, by your example, able to help others in it. But in case you have not been a novice, nor as yet have learned to speak, it is necessary you should become novice, that by this means you may learn of what and when you are to speak.

———o———

CHAPTER V.

That silence is a very great help to prayer.

SILENCE not only teaches us to speak with men, but with God also, and makes us men of prayer. This is St. Jerome's opinion, who says, that "this was the reason why the holy fathers of the desert, who were instructed by the Holy Ghost, were so careful in the observance of silence; which they looked upon to be the author and preserver of contemplation." (Hier. in Reg. Mon. c. xxii.) St. Diadocus says, "silence is an admirable virtue, being the mother of our best and most holy thoughts." (De Perf. Spir.) Do you wish to be a man of prayer, to converse familiarly with God, to be freed from bad thoughts, and always be in a disposition to receive divine inspirations? Take care to live in recollection and silence. A great noise hinders us from hearing what is said to us; in like manner, secular business and much idle talk permit us not to listen to divine inspirations, nor to conceive in our hearts what they would urge us to. When God wishes to converse with a soul, he desires to be alone with her. "I will lead her" says he, "into solitude, and speak to her heart." (Osee ii. 14.) "There I will feed her with the sweet milk of spiritual comfort." (Ibid.) God is a spirit, and it is a spiritual retreat he asks of us. "What signifies," says St. Gregory, "the solitude of the body, if the mind be not also in solitude?" (In Job. i. 30, c. xii.) God requires a closet in your heart to con-

verse with you in ; at which time you may truly say with the
Psalmist—"I have fled from the world and retired to the
desert." (Ps. liv. 8.) But to do this, you need not make yourself an hermit, nor quit those places where charity to your neighbour requires your presence. If, then, you desire to maintain
devotion in your heart, and to be always in a good disposition for
prayer, live in silence and recollection, when obedience and
charity permits. It is a good observation of St. Diadocus, that
as by often opening the door of a hot bath the heat is exhaled ;
so a frequent and unprofitable opening of the mouth, emits the
fervour of devotion, divides the heart between many objects, and
leaves a soul so destitute of good thoughts, that it is even very
surprising to see how instantaneously the spirit of devotion evaporates thereby. If, then, you desire to be free, and to manage
your time so that you may still find a vacant hour for prayer,
keep silence, and you will find sufficient time wherein to entertain both God and yourself. Thomas-à-Kempis says : "That if
we bid adieu to all unprofitable conversations, if we employ ourselves no more than necessity requires, and disengage ourselves
from the vain curiosities of the world, we shall find sufficient
leisure to admit holy inspirations ; but if we love to talk much,
and to fix our hearts upon all those objects that strike or please
our senses, we must not wonder that time is too short, and that
we scarce ever find enough for our ordinary actions. Hence it
was that the children of Israel, being dispersed all over Egypt
to seek straw, could never perform the task set them ; so that
Pharao's officers treated them harshly.

There is still another thing very necessary to be observed,
which is, that silence naturally disposes to prayer, as well as
prayer to silence : " I have more impediment and slowness of
tongue," said Moses to God, "ever since you were pleased to
speak to me." (Exod. iv. 10.) The prophet Jeremias also, after
he began to speak to God, looked upon himself as an infant, and
as one that knew not how to speak. St. Gregory takes notice,
that those who give themselves to spirituality, and who frequently converse with God, grow deaf and dumb to all earthly
things, and can neither speak themselves, nor bear to hear others
speak of them : " For being unwilling to speak of anything but
what they love, all other things become very tedious and intol-
erable to them." (Lib. vii. in Job.) This we ourselves sometimes experience, when God is pleased to shower down his graces
upon us in prayer, and when we come from it full of devotion ;

for then we do not desire to speak to any body, but keep our eyes so modestly cast down that we seem to have lost all curiosity; insomuch, that those who should see us then would think us tongue-tied, and bereft of every sense. From what does this come, but from our interior conversation with God, and from our being in such a condition as diverts us from seeking any satisfaction from creatures? On the contrary, when we love to talk, and when the mind is spread on external objects, it is a proof that we have no interior fervour. "How comes it to pass," says the author of the Following of Christ; "that we so much love to converse with one another, since we rarely do it without hurt to our conscience? The reason is, because we desire to be comforted by one another—because we are willing to disburthen our hearts of a multitude of thoughts that oppress it—and because we take pleasure in speaking of what we love, or of what we are afraid of, as being opposite to our natural inclinations." We cannot find in our hearts to live without some little contentment or other, and having none within ourselves, or from God, we endeavour to find it abroad in creatures. Hence it is, that our exterior failings, for example, our violation of silence, loss of time, and many other irregularities, are so much taken notice of in religion, and so severely punished. For these faults, though they seem small in themselves, yet are a great sign of a soul's being very little advanced in virtue, and show that the person who commits them wants the qualities requisite for a spiritual life, and that he has not as yet tasted how sweet God is; because he knows not how to entertain himself with him, when alone in his cell. When a chest has no lock upon it, we easily conclude that there is nothing in it of any considerable value; in like manner, where silence and custody of senses are wanting, there is seldom any considerable virtue to be found; and therefore when we perceive any one to be deficient in these, we form a judgment of him accordingly.

————o————

CHAPTER VI.

That silence is one of the chief means to obtain perfection.

A CERTAIN religious, no less versed in spiritual than in human learning, said, what is so very much to the praise of silence, that it may perhaps seem an exaggeration, though it is a truth experimentally certain. These are his words: "Silence well observed is sufficient to reform, not only one religious house, but even a whole order. Keep silence well, and I pledge myself for the reformation of all irregularities. The reason is this, when silence is strictly kept in a community, all are employed in their spiritual advancement, which is the only object they had in view in embracing religion. But if silence is not kept, there is nothing heard but complaints, idle stories, murmurings, detraction, and particular disgusts; which are not only introduced, but fomented by too great liberty of conversation. It is hereby that one man makes many lose their time, and one inconvenience draws on another, till at length all regular observance decays, and the whole house in a very short time loses the name of being religious, and becomes both secular and profane. On the contrary, where silence is observed, it consecrates the house to God, causes all to breathe an air of sanctity, and fills it with an odour of virtue and recollection, which excites all strangers to piety, and makes them cry out—" God is truly here, this is the house of God, and gate of heaven." (Gen. xxviii. 16.) What we say here of a house in general, may be applied to every person in particular. Let any one religious observe his rule of silence exactly, and I pledge myself he shall soon amend his imperfections. For, let us upon those days we have spoken much examine ourselves at night, and we shall find that we have fallen into a great many faults. "Much misery," says Solomon, " attends much talk." (Prov. xiv. 23.) Whereas, if we had strictly observed silence, we should scarce find matter for our examen. " For," as the same wise man says, " he that guards his mouth, defends his soul;" (Prov. xiii. 3), of which truth the heathens themselves were not ignorant ; wherefore a Lacedemonian philosopher being asked why Lycurgus had enacted so few laws for that commonwealth, answered, " those that speak little need not many laws to keep them in due subjection." (Pluta.) This is the reason why silence is sufficient to work an entire reformation, not only in one particular person or house, but in the whole body of a religious order, and even in kingdoms and commonwealths also. Hence we can easily infer why the ancient fathers of the desert had so high an esteem of the practice of silence, and why it is made so important a rule in all religious orders. Denis, the Carthusian, assures us that this was the reason why the apostle taught us this great moral above cited. " He that offends not in his tongue is perfect. He that thinks himself religious, and does not bridle his tongue, his religion is vain and unprofitable." (James v. 2.)

Let every man, then, consider attentively at how little expense he may be perfect, and how easy are the means prescribed. Do you desire to be a virtuous and perfect man? St. James the apostle assures you that silence will accomplish your desires. Do you wish to be a spiritual contemplative? The saints engage that silence will make you so. On the contrary, if you are careless in the observance of this virtue you will never arrive to perfection : and, as for contemplation, you will always be a stranger to it. Pray tell me if ever you saw a great talker much given to prayer, or to any other spiritual duty? No, certainly, such a one will scarce ever advance in virtue ; since the scripture, not without reason, doubts of it, when it says, "shall the man that talks much be justified?" (Job. xi. 2.) Wherefore, St. Gregory, writing upon this passage says, that "a man much given to talk will never make any great progress in virtue ;" in proof of which assertion he quotes many texts from scripture, and this among the rest, "a talkative man shall miss his way upon earth ;" (Ps. cxxxix. 13), that is to say, he shall not advance in virtue, but Jacob's malediction to Ruben shall fall upon his head ; " you are poured out like water, you shall not increase." (Gen. xlix. 4.) Your heart is always taken up with vain and unprofitable entertainments, it is always wandering abroad and absent from you; wherefore you shall never make any great advancement in perfection, nor shall you increase in virtue.

The saints justly compare a talkative man to a vessel without cover, which God in the book of Numbers, commanded to be looked upon as unclean. "A vessel," says he, "that is open, and has no cover, shall be unclean ;" (Num. xix. 15), it being always exposed to receive all kind of dirt and filth. In the same manner the heart of a man, by keeping his mouth always open, is defiled with sins and imperfections. The Holy Ghost confirms this in several other places of scripture: "He that uses many words, wounds his own soul." (Eccl. xx.) "Where there is much talk, sin will not be wanting." (Prov. x. 19.) And lastly, "to speak much is a very great folly." (Eccl. v. 2.)

I wish to God that we had not daily experience of this truth. St. Gregory taking notice of this inconvenience, says thus: " your discourse is good at the beginning, but presently it degenerates into idle talk, than raillery succeeds, which is sometimes too sharp and reflecting : at last the company grows warm, and you become too hot also in proving what you said ; and to make it appear the more probable, rather than fail you would not stick at a lie, nor perhaps at something still worse. Thus what is little in the beginning, grows great in the end, and jest is turned into earnest."

Albertus Magnus goes farther yet, and says, that "the devil easily overcomes where silence is not kept;" (Lib. de virt. cap. 31), and proves it from the Proverbs: "a man that is profuse, and cannot contain himself in speaking, is like an open and unwalled town." (Prov. xxv. 28.) St. Jerome says upon this passage that "as a city without walls is continually exposed to the enemy's incursions, and in great danger of being plundered, so a Christian who is not sheltered and defended by silence lies open to all the temptations of the devil, and is in very great danger of surrendering." We may add to this the following comparison, which comes more home to my design, and confirms what I have said:—"It is easy to surprise a careless and negligent man, but very hard to do so to a person that is valiant and always upon his guard. Thus the devil finds no great difficulty in deceiving a man that talks much, and whose thoughts are quite taken up with vain and impertinent objects. Whereas, he that is recollected, and lives in silence, is never unprovided, but is always in readiness, to resist his attempts, so that his enemy has a great deal to do before he can surprise him."

---o---

CHAPTER VII.

That modesty, recollection, and silence do not make us melancholy, but rather pleasant and agreeable.

THE consequence which ought to be drawn from the preceding discourse is very remarkable, which is, that this retired way of living, in which we have our eyes modestly cast down; in which nothing but mere necessity forces us to speak, or to hear others; in which the love of God makes us blind, deaf, and dumb; is not an uneasy, melancholy life, but is so much the more sweet and pleasant, as the conversation with God, to which it exalts us, is above all the satisfaction and charms that human conversation can impart. "Let others think what they please," says St. Jerome, "for my part the world is a prison to me, but solitude a paradise." (Ep. v. ad Rust. Mon.) St. Bernard showed himself to be of the same mind when he said: "I am never less alone, than when alone," (Ad. frat. de. mon. Dei), for it was then he found the best company, and was most of all contented;

God being still with him, who alone can give the most solid comfort to a soul. Those persons that are unacquainted with these private entertainments and conversations with God, and have never yet relished the sweets of prayer, and of a spiritual life, will meet with a great deal of discontent and sadness in this sort of life ; but a good religious man will find therein much comfort and content of mind.

From what has been said, we may discover how great is the error of those, who, judging other persons by themselves, and seeing one of their brethren grave and modest, walking with his eyes fixed upon the ground, without stopping to talk with all he meets, presently concludes that he is troubled with some temptation or other, or is in some great affliction. And by frequently mentioning these their suspicions, they sometimes cause the parties to become so uneasy, that several, through an imprudent bashfulness, have afterwards never dared to observe that silence and modesty they were even obliged to, and which otherwise they would have observed. We ought to be extremely careful in this particular, that the indiscretion and want of recollection in one, may not turn to the prejudice of many. When you yourself find no satisfaction in modesty and silence, you presently think your brother to have a similar disposition ; or perhaps it may also happen, that you have no mind to suffer these good qualities in another, because they are a continual censure on your own conduct. But do not trouble yourself, nor disturb your brother in so holy a practice, since he feels more content in it than you ; for his joy is interior, and truly spiritual. Hence the apostle takes notice, that the servants of God " carry indeed a kind of sorrowfulness in their looks, but always possess a joy in their hearts." (2 Cor. vi. 10.) Their outward appearance seems the more sad and full of sorrow, because their sole delight lies hid within. Heathens as well as Christians are of opinion, that there is no joy so true and lasting as that which is interior. That gold which is found upon the surface of the earth is not comparable to that which lies deep and hid within the veins and bowels thereof ; nor is that content true and solid which shows itself only in words and exterior signs, wherein the soul has no part or share at all. True and solid joy lies low in the bottom of the heart ; and this true contentment can only be found in the peace of a good conscience, in a generous disdain of all perishable and fading objects, and in a mind that soars above the earth, and above all goods that are transitory.

CHAPTER VIII.

What is to be observed in speaking.

" LORD, put a guard upon my mouth, and shut up my lips with a door," (Ps. cxl. 3,) says the royal prophet. St. Gregory and St. Ambrose, speaking of the great inconveniences which are caused by the tongue, and prescribing silence as the best way to avoid them, start this objection :—" Alas! are we then to remain dumb ?" They answer, by no means ; since the virtue of silence does not consist in not speaking, but in speaking when we ought to speak, and in being silent when we ought to be silent ; just as the virtue of temperance consists not in a continual fast, but in eating what is necessary, and when it is necessary, and in abstaining from everything else. " There is a time to speak, and a time to be silent ; (Eccl. iii. 7) ; but to do both well, requires a great deal of prudence ; since unseasonable silence is as improper as ill-timed speaking. We are taught how to behave ourselves in both occasions, by the words above cited ; " Lord, put a guard upon my mouth, and shut up my lips with a door." " David," says St. Gregory, "did not ask of God, that he would wall up his mouth, or shut it so that he should never be able to open it ; but only desired that it might be so secured, that he might always have the liberty and free use of it, as necessity should require ; to inform us that the virtue of silence consists no less in speaking, than in holding our peace when necessity requires either the one or the other." Solomon, following his royal father's steps, begs the same favour in these words : " Who will give a guard to my mouth, and set the seal of prudence upon my lips, that I may never offend by them, nor be ruined by my tongue ?" (Eccl. xxii. 33.) So difficult is it to speak seasonably and to the purpose, that Solomon, the wisest of men, petitions heaven that he might be able to discern the proper time, both of speaking and of being silent. For, in speaking, the omission of a single circumstance constitutes a fault ; there being this difference between good and evil, that in order to constitute a good action, all the requisite conditions must concur at the same time ; but to render an action bad, a single defect is sufficient.

Now let us come to these circumstances that are indispensably required to speak well : they are handed down to us by St. Basil,

St. Ambrose, St. Bernard, and many other holy men. The first and chief is to consider very well beforehand what we are to say. This lesson is taught us by nature itself, which has so ordered that our ears should be always open, and ready to receive every sound, but has wisely placed our lips and teeth as a double barrier for the defence of our tongue. By this means she teaches us to be forward and ready in hearing, but very moderate and reserved in speaking, according to what St. James prescribes, "let every one be quick to hear but slow to speak." (James i. 19.) The anatomy and structure of the tongue teaches us the same thing ; it has two veins or branches in it, one of which goes to the heart, the source of all our passions, the other mounts to the brain, the seat of reason, in order to show us that our words should come from the heart, and be regulated by reason. St. Austin made the same remark, when he advised us, " to call our words to the test before we speak them ;" that reason might first correct and polish our thoughts, before they come to the tongue. It is in this that the scripture places the difference between wise men and fools, when it says, " the heart of a fool is in his mouth, but the mouth of a wise man is in his heart." (Eccl. xxi. 29.) Because the heart of a fool suffers itself to be carried away with the violence of his tongue, and permits it to vent whatsoever occurs, acting hereby as if the tongue and heart were only one member ; when, on the contrary, the wise man has his mouth in his heart, because all he says has first been seriously considered, and found conformable to reason, he makes his tongue depend upon his heart for every word it speaks.

St. Cyprian says, " that as a temperate man does not swallow his meat before he has chewed it well, so a prudent man never utters anything which he has not beforehand nicely weighed in his heart, knowing that rash and inconsiderate language is often the occasion of quarrel and dissension." Another saint advises us to be as long in bringing a word out of our mouths, as we are in taking money out of our purse to discharge a debt. " How slow and dull are we in opening our purse? How often do we consider whether the debt be due, and how much money it comes to? Use the same caution in opening your mouth," says the same saint. Consider first whether you ought to speak at all, and when in what manner; and be sure to overshoot yourself no more in speaking, than you would do in paying more than is due to your creditor. St. Bonaventure also counsels us to become misers in our words, and to part with them as warily as they do with their money.

St. Bernard in this is more rigorous than St. Austin, who only required that every word should be once examined before it was spoken ; but he will have it " be called twice to the test of a serious examen, before it comes to the tongue to be uttered." (In spec. Monach.) St. Bonaventure's sentiment is the same ; and the abbot Amon, as St. Ephrem tells us, was of opinion, that we should first communicate our thought to God, and tell him what we would say, and what reasons we designed to make use of in our discourse, which having done we might then venture to speak, and by so doing believe we put God's will in execution, having consulted him beforehand. Here you see the first circumstance of speaking well clearly laid down ; which, if you observe well, you will succeed in all the rest.

The second circumstance recommended to us is the end and intent of speaking. For it is not sufficient to discourse of what is proper and good in itself, but the design and intent of our discourse ought equally to be good and virtuous. There are several that talk like saints, but it is only to deceive their auditors, and make them think them devout or able men ; whereas they manifest their folly by the one, and disguise their hypocrisy by the other.

St Basil points out the third circumstance, which is to consider the person that speaks, the person spoken to, and the company in whose presence we speak. In pursuance of this rule the saint gives a great many good documents in order to instruct young people how they ought to behave themselves before aged persons, and to show those in orders how they should behave before priests; alleging these words of scripture, " do not speak much in the presence of priests and elders." (Eccl. vii. 15.) " Youth," says St. Bernard, " shows its submission, deference, and veneration to old age by silence ; that being the greatest testimony of the honour and respect they pay it." St. Bonaventure renders this still clearer by the following comparison : " the fear of God," says he, " makes us appear with modesty and respect in his presence, and brings us into favour with him ; even so, venerable old age commands duty and veneration from us, and even obliges us to respectful silence, and a modest behaviour."

The proper time of speaking is the fourth circumstance recommended to us by St. Ambrose, as the chief part of prudence. "The wise man," says Ecclesiasticus, "will not speak but in a due time, but the impudent and imprudent observe no order or method in their words." (Eccl. xx. 7.) To make us the more observant of this circumstance, the holy scripture give this high commen-

dation of those that use it, " a word in season is like a golden
apple upon a bed of silver." (Prov. xxv. 11.) Where this caution is not used, confusion follows, and the best things lose their
value and become disagreeable ; for, according to the Wise man,
" a parable never comes well, or has any force, out of the mouth
of a fool ; because he pronounces it not in due season." (Eccl.
xx. 22.) This circumstance requires of us never to interrupt
another's discourse ; it being not only against the rules of common civility, but even of Christianity. " Interrupt not another
whilst he is speaking," (Eccl. xi. 8.) says Ecclesiasticus, " have
patience till he has done, and then speak in your turn ;" and the
Wise man gives us still another instruction, when he says, " he
that answers before he understands what is said to him, shows
himself a fool, and deserves to be confounded." (Prov. xviii. 13.)
He answers to he knows not what, and therefore meets with confusion corresponding to his folly. He imagines them to say what
they never thought of, which makes his answer impertinent, and
though he designed to show his quickness of apprehension, yet
instead thereof he discovers his own extravagance. St. Basil
gives us very good counsel on this point, and advises us to be
silent when a question is asked another ; nay, suppose that we
be engaged in company, and some one starts a question to all in
general, we must never take it as addressed to us in particular,
nor presume to be the first in answering. Humility forbids so
great an arrogance as to look upon yourself as the best man in
the company. It is better to be silent till your opinion be asked
in particular, and then offer what prudence shall suggest.

The tone or manner of speaking is the fifth circumstance.
This is prescribed us by our holy rule, when it ordains us to
speak in that low voice which becomes a religious. This is not
only a very material circumstance, but is one of the chief parts
of silence ; wherefore the gospel takes particular notice of the
manner of Martha's addressing herself to her sister upon the
coming of our Saviour to raise Lazarus. The text says, " she
called her sister Mary in silence, and told her that their Master
was come, and asked for her." (John xi. 28.) " How could she
do this in silence," says St. Austin, on this place, " when she
expressly said, ' our Master is come and asks for you ?' Yes,
she did it," says the saint, " and in silence ; because she spoke
softly and in a low voice." The same happens among religious,
who though they be together at work, and speak to one another,
yet there is no breach of silence amongst them so long as they

speak in a low voice. Whereas, should they change their tone and talk aloud, let their necessity be ever so great, it would not excuse them from a breach of silence ; so necessary is it upon all occasions, and in all places, to speak softly, and to observe a decorum in our words, that we may appear true religious, and make our house appear so too. St. Bonaventure esteems it a great fault for a religious to speak loud, and would have us speak so as to make those only hear us who are close by us. If anything presses you to speak to one that is at a distance, go to him, it being an injury to religious modesty to speak at a distance or to call out aloud. The same saint bids us also speak more softly than ordinary when it is night, or when we are retired to go to rest, for fear of disturbing others, which caution is also to be used in the sacristy, refectory, chapter-house and other places of respect and silence.

An engaging behaviour, and a pleasant and serene countenance, are also reduced by St. Bonaventure to this circumstance. We must not put on a dark and austere look, wry mouths, rolling and staring eyes; and the contraction of our nose and eye-brows must be avoided ; we must not shake our head, or use any other light or unbecoming gesture. This is what our holy founder commands in those admirable rules which he wrote on modesty. As to our voice St. Ambrose "would have it even, and of an equal and constant tone, without any languishing stops or interruptions, free from all affectation and effeminacy, but grave and masculine as becomes a man, yet, at the same time, so governed as neither to appear harsh nor rude." (Lib. i. Off. c. 19.) And St. Bernard is of the same opinion when he says, that "as a whining and effeminate voice or gestures are not to be used, so such as are clownish and unmannerly are equally to be avoided." (De. ord. Vit. et Mor.) A religious ought in all his words to aim at a happy composition of sweetness and gravity, but most of all when he reprehends another, otherwise his words will gain no credit, and all his labour will be lost. Nay, St. Bonaventure does not stick to say, that he who discovers the passion of anger in correcting another shows that he is more ready to afflict than charitably to help the party. " Vice can never teach us virtue," impatience cannot instruct us how to suffer patiently, and pride can never teach us humility. Whereas, patience and mildness would at once both have edified and prevailed upon the offender, far beyond the best discourse in which the least heat appears. The following excellent sentence of St. Ambrose suits our purpose

very well :—" Tell a man," says he, " his fault, but do not up-
braid him, advise him so that he may perceive his error without
his receiving the least offence ; " which is confirmed by what St.
Paul advises Timothy—" In your corrections," says he, " be
mild and gentle, treat old men as your fathers, young men as
your brethren ; aged women as your mothers, and young ones
as your sisters." (1 Tim. v. 1.)

An affected style by which a man would be thought learned
or eloquent, is extremely improper; and without doubt those
preachers who make it their study to be masters of a quaint and
elegant style are censurable. Their diligence in seeking after
proper terms makes them neglect their matter. Their words
are empty, they want the force and energy of the Holy Ghost,
and produce not the fruit that might be expected from sermons.
Water that is good has no taste ; in like manner, good language
should never relish of affectation.

To conclude, there are so many circumstances to be observed,
so many conditions requisite to speak well, that it would be a
wonder not to fail in some of them. For this reason silence is
the securest harbour we can put into. It protects us from all
the inconveniences and dangers to which our words expose us.
" He who is cautious and careful in his words, frees his soul from
many afflictions " (Prov. xxi. 23), says the Wise man. And an
ancient father assures us that, " wheresoever we live, if we keep
silence and are sparing of our words, we shall live in peace."
Seneca also says to his friend in one of his epistles, that " there
was nothing more profitable than to be retired, and to converse
little with others, but much with one's self." (Ep. civ.) All
applaud that frequent saying of Arsenius, "I have often repented to have spoken, but never to have held my peace." The
same is related of Socrates ; and the wise Seneca gives the following reason for what I just now quoted from him : " though
you are not permitted," says he, "to speak now, yet you may
do it afterwards, but when you have once spoken, it is not then
in your power to recall it, according to the common saying,
' words are irrevocable. ' " St. Jerome compares a word when
once uttered to a stone cast out of a man's hand, which being
once thrown, he cannot hinder from doing all the mischief it is
capable of doing, and therefore he advises us to be very wary,
and consider seriously before we speak ; because afterwards it
will be too late to do so. This advice attaches to the first circumstance we spoke of in the beginning.

Let us therefore resolve to stand upon our guard, and watchful over our tongue, with the royal prophet, who said, "I am now determined to take care of my ways, that I may not offend with my tongue." (Ps. xxxviii. 1.) St. Ambrose, commenting upon these words, says : "there are some ways which we may follow safely, and others in which we ought to be very wary and cautious. The first are the ways of God, the others are our own. Those are secure, these lead to destruction, and cause us quickly to lose ourselves, unless silence be our guard and safeguard." When St. Pambo first retired into the wilderness, his ignorance of that way of living obliged him to ask help and instruction of an old experienced hermit, who had lived there for a long time. The good old man received him very kindly, and, out of a charitable condescension to his request, began his instructions from those words of the prophet I before cited ; "I am resolved to take heed of my ways, lest I should offend with my tongue." Here St. Pambo interrupted him, telling him that this one point was sufficient for the present, could he but well comply with its practice. Six months after, the old hermit meeting him, gave him a check for his not coming all that time to take another lesson ; to which he replied, " Father, permit me to confess the truth, and to assure you that I am not as yet perfect in the first you taught me." Many years after, some others asked him whether he had as yet learned his lesson? He returned this answer : "It is now five-and-forty years since I first heard it: yet I still find very great difficulty in its practice." But it was humility that forced him to this modest confession ; For Palladius assures us that he had got this lesson so well, and practised it so diligently, that he always raised his thoughts to God, and consulted him about what he was to say, before he could either speak, or make answer to any one. Which laudable custom drew so many graces from heaven upon him, and preserved him in that innocency, that being upon his death-bed, he owned, that he could not call to mind any one one word of his whole life which he now repented to have spoken. Surius, in his history, tells us of a holy virgin, who lived in such rigid and continual silence, from the exaltation of the holy cross till Christmas, that in all that time she did not speak one word. And Almighty God was so pleased with this her mortification, that he vouchsafed to assure her by a revelation, that at her death, she should in recompense thereof, go straight to heaven without passing through purgatory.

CHAPTER IX.

Of Detraction.

" BRETHREN, do not traduce one another," (James iv. 11), says St. James the Apostle. "Detractors are odious to God," (Rom. i. 30), according to St. Paul ; and Solomon says, that " they are abominable to men." (Prov. xxiv. 9.) For though there are some that outwardly seem to take pleasure in hearing a detractor, yet they detest him in their hearts, and are very reserved and cautious in his company, justly fearing to be treated one day by him in the same unchristian manner he treats others. This alone is sufficient to create in us a horror of this vice. For what can we imagine worse than what is abominable in the sight both of God and man ? But, waving this consideration at present, I will endeavour to make you sensible of the enormity and danger of this sin, in order to preserve you from ever falling into it. It discovers its enormity by the ruin of our neighbour's reputation, which is of greater value than all the goods of fortune, as Solomon assures us in these words : "A good name is better than the greatest riches." (Prov. xxii. 1.) "Be industrious in purchasing to yourself a good reputation, which will last longer than all the treasures of the world." (Eccl. xli. 15.) This makes divines say, that the sin of detraction is so far greater than the sin of theft, as a good name is better than riches. And, when they come to consider whether it be a mortal or a venial sin in some particular cases, they speak of this as of other sins which of their own nature are mortal. They say, that as though theft is in itself a mortal sin, yet the thing stolen being of inconsiderable value, for example, an apple, this extenuates it, and makes it only venial ; so detraction, though it be of its own nature a mortal sin, may prove only venial, when its subject is trivial, and of little or no moment.

Here we are to take notice, that divines, reflecting upon the great danger of falling into this sin, advise us to abstain from the least shadow of it, and not to think anything little, that has any tendency to it, lest, as too often happens, we be deceived in our judgment. For instance, suppose one should say, that a secular person told a lie, which amounts to no more than a venial sin ; and should say the same thing, or only relate one single

imperfection of a religious ; this last may prove a mortal sin, for
the religious man's reputation is much more wounded than the
secular person's is, although you should have fixed a greater
crime upon him.   For, it is certain that the credit of a religious
would suffer more in the opinion of the world by being held up
as a liar, than a secular's would, though you should charge him
with not keeping Lent, and with being a night-walker.   Therefore, to form a true judgment of detraction, we must not look
upon it barely in itself, but with relation to the ill consequences
it produces.   An example will make this doctrine evident ; it is
no crime to be of the race of a Moor or Jew, yet divines look
upon it as a mortal sin to fix that infamy upon one who is already
a Christian.   In like manner, to say that such a religious is silly,
that he is not a man of judgment, (it is the example which
doctors bring upon this matter), is a far greater injury to his
reputation than to charge a secular with a mortal sin, and consequently brings a greater inconvenience along with it than is
generally imagined.   Again, I have a very good opinion of a
certain religious, and look upon him as a prudent discreet man ;
you, on the other hand, tell me, that he is not the man I took
him for, and that he did this and that imprudent action.   By
this you do him a very great prejudice, since, by what you have
told me, he has lost the credit he had with me before.   Likewise, when a religious changes his convent, and is sent to live
in another, ordinarily, the first news he tells is how much he
was disedified in the place he left ; where, says he, such a one is
vain ; another fantastic in his opinion ; another troublesome ;
which things, though they are of no very great moment, yet
they lessen the reputation of the religious house he came from,
and of the persons in it.   Every one may best judge of this by
himself, and see if he would not take it extremely ill, to have
these things said of him, or to pass for such a one as detraction
has described him to be ?   The charity therefore we have for
our own, should show us what we ought to have for our neighbour's reputation,   And since we pretend to perfection, we
should never run the risk, even of doubting whether we have
injured our neighbour in the opinion of another by what we
said, or whether the injury be a mortal sin or not.   Why should
we deliberately plunge ourselves into such inconveniences, from
which very often we cannot emerge without great trouble, disquiet, and difficulty ?   If the doubt remains in a religious man's
breast, it must needs disturb him so far as to make him resolve,

not for the gaining of the whole world, to expose himself hereafter to so cruel an uncertainty. / Therefore, to free ourselves from scruples, anxiety, and remorse of conscience, we must be extraordinary cautious of speaking even of the smallest faults of others, and take most particular care to avoid detraction, to which our tongue is but too much inclined, and to which we ourselves are naturally prone. / There is this difference between those who aspire to perfection, and those who never seek after it, that the former think that to be a great sin, which the latter look upon as a light and trivial imperfection, and by this it is easily known, whether or not a man applies himself seriously to his advancement in virtue.

St. Ignatius was most particularly careful in hiding the faults of his subjects, as we read in the fifth book of his life. For when any disorder happened, he never discovered it to any but to the person whose office it was to see it remedied. And, in discovering it, he was so tender of the reputation of the party concerned, that he never imparted it to two, if he judged one person's knowing of it were sufficient to correct it. Let us learn hence to treat our brethren after the like manner. You see how private and secret St. Ignatius was concerning the least faults of his subjects, although it was in his power to order them a public penance—with how much greater reason ought we abstain from publishing the faults of our brethren?

St. Bonaventure prescribes us an excellent rule for speaking of the absent :—" Be ashamed," says he, " to say that of a man in his absence, which you would not say in his presence," and hereby let every body know their reputation is at all times secure in your hands. This rule is, no doubt, a very good one to guide us, as well in important matters, as in those which appear to us to be trivial ; for, we are often mistaken in the latter, they being more important than they appear to us. Hence, we must not allege that these things are of no consequence, that they are not noticed by others, and that they are public. For the perfection we pretend to admits not of such excuses as these. This our holy founder taught us by his own example : he never spoke of the vices and imperfections of others, though they were public, and recommended the same to be done by us. Let us adopt this practice then, since it is full of wisdom and piety. Let all men be virtuous, honest, and of good reputation in our mouths, and let the world know that our words shall never lesson the honour or reputation of any man.

If by chance you have heard of any one's misdemeanour, do as Solomon bids you : "Have you heard one speak against your neighbour? Let it die within you, and find its grave in your breast, and be asssured that it will do you no harm, nor stifle you." (Eccl. xix. 10.) The Scripture alludes here to one that has drunk poison, who, finding great suffocations in his stomach, and most cruel torments in his bowels, is incapable of ease or relief till he has vomited up all the poison. And the same wise man, for farther evidence in this matter, brings these two following comparisons :—"When a fool has anything to say, he is seized, as it were, with the pangs of child-bed, and he can no more abstain from speaking, than a woman in labour from bringing forth. A word in a fool's heart is like an arrow that sticks in the body of a wild beast." (Eccl. xix. 11, 12.) Whilst the arrow is in the wound, the wild beast tosses and flings about with all its force to get it out. In the like brutish manner a detractor, when once he knows any ill of his neighbour, can never be at rest, nor enjoy any quiet till he has discovered it, and made it public. Let us by no means rank ourselves amongst fools ; but let us imitate the wise, who bury in silence in their hearts whatever they hear to the prejudice of their neighbour.

Father Aquaviva, general of the society, in the treatise he composed to cure the maladies of the soul, has a particular chapter on detraction, where, amongst many other excellent things, he gives us this counsel; and if any one has forgotten himself so far as to fall into this sin, he must not sleep before he has confessed it. And he subjoins these two following reasons for it ; first, because the thing may be very considerable, and consequently dangerous to sleep upon, since a Christian ought never to go to rest, without having prepared himself to go from his bed to his grave. Secondly, though the thing should not be so considerable, yet confession is not only a remedy for the present evil, whatever it be, but also an antidote against it for the future. This counsel is not only profitable for us in the case here proposed, but the practice of it is likewise highly beneficial in all doubts and troubles of conscience ; and the authority of so great a man ought to be no small encouragement to us of the society to make use of it.

CHAPTER X.

We are never to give ear to detraction.

" We are not only," says St. Bernard, " to forbear speaking anything against charity or good manners, but obliged to refrain from even the hearing of such discourse ; because our willingness to hear encourages the other to speak, and we ought to be ashamed to hear what we would be ashamed to speak." (De Ord. Vit. et Mor.) St. Basil, speaking of the punishment merited by the religious who detracts, and by him who willingly listens to detraction, says, that both ought to be separated from the community. He adjudges them equal punishment ; for if the one had not taken pleasure in hearing, the other would not have had confidence to speak what he did ; since no man living is fond of speaking, when he thinks he shall not willingly be heard, or that what he says is disliked.

Here divines discuss the following question, *i.e.*, whether or not the person that willingly hears a detractor, and does not contradict what he says, sins mortally ? They answer, that such person sins mortally in many cases : if it is he, for example, who gives occasion to the detraction, either by encouraging it, or asking some questions which will necessarily introduce it ; if, being at variance with the party ill spoken of, he lends a more willing ear to the detraction ; or seeing that the discourse may prove prejudicial to his neighbour, he does not prevent it, though it is in his power to do so. For, as he that looks on and warms himself, when he might and ought to put out the fire, sins mortally as well as he that sets fire to a house ; even so the offence is mortal both in a detractor, and in him that willingly listens when he ought and should prevent the detraction. For charity obliges him then to help and succour his neighbour ; and, instead of doing this, it is he, perhaps, who by his looks, approves of the detraction and urges its continuance. There are other circumstances wherein by your silence you commit only venial sin ; as when the detractor is a man of great authority, and the respect due to his rank and quality will not permit you to contradict him. Divines make one observation here, highly deserving the attention of religious, it is, that when a superior hears his subjects detracting, he is particularly bound to prevent them, and to defend the neighbour's honour ; and the greater his authority is, the greater is his obligation.

From this doctrine we can infer how we are to behave on similar occasions, and how dangerous it is to dissemble, or to remain silent, through weakness or complaisance. And whereas the corruption of the age is now so great that worldlings can scarce entertain each other without detraction, we ought to feel many scruples on this head—we, who by our institute are obliged to be so much in the world. For may there not be reason to fear that we countenance this vice, either by our asking questions, or by our approving looks and gestures? But abstracting from these scruples, (as every man may say, that he knows well how far he has offended in this point, and whether his sin be mortal or venial,) I fix on this principle—viz., that the persons I am addressing are religious, who labour to be perfect, who pretend to avoid not only mortal and venial sin, but even the least imperfections, and who generously aspire to what is best for themselves, and most profitable to their neighbour. This premised, let me suppose that we are in a company where our neighbour is spoken ill of, and that either out of curiosity we take some little satisfaction in the discourse, or through shame or weakness we seem to consent to it ; pray tell me, is this edifying to the very detractors themselves? When they see a religious, a servant of God, whose profession gives him authority over them, say nothing to the contrary, do they not look upon his silence as an approbation of what they are saying? On the other hand, if they think their discourse sinful and still continue it, they show a disrespect both to you and your order, by presuming that you have neither the courage nor the virtue to contradict them.

To suppress the vice of detraction, St. Austin wrote, and ordered to be hung up in his dining-room, these words :—" BE IT KNOWN TO DETRACTORS THAT THEY ARE FORBIDDEN THIS TABLE." And it is related that when some bishops of his acquaintance who dined with him took the liberty of speaking too freely of their neighbour, he interrupted them, saying : "if they did not cease, he should either blot out those words or rise from table." Here indeed was a display of Christian courage, and an example we should follow on similar occasions. St. Jerome advises us to it in these words : " when you hear any one backbiting another, fly from him as from a serpent." (In Reg. Monach. c. 2.) What a confusion would this be to the detractor. For which reason the same saint adds, " we

ought to do this immediately, that the detractor being put to
confusion, may learn hereafter to treat his neighbours better."
According to this, then, whenever we are in company with a
detractor, we are to request of him to desist ; and if he does not,
we are to retire.

But in case we cannot withdraw on account of the respect due
to the detractor, who is a great personage, we are then to adopt a
gentler method—we are to put on a grave countenance, indica-
tive of our displeasure.   This we are taught by the Holy
Ghost in these words : " as the north wind drives away rain, so
does a severe look drive away detraction ; (Prov. xxv. 23,) and
in these other words also : " Hedge your ears with thorns that
you may not hear any evil tongue." (Eccl. xxviii. 28.)   These
looks of displeasure and this holy change visible in the countenance of a good Christian, who is present at detraction, are the
thorns which defend his own ears, but which pierce the detractor's,
and make him reflect on the harm he has done by censuring his
neighbour's actions.   It is for this reason that the holy scripture
does not command us to stop our ears with cotton, or anything
else that is soft, which would hinder only ourselves from hearing,
but to make use of thorns which may pierce the heart of the
detractor, and correct him.   For as the Wise man says, "a grave
look chastises a delinquent;" (Ibid. vii. 4,) and gives him a sense
of his failings.   When a religious said or did anything disedifying
in company, St. Ignatius, if he were there, made use of this
remedy, and by the grave looks he put on, gave a secret reprehension to the party, and made him sensible he had done amiss.
Nay, when they were but imperfections, visible to no one but
himself, he did the same ; for he was not content with being on
his guard himself, but he earnestly wished that every one else
should be equally on their guard.

To interrupt the detractor by changing the subject of discourse
is another very good remedy against this evil.   In order to do
this, we need not wait for an opportunity of speaking ; the best
time is to do it out of time.   By this the guilty person and all
the company will readily see that the conversation is disapproved
of, and that, unwilling to bring public shame on the detractor,
you, through a motive of charity, abstain from open reprehension.   But if you wait till the conversation takes a different turn,
or till it ends of itself, perhaps you will not be listened to, and
consequently, you will not apply a remedy to the evil.   When a
bull pursues a man, ordinarily, the best way to stop his career

is to throw a cloak before him, to engage his attention, and thus to favour the man's escape ; in like manner, when one is bent on defaming his neighbour throw a cloak before him : *i. e.* introduce some other subject to divert and hinder him from proceeding farther.   And as the person pursued by the bull is obliged to him that threw the cloak for the preservation of his life, so the party defamed owes the preservation of his honour and reputation to him who kindly interrupted the discourse.

—— o ——

CHAPTER XI.

Against Lying.

"ABOVE all things," says the Wise man, " speak truth." (Eccl. xxxvii. 20.)   Methinks there should be no need to reccommend this to religious, since truth carries a sufficient recommendation along with it. Even in the world lying is considered so degrading a vice, that you cannot affront or dishonour a man more than by upbraiding him with a lie.   Judge then how great a crime it must be in a religious, whose reputation is much more easily tarnished in religion, than that of a secular is in the world. Hence we infer, that it is exceedingly base and shameful in a religious to tell a lie ; and, consequently, that he ought never to be guilty of it, though it were even to conceal or excuse his faults. He that will tell a lie to save his credit, or cover his frailties, is far from being a humble mortified man. By our rule we are to seek humiliations, and to embrace all occasions of mortifying ourselves ; yet, when we lie, we not only do not embrace these occasions, but in order to fly them we commit sin. This surely is to keep at a distance from the perfection we have embraced. Divines teach that it is not lawful to tell a lie to save the world ; and will you tell one to prevent the discovery of a small fault, and to save yourself from the confusion of a moment?   There are seven things which God hates, and a " lying tongue is one of them." (Prov. vi. 17.)

Another mode of telling a lie, which does not argue so determined a will, is, when in relating anything we make additions to it.   These additions, whatsoever they are, deviate from truth, which, being one and indivisible, admits not of increase or diminution.   This, however, is a fault very frequently commited by persons who, naturally fond of enhancing the value of the things they speak of, are very apt to exaggerate : and hence, in this particular, we cannot be too much on our guard.

St. Bonaventure adds, that religious in particular ought never use exaggerating terms, as being entirely foreign to religious gravity and modesty. The reason is, that those extravagant expressions raising things above not only what they are, but even above what they can be, their falsehood is plain to every one, and consequently whoever uses these expressions will quickly forfeit all his credit. St. Ignatius very rarely used any words in the superlative degree; because frequently things were thereby exaggerated and made greater than in reality they were; but he always contented himself to relate things simply as they were, without any amplification at all, and his modesty was such, that he never would boldly affirm even what he knew for certain.

It is an admirable lesson, which St. Bernard and many other saints teach us:—"never," says he, " be pertinacious or obstinate in what you affirm or deny ; but whether you be for the negative or affirmative, still modestly seem to doubt." (In form. hon. vit.) Wherefore express yourself thus : if I am not deceived, it is so ; I believe it is so ; or methinks I have heard somebody say so. This way of speaking is prudent, modest, obliging, and proper, both for a Christian and a religious, who ought not to be too confident of themselves, nor judge too favourably of their own opinion. Holy men that are truly humble, are still wont to mistrust themselves, and therefore speak always after this manner. It is related of a great saint, when asked what o'clock it was, that he never answered exactly, it is eight o'clock, it is nine o'clock ; but it is about eight, about nine. On being asked, why he answered in that manner, he said, it was to avoid telling a lie ; which he did, whether the clock had struck or not. And this is another reason why it is both prudent and religious to leave place for an apparant doubt in your answers, and never to press them too home ; as by this means, be the matter as it will, we shall not offend against truth. But if we be very positive in affirming that to be true which, as often happens, afterwards proves false, we are not only confounded, but sometimes give scandal to the person we spoke to, as soon as he has discovered the falsity. I speak here of things which we look upon as certain. For should we boldly affirm the truth of what we are not fully certain, and which appears to us doubtful, we should tell a lie, though the thing were as we affirmed it to be ; at least we should evidently expose ourselves to the danger of telling one, which is almost the same thing.

St. Bonaventure goes farther, and says, "that "in our words we should be candid and sincere;" for we are not only bound to speak truth, but we must also practise candour and sincerity. Religious probity and simplicity ought to be a stranger to equivocations and words of double meaning, which St. Austin pronounces to be lies. "There are some people," says he, "who are unwilling to tell a lie, and and yet are uuwilling to tell the truth ; and will, with this view, make use of such equivocations as induce you to believe one thing, whilst they mean another." (De util. cred.) I own indeed that in some cases of importance it is certainly lawful to make use of equivocations, in order to conceal something necessary to be concealed ; but in ordinary conversation, this is never lawful—it shows a duplicity directly contrary to that candour, which a Christian as well as religious ought to practise, and which even the social duties require of us. For it is very certain that the fidelity which should subsist between man and man, receives as deep a wound from this manner of speaking as it does from evident falsehood; and were it once permitted in the world, we might bid adieu to all integrity and sincerity. Hence, if a man is given to this fault, though he be very honest in other things, yet no one would trust him, nor without fear and trembling hold any commerce with him. Soloman says, "he that speaks sophistically, is to be hated," (Eccl. xxxvii. 23), meaning one that dissembles, equivocates, or uses ambiguous terms, because he is looked upon as a faithless and deceitful man. Let us then carefully avoid all language of this sort ; and let us never leave it in the power of any one to say of us, what is said of so many others ; *i.e.*, that though we do not tell lies, yet we know not what it is to tell the truth.

———o———

CHAPTER XII.

That a religious ought to abstain from all kind of bantering and raillery.

"Do not trifle away your time," says St. Basil, "in childish jests, very unbecoming one that aspires to perfection." (Exhort. ad. fil. spir. a xiii.) He adds, that a Christian who jests and turns things into ridicule must needs be negligent and very tepid in the service of God ; since all devotion and true compunction of heart are thereby destroyed. And he particularly advises us never to disgrace ourselves, who are religious, by playing the buffoon or jester.

St. Bernard urges this point home, and says very well, that "jesting or raillery in a secular man's mouth passes for what it is, but in the mouth of a priest it is is a kind of blasphemy. His mouth is consecrated, and ought to speak what is holy ; in him it is a crime to utter a jest, but to accustom himself to them is a sacrilege." (Lib. de consid. ad Eugen.) For it is the same as to apply what is dedicated to God and his church to profane uses. The saint still prosecutes this matter in the words of Malachy ; "the lips of a priest shall be the treasury of knowledge, it is from his mouth we must learn the law of God (Mal. ii. 7), not foolish, idle jests and stories." St. Bernard would not only have "all scurrilous jests and drollery, which some pretenders to this art call by a softer name, and wish to have pass for innocent wit, be banished from the mouth, but from the ears also ; " and bids us, if we chance to fall into company where it is practised, to behave ourselves as if we were amongst detractors, showing our dislike of it by our looks, and endeavouring to turn the discourse, by introducing something more grave and profitable. If the very hearing of these trifles be a fault, what must it be to speak them ? "It is a shame," says St. Bernard, "to applaud these follies by laughing at them, but it is a greater shame to be guilty of them, and to move others to laughter."

Clement of Alexandria agrees with the saints, Basil, Bernard, and Bonaventure in saying, "that all our words take their source from our hearts and manners ; our tongue discovers both our thoughts and actions, and consequently all vain and idle discourse shows a levity of mind, and a tendency to immorality." The gospel tells us, that "the mouth speaks from the abundance of the heart." (Matt. xii. 34.) We know by the sound when a bell is cracked, or a vessel is empty ; in the same manner, "we know by a man's words how his head and heart are affected. St. Chrysostom, upon the words of the apostle, "let nothing that is bad come out of your mouth " (Eph. iv. 29) says, that "such as your heart is, such are your words and deeds." St. Ignatius the martyr, being asked why he pronounced the name of Jesus so often in the middle of his torments ? answered, that he could not hinder himself from naming what was engraven in his heart ; and opening his breast after his death, they found this sacred name of Jesus written on both sides of his heart in golden letters. He that loves jesting and raillery has the world and its follies, not the name of Jesus, written in his heart ; and hence it is that such as pride themselves on showing their wit and exciting laughter, are so far from being spiritual men, that they deserve not the name even of religious. Father Avila is of the same opinion. Interpreting these words of St. Paul, "scurrility which is always impertinent" (Ibid. v. 4), he says, that scurrility does not at all become either religious modesty or Christian gravity ; and the author of his life tells us, that he was never guilty of it himself. Metaphrastes says, that St. Chrysostom never spoke himself, nor permitted any other in his presence to speak a scurrilous or bantering word: and the ancient fathers were so averse from this kind of language, that St. Basil would have a religious found guilty of this fault, to be shut up in his cell and deprived of all conversation for a week together. This penance was a kind of excommunication, and made use of to this end ; and that those who had committed this misdemeanor should not infect others by their bad company, but should live alone to their confusion, and be made to feel, that he deserves not to converse with religious who does not behave himself like a religious.

We read in the life of St. Hugh, abbot of Cluny, that M. Durant, archbishop of Toulouse, who had formerly been one of his monks, and who was fond of bantering and exercising his wit, was frequently told of this fault by the abbot, who assured him that he would suffer for it in the other world. The Archbishop died, and soon after appeared to a holy monk of Cluny called Seguinus, with his mouth all swelled and full of ulcers. and begged with many tears that he would desire his abbot Hugh to pray for his deliverance from those cruel torments he was suffering in purgatory, upon account of his jests, which he had not left off before he died. As soon as Seguinus had told this vision to the abbot, he appointed seven days' silence to seven of his religious, in order to satisfy for the archbishop's fault. One of the seven religious broke silence, which made the archbishop appear once more to Seguinus, and complain that the disobedience of that one monk was the cause why his release from purgatory was deferred. The abbot being informed of this, and finding that one of his religious had failed in obeying his orders, commanded another to keep seven days' silence : which being done the archbishop appeared the third time to Seguinus in his pontifical robes, with his mouth perfectly cured, and his looks serene and cheerful ; and having requested of Seguinus to return his thanks to the good abbot and his religious, he disappeared.

Above all, we must have a particular care to avoid offensive jests, which though they be uttered only as witticisms, yet fail not to wound the neighbour ; because, under cover, they attack his temper, which is not of the best ; or his parts, which are not the most brilliant, or something else in which he is defective.   This is the worst sort of bantering, and the more witty, the more injurious ; because it makes the deeper impression on the minds of the hearers, and is, in consequence, longer remembered by them. There are even secular persons pleasant, facetious, and esteemed men of parts and good humour, who can be cheerful without doing prejudice to any one.   While they continue to excite this innocent mirth, their company is courted, but if in their bon mots they become sharp and satirical, they are hated ; and, sooner or later, they will meet some one who will retort on them, and repay them with usury.   I shall not enlarge upon this subject, having sufficiently treated of it in the first volume; where I spoke of all such language as is contrary to fraternal charity.

———o———

CHAPTER XIII.

That all our entertainments and discourses ought to be of God ; how we are to make them so.

St. Paul forbids us to " let any bad discourse come out of our mouths, but would have all our discourse so edifying, that it may inspire piety into our hearers. (Eph. iv. 29.)   We, who are obliged by our institute to labour for our neighbour's salvation as well as for our own, ought to take these words of the apostle as particularly addressed to us, since they concern us so nearly. There is nothing that edifies the neighbour, or produces greater fruit in him, than to entertain him with pious discourse.   For, besides those advantages that these spiritual conversations carry along with them, it is certain, that worldly persons perceiving that a religious never gives them any other entertainment than this, conceive a high esteem of him, and have a particular veneration for him, believing such a one to be replenished with God, who can speak of nothing else but of him.   Hence the functions of charity they have occasion to exercise, either in private or public, become more efficacious.   St. Xaverius is said to have done more good by his ordinary familiar discourses than by his sermons. And St. Ignatius, in his Constitutions, looks upon pious discourses as extremely beneficial to our neighbour, and enjoins the practice of it to all ; even to the meanest brother.

But, to succeed in this practice abroad, it will be extremely requisite that we accustom ourselves to talk spiritually at home. St. Francis obliged his religious to frequent spiritual conferences in their convents, that being well versed in this divine language, they might make use of it when they met with worldly persons. In time of one of these conferences our blessed Saviour appeared to them in the form of an infant, and giving his blessing to all there assembled, showed how agreeable such pious entertainments were to him. The society of Jesus still upholds this pious custom, by appointing for the novices several meetings, which admit of none but spiritual discourse. Having finished the noviceship, we frequently practise the like spiritual conferences, thereby to render ourselves the better able to speak this language of saints: and, besides all this, we have an expressed rule which enjoins us to mingle spiritual discourse with our ordinary conversation.

St. Bernard severely reprimanded some of his religious, who in his time were not observant of this custom; and objecting to them the practice of the primitive Christians, cries out—"How much difference is there between us and those holy men who lived in St. Anthony's days? "—(Apol. ad Guliel. Abb.) They no sooner met but they began to speak of God. The desire they had to feed their souls, made them forget even for several days to feed their bodies, and in this they observed a due order, for the noble part ought to be served in the first place. But our meeting together, to use the apostle's words, is not to eat the Lord's supper; because nobody asks for this bread of life, and nobody also thinks of giving it. Not a word of the holy scripture is heard amongst us, nor any discourse tending to the salvation of our souls; but all our discourse is filled with jests and laughter, and with vain and idle words. But what is worst of all, this neglect being now called affability, prudence, and charity, the contrary is looked upon as a want of breeding; and those who love to speak of God and good things, are censured as melancholy and ill-bred persons, whose conversation should be avoided. Surely this sort of worldly charity and prudence destroys all that is truly Christian. For how can that be true charity which, obsequious to flesh and blood, neglects the soul? Or how can that be called prudence, which obliges the body at the expense of the mind? To glut your body, and let your soul starve, is no less foolish than cruel, and therefore is far from being charitable. Taulerus relates a vision which happened to a holy man, in which our blessed Saviour himself complained of six defects which he found in his servants; one of which was, that they entertained themselves with trifles in their ordinary recreations, and seldom spoke of him, which he resented very much. Let us hence take warning, and endeavour not to merit the like reproach.

St. Bernard and St. Bonaventure teach us in the following words how to edify our neighbours by good discourse. " Consider," say they, " before you go to speak with your neighbour, what subject is the most profitable and edifying for you to introduce ; and be ever prepared to divert the conversation, if it should become vain or trifling." Our holy rule, also advises us to this, and certainly it ought not to seem painful and troublesome to us, who are religious, to comply with so necessary a duty, prescribed us by our rule, and taught us by our profession ; when even seculars adopt the same method to introduce and keep up profane and idle conversation ; but in order to divert impertinent discourse, and introduce what is more solid and substantial in place of it, I own that a great deal of prudence and discretion is necessary.

The third means is the love of God and of heavenly things. Were we but once masters of this love, we should never be weary of speaking or hearing of spiritual things. For can it be painful to hear what we love spoken of ? No ! but such conversation must ever impart new pleasure and new delight to us. Take notice how solicitous a merchant is about his affairs ; how feelingly he talks of them at all times, and in all places ; and with what satisfaction he hears others speak of buying and selling, and of all kind of traffic. " He that drives the plough, and holds the goad in his hand," says Soloman, " speaks of nothing but of oxen and their labour ; and his whole talk is of the offspring of his bulls." (Eccl. xxxviii. 36.) In fine, every one likes to speak of his own profession. Perfection is what we profess ; for this we left the world, and if we love either God or the profession we have embraced, it is certain we shall feel very great delight in spiritual discourse, and we shall never be at a loss for a subject. It is a good sign when we love to speak of God, but a bad one when we do not. St. John says—" The reason why people speak so much of worldly things is because they are of the world themselves." (John iv. 5.) St. Austin, in his comment upon these words of wisdom—" Thou hast fed thy people with the food of angels, and given them bread from heaven ready made, without any labour of theirs, having in it all that is delicious, and the sweetness of every taste (Wisd. xvi. 20), says that this manna which the children of Israel ate in the desert was such, that to the good it was most delicious, but the bad relished it not; and hence they importuned Almighty God for other food, in these words—" Who will give us some flesh to eat? Now have we cause to remember the fish we ate for nothing in Egypt. How can we forget the melons, leeks, onions, garlick, and cucumbers we had there? Now we are ready to faint and starve, having nothing but a little manna." (Numb. xi. 4.) These persons not only did not find in the manna all that variety of taste which it possessed, but they looked upon it as very insipid, and even loathed it; otherwise they would never have languished after the flesh-pots of Egypt. But as for the good, they found all manner of sweetness and content in it, they wished for nothing else, and never so much as thought of their Egyptian fare. This difference is still found amongst religious. The good feel incomparable satisfaction in speaking of God and of heavenly things. This is their most delicious manna—God is their all, and in him they find all things they wish for. But the tepid and imperfect feel no gust at all in it; nay, they find it unpleasant, and therefore reject it as such, and, contenting themselves with the leeks and garlick of idle words, they loathe the heavenly manna of pious discourse. " Happy the tongue," says St. Jerome, " that knows no other language than that of saints ! " " Do not give ear to vain and insignificant discourse," says St. Basil, " but if anything is taken from Scripture, or if it concerns your soul's welfare, listen to it, and dwell upon it. Let the bare mention of things of the world be bitter unto you, but think it a comfort to hear discourses of devotion and piety." A faithful servant of God cannot bear the vain entertainments of the world; he loves to speak but of God. Hence it is that in all his infirmities and afflictions he never looks for comfort in worldly amusements and entertainment— no ! they would only augment his pain ; for, loving but his God, he finds no satisfaction but in hearing and speaking of him who is the object of his love. It is related of St. Cathrine of Sienna, that she never felt weary in speaking or hearing others speak of God. On the contrary, she took a particular satisfaction in it ; she declared that it preserved her strength and health, and that it was her greatest comfort in sickness and troubles. We read of a great number of saints, who in their conversation with God, felt effects similar to those felt by St. Catherine.

CHAPTER XIV.

Another weighty reason, that proves the great importance of conversing on spiritual subjects.

It is not only for the good of the neighbour, but likewise to promote our own advancement in virtue, that we should often speak of God. One of its effects is to inflame our hearts with divine love, as happened to the two disciples who, going to Emmaus, and discoursing of the passion of our Saviour, confessed that "their hearts were all on fire whilst he spoke." (Luke xxiv. 22.) This we find sometimes by experience when, on leaving a company where piety and devotion were the sole entertainment, we feel ourselves impressed with a deeper sense of virtue than we are after a sermon. St. Thomas of Aquin's discourse, whenever he conversed with any body of what rank soever, was always pious, and relative to their salvation. This was the reason why, on leaving company, he could easily recollect himself, go to prayer, and meditate upon the sublimest points in divinity ; for his discourses being of God, they left behind no ideas which could distract him in his meditations. It is admirable to read in the life of St. Xaverius, how well he united action with contemplation, and recollection with business. For though he was constantly engaged, and even in the business of the first importance ; though he was almost ever travelling by sea or by land, sinking under fatigue and exposed to peril ; and what is more, though to all he was easy of access ; yet he was ever interiorly recollected—he ever kept himself in the presence of God. Hence the business he was engaged in for the neighbour being dispatched, he resumed prayer, and in a moment his prayer was most fervent—his union with the heavenly spouse most intimate; for his exterior employments never alienated his mind from God, and hence he readily assumed the devotions he had left for the good of his neighbour. But if we neglect to keep our minds steadily fixed upon God ; if, in our intercourse with the neighbour, we speak not of spiritual but of unprofitable things, we shall feel it very difficult to bring ourselves peaceably back to prayer and meditation. Our holy founder said that our conversation would prove edifying to our neighbour and advantageous to ourselves so long as we carried the spirit of God along with us; but that it would be scandalous to our neighbour and dangerous to ourselves if we carried with us the spirit of the world.   St. Bernard says, " that bad discourse defiles the mind, and that we easily reduce that to practice which we hear with pleasure."

It is true that, in our conversations with persons of the world, we may sometimes show condescension to them ; but this should be ever done in order to render them condescending to us.   But let us not allow ourselves to be carried too far by them; let us not suffer them to begin and end any discourse as they please ; but, having our object ever in view, let us gradually draw them to ourselves and to God by pious and edifying language.   We need not be long in doing this, nor is it necessary to wait for a favourable opportunity.   If we do, perhaps we will find no opportunity, and nothing will be heard but vain and unprofitable discourse—not one word will be spoken of the Almighty. Let us endeavour to make all men know that we are true religious ; that our conversation is suitable to our profession ; and that in our intercourse with seculars we do not speak of worldly affairs, but of God and of the great affair of salvation.   Let those who disapprove of this our conduct neither receive nor invite us. When St. Ignatius was visited by persons who misspent their time in idle conversation, he received them kindly for the first and second time ; but if they continued their visits, he immediately began a discourse on death, judgment, or hell.   " For," said he, " if they dislike these topics, there is an end to their useless visits ; but if they feel pleasure in hearing them discussed, their salvation will be thereby promoted."

St. Austin desires us to accommodate ourselves to all persons, that we may gain them to heaven.   This was done by the apostle of the Gentiles, who " made himself all to all." (1 Cor. ix. 22.)   It being most consoling to a man in distress to see another sympathising with him, and kindly sharing in his affliction, St. Paul was afflicted with the afflicted ; with the joyful, likewise, he was joyful ; and with the weak he was weak.   The same saint, however, cautions us not to do, on these occasions, more than is necessary to free our neighbour from the present misery he suffers, but never to venture so far as to fall into the like misery ourselves.   To elucidate this point, he makes use of the following comparison.   Observe how one man stoops to help another that is fallen ; he does not throw himself down, nor does he fall as the other did, but holds his feet firm, that the other may not pull him down, and only bends so far as is necessary to help the other up. Thus we are to act with secular persons; we must stoop a little to their inclination, and comply with their humour so far as to be able to gain them to God; but, at the same time, we must stand firm, that we may prevent them from pulling us down, and that we may attain our object. And let us be convinced of this truth, that nothing edifies the neighbour more than to let them see that we converse with them on spiritual subjects only. It is true there may be some who, in the beginning, will not relish these discourses; but they will soon relish them, and will esteem us the more when they come fully to comprehend that there is no business truly important save the business of salvation. On the contrary, if they see us join in their worldly conversation, and, like themselves, take pleasure therein, they will, perhaps, feel friendship for us, but they will have no great esteem for our piety; and, in consequence, losing all authority over them, we shall be able to render them little or no spiritual service. Let us, then, in imitation of our first fathers, strive to advance the reputation of our society. When persons came to pay a visit to St. Francis Borgia, and began to talk of vain and unprofitable matter, and when he could not avoid being with them, he paid no attention to their discourse, but kept his heart continually fixed upon God; insomuch that some of the fathers who were present, telling him he committed mistakes on that account, and gave answers that were not to the purpose, he replied, that he wished to appear stupid and impolite rather than to lose his time; for he counted as lost the time which was not given to God, or spent in his service. Cassian relates something like this of the abbot Maguet, who was so far blessed by God as never to fall asleep during spiritual conferences, and always to fall asleep the moment idle and useless conversation was introduced.

Let us conclude this treatise with the advice which St. Bernard gives to all religious. "Let a religious," says the saint, "behave in such manner that he may truly edify all that see him, and that nobody, who shall either hear or see him, may doubt of his being religious." (In spec. Monach.) St. Paul said the same to Titus, in these words, "in all things show yourself an example of good works, in doctrine, in integrity, in gravity, sound speech, unblameable, that your enemies may be confounded, not having anything to lay to your charge." (Tit. ii. 7.) Let us follow these counsels; let our conduct be so exemplary and edifying, that not only our friends may see nothing reprehensible therein, but that our enemies, and those envious of us, may blush for shame, having nothing to reproach us with.

It is said of a philosopher, that, on being informed that a man spoke ill of him, he answered, " I will live in such manner that no one will believe what he says against me." Thus ought we live : that is, our words and actions ought not only to be blameless, but, in case any body should speak ill of us, we should endeavour that our whole conduct through life may be a convincing argument that the charges against us are false. The best reply to a detractor is, to hold our tongue and to let our actions speak.

THE THIRD TREATISE.

———o———

ON HUMILITY.

———o———

CHAPTER I.

Excellence and necessity of humility.

"Learn of me," says our Saviour, "because I am meek and humble of heart." (Matt. xi. 29.) And St. Austin hereupon says, that "the whole life of our Saviour upon earth was a continual lesson of morality, but that he, in a special manner, proposed his humility for our imitation." To comprehend well the excellence of this virtue, and the need we have thereof, we are to consider, that the Son of God descended from heaven to teach it us, not only by his words, but more especially by his actions ; and that his whole life was nothing else than a long example and living model of humility. St. Basil, to prove this proposition, takes a view of the whole life of our Saviour, and after having examined the chief circumstances thereof, from his very birth to his death, shows that all his actions teach us particularly the virtue of humility. His will was to be circumcised as a sinner ; to fly into Egypt as too weak and unable to resist ; and to be baptized with sinners and publicans as one of them. When the people wish to honour and make him king, he hides himself ; when they wish to cover him with reproaches, he shows himself. Men praise him, and even the devils themselves do so by the mouths of the possessed, and he commands them to silence. They load him with outrage and injury, and he answers not a word. After all this, to recommend humility to us, as it were by his last will and testament, at the close of life he stoops so low as to wash his disciples' feet ; and, in fine, he crowns so many examples by the most shameful death of the cross. "He wishes to annihilate himself," says St. Bernard, " to show first by his

example what he was afterwards to teach by his words."
(Serm. de Nat. Dom.)   But why, O Lord, does majesty so exalted
stoop so low?   It is "that none should henceforth presume to
magnify themselves upon earth." (Ps. ix. 30.)   At all times it
argued an extravagance in man to yield to vanity; but now, as
St. Bernard adds, " it would be an insufferable imprudence for a
worm to swell with pride, when the majesty of the eternal God
has humbled and annihilated himself." (Ubi. supra.)   The Son
of God, equal to his Father, takes the form of a servant—he
wishes to be humbled and dispised, and shall I, who am but
dust and ashes, seek to be honoured and respected?

It is with reason the Saviour of the world says "that he is
master of this virtue, and that it is of him we ought to learn it."
For not Socrates, nor Plato, nor Aristotle, nor any other philosopher, ever knew how to teach it.   When they valued themselves
upon other virtues, as fortitude, temperance, and justice, they
were so far from being humble, that they aimed at nothing but
reputation and vain-glory.   It is true that Diogenes and some
others, who made open profession of despising whatever the world
valued, seemed indeed to despise the world and themselves too ;
but in that very thing they only sought vain-glory, though in a
way different from others, as they have been all reproached with
since ; and as Plato reproached Diogenes with in his own days.
Plato had, it seems, invited him with some other philosophers to
dinner, and ordered the diningroom to be hung with rich tapes-
try.   Diogenes enters in his filth and dirt : he pulls down a
piece of the hangings and tramples it under foot.   Plato asked
him what he was doing?   " I am trampling," quoth he, " on
the pride of Plato."   " You are indeed," answered Plato ; "but
in doing so, you are showing your own pride, though in another
way."   But so far were the philosophers from knowing what was
meant by the contempt of one's self, in which Christian humility
consists—so far were they from knowing what true humility was,
that they were ignorant of its name.   It is a virtue peculiar to
Christians, which was never taught before Jesus Christ preached it.

St. Austin remarks that, in the very first words of his admirable sermon on the mount, our Saviour recommended humility.
For, by the words, "blessed are the poor in spirit " (Matt. v. 3),
are understood the humble, as not only St. Austin, but St.
Jerome, St. Gregory, and several others affirm.   He begins, continues, and ends his sermon with humility ; he teaches nothing
else in the whole course of his life ; and, it is it in particular he

will have us to learn of him. " He says not," continues St. Austin, " learn of me to make heaven and earth, to create all visible things, to work miracles, to raise the dead, but learn of me to be weak and humble; for solid humility," as the same saint adds, " is much more powerful and safe than empty grandeur." It is better to be humble and serve God with fear than to work miracles. The first is an even and sure way, the other a very difficult and dangerous one.

To speak now more particularly—the necessity of this virtue is so great, that without it we cannot hope to advance one step in the way of perfection. " Humility," says St. Austin, "must precede, accompany, and follow all the good we do ; for, from the very moment that pride enters, it snatches all merit from us." Nay, it is for that very reason, that pride and vain-glory are the more to be feared ; for other vices spring from bad actions, but pride springs from good ones ; so that we are to be more on our guard against pride in our good actions, lest by too great desire of praise we come to lose the fruit of all we have done that was praiseworthy." (Ep. 56, ad Discor.) It is easy for us, if we will, to keep ourselves from other vices; they have certain marks which discover them—they are accompanied with other sins : but pride takes his place in the midst of good works, and continually endeavours to destroy them. Yet! let a Christian be steering a happy course on the sea of the world, and thinking of nothing but heaven, where from the beginning he intended to land, yet, if there comes a sudden puff of pride, a desire to please men, a self-complacency, *this* will send him to the bottom, in the midst of his voyage. St. Gregory and St. Bernard say, " that he who treasures up other virtues without humility, does nothing more than throw dust before the wind—the first puff blows all away."

---o---

CHAPTER II.

That humility is the foundation of all other virtues.

St. Cyprian says, that humility is the foundation of sanctity;" St. Jerome, that " it is the first Christian virtue;" St. Bernard calls it " the foundation and preservation of the virtues;" and all three, in fine, agree that it is the basis of the rest. St. Gregory at one time calls it " the mistress and mother ;" at another, " the spring and root of all other virtues." This metaphor of the root agrees exactly with it, and explains very well the properties and conditions thereof; for first, in the words of St. Gregory, just as a flower draws all its freshness and beauty from the root, and quickly fades as soon as it is plucked; even so, if any virtue whatsoever be but separated from the root of humility, it withers presently, and is quite lost. Again—as the root lies deep under ground, and is trodden under foot, and has ordinarily neither beauty nor smell, yet is nevertheless the principle both of the plant's life and nourishment; so, humility makes man who is humble love to lie hid, as it were, under ground, and to be trod upon and despised. It shuns noise and splendour, and seeks only the obscurity of retirement; and nevertheless it is it which preserves in itself all the other virtues, and makes them daily grow more and more. Lastly, as a tree must take deep root, in order to bear well, and to live long—and the deeper the root, the longer the tree lives, and the more fruit it bears, according to the words of Isaias, "It shall shoot its root downwards, and bear fruit upwards" (4 Kings xix. 30)—so, in order that other virtues should thrive and fructify in our hearts, it is necessary that humility be deeply rooted there; and the deeper the root is, the more will these virtues increase, and the stronger will they grow. I shall conclude then, with asserting, as I did in the beginning, that humility, according to the doctrine of all the holy fathers, is the source, foundation, and root of all virtues, "as pride is the beginning and origin of all sins" (Eccl. x. 15), according to the words of the Wise man.

But some perhaps may say, how can humility be the foundation of all other virtues, and of the whole spiritual edifice, since it is certain that faith is the foundation thereof, and that according to the words of the apostle, "none can lay any other foundation than that already laid, which is Jesus Christ?" (1 Cor. iii. 11.) St. Thomas answers this objection very well. "Two things," says he, "are requisite to lay the foundation of a house well; first, the ground must be dug, everything light and sandy must be thrown out, and persons must continue to sink, till the ground is felt firm enough to build upon. In the second place, after having cleared away the sand, and sunk deep, they must lay the first stone, which, together with the other stones laid in the same line, makes the principal foundation of the building. Here," continues the saint, "we have a representation of what humility and faith do in the spiritual building. Humility opens the ground, digs the foundation, and throws out all the sand; that is to say, the weakness of human strength." For you must not build upon your own strength, which is but a quicksand, and which you must remove by having a diffidence in yourself, and by digging always till you find sure and solid ground to lay the first stone, " and that stone is Jesus Christ," (1 Cor. v. 4,) who is the chief foundation of all the building. But because, in order to lay this foundation well, we must first of all dig with humility, it is for this reason that humility is called the foundation of this edifice. Now, if humility opens the ground well, if it penetrates into the knowledge of our own nothingness, if it throws out all the quicksand in us, I mean, all the confidence we have in ourselves—if it does this, in order to lay there the foundation-stone, Jesus Christ, the building reared thereon shall never be shaken, neither shall the wind or the rain be ever able to overthrow it, because the foundations thereof are solid. But if we build without humility all the edifice will quickly fall to the ground, because it was built on sand.

All virtues which are not founded upon humility are not real virtues; they are virtues only in appearance. St. Austin, speaking of those of the ancient Romans and philosophers, asserts, that they were not real virtues; not only because they were not animated by charity, which gives spirit and life to all other virtues, but because they had not the foundation of humility. For in fortitude, justice, temperance, and all their acts of virtue, these persons sought only worldly esteem and reputation, so that their virtues were rather the ghosts or phantoms of virtue than real ones. Treating likewise particularly of the ancient Romans, he says, " that as they were virtuous only in appearance, so God rewarded them with the good things of this world only, which also are apparent goods." If therefore you desire that real virtues should raise up a spiritual edifice in your souls, endeavour first of all to lay a solid foundation of humility. " You aspire," says St. Austin, " to great things, begin with little ones ; you desire to erect a very high building, think first of the foundation of humility. The foundations are always sunk proportionably to the intended weight of the building ; and the higher one intends it, the deeper must the foundations thereof be laid." (Serm. x. de verb. Dom.) The height must answer to the depth, so that you cannot raise the edifice of evangelical perfection which you intend to build, but proportionally to the depth of humility you shall give to the foundations. It is related of St. Thomas of Aquin that, speaking of humility, he was wont to say, that if a man who loves to be honoured, who shuns contempt, and who bears it with chagrin, does ever so many good works, yet he is far from perfection, because all his virtue has no foundation.

———o———

CHAPTER III.

A view of the principal virtues, to show more particularly how humility is the foundation of them all.

I SHALL now take a cursory view of the principal virtues, in order to show more plainly the truth of this maxim of the saints —that humility is the foundation of all other virtues ; and to show how necessary this foundation is for us.

First of all, faith stands in need of humility. I speak not of infants who receive faith in baptism, without exercising any act thereof, but I speak of those who have the use of reason. Faith requires an humble and submissive spirit, according to St. Paul, "bringing into captivity every understanding to the obedience of Christ." (2 Cor. x. 5.) On the contrary, the spirit of pride hinders the receiving of faith, according to the words of our Saviour :—"How can you believe, who give honour to one another, and who seeks not the honour which comes from God alone ?" (John v. 44.) Now, as humility is necessary for the receiving of faith, it is equally so for the preserving it ; for all holy writers hold, that heresies spring from the pride we manifest in preferring our own light to the decisions of the whole church. It is this the apostle alludes to, when he says, " this know also, that in the last days, perilous times shall come : men shall be lovers of themselves, covetous, haughty and proud :" (2 Tim. iii. 1 ;) and St. Austin observes on this place, that the apostle attributes the cause of all heresies and errors particularly to pride and arrogance. Hope likewise is supported by humility, because he who is humble knows his misery and weakness ; he is sensible that of himself he can do nothing, and so flies with greater ardour to God, and fixes all his hope in him. Charity, which consists in loving God, is very much increased also by means of humility ; for one of an humble spirit, seeing that he receives whatever he has from the hand of God, and that he is very far from meriting it, feels himself excited thereby to love his benefactor more and more. " What is man," says Job to God, "that thou shouldst magnify him, and that thou shouldst set thy heart upon him ?" (Job vii. 17.) Shall I, O Lord, remain thus rebellious to thee, and thou so good to me ? Shall

I go on, still offending thee, whilst thou continuest to heap thy
favours upon me ? This is one of the considerations which the
saints have made use of, to inflame themselves with the love of
God. The more they reflected upon their own unworthiness,
the more they thought themselves obliged to love him, who had
condescended to cast his eyes upon their meanness. " My soul
doth magnify the Lord," says the holy virgin, " because he hath
regarded the humility of his handmaid." (Luke i. 46.) As to
the charity which we exercise towards our neighbour, it is easily
seen how necessary humility is thereunto ; because one of the
things which usually make us so cold to our brethren is some
judgment we form to their disadvantage—some impression made
on us by their faults. An humble man is very far from all this ;
he looks upon his own errors, and never minds those of
others ; he sees nothing in his neighbour but what is good and
virtuous, and thence it comes, that whilst he imagines every one
else perfect, and himself alone imperfect, he thinks himself unworthy to live among his brethren, and is, in consequence, full
of love, esteem, and veneration for them. Moreover, the humble
man is not angry at others being preferred to him—at others
being esteemed, and himself despised. He feels no pain that
they should get the highest and himself the lowest place. There
is no envy among the humble, because envy springs from pride ;
so that wherever humility reigns, you will find neither envy,
dispute, quarrel, nor anything to cool fraternal charity.

Patience, a virtue so necessary for a Christian, arises likewise
from humility ; because he who is humble knows his own faults,
and is sensible at the same time, that he deserves all manner of
chastisement. He therefore meets with no mortifications which
he looks not upon as less than what he has deserved, and instead
of complaining thereof, he says with the prophet Micheas, "I
will bear the indignation of the Lord, because I have sinned
against him." (Mich. vii. 9.) A proud man complains of every
thing, and suspects still without reason that he is wronged, and
not treated according to his merit. On the contrary, whatever
injury is done the humble man, he minds it not, nor takes it for
an injury : nay, so far is he from imagining that an injury can
be done him in anything, that he still reckons all as kindness ;
and however he is treated he is always satisfied, because he believes he is treated better than he deserves. In fine, humility is
a great disposition to patience ; and hence after the Wise man had
admonished him who will engage in the service of God, to pre-

pare himself for a great many mortifications, and to arm himself with patience ; the means he proposes for that end is to humble himself. " Humble thy heart," says he, " and have patience ; receive all that shall befall thee, and bear afflictions patiently ;" (Eccl. ii. 2,) but what arms does he give him to ward off pain or to make him at least bear it courageously ? " Be patient." says he, " in your humility," (Ibid. ii. 4,) that is say, be humble, and then you will be patient.

Peace also, the blessing so much desired by all the world, springs from humility ; and Jesus Christ himself teaches us this truth, when he says, " learn of me who are meek and humble of heart, and you will find peace in your souls." (Matt. xi. 29.) Be humble and you will be at peace both with yourselves and your brethren. " There are always contentions among the proud;" says Solomon ; (Prov. xiii. 10;) but, as much as they are exposed to them, the humble are free from them. There is but one contest between these : it is to decide who shall be lowest, and pay the greatest deference to his companion. The strife between St. Paul the hermit and St. Anthony was of this nature ; it was who should break and divide the bread which the raven had brought them. Paul would have Anthony do it, as being the elder ; each of them sought reasons to yield and give place to the other. It is good to have such contests, and as they spring from true humility, they are so far from troubling and destroying fraternal charity, that they nourish and confirm it.

Let us now come to the three virtues which are peculiar and essential to a religious, and to which we oblige ourselves by the three vows we make, of poverty, chastity, and obedience. Poverty is so nearly allied to humility, that they seem to be two sisters ; and by poverty of spirit, which our Saviour pronounced as the first beatitude, some holy writers understand humility, and others, voluntary poverty, such as religious profess. But be it as it will, poverty must be always accompanied with humility ; for a coarse and mean habit gives occasion oftentimes of pride to him that wears it, and raises in him a contempt of others : and it is for this reason St. Austin did not relish poverty of dress, and would have the religious of his order decently clad. Humility is moreover necessary to hinder us from loving our own ease and an abundance of all things, and to make us content with whatever is given us, even though it should be unequally divided ; because we are poor and profess poverty.

As for chastity, we cannot doubt but humility is necessary to preserve it, after the many examples we have in the lives of the fathers of the desert of persons, who, though they had led a most penitential and solitary life, yet fell most shamefully. For it is by permitting falls like these that God punishes those who have too great confidence in themselves. In fine, humility is so great an ornament to chastity and purity, that St. Bernard says, "he dares take upon him to assert, that the purity of the Virgin Mary herself would not have been agreeable to God without humility." (Hom. sup. Missas est.)

As to the virtue of obedience, wherein our holy founder would have us particularly signalise ourselves, it is certain that the proud will never be obedient; and on the contrary, the truly humble will be always obedient. One may command an humble man to do anything; he never shows opposition; he conforms himself entirely to his superior; and he submits not only his conduct and actions to him, but even his will and judgment : in fine, you will never find any contradiction or repugnance in him. But it is not so with others.

Now if we consider prayer, which is the foundation of a spiritual and religious life, it is certain that it is of no effect without humility, and with humility it pierces the heavens, according to the words of the Wise man—"The prayer of him who humbles himself shall penetrate the clouds, nor will he be comforted till it mounts up to God, nor will he depart till the Most High behold." (Eccl. xxxv. 21.) The holy and humble Judith, shut up in her closet, clothed with a hair-cloth, covered with ashes, and prostrate on the ground, cries out—"The prayer of the humble and meek has been always pleasing to thee, O Lord." (Jud. ix. 16.) And the royal prophet says that " God has regard to the supplication of the humble, and despises not their prayer." (Ps. ci. 18.) " Fear not, therefore, that an humble man will be rejected." (Ps. lxxiii. 21.) He will obtain what he asks. Consider, too, how agreeable the prayer of the publican was to God—he durst not lift up his eyes to heaven, nor approach the altar, but getting into a corner of the temple, he struck his breast saying—" O my God be merciful to me a sinner " (Luke xviii. 13,) whereupon Jesus Christ declared that he went down to his house justified, rather than the proud pharisee. We might thus run over all the other virtues, and show that they all depend upon humility; so that if you seek a ready way to acquire them, and a short lesson for attaining perfection, you have it in two words—be humble.

CHAPTER IV.

That they whose profession it is to labour for the salvation of others,
have particular need of humility.

" THE greater you are," says the Wise man, " the more ought
you to humble yourself in all things, and you will find grace in
the eyes of God." (Eccl. iii. 20.) Great, doubtless, is the dignity annexed to the profession we have of labouring for the salvation of souls. We may truly say, that God has therein called us
to a very eminent employment. For we are ordained to exercise
in the Church the same functions our Saviour assigned the
apostles, which are preaching the gospel, administering the
sacraments, and distributing his precious body and blood; so that
we can say with St. Paul, " that he has given us a ministry of
reconciliation" (2 Cor. v. 18), for so the apostle calls the preaching of the gospel, and administration of the sacraments, whereby
the grace of salvation is communicated. " He has given to us,"
says he, "the ministry of reconciliation ; we therefore speak as
ambassadors of Christ, and as though God did exhort you by us."
It is by us, it is by those tongues of flesh which he has given us,
he is pleased to speak to souls, and to touch men's hearts ; and
hence we have far more need of humility than others, and that
for two principal reasons. The first is, that the more sublime
our vocation and employment are, the more are we exposed to
the attacks of pride and vanity. The highest mountain is most
exposed to the storm. The sublimity of our functions makes us
be respected and honoured by every one—it makes us be looked
upon as saints and new apostles, and even as persons who sanctify
those that approach them. Now there must be a very deep
foundation of humility to hinder so lofty an edifice from tumbling
down ; there must be a great stock and solidity of virtue to
keep one from falling under so weighty a charge, as it is very
hard without being proud to see one's self universally honoured.
There are but few who can look down from a very high place
without getting a dizziness ; and how many, through want of
humility, have fallen from the height whereon they were sta-
tioned ? How many, also, have been seen to soar aloft, like the
eagle on the wings of virtue, and to become afterwards no better
than night birds, by reason of their pride ? That solitary, who is

spoken of in the "Lives of the Saints" Pocomus and Palemon, who walked upon glowing coals without burning himself, wrought, without doubt, many miracles; but he happened unfortunately to grow proud thereupon, and to despise others so much, that looking upon himself as infinitely above them, he said to them—" He indeed is holy who walks on fire without burning himself, which of you could do that?" For this vanity St. Palemon reproved him very severely, but without effect; for the unhappy man, a little while after, fell into debauchery, and met a very deplorable end. Sacred history abounds in similar examples.

We have therefore particular need of the foundation of humility, for without it, we run the hazard of falling into pride, and into the greatest of all, which is spiritual pride. St. Bonaventure illustrates this doctrine still more when he says, " that there are two sorts of pride; the carnal, which arises from temporal things, and the spiritual, which proceeds from spiritual things, and that the latter is much greater and more criminal than the former." The reason he gives for it is clear : " It is," he says, " because the proud man is properly a robber, for he takes away what is another's against the will of him to whom it belongs ; he takes away the glory which belongs only to God, which God has particularly reserved to himself, and which he declares by the prophet Isaias, 'he will not give unto another.'" (Isa. xlii. 8.) He, I say, takes this away, as much as depends on him, and appropriates it to himself, as his own. Now he who is proud of the goods of nature, as of his strong constitution, his birth, brilliancy of wit, knowledge, and all other like qualities, does without doubt commit robbery; because all these things belong to God; but since these things are of but little value, and are, as it were, useless and cast-off furniture, his crime is so much the less. But he who prides himself in the spiritual gifts which God has bestowed on him, and in the fruit, which through his means, God produces in souls; he, I say, is a great criminal, and robs God of his glory; he is a notorious robber, who takes away the most precious treasures of the house of God, and which God has purchased at the price of his blood and life. St. Francis was so much afraid of falling into this sort of pride, that he addressed himself often to God in this manner—" O Lord, if thou art pleased to bestow thy gifts upon me, be thou the guardian thereof thyself, for I have a diffidence in myself, and I am a great robber, who may perhaps prove bankrupt to thee." Let us manifest a similar fear; we have much more reason to do so than this great saint, because we are not so humble as he ; and let us beware of falling into so dangerous a pride. God has put his treasures into our hands, as things committed to our trust and charge; let us not become bankrupts; let us not retain any part of them, so as to appropriate it to ourselves, but let us faithfully restore whatever belongs to him.

It is not without a great mystery that the Saviour of the world, when he appeared to his disciples on the day of his ascension, reproached them first with their incredulity and hardness of heart, and commanded them afterwards to go and preach the gospel all over the earth, and gave them power to work miracles. He gave us to understand thereby, that he who is to be raised to great employments of grace, ought first humble and abase himself, from the sense he has of his own weakness and misery, in order that though he should afterwards work miracles, and soar to heaven, he may still remain impressed with the sense of his own meanness and nothingness, without attributing to himself anything but his own unworthiness. Theodoret observes to this purpose, that it was for the same reason, that when God was pleased to choose Moses to be the leader and conductor of his people, and to work so many miracles by him, he commanded him first to put his hand into his bosom, and was pleased that he should draw it out all covered with leprosy—even that very hand which was to divide the waters of the Red Sea, and perform afterwards so many other miracles.

The second reason why we have more need of humility than others is, that we may thereby render our ministry more useful for the salvation of souls; so that it is not only necessary for our own perfection, and to hinder pride and vanity from destroying us ; but also to win our neighbour more easily to God, and to make greater progress in the conversion of souls. Now one of the means most conducive to this is humility ; that we may know how to have a diffidence in ourselves, and that instead of laying any stress upon our own strength, ability, and prudence, we may place all our confidence in God, according to the words of the Wise man; "trust in the Lord with all thy heart, and lean not unto thine own understanding." (Prov. iii. 5.) The reason of this is, as I shall hereafter show more at large, that by diffidence in ourselves, we place all our confidence in God alone, and we lay all upon him; so that he is obliged more particularly to help us. The conversion of souls, O Lord, is thy work, and not ours; put thy hand therefore unto it, since we can do nothing of ourselves. This is what we ought to say to Almighty God if we would have him bless our endeavours ; but when we trust to such means as our own reason furnishes us with, we then give ourselves a share therein ; and we cannot attribute anything to ourselves without taking it from God. It is with this as with the two scales of a balance, when one rises the other sinks; whatever we attribute to ourselves we take from God, and thereby we rob him of the glory and honour of which he is the true owner; and who knows but this may be often the cause of our reaping so little fruit in the conversion of souls ?

We read in the life of St. Ignatius, that being at Rome, and knowing little of the Italian language, he profited so much in gaining souls by the Christian exhortations which he made in a plain and homely way, that often when the exhortation was ended the auditors went to throw themselves down at their confessors' feet, and their hearts were so touched with sorrow—such were their sighs and groans, that they could scarce utter a word. The reason was, that he founded all the strength of his discourse, " not on the persuasive words of human wisdom, but on demonstration of the spirit, and of the power of the Holy Ghost." (1 Cor. ii. 4.) Now as he had a diffidence in himself, and put all his confidence in God, God also gave so great power and virtue to what he said, that all his words seemed as so many burning arrows, wherewith he pierced the hearts of his hearers. And the reason why we convert so few souls is, perhaps, because we think too much of our talents—because we rely too much on human means; on the strength of our reasoning—on our elegance of style, and our flowery discourse, and because, in consequence, we yield to self-complacency."

Well! says the Almighty God, I will so order it, that you shall believe you have said the best things in the world, and the best adapted to your purpose, but when you shall find most satisfaction in yourselves, and think you have succeeded most, then shall it be that you shall have least success, and that the words of the prophet Osee shall be verified in you—"Give them, O Lord; what wilt thou give ?" " Give them a womb without children, and dry breasts." (Osee ix. 14.) That same name of Fathers, which is given you when you are called father-preacher, will be to yourself a vain and useless name ; for you shall have no spiritual children, you shall have no milk to give them ; at least the milk which you shall give them shall not nourish them. This is the chastisement which he deserves, who usurps what belongs only to

God, and appropriates it to himself. I do not, say, however, that you should not study, and weigh exactly all that you are to preach ; but that is not enough—you must also carefully recommend it to God with tears, and after you have laboured and taken a great deal of pains to examine and digest it, you must still say ; " We are unprofitable servants, we have done that which was but our duty to do." (Luke xvii. 20.) And after all, what is it that I can do? I can make a little noise with my words at most, like that of a musket charged only with powder ; but it belongs to thee, O Lord, to touch the heart. " The king's heart is in the hand of the Lord, he turneth it wheresoever he listeth ;" (Prov. xxi. 1) ; it is thy part alone, O Lord, to touch hearts ; for how are we able to succeed therein of ourselves ; and without thy grace of what effect can all discourses be, and all the human means we use, to attain so supernatural an end as is the conversion of souls ? When therefore we think that we promote the good of souls, and are successful, on what do we then ground that vain complacency which we give way to, as if that success were our own work ? " Shall the axe," says our Lord by the prophet Isaias, " boast itself against him that heweth therewith, or shall the saw magnify itself against him that draweth it ? As if the rod should shake against him that lifts it up, or as if the staff should take pride and exalt itself, which is but a piece of wood." (Isa. x. 15.) This is a representation of what we are as to the conversion of souls. We are but pieces of wood, who have no motion in ourselves, but what it pleases God to give us. We have no reason, therefore, to pride ourselves on anything ; and it is to him alone that we ought to attribute the success of what we do.

He is so jealous lest we should lay any stress on our own strength, or upon human helps, and will have us so absolutely give him the glory of everything, that it was for that reason he was pleased to choose for the preaching of the gospel and conversion of the world, not learned and eloquent men, but simple fishermen, and those who were uncouth and ignorant. "God had chosen," says St. Paul, " the foolish things of the world to confound the wise, and the weak things of the world to confound the strong." Would you know why he has done so ? "It is," adds the apostle, " that no flesh should glory in his presence, but that according as it is written, he that glories, let him glory in the Lord." (1 Cor. i. 27, 28.) If the preachers of the gospel had been powerful princes, and had planted it all over the earth with an armed force, the conversion of the world might have been attributed to the terror of their arms. Or if, for that purpose, God had chosen great orators, who by their profound knowledge and great eloquence would convince the philosophers, the success might have been attributed to the force of their rhetoric and learning, and the glory of Jesus had been thereby so much diminished; but he has done otherwise, and would not suffer that "the wisdom and eloquence of man should share in preaching the gospel, lest the cross of Christ should thereby be made of no effect." (1 Cor. i. 17.) St. Austin says, "that the Saviour of our souls, with a view to put down the pride of the haughty, employed not orators to draw sinners to him, but by the means of a simple fisherman he gained even emperors. Cyprian," he adds, "was a great orator, but before him Peter had been a fisherman, and it was by the means of that fisherman, that not only orators but emperors also submitted to the faith." (Tract. xi. sup. Joan.)

The holy scripture is full of examples by which we see that God made use of weak instruments for the execution of the greatest things, that he might the better imprint this truth in our hearts, that we ought never glorify ourselves in anything, but attribute the glory of all to God alone. This we learn from the famous victory which Judith, a weak woman, and all alone, gained over an army of above forty thousand men. And we are taught this by the victory David gained over Goliah when, very young, and with no other arms than his sling, he laid him on the ground with one blow, and triumphed over the Philistines, "that all the earth should know," says the scripture, "that there is one God who takes care of Israel, and that all this assembly should find that it is not by the sword or the spear that the Lord gives victory in battles, but that it proceeds from him alone." (1 Reg. xvii. 46, 47.) Those are the words God said to Gedeon, who had brought together two and thirty thousand men against the Madianites, whose army consisted of above an hundred and thirty thousand. He expresses further the same thing—"You have," says God, "too many men with you to make me deliver the Madianites into your hands." (Judg. vii. 2.) Let us reflect a little with admiration upon the reason which God assigns. You shall not conquer, because you have too many men with you. If he had said, you will not be able to conquer because they have a great number of men and you but few, that, one would think, had been more conformable to reason. But, no! this would be to reason like man; whereas to reason

like God is to say, you will not be able to conquer because you
are too numerous.   And why so ?   " Lest," continues the Lord,
"Israel should glorify itself therein, and say that it was delivered
by its own strength. (Judg. v. 2.)   Wherefore God commands
Gedeon to take only three hundred men with him, and to fight
the enemy, and gives him a signal victory, without putting him
to the necessity of even drawing a sword,   The sound of the
trumpets which they carried in one hand, and the clashing of the
water-pots, and the light of the torches which they carried in
the other, were the means used by God to render the enemy so
panic-struck, that breaking their own ranks, they defeated themselves, and killed one the other in great numbers.   Now the
Israelites could not say that they overcame by their own strength;
and that was all the acknowledgment that God designed to bring
them to.   If then in temporal things, wherein there is some proportion between the means we use and the end we propose to
ourselves, between the forces we have and the victory, God will
not have us give the glory of anything to ourselves, but acknowledge that the gaining of battles and the good success of affairs
proceed from him.   If, in the order of natural things, neither he
who plants, nor he who waters, is properly anything ; if it is not
the gardener but God alone that makes the plants grow and the
trees bear fruit, what must it be in the order of grace, in the
conversion of souls, in the progress of virtue, and in all other
spiritual affairs, where human strength is so bounded and our
means so limited that they bear no proportion to so sublime an
end ?   " Wherefore, neither he that plants is anything, nor he
that waters, but God that gives the increase." (1 Cor. iii. 7.)
He alone by his grace makes the plants we cultivate increase
aud fructify ; he alone can strike men with fear and terror ; he
alone can make them detest sin, and quit their wicked ways.   For,
as for us, what can we do but make a little sound with the
trumpet of the Gospel?   Nevertheless, if we do at the same time
keep down our body by mortification, and make our light shine
before men by an exemplary life, we shall do a great deal, for
by that means God will give us the victory.

Let us draw from all this two maxims, which will be of great
comfort to us in the exercise of our ministry, and which will
serve very much to render it useful both for our own particular
advancement, and that of our neighbours also.   The first is, to
have a diffidence in ourselves, as has been already said ; to put
all our confidence in God, and to attribute all our good success

to him alone. " Let us not be elated with anything," says St. Chrysostom, " but let us acknowledge ourselves to be useless, that we may prove useful both to ourselves and others" (Hom. xxxviii. ad pop. Antioch) ; and St. Ambrose admonishes us, if we will advance the good of souls to practise what St. Peter teaches—" If any man speaks, let him speak as the words of God ; if any man minister, let it be as from the power that God administereth, that God may in all things be glorified through Jesus Christ, to whom appertains praise and dominion for ever and ever. (1 Pet. iv. 11.) Let us attribute nothing to ourselves, let us rob God of nothing, and let us not have any vain complacency in anything whatsoever.

The second maxim, which we ought to draw from what has been said, and which is very necessary for us, is, " not to be discouraged on account of our own weakness and misery." For who is it, that seeing himself called to a charge so high, and an end so sublime, as is that of converting souls, of delivering them from the bondage of sin, and from the darkness of heresy and infidelity—who is it, I say, that considering these things, and reflecting upon himself, would not lose courage when he is sensible of the disproportion between his own strength and so great an undertaking ? He may say, perhaps, this concerns not me, I have more need to be converted than anyone ; I am very sensible of my own weakness, and I am the least and most incapable of all : but he is mistaken when he reasons thus ; it is even by reason of his weakness that God designs him for so great a work. Moses could not be persuaded that he was the person who should perform so marvellous an action as to deliver the children of Israel from the bondage of Egypt, so that, excusing himself to Almighty God, who gave him that commission, "Who am I," says he, " that I should go unto Pharao, and that I should bring forth the children of Israel out of Egypt ? I beseech of thee, O Lord, send whom thou wilt send; I am slow of speech, and a slow tongue." Listen now to what God says : "Go, I will be with thy mouth, and teach thee what thou shalt say." (Exod. iv. 12.) The same thing happened to the prophet Jeremias. God sent him to prophesy to the nations: whereupon he excused himself and said : " Ah, Lord ! behold I cannot speak, for I am a child !" (Jer. i. 6.) And it is for that very reason that thou must go, and it is such a one that God seeks ; whereas, if thou hadst great parts, he would not perhaps have chosen thee, lest thou shouldst rob him of the glory of what thou doest, and attribute it partly to thyself. God seeks out the humble, who cannot attribute anything to themselves, and it is by them he accomplishes the greatest objects.

The holy scripture tells us, that when the disciples were returned from their mission the Saviour of souls, seeing the fruit they had reaped, and the miracles they had wrought, rejoiced and said, " I thank thee, O Father, Lord of heaven and earth, because thou hast hid these things from the wise and prudent, and hast revealed them unto little ones : Yea, Father, for so it hath pleased thee." (Matt. xi. 25.) Happy the simple, happy the humble, and happy they who do not attribute anything to themselves. They are those whom God raises ; it is by them that he performs the wonders of his grace ; those he chooses for instruments of the greatest things, to work great conversions, and to promote exceedingly the good of souls. Let nobody, therefore, lose courage : " Fear not, little flock, for it is your father's good pleasure to give you the kingdom of heaven." (Luke xii. 32.) And you who compose the society of Jesus, who are at present the weakest and the least numerous of all, be not discouraged on that account; for it has pleased your heavenly father to give you power over the souls and hearts of men. "I will be favourable to you at Rome," (In ejus vita, 1, 2, c. xi.) said Jesus Christ when he appeared to our holy founder as he was going thither, and from which miraculous apparition our order, which was then forming, took afterwards the name of the Society of Jesus. This name shows us, that it is not only to the order of St. Ignatius we are called, but even to the Society of Jesus, and it assures us at the same time of the protection which he pro- mised to our founder. So that since it is Jesus Christ who is properly our head and leader, we must not be weary nor lose courage in so great an enterprise as that of the salvation of souls, to which it has pleased God to call us.

——o——

CHAPTER V.

Of the first degree of humility, which is to have an humble opinion of one's self.

St. Laurence Justinian says, that " nobody knows well what humility is, but he who has received the gift thereof from God ; that it is of itself very hard to be known, and that there is nothing in which man deceives himself so much as in the knowing what true humility is. "You think," says he, "that it consists in saying you are a sinner, and a miserable creature." If it consisted in that nothing in the world would be easier; we should all be humble, for we all speak in that manner, and God grant we believe what we say, and that our words on the occasion are not mere matter of form. You think that humility consists also in wearing plain clothes, and in employing yourself in mean and despicable offices; by no means—there may still lurk a great deal of pride at bottom. It may very well happen, that by adopting this mode you wish to distinguish yourself from others, and to pass for a better and more humble man than they, and so all may be a sort of refined pride. Not but that these exterior things, as I shall hereafter show, contribute much to true humility, when they are made use of as they ought, but, after all, it does not consist therein. "Many," says St. Jerome, "embrace the shadow and appearance of humility, but few embrace humility itself." (Ep. ii.) It is very easy to look down upon the ground, to speak in an humble tone, to fetch a sigh or two, now and then, and to own one's self a sinner and a miserable creature at every word; but if you say anything to these persons which may hurt their feelings in the least, you will see how far they are from true humility. "Let therefore," adds St. Jerome, "all feigned and affected language be dropped; it is patience that shews a man to be truly humble" (Ibid.); it is that which is the touch-stone of humility.

St. Bernard explains more particularly in what this virtue consists, and gives this definition of it. "Humility," says he, "is a virtue whereby a man, from a true knowledge of himself, becomes vile in his own eyes." (Ibid.) Humility consists not, therefore, in words, nor in the exterior; it consists in the sentiments of the heart, in having a low and mean opinion of ourselves founded on the deep sense we have of our own nothingness; and in desiring to be despised by all the world.

Holy writers who have more particularly treated on this subject lay down several degrees of humility. St. Benedict, who was followed therein by St. Thomas and several others, reckons twelve; St. Anselm but seven; St. Bonaventure reduces them to three, whom I shall follow, both for brevity's sake, and that this doctrine being reduced to fewer points, we may have it easily before our eyes, in order to practise it. "The first degree of humility," says St. Bonaventure, "is to have a low and mean opinion of ourselves; and the only means of acquiring that is to know ourselves." St. Bernard's definition comprises these two points only ; and therefore it contains only the first degree we speak of. Humility is a virtue which makes man become vile in his own eyes, that is the other. And thence it comes, that some authors place the knowledge of one's self as the first degree of humility, and not without reason; but because here we reduce them all to three, with St. Bonaventure, we reckon the first degree of humility to consist in having a mean and low opinion of ourselves, and we look upon the knowledge of ourselves as the necessary means to come to this degree. Nevertheless it is all one at the bottom, and we all agree, that the knowledge of ourselves is the principal foundation of humility, and of the opinion we ought to frame of ourselves. For how can we know what we ought to believe precisely of any one, if we know him not ? It is a thing impossible; you must first know him, and thereupon you will be able to frame the opinion you ought to have of him. It is needful, therefore, that before all things you should know yourself thoroughly; and, after that, esteem yourself according to what you are, and this you may lawfully do. For you will be humble enough as soon as you shall know yourself ; as then you will plainly see how little you are. St. Isadore in his Etymologies, says. that the word "superbus, in Latin, is so called because he whom we styled proud would be esteemed above what he is in effect." According to some, one of the reasons why God loves humility is, because he loves the truth above all things. Now humility is truth itself; whereas, pride is a mere deceit and a lie, for you are not in effect what you think you are, nor what you would have others think you to be. If then you would walk in the paths of truth and humility, reckon yourself for what you are; and surely that is not to require too much of you. For what reason can you have to believe yourself any other than what you are ? Nay, what a strange and dangerous cheat would you here practise upon yourself ?

——o——

CHAPTER VI.

Of the knowledge of one's self, which is the source of humility, and the only means of acquiring it.

LET us now begin by enquiring minutely into what we are, and as it were by digging deep into the knowledge of our misery and weakness, that we may there find the treasure of humility.

"One has lost," says St. Jerome, "a drachm, and it is in dirt and dung it is found again." (Ad. Rustio.) In the dung-hill and filth of your sins and miseries you shall find the jewel of humility. Now, to observe method in our inquiry, let us see in the first place what man is in his natural being. Let this be our first search. "Have these three things always present in your mind," says St. Bernard, "what you were, what you are, and what you shall be. Now what were you, but impure seed? What are you, but a vessel of uncleanness? And what shall you be, but rottenness and the food of worms?" (In form. hon. vit.) Here is already matter enough to meditate upon, and it is with good reason that St. Innocent cries out: "O the vile and miserable condition of human nature! Behold the herbs and the plants, they bring forth leaves, flowers, and fruit; and man's body breeds nothing but vermin, worms, and filth; they produce oil, wine, and balm, and send forth a delightful smell, and man's body is a sink of stench and ordure. In a word, such as the tree is, such is the fruit." (Innoc. de contem. mun.) "For a bad tree never bears good fruit." (Matt. vii. 17.) It is a very just comparison which the holy writers make of a man's body, to a dung-hill covered over with snow, which appears fair and white on the outside, but within is nothing but dirt and filth. "If you do but observe," says St. Bernard, "all the filth that comes out of the nose, mouth, and other parts of a man's body, there is no dung-hill or common sewer so foul." (C. 3, Med.) It is this consideration which made Job cry out: "I have said to corruption, thou art my father, and to the worms, thou art my sister and my mother." (Job xvii. 14.) For indeed what else is man but a source of corruption, and a sack of worms, and rottenness? What have we therefore to raise our vanity on? "What can dust and ashes be proud of?" (Eccl. x. 9.) At least it cannot boast of what we have described; for we can find nothing therein but subjects for the humiliation and greater contempt of ourselves. "The remembrance of the infirmities and miseries of man is a good preservative of humility," says St. Gregory; under the dung-hill this plant is kept perfectly well.

But let us examine a little farther. Consider what you were before God created you; you will find that you were nothing, and that you could not of yourself draw yourself out of the abyss of nothing; but that it was God who by his great bounty drew you thence, in giving you the being which you have. So that on our side we are nothing, and therefore ought not to esteem ourselves more than things which are not; it is to God alone to whom we are to attribute whatever we are more than nothing. "If any one," says St. Paul, "thinks himself to be something, when he is nothing, he deceives himself." (Gal. vi. 3.) This is a great discovery we have made—it is sufficient to enrich us with humility all our life-time.

But there is yet more to be considered, which is, that even after we have received our being we do not subsist of ourselves. It is not with us as with a house, which the architect leaves after he has built, and which stands of itself without any need of his help. We have after our creation and at every moment of our life, as much need of God to preserve our being, as we had to obtain it when we were nothing. He continually upholds us with his almighty hand, to hinder our falling again into the abyss of nothing, from whence he has drawn us; wherefore the royal prophet says, "Thou, O Lord hast formed me, and stretched thy hand over me." (Psal. cxxxviii.) It is that hand that holds me up, that preserves and hinders me from falling back into the nothing from which I came. We do so depend on the help of God, and our preservation is so much linked thereunto, that if he should withdraw his hand one moment, we should fall that very instant ; we should cease to be, and should return to our first nothing." "All nations," says the prophet Isaias, "are before him as if they were not, and are counted as nothing." (Isa. xl. 17.) We also say of ourselves every day that we are nothing, but it is to be feared we say it only with our lips, and understand not what we say. God grant that we may understand and be as sensible of it as the prophet was when he said, "all that I am is as nothing before thee." (Psal. xxxviii. 6.) I am indeed nothing of myself; for I was nothing, and what I am I hold it not of myself. It is thou, O Lord, who hast given me my being, and it is of thee that I hold it ; and what reason can I have to glory therein, since I contributed nothing thereunto, and it is thou alone who preservest it ; and givest me the power to act ? Our being, breath, and action, all come from thy hand ; as for us, we can do nothing, because we are nothing of ourselves. Of what then can we be proud ? Perhaps of our nothing. We have said with the Wise man; "what can dust and ashes be proud of ?" But we may now say, what can nothing be proud of, which is less than dust and ashes ? What reason, what occasion can it have to be puffed up with pride, and to believe itself something ? There can certainly be none.

CHAPTER VII.

*The consideration of our sins is very proper to make us know our-
selves and acquire humility.*

LET us go on with our inquiry, and, as it were, dig deeper still
into the knowledge of ourselves ; but what or where can we now
dig ? Is there anything beyond nothing? Yes, doubtless, there
is something—there is sin which you have added thereunto.
And what an abyss is that ? It is much greater than the abyss
of nothing, because sin is worse than nothing. Jesus Christ,
speaking of Judas, who designed to betray him, says, " it would
have been better for him that he had never been born." (Matt.
xxvi. 24.) There is nothing so vile and despicable in the eyes
of God, within the whole extent of existence, and of nothing, as a
man in mortal sin, who is banished from heaven, the declared
enemy of God, and condemned to the eternal pains of hell. Let
us always have this consideration in our mind, even when we do
not find our conscience charged with any mortal sin ; and as, for
the better knowing of our nothingness, we have represented to
ourselves the time when we were nothing ; so, for the further
knowledge of our meanness and misery, let us call to mind the
time when we were in sin. Think what a miserable condition
you were in when, having yourself disagreeable in the eyes of
God by the enormity of your sins, he looked upon you as his
enemy, as the child of wrath, and as a criminal destined to everlasting flames. After that, cover yourself with confusion, and
prostrate yourself as low as you can ; for you ought to believe,
that, put yourself in ever so low a situation, you can never render
yourself so contemptible as he deserves to be who has offended
the sovereign good, which is God. This meditation is an infinite
abyss. For, till we can see in heaven how great the bounty of
God is, it is impossible for us fully to comprehend how enormous
sin is which makes us rebels to him, and what punishment he
deserves who offends him.

Now did we but think well of this, and search thoroughly into
our sins and miseries, how humble should we be ? How little
should we esteem ourselves, and with what joy should we receive
contempt and reproach ? What ought not he who has been unfaithful to God suffer for the love of him after he is restored to

his favour? And he who has left God to follow his passions, who has offended his Creator and Master for a transient pleasure, and who has deserved thereupon eternal punishment, to what injuries and affronts ought he not heartily submit in atonement for the sins which he committed against the majesty of God? "I went astray," says David, (addressing himself to God) "before I was humbled by afflictions, but now have I kept thy commands." (Ps. cxviii. 67.) It is that makes me hold my peace, and not dare to complain, for what I suffer is nothing in comparison to what my sins deserved. Thou hast not punished me, O Lord, according to my deserts, and whatever we can suffer in this life is nothing in proportion to what one sin deserves. Is it not just that the sinner who has despised God should be despised—that there should be little esteem made of him who has made so little of his master, and that the man who had the will and insolence to offend his Creator, should be punished in not being able ever to do anything that he has the least mind to do?

But on this point we are still farther to reflect, that though the confidence we ought to have in God's mercy may give us grounds to hope that he has forgiven us our sins : yet, nevertheless, we have no certainty thereof. "Man," says Solomon, "knows not whether he deserves love or hatred." (Eccl. ix. 1.) And the apostle, speaking in the same sense—"I am conscious of nothing," says he, "but I am not thereby justified." 1 Cor. ix. 4.) Now, if unfortunately I am not justified, what shall I gain by having embraced a religious life, and converted souls to God? "Though I speak with the tongues of men and angels, and have not charity, I am become as sounding brass or a tinkling cymbal; and though I have the gift of prophecy, and understand all mysteries and all knowledge, and though I have all faith, so that I could remove mountains, and have not charity, I am nothing ; and though I bestow all my goods to feed the poor, and give my body to be burned, and have not charity, it profits me nothing." (1 Cor. xiii. 1.) Wo be to thee, then, if thou hast not charity, if thou art not in the grace of God, for without that thou art nothing, nay, thou art less than nothing. Not to know whether or not we are in the state of grace is a great means to keep us always humble, and to make us have a low opinion of ourselves. We know most certainly that we have offended God, but we have no certainty that God has pardoned us. Now, who dares look up, who will not be covered with confusion, who will not sink even to the centre of the earth, whilst he is in this incertitude ?

It is this made St. Gregory say, that "it has pleased God we should not be certain of his grace, to the end that we should always have one grace certain, which is that of humility." And, indeed, how grievous soever the fear and incertitude he has left us in seems unto us, his conduct therein is full of mercy and bounty; it is a fear which is profitable to us for the acquiring of humility, for the preservation thereof, and which hinders us from despising our neighbour, whatever sins he may have committed. The thought that God has perhaps received him into grace, and that we know not whether we are in his grace or not, is indeed a powerful motive to excite us always to do good, without ever being weary, and to make us still walk with fear and humility before God. Wherefore, the Holy Ghost, by the mouth of the Wise man says—"Happy is the man that is always in fear;" (Prov. xxviii. 14) and he admonishes us in another place, "not to reckon ourselves too sure as to the remission of our sins." (Eccl. v. 5.) Hence, the sight of our sins is very useful to keep us in humility, and in a contempt of ourselves. Oh! what a subject of inquiry do they not furnish us with.

Moreover, the misfortunes and wounds inflicted on us by original sin will supply sufficient matter to humble us, if we reflect how much nature has been corrupted in us by sin. For, as a stone is drawn downward by its own weight, so are we carried by the corruption of original sin to whatever regards our flesh, our vanity, and our interest. We have a most lively relish for earthly things, little or no relish for heavenly ones. What should obey in us, commands; and, in fine, we are so miserable, that though we are men and born for heaven, we have the inclinations of beasts, and hearts that tend only to the earth. "The heart of man is deceitful above all things; who can know it?" says Jeremias. (Jer. xvii. 9.) It is that wall of the vision of Ezechiel; the more you dig there the more abominations you will discover. But if we will cast our eyes next upon our faults, which spring from our own stock or fund, how many subjects of confusion shall we find there? Whither does not intemperance of tongue carry us? How negligent are we in not guarding our hearts? How inconstant are we in our good designs? How great lovers of our interest and convenience? How eager to do what pleases us? How full of self-love? How wedded to our own will and opinion? How violent in our passions? How steady in our ill habits, and how prone to gratify our corrupt inclinations? St. Gregory, writing upon these words of Job,

" wilt thou show thy power against a leaf, which is carried to and fro by the wind," (Job xiii. 25,) says, it is with reason that man is compared to a leaf, because just as a leaf moves at the least breath, so man lets himself easily be tossed up and down by all the winds and passions of temptations. One while he lets himself be transported with anger; another while he abandons himself to vain joy; to-day avarice and ambition torment him; to-morrow pleasure and sensuality carry him away; sometimes pride elevates him, and sometimes fear and trouble deject and cast him down. Wherefore, the prophet Isaias says very well, that, " we are all fallen like the leaves, and our inquities like the wind have carried us away." (Isa. lxiv. 16.) The least wind of temptation throws us down and carries us away; we have no steadiness in virtue and good resolutions; so that here is enough in this matter wherewith to humble and confound ourselves. But they are not only our sins and faults which should humble us, even our good actions should produce that effect, if we examine them carefully and see with how many faults and imperfections they are ordinarily mingled according to the words of the same prophet, " we are all become as unclean, and all our good works as filthy rags." (Isa. lxiv. 6.) But we have already spoken of that elsewhere, so that there is no need to enlarge on it here.

———o———

CHAPTER VIII.

How we are to exercise ourselves in the knowledge of ourselves, so as not to lose courage and confidence.

OUR misery is so great, the causes we have to humble ourselves are so numerous, and we know them so well from our own experience, that methinks we should have more need to be encouraged not to let ourselves be cast down at the sight of our imperfections, than exhorted to use endeavours to be well acquainted with them. This is indeed so certain a truth, that all spiritual directors teach us that when we have been searching into the knowledge of our misery and weakness we should not stop there, lest the prospect may cast us down and make us despair, but that we should immediately pass on to the consideration of God's goodness, and so put all our confidence in him. As the sorrow for having sinned ought not to be so great as to make us fall into despair, but should be moderated through hope of pardon, by casting our eyes sometimes upon the mercy of God, and taking them off from the view of our sins, " lest he," as the apostle says, " who is in that condition should fall into excessive grief," (2 Cor. ii. 7), so we ought not dwell upon the consideration of our weakness and infirmities, for fear that our courage and confidence should fail us. But after having searched well into the knowledge of ourselves, after having seen that there is nothing in us whereupon we can rely, and having learned thereby to have a diffidence in our own strength, we ought forthwith to cast our eyes upon the infinite goodness of God.   Thus we shall not only not lose courage, but shall, on the contrary, find ourselves more animated ; because the same thing which serves to cast us down, when we turn our eyes only on ourselves, serves to strengthen us when we fix them upon God ; and the more you know your own weakness, and the little stress you can lay upon yourself, you will find yourself the more fortified when you shall contemplate God, and put all your confidence in him.

But the holy writers make here a remark of great importance, which is, that as, for the reason we have given, we must not fix too much upon the consideration of our misery and weakness, but go on to the knowledge of the goodness and liberality of God, in order to put all our confidence in him ; so ought we not rest altogether upon this last consideration, but return forthwith again to reflect upon ourselves and our infirmities.   For, if we dwell upon the contemplation of the bounty and liberality of God, and forget what we ourselves are, it is to be feared we may fall into presumption and pride, by taking occasion from thence to have too great confidence in ourselves, and to walk with too little diffidence and foresight, which has often been the cause of several terrible falls.   How many spiritual persons have cast themselves down by this means, who seemed to soar up even to heaven itself by prayer and contemplation ?   How many saints, and great ones too, have fallen for having forgotten that they were sinners, and for confiding too much in the favour God had shown them ?   They hazarded themselves, and trusted to it as if they had been out of danger, and therefore they have shamefully fallen.   St. Basil attributes the fall of David, when he made himself guilty of adultery and murder, to the presumption which he had once ; when, God having heaped favours and blessings upon him, he let these words slip from him : " I said in my prosperity, nothing shall ever move me." (Ps. xxix. 7.)   But stay a little ; God will withdraw his hand ;

he will deprive you of his favours, and then you will see the consequence. " Thou hast turned thy face from me, and I was grievously troubled." (Ibid.) God will leave you to your weakness ; you will fall into a thousand disorders, and you will know to your cost, after your fall, what you would not know when he favoured thee with his grace. The same St. Basil attributes further the fall of St. Peter to the same cause, which was for having too much presumed upon himself, when he said to our Saviour : " When all shall be scandalized at thee, I shall never be scandalized. Nay, though I should die with thee, I would never deny thee." (Matt. xxvi. 33.) So that it pleased God to punish his presumption and permit him to fall, thereby to humble and make him know himself. Wherefore, we ought never to lose sight of ourselves, or think we are wholly secure in this life ; but, considering what we are, we must always have a diffidence in ourselves, and stand in fear lest the enemy we have within should deceive and betray us.

Hence, as we must not dwell too much upon the knowledge of our weakness and misery, but pass forthwith to that of the bounty of God, so we ought not dwell on that either, but presently cast our eyes again upon ourselves. This exercise ought to be like Jacob's ladder, of which one end touched the earth and the other reached up to heaven. It is by it you are to ascend and descend as the angels did. Ascend till you arrive at the knowledge of the goodness of God ; but rest not there, for fear of falling into presumption. Go down again forthwith to the knowledge of thyself, and not rest there either, for fear of being faint-hearted, but return up again to the knowledge of God, to place all your confidence in him. In fine, all you have to do is to go continually up and down this ladder.

St. Catherine of Sienna says, " she used to do this to deliver herself from the temptations of the devil." For when, to discourage her, he endeavoured to make her believe that all her life had been only a deception, she took courage at the consideration of the mercy of God, and expressed herself thus : " I confess, O my Creator, that all my life has been nothing but darkness, but I will hide myself in the wounds of Jesus crucified ; and I will bathe myself in his blood, which will wash off all my sins ; and I will rejoice in my Creator and my God." " Thou shalt wash me, O Lord, and I shall become whiter than snow." (Ps. i. 9.) On the other hand, if the devil by a contrary temptation tried to puff her up with pride, by representing to her that she was already perfect, and that she had no further need to bewail her sins, or to be afflicted ; she most profoundly humbled herself, and thus reasoned with herself : " What ! unhappy creature that I am !—St. John Baptist never sinned, he nevertheless failed not to do severe penance ; what then must I do, who have committed so many sins, and never acknowledged and bewailed them as I ought ?" The devil, then, enraged to see so much humility on one side, and so much confidence in God on the other, thus cried out ; " Cursed be thou, and they who have so well instructed thee ! I know not where to attack thee :—If I cast thee down to make thee lose courage, thou raisest thyself again by contemplating the mercy of God ; and if I exalt thee, thereby to fill thee with vanity, thou castest thyself down by humility, even to the bottom of hell." After this he let her alone, seeing he came off so shamefully from all the assaults he made upon her. Thus ought we to exercise ourselves—on the one hand we must have great diffidence and fear, on the other, much confidence, joy, and courage ; a great deal of diffidence in ourselves, and a great deal of confidence in God. These are the two lessons which a holy man says that God gives every day to his elect : one to consider their own faults ; and the other, to consider the goodness of God, who with so much bounty and affection pardons them.

————o————

CHAPTER IX.

Of the advantages found in the exercise of self-knowledge.

To excite us more and more in the exercise of the knowledge of ourselves, I shall here speak of some considerable advantages which are found therein. I have already touched upon a very important one, which is that this knowledge of ourselves is the basis and foundation of humility, and the necessary means to acquire and preserve it. An ancient father of the desert was asked, how true humility was to be acquired ? He replied, " by reflecting upon one's own faults only, and not looking upon those of another." It is by this self-knowledge that true humility is acquired ; it is by sounding ourselves that it is found ; and this alone ought to suffice to make us apply ourselves to this exercise, because it is so much our interest to acquire humility.

But the holy writers proceed farther, and say, that the humble sense and knowledge of ourselves is a more certain way to arrive at the knowledge of God, than the most profound study of all other sciences ; and the reason which St. Bernard gives for it is, that this science being more sublime than any other leads us also straighter to God. St. Bonaventure says ; it is this which the Saviour of the world would have us understand by the curing of the man who was born blind, when rubbing his eyes with a little dirt, he gave him at the same time both the sight of the body to see himself, and that of the soul to know and adore God. "It is thus," continues he, "that as we are born blind, and ignorant of God and ourselves, the Lord enlightens us by rubbing our eyes with the clay of which we are composed, that we may begin first to know ourselves, and then adore with a lively faith him from whom we have received light." (Proc. v. Rel. c. xviii.) It is this also which the Church teaches us in the ceremony which it practises at the beginning of Lent, of putting ashes on our fore-heads, saying, "Remember, O man, that thou art dust, and shalt return again to dust." (Gen. iii. 19.) For she thus sets before our eyes what we are, that by the knowledge of ourselves we may come to know God, to repent for having offended him, and to do penance for our sins. So that self-knowledge is a means to come to the knowledge of God, and the more a creature shall consider the dust he is originally made of, the more will he know the greatness and elevation of God, according to the axiom, "that nothing gives us a better knowledge of things that are opposite to one another, than to place them by one another." White never appears and shines more, than when it is placed near black. Now, man is everything that is low, and God every thing that is elevated—these are contraries ; and therefore the more man knows himself and understands that he is nothing of himself but misery and sin, the more sensibly he feels what the goodness and mercy of God is, to love a thing so vile and despic-able as man.

But what consideration still further produces is, that the soul by this means is inflamed more and more with the love of God, not being able to cease from giving him thanks for so many benefits which he bestows on so miserable a creature ; nor from wondering that men having so much difficulty in bearing one with another, God should not only have the goodness to bear with them, but that he should himself say, "That it is his delight to be and converse with the sons of men." (Prov. viii. 31.) Hence the Psalmist could not forbear to cry out with admiration :— "What is man that thou shouldst be mindful of him ? Or the son of man that thou shouldst visit him ?" (Psal. viii. 5.) For this reason it is the saints study to know themselves, that thereby they might come to a greater knowledge and love of God. It was for the same reason St. Austin was wont to say :—" O my God, who art always the same, let me know myself, and I shall know thee !" (Lib. de vitâ beatâ.) It is this made St. Francis cry out, night and day, " Who art thou, my God, and who am I ?" And lastly, it is by this means that so many saints have attained so great a knowledge of God. This, therefore, is an infallible way ; because the more you humble yourself in the knowledge of yourself, the more will you be exalted in the knowledge of God, and the more you increase in knowing God, the more you will advance in self-knowledge ; because the heavenly light pierces into the most secret and hidden corners of the heart, and makes us find out subjects of confusion, even in such things as appear best in the eyes of the world. St. Bonaventure says, that, as when the rays of the sun enter into a chamber, we immediately discover a thousand atoms which we saw not before ; so when our heart is touched with the rays of divine grace, the soul perceives even the least imperfections, and sees a thousand faults in those things which seem perfect to such as are not enlightened with so bright and piercing a light as this.

This is therefore the cause why the saints are so humble, and have so low an opinion of themselves, and that as they increase in sanctity, they increase in humility, and in a contempt of themselves. The more God enlightens them, and communicates himself to them, the more they perceive that they have of their own only nothingness and sin ; and the more defects this self-knowledge makes them discover in themselves, the more they believe there are still to be discovered, and that they see but the least part of them. In fine, as they are persuaded that the goodness of God exceeds all the knowledge they have of it, so they are also convinced that their own wickedness far surpasses all the knowledge they have thereof. For as, whatever knowledge we have of God, we can never comprehend him, but there always is something in him to be more and more known and admired; so, whatever knowledge and contempt we may have of ourselves, there also remains something more to be despised, and therefore we can never know fully the excess of our misery. This is no exaggeration, it is a plain truth ; because, it being certain that man is of himself but nothing and sin, it is consequently certain that he can never humble himself so much as these two qualities require.

We read that a holy woman begged of God the grace to know herself, and having obtained it, she had so much horror of her deformity and misery, that unable to bear longer the sight thereof, she prayed again, that he would hide some part of it from her, lest she should be too much dejected. Father Avila tells us also, that he knew a certain person, who had often made a similar request of God, and that God having one day opened his eyes, to let him see his misery ; he was struck thereupon with so much horror, that he cried out,—take away, O Lord, for thy mercies' sake, this looking-glass from before me ; I am not able to bear any longer the sight of so abominable an object.

This is the cause, also, why there arises in the servants of God that holy hatred and horror of themselves, of which we have already spoken of elsewhere. For, looking upon themselves as enemies of God, the more they come to know his goodness, and to love him, the greater aversion they have for themselves, according to the words of Job :—" thou hast set me opposite to thee, so that I am become a burden to myself." (Job vii 20.) They see that they have in themselves the root of all sorts of evil, which is the corrupt inclination of the flesh, and the knowledge of all this makes them rise up and revolt against themselves. Is it not just, then, to abhor him who has made you quit so great a good as God himself is, and that for a pleasure of so short duration ? Is it not just to hate him who has made you deserve hell, and put you in hazard of losing glory, and that for ever. Him who, in fine, has been the cause of so much evil to you, and will be so continually to you. Now, it is you yourself who are an enemy to God and to yourself, an enemy to your own good and to your eternal salvation.

———o———

CHAPTER X.

That the knowledge of one's self, instead of making us lose courage, adds new strength.

THERE is yet another advantage in this self-knowledge, which is, that not only it does not put down our courage, as might easily perhaps be imagined, but on the contrary, it raises and fortifies it. The reason of this is, that a man cannot know himself without seeing that he cannot rely or lay any stress upon his own endeavours, so that diffiding in himself, he puts his whole confidence in God, in whom he is able to do all things. Nor does it properly belong to any but those who thus know themselves to undertake and execute the greatest things; because, as they attribute all to God, and nothing to themselves, so God gives them his helping hand, makes it his own business, and is pleased to work wonders by very weak instruments, " to shew," as the apostle says, "the riches of his glory upon those vessels of mercy he had before prepared for his glory." (Rom. iv. 23.) It is to make his glory appear the more, that he puts the treasure of his power and strength in the frailest vessels, and therefore when this great saint prayed to be delivered from the temptations which tormented him :—" my grace is sufficient for thee," says our Lord to him, "for my power appears most in weakness." (2 Cor. xii. 9.) For as the greater and more dangerous the disease is, the more honour the physician gains by curing it : so the greater our weakness is, the more the power of God is displayed. Thus St. Austin and St. Ambrose explain this passage ; and it is for this reason that God does powerfully assist those, who, knowing themselves, have a diffidence in their own strength, and place all their confidence in him ; whereas he always abandons those who presume upon themselves, and confide in their own strength and ability. St. Basil also says, that we sometimes find by experience, that on some certain principal feasts, when we expected to have more than ordinary devotion and fervour, we feel less because we had too much confidence in our own preparations. On the contrary, God heaps sometimes upon us the most sweet consolations of heaven, when we think least thereof, to make us sensible that fervour of devotion is a pure grace and mercy of God, and not an effect of our own endeavours and merit. The knowledge of our misery, therefore, serves rather to raise our courage than to cast us down ; because it makes us put all our confidence in God ; and it is this the apostle would express by these words, " when I am weak, I am strong ;" (2 Cor. xii. 10,) that is to say, as St. Austin and St. Ambrose explain it, when I humble myself, in the knowledge of my weakness and nothingness, then it is that I am elevated and exalted ; and the more infirmity and weakness I discover in myself, the more I find myself strengthened in the sight of God, in whom I have put all my hope and confidence.

We may learn from hence that neither certain discouragements, which we feel sometimes in our spiritual advancement, nor certain diffidence which we sometimes have, of being able to overcome our corrupt inclinations, acquire perfection, or acquit ourselves of the functions which obedience may call us to, proceed from humility. Nor does it always argue humility in us to say, we are not fit to be confessors, missioners, and the like : on the contrary, expressions of this kind very often betray our pride. For why do we make use of them ? It is because we look upon ourselves as if the execution and success of these things were to depend on our own strength, instead of turning our eyes upon God as we ought to do, in whom we shall be sufficiently encouraged and strengthened. " The Lord is my light and salvation, whom then shall I fear ? the Lord is the protector of my life, of whom shall I be afraid ? If a whole army stands against me I will not fear ; and in the greatest heat of the battle I will hope in him." (Ps. xxvi. 1, 3.) Though I should walk in the midst of the shades of death, I will fear nothing, because thou art with me." (Ps. xxii. 4.) Let us admire the variety of words wherein the holy prophet expresses the same thing. The whole book of Psalms is full of these sentiments, whereby the prophet shews us how much confidence he had in God, and how much we ought to have. " By the help of my God I will leap over a wall." (Ps. xvii. 30.) Nothing will be able to oppose me ; he it is who to overcome giants makes use of men, who are but locusts in comparison of them ; " In his name it is that I will crush lions and dragons. It is he who teacheth my hands to war, and gives me strength to break a bow of steel." (Ps. xvii. 35.) We shall indeed be strong enough with his grace and assistance.

——o——

CHAPTER XI.

Some other advantages which accompany self-knowledge.

One of the chief things which we can do on our part to oblige God to communicate his favours, and to shower his graces more abundantly upon us, is to humble ourselves at the sight of our weakness and misery. The apostle, therefore, says, "I will glory willingly in my infirmities that the power of Jesus Christ may dwell in me." (2 Cor. xii. 9.) And St. Ambrose, writing upon the words of the same apostle, "I take pleasure in my infirmities," says, " that if a Christian ought to glory, he ought not to do it but in humility, whereby he becomes greater in the sight of God." St. Austin also applies to the same subject these words of the royal prophet : " Thou, O God, didst send a plentiful rain whereby thou didst confirm thine inheritance, when it was weary." (Ps. lxvii. 10.) "When do you believe," says he, "that God will pour down upon his inheritance, which is the soul, the plentiful showers of his grace?" When it shall become weak or weary : that is, when it shall be sensible of its weakness and infirmity, then God shall strengthen it, and shall heap his gifts and favours upon it. As the more a poor man exposes his sores and misery the more he moves compassion and charity ; even so, the more a Christian humbles himself before God by the acknowledgment of his infirmity and weakness, the more he moves the mercy of God to have pity on him, and to communicate to him abundantly the inexhaustible treasures of grace. " It is he who giveth power to the weary, and he increaseth strength and might to them that are not." (Ps. xl. 29.)

To comprehend in a few words all the advantages and profit which may be drawn from this exercise—I say, that self-knowledge is an universal remedy for everything ; so that to the greatest part of the questions which are asked us in our spiritual conferences, as whence proceed such and such a disorder, and what remedy may be applied to it, we may always answer, that it proceeds only from the want of self-knowledge, for if you attend well to the knowledge of yourself, it will be business enough for you to consider and deplore your own misery without being curious in examining that of others. If you ask me whence comes it that you are satirical in your discourse, I must make you the same answer—for if you knew yourself well, so as to reckon yourself the least of all, and every one else your superior, you would not have presumption to speak to them in that manner. If you ask me whence arise bad excuses, and those complaints and murmurings which are so ordinary, as— Why have not I such or such a thing? Why am I treated so ill? It is certain that all proceeds from the same cause. If you would know whence comes the trouble and excessive oppression you feel when tormented with certain temptations, and that discouragement you lie under when you see how often you relapse into the same faults, the answer will always be, because you know not yourself. For if you had but humility, and knew well the deceitfulness of your own heart, you would not be uneasy or lose courage. But, on the contrary, you would wonder that there happens no worse to you, and that you fall not oftener; and you would not cease praising and blessing God who upholds you with his hand, and saves you from the disorders you would infallibly fall into without him. For, from a common sewer of all sorts of vices what can come but vice? What can be expected from a dunghill but noisome exhalations; and from so cursed a tree what can we promise ourselves but cursed fruit? "What wonder is it that the wind carries away the dust," says St. Anselm, speaking on the passage of the prophet, 'he remembers that we are dust.'" (Ps. cii. 14.) If, therefore, you seek means to become charitable towards your brethren, to be meek, submissive, patient, and mortified in everything, you will find a remedy for all your maladies in the knowledge of yourself.

We read of St. Francis of Borgia, that, being one day on a journey, he was met by one of his friends, a man of quality, who seeing him destitute of all the conveniences which he enjoyed before in the world, and feeling for him, begged of him to take a little more care of himself. The saint answered, with a cheerful countenance and holy dissimulation, thus: " Let not the condition in which you see me in the least trouble you; I am not so unprovided of all things as you think; for I always send a harbinger who takes care to have everything ready before me." The person asking who was that harbinger—" It is," replied the saint, " the knowledge of myself and the consideration of the pains of hell, which I have deserved for my sins, and with this self-knowledge wherever I arrive, and whatever bad lodging I find, I always think I am better treated than I deserve."

The Chronicles of the order of St. Dominick tell us, that one of their religious, a great servant of God, conversing one day with St. Margaret, who was of the same order, told her, among other things, that he had often begged of God to show him the way which the ancient fathers had walked, in order to make themselves amiable in his eyes, and to obtain all the favours they had received; and that one night he dreamed that a book, written in golden letters, was set before him, and that a voice awoke him, saying, "arise, and read." Then, rising immediately, he read in that book these divine words: the perfection of the ancient fathers consisted in loving God, in despising themselves and in neither judging or contemning any body." And so the vision forthwith disappeared.

CHAPTER XII.

Of what importance it is to practise the knowledge of ourselves.

FROM all that we have said, it may be inferred how important it is to practise the knowledge of ourselves. Thales, one of those whom ancient Greece called the seven Wise men, being asked, which of all the natural sciences was the hardest to be acquired? answered : " it was that of one's self, because self-love continually obstructs that knowledge." Hence came that so famous saying among the ancients, "know thyself." And another philosopher meant the same thing when intending to give a short lesson of wisdom, he was wont to say, " live at home." But laying aside the instructions which the pagan philosophers have given upon this subject, let us come to those which have been left us by the Christian philosophers, who are much better masters than the others in this matter. St. Austin and St. Bernard say, that the knowledge of one's self is the most sublime and useful of all sciences that have ever yet been discovered, " Men," says St. Austin, " esteem very much sciences which treat of the heavens and the earth—which point out the motion of the heavenly bodies, the course of the planets, their influences and virtues ; but self-knowledge is a more sublime and useful science." The other sciences puff us up and destroy us, as St. Paul says, but this humbles and edifies us. The spiritual directors, therefore, very much reccommend this exercise whilst we are at prayer, and blame as an abuse what some persons do, who passing slightly over their faults, which are painful to look upon, spend a good deal of time upon some pious meditation, in which they feel comfort and delight. They are ashamed of being so disagreeable to themselves, and imitate an ugly woman, who dares not look herself in the glass. " But if thou didst but behold, O man, what thou art," says St. Bernard, speaking as in the presence of God, " thou wouldst be disagreeable to thyself, and pleasing to me : but because thou seest not thyself, thou art agreeable to thyself and displeasing to me. The time will come when thou shalt neither please thyself or me ; thou shalt not please me, because thou hast sinned ; thou shalt not please thyself, because thou shalt be the cause of thy eternal destruction." (Bern. de inter. dom.)

St. Gregory speaking of this, says, "that there are some people who think themselves holy as soon as they begin to serve God, and to do some virtuous actions; and they are so intent in looking upon the good they do that they entirely lose sight of the sins they have committed: nay, and sometimes they see not even those which they do commit. But the elect, and such as are truly good, do the contrary; for, abounding in virtue and good works, they look only on what is evil in them, and have their eyes continually on their own faults and imperfections." It is easy to see the consequence which this different manner of viewing one's self brings with it; for it happens from thence, that some, whilst they humble themselves at the sight of their faults, preserve the virtues which they have, and others whilst they glory in the good they perceive in themselves, lose both it and themselves also by their pride. Thus some make good use of what ill they have in them that they profit thereby; and others make such bad use of the good they have that it turns to their disadvantage. What happens in eating is a representation of what we say. How good soever the food may be it will do harm, if one eats thereof to excess; and, on the contrary, however dangerous some poisons are they may serve for a remedy and antidote, when they are well prepared and taken as they ought. "When the devil," as the same saint says, "raises vanity in you, in representing to you your good works, set the remembrance of your sins against that temptation." Thus the apostle used to do, when fearing lest the great revelations and miracles which God had wrought by him, should cause too much vanity in him; "he called to mind his having been a blasphemer, his having persecuted and injured the servants of Jesus Christ;" (Tim. i. 13,) and said, "I am not worthy to be called an apostle because I have persecuted the Church of God." (1 Cor. xv. 9.) Against such attacks there is no better counter-battery and counter-mine than to call to mind our past sins.

St. Jerome, writing upon these words of the archangel Gabriel to the prophet Daniel, "hear, O son of man, what will I say unto thee," says, that the ancient prophets, Daniel, Ezechiel, and the rest, seemed to be already angels by the sublimity of their continual revelations. For fear therefore they might be puffed up more than they ought, by forgetting their condition, and believing themselves altogether of an angelical nature, the angel sent from God set before their eyes their miserable and frail original, by calling them "sons of men;" in order that considering they were but weak and miserable men, like others, they should humble themselves under the knowledge of what they were. We have a great many examples, both in ecclesiastical and profane history, of several saints, great persons, kings, popes, and emperors, who used some such means to defend themselves from the attacks of vanity ; and who kept a person on purpose near them, to put them in mind from time to time, "that they were but men."

When St. Francis of Borgia was yet a secular, he was told by a holy man that if he wished to make good progress in the service of God, he must let no day pass without reflecting upon something which might excite in him shame and a contempt of himself— He embraced this counsel with so much fervour, that after he had given himself to mental prayer, he never failed to employ the first two hours thereof to know and despise himself, and to turn whatever he heard, read, or saw, to his own confusion. Besides this, he practised another devotion, which was, that every morning when he rose the first thing he did was to fall down on his knees and kiss the ground three times, to remind himself that he was but dust and ashes, and that he should again return to dust and ashes, And the great and many examples which he has left us of humility and sanctity, shew plainly what fruit he reaped from those exercises of piety. Let us take the same counsel, and let no day pass without employing one part of our prayer in the consideration of something which may move us to a contempt of ourselves ; and never leave off till it sinks thoroughly and very deeply into our soul, and till the continual view of our misery and meanness shall have covered us all over with holy shame and confusion before God. We have great need thus to exercise ourselves ; for we are naturally so full of pride, and so inclined to the desire of being esteemed, that if we take not care to humble ourselves continually, by the consideration of our weakness, we shall always be exalted above ourselves, being like unto cork, which still lifts itself above the water, if you keep it not under by main force. We must, therefore, always keep down the swelling which the good opinion of ourselves raises in our hearts ; and looking upon our weakness and faults, as the peacock does upon his feet, beat down that vanity which self-complacency raises in us. Let us remember the parable of the fig tree planted in the vineyard ; the master of the vineyard would have it cut down, because in three years' time it bore no fruit ; but the dresser of the vineyard said to him, "my Lord, pray let it alone for one year more, till I shall dig about it and dung it ; and if it bear fruit, well : but if not, then after that if you please I shall cut it down." (Luke xiii. 8.)   Do you like-wise dig well the earth about the dry and fruitless plant of your souls ; spread about it the dung of your sins and miseries, and so it will bring forth the fruit of humility and righteousness.

But to encourage us farther in this exercise, and to hinder our taking occasion to leave it off upon ill-grounded apprehensions, it is good to remark here two things.   The first is, that we must not imagine that it is an exercise for new beginners only, for it suits those equally well who are already most advanced in the way of perfection, since we see that the saints and apostles them-selves have practised it.   The second is, that we must not fancy to ourselves that it is a sad and melancholy business which fills the mind with disquiet and trouble.   On the contrary, it brings with it a great deal of tranquillity and delight, in spite of all the weaknesses and faults it makes us discover in ourselves, and of the sense it gives us that we deserved to be contemned and abhorred by all the world,   For when this sense arises from true humility, the pain that gives us is so pleasing that we would not be without it.   And as to certain vexations we sometimes have at the view of our faults and misery, they proceed from the temptation of the devil, who would thereby make us, on the one hand, believe that we are very humble, and on the other, make us despair of the mercy of God, and discourage us from his service. If indeed we were to dwell wholly upon the sense of our own weakness and infirmity, there would be reason to sink under our sorrow, and to lose all courage ; but we must not stop there, we must forthwith pass on to the consideration of God's infinite goodness and mercy, of the love he bears us, of what he has suffered for us, and therein place all our confidence.   Thus what serves to deject us when we look upon ourselves, serves to raise us up again when we look upon God.   In ourselves we see nothing but subject of tears and apprehension, in God we see nothing but subject of joy and confidence, which, notwithstand-ing the excess of our weakness and multitude of our faults, will not permit us to fear that he will abandon us.   Because the greatness of his bounty and mercy which we look upon surpasses infinitely that of our misery and sins.   Thus, by a profound con-sideration of these two things, we come to see at the same time that we ought not to lay any more stress upon ourselves than upon weak reeds, and that we must fix our confidence in God alone, according to the words of Daniel: " For we do not present our supplications before thee, confiding in our own righteousness, but in thy great mercies." (Dan. ix. 18.)

——o——

CHAPTER XIII.

Of the second degree of humility, and in what it consists.

THE second degree of humility consists in our being glad that we are despised. " Love to be unknown," says St, Bonaventure, "and to be contemned." (Proces. 6, Rel. c. 22.) If we were well established in the first degree of humility, we should have but a little way to get to the second. If we truly had a contempt for ourselves, we should not be concerned that others had so too ; but, on the contrary, we should be glad of it. " Will you have a proof thereof ?" says the same saint. " Is it not true that we are naturally glad to have others of our opinion ? If so, why are not we glad to have them slight us ? It is because we do not indeed slight ourselves, but have too good an opinion of ourselves." St. Gregory, upon these words of Job, " I have sinned and indeed done amiss, and have not yet received the punishment which I deserved," (Job xxxv. 27,) says that many express as much with their lips, and speak with contempt of themselves ; but when others repeat the very same things which they have heard them say of themselves, or even far less, they cannot bear with it. The reason is, because when they speak ill of themselves they speak not in the spirit of truth, and according to the sentiments of their heart, as Job did, and because they have only the exterior of humility. They would fain be thought humble, but in reality they are not ; for if they were really humble, they would not, when reprimanded, show so much resentment as they do, nor take such great care to excuse and defend themselves, nor would they show so much trouble and uneasiness.

Cassian tells that an abbot called Serapion had one day a visit paid him by a hermit who, in his dress, his countenance, and his discourse, was very humble, and who seemed to have a great contempt of himself. He was continually saying that he was a great sinner, that he deserved not to breathe the air, and that he was unworthy the ground should bear him, nor would he sit down anywhere but upon the floor, nor let anyone wash his feet. The abbot introducing after dinner, some discourse which related to a spiritual life, and desiring to entertain his guest with some good counsel, told him, with a great deal of sweetness and charity, that as he was young and healthy, he would do better to remain in his cell, and to live there upon the work of his hands like the other hermits, than to be going here and there as he was. The hermit took this advice so very ill, that he could not help changing colour upon it; whereupon Serapion said :— " What! friend, just now you did nothing but speak ill and show contempt of yourself ; yet you cannot take in good part a simple advice given you with all imaginable charity and sweetness. Did you not understand that what you said against yourself obliged us to apply to you that sentence of the Wise man—' the just is the first accuser of himself ?' (Prov. xviii. 17)—or did you aim at nothing but praise by your despising yourself ? " " Unhappy that we are," says St. Gregory, " that all we aspire to by our hypocrisy and dissimulation is ordinarily the esteem of the world ; what appears humility in us is sometimes great pride, and we often seem to stoop before men, that we may be the more extolled and praised by them." If this were not so, why should you say that of yourself, which you would not have others believe of you. If you say it from the bottom of your heart, and in testimony of the truth, you should be glad that you are believed ; but if you are angry at it, it is a sign that by humbling yourself, you have no other design than to gain the esteem of men. It is this the wise man teaches us when he says, " there is one who humbleth himself wickedly, and his interior is full of deceit." (Eccl. xix. 23.) What greater hypocrisy and deceit can there be than to seek the esteem of men by the means of humbling and despising ourselves ? And what greater pride is there than that of desiring to pass for humble ? St. Bernard says, that " the desire to acquire by humility the praise of being humble is no virtue, but it is the overthrowing of virtue ; for what is more corrupt and unworthy than to desire to appear better by the very way whereby thou appearest worst of all ? " (Ser. 16, sup. Cant.) To desire that the ill which thou sayest of thyself should only serve to make others think well of thee, St. Ambrose, speaking of such persons, says, " several have the image of humility, without having the real virtue—they show it without, but contradict it within." (Lib. 7, Ep. 44.)

In fine, our vanity is so great, and our desire of being esteemed is so violent, that we find out a thousand expedients to gratify our pride ; and whether it be by direct or indirect means, we still endeavour to turn all to our own praise. " The proud," says St. Gregory, " when they think they have succeeded in anything, request to have their faults pointed out in order to make others say they have done well. One would think that it were humility in them to desire that their faults should be shown them; but it is not humility, it is pride; because they have no other aim therein but to attract praise to themselves. There are others who find fault with what they have done, and express how discontented they are therewith, which is only to extort the approbation of others, and to have the pleasure of hearing that nothing could be done better, and that they are to blame not to be satisfied therewith. A grave religious used to call this sort of humility, humility with a hook; for, as we sometimes make use of a hook to pull things to us which we cannot otherwise reach, so this false humility is used to hook in, as it were, the praise which we could not otherwise attain. A preacher, for example, will come out of the pulpit fully persuaded that he has done marvellously well, and then will ask some of his friends to tell him, in charity, wherein he failed. To what end is all this dissembling? For you do not believe you have failed in any thing, nor is it your intention to be found fault with, but to be praised, and to have others of the same opinion with yourself; it is that which you seek, and that which tickles your vanity. But if any one more sincere than the rest happens to hint to you some small fault, you are not pleased thereat, but warmly defend the point, and often judge that he who has told you of this same fault, has no judgment, and understands nothing at all, whereas he blames what seemed to you to be a very good thought, and extremely well expressed. Nothing, therefore, but pride and vanity move you, and the praise of men is all you seek by this affected humility. It is also with the same spirit that we some-times confess frankly the faults which we cannot hide; yes! we wish, by acknowledging these faults, to regain what we have lost in the opinion of the world by committing them. At other times we exaggerate them beyond what they are, that the world, seeing it impossible that they should be so great as we say, should conclude that we accuse ourselves of what we have not done, and so attribute it to an excess of humility, and thus by magnifying what is not, we endeavour dexterously to hide what is. In fine, we make use of every artifice and invention to hide our pride under the cloak of humility."

" Thus you may judge," says St. Bernard, " how excellent and sublime humility is; and, on the contrary, how shameful and despicable pride is. For certainly humility must be a thing of great value, since even pride seeks to deck itself therewith, lest it should become contemptible." (De grad. humil.) As, on the contrary, pride must needs be a very shameful thing in itself, since it dares not appear naked, and is forced to hide itself under the veil of humility. For, in fine you would be ashamed to have it known that you seek to be esteemed and commended; because you would pass for a vain and weak person, which is the meanest opinion one can have of a man ; and therefore it is that you try to disguise pride under an apparent humility. But why would you be what you are ashamed to appear to be? And why are not you ashamed to hunt after praise, since you are ashamed to be thought to hunt after it ? The mischief is not that any one believes this of you, but it is really true, and since you would be ashamed that men should know it, why are you not ashamed that God should know it, " whose eyes behold all our imperfections ?"

The reason of all this is, that we are not well established in the first degree of humility, and, consequently, that we are at a great distance from the second. We must undertake this business at the source ; we must begin to know our misery and nothingness, that, when this knowledge shall have produced in us a contempt of ourselves, which is the first degree of humility, we may arise ourselves, afterwards to the second. It is not enough, therefore, to have a contempt of yourself, and to speak ill of yourself even from your heart, you must endeavour to attain the point of being willing that others should think and say of you what you think and say of yourself, and be content that they effectually despise you. " To contemn and speak ill of one's self," says St. John Climachus, " is not to be humble ; for who is there that suffers not everything from himself with patience ? But to receive joyfully the scoffs and ill-treatment of the world is to be truly humble." It is good to speak ill of ourselves—to say that we are proud, slothful, impatient, negligent, and inconsiderate ; but it would be better to reserve that acknowledgment till others reproach us with these faults. If, indeed, you sincerely desire that others should entertain this opinion of you, and that they should occasionally make known this opinion, you are truly humble."

CHAPTER XIV.

The steps we must ascend by in order to attain the second degree of humility.

SINCE this second degree of humility is the most difficult in the practice of this virtue, I shall divide it, as some holy writers do, into four other degrees or steps, so that by little and little, step by step, we may ascend to the highest perfection of humility that this degree reaches to. The first step, therefore, is not to seek the glory and esteem of the world, but, on the contrary, to shun it very carefully. Whole volumes are full of examples left us by the saints, who were so far from seeking this esteem, that they avoided worldly honours, and whatever could gain them any reputation before men, as a most dangerous rock. Was not Jesus Christ himself the first who did this? For, knowing that after the famous miracle of the five loaves the people would carry him away and make him king, he retired into the mountain, to teach us by his own example to shun honours, though he had no cause to fear, had he been exalted to the highest station. It was from the same motive, that his having manifested his glory to three of his disciples in transfiguration, he forbade them ever to speak of it till after his resurrection ; and it was for this reason also that, in giving sight to the blind, and in working so many other miracles, he recommended secrecy to those whom he had cured. His intention was to teach us to shun the esteem and praise of men, which might render us vain, and be the cause of our ruin.

The registers of the order of St. Francis tell us that a holy religious, called brother Giles, having heard of the fall of father Elias, who had been general of the order, and who then stood excommunicated for adhering to the emperor Frederick II, an enemy to the Church, threw himself upon the ground, and lay there a long time clinging to it with all his force. On being asked why he did so, he answered, that as Elias fell for having been too much elevated, he wished, if it were possible, to lower himself to the very centre of the earth. Gerson makes an ingenious application of the fable of Anteus to the subject we speak of. The poets feign that Anteus was a giant and son of the earth, who having been thrice thrown to the ground, whilst he wrestled with Hercules, regained additional strength every time he touched the earth. Hercules perceiving this, raised him up from thence, and squeezed him to death in his arms. "This is," says he, "a figure of what the devil does when he fights with us ; he endeavours to lift us up very high by means of the esteem and praise of men, that so he may the more easily overcome us.." Hence, whoever is truly humble continually lies low in the knowledge of himself, and is afraid of nothing more than of being exalted.

"The second step," says St. Anselm, "is to suffer contempt with patience ;" that is to say, if it happens that you receive any slight or affront, you must bear it with meekness ; for I do not now require of you to desire injuries, to seek them industriously, or to receive them joyfully ; that would be yet too much, and very difficult for you to undertake. I only desire, that, whenever you receive contempt, you will bear it patiently, according to the words of the Wise man—"Take well all that shall happen to you ; how great pain soever it may cost you, bear it with patience and humility." (Eccl. ii. 4.) This is a very proper means to acquire and preserve humility ; for, as the honour and esteem of the world tend to make us proud and vain, so whatever turns to our contempt is an occasion of making us humble, and fortifies and advances us in the practice of humility. St. Laurence Justinian compared humility to a river, which has a great deal of water in winter, and scarce any at all in summer ; and, indeed, humility usually decreases in prosperity, and increases in adversity.

If we think proper to embrace them, we have, every day, opportunities of practising humility. "That which is pleasing to others shall go forward," says Thomas à Kempis; "that which is pleasing to thee shall not succeed. Others shall be heard, and what you shall not be regarded ; everything shall be granted to others, and nothing to you ; others shall be respected, and you slighted ; in fine, others shall be employed in business, and you accounted as fit for nothing. At this nature will sometimes repine, and it will be no small matter if you bear it in silence." Let every one, then, examine himself ; let him run over the different occasions which daily happen, and see how he behaves himself therein. How do you feel when you are commanded imperiously to do a thing ? How do you take the reproof and advice which is given you ! What are your feelings when you think that your superior treats you with little confidence, and shows himself too reserved to you? "Of so many occasions which daily occur, whatever humiliation offers itself to you, take it," says St. Dorotheus, "as a proper remedy to cure your pride; pray for him who gives it you, as for the physician of your soul; and assure yourself that you have not humility when you take these things otherwise."

The third step by which you must ascend, is, not to be affected or touched with the praise and esteem of men; and this is harder to practise than the other. "For, though it be easy," says St. Austin, "to be indifferent as to the commendations we are deprived of, yet it is hard to be insensible to those given us." (Epis. lxiv.) St. Gregory treats this matter exceedingly well, and applying thereto these words of Job, "if I beheld the sun in its splendour, and the moon in its brightness, and my heart was secretly overjoyed," (Job xxxi. 26, 27,) says, "that by looking upon the sun and moon with pleasure when they shine, may be understood looking with pleasure and delight upon the glory and reputation which we have acquired in the world; and that Job would teach us thereby, that he felt no vanity from the esteem and praise of men. There is this difference," continues he, "between the proud and the humble: the proud are always overjoyed with the praises given them, and even with false praises; for they care not what they are in themselves and in the sight of God, but only what they are in the opinion of men; therefore, when they see themselves esteemed according to their desire, they are transported with joy and vanity, as having obtained all they expected. But the man of a truly humble heart, as soon as he sees himself praised and esteemed, reflects and covers himself with confusion." According to the words of the royal prophet, "When I was exalted I humbled myself, and was troubled." (Ps. lxxxvii. 16.) "Nor is it without reason that he is troubled," as the same St. Austin continues, "for he trembles when he reflects that if the things he is praised for are counterfeit, he may be the more severely punished by Almighty God; and if they are true he may lose the recompense he was to expect, and may one day hear these words;" (Ps. lxxxvii. 16,) "thou hast received thy good things in this life;" (Luke xvi. 25,) thou hast had the reward of your good works. So that the praise which gives occasion to the proud to become more vain and haughty, causes the humble to humble themselves still more. "And it is this," says St. Gregory, "that the Wise man teaches us, when he says, 'As the silver is tried in the crucible, and the

gold in the furnace, so is a man by the mouth that praises him.'"
(Prov. xxvii. 21.)   When the gold and silver are good the fire
refines them ; when they are good for nothing it consumes them.
" Praise," says the Wise man, " works the same effect upon
man : if he be puffed up with the honour given, he is not gold
and silver of a good alloy, because he cannot bear the crucible of
the tongue ; but, if he humbles himself when he is praised he is
very fine gold ; because the fire of praise destroys him not, but,
on the contrary, purifies and refines him the more."   Make use
therefore of this mark which the Holy Ghost gives thee to know
whether or not thou dost advance in humility, see whether thou
art troubled or joyful at being praised, and thereby thou wilt
know whether thy humility is true or false.

We read of St. Francis of Borgia that nothing gave him so
much pain as when he saw that he was honoured as a saint; and
being one day asked why he troubled himself so much for a thing
he had no hand in, he answered, " that being so unlike to
what he was believed to be, he feared that he should be called
to a more severe account by God."   And this altogether agrees
with the passage of St. Gregory which we just now quoted.

Let us, therefore be so established in the knowledge of ourselves, that the wind of man's praise and applause may not raise
us from the earth, and make us lose the sight of our misery.
But, on the contrary, let us then humble ourselves the more and
be clothed with new confusion, seeing that the praise given us is
undeserved, and that we are not masters of the good qualities
ascribed to us ; and that, in fine, we are not the persons we are
taken for, nor such as we ought to be.

——o——

CHAPTER XV.

*Of the fourth step, which is to wish to be despised and to rejoice
thereat.*

THE fourth step to arrive at the perfection of humility is, to
desire to be despised by men, and to take pleasure in being injured and reproached.   "He who is truly humble," says St.
Bernard, " desires to pass for a despicable person and not for an
humble one, and he rejoices at the contempt he is treated with."
(Bern. Serm. xvi. sup. Cant.)   This is that which is most
excellent in the second degree of humility ; and therefore it is,
as he adds, that the spikenard, which is a very small herb, but

a very fragrant one, is taken for the symbol of humility, according to the words of Solomon's song, " My spikenard sends forth its odour." (Cant. i. 11.)   For when you have not only a contempt for yourself, but would have others contemn you also, then is your humility as a kind of spikenard whose odour spreads itself all round.

St. Bernard observes, "that there are two sorts of humility : one in the understanding, whereby man, considering his misery and lowliness, is so convinced thereof, that he despises himself, and believes that he deserves to be altogether contemned ; the other in the will, which makes him desire to be despised and disesteemed by all the world." Jesus Christ could not have humility of the first description, which is that of the understanding ; because, says the saint, " he knew himself, and thinking it no robbery to be equal to God," (Phil. ii. 6,) he could not despise himself, nor believe himself worthy of contempt.   But he had the second sort of humility, which is, that of the will and heart ; " when he made himself of no reputation, taking upon him the form of a servant " (Phil. ii. 7), and when, for the love he bore to men, he was pleased to humble himself, and appear contemptible in their eyes, and therefore, he says to us, " Learn of me who am meek and humble of heart." (Matt. xi. 29.)   But as for us, we ought to have humility of both kinds ; for the first without the second is false and deceitful, there being nothing more unjust than to desire to pass for what we are not,   He, therefore, who is truly humble, and has a real disesteem of himself, ought to be pleased that others disesteem him also.

It is this that our Saviour has taught us by his own example. Consider with what affection and ardour he embraced contempt and reproach for the love of us.   He the Lord of heaven and earth, was not content with humbling himself so far as to make himself man, and take the form of a servant, but even clothed himself with the form of a sinner, and appeared, as the apostle says, " in the likeness of sinful flesh." (Rom. viii. 3.)   He took not sin upon him, because sin is incompatible with God ; but he took the mark and character of sinners, being pleased to be circumcised as a sinner ; to be baptized among sinners and publicans, as if he had been one of them ; to be put in competition with Barabbas, and judged more wicked and more unworthy to live than he.   In fine the eagerness which he had to suffer all sorts of affronts and reproaches for the love of us, was so excessively great, that he thought it long till he saw the time, wherein,

inebriated with love, he was like another Noah, exposed all
naked to the raillery and insolence of men. "I have," says he,
"a baptism of blood to be baptised with, and how am I strait-
ened till it be accomplished." (Luke xii. 50.)   "With desire
have I desired to eat this passover with you." (Luke xxii. 15.)
He thought it long, I say, to see the hour wherein he was to be
abandoned to all sorts of indignities—to be buffeted as a slave ;
to be spit upon as a blasphemer; to be clothed in white as a
fool; and with purple as a mock-king; and, more than all this,
to be cruelly scourged like a public highwayman, and, in fine,
to suffer between two thieves the most shameful and ignominious
death.   This is what the divine Saviour of our souls desired so
earnestly, and what made him say by the mouth of David :
"reproach has broken my heart, and I am full of misery."
(Ps. lxviii, 21.)   He loves reproach and ignominy so much that
he longs for them with the same impatience as others do for
things which are the most pleasing.   And, therefore, Jeremiah,
speaking of him, says, "he shall be satiated with reproaches,"
(Thren. iii. 30,) to show us by this expression the violent hunger
and thirst which he had to endure—all sorts of contempt and
affronts for the love of us.   Now, if for love of us the Son of
God, so worthy of all veneration, has desired so ardently and
received with so much joy scorns and affronts, shall we think
we do much, who deserve all manner of contempt, when we
shall desire for the love of him to pass at least for what we
really are, and to suffer with pleasure the reproaches and affronts
we deserve?

It was that which the apostle practised, when he said, "therefore, I take pleasure in infirmities, in reproaches, in necessities,
in persecutions, in distresses, for Christ's sake." (2 Cor. xii. 10.)
And it is in the same spirit that, writing from the place of his
imprisonment to the Philippians, and not being able to contain
the satisfaction he had to suffer for Jesus Christ, he tells them
that it is just that they should share in his joy.   It is with this
milk that the Saviour of the world nourished his apostles, and it
was the cause, that when they were beaten with rods by the
command of the synagogue, "they departed from the presence of
the council, rejoicing that they were accounted worthy to suffer
contempt for his name." (Acts v. 41.)   And it is this which
several martyrs have imitated ; and among others St. Ignatius,
when being brought to Rome to be exposed there to the wild
beasts, and seeing himself loaded with all manner of affronts and

reproaches by those who led him along, he cried out joyfully, "I begin now to be a disciple of Jesus Christ." (In ejus vita. cap. 4.) In fine, it is this our holy founder would have us imitate, and what he recommends to us in express terms, and in the most pressing manner possible. "They," says he, "who shall enter into the Society, or who are already of it, ought to examine carefully before God, how important and how useful it is for a spiritual life to abhor wholly, and not in part, whatever the world loves, and to embrace and seek ardently whatever Jesus Christ had loved and embraced. For, as worldings, who follow the maxims of the world, seek earnestly after the honour, glory, and reputation which the world gives; so they who have renounced the world, and truly follow Jesus Christ, ought fervently to desire whatever is opposite to the spirit of the world, and ought to take delight to wear the livery of their divine Master, out of the love they bear him ; so that to become in a manner like unto him, they ought to wish themselves to be overwhelmed with injuries, affronts, false testimonies, and all sorts of ignominy, so God were not thereby offended, and if the inflicting them were no sin in their neighbour." (Examen. xliv. & Reg. xi. sum.) All that can be said of humility is comprised in this rule. A true renouncing of the world is to renounce what is most excellent in the world, which is reputation and glory; to wish for ignominy and affronts as eagerly as worldlings wish for honour and praise, is to be truly religious, and to be dead to the world. To be truly of the Society of Jesus, and to become indeed his companions, is to desire to keep him company in affronts and reproaches, to put on his livery, to seek after, and receive injuries and contempt with joy for the love of him. Thou, O Lord, hast been looked upon by all the world as a wicked person, and thou wert placed as a criminal between two thieves—suffer not, therefore, that I should pass for a good man in the opinion of men ; for it is not just that the servant should be thought better than the master, and that the scholar should be preferred to his teacher. But since the world has persecuted and despised thee, let the world persecute and despise me; so that I may imitate thee in all things, and be truly thy companion and disciple. St. Francis Xaverius thought it very unworthy that a Christian, for whom Jesus Christ has suffered so many reproaches, and who ought always to have the remembrance thereof present in his mind, should be pleased in being honoured and respected by men.

CHAPTER XVI.

That the perfection of humility, and of all other virtues consists in performing the acts thereof with pleasure ; and of how great importance this is for our preserverance in virtue.

It is the general opinion of philosophers that the perfection of any virtue consists in performing the acts thereof with pleasure ; and when they speak of the signs whereby it may be known whether any one has acquired the habit of any virtue, they say, that is known when a person performs the acts thereof " readily, easily, and with pleasure." He who has acquired the habit of some art or science, knows how to reduce the art or science to practice with a marvellous readiness and facility. An excellent lutanist, who understands music perfectly well, has no need to prepare himself or to consider how to play what he knows ; it is so easy to him, that even when he thinks of something else, he plays admirably well. It is the same with those who have acquired the habit of any virtue, they practise it without any pain at all. Would you know, therefore, if you have acquired the habit of humility,—see first of all, if you perform the acts thereof " readily and easily," for, if you feel any repugnance and difficulty in the occasions which present themselves to practise it. it is a sign that you have not yet acquired the perfect habit thereof ; and if to make use of them as you ought, you have need of preparations and reflections, those reflections and preparations are indeed a good means of attaining the perfection you aim at ; but they always show that you have not as yet attained it. When a man, before he plays upon a lute, considers where he must sometimes put one finger and sometimes another, what string he is to touch, and what rules have been given him, he does what ought to be done to learn to play well upon the lute ; but it shows that he has not acquired the habit of playing upon it, because he who has acquired that, has no need of considering in order to be able to play well. Wherefore Aristotle says, that " when a man is master of any art in perfection, he can so easily reduce it to practise that he deliberates no more upon the means," (Arist. iii. Ethic. ca. 8,) and philosophers hold likewise, as well as he, that the habit of virtue appears not in the actions which are performed with reflection, but only in those which are done without musing thereon ; so that in all sudden and unforeseen actions, we act always according to the habit we have acquired.

Nay, they go still further ; for Plutarch, showing how one may know if a man has acquired the habit and perfection of virtue, points out twelve ways, one of which is that of dreams. " If even in a dream you have no idea but what is modest and regular, or if when others come upon you, you find even whilst you are asleep that you are troubled thereat, and that you struggle to resist them, as if you were awake, it is a sign that virtue is deeply rooted in you ; because not only the will, but even the imagination and senses, are in you made subject to reason. Even as horses," says he, " when they are broken and taught well to draw, still go on in their ordinary pace, though he that drives them leaves them to themselves, or sleeps, so when any one has perfectly acquired virtue, and has thoroughly subjected his senses to reason, the senses remain still under subjection, even when reason is drowned in sleep." St. Austin teaches us the same doctrine when he says, " thy commandments, O Lord, are so deeply engraven in us, that we resist temptations even in dreams." (Aug. lib. 12.) And indeed there are some who have so much zeal for the law of God, so much zeal for virtue, and so much abhorrence for vice, and who are so used to resist temptations when they are awake, that they resist them even when they are asleep. We read in the life of St. Francis Xaverius, that when he was asleep one night, he struggled so much in resisting the impure illusion of a dream, that by the resistance he made, he threw up a great deal of blood at his mouth. This agrees with the explanation of authors, upon the passage of St. Paul, " whether we are awake or asleep, let us live together with God." (1 Thes. v. 10.) For, according to them, these words do not only signify, " whether we live, or whether we die," which is the common exposition of the interpreters ; but they signify also, that they who are very fervent in the service of God ought always to be inseparably united to Jesus Christ, not only when they are awake, but even when sleep suspends in them all the functions of their will and reason.

The third and principal mark whereby is known whether one has acquired virtue in perfection is, when the acts thereof are performed with delight, and therein consists properly the perfection of virtue in us. Will you know then if you have acquired

the perfection of humility ? Examine yourself upon the rule,
which we have set down in the foregoing chapter ; see whether
injuries and contempt raise as much joy in you as the people of
the world find in the esteem and praise of men. Nay, further, so
far from being perfect in virtue without such a disposition, you
can scarce persevere therein ; perseverance being in a manner
utterly impossible in a thing wherein you take no pleasure.
" The ancient fathers," says St. Dorotheus, " held for a constant
maxim, that what the mind does not joyfully embrace cannot be
of any continuance." (Dor. doc. seu serm. 10.) You may perhaps keep silence and remain for some time in great recollection ;
but till it proceeds from the bottom of your heart, and habit has
made it natural to you, so that you take pleasure therein, you
will be in danger of not persevering ; " you will be in a kind of
violent state, which consequently cannot last." Wherefore, it
is of great importance to exercise ourselves in virtue, till it has
taken so deep root in us, as to seem natural to us and to proceed
from our inclination, that we may perform the acts thereof with
delight : for so we may be, in a manner, assured of persevering.
" Blessed is he," says the Psalmist, " whose delight is in the law
of the Lord." Another text has it, " he whose pleasure is
wholly in the law of the Lord ; he shall be like a tree planted
by the river's side, and shall bring forth the fruit of virtue and
righteousness in due season." (Psal. i. 2, 3.)

----o----

CHAPTER XVII.

*Wherein is more particularly explained what that perfection is
which we must try to raise ourselves to, in this second degree of
humility.*

St. John Climachus adds another thing to what we have already
said ; it is, that as the proud value the esteem of the world so
much, that, to acquire it, they falsely attribute to themselves
several gifts and advantages which they have not, and announce
themselves to be of higher birth, to be possessed of more wealth
and talents than they are ; so they who are extremely humble so
far show the desire they have of being despised by the world, that
to make themselves the more despicable, they wish to have im-
puted to them some defects which they really have not. We
have, says he, an example thereof in Simeon the hermit, who
knowing that the president of the province, moved by the repu-

tation of his sanctity, was coming to see him, sat down on the threshold of his door, with a piece of bread and cheese in his hand, which he began to eat, assuming all the appearance of a simpleton. The president on seeing him felt contempt for him, and returned; but the hermit remained quite happy, because he obtained what he desired. We have several examples of the same kind; as that of St. Francis, who, to avoid the honour and reception intended him, began to knead the dirt with his feet ; and that of brother Juniper, who was found playing at see-saw on a beam with little children, in order to render himself despicable.

Those great saints did doubtless then consider, that the world had despised Jesus Christ, who is the sovereign good ; and this blindness of the world in not having known the true light, nor having honoured the Son of God, had given them such an aversion to the world, and such a contempt of whatever it esteems, and so much esteem for whatever it despises, that they thought they were carefully to avoid being honoured by the world, and looked upon their being despised by the world with him, and for the love of him, as a great mark of love of Jesus Christ for them. It was that which made them feel so much pleasure in reproach and contempt, and urged them to disguise themselves in so many ways, that they might be despised. It is true, says St. John Climachus, that what the saints have done therein has often come from a particular inspiration of the Holy Ghost, and that consequently they are more to be admired than imitated; but if we do not imitate them in their holy follies, we ought endeavour, at least, to imitate them in the zeal which made them commit them, and in the ardent desire they had to be despised by the world.

St. Diadocus goes further yet, and says, "there are two sorts of humility. The first is the humility of the indifferent, that is to say, of those who indeed make some progress, but have yet some battles to give, and who are attacked by motions of pride, which they endeavour to overcome by the grace of God, in humbling themselves. The other sort of humility is that of the perfect, to whom God communicates his light so abundantly, and gives so great a knowledge of themselves, that nothing seems capable to give them any further motion of pride and vain glory. In this state, humility is as it were natural in the soul, so that whatever good works a person performs, he has always a mean opinion of himself, and believes himself the least of all. Now there is this difference," continues the saint, " between these two kinds, that the humility of the indifferent, who have not yet gained an entire victory over themselves, but who feel still some contradiction within them, is ordinarily accompanied with some pain; and that though they bear with patience the occasions of humiliation, they nevertheless receive them not with joy, because the passions being not fully vanquished in them there is always something within which still makes resistance. But the humility of the perfect is not only free from pain, but full of joy; because their passions being wholly overcome, and there being nothing in them which makes further resistance, they humble themselves before God with pleasure, and find delight in the contempt shown them. Wherefore," still adds the saint, "they who have only the first humility let themselves be easily troubled by good and bad success, and by all the different accidents of life; whereas those who have the other kind of humility, never let themselves be cast down by adversity, nor elevated by prosperity, but remain always in the same frame and temper of mind, and enjoy a perfect peace and tranquillity, as persons whom virtue has raised above all that can happen in the world. Nothing puts him in pain who is glad to be despised; for what can do it, since the scorn of men, which is the only thing that could vex him, is what makes him rejoice? What, also, can make him lose his peace, if he finds it in the very thing which one would think could be done to disturb it? "He who has brought himself to this state," says St. Chrysostom, "makes even this world a paradise; for what can be more happy than a soul which lives thus, which is always in the harbour sheltered from all storms, and enjoys itself in peace?" (Chrys. hom. sup. Gen.)

Now, it is this height of humility which we should endeavour to attain, and let it not seem impossible to us. "For if we will," says St. Austin, " we can, with the grace of God, imitate not only the saints, but the Saint of saints; since he himself says to us, ' Learn of me, for I am meek and humble;'" (Matt. xi. 29;) and St. Peter teaches us also, that "Jesus Christ has suffered for us, leaving us an example that we might follow his footsteps." (1 Pet. ii. 21.) St. Jerome, upon these words of our Saviour, "if you will be perfect," says, " we plainly see that we may, if we will, be perfect, because Jesus Christ says, 'if you will.' For if you pretend to be excused on account of the weakness of your strength, does not he that sees the very bottom of your heart know it better than you? Nevertheless he says you can if you will, for he is always ready to help us; and if we will, we can do all things with his assistance. Jacob," as St. Jerome continues,

" saw a ladder which reached from earth to heaven, upon which there were angels, who went up and down, and God sat at the top of the ladder to give, as it were, his hand to those who went up, and to encourage them by his presence." Get up this ladder— endeavour to do it by mounting the steps we have shown you, and he will reach out his hand to help you to the top. A traveller who sees a steep place a great way off, believes it not possible to get up thither, but when he comes near to it, and sees the beaten road, he judges thereof after another manner.

———o———

CHAPTER XVIII.

Of some means which may be made use of to attain this second degree of humility, and particularly of the example of Jesus Christ.

THERE are ordinarily two ways pointed out for acquiring moral virtues. One directs us to the reasons which may excite us thereunto ; the other to the practice of the acts which may make us contract the habit thereof. To begin with the first, I say, that the example of Jesus Christ is one of the principal and most efficacious considerations which we can make use of to become humble, or, in better terms, it is the principal and most efficacious of all. All the life of the Saviour of the world, from his very birth to his death, has been a perfect model of humility ; but among so many examples which he has given us of his virtue, St. Austin fixes particularly upon the consideration of that he has given us by washing the feet of his apostles upon the eve of his passion. "He was not contented," says he, "with the examples he had given during the whole course of his life, nor with those which he was quickly going to give further, and which were to make him be looked upon as 'the meanest of men,' as Isaias says, and according to the royal prophet, 'the reproach of men, and the refuse of the people,' but 'knowing that his hour was come that he should pass out of this world to his Father, having loved his own which were in the world, he loved them unto the end,' (John xiii. 1,) and would give them yet a further mark thereof. Wherefore, 'supper being ended, he rises from the table, lays aside his garments, and girds a towel about him, pours water into a basin, and begins to wash his disciples' feet, and to wipe them with a towel wherewith he was girded,'" (John xiii. 4, 5.) What a mystery of humility was this, which the apostles themselves did not yet comprehend

"How, O Lord, dost thou wash my feet?" says St. Peter to him.
Jesus answered, "What I do thou knowest not now, but thou
shalt know hereafter." (John xiii. 6, 7.)   After that he returns
to his place, and to explain this mystery to them, he told them—
"Ye call me master and Lord, and ye say well, for so I am.   If
then your Lord and master has washed your feet, you ought also
to wash one another's feet, for I have given you an example, that
you should do as I have done to you." (John xiii. 13-15.)
What he means by this mystery is to teach us to humble ourselves
as he has humbled himself.   And, doubtless, humility must be a
virtue of great importance and difficult to practise, since Jesus
Christ is not content with so many examples which he had already
given us, nor with so many others which he was about to give :
but that knowing well our infirmity, and the malignity of the
humour of pride, which is predominant in us, he does so many
things to cure it; and that, in fine, to make a stronger impression
of humility on our hearts, he yet reccommends it to us, as it
were, by a declaration of his last will.

St. Austin, explaining these words of our Saviour, "learn of me
who am meek and humble," cries out : " O wholesome doctrine,
O master and Lord of men, who hast swallowed death in a cup
full of the poison of pride, what wouldst thou have us learn of
thee ?   That I am meek and humble of heart.   What! are all
the treasures of the wisdom and knowledge which are lodged in
thee, reduced to this ?—to teach us, that thou art meek and
humble of heart.   Is it so great a thing to be little, that nobody
can teach it us, except thou who art so great takest care thereof ?
Yea," adds the saint, " so great and difficult a thing it is to
humble and make one's self little, that men could not have
arrived thereto if the great God himself had not set them the
example ;" (De Sanct. virg. ca. lii.) ; because nothing is more
deeply rooted in the heart than the desire of the glory and
esteem of the world ; so that no less was required to humble us ;
and no less remedy than this was requisite to cure the pride of
which we were all sick.   "And if this remedy " he made use of
in making himself man, and of no account, for the love of us,
" cures it not, I know not what else can ever be able to do it."
If the sight of a God humbled and despised, is not sufficient to
makes us ashamed of desiring to be honoured and esteemed, and
to make us wish to be despised with him and for him, I know
not what can be sufficient.   Wherefore Guerry the abbot, finding
himself forced to admire and follow so great an example of

humility, cries out, addressing himself to God in these words, in which we all ought to address ourselves to him :—" Thou hast overcome, O Lord—thou hast overcome my pride. Lo! I voluntarily put on again thy chains, receive me for thy slave." (Serm. i. de Adventu.)

St. Bernard's thoughts upon this subject are admirable. " The Son of God," says he, "considered, that two sorts of creatures, who had been created capable of eternal happiness, had destroyed themselves by having a mind to be like him. God no sooner created the angels, but Lucifer would be equal to him. 'I will ascend,' says he, 'into heaven—I will exalt my throne above the stars of God, I will sit also upon the mount of the congregation, on the side of the north. I will ascend above the heights of the clouds, and I will be like the most High.' (Isa. xiv. 14.) At the same time he draws several others to his party, but God throws them down headlong into hell. 'Thou shalt be thrown to hell,' says he to him, 'to the bottom of the pit;' (Isa. xiv. 15,) and so, angels of light as they were, they become spirits of darkness. After this, God creates man; and the infernal serpent having forthwith conveyed his poison into him by these words : 'Ye shall be gods, knowing good and evil;' (Gen iii. 5,) man receives this proposal greedily, breaks the commandments of his God ; and for endeavouring to make himself like unto him, becomes like the devil. Eliseus' servant having run after Naaman the leper, to take the presents of him, which his master had refused : 'You would have had share of the riches of Naaman,' says the prophet to him, 'you shall also have share of his leprosy, even you and all your posterity." (4 Kings v. 26.) God's judgment against man is like this. Thou wouldst, O man, partake of the riches of the devil, that is to say, of his pride ; thou shalt also partake of his punishment. So that you see man is lost as well as the devil, and made like unto him, because he endeavoured to become like unto God. What will the Son of God do now?—'I see,' says he, 'how jealous my father is of my honour;' (Serm. i. de Adventu.) ; I see that he destroys his most noble creatures on my account—the destruction of the angels came from their endeavouring to be like me ; man lost himself also for the same reason ; every one, in fine, envies me, and would be like me—'Well then, I will appear to men under so mean a figure, that whoever shall envy me, and aspire to be like me, shall thereby find his salvation.'" Oh! the excessive greatness of the infinite mercy and goodness of God, who has been pleased to come down from heaven, and make himself man, in order to satisfy the ardent desire we have of resembling him. It is henceforth, indeed, we may, not falsely and through a punishable pride, but truly and in holy humility, flatter ourselves with the hopes of being like unto him.

The same St. Bernard, interpreting these words, " unto us a child is born," (Isa. ix. 6,) " let us endeavour all we can," says he, " to become like this little child ; let us learn of him who is meek and humble of heart, so that it may not be to no purpose for us that the great God is become a little child. For if you become not as this little child, you shall not enter into the kingdom of heaven." (Hom. iii. sup. Missus est.)

---o---

CHAPTER XIX.

Of some reflections which may serve to make us humble.

FROM the beginning of this treatise we have laid down several reasons which may excite us to humility.   We have said that it is the root and foundation of all other virtues ; that it is the way to acquire and preserve them ; that we shall possess them all provided we are humble; and we have spoken of several other such like motives.   But that we may not seem to rest solely on such spiritual considerations as these, it will not be amiss to touch here upon some reasons which are more plain and more proportionate to our weakness ; that, being convinced, not only by spiritual principles, but also by the light of natural reason, we shall be induced more zealously to despise the glory and honour of the world, and to follow the paths of humility.   But it is so difficult a thing to do this, that we have need to use all possible means and helps in order thereunto.

Let us begin by examining carefully what really is that opinion of men which does so disquiet and trouble us ; let us look upon and consider it on every side, that being able to make a sound and solid judgment thereof, we may be encouraged to despise it, and remain no longer in so great an error.   " There are several things," says Seneca, " which we look upon as great, not because they are really so, but because our weakness makes them appear so to us; like the burthens of ants, which are, indeed, very heavy in respect of their little bodies, but are, nevertheless, in themselves very light.   And thus it is as to the opinion and esteem of the world.   But that it may not be so, let me ask you whether the good or bad opinion which men have of you makes you in reality either better or worse? "No, certainly," says St. Austin; "for neither praise cures a sick conscience, nor does calumny hurt a sound one. Wherefore, believe of Austin whatever you please: provided his conscience reproaches him with nothing in the sight of God, he is satisfied."

This is, indeed, the only thing of importance; all the rest is but vanity; because it neither gives nor takes away anything. "Not praise," says the author of the Imitation of Jesus, "but a good conscience adds to the merit of a good man." Nobody is more than what he appears in God's sight: "For it is not he," says the apostle, "that esteems himself who is approved, but whom God esteems." (2 Cor. x. 18.)

St. Austin makes an excellent comparison upon this occasion. "Pride," says he, "is not true greatness, it is only a swelling; and as what is swelled seems great on the outside, but is not sound within; so they whom the praise of men makes proud seem great, but indeed are not so." (Serm. xvi. de Temp.) The pride which that praise causes is no true greatness; it is a dangerous swelling. "There are," continues he, "sick people who appear fat, and to be in good plight; but it is not fat, it is a swelling and a kind of dropsy." Thus it is as to the opinion of men; it may swell and puff us up, but cannot make us great. Now if this be true, why are we always, like chameleons, gaping to suck in air to blow or bloat us up? For, as it is far better to be well and seem sick, than to be sick and seem well; so it is also better to be a good man, and pass for a bad one, than to be a bad man, and pass for a good one. What will you get by being thought virtuous, if you are not really so? St. Jerome, upon these words of the Proverbs, "and let his actions praise him in the gates," (Prov. xxxi. 31,) says, "not the vain praise of men, but your actions shall commend and witness for you, when you are to appear in judgment before God."

St. Gregory tells us that there lived in a convent of Iconia a religious, who was highly esteemed for sanctity, and who, above all, was applauded for his exemplary abstinence and mortification. Being upon his death-bed, he desired all the religious to be called in, who were very much overjoyed hereupon, hoping to hear something from him which might serve for their instruction. But he, seized with terror, was tormented in conscience, and finding himself inwardly forced to declare the state he was in, told them that his whole life had been nothing but disguise and hypocrisy ; that when he was believed to fast and abstain most he made good cheer in private, and that in punishment thereof he was now delivered up to a horrible dragon, whose tail was already twisted about his legs. " Behold ! there it is," cried he, on a sudden ; " now it puts its head in my mouth to snatch and carry away my soul ;" and having ended these words he expired, to the great astonishment of all. What advantage had that miserable wretch gained by passing for a saint ?

St. Athanasius compares those who seek after the approbation and praise of men to children who run after butterflies ; others compare them to spiders, and, applying to them these words of Isaias, " they have woven spiders' webs," (Isa. lix. 2,) say, that as those insects spend the very substance of their bowels in making webs to catch flies, so the proud spend themselves in working continually to acquire a little esteem in the world. We read in the life of St. Xaverius, that he always showed a particular aversion to the esteem of the world ; " because," says he, " it produces great evil, and hinders great good." And this truth had made so great an impression on his mind that he some-times groaned, and cried out, " O worldly esteem ! what mis-chief hast thou done ; what mischief dost thou do ; and what mischief wilt thou yet do ?"

——o——

CHAPTER XXII.

Of some other human considerations which may help to make us humble.

St. Chrysostom, explaining these words of the apostle, " that one is not to think of himself more highly than he ought, but to think soberly and modestly," (Rom. xii. 3,) goes into a detail, in order to prove that a proud man is not only wicked but a fool. He cites for this purpose that passage of Isaias, " the fool shall utter foolish things." (Isa. xxxii. 6.) "For," says he, "you shall know him to be a fool by the follies he shall utter. Attend to the extravagant things pride makes persons say—it made the first proud creature deliver himself thus : ' I will ascend to heaven, I will exalt my throne above the stars of God, I will sit also upon the mount of the congregation, on the side of the north, I will ascend above the height of the clouds, I will be like the most High. (Isa. xiv. 13.) What more extravagant expressions can be imagined? Now hear with what arrogance another boasts to have subjected the whole earth unto himself. ' My hand,' says he, ' has found the strength of the people as a nest, and I have taken all the nations of the earth, as one who takes eggs that are left therein, and there was none that moved a wing, or opened the mouth, or made the least noise.' (Isa. x. 14.) Can there be anything," continues the same St. Chrysostom, "more extravagant than this?" He relates also two other examples of such like discourses, wherein the proud show so much folly that you may well conclude that they really talk like men who have quite lost their senses. We see, moreover, that as fools make us laugh sometimes by their extravagant words, so the proud often do the same by their vain discourses; by their affected gestures; by their haughty looks ; by the studied gravity of their gait; by the excessive desire they show to be esteemed in all things ; and by the great opinion they have of themselves, and of all that comes from them. " This sort of folly is even worse and more shameful," says St. Chrysostom, " than the other : and thence proceeds another difference which is made between these two, which is, that real fools are pitied, whereas proud fools rather move us to laughter and scorn than to compassion."

It is therefore very true, that the proud are fools ; and it is also true that we deal with them as we usually do with fools, for whatever extravagance a fool utters, we seem to agree to it all, in order to be at peace with him, and therefore we will not go about to contradict him ; so, for the same reason, we are still very cautious not to contradict a vain and proud man.

Now this disease and folly of pride reigns so generally among men, that you can hardly speak to them without flattering, and telling them things which are false, and which you yourself believe to be so. They are so pleased at being esteemed and approved of in everything, that there is no surer way to gain their good will than to praise them ; and this is one of the vanities which Solomon observes in the world when he says : " I saw the wicked buried, who when they were yet alive were in a holy station, and were praised in the city as just men, but this also is vanity." (Eccl. viii. 10.)   And indeed what vanity and folly is greater than to praise a man for a good quality which it is very well known he has not; nay, oftentimes for what is bad, and what you know to be so ?   But the best of it is, they will make known to others their opinion of you—indeed, in order to please you, they will either not stick at telling yourself a lie ; or

to avoid a lie, they will use evasions, whilst they praise you for
a thing which they believe not to be praiseworthy.   Thus you
are treated like a fool when you must be humoured after this
manner.   It is known where your weakness lies, and that it is
the greatest pleasure which can be done you, when you have
preached, for example, or performed any other public exercise,
to tell you that you came off very well, and that every body was
wonderfully satisfied with you ; it is nevertheless only to please
you that you are thus dealt with ; or because, as you may be
of some use to the flatterer, he wishes by this praise to gain you.
But at the bottom, all this serves to make a greater fool of you ;
for false praises, keeping you still in your error, cause you to relapse into the same faults.

We are very cautious now-a-days even in speaking what we
think ; " because truth is become odious, and begets enemies ;"
and because we know that the proud, when they have any
charitable advice given them, in order to their amendment, show
themselves like madmen, who spit in the faces of those who
bring them physic to cure them.   Since nobody therefore wishes
to draw ill will and quarrels upon himself, we say nothing which
may displease him to whom we speak.   Nay, we dissemble so
well before him, that having a very good opinion of himself, he
considers all the false praises we give him to be true.   By this
may be seen what folly it is to reckon upon the praises of men,
since we know they are only compliments ; that is to say, dissimulation and flattery, if not downright lies.

But let us farther observe that the proud, as St. Chrysostom
says, are hated by God, according to the saying of the Wise man,
" every proud man is an abomination to the Lord," (Prov. xvi.
5,) and among the seven things which God hates, he puts in the
first place " a proud look." (Prov. vi. 17.)   The proud are
hated by men also according to these words : "pride makes itself be hated both by God and man, and the heart of the proud
is like the breath of those whose lungs are corrupted." (Eccl. x.
7,) nobody can come near them.   And certainly the world repays
them for their pride ; because people cross and mortify them in
the most sensible part, and in things which are most opposite to
what they desire.   They seek to be esteemed and respected by
every one ; and every one looks upon them as fools ; they would
be loved and sought after by every one, and every one hates and
shuns them.   They who are above them, use them thus, because
they endeavour to make them their equals ; their equals also

treat them after this manner, because they would set themselves above them ; and their inferiors do the same, because they look for that respect from them, which they do not at all owe them ; nay, there is not so much as a servant of theirs but hates them, and finds them insupportable. In fine, wheresoever we meet pride, we hate and contemn it. On the other hand, the humble are esteemed, beloved, and caressed by all. For as the goodness, innocence, and simplicity of little children make every body love them ; so the same qualities make every body love the humble ; for their easy, sincere, and modest way of behaviour gains the hearts of all ; it is a loadstone which attracts affections, and a charm which makes them be beloved by every one.

To convince you, in fine, that it is a folly to seek the esteem and approbation of men, St. Bernard lays down a most powerful argument. " Either," says he, "it was a folly for the Son of God to have humbled and made himself an object of reproach and contempt as he did ; or it is a great folly in us to have so much passion for the esteem of the world; but it was not a folly in the Son of God, though it seemed so to the world, according to the words of St. Paul : " But we must preach Christ crucified, to the Jews a stumbling-block, and unto the Gentiles foolishness ; but to them who are called, both Jews and Gentiles, we preach Christ, the power and wisdom of God." (1 Cor. i. 23.) If then humility and lowliness was wisdom in the Son of God, vanity and pride must be folly in us, and we are indeed fools to esteem so much the glory and reputation of the world.

——o——

CHAPTER XXI.

That a most sure way to gain the esteem of men, is to become virtuous and humble.

If, notwithstanding all we have said, you cannot yet forbear to love so vain a thing as the opinion of the world is; and to attach a value to a little smoke—if, to defend your own sentiment therein, you say, that to be esteemed by men is of value, and of importance for the edification of your neighbour, and for several other things, and that the Wise man himself counsels you, " to take care of your reputation ;" (Ecclus. xli. 13) ; well then do so in God's name. I will grant that you ought to take care of it, and endeavour to acquire esteem in the world ; but I beg to tell you at the same time, that you deceive yourself if you hope to

succeed therein ; for by the way you take you will never obtain
what you aim at. " The infallible way to be esteemed by men,"
says St. Chrysostom, "is that of virtue and humility." Endeavour
to be a good religious, labour to be and to show yourself the
humblest of all in the way you are, and on all occasions which
shall offer themselves, and so you will gain the esteem of every
one ; for herein consists the honour of a religious, who has truly
renounced the world. A plain and coarse habit, and a mean
office, which through humility he takes upon him, becomes him
as well as rich and fine clothes do worldly people. Nay, he
would otherwise be laughed at as one " who had begun to build,
without being able to finish ;" (Luke xiv. 30) ; nay it would be
a shame for him to aim at the esteem and praise of men; because
to adopt again the sentiments of the world, which a man had
quitted at his entrance into a religious life, is a kind of returning to the world.

Would you see clearly what a shame it is to him, who pro-
fesses to aspire after perfection, to desire to be esteemed of men,
let but any body know this your design, and you will find how
ashamed you will be as soon as ever it is perceived. We have a
very good example hereof in the gospel. The apostles, walking
once at a little distance from our Saviour, so that they thought
he could not hear them, began to dispute, " who was the
greatest among them :" and when they came home, he asked
them, " what was the subject of their discourse upon the way?"
(Mark ix. 32.) They were so ashamed to find their ambition
and vanity discovered, that they all held their peace; "because,"
says the gospel, " they had disputed who was the greatest
amongst them." Then Jesus, calling them to him, said, " those
who command others in the world are looked upon as the greatest,
but it is not so with you." (Matt. xx. 25.) " For he that would
be great among you, let him be as the least, and let him who
would be chief, be your servant." (Luke xxii. 26.) " He who
would be the first let him be the last, and become the servant of
all." (Mark ix. 34.) To be great in the house of God, and in
a religious life, is to be humble, and to make one's self little ;
and to give place to all is to raise one's self above all. In this
kind of honour a religious life consists ; for that honour which
you seek is no true honour at all, but rather a subject of confusion ; and instead of acquiring thereby the esteem of the world,
you make yourself despicable, because you pass for a proud man,
which is the worst opinion can be had of you. You cannot

injure your reputation more than when you give occasion to make others believe that you would fain be honoured and esteemed; or when you stand much upon your honour, and are touched in what relates thereunto.

Upon this account it is that St. John Climachus says, that vanity has been often the cause of shame and confusion to the proud, because it makes them do things which betray their pride, and bring them into contempt. They are not aware that all they say and do to make themselves esteemed and respected, serves many times only to lay open the vanity of their pride, and to render them despicable by the very means they adopt to attract esteem.

" Pride," says St. Bonaventure, " is a blindness of our understanding, which is never greater in us than when we perceive it least; and hence it is, that a vain man is moved sometimes to say and do things which he would be sure never to say or do, if he did but ever so little reflect thereupon; nay, though he should consider therein only the esteem of the world, without any regard either to God or his own duty." How oftens happens it, that a man, finding himself disquieted because he has not been regarded; or because some other has been preferred to him; and imagining that he is wronged, and that his honour is affected, and that justice will be done him upon his complaint, goes so far as to make a discovery of his whole heart? The effect of all which is, that this very person is hereupon less esteemed than he was before; because he is now looked upon as a proud man, since he stands so much upon punctilios; which is very odious, especially in a religious: whereas, had he lightly passed over the business, and left the superiors at liberty to do what they thought fit, he would no less have gained their esteem, than the friendship of every body else.

So that if we consult only prudence, common sense, and even worldly principles, without any regard to those of a spiritual life, the surest way to attract the love and esteem of men is to become really virtuous and humble. Agesilaus, one of the wisest kings of Sparta, being asked by Socrates how he could gain esteem in the world, answered, "you will gain it by endeavouring to be such a one indeed as you would be thought to be." And at another time, when some one else asked the same question; " you will be esteemed," says he, " if you say only good things, and do nothing else but what is also good." There is a story also, that a great philosopher had a friend, who was used in all places to speak well of him, and that his friend took once occasion to tell him how much he was obiged to him, because in whatever company he went he praised still his virtue and merit : the philosopher answered, that he sufficiently requited him, by living so, that in the praises he gave him he could not be accused of having said anything that was false.

But all this while it is not my intent, that you should pursue virtue with the prospect only of acquiring esteem among men ; for that would be to pervert and destroy the best thing in the world by a motive of pride.   What I say is, that if you endeavour to be truly humble, you will undoubtedly gain esteem, even though you seek it not; and the more you avoid being esteemed and are despised, the greater account will be made of you ; for glory is like a shadow, which follows always when you go from it, and is never to be caught when you run after it.   Hence St. Jerome, speaking of St. Paula, says, "that in shunning glory she deserved glory, which always follows virtue as the shadow follows the body, and flying from those that seek it, seeks those that despise it."

Jesus Christ himself has taught us this in the gospel, when speaking to the Pharisees, who chose always the best places in the assemblies :—" When thou shalt be invited to a wedding," says he, " sit not down in the first place, lest a more considerable man than thyself be also invited, and that he who invited both of you, comes and says to thee, give this man place, and thou findest thyself put down with shame to a lower place ; but when thou art invited, go and sit down in the lowest place, that when he comes that invited thee, he may say unto thee : friend, go up higher ; then shalt thou be respected in the presence of all about thee." (Luke xiv. 8, 9.)   The Holy Ghost teaches us the same thing by the mouth of the Wise man, when he says, " Put not thyself too forward before the king, and stand not in the place of great men, for it is far better that it should be said unto thee : come up hither, than that thou shouldst be put down lower in the prince's presence." (Prov. xxv. 6.)

To conclude, " whoever exalts himself shall be humbled," says the Saviour of the world, " and whosoever humbles himself shall be exalted." (Luke xiv. 11.)   You see, then, that he who is humble and stoops to others becomes thereby more esteemed, not only before God, but men also ; and on the contrary, that he who is proud and will have the preference everywhere, exposes himself to contempt and affronts, even by behaving himself after this manner. "O holy humility," cries out the great St. Austin, "how different art thou from pride? It was pride, my brethren, which threw down Lucifer from heaven, and it was humility that made the Son of God descend from thence, to take our flesh upon him; it was pride that drove Adam from paradise, and humility that gave the good thief a place there. Pride caused the confusion of tongues, and humility re-united people of different languages. Pride transformed Nebuchodnosor into a beast, and humility raised Joseph not only above all the Egyptians, but even above all the children of Jacob. Pride caused the destruction of Pharao; and humility exalted Moses." (Serm. 12. ad frat in Erem.)

———o———

CHAPTER XXII.

That humility is the means to acquire inward peace of mind, and that we cannot have peace without humility.

"LEARN of me, for I am meek and humble of heart, and you shall find rest for your souls." (Matt. xi. 29.) The peace of mind which St. Paul reckons among the fruits of the Holy Ghost, is so desirable and precious a blessing, that one of the strongest reasons to make us humble, and despise the esteem of the world, is that which our Saviour proposes to us in the above words; whereby he teaches us, that humility is the only means to acquire inward peace. But as everything becomes more intelligible by comparing it with its contrary, so let us see, in the first place, with what trouble and restlessness the heart of the proud are tormented, that we may the better comprehend the peace and tranquillity which the humble enjoy. The Holy Scripture is full of passages which show us, that the wicked have no peace. "There is no peace, says the Lord, "unto the wicked." (Isa. xlviii. 22.) "They said peace, peace, but there was no peace." (Jerem. vi. 14.) "They find nothing but trouble of mind and unhappiness wheresoever they go, and they know not what peace is." (Ps. xiii. 3.) Their conscience is always at war with them, and even their very peace, if they have any, "is full of bitterness." (Isa. xxxviii. 17.) But the proud, in particular, are in continual disquiet; and St. Austin gives us a reason for it, when he says, "that pride never goes withou envy, and that it is by these two things that the devil is what he is, a devil;" (Lib. de 8. Virg. c. 55); so that we may judge what effects they produce in man since they make the devil to be what he is.

It is impossible for a man who is possessed of pride, and envy, its inseparable companion, and who seeks in vain to be honoured by every body, but to have a heart full of gall and bitterness, and not to be in continual agitation of mind. For what can more sensibly disturb a proud man than to see himself despised, and others preferred to him?

The Holy Scripture gives us an admirable description of the nature and effects of pride, in the person of Aman. He was the great favourite of King Assuerus; and by him was made rich, and placed above all the grandees of the kingdom; he was respected by all, and nothing seemed wanting to his wishes; yet nevertheless, he was so disquieted because Mardochai the Jew, who sat usually at the king's gate, did not rise up and show him respect when he passed by, that he could enjoy no content upon that account, as he confessed one day to his wife and friends; for after having set forth the happy state of his fortune, the high place he was in, and the favours he received every day from the king; "yet all this I reckon as nothing," said he, "so long as I see Mardochai sitting at the king's gate." (Esther v. 13.) What trouble and disquiet does not this express; and does it not prove, that pride raises many storms in the breast of man? According to the words of Isaias, "the wicked are as a troubled sea which cannot rest." (Isa. lvii. 29.) So great a rage did he conceive against Mardochai, that thinking it too little to be revenged on him, he resolved to extend his vengeance to all the Jews; and obtained an edict of King Assuerus to put them all to death. His fury, in the mean time, not permitting him to wait the day appointed for its execution, he caused a gallows to be set up to hang Mardochai upon, and went to the king for orders to that effect; but divine providence frustrated all his measures, covered him with confusion, and brought upon his own head the vengeance which he contrived against so innocent a man. For the king, not able to sleep that night, ordered the book of records to be brought to him, where all the remarkable things of his reign were written, and as they were read before him, there was a passage which showed that Mardochai had discovered a plot which had been made against his royal person. He then asked what reward Mardochai had received for so considerable a service? It was answered, none at all; then the king, inquiring who waited without, he was told, Aman; whereupon he commanded that he

should be called in, and as soon as he saw him he asked him:—
"What should be done to the man whom the king would
honour?" He then, thinking that his majesty would honour no
one but himself, answered, "that he whom the king had a mind
to honour was to be clothed with his royal robes, and put upon
the horse which the king himself used to ride, and have the
crown put upon his head, and that one of the greatest nobles of
the kingdom should hold the horse by the bridle and go before
him, proclaiming through the streets:—'Thus shall he be
treated, whom the king pleases to honour.'" "Go then," said
the king, "take my royal robes, and treat as you have said
Mardochai the Jew, who sits at the gate of my palace, and look
that you do not fail in the least circumstance thereof." What a
heart-breaking was this to a man puffed up with pride What
more terrible mortification could be thought of? But he was
obliged to obey all to the letter, and to complete his punishment,
he himself was hanged a little after on the same gallows he had
prepared for Mardochai. This is what one gets by giving way
to the motions of pride and vanity. And admire, I pray, the
occasion which makes Aman so furious against poor Mardochai,
it is because he bows not to him when he passes by. Any little
trifle is enough to trouble the rest of a proud man, and to make
him pine away continually with vexation. We have great
examples thereof in the people of the world, especially those who
are in high posts ; whatever touches their pride pierces them to
the quick ; the trust of a sword would be less sensible to them.
And because there is no favour or preferment which can defend
them from the affronts of this kind, therefore they live in continual bitterness of heart, and in great agitation of mind.

As much will happen even to a religious, if he is proud ; for
he will be sure to feel hurt if less esteem is made of him than
of others : if such a one is chosen for such or such business, whilst
he is not thought of ; and things of that nature will excite more
uneasiness in him, than even worldings feel when their vanity
is touched. How many religious have thus run the hazard of
losing their vocation ? How many have quitted their convent,
thinking they could no longer stay there without exposing themselves to affronts, not being looked upon with any consideration?
Nay, how many have hereby hazarded even their salvation? For
humility is not only necessary for perfection, but very often for
salvation. "If you become not as one of these little children,
you shall not enter into the kingdon of heaven." (Matt. xviii. 3.)

With what reason then was St. Xaverius used to cry out :—
"O esteem of the world, what evil hast thou done, what evil
dost thou do, and what evil wilt thou yet do ?"

This may serve to convince us of the truth of one thing we too
often experience—namely, that though we may be sometimes
sick of melancholy from the overflow of bile, yet what makes us
melancholy is very often neither bile nor any indisposition of the
body. It is only a motion of pride, which is a disease of the
mind. You are melancholy because you believe that people
don't think of nor respect you. You are melancholy because
you came off ill upon an occasion ; and where you expected
honour, have met with confusion. That sermon, that public
exercise, was not applauded as you expected : nay, on the contrary, you think you have thereby lost your credit, and that is
your real disease. You are melancholy only through pride ; just
as you feel agitated through pride, when you are to do some
action upon which your honour depends, and of which you doubt
the success. In fine, when a proud man is sick and melancholy,
you must seek for the cause thereof only in his pride. But it is
not so with a man truly humble of heart; for as he seeks not the
esteem of the world, and is contented with the last place every
where, so is he free from all sort of disquiet, and enjoys an entire
peace which nothing can disturb ; so that though we should not
regard our spiritual welfare, and what tends to perfection, but
consider only our own interest, and the pleasure of having peace
within that alone ought to suffice to make us humble ; for to live
in a perfect tranquillity of mind, is properly to live ; and to live
in perpetual uneasiness every moment, is to die.

St. Austin hereupon relates a passage of himself, whereby he
says, God showed him the blindness and misery he was under.
"I was," says he, "to make a speech in praise of the Emperor,
in which I had introduced a great many flatteries and unmerited
praises. But the folly and vanity of the world are so great that
these very praises would not have failed to have pleased even
those very persons who knew them to be false. Upon a certain
day, therefore, when my head was engaged with these thoughts,
and the uncertainty of success tormented me to that degree that
I was even in a kind of burning fever, it happened that, passing
by a street in Milan, I saw a poor fellow who was merry with
drink. Looking upon him, I sighed, and turning to some of my
friends, said : "Oh, how highly I blame our folly ! For, in a
profession like ours, where we bend continually under the weight

of our miseries, and where the goads of ambition force us on still to increase our burden, we have no other end in all the pains we take than to gain sure and certain joy, which we shall never perhaps arrive to, and which this poor man has compassed—so that what he has already purchased with a little money he begged, I mean a little temporal happiness, we seek, perhaps in vain, though with great care and labour. It is true," adds that great saint, " his joy was no true joy, but what I aimed at by my ambition was yet more false than his; and, after all, he was gay and I was sad—he was in great peace and tranquillity and I in deadly disquiet. Now, if any one had asked me, whether I had rather be joyful, and if I had been asked yet further, whether I had rather have been as that poor man was, or as I was myself, I had certainly chosen to have remained as I was, though I was tormented with a thousand anxieties. Yet I should, nevertheless, have made that choice without any reason; for, what motive had I to prefer myself to him? Was it because I was more learned than he? But my learning excited no joy in me; and I thereby sought only to please men and not to instruct them. Without doubt," continues he, " that poor creature was happier than I, not only because he was merry and I was vexed with a multitude of cares, but because the means he used to have, wherewith to buy a little wine, which had made him so merry, were innocent; whereas I sought to gain a vain reputation by pronouncing lies."

———o———

CHAPTER XXIII.

Another more efficacious way to acquire the virtue of humility, which is to practise it.

OF the first way or means usually proposed to acquire this virtue, which consists in searching all divine and human reasons which may bring us to it, we have already spoken. But the presumptuous hope which our first parents conceived, " to be as gods " has so deeply rooted pride in our hearts that reason alone is not able to destroy it.

In this we are are always like those who are naturally fearful : whatever reasons you may advance, in order to persuade them there is no cause for their fear, they answer, that they see very well that it is so, and that they would fain take courage but that they cannot. I agree with you, say some, that all you say of the esteem and opinion of the world is very true, and I am thoroughly convinced that it is only wind and smoke, nevertheless, I cannot overcome myself so far as to slight it ; I would fain do it, but I know not how it happens, for, whether I will or not, it carries me away and makes me very uneasy. Now, just as when we would cure one of fear and reason is not sufficient to give him courage, we make him come up close and touch the things which cause his apprehension ; and advise him to go alone in the dark that he may be convinced, by his own experience, that what affrights him is only an effect of his troubled imagination—so wholly to cure and disabuse a man of the impressions which he has of the opinion of the world, " it is not enough," says the holy father, " to represent the vanity of it by solid and convincing reasons, but you must make him practise humility, which is the most effectual means he can adopt."

" Moral virtues," says St. Basil, " are not to be acquired any more than arts and sciences, but by exercise and practice. To be a good artist, a good musician, a good orator, and a good philosopher, you must exercise yourself often in the actions proper to each of these professions ; because there is no good success to be had but by exercise thereof : so to acquire humility and other moral virtues, you must practise the acts belonging to them, and it is only by this means you can acquire a habit thereof."

Now, if any one says that reason and discussion, joined with the instructions and counsel of scripture, suffice to moderate and govern the motions of our passions, " he is deceived," says St. Basil, "and does like a man who learns all his lifetime to build, or to coin money, without ever actually doing either." (In reg. fusius disput. vii.) And sure it is, that he who employs all his time in filling his head with rules and precepts of any art, without ever reducing them to practice, will never be a good artist ; so it is certain that humility and other virtues will never be acquired without practising them. " For as those who hear the law," says St. Paul, " are not just before God but those who practise it," (Rom. ii. 13,) so it is to no purpose to give ear to wholesome instructions if they are not reduced to practice ; for the practice thereof is better than all the speculation in the world.

It is true that all virtue, and whatever is good in us must come to us from the hand of God, and it is also very certain we can do nothing of ourselves ; but it is true also that the same

God without whom we can do nothing, will have us also cooperate on our part.

St. Austin, upon these words of our Saviour, " If I, therefore, have washed your feet, I, who am your Lord and master, ye ought also to wash one another's feet," (John xiii. 14,) says, that what Jesus Christ would teach us by washing his apostles' feet is, that we must practise humility. "It was that," continues he, " O blessed Peter, that thou understoodest not, when thou wouldst not suffer our Saviour to wash thy feet, but he promised that thou shouldst understand it afterwards ; and see how he teaches it thee ; ' for I have given thee an example,' says he, ' that thou mightest do what I have done.' Since, therefore, we have learned humility from the Most High," as that great doctor of the Church adds, " let us who are but poor creatures, practise what the Most High practised with such exceeding humility. Since the sovereign and omnipotent Lord of all things has humbled himself—since the Son of God has condescended so far as to wash his disciples' feet—has lived with a submission to all that his mother and St. Joseph commanded him, and subjected himself to the vilest and lowest service, let us learn from him to exercise ourselves, after the same manner, in the exterior actions of humility, and hereby we shall acquire this virtue in perfection.

St. Bernard is of the same opinion when he tells us that " humiliation is the way to humility, as patience is to peace of mind, and study to learning. If you will, then, acquire humility," continues he, " put yourself in the way of humility, for if you cannot pass over a humiliation, you cannot attain humility." (Ep. lxxxvii.) St. Austin gives a very good reason why the exterior practise of humility is so necessary to acquire true humility of heart. " It is," says he, " when you prostrate yourself at the feet of your brother, that humble thoughts are raised in your heart, or if those thoughts were there already, they are the more fortified thereby." There is so great a connection and relation between the outward and inward man, and they have such a dependence one upon the other, that as soon as the body humbles itself, humble thoughts are stirred up in the heart. The submission which a man shows to his brother, by serving him and kissing his feet, by the coarse habit which he wears, and the mean office he performs, have all a something in them which stirs up humility in the heart, or preserves or increases it when it is already there. This was St. Dorotheus' answer, when he was asked, "how is it possible that the mind should acquire humility by means of a coarse habit which the body is clothed with?" Is it not certain," says he, "that the good or bad disposition of the body has an influence upon the mind— and do we not see that when the body is at ease, the mind is at ease? And is it not plain, when the body is satisfied with meat, that the feelings of the mind are different from those it has when the body is kept low with hunger? Likewise, when a man is mounted upon a mettlesome horse, or seated upon a throne, his mind is more elevated than when he rides a lazy horse, or sits upon the ground; and when he has rich clothes he is otherwise disposed than when he is poorly clad."

The same observation is also made by St. Basil; "for," says he, "as rich clothes raise proud and presumptuous thoughts in worldly people; so a plain and coarse habit inspires the servants of God and religious men with such thoughts of humility and contempt of themselves, as if it made them really despicable. And as worldly people," adds the same saint, "love to set themselves off with rich clothes, to be thereby esteemed, so the servants of God and the truly humble are pleased with plain and coarse clothing, thereby to render themselves the more despicable in the eyes of men; and to preserve and fortify true humility within ourselves." We read in the life of St. Xaverius that he was always very poorly clad, because he would thereby keep himself humble; fearing that should he put on better clothing, he should, as it often happens, be puffed up with pride and presumption.

Another proof that exterior practice contributes much to acquire humility of heart, or any other interior virtue whatsoever, is this, that practice makes far greater impression upon the will than a simple desire. Because the object, when it is present, moves us much more than when it is absent; and what we see moves us more than what we hear. In like manner, what we set before our eyes by practice, has much more power to move our will than the desires we may frame thereof upon the idea we have of it. An actual affront, for example, which you shall willingly bear, strengthens much more your patience than all those you are able to suffer in your mind and thought. And a single day that you are actually employed in some mean office or that you put on an old torn habit, will fortify you more in humility than the spending many days in framing desires and fancies of the self-same things. We experience this every day in the mortifications in use among us. How passionately soever you may pretend to desire them, you will feel always a repugnance the first time you put them in practice ; but the second time you will scarce feel any difficulty at all. And for this reason the use of public penances and mortifications, formerly practised by many saints, has been introduced into the Society of Jesus; as a remedy which, having been once applied, makes a man afterwards master of himself, and of all other things which before seemed very difficult. We may add to this, that according to the opinion of all divines the interior act of any virtue is, commonly speaking, much more perfect and efficacious when it is accompanied with the exterior practice ; so that let the matter be taken as it will, exterior acts of humility, are always a very great help to acquire the virtue of humility.

Now, since the same means which serve to acquire a virtue serve also to preserve and increase it, we may truly say, that the exterior practice of humility is no less necessary to preserve and increase humility in us than to acquire it ; whence it follows, that this exercise, as we have already said when speaking of mortifications, is of great importance not only to beginners, but even to those who are advanced in virtue, as well as to all persons in general.

St. Ignatius in his Constitutions earnestly reccommends this to us. "It is a great help," says he in one place, " to employ one's self with all possible devotion in those offices wherein humility and charity are most exercised." In another place he says, "we must prevent and overcome temptations by their contraries ; as when we know that any one is given to pride, he must be employed in such vile and mean offices as we think may serve to humble him, and so of the rest." And in another place, " we must," says he, " if obedience enjoins it, readily embrace those offices which seem mean and despicable, and to which we have the greatest repugnance ;" (3 P. Const. c. i. § 13 & 23) ; so that humility and humiliation must, as it were, go hand in hand, in such a manner that interior humility, which consists in contemptible thoughts of one's self and in a desire of being contemned by others, may raise up exterior humiliation, which consists in showing one's self outwardly such as one ought to be inwardly. I say, that as he who is truly humble has a contempt of himself, and thinks he is unworthy of any honour ; so ought all his exterior actions to correspond with these thoughts, and his exterior behaviour must give testimony of his interior humility.   Wherefore choose everywhere the last place, as our Saviour counsels—disdain not to converse with the poor and little ones—exercise yourself in the meanest offices, and you will see that the exterior humility, which comes from inward humility, will serve to increase the source and fountain whence it springs.

———o———

CHAPTER XXIV.

The preceding doctrine confirmed by some examples.

PETER of Cluny tells us of a Carthusian who having led a holy life, and always so chaste a one, that God had kept him even from the very illusion of impure dreams, was attacked by a disease of which he died.   As his death was approaching, and all the religious of the house were around his bed, the prior commanded him to tell in what things he believed he had most pleased Almighty God.   The Carthusian answered : what you ask, reverend father, I feel great difficulty in answering ; and I would never do it were I not obliged thereunto by obedience. From my infancy," continued he, " the devil still pursued and persecuted me, but in proportion to his afflicting me the Blessed Virgin still comforted me ; and as I found myself one day tormented with stronger and more than usual temptations, she appeared to me and chased away the devil by her presence ; and after giving me comfort and encouragement to persevere in virtue, she said: "that I may point out an easy way, and discover something of the immense treasures of my Son, I will teach you three exercises of humility, which, if you practise well, will render you acceptable in the sight of God, and give you victory over your enemy.   You are therefore to humble yourself in three things—your diet, your clothing, and your employment ; so that, in your eating, you must desire and seek always ordinary fare ; in your clothing, the coarsest habit ; and in your employment, those functions which are the lowest and most humbling."   The Blessed Virgin hereupon disappeared—but the virtue and efficacy of these holy words made then such an impression upon my heart as to make me practise ever after what she had taught, and I received thereby great help and advantage towards my spiritual advancement.

Cassian relates, that a holy old man called Pinuphius, wishing to shun the respect and honour which were given him in the monastery where he presided, resolved to go away and retire to some place where he might live neglected and without being at all taken notice of. To this end he privately left his own convent, and knowing that in the part where St. Pacomius lived, which was a great way off, discipline and zeal did then most flourish, he in a secular habit went thither, so that not being known there he might be treated as a novice, and no regard had of him. Several days he stayed there at the gate, asking with all humility the habit, and prostrating himself at the feet of the monks ; who on purpose showed a contempt of him, reproaching him, that after being glutted with the world he came to give himself to God in his old age ; and that it was more out of necessity, and to be sure of a livelihood, than to serve God by his own choice and inclination, that he begged admission. He was nevertheless at last received, and made under-gardener to another brother, whom he was to obey in all things. And he not only did his duty herein with great exactness and humility, but he endeavoured moreover to do the most troublesome work of all the house, and that to which others had the greatest aversion. In the night he rose privately, as if he had not worked enough in the day, and put everything he could in order without being perceived ; so that the religious who knew not how, nor by whom, all that was done, were hereby every morning in a very great surprise. Three years he remained in that condition, very well content with the opportunity he had to work and render himself contemptible, which was the thing he so much desired. His own religious, much troubled in the mean time at his absence, inquired after him in several places, and at the end of three years, when they despaired of finding him, one of them passing by a monastery of St. Pacomius, little thinking of meeting him there whom he sought after, found him spreading dung on the ground ; so that knowing him very well, he threw himself presently at his feet, to the great wonder of all present ; but when they learned who he was, their wonder increased, for they knew him well enough by fame, and begged his pardon for using him as they had for so long a time. The good old man, bewailing his misfortune of being thus discovered by the envy of the devil, and losing thereby the treasure he had found in the obscurity of a private life, was forced to return to his own monastery, where being received with very great joy by all the religious, they took great care that he should not get away from them any more. But their precaution was however to no purpose, for he had still so great a desire of becoming very contemptible, and was so taken with the

pleasure he found during the three years he had passed in an
humble and private way of living, that having taken measures
privately to get on board a ship, which was bound for Palestine,
he found means to steal away once more from his monastery, and
embarked.   But God, who takes care of exalting the humble,
permitted him, being arrived at the monastery where Cassian
was, to be known by some of the religious, who went thither to
visit the Holy Land, and thus what he did to render himself contemptible, served only to make him the more esteemed and respected.

We read in the lives of the fathers of the desert, that a certain
hermit having lived a long time in the continual exercise of
penance and prayer, and imagining himself to be already in a
high degree of perfection, prayed one day, that God would let
him know if he wanted anything whereby he might become more
perfect.   God, intending to humble him, caused him to hear a
voice which commanded him to go and find out a man who kept
hogs hard by, and then to do what he should bid him.   He immediately obeyed, found him out, saluted him, and prayed him
to tell him what he was to do to please God.   He knowing, it
seems, by revelation what he was to answer; " will you do,"
quoth he, " what I shall bid you ?"   The hermit answering, that
he would ; "take the whip then," replied the other, " and go
and keep the hogs."   The holy man, desiring ardently to serve
God, and to make himself agreeable and more perfect in his sight,
went immediately to do what the hogherd bade him.   Now as
the fame of his sanctity was spread all over that country, those
who knew and saw him so employed said to one another ; " have
you observed that the good old man of whom so many wonderful
things have been related is turned fool, and gone to keep hogs; his
continual fastings and great austerities have turned his head ?"
The holy man, who heard all this, took it patiently, and went on
yet some days in the same employment, till Almighty God seeing
his humility, and the spirit with which he bore affronts and injuries, commanded him to return to his own hermitage.

It is related in the "Spiritual Meadow," that a holy bishop
having left his bishopric, where he was much esteemed and
honoured by every body, went his way to Jerusalem, where he
was not known, and having put on poor clothes, he took upon him
to serve a mason.   It happened in the meantime, that a good
man called Ephraim, who was superintendent of all the public
buildings, went to oversee them twice or thrice when the work-

men reposed ; and having all these times beheld upon the head of the holy man, who slept upon the ground, a pillar of fire, which seemed to reach up to heaven, he was the more surprised, because he saw the old man in a very miserable condition and employment. To inform himself further thereupon, he made him be called, and asked him who he was? The saint answered, that he was a poor man who got his livelihood by his labour. Ephraim was not satisfied with this answer, but, by a secret inspiration of God, who permitted it should be thus the more to honour the humility of his servant, pressed him anew with such earnestness to tell him who he was, that the holy man, unable to deny him any longer replied ; I will tell you upon condition that you will never speak of it to any body whilst I am alive, nor ask my name. The superintendent consented, and hereupon gave him his word. The saint then owned that he was a bishop, and that to shun the esteem and honour of the world he had quitted his bishopric.

St. John Climachus tells us that a man of quality, who lived at Alexandria, went to request admission into a certain monastery. The abbot thereof believing by his looks and other outward marks that he was a vain-glorious man, and one who was yet puffed up with the pride, and vanity of the world, wished to put him into the sure path of humility, and therefore told him, that if he was resolved to carry in good earnest the yoke of Jesus Christ, he must oblige himself to exercise obedience. " I am, father, very willing," said the gentleman,; "and I put myself into your hands to do with me, just as the smith does with the iron, which he forges into what shape he pleases." Since it is so," replied the abbot, "I will have you stand at the monastery gate as under-porter, still prostrating yourself at the feet of all who come in or go out, and begging of them to pray to God for you, because you are a great sinner." The gentleman obeyed most punctually, and after he had lived seven years in this exercise, and had acquired a great fund of humility, they were willing to receive him into the monastery, and admit him even to holy orders ; but having got several persons, and among the rest St. John Climachus, to intercede that he might finish the course he had began in the station where he was, he obtained what he desired, and seemed in asking that favour, to have had some foresight of his approaching death ; for, in ten days after, it happened that God called him to himself ; and seven days after him, the porter of the monastery died also ; whom the gentleman, when he was alive, had promised, that if he should have any interest in heaven after his death, he would make use of it, that he might be quickly his companion in glory.   This was the reward of his continual humiliations, which had made him so humble, that when the forementioned St. Climachus asked him what he still thought of, whilst he practised those acts of humility, he answered, that he was always thinking how unworthy he was of the conversation, and even of the sight of the religious ; and that he deserved not so much as to behold them.

It is stated in the lives of the ancient fathers, that an abbot, whose name was John, told a story one day how a certain philosopher having a scholar who had committed a fault, told him he would not pardon it, till he had for the space of three years suffered patiently whatsoever bad language should be given him. The scholar consented to it, and at the end of three years came to him to have his pardon.   The master told him he would not yet pardon him unless that during three years more he would hire people to give him ill language ; the scholar again consented to this second trial ; and after having completed that time also, his master told him that he pardoned him, and that now he might go and learn wisdom at Athens.   He went accordingly ; and hearing there another philosopher, who still was wont to give bad language to his new auditors to try their patience, upon his entrance, he fell laughing at what he also gave him. "How now," quoth the philosopher, "I give you bad language, and do you laugh ?"   And ought I not do so," replied the other ; since I have given money these three years to hire people to give me such language, and now I find one that gives it me for nothing. would you not have me rejoice at this?"   "Come in," replied the philosopher, "you are fit for the study we here make profession of."   So that the abbot concluded from this example, that patience was the gate of wisdom.

In the life of St. Ignatius, father Maffeus, says, that, "the saint going one day in pilgrimage from Venice to Padua with father James Lainez, and both of them having nothing but old patched clothes on, they met in the way a young country boy, who seeing them thus dressed, came close up to them, to view them nearer ; and then fell jeering and laughing at them ; sometimes at one, and sometimes at the other.   St. Ignatius, being overjoyed at what had thus happened, stood still, and when his companion asked him why he did not go on, and rid himself of that rude and idle lad—' Why would you,' replied the saint, ' deprive the poor

youth of the diversion he has met with?' Wherefore he stayed in
that posture till the boy was weary of staring and laughing at
him ; and he himself received these scoffs with far greater satisfaction than the people of the world do the honours and respects
which are shown them."

We read also in the life of St. Francis of Borgia, that he and
father Bustimantius, travelling together, arrived at a very poor
inn, where they found nothing to lie upon but a truss or two of
straw in a little dirty corner.   Father Bustimantius, who was
very old, and had an attack on his lungs, did nothing but cough
and spit all night long ; but when he thought still to spit upon
the wall, he spat upon St. Francis's face, who notwithstanding
said not a word, nor so much as turned aside.   When it was day,
and the good father perceiving what he had done in the dark, he
was so concerned and confounded, that he was not to be comforted ; but the saint, being as joyful as the other was ashamed
and troubled, said, " pray, father, bo not in pain, for I assure
you, that there was nothing in the room deserved more to be
spit upon than myself."

————o————

CHAPTER XXV.

*The exercises of humility, which are practised among us of the
Society.*

ONE of the reasons which St. Basil lays down to show that the
life of religious, who live in community, is preferable to that led
in solitude, is, that the life of hermits is not only exposed to great
dangers, but is deprived of those exercises of virtues, which are
necessary for Christian perfection, and consequently is less proper
than the other for the acquiring of them.   For how can he exercise humility who meets with no one before whom he can humble
himself ?   Or how can he perform works of charity and mercy
who has no communication with others?   Or how can he show
patience who meets with no one to vex him ?   But it is not so
with a religious who lives in community.   The frequent occasions he has to exercise all sorts of virtue, are a great means to
acquire them.   If you consider humility, he meets with those
before whom he may humble himself : if charity, he has objects
thereof : if patience, the commerce he has with all his brethren
gives him a thousand occasions to practice that also ; and so it
is as to all other virtues.

All religious in general owe doubtless great obligations to Almighty God for the grace whereby he has called them to a religious life, which furnishes so many ways to acquire virtue, and which, in fine, is a school of perfection; but we of the Society are more obliged to him than all the rest; because, besides the means which are common to us with others, he has given us particular ones, especially in what relates to humility. For our constitutions have taken such care herein, and the rules of them are so express, that provided we keep them well, we shall never want wherewith to exercise ourselves in humility. One very profitable rule, for example, is that which enjoins us to lay open the very bottom of our heart and conscience to our superior, by giving him an exact account of our temptations, passions, bad inclinations, and generally of all our defects and indispositions of mind. For though this is ordered to us upon another account than that of humbling us, as we shall show in its proper place; it is nevertheless very certain that it contributes very much to humility, and is a great practice thereof. Another very profitable rule is that, which for the making a greater progress in spiritual things, and for the entering into deeper sentiments of confusion and humility, enjoins us to rejoice that all our faults, and whatever is perceived amiss in us, should be carried to our superiors; and that, by any one who should know them out of confession. Take notice of this, and thereby you may be the more confounded and humbled; for this is the end of its practice. So that if you desire to acquire true humility, you will rejoice to have all your faults exposed to your superiors; or if you have already acquired it, you yourself will go and tell those faults, and desire a penance for them; and as you are the first in knowing them, so you will also be the first in discovering them. But we have yet another and greater exercise of humility required of us, which is to accuse ourselves of our own faults in public, to be thereby the more despised. For it is only with that view you are to do all this; and not that you may be taken for an humble and mortified man; as then it would be an act of pride, rather than an exercise of humility. It is also with the same intention we must receive reproofs, whether they be made in private or public; being glad in good earnest they are given us, and that every body should be fully convinced that what is said of us is true. In fine, it is with the same spirit that we are to undergo all exterior mortifications which are used among us: as kissing the feet of our brethren; eating under the table, or upon our knees; lying prostrate at the door of the refectory, and a great many others; which conduce much to acquire and preserve humility; provided that we perform them with such disposition of mind as is necessary to perform them well. So that when you eat upon the ground; when you kiss your brother's feet, and when you lie prostrate for them to pass over you; you are then to think, how unworthy you indeed are to sit at the table with them; how you ought to kiss the ground they tread upon; and how you deserve to be under the foot of every one. Nor are you only to think thus yourself, but to be willing also that every body else should think the same of you; and thus you are to entertain yourself with such reflections as these, after the example of those holy men, whom we have spoken of in the foregoing chapter. For when mortifications are thus taken, it is impossible but they should produce profound humility in the heart; if, on the contrary, you perform them only outwardly, and without any interior submission of mind, they will be good for nothing; because, as the apostle teaches us, " bodily exercise profits little," (1 Tim. iv. 8,) and the doing things without aiming at the end for which they were instituted, is to do them only out of form and custom. If, therefore, after having kissed your brethren's feet, and lain down for them to walk on you, you should speak rudely and after a surly manner to them, how can you reconcile such behaviour that so much contradicts itself; and how can you hinder people from believing that all you did was mere dissimulation and hypocrisy.

Thus have I shown you one part of the exercises of humility to which our rules oblige us; and though I have elsewhere spoken of them upon another occasion, yet I wished to take notice of them here also; that every one may again consider them, and so set themselves to the practice of humility. For the progress and perfection of a religious man consisting in the exact observance of his rules; the practice of virtue to which he is most to apply himself is that which his rules prescribe to him; so that if he performs not the exercise of humility and morti-fication, to which they oblige, he may reckon all which he does of himself as nothing. We may say as much of Christians in general: the things in which every one of them has most need of humility, are those where humility is necessary to keep God's commands. If he has no humility in them, it will be to no purpose to have it in other actions. For if he has not humility enough to confess a great sin, which through shame or rather pride he hides from his confessor, and hereby fails in so essential a point, what will all other actions of humility signify, since he will be condemned for failing in this ? It is the same with a religious, in all other things that are of obligation. If you have not humility enough to discover the bottom of your conscience to your superior, thereby to comply with your rules; if you˙cannot endure to be put in mind of your faults, that you may mend them ; if you receive correction and penances with trouble and disquiet; if you will not be employed in mean and humble offices and submit to all the functions the Society has appointed; where is your humility ?—Where is that indifference of will which your superiors require of you ? And why do they require it of you, if not for things of this nature ? Every religious may thus run over with himself what belongs to the obligations of his rule, and each particular person may do the same according to what the condition and profession he has embraced require of him.

———o———

CHAPTER XXVI.

That we must beware of saying anything that may tend to our own praise.

St. Basil, St. Gregory, St. Bernard, and many other teachers of a spiritual life who have laid down rules, put us in mind of taking great heed lest we say anything which may turn to our own praise. And this counsel agrees with that which good old Tobias gave his son, when he said, "suffer not pride to reign either in your heart or words." (Tob. iv. 14.) It is this which the apostle also has taught us by his example, when having said great things of himself, which were necessary for him to utter, for the glory of God and edification of the faithful, because " he he had been taken up to the third heaven,"he adds, "but I forbear, lest any man should think of me above that which he sees in me or hears of me." (2 Cor. xxxii. 6.)

St. Bernard, examining these words, cries out, "how well was it said, I forbear to and any more. The presumptuous, the proud, and they who boast of their actions, are not sparing, for they puff up themselves vainly with what they have, or falsely glory in what they have not." (Epis. 87.) None but he who is truly humble is sparing of his words ; for, fearing that he should be believed to be what he is not, he endeavours always not to let it be known what he is. The same saint, in another place, descends to particulars, and admonishes us "to say nothing of ourselves which may make us pass for men of profound knowledge, or eminent virtue." (In spec. Mon.) For as soon as ever a thing may turn to our praise, although it may be true, and edify our neighbour, and though we may have ever so good an intention in telling it, it is always dangerous to speak of it. It suffices that the good action is yours without speaking thereof, and you ought always to be extremely reserved, lest by declaring the good you have done, you thereby lose all the merit thereof.

"A religious must not," says St. Bonaventure, "boast either of his knowledge, or of what he was when he lived in the world." In fine, what is more unbecoming a religious man than to show vanity on account of his nobility, or the rank his relations hold in the world? For what is the lustre of birth, grandeur, and dignity, but a little wind and smoke? "And," as a certain author said very well, "do you know what nobility in a religious man is good for? For nothing else than to despise it, as he does riches." For that which is esteemed in him is virtue and humility. As to what he was or was not in the world, it is reckoned for nothing; and whoever makes account of these things in a religious life, and prides himself thereupon, shows very much his vanity, and the little relish he has for spiritual things; he discovers plainly that he has not despised or truly renounced the world. "For he," says St. Basil, "who, by a new spiritual birth, has received the honour to become the child of God, is ashamed of his relations according to the flesh." (In reg. brevoir, 90.)

It is improper for any one to praise himself; nay, it is a very old and common saying that praise sounds very ill in the mouth of him who commends himself; and the Wise man teaches us the same when he says, "let another praise thee, and not thy own mouth." (Prov. xxvii. 2.) Now, if this becomes every body so ill, it becomes far less a religious, who ought to profess humility; and that, indeed, which should make all mend this fault is, that when a man thinks to have himself esteemed, he even, by so doing, renders himself contemptible.

St. Ambrose, upon these words of the prophet, "behold my humility, and deliver me," (Serm. xx,) says, that "let a man be ever so little in himself, and reduced to ever so miserable condition, provided he has no pride, nor prefers himself to others, he is always commendable by his humility." That makes him be beloved; that makes him esteemed; and that supplies him in the defect of all other qualities. On the contrary, whatever merit a proud man may have—however rich, noble, powerful, able, and learned he may be, pride ruins all, and makes him to be hated and contemned.

In the life of St. Arsenius, who had been preceptor to Arcadius and Honorius, sons of the Emperor Theodosius, and emperors themselves after his death, we read that whatever rank he had held in the world, and how much soever he had been esteemed for his learning, yet, after he had made himself a religious, he was never heard to say anything which seemed haughty, or showed any learning he had. But, on the contrary, he lived and conversed with all the other religious with such a spirit of simplicity and humility as if he had never known anything; and he addressed himself usually to the most simple, to learn of them a spiritual life; saying that he deserved not to be their scholar in so elevated a science.

It is observed also in the life of St. Jerome, that, though he was of very great quality, yet, nevertheless, there is not so much as one passage in all his works where he has taken any notice of it.

To hinder us from speaking to our own advantage, St. Bonaventure lays down a very good motive. "Be persuaded," says he, "that it is very hard for you to have any good quality but others will perceive it; if you take no notice of it yourself you will be better loved for it, and deserve a double praise; as well for being master of so good a quality as for being willing to conceal it. But if you make a show of it you will be laughed at, and instead of being esteemed and giving edification, you will be despised, and give scandal. Virtue is like an excellent perfume, the more close you keep it the greater is its odour; but if you expose it to the air it quickly evaporates and loses its scent."

St. Gregory tells us how a holy abbot, called Eleutherius, being once on a journey, stopped at a nunnery, where he was lodged in a chamber in which there was a youth who was wont to be very much tormented by an evil spirit. When it was day the nuns asked the holy man whether anything had happened in the night to the said youth? He answered, that nothing at all had happened; they then told him how the case was with him, and so conjured him to take him along with him. The good old man kept him a good while in his company, in all which time the devil durst not approach him. This at length excited a vain complacency and satisfaction in him, and not being able to abstain from showing it, one day as he was with his monks he told them that he believed the devil had tormented this boy at the nunnery only to make sport with the nuns, by reason he had not had the confidence to come near him since he had been there among the servants of God. Scarce were those words out of his mouth when the devil began anew to torment the youth in presence of them all. The abbot, hereupon, attributing the cause thereof to his own vain-glory, wept very bitterly. And when his monks endeavoured to comfort him, he told them, that they should neither eat nor drink till they had obtained of Almighty God to restore the youth to himself; whereupon going all to their prayers, they ceased not till he was quiet again. By this example may be seen the aversion which God has to all words which tend in the least to the praise of him who pronounces them; nay, even to those which are said only in jest, as these of the holy abbot seemed to have been.

———o———

CHAPTER XXVII.

How we are to exercise ourselves in the second degree of humility by means of prayer.

ONE of the most important rules of the Constitutions of the Society is that we have spoken of in one of the foregoing chapters, wherein our holy founder tells us, " that as the people of the world seek earnestly the honour, glory, and reputation which the world gives, so they who truly follow Jesus Christ ought ardently to desire whatever is opposite to this spirit of the world ; thereby to become, in a manner, like their Divine Master : wherefore they must desire always to be covered with injuries, affronts, false accusations, and all sorts of ignominy." Nay, he requires further, " that all they who offer themselves to be admitted into the Society should be examined whether they truly have such a desire." It seems indeed harsh enough that a man who has offered violence to himself in leaving the world, and whose wounds which he has received in it are still fresh, should be questioned by so strict and so severe a rule. But this shows what perfection our institutions requires of us; since it is for admitting those only who are altogether weaned from themselves, and truly dead to the world ; and, although this is very hard, and supposes great perfection, yet the rule requires still further, " that should it happen that any one, through human frailty, feels not yet this desire, he is to be examined whether he has not at least a longing to have such a one ;" and provided he has, and is disposed to suffer everything patiently on all occasions, it orders him to be received. And, indeed, what better disposition can be wished for, in order to learn or make progress, than to have a will of doing so ? To learn any art whatsoever it is sufficient to have really a desire for it, and to apply our-selves to it in good earnest. A religious life is a school of virtue and perfection; wherefore enter into it with an intention to do your duty well, and, with Almighty God's grace, you will in-fallibly succeed therein.

Let us do the same as to the exercise we speak of, and let us proceed step by step. You say that you feel not in yourself, as yet, a desire of being despised, but that you would fain have that desire. Begin, therefore, with that desire in your prayer to exercise yourself in the virtue of humility, and say with the prophet : "My soul has longed always to desire thy justifica-tions." (Ps. cxviii. 20.) Oh, how far am I from having these ardent desires which so many have had to be despised ! But I would fain, O my God, come to the point at least of wishing earnestly to have these desires. Thus you will be in the right way ; for this is a good beginning and disposition to obtain them. Persevere in your prayers, insist still thereon, beg of God to soften your heart, and remain some days in such desires as these, which are very agreeable unto him, and which he attends most willingly : " The Lord has heard the desire of the poor ; he has given ear to the inclination of their hearts." (Ps. x. 41.) God will quickly give you the desire of suffering something for the love of him, and of doing penance for so many sins you have committed ; and when he shall have inspired you with so good a disposition, can you better employ that desire to suffer than to be despised for his sake? And can you better bestow your penance than in making reparation for your sins ? It was in this spirit that David expressed himself to his servants, who urged him to revenge himself upon Simei, that cursed him—"Let him alone," said he, " the Lord, for his cursing me, will perhaps bestow some favour upon me this day ; it may be he will receive the injuries done me as a part of that satisfaction and chastisement which my offences deserve." (2 Kings xvi. 11, 12.)

But when, by the mercy of God, you begin to feel these desires of being despised for the love of him, that thereby you may be made like to Jesus Christ ; believe not that then the work is done, and that you have already acquired humility. On the contrary, reckon that you are then to begin to plant and to root it in your heart. You must, therefore, endeavour not to pass slightly over such desires, but to fix your mind as much as you can upon them, and continue a long time in prayer till these thoughts become strong enough to be reduced to acts ; when you shall arrive so far, and seem to bear patiently the occasions of being despised, there will yet occur in the act itself several occasions of being despised, several degrees and steps will still remain before you can get to the top of humility.

In the first place, you must accustom yourself to suffer patiently all the different occasions of humiliation which may present themselves ; whereby you will have enough to do for some time, and it may be even for a very long time. After this you must go forward, and never stop till you are come to that pass as to receive contempt and injuries with as much joy as the people of the world receive riches and honours ; so that you may truly say with the prophet—" I have rejoiced in the way of thy testimonies, as much as in all riches." (Ps. cxviii. 14.)

It is natural for us to rejoice when we obtain something which we have desired, and to rejoice more or less as we have desired that thing with more or less passion. Examine yourself upon this rule, you will thereby be able to judge whether you really desire to be despised, and whether you make any progress in humility. One may use also the same rule in order to all other virtues.

But that humility may make a greater impression upon our hearts by means of prayer, and that these means may be more advantageous to us, we must in our meditation descend to the particular causes of humiliation which every day may happen to us ; we must make a lively representation of them to ourselves, and so, by the prospect of them, be encouraged to form acts of humility. We must strongly insist and fix ourselves thereupon till we have entirely overcome the aversion we feel thereunto, and have fully gained what we aimed at. For thus vice is rooted out of our heart, and virtue fixes itself therein, and flourishes more and more. What goldsmiths do in refining gold may serve us for a very good comparison in this point. When they have melted the gold in the crucible they throw into it a grain of sublimate, whereupon the gold begins immediately to rise in large bubbles till the sublimate is consumed ; and then what boiled up falls again, and the gold is reduced to what it was before. They then throw in a second grain of sublimate, and the gold begins again to boil up, but with less force than at first; and as soon as the sublimate is again consumed the agitation presently ceases. They then put in a little more of it, which causes only a bare fuming or heaving in the gold. In fine, some more is put in the fourth time, but that works no more effect upon the gold than if none at all had been thrown in; because it is then wholly refined and purified, and that is an infallible sign it is so. This shows what we must do in prayer. Throw in a grain of sublimate; image to yourself, in a lively manner, an occasion of suffering some mortification and contempt, and if you then begin to foam and be troubled, dwell upon that idea till the fervour of prayer has wholly consumed this grain of sublimate—till you have mastered what disturbs you and are become quite calm. The day after throw in a new grain of sublimate, and fancy some mortification and humiliation; if you then feel that nature rises and boils up in you, persist in considering of the affront, till you have wholly digested it, and are become quite calm; continue afterwards to practise the same thing several times, and when that grain of sublimate, that lovely idea of an affront of injury, raises no more trouble or foaming in your breast, and that at the sight of all affronts and injuries which you can imagine, you shall find yourself in an equal temper and tranquillity of mind, then you may stop; for that is a sign that the gold is refined and purified, and that the perfection of humility is acquired.

———o———

CHAPTER XXVIII.

How the particular examen of the virtue of humility is to be made.

A PARTICULAR examen, as we have observed in its proper place, must be on one thing at a time; because it is more efficacious than if it included many things at once; and the proper reason why it is called particular is, because it is intent only upon one thing. Now, this practice is of very great importance; and to succeed more easily therein, you must ordinarily divide the vice or the virtue which you intend to make the subject of your examen into several parts. If, then, you will root pride out of your heart, and plant humility in the room of it, consider not the thing in general. For pride and humility being of vast extent, if you propose to yourself in general to be proud in nothing, and to be humble in all things, it is a purpose of far greater extent than if you formed two or three other designs together, and so, by proposing too much, you will do nothing at all. Descend to particulars ; consider wherein you have been used chiefly to fail in humility, and in what you have been touched with pride, and begin in that particular thing to correct yourself. Afterwards, when you have compassed one thing, begin with another, and after that with a third, and so you will by little and little root up the pride you took in things you loved most, and thereby acquire humility. But that you may examine yourself more profitably upon so necessary a virtue, I shall here run over these several points which may be made the subject of your particu-examen.

Let us purpose, in the first place, to say nothing that may turn on our own praise ; for, since the desire of being esteemed is so natural, and so rooted in our heart, and that " out of the abundance of the heart the mouth speaks" (Luke vi. 45), we often happen to say things which may directly or indirectly turn to our advantage, without thinking thereof. If, for example, on a person speaking before you of something in which you participated ever so little, but which may be to your honour, you should immediately attribute all the glory of it to yourself: "I was concerned," you will say, " in that business : nay, it was through my influence it succeeded so well, and without me it had come to nothing." And as soon as ever you opened your mouth your hearers judged that, though you had had a greater share in it, yet you would not have said a word if it had not succeeded. Thus, many things drop from our mouths which we ourselves are not aware of till we have said them ; so that it is good to use ourselves to make a particular examen of them, that by taking great care to let nothing of this nature fall from us, we may overcome this ill habit, which is in a manner natural to us.

For the second subject of our examen let us take what St. Basil, St. Jerome, St. Austin, and St. Bernard recommend to us, which is, not to take pleasure in hearing people praise and speak well of us, for it is dangerous to take pleasure therein.

St. Ambrose says that when the devil sees that he cannot effect our ruin by discouraging us, he endeavours to effect it by raising presumption in us : when he has set upon us to no purpose by reproaches and contempt, he causes us to be honoured and praised that he may this way destroy us.

In the life of St Pacomius it is related, that when he wished to pray, he was used to go out of his convent, and to retire into a solitary place ; and that often at his return many devils went before him with a great deal of bustle, as when people go before a great prince ; and that several of them, who seemed as it were to make way for him, cried out aloud—"make way there for the man of God," to try if they could make him yield to some temptation of vain-glory. But the holy man, who knew that all these their stratagems were vain, smiled at them. Do you, in like manner, when you shall hear yourself praised, or when any thought of vanity or self-esteem comes into your head, think that you hear the devil speak to you; scorn him accordingly, and you will overcome the temptation.

To this purpose St. Climachus tells us a very particular story of how the devil discovered to a hermit the bad thoughts he tormented another hermit with, to the end, that what the one had most hidden in his heart being told him by the other, he who was tempted should take the other for a prophet and a saint, that so the praises which he gave him might be an occasion of his fall. We may infer from hence, how advantageous the devil must believe it is for him to instil into us some thoughts of pride and self-satisfaction, since for that purpose he makes use of so much craft and cunning. It is for this reason, St. Jerome tells us, that, "if we wish to advance towards our native country, we must shut our ears against the destructively melodious voice of the syrens." (Epis. 84.) For the sound of our own praise is a music so pleasing to our ears, that whatever the poets have invented of the singing of the syrens comes not near it ; but this music at the same time is so dangerous to our soul, that we must stop our ears if we have not a mind to be destroyed.

St. John Climachus says, that when we are praised we ought to cast our eyes upon our sins, for then we shall find ourselves unworthy of those praises ; and so they will serve only to raise in us greater sentiments of confusion and humility. And to this second practice of not taking pleasure in hearing yourselves praised, you may add another very important one, which is, to take pleasure in hearing others praised. Whenever, then, the good which you shall hear of your neighbour excites envy in you, or what you shall hear said of yourself raises any self-satisfaction in you, be sure to look upon it as a fault.

The third point of our particular examen may be, to do nothing to be seen and esteemed by men ; and of this our Saviour gives us warning in the gospel when he says, "Take heed that you do not your good works before men, to be seen by them, otherwise you will have no reward of your Father who is in heaven." (Matt. vi. 1.) This examen is very useful, and may be divided into several parts; we may, in the first place, propose to ourselves not to do things through human respect; afterwards to do them purely for God's sake; and then to do them very well, as doing them really in the presence of God; and in fine, so to do them that it may seem, as we have said elsewhere when speaking of the uprightness and purity of the intention, that all our actions are only a sequel and effect of a motion of love which impels us to act.

The fourth point of our examen may be, not to excuse ourselves when we are in fault; for it is pride that makes us, as soon as we have committed one, or as soon as we are reproved for it, stand upon our defence; and it is pride that furnishes us with words "even to add excuses to excuses as to our sins." (Ps. cxl. 4.) In this passage of Job, "if I have covered my sins as a man, and if I have hidden my iniquity in my bosom," (Job xxxi. 33,) St. Gregory dwells very particularly on the words, "as a man." saying, that it is the nature of a man to hide and excuse his sin, and that it is a thing which he derives from his first parents. Scarce had man sinned than he went to hide himself behind the trees in paradise, and when God reproaches him for his disobedience he immediately lays the fault thereof upon his wife. "The woman," says he, "whom thou gavest to me for a companion, gave me of the fruit of the tree, and I did eat thereof." (Gen. iii. 12.) The woman then lays the fault upon the serpent: "the serpent," says she, "beguiled me, and I did eat." "God examines them upon their sin," says St. Gregory, "that acknowledging and confessing it, they might obtain pardon thereof; but he questions not the serpent thereupon, because he intends not to pardon him. But they, instead of humbling themselves by the acknowledgment of their fault, increase it by excusing it; for they seem to endeavour in a manner to throw the fault upon God himself. 'The woman whom thou hast given me,' says one, 'made me sin;' which was as much as to say, that if God had not given her for a companion to him, it would not have happened. 'The serpent which thou hast created,' says the other, 'has deceived me;' as if she would also say, that she had not sinned if God had not created that serpent, and placed it in the garden."

"They let themselves be persuaded," says St. Gregory, "that they should be like unto God, and seeing that they could not make themselves like unto him by participation of the divinity, they endeavoured to make him like themselves by the participation of their fault; and thus, intending to excuse it, they aggravate it. Now, all men being descended from them, they all feel this fault of their forefathers; and hence it is, that as soon as ever they are reproved for a fault, they immediately seek a thousand excuses to hide it; nay, often not content with excusing themselves, they attach the blame to their neighbour."

A holy writer compares those who are always excusing themselves when they are reproved, to a hedge-hog, which as soon as one goes to touch it turns itself into the form of a bowl, and thrusts out its prickles on all sides, so that you cannot touch it without pricking yourself; you cannot see its body without first seeing your own blood. "Even so it is with those," says he, "who excuse themselves: if you think of touching them ever so little, or of telling them any fault they have committed, they bristle up and defend themselves like the hedge-hog, and sometimes do as it were prick you, by telling you that you yourself have also need of being corrected; sometimes by shewing you that there is a rule which forbids the reproving your brother; and sometimes, in fine, by observing that others commit greater faults and have nothing at all said of them. All this proceeds only from an excess of pride; for we would fain hide from the eyes of men whatever is defective in us; and we are less concerned for having committed faults than for having them discovered, and the good opinion lessened which people had of us; and this is the reason why we hide them with so great care, and excuse them with so much artifice and obstinacy. Nay, we sometimes meet with persons who are so far from having the spirit of mortification, that when you say not one word to them of their faults they anticipate all you can say, and prevent beforehand whatever you can accuse them of. They will tell you, if they have done such or such a thing it is for such and such a reason; they are never upon any occasion at a loss for an excuse; but what is it that disquiets and makes them thus uneasy? It is pride indeed that torments them; it is that disquiets them before you speak to them; and makes them defend themselves before you attack them. It is fit, that they who find themselves subject to this temper, should be very intent in examining themselves hereupon, till they have overcome the desire they have to hide their faults; and are become so much masters of themselves as to be glad that since they have committed them others should believe them, and that they should make satisfaction for what they ought to believe themselves; that so they may be in a manner punished for them. I will yet go further, and say, that when you are reproved even for a thing which you have not done, it is always good not to excuse yourself; for when your superior wishes to find the truth, he will know how to do it, and it may be he even knows it already, but intends to try your humility, and see how you will receive a reproof.

To prevent our imagination from indulging too freely in proud thoughts, wherein it often strays, is, in the fifth place, another examen of a very useful kind. For sometimes our fancy exalts us to the first and most important employments; sometimes it sends us into our own country to preach with wonderful success; sometimes we imagine we teach in the public schools, and defend our conclusions with general applause; and a thousand such things as these come into our head. Now, since all this springs from inward pride, which, being unable to contain itself, breaks out into these extravagant thoughts, you must take no less care in suppressing them than in rejecting those against purity, charity, or any other Christian or religious duty.

The sixth subject of this particular examen may be, to look on ourselves as inferior to every one, according to what our rule enjoins, which prescribes the exciting ourselves to humility by preferring our brethren to ourselves, by imagining them as if they were indeed our superiors; and by respecting them outwardly with a religious frankness and simplicity, as far as the condition of each of them can well permit. For though there ought to be an exterior difference between persons, according to the difference of their condition, yet, as to what concerns interior humility, our holy founder, who called our Society the least of all orders, will also have every one of us look upon himself as the least of all his brethren, and this is founded upon the sentiment of the apostle, "who will have every one through humility believe orders to be above him." (Philip. ii. 3.) This examen will be very profitable, provided we do not rest in the sole speculation thereof, but endeavour really to behave towards our brethren with the same humility and respect as if they were all our superiors. For if we did look upon them really as such, we should be very far from speaking to them with so much sharpness and roughness as we do—we should forbear saying anything to them which might displease and mortify them—we should not judge of their conduct with such freedom and rashness; and we should not be so easily offended at their language or behaviour to us. In the examen, therefore, which we shall make, we ought to observe all these things, and correct them, as so many faults.

For the seventh point of this particular examen, we may make a resolution to bear quietly all occasions of humiliation which may be offered us. You have been used, for example, to be offended when a sharp word is said to you—when you are haughtily or imperiously commanded to do anything, and when you think that you are not regarded so much as others. Let then the subject of your examen be, a resolution to bear quietly all things of this kind, and all others which may tend to a contempt of you; and be persuaded that you cannot make a more proper and profitable examen than this, to acquire the virtue of humility; for besides its being a very wise precaution against whatever may happen to you at all times, it is also a very efficacious way to raise you by degrees to the summit of virtue and perfection. You may then propose to yourself in your examen, first, to bear with patience all these things; afterwards to bear them easily and without repugnance; and lastly, to receive them with joy and to be glad at being despised; wherein, as we have already said, consists the perfection of humility.

In the last place, we may employ our particular examen in making both interior and exterior acts of humility; obliging ourselves to form so many in the morning, and so many in the evening; beginning at first with a few, but increasing every day the number, till we have acquired a perfect habit of humility. What I now say of this virtue may be easily applied to all other virtues; and thus the address and care which we shall use in dividing our enemies, and falling upon them separately, will make us get a speedier and easier victory.

———o———

CHAPTER XXIX.

Humility compatible with the desire of reputation.

A DOUBT which ordinarily occurs concerning humility, and which it is of great importance to solve, that we may hereupon know how to behave ourselves, is, whether according to the common opinion of all the holy fathers, we ought to wish to be contemned? The objection against it is, how, if we are despised, shall we be able to bring forth fruit for the good of souls? For to make an impression by what we say, and to gain credit with our audience, we must be in esteem with them; so that upon this account it seems even necessary to desire the esteem of men. St. Basil, St. Gregory, and St. Bernard, thoroughly and solidly discuss this question, and the solution they give to it is, that though the great danger we run by being honoured and esteemed by men ought to oblige us to avoid such honour: and though when we regard only ourselves we ought to wish always to be despised; yet we may, nevertheless, with a view to God's greater glory and service, desire their approbation and seek their esteem. Wherefore St. Bernard says, "it is true, that in regard to ourselves, we should always be willing to have others know us to be what we are, and that we should know ourselves too, that is to say, how full of weakness and defects we are; but that in respect of others, it is not convenient it should be so; and thus we may be sometimes permitted to wish that they may not know our faults, for fear they may be scandalized thereby, and so hindered in their spiritual proficiency." But we must understand this with simplicity of spirit, and not practise it but with great prudence, and with an eye still upon God. For these truths are subject to great abuse and inconvenience when they are not understood as they ought to be. The same holy fathers further explain this doctrine to us, to take away all pretence of making ill use of it. "It happens sometimes," says St. Gregory, "that good people rejoice at the good opinion which others have of them; but that is when they believe they can thereby do more good to their souls; and then they do not so much rejoice at the esteem had for themselves, as at the benefit of their neighbour." (Lib. 22, Moral. c. 5.) For there is a great difference between seeking the applause of men and rejoicing at the salvation of souls. It is one thing to love the esteem of the world for its own sake, and to regard nothing therein but one's own satisfaction, and the pleasure of glory, which is always criminal; and another thing to seek this esteem upon account of a good motive, as that of the advantage and salvation of your neighbour; for that cannot but be very commendable. It is, therefore, permitted to desire the esteem of men, provided it be for the greater glory of God, and their edification, and thereby to be able to work the more good in their souls; because it is not then to love one's own reputation, but the advantage only of our neighbour and the greater glory of God. In this manner, when a man has an aversion to physic, and takes a potion for his health, it is his own health which he loves and not the potion; so he, who at the same time that he despises the esteem of the world in his heart, seeks it as advantageous to the service of God and the good of souls, seeks the glory of God and not his own reputation.

Let us now see how it may be made known whether, when one rejoices at the esteem of men, it is purely for the glory of God and the advantage of his neighbour, or whether vanity or self-love have not a great share it it; for this is a very nice point, in which all the difficulty of this affair consists. St. Gregory teaches us how to solve it, and says, that "when one rejoices at the esteem of man, it must be with such a regard only to God, that, at the very same moment that this esteem serves no further for God's glory, and the salvation of our neighbour, it ought rather to be a pain than a joy to us." (Lib. 22, Moral.) So that if we look no further than ourselves, we ought do desire always to be despised, and receive with joy all occasions to that purpose, as having met with what we sought for; for it is never permitted to desire the approbation of men, or to be glad to have it, except with a view to God, and the advantage of our neighbour.

We read in the life of St. Ignatius that he used to say, if he had but given way to his fervour he should have run about the streets naked, and all over dirty, whereby to pass for a fool; but the excess of his charity, and the ardent desire he had to be useful in the conversion of souls, repressed those motions; and obliged him still to behave himself with such gravity and decency as was proper for him. His inclination was, nevertheless, to be despised; nor did he only embrace all occasions with pleasure that he might be so, but he even sought them with great earnestness. Now it is this will show upon what motive you are glad to be esteemed and valued by men; whether it is for the love of yourself, and for your own glory: or for the glory of God, and the salvation of souls. For if you do cheerfully embrace humiliations and contempt upon all occasions, and if all those occasions are heartily welcome to you, it is a sign that when you have succeeded either in a sermon or any other such like function, and that you have thereby gained credit and esteem, you do not then rejoice for your own interest, but for that of Almighty God, and for the benefit which your neighbour may get thereby. But if, when any occasion is offered to humble and depress you you reject it, or receive it not as you ought;—if you seek the praise of men, and take pleasure therein, even when it brings no good to your neighbour; it is a sign that the joy you feel springs from the consideration you have for yourself, and not for God, and that you regard not his glory, but your own.

It is true, therefore, to say, that the esteem and praise of the world have nothing of harm in themselves, when we know how to make good use of them, and therefore, that one may with a good conscience seek and desire them, as St. Xaverius did, when accompanied by a numerous and splendid retinue, he went to wait upon the king of Congo; nay, it may be even sanctity to praise one's self, provided it be done in the spirit it ought to be; and thus St. Paul also did, who, writing to the Corinthians, praises himself, and glories in the favours God had done him; saying, he had laboured more than all the other apostles; and he relates the revelations he had had; and his being rapt to the third heaven. But he did this, because then it was proper for the glory of God, and the good of those to whom he wrote. It was that they should the more easily acknowledge him for a true apostle of Jesus Christ, receive his doctrine, and thereby profit the more. He said these things too with a spirit which not only despised the glory of the world, but embraced contempt and reproach for the sake of Jesus Christ. For he knew when it was necessary, for the salvation of others, to give so advantageous an account of himself, as also when and how to humble and make himself of no reputation; saying, " that he was not worthy to be called an apostle, because he had persecuted the church of God." (1 Cor. xv. 9.) He called himself " one born out of due time, a blasphemer, a violent persecutor;" (1 Tim. i. 13); and when any occasion of being despised offered he was delighted therewith. Wherefore, for those who are thus disposed there is no fear when they accept any honour, or even speak to their own advantage; for they never do it but when they judge it necessary for the glory of God; and as it is not their own, but the glory and the good of souls they seek; so the honours they receive, and the praises they assume to themselves, leave not the least impression of vanity upon their heart.

But because it is very hard that the honour which is done us should not puff us up, and raise in us a vain satisfaction, hence it is that several saints, knowing the danger which usually accompanies great reputation, dignities, and high employments, endeavour to avoid those rocks, by retiring from the world, and employing themselves in mean and despicable offices; and they found that to be the most profitable for their spiritual progress which was the most proper to keep them humble, and the surest for their salvation. "I am not a true religious," says St. Francis, "if I receive not the scorn of men with greater joy than their praise. For if, when I preach or do any other good action which is for their advantage, I rejoice at the praises which the interest of their salvation obliges them to give me, and which put my own in danger; how much more ought I to rejoice at their scorn, in which I find a far greater advantage for my own salvation?" Certain it is, that we ought to be much more concerned for our own salvation than for that of another, because well ordained charity begins at home. If then you rejoice at the advantage of your neighbour, when you have had success in a sermon or in a business of charity, and are praised for it; why rejoice you not at your own advantage, when having done on your part as you ought, you receive only scorn, since this is the safest way for you to walk in? If you are glad to find you have a talent for the great employments which relate to the salvation of souls, why, if you are not fit for them, do you not rejoice at the benefit which you may derive from the sense of your own unworthiness, by humbling yourself before God? If you are pleased with vigorous health, that you may be the better able to labour more profitably in the service of your neighbour, why are not you as much pleased with being weak, infirm, and useless, as if you were employed in the greatest offices of charity; because you may turn it to your own profit, make use thereof to become humble, and so render yourself more agreeable to God, who wishes you to be in that state?

From all this it may easily be perceived, how much they deceive themselves who have an eye continually upon the esteem and reputation of the world, on pretence that it is a necessary means for the doing good to souls, and under that cloak seek honourable employment, and whatever has an air of dignity; and on the contrary avoid mean and humble offices, as things which degrade them in the opinion of men. There is another mistake also in acting thus. For it often happens that what a man believes ought to ensure him the esteem of the world makes him lose it, and that which he believes may make him lose it is the very thing that makes him gain it.

Some imagine that if they were coarsely clad, and employed in mean offices, they would not be held in that esteem which is requisite to labour successfully for the good of their neighbour.

But it is their pride that deceives them. Because those very circumstances will ensure them respect ; and the contrary will make them lose the esteem they expected. St. Ignatius was deeply convinced of this.—He says that " an humble, simple, and kind way of acting, contributes more to the conversion of souls than one that is grave and supercilious ; in which appears still some tincture of a worldly spirit." And he not only practised this himself, but when he sent forth labourers into the Lord's vineyard, he always counselled them to walk in the path of humility ; because whatever they should do would be firm and sure, when they built upon so solid a foundation ; and that God was wont to make use of such means to work the greatest things. Wherefore in all occasions he acted according to this principle; for when he sent St. Xaverius and Father Simon Rodriguez into Portugal, he enjoined them to beg alms as soon as they should arrive there in order that through poverty and humility they might make way for themselves to everything else. He also directed Father Salmeron and Father Pascasius, when they went afterwards as apostolic nuncios into Ireland, to catechise the children and common people. And when the same Salmeron and Father Laynez were sent the first time by Paul III. to the Council of Trent, as his Holiness's divines, the instruction which our holy founder gave them was, that every day before they gave their opinion in the council they should go and serve the sick in the hospital, and teach children the principles of the Catholic faith ; and that after that preparation they might give it freely; and that it would then be sure to be received with greater advantage ; as by the mercy of God it indeed was. And shall we, after all this, amuse ourselves in examining by the false rules of human prudence, whether or not it may be prejudicial to us to practise the same things ? No, no, let us not fear that by teaching the catechism, that by making exhortations in public places, in hospitals, or prisons, we detract from the dignity of the ministry of the gospel. Let us not fear to be less esteemed for having been seen to hear the confessions of poor people, or for wearing a habit suitable to the poverty of a religious. We shall on the contrary be the more esteemed for this, and by these means do more good to souls ; for God is pleased to exalt the humble, and it is by them that he usually accomplishes the greatest designs of his providence.

But though we should not attend to this reason, which nevertheless is the principal one, and should look upon things only

according to the true rules of human prudence, yet we can do
nothing more proper for gaining the esteem and favour of men,
and working successfully for the salvation of souls, than by being
employed in mean and humble offices ; and the more capable we
shall be of great things, it will be the more advantageous for our
reputation, and the edification of our neighbour, to stoop to little
ones.   The reason of this is, that the world makes so great an
account of marks of honour, esteem, and of great employments,
that it admires nothing more than to see any one make no account
thereof ; and to behold a man who is capable of the highest
things stoop to the lowest ; and hence it looks on persons of this
description as saints ; and receives their instructions as doctrine
that comes from heaven.

We read in the life of St. Xaverius, that being ready to embark for the Indies he would take no provisions with him for so
long a voyage ; and when the Earl of Castagnede, who was then
intendant of sea affairs for those parts, pressed him to take at
least somebody along with him to serve him on shipboard ; and
urged, among other things, that he would have less credit with
those for whose instruction he undertook the voyage if they
should see him wash his own linen and dress his own meat, he
answered, " Sir, that which has reduced the Church of God and
its prelates to the condition they are in at this day, is the esteem
and authority they endeavour to acquire by pomp and parade ;
and the true means which I must use to make myself be esteemed
is, to wash my old rags and to dress my meat myself, with out
giving any one else that trouble ; and, besides all this, to be continually busied in instructing and procuring the salvation of my
neighbour."   The Earl was so surprised, and edified at the same
time, at this answer, that he knew not what to reply.   It is therefore by the practice of humility that we obtain the esteem of
men and gain souls to God ; and, indeed, how many did this holy
man gain in the Indies by teaching the catechism to little children ; by ringing the bell in the night for the souls in purgatory ;
by serving and comforting the sick ; and by exercising himself
continually in the meanest and humblest offices of charity?   By
these means he acquired so great credit and reputation that he
won the hearts of all, and was called by no other name than that
of the holy man.   It is this sort of reputation we want for the
advancement and good of souls : reputation of humility, sanctity,
and zeal in the ministry of the gospel ; and we are only to endeavour and seek after such a reputation as this.   For, as to the

esteem we may pretend to gain by dignities and great employments, where something of the spirit of the world enters, it is
more prejudicial than profitable, and scandalizes rather than
edifies our neighbour.

A pious and learned author makes an excellent reflection upon
these words of our Saviour : " and I seek not my own glory :
there is one that seeks and judges." (John viii. 50.) " If our
heavenly Father," says he, " takes care himself to seek and procure our glory, it is to no purpose that we should seek it.   Let
us take care to humble ourselves, and to be what we ought to be,
and leave to God the care of our reputation, so far as he sees it
necessary for the good of souls."   The very thing we do for our
humiliation are those which he will make serviceable to acquire
an esteem for us, beyond that which we ourselves could have acquired by human ways.

And let us not imagine that the glory of our order is at stake;
for this is another kind of illusion, that serves only to give a
colour to self-love and vanity, which chiefly move us.   I do not
care at all for myself, you will say, but only for my order, for
which it is but just in me to have respect.   Fear nothing, your
order will never be in better repute than when you are humble,
reserved, and patient ; for what renders an order truly considerable is, to have those who belong to it humble, modest, mortified, and wholly weaned from all worldly things.

Father Maffeus, in his history of the Indies, tells us, that when
one of the fathers of the Society was preaching upon a certain
day the Christian faith in a public piazza of Firando, a city of
Japan, one of the idolaters of that place who was passing by fell
laughing both at him and what he said, and then spat full in
his face.   The preacher, without showing the least alteration, or
saying anything, wiped it off with his handkerchief and went
on with his sermon as if nothing had happened to him ; which
one of his auditors observing, began to reflect that a doctrine
which taught us to be so patient, so humble, and so composed,
could not but come from heaven ; and this affair made so strong
an impression upon him, that as soon as ever the good father
had concluded his sermon he went to him, and most earnestly
begged of him to instruct and baptise him.

—— o ——

CHAPTER XXX.

The third degree of humility.

THE third degree of humility is attained by him who having received great gifts from God, and seeing himself honoured and
esteemed, is so far from being puffed up thereby, that he attributes nothing to himself, but everything to the fountain of all
good, which is God. "And this third degree," says St. Bonaventure, "is attained by those only, who being already great
proficients in virtue, make their humility keep pace with their
perfection. That a man full of faults and imperfections should
acknowledge himself imperfect is always commendable, but no
great wonder ; no more than it is for the son of a peasant to say
he is not the son of a king. That a poor man should believe he
is poor, a sick man believe himself sick ; or that every one should
pass for what he is, is not to be wondered at ; but what is strange
indeed is, that he who is rich should rank himself among the
poor ; and that he who is above others, should descend to a level
with them." " We must not wonder then," says the same St.
Bonaventure, "that a wicked man believes himself wicked ; but
we ought, on the contrary, to wonder at him should he look upon
himself to be just and perfect ; as much as we wonder at a man
who, covered all over with leprosy, yet believes himself very
sound and healthy. But that a man of eminent virtue, replenished with Almighty God's grace, and truly great in his sight,
should reckon himself the least of all his brethren, is a true subject of admiration, and an extraordinary effect of humility.

" It is a great and rare virtue," says St. Bernard, " to do great
things, and yet not to think thyself great—to have thy sanctity
known to every one but to thyself—to appear an admirable man
to all, and yet a vile one in thy own sight; this," continues the
saint, " seems more to be admired than all other virtues."
(Serm. xiii. sup. Cant.) This humility the holy Virgin possessed
in a sovereign degree of perfection. For when she understood
that she was chosen to be the mother of God, she still acknowledged her own origin, and called herself " the handmaid of the
Lord;" (Luke i. 38), and when St. Elizabeth called her " blessed
among women," she did not ascribe to herself the glory of these
prerogatives she enjoyed, but gave all to God ; and taken up

wholly with thoughts of a most profound humility, offered up
her thanks to him for the favours he had showered down upon
her. "My soul," said she, "magnifies the Lord, and my spirit
rejoices in God my Saviour; for he has regarded the humility of
his handmaid." (Luke i. 46.) "This humility is practised even
in heaven itself, and this appears," says St. Gregory, "by the
vision which St. John had, 'of the four and twenty elders, who
fell down before him who sat on the throne; and worshipping
him, cast their crowns at the foot thereof;' for to 'cast thy
crown at the foot of the throne of God,' (Apoc. iv. 10), is not to
attribute thy victories to thyself, but to acknowledge that they
proceed wholly from him, and to give him all glory thereof as
they did, saying, 'thou art worthy, O Lord, to receive all glory,
honour and power, for thou hast created all things, and by thy
will they were and are created. It is but just for us to cast our
crowns at thy feet, because all that we have comes from thee,
and whatever good there is in us is the work of thy will, and
the effect of thy divine grace.' (Apoc. iv. 11.)" Thus, then, we
see that the third degree of humility consists in not being exalted
with the gifts we have received from God, and in not ascribing
the glory of them to ourselves, but wholly to him as the author
and dispenser of all good.

But, if it be in this that humility consists, some may say, we
are then all humble; for do we not acknowledge that what is
good in us comes from God, and that of ourselves we are nothing
but sin and misery? Who is there that will not say, that he
should be the worst man in the world if God abandoned him but
for one moment? "Thy destruction, O Israel, comes from thyself," says the Lord, by the prophet Osee, "but in me is thy
help." (Osee xiii. 9.) It is an article of faith that we have
nothing of our own stock but sin, and that we hold all the rest
from God's bounty; and thus we all seem to have that humility
of which we speak, because we all believe this evident truth,
which is to be seen in almost every page of holy writ. "Every
good and perfect gift," says the apostle St. James, "comes from
above and descends from the Father of lights." (Jam. i. 17.)
The same thing St. Paul expresses in several places of his epistles;
"what hast thou," says he, "that thou didst not receive? Of
ourselves we are not sufficient to think any good as of ourselves;
but our sufficiency is of God: it is God that works in you, both
to will and to do, according to his good pasture." (1 Cor. iv. 7.
&c.) Without him we cannot either do, or speak; begin or end;

or even will or think anything for our salvation; but all must come from God. And what clearer comparison can be given, to make us sensible of this truth, than that which our Saviour himself makes use of in St. John? "As the branch," says he, "cannot bear fruit of itself, except it remain in the vine, no more can ye, except you abide in me." (John xv. 4.) "I am the vine, ye are branches, he that abides in me and I in him, brings forth much fruit, for without me you can do nothing." What brings forth more fruit than the branch joined to the vine, and what is more useless when separated from it? What is it good for? "What shall be done with the vine tree," says the Lord to Ezechiel, "shall its wood be made use of to do any work, or can a pin be made of it to hang anything upon? It is good for nothing but to be thrown into the fire." (Ezech. xv. 2, 3.) This shows what we are when separated from the true vine, which is Jesus Christ. "If any one," says he, "abides not in me, he shall be cast forth as a branch, and shall wither, and then shall be gathered up and thrown into the fire to be burned." (John xv. 6.) Of ourselves, therefore, we are good for nothing but to be burned; or if we are anything, "it is by the grace of God that we are what we are." (1 Cor. xv. 10.) But every one being, as we have already said, fully convinced of all this, we must acknowledge that all that is good in us comes from God; that we have nothing of ourselves but sin; that we cannot ascribe the glory of anything to ourselves; and that it is due to God alone. Now, this truth being so evident and so universally admitted, and the disposition of mind it requires appearing at the same time so easy to a man of faith, we should not, one would think, have made the chief degree of humility to consist therein.

True, it is that it is a thing which seems easy at first sight, yet when it is considered not superficially, but at bottom, it is very hard and difficult. "It seems easy to beginners," says Cassian, "not to impute anything to themselves, nor to rely any way upon their own strength; to ascribe all to God, and to expect everything from him; but to do so, there is found indeed more difficulty than is imagined. For as we contribute something to our own good actions "which we perform, and in which we co-operate with God," (1 Cor. iii. 19,) it happens that we come unawares to rely too much upon ourselves, and presumption and pride gliding afterwards secretly into our heart, and representing our good deeds to us as our own work, we proceed so far as to be exalted thereupon, and to assume all the glory thereof to ourselves. Lastly, it is not so easy a business as it seems to restrain one's self herein; and we ought to be sufficiently convinced hereof, since the holy fathers have fixed in this self-restraint the chief degree of humility, and assert that the perfect only can attain it. For when we find favours heaped upon us, and consider the mighty things we perform, great perfection is, in good truth, required to give the glory to God, to whom it belongs, without assuming any of it or giving way to vain thoughts of complacency in ourselves. We must be endowed with very extraordinary virtue, and such as is very hard to be acquired, to see ourselves esteemed as saints by every one without receiving thereby some impression upon our heart.

"To be surrounded with honours without being any way moved, is," says St. Chrysostom, "as if a man should be among beautiful women without ever looking upon them otherwise than he should do." It is, therefore a difficult thing, and such as requires long-tried virtue. To look down from a very high place, and not have a giddiness, requires a good head; nor is every constitution adequate to that; for even Lucifer and his companions, when they saw themselves on so high a station as they were, became so giddy that they fell down into the bottomless pit. What destroyed him and them was that "he abode not in the truth," (John viii. 24,) that is to say, he abode not in his duty of acknowledging what he owed to God, but began to please himself with his own perfections; not that he believed that they proceeded from himself, for he knew very well that they all came from and depended upon God, who created him; but "by reason of his own beauty his heart was puffed up," says Ezechiel, "and he lost his wisdom because of his brightness." (Ezech. xxviii. 17.) Of the gifts of God he made to himself trophies of pride, as if he had not received them; and instead of ascribing all the honour and glory thereof to God, he himself gloried in them as if he had had them only of himself; so that though he knew by his understanding that the glory belonged to God, by his will, nevertheless, he robbed God of it, and attributed it to himself. The degree then of humility of which we speak is not so easy to arrive to as it seems; since the angels themselves have found it so difficult that, not knowing how to keep within bounds, they fell from the high station where God had placed them. Now if the angels could not see themselves so high without falling, how much more cause have we to fear; we, who are but miserable men, to whom with great reason these words of the prophet may be applied : "as soon as they shall find themselves honoured and exalted, they shall consume as the smoke that vanishes." (Psal. xxxvi. 20.) And, as smoke, the more it ascends the more it dissipates itself and vanishes; in like manner the more men find themselves exalted, the more they evaporate in thoughts of pride and vanity.

The Saviour of the world gives us warning himself to evade these rocks. He had sent forth his disciples to preach, and the gospel says that they returned full of joy, telling him that "the devils themselves became subject to them in his name." Where-upon he said to them, that "he saw Satan fall from heaven like lightning," (Luke x. 18,) as if he would have expressed himself thus : take heed, for it was pride which made Lucifer fall from heaven ; for, seeing himself so perfect, he fell into a vain conceit of himself, and instead of ascribing to God the glory of the gifts he had received of him, he made use of them as steps to his pride and rebellion : beware, lest something equally bad should happen to you. Beware, lest the miracles you work in my name should possess you with vain joy, and make you forget what you are. These words are directed to all those who are employed in the ministry of the gospel. Grow not proud because it hath pleased God to make use of you to benefit your neighbour, and to gain souls for heaven. Yield not to thoughts of vain-glory, when you see yourselves esteemed, honoured, and applauded. Take heed of being exalted at anything, or of suffering either the honour or praises given you to make the least impression upon your heart; for it was pride that destroyed Lucifer, and from an angel of light changed him into a spirit of darkness. "By this," says St. Austin, "may be seen how dangerous pride is, since it changes angels into devils ; and how estimable, on the contrary, humility is, since it makes men like unto angels."

---o---

CHAPTER XXXI.

In what the third degree of humility consists.

WE have not yet sufficiently explained in what the third degree of humility consists, so that it is necessary to explain it a little more fully, that the practice thereof may be made easier, which is all we pretend to. The holy fathers say, that it consists in knowing how to distinguish what we are by the mercy of God, from what we are by the corruption of our own nature ; thereby to give to every one what is his own; to God what proceeds from him ; and to ourselves, what is purely ours. And hence this degree consists, not in simply knowing that we cannot either do or merit anything as of ourselves ; that whatever good there is in us, comes from God; and that it is "God that works in us, both to will and to do according to his good pleasure ;" (Phil. i. 13) ; for this truth being taught us by faith, if we are Christians we must be convinced thereof; but it consists in having this know-ledge so imprinted in our hearts, that we never fail upon all occasions to reduce it to practice. And St. Ambrose says it is that which cannot be done without Almighty God's particular grace ; and thereupon he quotes this passage of St. Paul, "but we have received not the spirit of this world, but the spirit which is of God, that we may know the things that are given to us by God." (1 Cor. ii. 12.) It is, according to the apostle, a most particular grace of Almighty God, to know how to discern the gifts which we have received of him, and to attribute them purely unto his bounty : and according to Solomon, it is great wisdom to do so. "I knew," says he, "that I could not keep myself con-tinent, if God had not given me the grace to do it, and even that was great wisdom, to know from whom it proceeded." (Wisd. viii. 21.) Now, it is in what St. Paul looks upon as "a most particular gift of the Spirit of God," and in what Solomon calls "the greatest wisdom," that the third degree of humility consists. "What hast thou that thou didst not receive ; and if thou didst receive it, why dost thou glory, as if thou hadst not received it?" (1 Cor. iv. 7.)

This is the humility that was practised by the saints, who, though enriched by the gifts of heaven, raised to the top of perfection, esteemed and honoured by every one, looked never-theless upon themselves as despicable in the sight of God, and remained always steadfast in the knowledge of their own empty and mean condition. Applause and honours raised in them no vain thoughts ; because they knew how to distinguish what did and what did not belong to them ; so that looking upon the favours which were heaped upon them, and the honours and respects which were paid them, as things received from God, they gave him all the glory ; and considering at the same time that of themselves they neither had or could do anything, they humbled themselves before him under the sense of their own meanness. From thence it was, that although they saw them-selves honoured and respected, it made no impression upon them, nor did they thereupon set a higher value and esteem upon themselves ; nay, on the contrary, they looked upon the honours which were given them not to be directed to them, but to God, whom they belonged to ; and in his glory they placed all their joy and content.

It is then with great reason that the perfect only are said to be capable of this kind of humility ; because in the first place, it presupposes great gifts and favours of God, which is what makes men truly great in his sight.   And secondly, because to be really great before God and in the sight of men, and to be nevertheless contemptible in our own eyes, is a very rare and sublime perfection. It is that which St. Chrysostom and St. Bernard admired particularly in the apostles, and several other great saints, who being replenished with the gifts of God, raising the dead, and working daily an infinity of other miracles, which made them be esteemed by every one, preserved nevertheless, in the midst of all honours done them, as deep a sense of their own meanness as if they had had none of those advantages at all; but as if another had been the instrument of what they did; or as if the honours which were given them had been given to others.   " To be humble when we are low and despicable is not," says St. Bernard, " a strange thing ; for a low condition, and contempt, serve to make us know what we are; but to be honoured and esteemed by all, to be looked upon as a saint and as a man come down from heaven, and yet remain as sensible of our mean and low condition and nothingness as if we possessed no advantage above others, is a very eminent and extraordinary virtue indeed." (Hom. 4 sup. missus est.) " Thus they do," says the same saint, "who perform as they ought what our Saviour commands in these words : 'let your light so shine before men, that they may see your good works and glorify your Father who is in heaven ;' (Matt. v. 16,) and these are they who truly imitate the apostle, and are true preachers of the gospel, 'and who preach not to themselves, but Christ Jesus.' " (2 Cor. iv. 5.)   These, in fine, are the good and faithful servants, " who seek not their own interest," (1 Cor. xiii. 5,) who rob God of nothing, and attribute nothing to themselves, but render faithfully all things to him, and give him the glory of all.   And therefore they shall one day hear from the mouth of our Lord, these words : " well done, thou good and faithful servant; because thou hast been faithful over a few things, I will make thee ruler over many." (Matt. xxv. 21.)

——o——

CHAPTER XXXII.

A more ample explanation of the same subject.

WE have shown that a man attains the third degree of humility when, having received great gifts from God, and seeing himself honoured and esteemed, he is neither puffed up, nor does he attribute anything to himself; but ascribes all to the fountain of all things, which is God; giving him the glory of everything, and retaining as deep a sense of humility and lowliness as if he did nothing, and were not endowed with any virtue at all. Our intention, nevertheless, is not to assert that we should not act on our part, or that we have no share in the good works we do. For that would be a very erroneous proposition; since it is very certain that our free will concurs and operates jointly with God in every good work, by reason that the assent we give thereunto, whereby we put ourselves upon acting, is a free consent; since all that we will, and all that we do, we do it by a free motion of our will; and it is in our power to do or not to do it. On the contrary, even that which makes this third degree of humility so hard to attain is, that on the one hand, we must use all care and diligence imaginable to acquire virtue, to resist temptations, and to be successful in all our pious undertakings, as if our own strength were sufficient to ensure success; and on the other hand, that we may, after having done all that depended on us, be obliged to confide no more therein than as if we had done nothing we must look upon ourselves as unprofitable servants, and put our confidence in God alone, according to these words of our Saviour: "When ye shall have done all that is commanded ye, say still, we are unprofitable servants, we have done nothing but what we ought to have done." He does not say, "when ye shall have done part of what is commanded ye, but when ye shall have done all that is commanded ye." (Luke xvii. 10.) Now, to look upon one's self as unprofitable after that, there is very great need of a most profound humility. "He that is sensible that he is but an unprofitable servant, and that all he can do is not sufficient to make him master of any virtue, but that virtue is a gift of God's pure bounty, he," says Cassian, "will not be puffed up, when he has acquired it; because he will be very sensible that he gained it, not by his own care but by an effect

of the mercy of God to him, according to the words of the apostle,
' what have you, which you have not received ?' "

St. Austin explains this by an excellent comparison, where he
says, "that without the grace of God, we are like a body without
a soul." As a dead body is incapable of motion; so we, without
the grace of God, are incapable of any meritorious action in his
sight; and as life and motion are not to be attributed to the body,
but to the soul that animates it ; so the soul must not ascribe to
itself the good actions which it does, but to God alone, who
quickens it by his grace, and gives it the means to perform them.
In another place he says further, "that as the eyes of the body,
let them be ever so well disposed, cannot see anything without
the help of light ; so, how righteous soever a man may be, he can
do no good, without being assisted by the divine light of grace."
"If the Lord keeps not the city, the watchman wakes but in
vain." (Ps. cxxvi. 1.) "Oh what a happiness would it be for
men," the same St. Austin cries out, "if they did but know
themselves, and if they who glory, did glory in the Lord?"
(Confes. Lib. ix.) If God, by dissipating the clouds of their
mind by a ray of his light, made them fully sensible that whatever is created has its being from him, subsists only by him, and
has no good in itself but that which it pleases the divine mercy
to shower down upon and preserve in it. Now this is properly
the third degree of humility ; though after all we can say to
make it rightly understood, we must own that our words still
fall short in expressing its perfection ; because the theory or
speculation thereof is as sublime as its practice is difficult.

We may add further, that it consists " in the reckoning ourselves as nothing,"which is so much recommended by all masters
of a spiritual life. It consists, according to St. Benedict and
other saints, in a deep sense of our own unworthiness in all
things ; in the continual diffidence of ourselves, and our entire
confidence in God, of which the scripture so often speaks ; and,
in fine, in that real contempt of one's self, which it is to be
wished we had as often in our heart as in our mouth ; it being
that which so palpably convinces us, that of ourselves we share
in nothing but sin and misery, and that whatever good we have
or do, we neither have it or do it as of ourselves, but hold it all
from God, and to him we ought to ascribe all the glory.

If now, after all this, you do not yet comprehend well what
this degree of humility is, be not surprised : for the theory, as
we have already said, is so very sublime, that it is not strange if

we do not easily conceive what it is. Thus it happens in all arts and sciences, that what is most common in every art and science is easily understood by everybody; but none but such as are masters in it are well versed in the secrets and niceties thereof. So every one conceives easily what is most common and ordinary in virtue, but the perfect only are well acquainted with the whole excellence of it. Wherefore St. Laurence Justinian said, " that nobody knows well what humility is but he who has received it from God;" and thence it comes, that the saints who were endowed with profound humility said things of themselves which we, who are not arrived at so high a degree of virtue, cannot well comprehend, and such as seem to us mere exaggerations; as for example, that they were the greatest sinners in the world, and several such like expressions. For so far are we from saying or thinking such things of ourselves, that we cannot so much as comprehend how others could say so; the reason is, because we are not endowed with so profound humility as they were, and so know not the excellence and secrets thereof. Wherefore endeavour to become humble, and to profit every day more and more in the science of humility, and you will then comprehend how things of this kind may be said with truth of one's self.

----o----

CHAPTER XXXIII.

A further explanation of the third degree of humility; and whence it comes that they who are truly humble still look upon themselves as the least and worst of all.

THAT we may conceive yet better the excellence of this third degree of humility, and fortify ourselves in it, we must ascend higher to take a view of things. We have already shown that we hold our natural being and faculties from God; because of ourselves we were nothing, and therefore incapable either of the operations of our senses, or of those of our memory, will, or understanding; it being God alone that has made us capable of them, by giving us our being; and, consequently, it is to him we ought to ascribe both the being we have and the natural faculties which accompany it. The same may be said of our supernatural being, and of the operations of grace; and with so much the more reason, as grace is infinitely above nature; for we hold not from ourselves supernatural being, but from God;

which is a being of grace, that he has freely added to our natural being. "By nature we were the children of wrath," (Eph. ii. 3,) born in sin, and enemies of God. "God has called you out of darkness to his marvellous light." (1 Pet. ii. 9.) Of enemies, he has made us friends; and of slaves, children; of objects of hatred and anger, which we were, he has rendered us acceptable in his sight. Nor was he moved thereunto either in consideration of our former merits or future services, but out of his own pure mercy and the merits of our only mediator, Jesus Christ; since, according to the words of the apostle, "we are justified freely by the grace of God, and by the redemption that is in Jesus Christ." (Rom. iii. 14.) Now, as we cannot make ourselves out of nothing, nor give ourselves the natural faculties we enjoy, all which are the pure gift of the liberality of God, to whom alone we owe entirely the glory thereof; so cannot we of ourselves get out of the darkness of sin, in which we were, and in which we have been conceived, except God by his infinite goodness draws us out of it; and it is impossible to do any meritorious action for the gaining everlasting life, if he gives us not the grace to do it. For it is the grace of God which stamps a merit upon our actions; as the coin of the prince gives value to money. Thus ought we to ascribe all the glory to God alone, who is the author of grace as well as of nature; and to have always in our mouths and hearts these words of the apostle, "by the grace of God I am what I am."

Moreover, as we have shown that in the order of nature it is God, who has not only given us our being, but continually preserves us in it—who, sustaining us by his Almighty hand, hinders us from relapsing into the abyss of nothing out of which he has drawn us; so also in the order of grace, it is not only God who has drawn us out of the darkness of sin to the marvellous light of his grace, but it is he who holds us continnally by the hand to hinder us from falling back into the abyss. So that should he withdraw his hand but one moment, and permit the devil to tempt us at his pleasure, we should at the same instant relapse into our former sins, and into several other more heinous ones. "Because the Lord is at my right hand," says David, "nothing can be able to move me." (Ps. xv. 8.) It is thy grace, O Lord, which draws us out of our sins, and it is that hinders us from relapsing into them. If I have risen again it is because thou hast reached out thy hand to me; and if I now stand it is because thou upholdest me.

Now, as I have shown that this consideration is sufficient to convince us in natural things that we are nothing, because in reality we are and were nothing of ourselves, and should be still so did not God preserve us every moment; so ought the same consideration suffice in the things of grace, to convince us that we are still sinners. Because we really are and were nothing of ourselves but sinners; nor should we be anything else, if God did not always hold us by the hand.

Albertus Magnus, therefore, says, that he who will acquire humility ought to plant the root of it in his heart; that is, he ought to make it his study to find out his own weakness and misery, and to comprehend not only how weak and miserable he is, but to what a degree of weakness he would be reduced, even in the very moment of his reflecting upon himself, did not God, through his infinite goodness, turn him from the occasions of sin, and help and succour him in temptations. Into what sins should not I have fallen, O my God, if by thy mercy thou hadst not delivered me? How many times hast thou removed from me the occasions of sin, which might have overcome me, since David himself yielded to them, if thou who knowest my weakness hadst not put them out of my way? How many times hast thou tied up the hands of the devil, to hinder him from tempting me so far as he could, or that he should not tempt me at least beyond my power to resist? How often might I have said with the prophet, " unless the Lord had helped me, my soul had almost descended into hell." (Ps. xciii. 17.) How often, when I was attacked and staggered, have I been upheld by thy Almighty hand ; " if I said, my foot slips, thy mercy, O Lord, succoured me." (Ps. xciii. 18.) How often, alas ! should I have been destroyed, had not God by his goodness and infinite mercy preserved me ! These are the thoughts we ought to have of our weakness and misery, as we are nothing of ourselves but weakness and misery ; and should fall into all manner of disorders if God did abandon us, or withdraw his hand from us but for a moment.

Hence it is that many holy men have sought occasions to enter into such thoughts of so profound humility that, not content to be reckoned barely wicked, they have looked upon themselves as the greatest sinners upon the face of the earth. God raised St. Francis to so high a degree of perfection, and designed so eminent a seat in glory for him, that he one day showed that saint's companion the place he had reserved for him in heaven, among the seraphims; yet the same religious asking the saint afterwards what opinion he had of himself—"I think," answered he, "that there is not in the world a greater sinner than myself." St. Paul believed the same thing of himself; "Jesus Christ came into the world," says he, " to save sinners, of whom I am the chief." (1 Tim. i. 15.) Thus he teaches us to abide in the same sentiments of humility as he did, to value ourselves less than any body, and to prefer every body to ourselves. "For the apostle deceives us not in this," says St. Austin, " nor teaches us flatteries, when he writes to the Philippians, that every one of them should in humility esteem others better than themselves;" and to the Romans also, " that they should in honour prevent one another." (Rom. xii. 10.) It was not out of feigned humility that the saints styled themselves the greatest sinners upon earth, it was because they really thought so; and when they recommend to us the practice of this exercise, it is because they wish us to think seriously that we are great sinners, and not to be content with pretending to think that we are so.

St. Bernard, examining these words of our Saviour, " when thou shalt be invited to a marriage, sit down in the lowest place;" observes, that " he says not sit down in one of the middle places, or in one of the lowest, but ' sit down in the last place ;' in order," says the saint, " that you may not pretend, not only not to prefer yourself, but not so much as to equal yourself to any body, he orders you to take the last place, that is to say, to look upon yourself as the most unworthy of all, and as the greatest sinner." Nor do you expose yourself to any danger in thus giving place to all; but you would run a great hazard by pre- ferring yourself to any one. For, as in passing through a low door there is no danger in stooping too much, but you may easily break your head should you stoop ever so little less than you ought; so there is no hazard in much humbling yourself, but a great peal in not doing it enough, and in preferring your- self to any one whomsoever.

How know you but that he whom you do not only think more wicked than yourself, but whom you look upon as the worst of all men, may become a better man than you or any one else; or whether he be not so already in the sight of God ? How know you whether God may not change his hand, and prefer him to you; as Jacob did, when he blessed Ephraim the younger bro- ther, before Manasses the elder? How know you what God may have wrought in his heart since yesterday ; nay, since the very last moment ? " For in an instant he can easily enrich the poor." (Ecclus. xi. 23.) He needs only to look with an eye of mercy upon him. Of a publican, and persecutor of his church, he can make an apostle and preacher of his name ; " of stones he can raise up children to Abraham ;" (Matt. iii. 9) ; and in a moment make hardened sinners become his own children. How much was the Pharisee mistaken who judged so ill of St. Mary Magdalen ? The parable which our Saviour made use of, to re-prove him for the censuring of her, made him sensible that she whom he believed a public sinner was become more righteous than himself. Wherefore St. Bennet, St. Thomas, and several other saints say, that one of the twelve degrees of humility is to believe and to own one's self the least of all ; and it is not suffi-cient only to express it with our lips, but it must also come from our very heart. " Believe not," says the author of the Imita-tion of Christ, " that you are a proficient in virtue if you look not on yourself as the least of all your brethren." (Lib. ii. c. 2.)

———o———

CHAPTER XXXIV.

How just and holy men may with truth look upon themselves as the worst and last of men ; and style themselves the greatest sinners in the world.

HAVING shown that we ought to try to arrive so far as to reckon ourselves the least of all, and to look upon ourselves as the greatest sinners in the world : it will not be a vain curiosity, but a very profitable inquiry, to explain how the greatest saints could truly have such thoughts of themselves as these. Some of them, being content to have these thoughts in their heart, were unwilling to answer questions put them on this subject—and thus the holy Abbot Zosimus expressed himself before a certain philosopher, saying, " he believed himself the greatest sinner in the world ; and being asked by him, how he could have so bad an opinion of himself, since he knew very well that he observed God's commands :—"All that I can tell you," answered he, " is that I know that I speak truth, and that I am very sensible of what I say ; ask me therefore no more." But St. Austin, St. Thomas, and several other saints answer the question, and solve it differently. St. Austin's and St. Thomas' solution thereof is, that when a man looks upon his own faults, and considers at the

same time the hidden favours which God does or can do his
neighbour, he may then with truth say of himself that he is the
greatest of sinners; because he is acquainted with his own faults,
but knows not the secret gifts which his brother has received of
God.   But you will say, I see him every day commit such and
such sins and imperfections which I commit not !   And how
know you what God may have wrought in his heart even since
the last moment ?   How know you but in that instant he may
have conferred upon him some particular grace, whereby he may
become more righeeous than you?   The Pharisee and the Publican
entered at the same time into the temple to pray.   The Pharisee
looked upon himself as righteous, and the publican on himself as a
sinner; our Saviour, nevertheless, says, "that the last went down
to his house justified, and the Pharisee departed out of the temple
with his own condemnation." (Luke xviii. 14.)   This example
ought to suffice for our instruction, never to prefer nor even to equal
ourselves to any one ; but to keep still in the last place, which
is the only one where we may with security put ourselves.

To him that is truly humble, it is easy to look upon himself as
the least of all.   For, in his brethren he sees nothing but what
is good, and nothing in himself but his own faults ; and he is so
taken up in considering and seeking how to amend them, that
believing he has cause enough to weep for them, he never looks
up to behold what is amiss in others ; and for that reason, he
has a good opinion of all his brethren, and an ill one of himself
alone ; nay, the more he increases in sanctity, the more easy he
finds it to humble himself in this manner ; not only because as
he makes proficiency in other virtues he does so in humility and
in the knowledge of himself, and comes thereby to have a greater
contempt of himself; but, also, because the more sensible he is of
the goodness and mercy of God, the more acquainted he is with
his own misery ; and thus, "one abyss carrying him into another," (Ps. xli. 8,) from the abyss of the greatness of God into
that of his own nothingness, he sees by the light of grace into
the very least of his own imperfections.   Now, if we set any
value upon ourselves, the reason is, because we have little knowledge of God and are not illuminated with light from heaven ;
the rays of the sun of justice have not yet penetrated into our
soul, and so far are we from being able to discover the least
atoms of dust, which are our small faults, that we become so
blind as not to discern the greatest imperfections.

To this may be added, that humility is so agreeable to God

that the better to preserve it in the heart of his servants he often so conceals the favours which he confers upon them and so secretly impart his gifts to them, that even he who receives them perceives them not; nor believes he has received anything. "All the beauty of the tabernacle," says St. Jerome, "was covered with the skins of beasts and goat's hair;" and thus it is, that God is sometimes wont to hide under temptations the excellency of his gifts and benefits, and to suffer even some small faults in his servants, that so humility may be preserved in them, as coals are kept alive under ashes.

St. John Climachus says, that the devil, who seeks nothing but our destruction, endeavours to set continually our virtues and good actions before our eyes, that so he may make us proud; and that God, on the contrary, who desires only our salvation, gives particular light to his elect, to make them perceive even the least of their imperfections; and hides the favours he bestows upon them in such manner, that often they perceive not when they receive them. All holy writers teach the same doctrine; and St. Bernard says, "that it is by a particular disposition of the divine goodness which is pleased to keep us humble, that the greater progress one ordinarily makes in perfection the less he thinks he has made; for when any one is arrived at the highest degree of virtue, God permits that something of the perfection of the lowest should yet remain to be acquired, that he may not think he is advanced so far as he is." (De quat. mod. oran.) Thus the comparison which is made between humility and the sun, is a very just one; for as the stars disappear, and hide themselves before the sun, so when humility shines truly in souls, all other virtues hide themselves before it in such manner, that they who are humble indeed seem to themselves to have no virtue at all. "They are the only persons," says St. Gregory, "who see not in themselves the exemplary virtues which all the world admires." (Lib. xxii. Mor. ca. 5.) When Moses came down from mount Sinai, where he had forty days conversed with God face to face, "his countenance shone so bright, that all the children of Israel," says the scripture, "beheld it, and he alone knew not that his face was shining, because of the conversation he had had with the Lord." (Exod xxxiv. 29.) So it is with the humble man; he alone sees not his own virtues; and whatever he does see in himself appears full of imperfections; nay, he even thinks that he sees but the least parts of his faults; and that those which he sees not are much more numerous; and thus can he easily look upon himself as the least of all his brethren, and believes that he alone is the greatest sinner in the world.

True it is, that though God leads many saints, in this way which we have shown, by hiding from them the favours he confers on them ; yet the means he makes use of for the conduct of his elect are different ; for he sometimes discovers his gifts to those upon whom he bestows them, that hereby they may esteem and acknowledge them as much as they ought to do. St. Paul therefore said, "but we have not received the spirit of the world, but the spirit which is of God, that we might know the things which are given to us by God." (1 Cor. ii. 12.) And does not the holy Virgin, in her spiritual song, say, "that she magnifies the Lord ; because the Almighty had done great things to her." (Luke i. 49.) This knowledge is so far from being contrary to humility and perfection, that it is even accompanied with so perfect a humility, that for that reason it is called the humility of the perfect.

In this, notwithstanding, there is so great danger of abuse, that holy writers warn us to beware thereof ; the abuse is, that sometimes one thinks he is more enriched with the favours of God than he really is. Witness that unfortunate man to whom the Lord directs these words of the Apocalypse : " Thou sayest, I am rich, and abound with all things, and have need of nothing, and knowest thou not that thou art miserable, poor, blind, and naked ?" (Apoc. iii. 17.) In the same error was the Pharisee in the gospel, "who gave God thanks that he was not as other men ;" (Luke xviii. 11) ; he thought that he had greater advantages above them which he had not ; and preferred himself to them for that very reason. Now this sort of pride sometimes creeps so secretly into our heart, that we are often full of ourselves without perceiving it ; wherefore it is good to have our eyes always open upon the virtues of others, and shut upon our own ; and to live thus in this holy fear will with more security preserve the gifts of God in us.

As God, nevertheless, has not obliged himself to conduct every one by this way, but leads his elect by several paths ; so it now and then happens that he does the favour to some which he did to St. Paul, to make them know the greatness of those gifts which they have received from him. Now this being so, how can it happen, it may be said, that they who see the divine favours heaped upon them can truly believe themselves the least of all men ; and assert that they are the greatest sinners in the world? That he, indeed, from whom God hides the gifts which he confers on him, and who finds no virtue in himself, but a great many imperfections and defects, should have these thoughts of himself, is not difficult to conceive; but that they who know to what a height God has raised them should have the like thoughts, is very hard to comprehend.—Yet all this may very well be. Wherefore be but as humble as St. Francis, and you will quickly conceive it. When he was one day pressed by his companion to tell him, how he could have so low an opinion, and speak of himself as he did?—"I am," said the saint, "fully convinced, that had the greatest sinner received the same favours that I have, he would have made better use of them than I have done; and, on the contrary, I firmly believe, that did God withdraw his hand from me but one moment, I should fall into the most extravagant enormities in the world, and be the worst of men; therefore do I look upon myself as the greatest and most ungrateful of all sinners. This answer is very just, and flows from a great stock of humility, and at the same time contains admirable doctrine. For it is thoughts of this kind moved the saints to humble themselves, and to stoop to the very centre of the earth; and made them fall down at every one's feet, and truly reckon themselves the greatest sinners. The knowledge of our own weakness, which is the root of humility, was so fixed in their hearts, that they easily distinguished what they were in themselves from what they were by grace; wherefore, considering that if God left them but one moment they might have grown the greatest sinners, they always looked upon themselves as such; and upon the gifts of God as borrowed favours, which, instead of making them less humble, did, on the contrary, inspire them with a more profound sense thereof. Because they always thought, that they made not that use they ought of the benefits they had received; so that on whatever side we turn our eyes, whether we cast them down upon what we have of ourselves, or lift them up to behold what we have received from God, we shall always find occasion to humble and esteem ourselves less than all others.

St. Gregory, upon this occasion, lays great weight upon the words of David, when it being in his power to kill Saul in the cave into which he was entered and letting him go out of it again without intending him any harm, he cried to him from afar: "Whom pursuest thou, O king of Israel?—thou pursuest a dead dog and a flea." (1 Kings xxiv. 15.) "David," says this saint,

" was already anointed king, and had been informed by Samuel, who had anointed him, that God intended to take the kingdom from Saul to confer it upon him ; he nevertheless humbles himself and bows to him, though he knew that even by the choice of God he was preferred to him ; and was more acceptable than he in the sight of the Most High. This shows us very well, that we ought, with much more reason, to place ourselves beneath our brethren ; because we know not in what degree of esteem they are in God's sight.

———o———

CHAPTER XXXV.

That the third degree of humility is a means to overcome all kind of temptations, and to acquire all virtues in perfection.

CASSIAN says, that it was a constant tradition and a sort of first principle among the fathers of the desert, that one could not acquire purity of heart, or the perfection of other virtues if he were not first convinced that all the care he could take of himself in order thereunto was to no purpose, without God's particular assistance, who is the author and giver of all good. " And the knowledge of this," adds he, " must not be a knowledge of speculation only, founded either on what we have heard, or what we have read, or on the revelations of faith ; it must be a knowledge of practice and experience that makes this truth so palpable that we may touch it as it were with our very finger ; so that this is, indeed, the third degree of humility, of which we speak. And of this sort of humility are those many passages of Scripture to be understood which promise the humble so great rewards ; wherefore with great reason it is that holy writers fix the chief degree of humility in this knowledge we speak of, and hold, that it is the foundation of all virtues, and a necessary disposition to receive all other gifts of God. Cassian afterwards treats more particularly this subject, and coming to speak of chastity, says, that all the endeavours we can make to acquire it signify nothing, till by experience we are sensible that we cannot acquire it by our own strength, but that it must be a gift of the liberality and mercy of God. With this the doctrine of St. Austin agrees very well. He says, that the chief way to obtain and preserve chastity is, not to believe that of ourselves we can acquire it or by our care, because we deserve to lose it, when we lay any stress on our own strength ; but by believing that it must be a gift of God, that it must come from above, and that from thence all must be expected."

This it is which made an ancient hermit say that one could never be delivered from temptations of impurity, till he were first thoroughly convinced that chastity is a gift of God, and not an effect of our own care. This is confirmed by the example which Palladius relates of an abbot called Moses, who being of a strong and vigorous constitution, and given to incontinence, suffered in the beginning of his conversion great temptations of impurity, which he endeavoured to overcome by all the means several holy fathers of the desert had counselled him to make use of. He was continually at his prayers, and gave himself so much thereunto for six years together, that he usually passed the greatest part of the night standing at them ; he laboured very much with his hands, ate nothing but a little bread, carried water up and down to the cells of the ancient fathers, and exercised himself continually in the practice of several other austerities. With all this, notwithstanding, he could not overcome the temptations which tormented him ; the attacks whereof were so violent that he was in danger of sinking under them, and of quitting the solitary life he led. Being thus troubled in mind, the holy abbot Isidore, coming to him as sent from God, told him, " I assure you in the name of Jesus Christ, that your temptations shall forthwith cease ;" as indeed they then did for good and all. " But, Moses, if thou wouldst know," continues the saint, " why God has not given thee a perfect victory over them till now, it is because he would not have thee attribute it to thyself, or become proud thereupon, as if thou hadst by thy own strength obtained it ; so that it is for thy good that he has permitted thee to be so long tempted." Moses had not as yet an entire diffidence in himself ; and Almighty God, that he might bring him to it, and hinder him from falling into proud and presumptuous thoughts, permitted him to be so long a time exposed to such strong and violent assaults ; and did not permit that the practice of so many holy exercises should ensure him an entire victory over a passion, which others had conquered with a great deal less pains.

The same Palladius says, that the like happened to abbot Pacomius, who was subject to temptations of impurity, even to the age of threescore and ten, and who once upon oath assured him, that after he was fifty years old, he had for twelve years together suffered such frequent and severe assaults, that not a day or night passed, wherein he had not to defend himself against some or other of that nature; for all that he could do to preserve or free himself availed nothing; so that complaining one day that he thought God had forsaken him, he heard a voice within him say —"know, that thou hast been so long exposed to such severe assaults that thou mightest be the better acquainted with thy own weakness and how little thou art able to perform of thyself; and that being thus stripped of all the confidence thou hadst in thyself, thou mightest fall down before me, and in all things have recourse only to me." After this he found himself so comforted and strengthened, that he never after had the like temptation. So that God will have us put all our trust in him alone, and none at all in ourselves.

Now, this doctrine is not only St. Austin's, Cassian's, and that of the ancient fathers of the desert, but it is also the Holy Ghost's; who speaks thereof in the book of Wisdom in terms, wherein the practise is joined to the speculation. "When I found," says Solomon, "that I could not be endowed with continency, otherwise than by the gift of God, and even that it was a point of great wisdom to know from whom the gift came, I prostrated myself before the Lord, and prayed to him with my whole heart." (Wisd. viii. 21.) The word continency is here a general word, whith signifies not only a resistence to motions contrary to chastity, but also the moderation of whatever is against reason; and in the same sense this other passage of Ecclesiasticus is to be understood: that "a continent soul is worth all the riches in the world;" (Ecclus. xxvi. 20); that is, he who keeps all his passions within the bounds of reason and virtue. Solomon hereby signifies, that knowing he could not contain his passions within the bounds of virtue without God's particular grace (and it was, as he said, great wisdom to know that without God's help one can do nothing,) he had recourse to God, and prayed to him with all his heart to be assisted by his grace. So that this knowledge is a proper means to keep us continent, to repress and regulate our passions; to get the victory over all temptations, and to acquire all virtues in perfection. This the royal prophet confesses when he says, "unless the Lord builds the house, they that build it labour in vain; and unless the Lord keeps the city, the watchman watches but in vain." (Ps. cxxvi. 1.) It is God must bestow gifts upon us; and it is he that must preserve them in us after having bestowed them; otherwise whatever we shall do will be to no purpose.

CHAPTER XXXVI.

That humility is not contrary to magnanimity, but is the source and foundation thereof.

ST. THOMAS, treating of magnanimity, proposes this difficulty : " holy writers, and the gospel," says he, "teach us on the one hand that humility is very necessary for Christians ; and on the other hand, that magnanimity is very necessary for them also; but more especially for those who are exalted to high employments. These two virtues, however, appear directly opposite ; for magnanimity is a greatness of courage, which urges us to undertake grand and glorious things ; yet nothing seems more contrary to humility than this. Because, in the first place, the undertaking of great things seems wholly repugnant to humility ; for one of the degrees of this virtue is to acknowledge and believe that we are unworthy of everything, and good for nothing ; and it is presumptuous to attempt what we are not capable to perform. In the second place, to attempt things which entitle us to honour seems still a further acting against humility ; because he who is truly humble ought to be far from so much as thinking how to attain honour." These objections St. Thomas answers well, and says, that though these two virtues seem contrary to one another if we look only to the exterior, yet they are not so ; not only because no virtue can be contrary to another, but because humility and magnanimity are very like, and depend upon each other.

First, as to the attempting great things, which is the property of magnanimity, it is so far from being contrary to humility, that it is what belongs properly to none but to him who is truly humble. To attempt great things upon our own strength would, indeed be presumption and pride ; for what can we do of ourselves, since, according to the apostle, " we are not able even to think anything as of ourselves ? " (2 Cor. iii. 5.) But likewise it is only upon the diffidence in ourselves, and our confidence in God, that Christian magnanimity lays the foundation of great enterprises ; and humility does the same. For, the reason why holy writers call it the foundation of all virtues is, as we have already said, because it is that which breaks the ground for the spiritual building ; which digs the foundations, and throws out the light and sandy earth, till coming to the solid stone, which is Christ Jesus, it begins to build thereupon.

Upon this passage of the Canticles, " who is she that comes up from the wilderness, breathing nothing but perfumes, and leaning on her beloved ? " (Cant. viii. 5,) St. Bernard shows how all our virtue and good works ought to lean upon Jesus Christ ; and upon this occasion he quotes these words of the apostle to the Corinthians : " By the grace of God I am what I am ; and his grace in me was not in vain, but I laboured more abundantly than all." (1 Cor. xv. 10.) " Have a care great saint, what you say," St. Bernard cries out, " and, that you may not lose the fruit of all your labours, lean upon your beloved." See, therefore, how he leans; " yet it is not I," says the apostle, " but the grace of God which was with me." (1 Cor. xv. 10.) After the same manner he expressed himself in his Epistle to the Philippians, for after having said, " I can do all things," he immediately leans upon his beloved, and adds, " in him who strengthens me." There is nothing but we can do with the help of God ; his grace can make us capable of everything ; upon that we ought to rely, and upon that the greatness of a Christian's courage ought to be founded. "For they who hope in God shall change their strength," (Isa. xl. 31,) says the prophet Isaias. They shall change earthly strength for that of heaven ; their own weak arm for the arm of the Almighty ; and so there will be nothing which they are not capable to undertake and perform, because they can do all things with God's help. " Nothing is difficult to the humble," (Serm. v. de Epiph.) says St. Leo. For he who is truly humble is magnanimous, courageous, and bold to attempt great things ; nothing seems impossible to him, because it is not in himself, but in God that he places his confidence; and when he turns his eyes upon God, he sees nothing that can be any obstacle to him. " Through God we shall do valiantly, and he it is who shall destroy those that afflict us." (Ps. lix. 14.) These are the thoughts which we, who are ministers of the gospel, ought most particularly to have—thoughts of courage, resolution, and confidence in God ; and not thoughts of fear and pusillanimity, which may take away from us the desire of labouring in our functions. So that we must be humble in ourselves, acknowledging that of ourselves we neither are, nor can do, anything ; but we must at the same time place our

courage and confidence in God, and believe that with his grace
and assistance we are capable of doing all things.

This is perfectly well explained by St. Basil upon these words
of Isaias, "here I am, send me." (Isa. vi. 8.) "God designed
to send somebody to his people; and because he will have a con-
currence of our consent in things which he designs to work in us
and by us, that Isaias might understand him, he said, 'whom
shall I send, and who will go from us?' The prophet answers,
'here am I, send me.' He says not," continues this father, "I will
be the man that shall go; I will perform all that is to be done;
for he was humble, he was sensible of his own weakness, and he
saw that it would have been presumptuous in him to promise to
do a thing that was above human strength; but he says only,
'here am I, O Lord, send me;' as if he said, I know that of myself I am not capable of so high an employment, but thou canst
make me capable thereof, thou canst put into my mouth words
powerful enough to soften the hardest hearts, and if thou sendest
me, there is nothing but I shall be able to do in thy name.
'Go then,' says our Lord to him." And St. Basil observes hereupon, that the reason why Isaias became the ambassador of
God, and minister of his word, was, because he knew how to
keep himself within the bounds of humility, and had not attributed to himself the power of "going," but acknowledging his
own incapacity and weakness, and convinced that he could do
everything with the help of God, he had placed his whole confidence in him alone. This, therefore, is the magnanimity we have
need of in great enterprises, and which will hinder our insuffi-
ciency and weakness from making us lose courage. "Say not,
I am a child, for thou shalt go to all that I shall send thee, and
whatsoever I command thee thou shalt speak; be not afraid of
their face; for I am with thee." (Jerem. i. 7.) So that as to
what concerns the greatness of an undertaking, humility is not
only not contrary therein to magnanimity, but is the very source
and foundation of it.

Now, as to our loving to do things which may deserve glory,
neither is that at all contrary to humility. For, as St. Thomas
says very well, though it is what the magnanimous man desires,
yet he desires it not for the glory that arises from it; he desires
only to deserve the glory, without caring to possess it. And on
the contrary, he has raised himself so high above the opinion of
the world, that he finds nothing estimable but virtue; and looking with the same eye upon the praise and the scorn of men, he

does nothing for the love of the one, or through fear of the other. And indeed virtue is a thing so excellent, that men cannot either honour or recompense it sufficiently; God only can do it. The magnanimous man therefore makes no account of the honours of the world; he looks upon them as what deserves not to be made the object of his desire; his flight is higher— it is for the love of God and of virtue that he is moved to the performance of great actions; all other motives have no influence upon him. Now there is need of very great humility to care as little for the honour or the scorn of men as the magnanimous person ought to do, and to be able to say with the apostle, "I know how to be humbled, and how to abound with honour, everywhere and in all things. I am instructed both to be full and to be hungry, both to abound and suffer want;" and to teach us how to show ourselves true ministers of the gospel, he adds, "by honour or dishonour, by bad and good report, as deceivers and yet true, as unknown and yet well known, as dying and behold we live." (Philip. iv. 12.) There is need, I say, of a great stock of humility and of heavenly wisdom to hinder winds, so violent and contrary to one another as those of esteem and contempt—of praise, and detraction—of favour and persecution are from tossing us; and to keep ourselves steady in same frame of spirit, and the same temper of mind, in the midst of the greatest storms. It is hard to preserve humility, as St. Paul did in the midst of plenty. You may preserve it, perhaps in poverty, banishment, reproaches, and affronts; but to preserve it in the midst of honour and applause; in the great offices and in the splendid exercise of the most eminent employments, is what, I doubt, you will not be able to perform. The angels themselves knew not how to preserve it even in heaven, and it was that caused the misfortune of their fall. "A wise man," says Boetius, "ought to fear both good and bad fortune, but the good is to be feared more than the bad;" and indeed it is far more difficult to be humble in promotion, than in disgrace; because the last leads naturally to humility, and the first to pride and vanity. "Knowledge puffeth up." (1 Cor. viii. 1.) And all other things which do any way exalt us produce the same effect; and upon that account it is that holy writers say, that none but the perfect know how to keep themselves humble in the midst of those signal favours which God bestows upon them, and the honours and respects which the world shows them.

There is an affair related of St Francis very different from

that we have already told of him, when to shun the honours de-
designed him at his reception, he began to tread mud as if it had
been mortar. The saint coming one day to a small village, the
people, who entertained an high opinion of his sanctity, showed
him all honour imaginable ; they kissed the hem of his garment,
and his hands and feet; whilst the saint in the meantime showed
no dislike thereof. His companion judged hereupon that he was
very well pleased with the honours he received, and being able
to dissemble his thoughts no longer, he imparted them to the
saint, who answered thus : " these people, dear brother, do nothing yet in comparison of what they ought to do ;" so that the
good brother was yet more scandalized at his answer than he was
before, the meaning of which he did not comprehend. At last
the saint told him, " I am not puffed up or exalted in my
thoughts with the honour they show me, nor do I attribute it to
myself; but swallowing up all in the depth of my own nothingness
and baseness, I ascribe all to God, to whom alone it belongs. So
that they who behave themselves thus are gainers by it; because
it is God whom they acknowledge and honour in his creatures.
" At which answer the good brother remained satisfied, and was
at the same time surprised at the perfection of the saint. And
without doubt he was justly so ; for to be thought a saint, which
is the greatest honour that can be done man, and to attribute
nothing thereof to one's self, or give way to any secret complacency therein, but to ascribe the glory of all to God alone ; to
contract one's self within one's own narrow bounds, as if nothing
happened, and as if the honour had been given to another ; it is
certainly a very high perfection, and a most profound humility.

Now it is this humility every one should endeavour to arrive
to, and they chiefly who are called not to lie hidden under a
bushel, but to be exposed to the sight of all, as a city upon a
high mountain, and to give light, like a candle in a candlestick.
But to do so, good and deep foundations must be laid ; there
must be an ardent desire of being despised by every body ; and
that desire must proceed from a deep sense of our own nothingness, such a one as St. Francis had, when he began to tread the
mud, that he might pass for a fool. For that deep knowledge of
himself, which made him desire to be contemned, was the cause
also that when one hem of his garment and feet were kissed, he
valued himself never the more, and was puffed up with no vanity
thereupon, but being as steadfast in the contempt of himself as if

no honour had been done him, he ascribed all to God alone. Thus, though these two actions of St. Francis seem contrery to one another, they proceed nevertheless from one and the same principle and spirit of humility.

—— o ——

CHAPTER XXXVII.

Of several other great advantages, which are found in the third degree of humility.

"ALL belongs to thee, O Lord—what we have received from thy hand we have given back unto thee," (1 Paral. xxix. 14,) said David to God, when he offered him the gold, silver, and other materials which he had amassed for the building of the temple. Thus also ought we to express ourselves when we do any good work; for as St. Austin says very well, " whoever enumerates his merits to thee, what else does he do but enumerate, O Lord, thy own merits?" It is by an effect of thy infinite goodness and liberality that thou ascribest anything to our merit, so that when thou rewardest our services, thou dost but crown thy own gifts, and heap upon us one favour after another. God deals with us as Joseph did with his brethren; he is not satisfied with giving us the corn we have need of for our subsistence, he gives us also the money that it costs. " He gives us grace and glory. (Ps. lxxxiii. 11.) Everything comes from him and we ought also to return everything to him, by ascribing still to him the honour of all things.

One of the greatest advantages of the third degree of humility is, that the action it produces expresses best our return of thanks to God for the gifts received. We know well enough that thanksgiving to him is exceedingly recommended in scripture; for we see that when he had done any signal favour to his people he commanded forthwith to have a feast of thanksgiving instituted, that hereby he might give us to understand, that to deserve new favours it is necessary to shew gratitude for the old. Now this is done in an eminent manner by the third degree of humility, which consists, as we have said, in attributing to one's self nothing of those gifts it has pleased God to bestow upon us, and in ascribing and giving the glory of all to him alone. For that is to be truly thankful, and not only to say with our lips: "we give thee thanks, O Lord, for all thy benefits;" though we ought also this way to give him thanks, but if we do it only with our lips it is no true thanksgiving, being only verbal thanks. Wherefore we must not only utter a few bare words, but heartily express our thanks, and that the heart may share therein as well as the lips, we must acknowledge that whatever good we have in ourselves comes from God; we must, by ascribing all the glory thereof to him, make entire restitution, without reserving the least part; and thus by stripping ourselves of an honour which we know belongs not to us, we restore it wholly to God, to whom alone it appertains. Our Saviour was pleased to instruct us to do this, when having healed the ten lepers, of whom one alone, who was a Samaritan, returning to give him thanks for his cure, " there is not found," says he, "one that returned to give glory to God, except this stranger." (Luke xvii. 18.) The same instruction is given also to the people of Israel in Deuteronomy, where God speaking by the mouth of Moses, "beware," says he, " that thou forgettest not the Lord thy God; beware, when thou hast plenty of all things, lest thy heart be exalted and puffed up, and thou rememberest not the Lord thy God, who has brought thee out of the land of Egypt. Say not, that it is my power, and the might of my own hand, that has procured me all this; but remember the Lord thy God, for it is he that gives the power, that he may accomplish his promise which he swore unto thy forefathers." (Deut. viii. 11, 14.) To attribute to ourselves the gifts we have received from God is to forget God, and to show him the greatest ingratitude in the world. On the other hand to acknowledge the benefits which we hold from his divine bounty is to return the true thanks required of us. This is the "sacrifice of praise whereby," he says, " he will be glorified;" (Ps. xlix. 23,) and this is the acknowledgment the apostle teaches us to express when he says; "to the King eternal, immortal, invisible, the only God, be honour and glory." (1 Tim. i. 17.)

Hence arises another advantage, which is, that whatever gifts he who is truly humble may have received, and whatever esteem he may have gained thereby, he values not himself the more for it, but remains as deeply impressed with the sense of his own baseness and nothingness, as if he had received none at all; because he knows how to distinguish between what belongs not to him; and what is properly his own; and understands how to attribute to every one what is his due. Thus, looking upon the favours he has received from God as foreign and borrowed goods, he never turns his eyes off his own meanness, and the condition he should be in if God abandoned him but for one moment, and did not hold him continually by the hand. But the more he is crowned with divine favours, the more he humbles himself before God. " When trees are much loaded with fruit," says St. Dorotheus, "the quantity bends, nay sometimes breaks the branches; whereas, those which are not so laden remain straight: and when the ears of corn are full they hang down so that the stalk seems ready to break, but when they stand straight up, it is a sign there is little in them. Just so it is as to spiritual things. They who bear no fruit shoot still upwards, but they who are loaden with the fruit of grace and good works are always hanging down their heads in an humble posture; they make the favours they have received from God a subject of further humiliation and fear." St. Gregory says, " that as a man who has borrowed a great sum feels his joy for having the money allayed by the obligation he lies under to restore it, and by the disquiet he is in, not knowing whether he shall be able to pay it at the time appointed : so he who is humble, the more gifts he receives from Almighty God the more he acknowledges himself a debtor, and that he has a stricter obligation to serve him ; and fancying still that his gratitude and services answer not, as they ought, the greatness of the favours and benefits he has received, he believes at the same time, that any one but himself would have made better use of them." And this it is which makes the servants of God more humble than all others; for they know that God will call them to account, not only for the sins they shall commit, but also for the benefits they shall receive. " That much shall be required of him to whom much shall have been given, and to whom much has been intrusted more shall be required and demanded of him." (Luke xii. 48.) St. Micharius was used to say, "that the humble man looked upon the gifts of God in himself as a man does upon things that are deposited in his hands; or as a faithful treasurer looks upon the money which he has in keeping. So far is he from being proud, that he is in continual fear of it ; because he knows that it is money which he must give an account of, and that if he loses it by his fault the loss will fall upon his own head."

There is yet another advantage in being humble, which is, that he who is truly so never despises his neighbour, whatever sins he sees him fall into, nor does he thereupon esteem himself the more; but on the contrary, he takes occasion the more to humble himself ; because he considers that he is framed of the same mass that he is who has fallen ; and because in his brother's fall he beholds his own. For, as St. Austin says very well, "our brother commits no sin which we should not also commit, if God by his mercy did not continually hold us up by the hand." And therefore an ancient father of the desert, when he heard of any one's fall, used to weep bitterly and say, "such a one is fallen to-day, as much may happen to me to-morrow, since I am a man like him; subject to all human weaknesses, and if I am not yet fallen, it is a particular grace of God which has supported me." For as when we look upon a blind, deaf, or lame man, or any one afflicted with any other distemper, we ought to reflect upon all those calamities in others as so many obligations which we have to God for having exempted us from them; so ought we in like manner to consider the sins of all men as so many gracious favours of God to us; since we might have fallen into the same, if by his infinite mercy he had not preserved us, Thus it is that the servants of God keep themselves humble, without ever despising, or being angry with their neighbour, by reason of his sins. "For true justice is full of compassion," says St. Gregory, "but pretended justice is full of disdain." (Hom. xxxiv. sup. Evang.) They, therefore, who are only angry at the faults of their neighbour, ought, as St. Paul says, "to consider themselves, for fear of being tempted" (Gal. vi. 1,) with the same things themselves, which they with so much severity condemn in others; and lest God should by a punishment, which falls usually on this sort of pride, permit them to find to their cost how great human weakness is. An ancient father of the desert was used to say, "that he had without pity judged his brethren upon three things, and that he happened to fall into the three himself." God, therefore, will "have us learn that we are men," (Ps. ix. 21,) and therefore ought not to take upon us to judge or despise any one.

—o—

CHAPTER XXXVIII.

Of the great favours God confers upon the humble, and why he raises them so high.

"ALL good things came to me with it," (Wisd. vii. 11,) says Solomon, speaking of wisdom; which words we may apply to humility and say also, that all good things come along with it. The same Solomon adds, "that where humility is, there is wisdom;" (Prov. xi. 9,) and David tells us, "that God gives

wisdom to little ones," (Ps. xviii. 8,) that is to those who become
little by humility.   But this truth is taught us expressly in
several places of the Old and New Testament, wherein God
promises great favours and benefits to the humble, to little ones,
and to the poor in spirit; calling those who have true humility of
heart indifferently by all these names.   "On whom shall I look,"
says the Lord in Isaias, " but on the man that is poor, and of a
contrite spirit, and who trembles at my word?" (Is. lxvi. 2.)
God casts his eyes upon such to crown them with benefits and
favours.   And St. Peter and St. James teach us that " God
resists the proud and gives grace to the humble." (1 Pet. v. 5.)
The same thing the Holy Virgin assures us of. "The Lord," says
she, " has cast down the mighty from their seat, and has exalted
the humble ; he has filled the hungry with good things, and the
rich he has sent empty away. (Luke i. 52.) The royal prophet says
likewise, "that the Lord will save the humble and will humble
the haughty looks of the proud." (Ps. xvii. 28.)   And our
Saviour, in fine, assures us, that "whosoever exalts himself shall
be humbled, and he who humbles himself shall be exalted."
(Luke xiv. 11.)   As " God sends rain upon the vallies whereby
they abound in corn ;" (Ps. ciii. 10 ; Ps. lxiv. 14); so the showers
of God's grace fall more plenteously upon the humble, and cause
them to bring forth a greater abundance of fruit than others.
St. Austin says that humility draws down God unto it.   " God
is high," says he ; '' if you humble yourself, he comes down to
you ; if you exalt yourself, he withdraws himself from you."
And why so ?   Because " God is high, and looks down upon
things that are lowly," (Ps. cxxxvii. 6,) that is humble persons ;
and showers down blessings upon them ; but " he sees afar off
things that are high," that is, the proud.   And as we know not
what is seen a great way off, so God knows not the proud so as
to confer any favours upon them, but assures them, " verily, I
say unto you, I know you not." (Matt. xxv. 12.)   St. Bonaventure says, " that the humble soul is disposed to receive from
God all kinds of favours, as soft wax is to receive all manner
of impressions."   In the entertainment which Joseph gave his
brethren, the least had the best share."
   But why is God so pleased to exalt the humble, and to confer
upon them so many favours ?   It is, because all the good he does
them returns to himself.   For they who are humble appropriate
to themselves nothing of what they receive ; they restore it all to
God, and acknowledging, " that there is nothing great but the

power of God alone, they ascribe to him the glory and honour of all." (Ecclus. iii. 11.) Now God, seeing the disposition of their heart, knows very well he may securely trust them with the treasures of his grace without fear of their closing in his debt, or keeping anything for themselves ; and so the good he does unto them he does unto himself, because the glory thereof remains his own. Moreover, do we not see that even the grandees of the world often please themselves by signalizing their power upon inconsiderable people, and by raising them out of the dust to heap their favours upon them, by making them, as we usually say, their creatures. And thus it is that God deals with us. "For we have," says the apostle, "the treasure of grace in earthen vessels ; that our advancement may be ascribed to the power of God, and not to ourselves." (2 Cor. iv. 7.) This then is the reason why God is pleased to exalt the humble, and to confer so many favours upon them ; and why, on the contrary, he abandons the proud, who attribute all to themselves ; who have a vanity in all their good actions and successes, as if they owed all to their own care ; and thus rob God of his glory, who is alone the true owner of it. For, alas ! in every little fervour we feel : for example, on shedding a tear or two at our prayers, we fail not presently to look upon ourselves as persons of great devotion, far advanced in spirituality. Yea ! we stick not even to prefer ourselves to others, and to look upon them as being a great way behind us. And thence it comes that God sometimes does not only not confer new favours upon us, but takes from us part of the former, lest we should turn good into evil, and antidotes into poison ; and lest his gifts and benefits, by the bad use of them, should become a greater cause of our temptation. Thus we do when a man has a weak stomach—let the meat be ever so good of itself, we give him but very little of it, because he has not strength enough to digest a great quantity ; for if more were given him it would all turn into corruption, phlegm, and choler. The holy scripture tells us that the oil ceased not to run from the widow's pot, "whilst there were any other vessels to receive it, but as soon as the vessels were full, the oil stopped." (4 Kings iv. 6). So it is with divine mercy. On God's side it has no limits ; "for the hand of the Lord is not shortened." (Isa. lix. 1.) God neither does nor can change ; he remains always in the same state, and desires more to impart his favours to us than we do to receive them. The fault is in us, we are so full of ourselves, and of the confidence we have in our own strength, that there remain no empty vessels for us to receive the oil of mercies. Nothing but humility and the knowledge of one's self can free a man from so unhappy a fulness, can give him a just diffidence of his own strength, and make God shower down his favours more plenteously upon his; according to these words of the Wise man —"Humble yourself before God, and expect all things from his hands." (Ecclus. xiii. 9.)

———o———

CHAPTER XXXIX.

How important it is to have recourse to humility, thereby to supply what we otherwise stand in need of, and to hinder God from humbling and chastising us.

"He is a fool," says St. Bernard, "who puts his confidence in anything else but in humility. For since we have all, dear brethren, offended God in many things; we cannot but plead guilty." (Serm. de diversis xxvi.) "If any body will contend with him, he cannot answer one word to a thousand things which God will accuse him of." (Job ix. 3.) "What, therefore, remains for us to do but to have recourse, with all our hearts, to the helps of humility, and to supply whatever may be otherwise wanting." (Serm. de Nat. St. J. Bap.) This way being of great importance, the same saint repeats the same doctrine to us in several places: "If you find not your conscience clear enough, make up what is deficient by a holy shame and confusion; and what is wanting of fervour endeavour to compensate by an humble and sincere confession." (De inter. domo. vi. 37.)

St. Dorotheus tells us of an abbot, called John, who did very often recommend the same thing; "let us humble ourselves," said he, "to save our souls, and if our weak constitution hinders us from labouring much, let us study, at least, how to humble ourselves;" (Doct. de humil.,) for hereby we shall make as great proficiency as they who have undergone great labours. If after having lived a long time in sin, we find not sufficient health and strength to walk in the path of austerities, let us take that of humility, and we shall find no securer way to lead us whither we desire to go. If we cannot apply ourselves to prayer, let us endeavour to be clothed with confusion because we cannot pray; and if we have no talent for great things, let us at least get humility, and thus shall we make up whatever is wanting.

Moreover, let us here consider how little God requires of us, and with how little he is contented. He requires that we should acknowledge ourselves to be what we are, and conceive thoughts of ourselves proportionable to our weakness. If he required of us to practise great austerities, and to soar afloat in sublime contemplations, some might excuse themselves on account of their weak constitution; and others upon that of their incapacity ; but is there anything that can hinder us to humble ourselves ? To do this there is no need of vigorous health or great wit, a good will only is requisite. For, as St. Bernard says ; " there is nothing more easy to him that wills it than to humble himself." (Serm. 2, in cap. jejun.) And it is easy enough for every one to humble hinself, because every one has reason to do so, since, according to the prophet, " the subject of our humiliation is within us." (Mich. vi. 14.) Let us therefore have recourse to humility, thereby to make up what is wanting towards our perfection, and thus we shall move the bowels of divine mercy to compassion. Thou art destitute of spiritual riches, thou art poor and indigent. Be humble, and God will be satisfied with thee. But he cannot suffer arrogance and poverty joined together; and of three things which the Wise man says that God abhors, the first is, " to be poor and proud." (Ecclus. xxv. 4.) It is one of the things also, that most of all shocks and disedifies secular persons.

Now if all this be not sufficient to make us humble, let us at least humble ourselves, lest God should humble us ; for so has he been used to do, according to these words of the gospel, " he who exhalts himself shall be humbled." (Luke xviii. 14.) If then you will not have him humble you, humble yourself ; and this point is doubtless of great importance, and highly deserves to be examined with care. "Though God," says St. Gregory " takes pleasure in purifying the heart of the just ; he often nevertheless permits some imperfections to remain there, that whatever eminent virtues shine in them, the sight of their imperfections may make them look down with humility, and hinder them from being too much exalted with great things, since they find themselves so weak in resisting little ones. And knowing, in fine, that they are unable to overcome themselves in lesser occasions, they may not grow vain by the victory they gain in greater, but walk still in fear and humility, imploring continually the grace of God without which they can do nothing." St. Bernard says as much, and so do all holy writers. St. Austin upon these words of St. John, "without him nothing was made ;" (John i. 3) ; and upon these words of the prophet Joel, " I will restore to you the years that the locust, the bruchus, and the mildew, and the palmer-worm have eaten," (Joel ii. 25,) says, " it is to humble man that God has created such a variety of insects which torment us. It would have been as easy for him to have sent bears, lions, and serpents, to punish the obstinacy of Pharao and the Egyptians ; but the more to humble them, he was pleased to bring down their pride by flies, grasshoppers, and frogs." He deals with us almost after the same manner. To humble us the more, he permits us to fall into small faults, and lets little flies and atoms attack and disquiet us ; for if we will but examine what usually makes us most uneasy, we shall find that they are things, which, if well considered, are almost nothing. It is per-haps the tone of voice with which a word is said to us—it is because we think we have been despised. Of a fly, in fine, we make an elephant, and picking up still whatever comes in our way, we create a thousand things to vex and trouble ourselves with. What should we do if God had let loose tigers and lions upon us, when a fly puts us to so much pain ? And what should we do if some great temptation came upon us ? Thus ought we to turn all these things to our profit, and make them serve for our greater humiliation and confusion. And when we make so good use of them as this, " it is an effect," says St. Bernard, " of God's mercy not to deliver us wholly from them." (Serm, in cæn. dom.)

But if these things suffice not to humble you, know that God will proceed yet further at your expense, as he usually does. He hates pride and presumption so much that holy writers say he often, by a secret but just judgment, permits the proud for their humiliation to fall into some mortal sin ; and not only into some of the least but into those which are the most shameful of all, I mean the sins of the flesh. The secret sins of pride he punishes, say they, by the public ones of impurity ; and they quote upon this occasion what St .Paul says of the pagan philoso-phers, whose pride God punished " by giving them up to the unclean desires of their own hearts, to dishonour their own bodies between themselves." (Rom. i. 24, 26.) After such a judgment as this, " who will not fear thee, O King of nations ! " (Jer. x. 7.) Who will not tremble at the recital of a punishment so great that there is not a greater except in hell ; if sin be not yet a punishment more cruel than hell itself ? " Who knows the power of thine anger, and who is he that fears thee not ?" (Ps. lxxxix. 11.)

Holy writers observe, that God shows two kinds of mercy towards us ; the one greater, the other lesser. The lesser is, when he assists in the miseries which are but temporal, and which relate only to the body ; and the greater is, when he assists us in the miseries which are purely spiritual and reach even to the soul. Wherefore, when David, after the adultery and murder he had committed, saw himself fallen into the great misery of being abandoned by God, he implores God's great mercy saying: "have pity, O God, upon me, according to thy great mercy." (Ps. l. 1.) There are also, say they, two kinds of God's anger, the one greater, the other lesser. The lesser is, when he chastises any one in temporal affairs, by the loss of estate, honour, wealth, and the like, which concern the body only ; and the greater, when he extends his chastisement even to the very soul, according to these words of Jeremiah, "the sword reaches unto the soul ;" (Jer. iv. 10) ; and as God himself says to Zachary, "I am much displeased with the nations that are rich," (Zach. i. 15,) that is, with the proud and haughty. When God forsakes any one, and to punish him for his sins lets him fall into some mortal sin, it is an effect of his great anger ; and then he chastises him in his fury, and not as a tender and indulgent father, but as a severe and rigorous judge. And of this kind of chastisement may be understood these words of Jeremiah, "I have wounded thee with the wound of an enemy, and with a cruel chastisement ;" (Jer. xxx. 14) ; as also those of the Wise man, "the mouth of the strange woman is a deep pit, he whom the Lord is angry with shall fall therein." (Prov. xxii. 14.)

Pride, in fine, is so bad a thing in itself, and such an abomination in the sight of God, that holy writers hold it to be an advantage sometimes to a proud man to be thus chastised, that he may thereby be cured of his pride. "I dare assert," says St. Austin, "that it is profitable for the proud to fall openly into some sin ; that so the shame of a public fall may cure them of the secret complacency they take in themselves, into which they were already fallen without knowing it." (De Civ. Dei.) "For pride goes before destruction, and the spirit becomes haughty before a fall." (Prov. xvi. 18.) The same doctrine St. Basil and St. Gregory hold ; the latter of whom, speaking of David's sin, asks why God permits sometimes that they whom he has always elected, and favoured with his grace, should fall into the shameful sin of impurity ? "It is," answers the saint, "because they who have received great gifts from God, let themselves be carried away by the thoughts of pride, which lie lurking so secretly in their breast that they perceive them not : but full of the complacency they take in themselves, they believe they have no object but God." Thus St. Peter took for courage and excess of love to his master, the presumption which made him say, " though all men should be scandalized at thee, yet I will never be scandalized." (Matt. xxvi. 33.) Now, when any one is fallen into this kind of secret and covered pride, it is to raise him that God permits him sometimes to fall into sins of impurity ; which being sins of the body, are easier perceived than those of the mind. For he who falls being thereby put in mind of his weakness, discovers the secret pride that lurked in him, which he did not think of remedying for want of perceiving it, and might have perished thereby. And thus from his fall he derives this advantage, that it induces him to humble himself before God, and to seek by penance the remedy for this his crime of pride. The evident fall of St. Peter made him know the presumption which lay hidden in his breast, and thereby was of advantage to him ; because it gave him occasion to bewail, and do penance at the same time for both the sins he was guilty of. The same advantage David obtained by his fall, and it was that made him say :—" It is good for me that thou hast humbled me, that I might learn thy statutes," (Ps. cxviii. 7,) and have greater diffidence in myself. As when a physician sees that medicines are not strong enough to cure the malignity of an inward disease, he, to cure it the more easily, endeavours to draw it outward; so when God is pleased to cure any of us, of our pride, he lets us fall into some great exterior fault, that so the sense of so manifest a sin may cover us with confusion ; and that this confusion may serve to purge and cure in us the internal disease of presumption. God tells us he used his people thus :—" Behold," says he, " I will do a thing in Israel, which whosoever shall hear both his ears shall tingle." (1 Kings iii. 11.) And who would not tremble at the hearing only of so terrible a punishment ?

But God, nevertheless, being so merciful, it is only in case of extremity that he makes use of so severe a chastisement, and so violent and deplorable a remedy, after having tried milder and easier ones. For, first of all, he endeavours to cure and bring us back to himself, sometimes by diseases and crosses, and sometimes by afflicting us in our estate or honour ; and when these temporal punishments suffice not to humble us, he has recourse to spiritual ones. He first begins with slight trials ; afterwards he permits us to be assaulted by violent temptations, which may bring us to the very point of yielding to them, and make us doubt whether we have not consented thereunto ; and this he does to show us by experience that of ourselves we are not able to overcome them, and that being sensible of our weakness and the need we have of God's help, we may become diffident of our own strength, and humble ourselves before him. Now if this be not yet sufficient, he then uses the dreadful remedy of letting a man fall into mortal sin, and suffering him to sink under the temptation, that he may at least learn to know himself after so fatal a proof, and that he who would not be humbled by grace should be humbled by sin.

By this may be seen, of how great importance it is to us to be humble, and not to presume too much on our own strength. Let everyone therefore call himself to account, and examine how he improves the occasions of humbling himself which God sends him as a father, and a charitable physician, that he may not be obliged to make use of more violent and dangerous remedies. Chastise me, O my God, with the tenderness of a father ! To cure me of pride make use of sufferings, sickness, affronts, injuries, and all the humiliations which thou thinkest fit ; but never suffer me to fall into mortal sin ! Give the devil power to attack my reputation, and my health, and to reduce me even to the miseries of Job, but hinder him from making any attempt upon my soul! Provided, O Lord, that thou dost not go far from me, and permittest me not to go far from thee, no affliction will be able to hurt me ; but, on the contrary, I shall derive advantage from whatever trouble happens to me, because I may make use of it to acquire humility, with which thou art so well pleased.

---o---

CHAPTER LX.

A confirmation of the foregoing doctrine by some examples.

SEVERUS SULPICIUS and Surius tell us that a holy man, who had received of God the gift of healing the sick, driving out devils, and performing several other miracles, finding that the great crowds of people, who flocked from all parts to see him, and to touch his clothes, and to receive his blessing, excited some thoughts of vanity in his heart, and not being able to banish them, nor to hinder the concourse of people from coming to him, he begged of God, that to free him from the temptation which tormented him and to keep him humble, he would for some time deliver him up to be possessed with the devil. God heard his prayer, permitted the devil to enter into him ; and it was a strange sight to see him, to whom the possessed were usually brought to be cured, dragged along like a madman, to be exorcised according to the practice of the Church. He was five months in this condition, at the end of which time God delivered him not only from the evil spirit that had taken possession of his body, but from all the thoughts of pride and presumption which had stolen into his mind.

The same Surius gives us another example almost like this, which is, that St. Severinus having in his monastery three religious who were very much puffed up with pride and vanity, and seeing that all his admonitions to them were of no avail, such was his zeal for their reformation, that it moved him one day to beseech God with tears that he would be pleased to inflict some punishment upon them, which might serve to humble and make them better. He had not finished his prayer when God, by a chastisement proportionable to their fault, gave up their bodies to three devils, that cruelly tormented them for forty days. After which time it pleased the divine goodness to deliver them at the prayer of the saint ; and the cure of their bodies was followed by that of their souls, the punishment having wholly allayed in them the vapours of pride and vanity.

Cæsarius relates that one possessed with a devil being brought to a monastery of the Cistercian monks to be cured, the prior, who was to exorcise him, took with him a young religious, who was in great reputation for his virtue, and who had always kept himself pure and chaste ; and having asked the evil spirit whether if that religious person commanded him to be gone, he durst still stay ? " Yes, " answered he, " for by reason of his pride, I fear him not."

We read in St. John Climachus, that a great servant of God purposing to walk in the path of humility, the devils, jealous of the progress he had made therein, wished to divert him from it, by sowing seeds of vain glory in his heart ; but, by a divine inspiration, he found out an easy remedy against their malice. He wrote upon the walls of his cell the names of some of the chief virtues, according to the most excellent idea that could be framed of them, as " perfect charity ! most profound humility ! angelical chastity ! continual fervour of prayer !" and so of the rest.   And when he found himself attacked by vain thoughts; "Let us come to the trial," said he, to the devils; and falling to read the inscriptions and titles he had written, as, "Most profound humility!" "I am not," said he, "come yet so far. I should think myself happy to come near it, but so far am I from being arrived at the last degree of humility, that I am not, it may be, even got to the first. ' Perfect charity :'—It is true I find that I have charity; but it is far from being perfect; for I speak sometimes very roughly to my brethren. ' Angelical chastity :'—It is not a thing I can flatter myself with, since I am subject to so many thoughts and motions contrary to purity. ' Continual fervour in prayer :'—I am far from having it, for therein I am very often either distracted or drowsy." Speaking afterwards to himself, he added—"when thou shalt have acquired all these virtues; thou oughtest yet to say, that thou art but an unprofitable servant, and must look upon thyself as such, according to those words of our Saviour—'When you shall have done all that is commanded you, say, we are unprofitable servants.' (Luke xvii. 10.)   And if it is so, what thoughts at present oughtest not thou to have of thyself, since thou art still so far from perfection ?"

THE FOURTH TREATISE.

——o——

ON TEMPTATIONS.

——o——

CHAPTER I.

That we are all in this life exposed to temptation.

"Son, applying yourself to the service of God, persevere in justice with fear, and prepare your soul for temptation." (Ecclus. ii. 1.) St. Jerome, upon these words of Ecclesiastes, "there is a time of war and a time of peace," (Eccl. iii. 8,) says, that as long as we are in this life it is a time of war ; and when we shall come to the other world it will be a time of peace, according to these words, " he has established his abode in peace ; " (Ps. lxxv. 2.) And it is for this reason that the name of Jerusalem, that is to say, the vision of peace, is given to this heavenly country to which we aspire. " Let nobody, therefore," adds he, " think himself at present secure in this time of war, in which we are continually to fight that at length we may rest in peace," such a peace as nothing shall be able to interrupt. St. Austin, upon these words of the apostle :—" I do not the good that I would do," (Serm. xlv. sup. Rom. vii. 15,) says, that the life of a just man is not a triumph but a combat; and therefore, at present we hear the cries of war, such as are expressed by the words which the apostle makes use of, when he complains of the repugnance of nature to what is good, and of its inclination to evil. " I do not," says he, " the good I would do; but I do the evil I would not. I see in my members another law, which is contrary to the law of my mind, and which subjects it to the law of concupiscence, which is in my members." But songs of triumph will be heard, when our mortal body shall be clothed with immortality, and then we shall cry out with the apostle, "Death is absorbed in victory. O death, where is your victory? O death, where is your sting ?" (1 Cor. xv. 54.) The same thoughts are very well expressed by these words of Job—"The life of man is a continual warfare, and his days are like those of a hireling." (Job vii. 1.) For, as a day workman labours from morning till night without ceasing, and then receives his day's wages; so our life is as a day's work, full of pain and temptations, after which each one will receive a reward according to what he shall have done.

But let us at present examine the cause of this continual war. The apostle St. James points it out in his canonical epistle—"From whence," says he, "proceed these combats and dissensions we feel in ourselves? Do they not proceed from concupiscence, which makes war against you?" (James iv. 1.) The source of all this is within ourselves; and the source is the repugnance we have to what is good, which has remained in our flesh since the entrance of sin. Because the earth of our flesh was no less cursed than the other; and therefore it produces so many thorns and thistles which prick and torment us. The saints compare us to that ship in the gospel which was no sooner launched into the sea but a tempest rose and covered it with waves. For our soul is in our body, as in a ship that leaks on all sides, and which the winds of a thousand different passions expose every moment to shipwreck.

The cause then of the continual temptations which torment us is our corrupt nature. "For the corruption of our body which clogs the soul," (Wis. ix. 15,) is that incentive to sin we carry about us, and that inclination to evil with which we are born. Our greatest enemy is within us, and wages continual war against us. Nor are we consequently to wonder at our being tempted. For since we are children of Adam, and "have been conceived in iniquity and brought forth in sin," (Ps. l, 7,) how can we be exempted from temptations, or how can we hinder our evil inclinations from making war continually against us? In the prayer therefore, which our Saviour taught us, St. Jerome observes, that he does not bid us beg of God, "to have no temptations, for that is impossible;" (Heir. in illud.); but only, that "he would not suffer us to fall or sink under them." (Matt. vi. 13.) After the same manner he taught his disciples, when he said to them, "watch and pray lest ye enter into temptation;" (Matt. xxvi. 41); "for to enter into temptation," says the same St. Jerome, "is not to be tempted, but to be overcome by temptation." Joseph was tempted to commit adultery, but he resisted the temptation; Susanna likewise was tempted after the same

manner, but God gave her also the grace of resisting. Now thus
it is we beg God in the Lord's prayer, that he would give us the
grace and strength to support ourselves in temptation, and not
to remove temptations wholly from us.   " Thou art mistaken,
brother," says the same saint, writing to Heliodorus, " thou art
mistaken if thou believest that a Christian is quite exempted from
temptation ; never art thou more strongly set upon, than when
thou believest that thou art not at all assaulted."   Never does
the devil make fiercer war upon thee than when thou thinkest
he is at peace with thee.   " Our adversary is as a roaring lion,
who goes about seeking whom he may devour, and canst thou
then think thou art secure ?   He lies in ambush for the rich,
and in hidden places to destroy the innocent.   His eyes are
always upon the poor ; as a lion in his den, he lays snares for
him in secret." (Ps. ix. 30.)   It is a mistake to think we can
live in peace here below.   We are in a time of war ; and to
startle at temptations is as if a soldier should startle at the
report of a musket, and thereupon quit the army ; or as if a man
should cease going to sea because the motion thereof raises some
qualms in his stomach.

St. Gregory says, many erroneously imagine that as soon as
they are attacked by any violent temptation all is lost, and that
God has forsaken them.   They are very much mistaken; for all
men are subject to temptations, and they who aim at perfection
are more subject than others ; as the Wise man tells us in the
words we have already cited.   The apostle teaches us the same.
" All," says he, " who will live piously in Jesus Christ, shall
suffer persecution." (2 Tim. iii. 12.)   All who will advance in
virtue shall be exposed to temptations ; as for others, they often
know not even what it is to be tempted: they are not sensible of
the rebellion and combat of the flesh against the spirit.

Upon this passage of the apostle, "the flesh lusteth against the
spirit," St. Austin says, " that it is in good people it so lusteth.
Because in the bad it has not anything to lust against, and that
it is only where the spirit is, that is to say, where there is a real
desire of virtue, that it lusteth against the spirit." (Serm. xliii.
in Evan. St. Joan.)   The wicked, therefore, having not the spirit
which fights against the flesh, are not sensible of the rebellion of
the flesh against the spirit, nor need the devil lose time in tempting them; since of themselves, and without resistance, they yield
to him.   We go not to hunt after tame animals, but after the
stag, and other wild beasts noted for their swiftness ; it is after

those whose feet God has made as swift as hart's feet, and those who keep upon the mountains, that the devil hunts: for, as for such as live like tame animals, he has no need to run after them; they are already his own; "and he minds not," says St. Gregory, "to disturb those of whom he enjoys a quiet possession." (Lib. xxiv. Moral. c. 7.) Wherefore we ought not only not to wonder at our having temptations, but should look upon them as a good sign, according to the words of St. John Climachus, who says "that the most infallible mark of having overcome the devil is that he assaults you violently." (Grad. xxvi. de Disc. art. 60.) For he attacks you only because you struggled with him, and shook off his yoke. This is the cause of his hating and persecuting you; and without this he would not so much torment you.

———o———

CHAPTER II.

That some are tempted at the beginning of their conversion and others afterwards.

St. Gregory observes, there are some persons who are never so sharply assaulted by temptations as in the beginning of their conversion. He says that our Saviour has been pleased by a wonderful providence to give us an example thereof in himself, by not having permitted the devil to tempt him till he retired, after his baptism, into the wilderness to fast and pray. "He intended thereby," adds the same saint, "to teach his children, that when they retire from the world to apply themselves wholly to virtue, they must be prepared to withstand strong attacks; because it is then usually that the devil makes his greatest attempts upon them." As soon as the children were gone out of Egypt, Pharao got his army together to follow them. When Laban saw that Jacob had gone finally away from him, then it was that he pursued him, with all the people he had about him. And when the devil went out of the man whom the gospel speaks of, he did like one who arms against a rebel to bring him back to a sense of duty; "he took seven other spirits more wicked than himself," (Luke xi. 26,) to return to the place whence he was driven. Thus it is, when the devil sees a man rebelling against him, and shaking off his yoke, he becomes more enraged, and attacks him with the greater fury. When our Saviour cast out the foul spirit which was deaf and dumb, "it came out of him crying," says the gospel, "and tearing him with great violence." (Mark

ix. 25.)   And St. Gregory well observes upon this occasion, "that when the devil possessed this man, he did not thus tear him ; but when by the divine power he was forced to quit him, then it was that he more cruelly tormented him ; (Greg. ubi. sup.); to make us comprehend," says the same father, "that when we forsake the devil, it is then we ought to expect our being assaulted by the most violent temptations." He says also, that " one of the reasons why God permits us to be tempted at the beginning of our conversion is, to hinder us from yielding too easily to thoughts of presumption, and from looking on ourselves as saints immediately on our leaving the road of perdition, and entering into the right way." And, as he further adds, " security being the mother of negligence," it is to hinder this security from making us fall into negligence and remissness God permits temptations to come upon us, to let us see the continual danger we are exposed to in this life, and oblige us to watch over ourselves with greater care and application. St. John Climachus says, that " the beginning of a holy and regular life seems ordinarily troublesome to him who has been accustomed to a licentious one: and that as a bird perceives not that it is taken in a net, till it wishes to get out ; so it is not till we renounce vice, that we are most sensible of our unhappy engagements, and feel the greatest strife within ourselves. We must not, therefore, be astonished or lose courage, whatever difficulties may be met with in the beginning, and whatever temptations may assault us ; for they who apply themselves to God's service are usually exposed to these trials."

St. Gregory adds, that it sometimes happens that a man who has renounced the world, to give himself wholly to the service of God, feels then much more violent temptations than all those that he had undergone before his conversion. Not, says he, that he had not then in him the root of all these temptations ; but the truth is, it did not then appear, but it showed itself afterwards. Thus it is, that a person distracted with many cares and thoughts, is not thoroughly acquainted with himself. He scarce knows what passes in his interior ; but when he comes to recollect and enter into himself, he then feels the disorder of his heart. Temptations, as the same St. Gregory moreover shows, are like thistles which grow on the highway but scarce appear, because every body that passes treads them down; the roots notwithstanding remain still on the ground, though the prickles show not themselves; but as soon as they are no more trampled upon they begin to shoot up. "The roots of temptations," continues he, "hidden thus in worldly people ; a variety of thoughts, cares, and business, produce in them the same effect that passengers do on thistles which grow on the highway. But when they reject all other occupations to employ their thoughts entirely in the service of God, then, as no one treads upon the thistles to prevent them from springing freely up, they begin to feel the thorns of temptations, the roots of which lay before covered in their hearts. This also is the reason why some feel greater temptations in time of retreat and prayer than when they are busied in exterior employments. Hence, though sometimes we feel them more violent in a religious life than before our conversion, yet we are not therefore in a worse state than when we lived in the world ; the reason of our feeling them is, because we are not so well acquainted with ourselves then, and because we now begin to discover the evil that before lurked in us. Wherefore we ought to be careful not barely to cover the root of our bad inclinations, but to pluck it up entirely.

"Those who feel a great deal of comfort and delight in the beginning of their conversion, and whom God tries not with temptations till afterwards, are indebted for this," says St. Gregory, "to divine providence, which would not have the path of virtue seem at first so rough and troublesome as to discourage them and make them turn back." And thus God dealt with his own people, when he delivered them from the bondage of Egypt. He led them not through the land of the Philistines, which was the nearest to the country they left, " lest," says the Scripture, " the people repent when they see war, and return back to Egypt ;" (Exod. xiii. 17); but when they had passed the Red Sea, and entered the wilderness, whence there was no apprehension of their return, God tried them with many sufferings and temptations before he put them in possession of the land of promise. He deals sometimes after the same manner with those who forsake the world. He hinders temptations from making war against them, lest being yet but weak in virtue they should be frightened, and return to the world. And in the beginning, he leads them through pleasant and comfortable ways, and after having tasted what God is, and known how much he deserves to be loved and served, they may with so much the more ease and courage support the temptations which war against the inward man. Nor did he suffer St. Peter to be tempted by a woman, who asked him whether he was not one of the disciples of Jesus Christ, till after he had shown him the majesty of his glory in his transfiguration; that when he had been humbled by temptation, he might, amidst his sighs of sorrow and tenderness, make use of what he had seen upon mount Thabor; and that as the fear of man had made him fall, so the consideration of the bounty of God, which he had already experienced, might help to raise him up again.

"This may show," says St. Gregory, "how much they are mistaken, who, beginning to serve God, and seeing that they find a great deal of pleasure therein, that God is pleased to give them fervour in prayer, and that all the exercises of virtue and mortification become easy to them, presently imagine that they have already attained perfection; whereas they ought to think, that these favours are only marks of Almighty God's kindness, which he shows to them as to children who begin to be weaned, and as persons whom he intends to sever wholly from the things of this world."

"It is sometimes," continues the same holy father, "to the less perfect, and to those who have made the smallest progress in virtue, that God communicates himself more abundantly; not because they merit more but because they have the greatest need thereof. In this he acts like a father, who having many children, and loving them all most tenderly, seems not much to mind those who are well; but if any one of them falls sick, he does not only take all care to restore him to his health, but seeks to caress and regale him with an hundred things. He acts also like a gardener, who is extremely careful to water continually the young plants, but as soon as they are strong and have taken root, he no longer waters them so constantly, nor takes so much pains about them."

Holy writers farther observe, that God sometimes sends more comforts to converted sinners, and bestows in appearance more special favours upon them, than upon those who have always lived as they ought. And this he does that the first may not fall into despair, nor the others yield to vanity. This conduct is perfectly well explained to us in the parable of the prodigal son. His father receives him with all expressions of joy, gives him a new garment, and sends for musicians; and this very father, though he never received anything but what was satisfactory from his eldest son, "had never given him a kid to eat with his friends," (Luke xv. 29,) yet he prepares a great feast, and orders a fatted calf to be killed for the return of a son who had been disobedient to him all his life. The reason is, "because they who are well," says our Saviour, " want not a physician, but the sick have need of one." (Matt. ix. 12.)

———o———

CHAPTER III.

Why God is pleased at our being tempted, and the advantages thereof.

" THE Lord your God tempts you, that it may be known whether or not you love him with all your heart, and with all your soul." (Deut. xiii. 3.) Upon these words of Deuteronomy, St. Austin asks, how what is said here by the Holy Ghost can be reconciled with the words of St. James, who says, that " God tempts no man." (James i. 13.) And answering his own objection, he says, that there are two ways of tempting; the one tends to deceive souls and make them fall into sin. Now it is not God makes use of this, but it is the devil, whose business it is to tempt after this manner, according to those words of the apostle, " lest he who tempts should have tempted you ?" (1 Thess. iii. 5,) that is to say, as it is interpreted, lest the devil should have tempted you. The other way of tempting goes no further than to try our hearts ; and in this sense it is that scripture says here, that God tempts us ; and in another place, that " God tempted Abraham." (Gen. xxii. 1.) God is pleased to try us, to make us sensible of our own strength, and to show how we love and fear him ; and therefore, as soon as Abraham had lifted up his hand to sacrifice his son, " I know now," said our Lord to him, " that thou fearest God," (Gen. xxii. 12,) that is, as St. Austin expresses it. " I have made thee know" that thou lovest him ; so that there are two sorts of temptations, the one, which God himself sends us ; and the other, which happens to us by his permission, and which proceeds from our enemies— the world, the flesh, and the devil.

But what is the reason that God permits us to be tempted by the last sort of temptation ? St. Gregory, Cassian, and several other great men, treating of this question say, first, that it is for our advantage to be tempted, and that God, sometimes to try us, withdraws his hand from us for a little while ; and if it were not so, neither he nor the prophet would have said, " O do not utterly forsake me !" (Ps. cxviii. 8.) But knowing well that God uses sometimes to forsake his servants, and to withdraw his hand from them for a little space, and for their greater good ;

thence it is, that he asks not of God that he would never forsake him, but only that he would not forsake him for ever.   After the same manner he addresses himself to God in the twenty-seventh Psalm : " Withdraw not thyself from thy servant in thy anger." (Ps. xxvi. 9.)   He asks not that God would never withdraw himself from him, but that he would not do it in his anger : that is, so that he might thereby fall into sin.   For with respect to that withdrawing which goes no further than to try us, and as to those temptations which God himself sends us, these are what the prophet asks for when he says : " Prove me, O Lord, and try me." (Ps. xxv. 2.)   And God himself says in Isaias, " for a small moment have I forsaken thee, but with great mercies will I gather thee.   In the moment of my wrath I hid my face a little from thee, but with everlasting kindness have I had pity on thee." (Isa. liv. 7, 8.)

But let us take a more particular view of the advantages we reap from temptations.   Cassian says, that God deals with us as he dealt with the children of Israel when he brought them into the land of promise ; he would not destroy their enemies wholly, but left there the Canaanites, the Amorites, and several others, " in order," says the Scripture, " that Israel might gain experience by them, and that her children might learn to fight with the enemy, and be accustomed to war." (Judg. iii. 1, 2.) " Thus it is," says he, " that God is pleased we should have enemies, and that we should be exposed to the assaults of temptations ; that, being continually engaged, we might not by softness and prosperity ruin ourselves." For, it has often happened, that they whom the enemy has not been able to overcome by an open war, have been afterwards easily vanquished, whilst they were seduced by the deceitful appearance of peace.

St. Gregory says, that God, by a secret and adorable providence, is pleased that the elect should be tempted and afflicted here ; because this world is only a place of pilgrimage, or rather of banishment, where we must be continually travelling till we arrive at our heavenly country.   And whereas travellers, on meeting with some agreeable meadow or grove, turn sometimes off the high road, God, who would not have anything put us out of ours, nor have us fix our minds upon earth, or take the place of our exile for that of our country, permits this life to be full of pain and torment, that the consideration of what we here suffer in it may make us more ardently sigh after the life to come. St. Austin delivers the same sentiment, saying, that temptations and afflictions serve to show us the misery of this life, and " to make us desire with greater ardour and seek more carefully the other," where we are to enjoy true happiness for all eternity. In another place he says, that " afflictions hinder the traveller who is going to his own country from looking upon his inn as the place of his abode, and from staying there too long." When we intend to wean a child, and use it to more solid diet, we rub the nurse's nipples with something bitter, which may make the child have an aversion to them. God deals with us almost after the same manner.—He diffuses a bitterness over all the things of this world that we may have an aversion to them, and that seeing nothing here worth our longing for, we should desire nothing but himself. And this it is which made St. Gregory say, that the " afflictions which oppress us here below force us to have recourse to God, and make us have an inclination for nothing but him." (Lib. xxiii. Moral. c. 15.)

———o———

CHAPTER IV.

Of some other advantages which temptations bring with them.

" BLESSED is the man that suffers temptation, for when he shall be proved, he shall receive the crown of life." (James i. 12.) St. Bernard, explaining these words of St. James, says, " it is necessary that temptations should happen, for who shall be crowned but he that shall lawfully have fought, and how shall a man fight, if there be none to attack him?" (Serm. lxiv. sup. Cant.) The scripture and holy writers show us, that a world of advantages are annexed to sufferings and adversities ; and the same are also annexed to temptations ; among which advantages one of the most considerable is that proposed to us in the words of St. James: " God sends us temptations, that our merits may be the greater, and our reward the more eminent." " For through many tribulations we must enter into the kingdom of God." (Acts xiv. 21.) So when the glory of the blessed souls was revealed to St. John, one of the elders that stood before the throne said to him : " These are they who came out of great tribulation, and have washed their robes, and made them white in the blood of the Lamb." (Apoc. vii. 14.) Hereupon St. Bernard asks, how is it that they are made white in the blood of the Lamb? For blood uses not to make what it touches white ; but, on the contrary, it makes it red. " They are made white,"

says he, " because with the blood that issued from the sacred side
of Jesus Christ there came forth water also, which made them
white ; or let us rather say that they are made white, because
the blood of this spotless Lamb is white and ruddy, according to
these words of the spouse in the Canticles : 'My beloved is white
and ruddy, the chief of ten thousand.' (Cant. v. 10.)" So that
it is through pains and sufferings we must enter into the kingdom of God. Here we must hew and polish the stones that are to
build the temple of the heavenly Jerusalem ; for not one stroke
of the hammer shall be given in that holy city. "When the
house of the Lord was building there was neither hammer nor
axe, nor any other tool of iron heard." (3 Kings vi. 7.) Now
the more considerable the place is where the stones are to be
put, the more strokes of the hammer and chisel are requisite to
polish them. Those, for example, that are to make up the
frontispiece of the gate of a building, must be more polished than
the others ; that so they may make the entrance of the building
more beautiful. Nor is it for this only that Jesus Christ, having
made himself for us the gate of heaven, was pleased to be afflicted
with so many sufferings and reproaches, but it is also, that being
to pass through a door where sufferings and reproaches, if we
may say so, had given so many strokes of the hammer and chisel
to him, we ought to be ashamed at not having received some
ourselves, that we might be made more fit for this heavenly
building. The stones that are to be thrown into foundations are
not cut with any care ; nor is it necessary that they who are to
be thrown headlong into hell should be tried by afflictions and
temptations. Let reprobates, therefore, think of nothing else
but diverting themselves—let them deny their sensuality nothing
—let them in all things follow their inclinations : but for such
as are designed to fill the places of the disobedient angels, they
must be exercised with temptations and sufferings. " For if we
are the children of God, we are consequently his heirs, heirs of
God and co-heirs of Jesus Christ, that provided we suffer with
him, we may with him also be glorified." (Rom. viii. 17.)

The necessity of being proved by temptations, is also manifested very well unto us by these words of the angel to Toby :
" Because you were acceptable to God, it was necessary for you
to have been proved by temptation." (Tob. xii. 13.) And the
Wise man says, " that it was temptation that made the faith of
Abraham appear." (Ecclus. xliv. 21.) And because he was
found steady in temptation, God forthwith lays before him the

reward of his virtue, and swears to him, "that he would multiply his posterity as the stars of heaven, and as the sand upon the sea-shore." (Ecclus. xxii. 17, 18.) So that one of the reasons why God sends temptations is to make us merit a greater reward and a richer crown. Holy writers therefore tell us, that God shows us great favours by sending us temptations, and giving us strength to overcome them, than if he should deliver us wholly from them; for so we should be deprived of the recompense of that glory which they give us an occasion to merit.

St. Bonaventure adds another reason, which is, that the love God has for us is the cause that he is not only pleased that we should come to glory, and to a high degree thereof; but, that we should also quickly possess it, without being obliged to stay a long time in the place he has appointed for the purifying us from our sins. With this view, he sends us here below temptations and sufferings, which cleanse our souls from the spots and rust of sin, and put them in a condition of enjoying sooner the presence of God. "Take away the dross from the silver, and a more pure vessel will come forth." (Prov. xxv. 4.) Thus it is that our soul must be purified from its uncleanness before it can be capable of glory; nor, is it, indeed, an ordinary favour which God shows us by thus putting us in a condition the sooner to enter into glory; nay, it is a very great one, that he is pleased the torments which we ought to suffer in purgatory should be changed into some slight pains, wherewith he chastises us in this life.

The holy scripture is full of examples which show us that prosperity does usually remove us far from God; and that adversity, on the contrary, brings us back again to him. Was it not prosperity that made Pharao's butler forget Joseph so soon? "All things prospering with the chief butler," says the scripture, "he remembered no more his interpreter." (Gen. xl. 23.) Was it not prosperity which made King Osias, after so good a beginning, make so ill an end? "When he found himself strong, his heart was lifted up to his destruction, and he neglected the Lord his God." (2 Paral. xxvi. 16.) Was not prosperity, in fine, the source of Nebuchodonosor's misfortunes? Was it not that which made Solomon transgress—which made David number his people; and made the children of Israel forget the benefits they had received from the hand of God? "My beloved waxed fat, and kicked, he is grown thick and blown up with fatness, and he has forsaken the Lord that made him, and gone far from the God who saved him." (Deut. xxxii. 15.) Afflictions, on the contrary, brought them back again to God, and it is that which made the prophet say, " with shame, O Lord, cover their faces, and they will seek thy name." (Ps. lxxxii. 17.) " They cried unto the Lord, when they were in trouble ;" (Ps. cvi. 13) ; " they sought him, they returned to him, and came to him betimes." (Ps. lxxvii. 34.)

When Nebuchodonosor was turned into a beast, however real or imaginary that change might be, it was then that he acknowledged God. And was not David more faithful when Saul persecuted him, when Absolom rebelled against him, and when Semei reviled him, than when all things went prosperously with him ? The experience also which he had of the advantages afflictions bring with them, made him thus address himself to God ; " we rejoiced," says he, " at the days wherein thou dost humble us, and the years when we were afflicted." (Ps. lxxxix. 15.) " It was good for me that thou hast humbled me." (Ps. xxxi. 4.) How many have been saved by adversity, who would have been lost by prosperity ? " I turned to thee, O Lord, in my affliction," says the Psalmist, " when I felt most the thorns thereof." When these thorns prick us, then it is that we enter into ourselves, and have recourse to God. It is a common maxim among the people of the world, " that chastisement makes fools wise." The same thing the Holy Ghost teaches us when he says by the mouth of the prophet Isaias, " that chastisement alone will give understanding," (Isa. xxviii. 19,) and explaining himself more clearly by the Wise man, he says that, " a great sickness makes the mind sober, and that the rod and correction give wisdom." (Ecclus. xxxi. 2.) Prosperity makes a man vain and insolent; it makes him like a bullock, which has not yet suffered the yoke ; and God to tame him, puts the yoke of afflictions and temptations upon him. "Thou hast chastised me ; and I was tamed as a bullock unaccustomed to the yoke." (Jer. xxxi. 18.) It was with gall that the angel cured Toby ; and with clay that our Saviour restored the blind man to his sight. And it is with the same design to heal us that God sends us temptations, which are the highest sufferings that they who truly serve him can be exposed to. For the loss of goods, sickness, and other things of that nature, are not very sensible afflictions to the true servants of God ; because they affect only the body, and do but touch the outside ; they are not therefore in great pain thereupon ; but when they are attacked with what pierces to the very soul, as with temptation, which tends to separate them from God, and seems to put them in danger of losing his grace ; then it is, that finding themselves touched to the quick, and agitated by the rebellion of the flesh, which would draw the spirit after it, they in the excess of their trouble cry out with the apostle, " O wretched man that I am, who will deliver me from the body of this death ? (Rom. vii. 24.) The corruption of the flesh draws me to evil ; I am full of good designs, which I put not in execution ; who will free me from the bonds of so deadly and dangerous a slavery ?

——o——

CHAPTER V.

That temptations serve to make us the more sensible of our weakness, and to have recourse to God.

TEMPTATION brings yet another advantage with it, which is, that it makes us know ourselves. Many times we know not ourselves, but temptation shows us what we are as Thomas à Kempis says very well : " temptations are very profitable though uneasy and troublesome to man ; because in them he is humbled, purified, and taught." This knowledge of ourselves is the foundation stone of the whole spiritual building ; without which nothing can be built that will last long ; and by the means of it the soul lays its whole stress upon God, through whom it can do all things, and becomes capable of raising itself to the height of Christian perfection. The effect then of temptation is that it shows us our weakness and ignorance. For, before that, man is not sufficiently acquainted with his misery ; and having not yet tried it, he has too good an opinion of himself. But when by experience he sees that the least puff blows him down, that little or nothing puts him quite out of heart, that a slight temptation confounds and dangerously wounds him, that his resolution and judgment fail him in time of need, and that darkness encompasses him ; then he begins to moderate his presumption and vanity, to be humbled, and to have no other thoughts of himself but such as suit his own meanness. " Were it not for temptation," says St. Gregory, " we should have too good an opinion of our own courage and strength : but when temptation comes, when we see ourselves just falling and as it were within an inch of shipwreck, then do we sincerely acknowledge our weakness, and enter into true thoughts of humility and lowliness. Wherefore the apostle, speaking of himself, says, "lest the multitude of revelations should exalt me, there was given to me a thorn in my flesh, the messenger of Satan, to torment me." (2 Cor. xii. 7.)

From hence follows another advantage, which is, that the knowledge of our weakness makes us know the need we have of God's assistance, of having recourse to him in prayer, and of cleaving fast to him only; according to these words of the Psalmist, "my soul cleaves unto thee; it is good for me to cleave unto God." (Ps. lxii. 9.) As a mother who would have her child go to nobody but herself makes it afraid of every one else, that so it may be forced to fly into her arms; so, the Lord permits the devil to frighten us with temptations, that so we may be obliged to run more readily to our heavenly Father. "He withdraws himself a little while from us," says Gerson, "as the eagle does from her little ones, to provoke them to fly after her; and as a mother that leaves her child for a moment that it may cry the more after her, look about for her with greater care, embrace her the more heartily after having found her, and that she herself may caress it with more than usual tenderness." (De Inst. Theol.) St. Bernard says, that "when God seems sometimes to withdraw himself from us, it is that we should, as it were, call him back again with more earnestness, and endeavour more carefully to keep him when we have him." Thus it was that being with his two disciples, who were going to Emaus, he pretended to leave them, and to be under a necessity of going on still further, that they should the more press him to stay with them, and say as they did; "abide with us, O Lord, for it grows late; and the day is much spent." (Luke xxiv. 9.)

By this means it happens also, that seeing the need we have of God's assistance, we esteem it the more. It is also this which makes St. Gregory say, that it is for our advantage God sometimes withdraws his hand from us: because if he should never leave us we might perhaps esteem his protection the less, and think it not so necessary as it is. Whereas, when he leaves us but for a time, and afterwards stretches out his hand to us, and that at the very moment we are ready to fall, we conceive much better the value of his favours. When we reflect with the Psalmist, that without him we had been lost: "had the Lord but deferred ever so little to help me, my soul had descended into hell;" (Ps. xciii. 17); we have then a more lively sense of his favours, and we enter into more deep reflections of his mercy and bounty. " Whensoever I call upon thee, I forthwith know that thou art my God," (Ps. iv. 10,) by the help that thou givest me. As soon as ever we have recourse to God in temptation we receive succour from him ; we find how faithful he is to assist us in time of necessity ; and that proof makes us, by looking then more particularly upon him as our father and defender, to be the more inflamed with his love, and to sing his praises, as the children of Israel did when they saw their enemies that pursued them perish in the Red Sea.

Another advantage that temptation causes is, that it teaches us not to attribute anything that is good to ourselves, but to give the glory of all to God ; and this advantage is so much the greater, because it is also a very effectual remedy against temptations, and a very proper means to obtain of God new favours.

———o———

CHAPTER VI.

That the just are proved and purified by temptations ; and that virtue thereby takes the deeper root.

HOLY writers say that God is pleased we should be the more tempted, thereby to prove our virtue. For as it is in great winds and storm that we find where a young tree has taken root ; and in war and battles, not in peace and repose, that we see the courage and valour of a soldier ; so it is in temptations and suffering, not in time of calm and still devotion, that we perceive the zeal and steadfastness of a true servant of God. Upon these words of the royal prophet, " I am prepared to keep thy commandments, without being disturbed at anything," (Ps. cxviii. 60,) St. Ambrose says that, " as a pilot must be of great ability to steer a ship well during a storm, and whilst one wave carries him, as it were, up to the skies, and then falling again, seems ready to swallow him up in the deep ; so we show ourselves skilful when we govern ourselves well in time of temptation, so that without being carried away by pride in prosperity, or pusillanimity in adversity, we can always say with the prophet : "I am prepared—without being disturbed at anything." Now, it is upon this account that God sends us temptations, to prove us, as he did his people, whom he left among many enemies "in order," says the scripture. "that by them he might prove Israel, and know whether they would hearken to the commandments of the Lord, which he commanded their fathers by Moses." (Judg. iii. 4.) Does not the apostle also tell us, "that heresies must be, that so those who have been proved may be made manifest." (1 Cor. xi. 19.) And does not the Wise man, speaking of the just say, "that God had tempted them, and found them worthy of him?" (Wisd. iii. 5.) Temptations are like strokes of the hammer, which show the goodness of the metal. They are the touchstones wherewith God proves his friends. For God, as well as men, will have friends proved, and therefore it is, that he puts them to the trial; according to these words, "the furnace proves the potter's vessels, and affliction the just." (Ecclus. xxvii. 6.) "And as silver is tried by the fire, and gold by the furnace, so the Lord tries our hearts by temptation. (Prov. xvii. 3.) "As when a mass of metal," says St. Jerome, "is thoroughly red hot it cannot be distinguished whether it is gold, silver, or copper; because whatsoever is so penetrated by the fire, seems like fire itself; so, in the ardour of devotion, and the fervour which spiritual consolations raise; we know not what any one is.—All is then fire. But take the metal out and let it but cool awhile, you will quickly see what it is—let the spiritual consolations and fervour pass, and let sufferings and temptations come, and then will appear what every one is in himself. When in a state of tranquillity and peace a man gives himself to virtue, it is hard to know whether he does it either purely out of love of virtue, or by reason of the goodness of his temper; whether for the pleasure he finds therein, or, in fine, because he is not then touched with anything else. But he who perseveres in spite of all the assaults which temptation makes upon him, shows indeed that it is for virtue's sake, and for the love of God alone, that he acts.

Temptation serves further to make us more pure. "Thou, O Lord, hast proved us," says the Psalmist, "as silver is tried in the fire." (Ps. lxv. 10.) God purifies his elect by temptation, as the goldsmith does gold and silver by the fire, "and I will make them pass through the fire," says he by Zachary, "and will refine them as silver is refined, and I will try them as gold is tried," (Zach. xiii. 9); and in Isaias, "I will purge away the dross, and take away all the tin." (Isa. i. 25.) It is thus temptation works in the just. It consumes whatever rust and impurity vice had left in them; it takes them off from self love, and the love of worldly things; and renders them most pure and agreeable in the sight of God. "it is true," says St. Austin, "that every body does not derive this benefit and comfort from temptations. Some things grow soft and melt before the fire, as wax; and other things, on the contrary, grow hard as clay. So it is with the just and the wicked; the just are softened by the fire of temptations and sufferings, by humbling themselves under the sense of their meanness; but the wicked, on the contrary, become hardened." Thus it was with the two thieves upon the cross. One made his punishment the means of his conversion, and the other made his a motive to blasphemy. This caused the same holy doctor, St. Austin, to say that, "temptation is a fire, in which gold shines, and straw consumes; the just is made perfect, and the sinner miserably perishes;" (Aug. in Psal. lxii. Exhort.); that it is a "storm from whence one gets ashore, and in which the other is drowned." The Almighty opened a way across the sea to the children of Israel, but the same waves which separated to save them, united again to swallow up the Egyptians.

St. Cyprian, desiring to encourage the faithful to suffer persecutions courageously, says, that "as the people of Israel did daily multiply more and more whilst the Egyptians oppressed them, so the church of God increases amidst the persecution of the unfaithful." And as the ark "was raised according to the swelling of the waters," (Gen. vii. 17,) so the true servants of God raise themselves up to heaven, according to the increase of temptations and sufferings. "And, as the agitation of the sea," says Gerson, "makes it in one instant throw up all the filth it had received by little and little in calm weather, so temptations and sufferings serve to purify the soul from all the imperfections it had contracted during the great peace it enjoyed."

The husbandman prunes the vine, that it may bear the more. And thus it is, say the holy writers, that God, who compares himself to the husbandman in the gospel, prunes his vines; that is, tempts and proves his elect, that they may more abundantly bring forth fruits of justice. "He will prune," says the scripture, "every branch which bears fruit, that it may bring forth more." (John xv. 2.) "The winds," says the holy abbot Nilus, "make the trees take stronger root, and temptation makes the soul more and more steadfast in virtue." (Nil. Abb. Tom. iii.) And it is in this sense that the holy interpreters understand these words of the apostle:—"Virtue is made perfect in weakness," (2 Cor. vii. 9,) as if he had said, that it is better established, grows more firm, and makes its solidity be better known. When any one disputes against the truth which you defend, the more reasons that are urged to oppose it the more also you endeavour to bring for the defence thereof. And so it happens, that by your answers to the objections made against you, you become more and more confirmed therein. It is so in temptations, the more endeavours that the devil uses to turn a servant of God from the practice of some virtue, the more the servant of God seeks by holy motives, by firm resolutions, and by new acts, to fortify himself therein; and thus that virtue becomes more firm, and takes deeper root in his heart. Where-fore it is very well said, that temptations are to the soul what the strokes of the hammer are to the anvil; they serve to make it stronger against all trials.

St. Bonaventure says, moreover, that those who finding them-selves strongly tempted by some vice remain faithful in the temptation, are ordinarily rewarded by God, in an eminent manner, with the possession of the virtue most opposite to the vice which they resisted. Thus St. Bennet, as St. Gregory tells us, having with great resolution overcome a violent temptation of the flesh, by rolling himself all naked upon thistles and thorns, received as a reward from God the gift of chastity; without ever feeling after that any motion against it. We read the same thing of St. Thomas of Aquin. A woman having a mind to entice him to sin, he drove her away with a firebrand; and, God crowned this his resistance by sending two angels, who strongly girt his loins, as a mark that he endowed him with the gift of perpetual chastity. God deals after the same manner with those who vigorously resist temptations against faith. He gives them afterwards pure and clear lights, which so illuminate their minds and inflame their hearts, that nothing any more troubles them. St. Bonaventure applies to this purpose the words of Isaias; "they shall lead them into captivity whose captives they were, and they shall bring into subjection their oppressors." (Isa. xiv. 2.) Wherefore, dear brother, comfort thyself when thou art tempted, and take courage; it is by this trial that God is pleased to strengthen in thee that virtue which temptations sets upon; it is by these rebellions of the flesh that he will have thee obtain the gift of angelical chastity. Sampson meets a lion in his way; attacks him and tears him in pieces; and in a while after returning by the same place, he finds a honeycomb in the body of the dead lion. Fall courageously upon the temptation and overcome it, and you will then see what pleasure you will reap thereby.

By this we may also learn, that to yield to a temptation is to give new force to it for the time to come; for hereby vice increases, and grows more hard to overcome; as St. Austin well observes upon this passage of Jeremias: "Jerusalem has sinned, and is therefore become weak." (Lament. i. 8.) The same truth the Wise man teaches us, in these words, "the sinner shall add sin to sin." (Ecclus. iii. 29.) And this remark is of great importance to those who are troubled with temptations; for the devil deceives some, by making them believe that they shall cause the temptation to cease by yielding to it. This is an error; for, on the contrary, it is the way to strengthen it, and to give concupiscence the greater power over you, thereby the more easily to overcome you upon all occasions. It is with that as it is with one that has a dropsy, who by drinking increases his thirst instead of quenching it: or as it is with a covetous man, who intending still to satisfy his avarice, makes it always the more insatiable. Take it therefore for a certain truth, that when you let yourself be carried away by temptation you add new strength to it against yourself; and you lose some of your own force, and so grow more easy to be overcome another time. Whereas when with resolution you resist, virtue does so much the more increase and grow strong in you. The way therefore to be rid of temptations, and to act so as not to be more disturbed by them, is not to yield to them, and never to suffer them to get ground upon us. For thus they so lose their strength, that they are brought in fine to give us no more trouble: and this is what ought greatly encourage us to make resistance.

———o———

CHAPTER VII.

That temptations serve to make us more careful and fervent.

ANOTHER advantage which temptation brings with it is, that it makes us more attentive to our duties of obligation, hinders us from being remiss in them, and causes us to stand more upon our guard; like men who are every hour on the point of engaging. As a long peace makes men negligent, takes away their strength, and softens their courage; so the exercise of war makes them valiant, robust and bold. Cato therefore asserted in the senate "that Carthage was not to be demolished, for fear the Romans

should then lose themselves in the idleness of peace.   For wo to
Rome," says he, " if once Cartharge is no more !"   The same
thoughts the Lacedemonians had as to their enemies.   For, one
of their kings having proposed utterly to destroy a city which
they were continually at war with, the Ephori opposed it, saying, they would not suffer the breaking of a "whetstone,"
which served to sharpen the virtue and courage of their citizens;
for so they called their enemy's city, which kept them still on
the alert, and alarmed them every hour : and thus they believed
that nothing was more prejudicial to them than the want of
occasions to fight and signalize themselves.   Just so it is in
things regarding our salvation ; the want of temptation makes
us careless and remiss, whilst to be tempted renders us more
careful and vigilant, and stirs up our fervour and courage.

A religious, for example, lets himself fall into a state of carelessness, which makes him negligent in all his duties and exercises.   He will wear no more haircloths, take no more disciplines;
he sleeps at prayer ; obeys but coldly, and seeks only pastime
and conversation.   Thereupon a violent temptation steals upon
him, wherein he has need of remedies, and of recourse to God ;
and then he starts out of his slumber, resumes new vigour and
fervour for mortification and prayer.   It is even a proverb
amongst worldly people, that to learn to pray to God, one must
as it were, turn seaman : and what does that signify but that
necessity and danger are great means to oblige us to have
recourse to God.   Upon this account it is, and in order to our
spiritual advancement, says, St. Chrysostom, that God permits
temptations.   "For when he sees us fall into carelessness and
lukewarmness ; when he finds that we leave off the communication we have with him in prayer, and make no more so great an
account of spiritual things ; he withdraws himself a little from
us, to oblige us thereby to return to him with more fervour.
When the devil," says the same saint, "possesses our soul with
fear and terror, then we may become more faithful, we are more
sensible of our own weakness, and we throw ourselves wholly
into the arms of God." (Hom. iv. ad Pop. Antioch.)   So that
temptations are so far from being an obstacle to us in the way of
virtue, that they on the contrary, forward us therein.   St. Paul
therefore, speaking of temptation, and intending to describe it by
a figurative expression, borrows not any term from the sword or
lance, but uses that of the goad.   The "goad or thorn of the
flesh," says he, "was given to me," (2 Cor. xii. 7,) to show, that

as the goad is not made to hurt or kill, but to quicken the pace, so temptation is not given us for our destruction, but to advance us, and to stir up our fervour; and so it is profitable even to those who have already made the greatest progress in virtue. For let a horse be ever so good and mettlesome, yet he goes always better when he feels the spur; so, let the servants of God be ever so perfect, they run more swiftly in the path of the Lord when they find themselves urged on by the goad of temptation.

"The intention of the devil in temptation is bad," says St. Gregory, " but God's design is good." Thus the leeches which are applied to a sick person would suck out all the blood to the last drop, if they could; but the physician uses them only to draw away that which is corrupted. In like manner, when fire is applied to a wound, the activity of the fire tends to burn the sound flesh as well as the other; but the intention of the surgeon being to heal, hinders it from acting anywhere but where it should. The design of the devil in temptation is, indeed to destroy virtue in our heart, and to rob us of the merit and reward of our good works; but God's design therein is quite opposite. The stones which the devil throws to overwhelm us are turned by God into precious ones, to make up a crown of glory for us. The Jews stone St. Stephen, and seek nothing but his death; and then it is that he sees the heavens open, and the Son of God calling him to him.

Upon this subject Gerson observes what ought to be of great consolation to us. He says, that it is the opinion of the holy fathers, that though in time of temptation we commit some little faults, and believe that we have been in some measure the cause thereof, through our own negligence; yet the patience and resignation, nevertheless, with which we may have suffered this trial, the resistance we may have made to the assaults of the temptation, and our endeavours to overcome it, do not only blot out all these faults and negligences, but make us increase in grace and merit in the eyes of God, according to the words of the apostle, "God will make you draw advantage out of the temptation." (1 Cor. x. 13.) When a mother or a nurse has a mind to teach a child to walk, she retires a little from it and then calls it to her; yet it is still afraid, and dares not to come forward; she, nevertheless, lets it alone; nay, sometimes exposes it to the hazard of falling, knowing that it is better it should have a little fall than not learn to walk. After the same manner God deals

with us.　"I am," says he, "as the nursing father of Ephraim."
(Osee. xi. 3.)　Those light faults which you believe you have
commited he makes no account of, in comparison of the profit
which you reap from temptations by resisting them.

Blosius tells us, that one day St. Gertrude, bewailing bitterly
a fault she was subject to, and begging of God most earnestly to
free her from it; our Lord, with great bounty, answered her thus:
"Why wouldst thou, my dear daughter, deprive me of great glory,
and thyself of great reward? Every time that thou art sensible
of thy fault, and dost purpose to amend it for the future, it is a
new merit thou acquirest; and as often as one endeavours, to
overcome any fault for the love of me, he does me the same
honour as a brave soldier does his king, in fighting courageously
against his enemies, and endeavouring to conquer them."

---o---

CHAPTER VIII.

*That the saints and servants of God, not only did not afflict them-
selves at temptations, but, on the contrary, rejoiced because of the
profit they derived from them.*

THE prospect of the great advantages annexed to temptations
was ths reason why the saints, instead of afflicting themselves
for having them, rejoiced thereat.　And it is to this purpose that
the apostle St. James exhorts in these words: "my dear brethren,
count it all joy, when ye fall into divers temptations." (Jam. i.
2.)　In the same spirit St. Paul speaks thereof; "it is not
only," says he, "in the hope of the children of God, that we
glory also in tribulations; knowing that tribulation worketh
patience; and patience, experience; and experience. hope."
(Rom. v. 3.)　St. Gregory, explaining this passage of Job, "if I
lie down, I say when shall I arise; and when I arise, I will be
still in expectation of the evening;" (Job. vii. 4); says, that the
expectation of the evening, in this place, is the expectation of
being tempted, as a good and advantageous thing.　For we are
in expectation of good things, as the same father adds, and in
apprehension of bad ones; and Job, by saying that he is in
expectation of temptation, shews sufficiently the esteem he has
thereof.

St. Dorotheus upon this occasion gives us an example of a
disciple of the ancient fathers of the desert, who being continually attacked by the spirit of impurity, did, through the mercy

of God, by means of prayer, fasting, labour, and several other austerities, courageously resist. His director, seeing him in that condition, told him one day, that if he pleased, he would pray to God to deliver him from that temptation. "I see very well, father," said he, "that the state I am in is very painful; but I find also that it furthers my progress in virtue; for it makes me give myself the more to prayer, mortification, and penance; so that all I desire you to beg of God for me is, that he would give me patience and strength that I may become victorious in the conflict." The good old man, overjoyed at the answer of his disciple, said to him; "now, my child, I see very well that thou dost truly advance in the path of virtue; for when a man is smartly attacked by temptation, which he strives to resist, he becomes more humble, more careful, and more mortified; and so the soul coming to rid itself of whatever is impure in it, ascends indeed to a high degree of purity and perfection." The same St. Dorotheus tells us of another hermit, who finding himself delivered from a temptation he was subject to, was very much afflicted thereat, and complained earnestly thereof to Almighty God; saying, "does this happen, O Lord, because thou hast not thought me worthy to suffer something for the love of thee?"

St. John Climachus says, that St. Ephrem, finding himself in that perfect state of tranquillity and peace which he calls impassibility, begged earnestly of God to re-engage him in the combat, that he might have more matter of merit, and wherewith to make up his crown. Palladius also tells us, that another hermit going to visit the abbot Pastor, and telling him that he was at last delivered from all the temptations which had tormented him, and that now by the divine mercy he enjoyed a profound peace, "go," said the holy man to him, "throw yourself at the feet of God, and beg of him to send you your temptations again, lest the state you are in should make you more lukewarm and negligent in his service. The hermit made his address anew to God, laid open his heart and soul before him, to know what was most convenient for him; and so God sent him back again his former temptations. In confirmation of all this, we see that when the apostle prayed to be delivered from the temptations which troubled him he was not heard, but God told him, "my grace is sufficient for thee; for virtue is made perfect in weakness." (2 Cor. xii. 9.)

———o———

CHAPTER IX.

That temptation serves both to instruct ourselves and others.

ANOTHER advantage which even spiritual directors may derive from temptations is, that those temptations making them feel in themselves what they are to see afterwards in others, they learn thereby what course they are to take. For he, we say, is the best surgeon who has been oftenest hurt; so he who is best exercised in the spiritual warfare knows by his own experience, (which is the best teacher,) all the artifices of the devil, whereby he becomes much more able to instruct his neighbour. "They who have been at sea," says Ecclesiasticus, "know the dangers thereof." (Ecclus. lxiii. 26.) And do we not every day see, that they who have been inured to the business of the world extricate themselves much better than others from the several emergencies thereof?

Now, temptations are as advantageous to us in reference to what regards our salvation; and this is what the Wise man teaches us by these words: "What does he know, who is not tempted? A man who has been tried in many things, makes many reflections. He that has not been tried knows very little." (Ecclus. xxxiv. 10.) A man, in fine, who has passed a long apprenticeship in this sort of warfare will, doubtless, be very proper for the direction of souls; and it is to make us expert in this science that God is pleased we should have temptations. He will have it so, likewise, that they may teach us to be sensible of those which our neighbour is exposed to; just as the diseases and infirmities of the body, with which we have been afflicted, teach us to compassionate those who are attacked with the like distempers.

Cassian tells us of a young hermit, who being tormented with continual temptations of the flesh, addressed himself to an ancient anchoret, and laid open unto him the state of his soul, hoping by the counsel and prayers of the old man to find a comfort and remedy for what thus perplexed him. But he found himself quite mistaken; for this person, who had neither that prudence nor discretion which age usually brings along with it, showed very great surprise at the recital he made of his temptation; reprimanded him sharply, and devoured him with words, calling him a wicked wretch, and telling him that he was unworthy the name of an hermit, since things of the nature he spoke of befell him ; lastly, he sent him away so disconsolate, by the roughness of this his reproach, that in the trouble and despair he was in he thought no more of resisting his temptations, but rather of executing what they suggested to him ; and already began to take measures for that purpose. The abbot called Apollo, who was then in great reputation in the desert for sanctity and prudence, met him on the high road to the adjacent town, and judging of his inward trouble by the gloominess of his countenance, asked him with great mildness what ailed him, and what was the cause of the discomposure and sadness which appeared in his countenance ? But the young man was so overwhelmed with his own thoughts that he answered him nothing ; the holy abbot thereby further knowing the confusion his mind was in, pressed him yet more earnestly, so that in fine he obliged him to declare the trouble of spirit he was in, and how the reproaches of the old man had so far discouraged him, that despairing of being able to overcome his temptations, and of living like a good hermit, he had resolved to quit the desert, and to return to the world to marry. The holy abbot began then to comfort and encourage him, by telling him that he himself was assaulted every day with the same temptations ; and that he was not, therefore, to lose courage, since for the overcoming of them we were not to rely so much upon our own strength as upon the grace and mercy of Almighty God. He, in fine, conjured him to defer but for one day his resolution, and to return in the meantime to his cell, to implore there God's assistance; and since the time was but short, he made him consent thereunto. After this the abbot went to the old man's cell ; and as soon as he was near it he fell prostrate to the earth, where, lifting his hands to heaven and bursting out into tears, he made this prayer to God: " Thou, O Lord, who knowest our strength and our weakness, and who art the sovereign physician of our souls, grant that the temptation which afflicts the young man may pass into the heart of this old man, that he may, at least at his age, learn to have compassion, and to pity the pains and weakness of his brethren." Scarce had he concluded his prayer when he saw the devil, in shape of a hideous negro, shoot a fiery dart into the old man's cell, who had no sooner felt the sensible stroke thereof, but he falls into so great trouble of mind as gives him no rest at all; he rises—he goes out—he comes back again ; and, after having been for some time doing continually the self-same thing over and over again, being at last unable to bear any longer the heat of lust which had seized upon him, he makes the same resolution the young hermit had made, and betakes himself to the same high road.

The holy abbot, who observed him, and who by the vision he had had knew the temptation that tormented him, comes up to him, asks him whither he was going, and what was the reason that, forgetting what he owed to the gravity of his age and profession, he walked with such great haste and disquiet? The old man, who believed himself discovered, and whose bad conscience had covered him with shame and confusion, answered nothing. Then the holy man, taking advantage of the trouble he saw him in, bade him return to his cell. "Believe," says he, "that if the devil has let thee alone hitherto, it is either because he did not know thee, or made no account of thee. See now thy own weakness; since, after having grown old in the desert, thou hast not being able to resist one temptation; nay, not so much as the first attacks of it; but hast permitted thyself to be immediately overcome; and without intending to wait one day only, hast thought of nothing else but the putting thy ill designs in execution. God hast thus permitted it, that at least in thy old age thou mayest learn to sympathise with thy brethren in their maladies and infirmities, and that thou mayest know by thy own experience that they are to be comforted and encouraged, and not to be disheartened and cast into despair, as the young hermit was who addressed himself unto thee. The devil did not attack him so violently, whilst he let thee alone, but because seeing more pity in him than in thyself, he was the more touched with jealousy and envy, thinking that so steady virtue could not be assaulted by too strong and too violent temptations. Learn then, by thyself, to pity others; to stretch out thy hand to him that is ready to fall; and to support him by words of compassion and comfort, and not to overwhelm him by too rough treatment, and thereby become the occasion of his greater fall. This is what the prophet Isaias teaches us by these words, ' the Lord hath given me a learned tongue that I might know how to support with a word him that is weary;' (Isa. l. 4); and it is what our Saviour himself has practised, to whom St. Matthew applies this passage of the same prophet Isaias, "the bruised reed he will not break, and the smoking flax he will not quench." (Isa. xliii. 3.) To conclude," continues the saint, "since we cannot, but by the help and grace of God, resist the motions and quench the heats of concupiscence, let us fly to him, and beseech him to deliver us from the temptations which torment us ; ' For he wounds and heals, he strikes and his hands make whole again.' (Job v. 18.) ' He kills and restores to life, he pulls down and sets up again.' " (1 Kings ii. 7.) They then fell to their prayers, and as it was through the prayers of the holy abbot that this temptation came upon the old man, so God delivered him from it by the same prayers ; and thus both the young hermit and the old one too met with such a remedy and instruction as they stood in need of.

———o———

CHAPTER X.

The remedies for temptations, and first that we must keep up our courage and be joyful in them.

" FINALLY, my brother, be strong in the Lord, and in the power of his might put on the armour of God, that you may withstand the snares of the devil.") Eph. vi. 10, 11.) St. Anthony, who was so well exercised in this warfare which the faithful are to carry on against the devil, was used to say, that one of the chief means to overcome him was to show resolution and joy in temptations ; because he is then troubled, and loses the hope of doing us harm. In the book of spiritual exercises, St. Ignatius hereupon gives us an instruction which agrees very well with this. He says that the devil deals with us in temptations as a woman that quarrels with a man ; if the woman sees that the man advances towards her, her heart fails and she retires ; but if she finds that he is afraid of her, she thereby becomes more bold and insolent ; so that she behaves more like a lioness than a woman ; in like manner, when the devil tempts us, if he sees us resolute and steady, he loses courage and is disheartened ; but if he perceives us yielding, he resumes new strength and becomes a formidable enemy. " Resist the devil," says St. James, "and he will fly from you." (James iv. 7.) And the observations which St. Gregory makes upon these words of Job, " the tiger perished because he had no prey," (Job. iv. 11,) agrees wholly with what has been said. " For what is called tiger in this place, is by the Septuagint or Seventy Interpreters called Myrmecoleon, that is, lion-pismire ; for the devil adds the saint, " is meant by this word." He is a lion and pismire both together ; a lion to those, who are to him but as pismires ; and a pismire to such as behave themselves to him as lions.   The holy writers therefore admonish us not to be troubled at temptations, lest thereby we may lose courage ; but to resist with joy, as the Maccabees did, of whom the scripture says, " that they fought with cheerfulness the battle of Israel ;" (1 Mác. iii. 2) ; for that is the true way to overcome as they did.

There is another reason for us to behave ourselves thus : because the devil, being the enemy of our happiness, is certainly troubled at our cheerfulness, and rejoices at our sorrow. So that, were it for nothing else, but to deprive him of so malicious a joy we ought always do our utmost to let him see our cheerfulness and courage.   The joy and constancy which the holy martyrs expressed in their torments was as cruel a punishment of their tyrants as all the pains which their extraordinary cruelty made them suffer.   And it is by this holy joy and resolution that we ought to be revenged upon the malice of the devil ; and because it is one of the best means we have to conquer him, I shall in the following chapters speak of some things that may conduce to the preservation of this joy and courage in our hearts.

———o———

CHAPTER XI.

That the devil is able to do but very little against us.

To encourage us in temptations, it will be a very great help to consider the weakness of our enemy ; and how little he is able to do against us, as he cannot make us fall into any sin against our own will.   "Behold, my brethren," says St. Bernard, "how weak our enemy is ; he cannot overcome but him who has a mind to be overcome." (Serm. lxxiii. in Cant.)   If a man who is going to fight were sure to overcome if he would, how joyful would he be ?   Would not he think himself sure of a victory which depended only upon his own will ?   With the same confidence and joy we might fight against the devil, for we know very well that he cannot conquer us, if we ourselves will it not. It is this that St. Jerome very well observes upon the words the evil spirit said to our Saviour, when, having carried him up to the pinnacle of the temple, he counselled him to throw himself down headlong.   "Cast thyself down," (Matt. iv. 6,) said the tempter ; "and this," adds the saint, "is the true language of the devil, who desires nothing so much as the fall of all men.

He can indeed persuade them to throw themselves down, but he cannot throw them down himself." The voice of the devil that tempts you says, throw yourself down into hell. You must answer him ; do so yourself ; you know the way ; as for me I will not do it : for he cannot have the power to make you if you have not the will to do it.

A certain person, finding that he was continually tempted by the devil to destroy himself, discovered to his confessor the trouble and perplexity he was in. His confessor having convinced him that the motions of the evil spirit could have no further power over him than what he himself would give him, advised him, that as often as he found himself troubled with that temptation, he should answer—"I am resolved I will not do what you would have me ;" and that he should come again to him eight days after. This man did what his confessor bid him, and by this means delivered himself from the temptation which tormented him, and so came to thank him afterwards for the remedy he had prescribed him. And it is of this remedy that I shall now speak.

The opinion of St. Austin agrees very well with what I have now asserted. He says, that the devil was not bound before the birth of our Saviour, and that till then he freely exercised his tyranny over men ; but that Jesus Christ by coming into the world chained him up, as St. John declares to us in the Apocalypse : "And I saw an angel coming down from heaven, having the key of the bottomless pit, and a great chain in his hand ; and he laid hold upon the dragon, that old serpent which is the devil and Satan, and bound him for a thousand years, and cast him into the bottomless pit, and shut him up, and set a seal upon him, that he should deceive the nations no more till the thousand years should be fulfilled, and after that he must be loosed for a little season." (Apoc. xx. 1.) "God has therefore chained up the devil," continues the holy doctor, "and do you know how he has done it ? After such manner that he permits him not to do the evil he might and would do, if he had the liberty of tempting and deceiving men by all those ways and artifices of which he is capable. But you may say, if he be chained, how comes it to pass that he still does so much mischief ? It is true," answers the father, "he does much indeed, but it is to those who take no care of themselves ; he is chained up like a dog, that is, so tied that he can bite none but those that come near him. He is able to bark, he is able to fawn and flatter, but he cannot at all bite any one, except such as will be bitten by him. (Lib. xx. de Civit. Deis, c. 8.) So that, as," adds the saint, "we laugh at a man that permits himself to be bitten by a dog in a chain, so we may also laugh at those who let themselves be overcome by the devil; because he is so fast tied that he can do no hurt to any but such as come near him." It is then your own fault if he does you any hurt in the state you are in; since he cannot hurt you unless you will yourself, so that you may even contemn him as much as you please. It is this the saint teaches us, explaining these words of the Psalmist, "the dragon which thou hast formed to serve us for sport:" (Ps. ciii. 26,) "have you not seen," says he, "how children feel pleasure in looking upon a bear, or any other wild beast that is chained, and how they amuse themselves with it : you may also mock the devil as often as he tempts you; for he is like a dog in a chain, who can only bark and make noise, but cannot bite you unless you will it yourself."

The devils once appeared to St. Anthony under several horrid and frightful shapes, and surrounded him as if they were ready to devour him; but the saint only laughed at them, saying, "if you have power to hurt me, the least of you is able to do it, but because you have not, you come in troops to affright me. If God has given you any power over me, behold here I am, devour me; but if he has not, all your endeavours are in vain." We may make the same answer in all our temptations; because since Jesus Christ became man, the devil has no power left; as he one day told St. Anthony; who answered him, "though you are the father of lies yet you have at present spoken truth against your will." For this reason our Saviour bids us confide and take courage. "I," says he, "have overcome the world:" (John xvi. 33,) and therefore let us say with St. Paul, "thanks be to God, who gives us the victory through our Lord Jesus Christ," (1 Cor. xv. 57.)

---o---

CHAPTER XII.

That it is a great help in temptations to think that we fight in God's presence.

THE consideration that God beholds us fighting is a further help to encourage us, and to give us new strength in temptations. A soldier that fights under his general's or prince's eye, thereby becomes more courageous. We truly fight in the presence of God in all our temptations ; wherefore, in all those attacks we have to sustain, we must make account that we are entered into the lists, and that all the saints and angels are spectators of the combat, and expect with impatience the success thereof ; and that God is the judge and rewarder of our victory. This thought the holy fathers had, which is founded upon the words of the gospel, where it takes notice, that after the devil had tempted our Saviour to no purpose, and had quitted him, " the angels came and served him." (Matt. iv. 11.) We read in the life of St. Anthony that one night, when the devils had beaten and bruised him with many blows, he lifted up his eyes and saw a bright light, which, piercing the top of his cell, dispersed the darkness thereof and drove away all the devils; and in a moment freed him from all the pain of those strokes he had received. Then presently addressing himself to our Saviour he said : " O Lord, where were you whilst your enemies so cruelly treated me ? Why came you not in the beginning of the combat to hinder them, and deliver me out of their hands ?" To whom a voice answered, " Anthony, I was present in the beginning of the combat, and all along have been a spectator of it ; and because thou hast fought with such courage, I will always continue to assist thee, and render thy name famous all over the world." Wherefore, in all our temptations we may assure ourselves that we have God and the angels witnesses of our resistance, and who is there that would not encourage himself to fight well before such spectators as these ?

Moreover, since with God it is the same thing to look upon us, and to help us ; we ought to consider that he regards us not only as our master and judge, to crown us if we become victorous, but as our father and protector, to help us if we stand in need of his assistance ; according to these words of the scripture ; " the eyes of the Lord contemplate the whole heart, and give strength and fortitude." (2 Par. xvi. 9.) " The Lord is upon my right hand, lest I should be moved." (Ps. xv. 8.) It is related in the fourth book of Kings, that the prophet Eliseus being in the city of Dothan, the king of Syria sent in the night part of his army to take him. Giezi, the prophet's servant, going out early in the morning sees the city quite surrounded with troops, runs presently to give notice to his master, believing himself lost, and cries out :—" Alas ! alas ! alas ! my lord, what shall we do ?" " Fear nothing," says the prophet, " for we have more for us,

than they have on their side." (4 Kings vi. 14.)   Whereupon
he betook himself to prayer, to beg of God that he would please
to open the eyes of Giezi, and presently he saw a mountain
covered with horsemen and fiery chariots, whereby he was freed
from his fear.   We have no less subject of confidence ; because
we know God is always ready to succour us.   " Set me by thee,"
says Job, "and let who will attack me." (Job xvii. 5.)   " The
Lord is with me," says Jeremias, "as a powerful warrior that
protects me.   Wherefore they who persecute me shall fall ; they
shall become weak against me, and remain covered with confusion." (Jer. xx. 11.)

St. Jerome, writing upon these words of the Psalmist, "Thou,
O Lord, hast crowned us with the buckler of thy good will,"
(Ps. v. 13,) says, that in the language of men there is a great
difference between a buckler and a crown, but in the language
of God they are one and the same thing ; because when he
covers us with the buckler of his love, the buckler which is our
protection and defence is also our crown and victory.   To conclude with the apostle, " if God be for us, who shall be against
us ?" (Rom. viii. 31.)

————o————

CHAPTER XIII.

*Of two reasons which may excite us to fight with confidence and
courage in temptation.*

St. Basil says, that the reason why the devil is so enraged
against us, comes not only from the envy he has to men, but
from the hatred he bears to God ; and since he is able to do
nothing against God, he turns all his fury against man his image ;
and thus, in some measure, endeavours to revenge himself upon
God.   " He does,'" says St. Basil, "as a man, who, being not
able to revenge himself upon his prince, tears his picture in
pieces ; or like a mad bull, who finding itself pricked on all
sides, and not being able to catch those that prick him, dis-
charges his rage upon a man made of pasteboard, which is on
purpose placed before him, and tears the image in pieces." From
this truth the saint deduces two reasons, very proper to excite us
to fight courageously in temptations.   First, because our glory is
not only concerned in it, but also the glory of God, whom the
devil endeavours to offend in our person ; and this consideration
ought to move us rather a thousand times to lose our lives than

to give the devil an occasion to revenge himself of God upon us. For then it is that we fight not only for ourselves but for God also; it is God's interest and cause we defend; and, therefore, we ought to die in the combat rather than suffer his glory to be diminished.

The second reason is, that since it is out of hatred to God that the devil makes war against us, we may assure ourselves that God will take our part against him, and help us to overcome him. Because, as in the world, when a prince or great man sees another engaged in a quarrel upon his account, he fails not ordinarily to take his part, and make his quarrel his own. It was out of hatred to Mardochai that Aman would have destroyed the Jews; and Mardochai took upon him so well their defence that he destroyed Aman himself. With how far greater reason ought we to expect the same thing from God? Wherefore, we may with David thus address ourselves to him with confidence, saying—"Arise, O Lord, judge thy own cause." (Ps. lxxiii. 22.) "Take up thy arms and buckler to defend me." (Ps. xxxiv. 2.)

———o———

CHAPTER XIV.

That God permits none to be tempted above their strength; and, therefore, we ought not to be discouraged, how long or violent soever the temptation may happen to be.

"God is faithful," says the apostle, "and will not permit you to be tempted above your strength, but, that you may be able to resist temptation, he will give you help proportionable to the attacks you shall have to sustain." (1 Cor. x. 13.) This ought to be a great subject of comfort and confidence to us in temptations. We already know that, on the one hand, the devil has no power but what God gives him, and can tempt us no farther than God permits; and, on the other, as St. Paul assures us, that God will not permit the devil to tempt us above our strength. Who is there to whom this assurance ought not to give comfort and courage? There is no physician that so proportions the drugs he prescribes, according to the strength and need of a sick person, as this heavenly physician proportions those temptations and afflictions with which he permits us to be tried. "If the potter," says St. Ephrem, "when he puts his vessels of clay which he has prepared into the fire, knows precisely how long he must leave them there to render them serviceable, and that if he leaves them too long in it they will fly in pieces, or if too short they will easily break only by touching them ;" with how far greater reason then ought we to believe that God, whose wisdom and bounty are infinite, knows how to keep the same measures towards us in temptations ?

St. Ambrose, upon these words of St. Matthew: "Jesus having ascended into the ship, his disciples followed him, and presently there arose a great tempest in the sea, so that the ship was all covered with waves, but he in the meantime slept ;" (Matt. viii. 23) ; says, " that the elect of our Lord, and those that accompany him, are tempted as well as others ; nay, it even sometimes happens," adds the saint, " that God feigns to sleep, thus industriously hiding the love he bears his children, that he may the more oblige them to have recourse to him." But he sleeps not, nor does he at all forget them. " If he makes any stay, expect him," says the prophet, " for he will soon come, and make no delay." (Hab. ii. 3.) It seems to a sick person that the night is longer than ordinary, and that the day is very long coming, notwithstanding there is no such thing, for the day comes at the ordinary time ; after the same manner, though God seems to you who are sick to stay longer than he should do, yet there is nothing of this, he knows at what time precisely he ought to come, and will not fail to come when he should.

St. Austin explains to this purpose our Saviour's conduct when the sisters of Lazarus sent him word that their brother was sick. " This sickness," says he, " is not unto death, but has happened for the glory of God, and that thereby the Son of God should be glorified." (John xi. 4.) After this he waited two days longer to render the miracle he designed to perform the greater. " It is after this manner," adds the saint, " that God sometimes treats his servants. He leaves them for some time in temptations and sufferings, and seems as if he had forgot them, but the reason for which he does this is thereby to procure greater advantgaes for them." After the same manner he had a long time let Joseph remain in prison, but he afterwards drew him out of it with greater glory to make him governor of all Egypt ; so, if he leave you for a long time in temptations and suffering, it is to draw you out of them after a manner more advantageous to his own glory and your salvation.

St. Chrysostom makes the same remark upon these words of the Psalmist : " thou who dost elevate me from the gates of death :"—" take notice," says he, " that the prophet does not say 'thou who dost deliver me;' but 'thou who dost elevate me from the gates of death;' because in effect, God is not contented with delivering his servants from temptations, but he makes temptations serve to their greater elevation and glory." Wherefore, though you feel yourself overwhelmed, and imagine yourself to be already within the gates of death, yet you ought firmly confide that God will draw you from thence. "For the Lord gives death, and gives life, he conducts even to the gates of hell, and brings back again." (1 Reg. ii. 6.) "And though he should kill me," says Job, "I will always hope in him." (Job xiii. 15.)

St. Jerome, reflecting upon Jonas's adventure—"take notice," says he, "that Jonas found his salvation where he thought himself assuredly lost." They cast him into the sea, and presently he was devoured by "a whale that God had placed there ready," not to devour him, "but to receive him into his belly," (Jonas ii. 8,) as into a vessel to carry him ashore. "Is after this manner," continues the saint, "it often happens that we think that to be the occasion of our destruction, which procures our salvation: 'and that we there meet with life where we thought we should certainly have found death.'" Moreover. the servants of God, who know by their own experience what his conduct is over men; and that he humbles to exalt ; that he wounds to cure ; and that he kills to give life; do not lose courage in dangers and adversities by the knowledge of their own weakness, but they entirely cast themselves into God's hands, and are satisfied by knowing that they are in too good hands to fear or apprehend anything from their own frailty.

It is related in ecclesiastical history that the abbot Isidore said, "I am now forty years attacked by a violent temptation and have never yet yielded to it." We see also a great many examples of divers fathers in the desert, who all their lives were attacked with violent temptations, which they always sustained with a steady and equal confidence. "These were those giants," according to the expression of the prophet, "who understood what belongs to war." (Baruch iii. 26.) It is in this we ought to imitate them. And St. Cyprian, desiring to inspire us with the same steadiness and confidence, makes use of the words of God in the prophet Isaias : "Fear nothing, because I have redeemed thee, and have called thee by thy name. Thou art mine, when thou shalt pass through the midst of the waters I will be with thee ; and the waves shall not cover thee. When thou shalt walk in the fire, thou shalt not burn, and the flame shall not burn thee ; because I am the Lord thy God, the holy One of Israel, thy Saviour ?" (Isai. xliii. 1, 2, 3.) These other words also of the same prophet are most proper to strengthen us in the same holy confidence : "You shall be as suckling children, carried on the breast of their mother, who are carressed upon their lap. So I will comfort you as a mother, that caresses and cherishes her child." (Isai. lxvi. 12, 13.)

Imagine with what marks of love a mother receives her infant when being frightened at anything it casts itself into her arms ; how she embraces it, how she presses it to her breast, how she kisses, flatters, and tenderly caresses it ; but the tenderness of God for those who have recourse to him in temptations and dangers is without comparison far greater. It was this that gave so much comfort to the Psalmist, when he cried out to God, " be mindful of the promise which thou hast made to thy servant, which thou hast given me hopes of. This comforted me in my humiliation, because thy promise gave me life." (Ps. cxviii. 49.) Let us animate ourselves with the same hope, and let us make it the subject of our comfort ; because, as the apostle says, " it is impossible that Almighty God should lie," (Heb. vi. 18,) or violate his word.

----o----

CHAPTER XV.

A good means of overcoming temptations is to diffide in ourselves, and to place all our confidence in God ; and why God particularly protects those who confide in his help alone.

ONE of the best means to overcome temptations is to diffide in ourselves, and to place all our confidence in God ; and, as the Scripture takes notice in several places, it is this which chiefly moves him to assist us in our temptations and sufferings. " I will deliver him ; because he has hoped in me." (Ps. xc. 14.) "Thou savest, O Lord, those that hope in thee." (Ps. xvi. 7.) " The Lord is a prophet of those that hope in him." (Ps. xvii. 31.) The prophet alleges no other reason to God than this to oblige him to have mercy on him, " have mercy on me, O God ; have mercy on me, because my soul puts its confidence in thee, and I will hope under the shadow of thy wings." (Ps. lvi. 1.) It was the same reason that Zarias made use of in the fiery furnace, when he begged of God to accept the sacrifice of his life ;

"because," says he, "those that confide in thee cannot suffer confusion." (Dan. iii. 40.) The Wise man, in like manner, assures us that "no one was ever confounded who trusted in God." (Ecclus. ii. 11.) And, lastly, the holy scripture is so full of declarations of this kind, that it is unnecessary to delay longer in proving so clear and known a truth.

But now let us see why this entire diffidence in ourselves, and confidence in God, is a means so proper to merit his help in our necessities. We have already touched on the reason in several places, and God himself has given it us, when he said by the mouth of David, "because he has hoped in me, I will deliver him. I will protect him, because he has known my name;" (Ps. xc. 14,) that is to say, according to St. Bernard, "I will protect him, and I will deliver him, on condition that acknowledging his deliverance to come from me he attributes it not to himself, but gives all the glory of it to my name." (Serm. xvii. sup. Ps. qui. habitat.) The reason therefore why God so particularly protects those that hope in him is because they attribute nothing to themselves, and give the glory of all to God. So that as they are regardless of their own honour, and attentive only to that of God, he takes their cause in hand, does his own work, and makes it his own business, as a thing that purely regards his own honour and glory. He acts not so towards those who confide in their own lights and rely upon their own strength, but since they attribute all to themselves, and thus usurp a glory which belongs to God alone, he leaves them to their blindness and weakness, and permits them not to succeed in anything. For according to the prophet, "he loves not him who confides in the strength of his horse, or in the swiftness of his legs. But the Lord loves those who fear him and hope in his mercy." (Ps. cxlvi. 10.) It is these he is pleased to protect, and abundantly to favour with his graces.

St. Austin says, that God sometimes defers the succours of his grace, and permits that for a long time there should remain in us an inclination to certain vices, without our being able to compass an entire victory over them. "And this not to damn, but to humble us—that we may more esteem his grace; and fear, also, that if we should find a facility in all things, we should believe that to belong to us which is his; which error is dangerous to religion, and very contrary to piety." (Lib. ii. de peccatis, c. 19.) Without doubt, if things became so very easy we should set less value on them, and believe we were indebted to none but ourselves for them. St. Gregory, explaining these words of Job, " behold there is no help to myself in me," (Job vi. 13,) says, that " it often happens that some virtue which we possess becomes a very dangerous instrument of our destruction; and that we should have been better without it. Because it happens to fill us with pride, by inspiring a vain confidence in ourselves, and by means of this pride it kills the soul, whilst it seems to give it new strength ; and thereby casts it into a precipice, after it has separated it by presumption from that interior confidence it ought to have had in God." (Lib. vii. Mor. c. 9.) It is this, our abuse of God's graces, which is the cause that he often refuses to give them unto us ; permitting in a thousand occasions, that we should know by experience how little ability we have of ourselves to do anything that is good; suffering us to remain a long time in this state to teach us humility, and not at all to confide in, or attribute anything to ourselves, but to render the glory of all to God alone. When we shall be in such a holy disposition of mind as this is, then we may assure ourselves of his divine assistance, and sing with the mother of Samuel, " the bow of the strong is broken, and the weak are armed with strength." (1 Kings ii. 4.)

——o——

CHAPTER XVI.

That prayer is a powerful remedy against temptation : some short and fervent prayers proper to be made in time of temptation.

PRAYER is another remedy of which we ought to make great account : and is a general one, recommended by both scripture and the holy fathers as one of the principal remedies we can use. Our Saviour himself teaches us the same truth in the gospel, not only by these words, " watch and pray, that ye enter not into temptation," (Matt. xxvi. 41,) but also by his own example. It was with prayer he prepared himself in the garden for all the pains and ignominies of his passion. He prayed not because he stood in need of prayer, but because he would teach us to have recourse to it in all the attacks we should meet with. The abbot John said, that a religious person ought to be as a man who carried fire in one hand, and water in the other, to cast upon it as occasion served ; even so, says he, when the fire of concupiscence begins to kindle in us, we ought presently to extinguish it by prayer. He made use of another comparison also to this purpose, saying, that as a man who lies at the foot of a tree, and sees wild beasts coming towards him to devour him, would presently climb to the top of it to save himself; so a religious who perceives himself beset with temptations ought to climb up to heaven, and retire into the bosom of God, by the help of prayer; and by this means he will be delivered from all the attacks and snares of the devil. "For it is in vain to cast a net in the presence of birds;" (Prov. i. 17,) and the devil will in vain set his snares to take us, if we raise ourselves to heaven upon the wings of prayer. "My eyes are always lifted up to the Lord," says the prophet, "it is he who will free my feet from snares." (Ps. xxiv. 15.)

I have spoken at large in the first part of this work of the advantage of prayer in temptations. It will therefore suffice at present to set down here some short and fervent prayers, which upon occasion we may make use of. The holy scripture is full of passages of this kind, and chiefly the psalms are filled with them. "O Lord, I suffer violence, answer for me." (Isa. xxxviii. 24.) "Arise, O Lord, why dost thou sleep, do not always reject me; why dost thou turn thy face from me, and forget my miseries and oppression?" (Ps. xliii. 23.) "Take up thy arms and buckler, arise to help me. Say to my soul, I am thy Saviour." (Ps. xxxiv. 2.) "How long, O Lord, wilt thou be forgetful of me? Wilt thou always be so? How long wilt thou, O Lord, hide thy beautiful face from me? How long shall my enemy be too strong for me? Cast thy eyes upon me and hear me, O my Lord, and my God. Illuminate my eyes and permit not the sleep of death to shut them; nor that my enemy should boast that he has prevailed against me." (Ps. xii. 1, 2, &c.) "It is thou, O Lord, who art my help in time of affliction." (Ps. ix. 10.) "I will hope under the shadow of thy wings; and when thou shalt cover me with them, I will rejoice." (Ps. lxii. 8.) St. Austin, touched with the idea this figure gave him, said to God, "Lord, place me in security under thy wings; because I am still so weak, that if thou dost not defend me, the kite will take me away." The beginning of the sixty-seventh psalm, is above all, of greater power in temptation; and St. Athanasius assures us that many servants of God have found in themselves miraculous effects of grace, by saying with the prophet, "let God arise and let his enemies be scattered, and let those that hate him fly before his face." (Ps. lxvii. 1.) It is because we then oppose the devils, not with our own strength, but with that of God, whose help we invoke against them; whereby they presently lose courage, seeing very well that God will not fail to espouse our cause and fight in behalf of his champions.

We may therefore help ourselves with those words which are very efficacious, or with any other like them taken from the scripture; or with those which our present necessity may dictate to us. But be it as it will, we must never fail in temptation to have recourse to God by means of prayer. It is for this reason that father Avila said, if temptation addresses itself to you, do you address yourself to God, and say, "I lifted up my eyes to the heavenly mountains, whence help will come unto me; my help is from the Lord who made heaven and earth." (Psal. cxxix. 1.) But above all, these prayers and cries which we address to God must come not only from our mouths, but from the bottom of our heart, according to the words of David, "O Lord, I addressed my cries unto thee from the bottom of my heart;" (Hom. i. sup.); upon which words St. Chrysostom takes notice, "that the prophet prayed not only with his mouth and tongue," because we often speak without thinking on what we say, "but he prayed from the bottom of his heart. He prayed with fervour, with joy and confidence, and, lastly, it was his whole heart and mind with which he prayed." (Psal. cxxix.)

——o——

CHAPTER XVII.

Of the two other remedies against temptations.

St. Bernard says, "that when the devil intends to deceive us, he beforehand examines our temper, our humour, and inclinations; and always attacks us in those things he finds us most inclined to. Those whom he finds of a sweet and easy nature, and who easily receive impressions of joy and pleasure, he attacks with vanity and impurity; and those whom he knows to be of a more rough and harsh temper, he sets upon with continual motions and provocations to anger, choler, indignation, and impatience."

St. Gregory makes the same remark, and says, "that as the greatest skill of those that take birds is to be well acquainted with the places they most haunt, in order to draw them the more easily into their nets, so the chief care of the devil is to know to what we are more naturally inclined, to make us thereby fall more easily into his snares."

Thus it was, that perceiving the great love Adam bore to his wife, he made use of her to tempt him ; he triumphed also over Sampson by means of Dalila, and thus found out the sense of the riddle, and the source of his strength. The devil imitates a skilful warrior, who before he attacks any place endeavours to find where it is weakest. He carefully observes which is the weakest part of our soul, what passion domineers in us, to what our natural inclination most of all carries us, and there he never fails to attack us. The best means to resist this craft is, with care to find out which is the weakest part of our soul, and the least fortified ; that is to say, what those things are to which we find our natural inclination, passion, or constitution of body leads us, and endeavour to fortify ourselves well on that side, where we fear to be most in danger.

Masters of a spiritual life propose another remedy, not unlike this ; they say that the general maxim to defend ourselves from any temptation is presently to have recourse to what is most contrary to it. Physicians use the same method in corporal diseases, according to their maxim, that, " contraries are cured by contraries." If the diseases come from cold, they make use of hot remedies; if they proceed from dryness and heat, they apply such remedies as are refreshing ; reducing after this manner the humours of the body to the just temper they ought to have. We ought to adopt a similar conduct in the diseases of the soul ; and this is what St. Ignatius teaches when he says we ought to cure those temptations we are subject unto by practising what is contrary to them : for example when we find ourselves carried away with vanity and pride we ought to exercise ourselves in servile work, and so, on all other occasions, always resist our bad inclinations.

———o———

CHAPTER XVIII.

Two other important remedies ; viz. : to crush temptations in the beginning, and to avoid idleness.

ANOTHER excellent remedy which the saints still propose to us, and which is not less general than profitable, is strongly to resist temptations in their beginning. Whilst " your enemy," says St. Jerome, " is still weak and feeble, kill him ; crush the serpent in the egg." For if you let him go and fortify himself, perhaps you will not be able afterwards to compass what you aim at. Temptation is "like a small spark, which still increases till it becomes a great fire," if it be not presently extinguished. "Apply a remedy to the diseases in the beginning;" otherwise, as an ancient poet says, "if you permit the disease to increase the remedy will come too late. It is in this sense that St. Jerome explains the words of the Psalmist: "happy is he that shall take thy children and dash them against a stone." (Ps. cxxxvi. 9); and those other words of the Canticles, "catch for us those little foxes which destroy the vineyards." (Cant. ii. 15.) When a thought of detraction, pride, or particular attachment, either to others or to yourself, begins to show itself in you, and is yet weak and tender, dash it against the corner-stone, which is Jesus Christ; chase presently away whatsoever may prejudice the Lord's vineyard. It is not in our power to hinder temptations or evil thoughts, but happy is he who knows how to cast them away as soon as they come. It is of great importance presently to resist them—when the enemy is yet weak it is easy to overcome him—but if you let him get strength, resistance and victory will become very hard.

St. Chrysostom explains this thought by a comparison: "When a sick person," says he, "has a mind to eat something that is hurtful to him, and he permits not himself to do so, he frees himself from that prejudice it would have done him, and also advances his cure. But if he has not so much power over himself as to abstain from it, his disease may become dangerous, nay, may prove mortal; which would not have happened if he had abstained from what did him hurt. The same thing happens," adds the father, "in temptations; if, for example, as soon as we feel inclined to look upon any object the sight of which may become dangerous to the soul, we use but a little violence, reject the thought, and withdraw our eyes from the object we would free ourselves from all that pain which this vain curiosity might fall into it by consenting to it. But if, on the contrary, we use no violence to ourselves at first, this pleasure of a moment, which we shall enjoy by permitting ourselves to be carried away with curiosity, is afterwards able to destroy our soul; or at least to engage it in a hard and long combat. So that what would in the beginning have cost us nothing, will afterwards prove very uneasy and toilsome. Hence, we see how important it is to resist temptations betimes."

It is related in the lives of the holy fathers, that the devil once appeared to St. Pacomius in the shape of a very handsome woman, and the saint having told him that all his endeavours against the servants of God were to no purpose—" but they are to some purpose," answered the devil, " if the first evil thoughts with which we tempt them make any impression on their hearts ; for then it is easy for us to increase the fire, and urge them to sin; but if they presently resist, and shut the door against those dangerous images we paint in their minds, we are then constrained to fly, and are dispersed before them, as smoke is in the air."

Another excellent remedy against temptations is to be always employed in doing something. Cassian observes that the hermits of his time taught continually to their disciples, and carefully practised themselves, this maxim which they had learned of the ancients, " let the devil always find you employed." (Cass. Instit. xx.) This employment is what God taught St. Anthony, in order to persevere in his solitary life, and to defend himself from the many temptations to which he was subject ; for one day complaining of the temptations he had in prayer, he said to God, " Lord, what shall I do ? I would wish to be better than I am ; and never to think on anything but yourself ; but an infinity of other thoughts molest me, and draw my imagination after them." Whereupon he heard a voice that said to him, "Anthony, if thou wouldst please God, pray ; and when thou canst not pray, work and labour with thy hands ; and always employ thyself in something ; do what thou art able to do on thy part ; and help from on high shall not be wanting to thee ?" (Aug. Serm. xvii. ad frat. in Erem.) Others say, that this lesson was taught him by an angel appearing to him in the shape of a young man, who did nothing else but work and pray ; going successively from work to prayer and from prayer to work. However it happened, it is certain that idleness is the source of many temptations and evils, and therefore it is of very great importance that the devil should never find us idle.

———o———

CHAPTER XIX.

Temptations that disguise themselves to us, under the appearance of good. To know them well is a great remedy against all sorts of temptations.

St. Bonaventure gives us a very necessary instruction upon the subject of temptations, which is, to take care that the devil does not sometimes disguise himself under the appearance of an angel of light, and make use of holy appearances to seduce the servants of God. "We are wont to mix poison," says St. Jerome, "with some other pleasant liquor; and we hide the hook under the bait." The devil does this also. "He secretly leaves his snares in paths in which the servants of God walk." (Ps. cxli. 4.) For should he attack them openly, under the appearance of vice, he would affright them, and gain nothing. "The good," as St. Bernard says, "are never deceived but under the appearance of good." But the devil is very subtile and industrious; he knows where to attack every one; and therefore, that he may attain his end, he acts with disguise towards the good. "He first begins," says St. Bonaventure, "to propose such things to them as are good in themselves; afterwards he mixes something that is bad with them; then, under the appearance of some false good, he presents what is truly bad; and, lastly, when he has so entangled them in his nets that they cannot without great difficulty free themselves, he discovers his venom and makes them fall into open sins. How many times have we seen friendships," continues the saint, "that appeared holy in the beginning; and which, perhaps, were so in effect, and in which was proposed nothing but to seek God and to advance in perfection? All, however, was but an artifice of the devil, as we discovered; 'for we are not ignorant of his designs.'" (2 Cor. ii. 11.) This friendship which he proposes to make, is at first innocent on both sides, and the motive even appears very holy. We speak only of God in the beginning, but afterwards we seek one another with eagerness, and make more frequent visits, and in the long conversation we have together we mix other discourses, and entertain ourselves with the affection we have for each other. We give mutual assurances by presents, and by a thousand other marks that a holy friendship is ignorant of. It is then the devil begins to mix some bad thoughts with good ones, and to draw us to evil under the deceitful appearance of good ; and it is after this manner in these friendships, and in many others, that he seduces an infinite number of persons, and artfully hides under the mask of virtue his interior suggestions, which are dangerous and criminal. He acts like Joab, who killed Amasa, pretending to embrace him ; and like Judas, who made use of a kiss of peace to betray his master, and deliver him into the hands of the Jews." We must therefore watch with great care these temptations that disguise themselves under the appearance of virtue, and mistrust them ; insomuch as the less they are known the more dangerous they are ; for, as the prophet says, it is God who will reveal " the works of the noonday devil." (Ps. xc. 6.) And St. Bernard takes notice, hereupon, that the devil is not content to transform himself into an angel of light, but he transforms himself into light itself, making what in itself is obscurity and darkness appear more clear and bright than noonday, and banishing all doubts and fears from things which in themselves are very bad and dangerous. There are some robbers whose dress and manners are such that we never suspect them to be robbers. For it cannot enter into our imagination, that persons having the appearance of honest men would be capable of robbing In order to believe them guilty of it we must detect them in the fact, and then we ask with astonishment how they could have led a life so ignominious ? The same may be said of temptations which disguise themselves under the false appearances of virtue.

It is the general opinion of the masters of a spiritual life, that, as to defend ourselves from an enemy it is a great advantage to know him to be one, so it is a great remedy against temptations to know that they are such. But the better to comprehend this truth, if, as soon as these evil thoughts and desires begin to rise in your mind and heart, you should see a frightful devil urging you to consent to them, what would you do ? Would you not presently have recourse to God ? And would it not be sufficient to resist them, to see that it was the devil who inspired them ? But it is certain that thus it happens in temptations. God has given to each of us an angel for the guard of our souls, as great persons in the world give their children a governor to superintend their conduct and education. This doctrine is grounded upon these words of our Saviour : " take care you contemn not one of these children, for I say unto you, that their angels in heaven

behold continually the face of my Father, who is in heaven."
(Matt. xviii. 10) And St. Jerome, explaining the same words,
says, " that the dignity of our souls must needs be very great,
since all have an angel assigned to guard them from the first
moment of their birth." (Hier. in idem.) But now to return to
our subject—since we have each of us an angel that guards us
from evil, so each of us has also a devil who continually solicits
us to what is bad; who excites ill thoughts and dangerous
motions continually in us ; who watches without ceasing for an
occasion to surprise us, and lets none escape. And the devils, to
compass their design, observe with study and care all our inclinations, and lastly make use even of ourselves, and our concupiscence to destroy us. It was for this reason that God said to the
devil, who tempted Job, "have you considered my servant Job?"
And hence we perceive that he speaks to him as to one that had
been a long time a spy upon Job, and had always been by his
side. So that when you shall have thoughts and motions that
incite you to sin, be as certain that it is a temptation of the devil
as if you then saw him using his endeavours to draw you to evil,
and presently have recourse to God, who alone is able to deliver
you from so cruel on enemy.

St. Gregory relates a story which very much confirms what I
here say. "There was a young man," says he, "who having
embraced the rule of St. Bennet, afterwards finding it too austere,
had an intention of leaving it. For this end he often addressed
himself to the saint, from whom he had received the habit ; who,
having always told him that it was a temptation of the devil,
and having endeavoured without success to withdraw him from
his design, was at last by his importunity constrained to yield to
him. However, as in his great charity he could not see him
depart without deep sorrow and regret, he betook himself to
pray for him, and the young man was scarce got to the doors of
the monastery when he saw a frightful dragon come towards
him with open mouth, ready to devour him. Then all trembling
with fear he began to cry out for help, saying, " Help ! help
my brethren, help, behold a dragon stands ready to devour me !"
the religious, running to him at his call, saw no dragon, but
found the young man half dead, whom they carried in this condition into the monastery. He no sooner entered, but he made
a vow never more to leave it ; and from that time forward he
never had the least temptation to return to the world. Upon
this St. Gregory observes, that the effect of St. Bennet's prayer

was to obtain that the religious should see the dragon which was ready to devour him ; and which he followed before, without seeing it. " He followed it," says this holy father, " because he did not see it ; but as soon as he perceived it he conceived a great horror, and cried out for help to be delivered from it." Now we see by this example, and by what has been already said, that it is not only in imagination the devil tempts us, but that he really does so ; and actually sets upon us by temptations. The apostle St. Peter, as a good pastor, warns us of this truth ; and the church, which knows of how great importance this warning is, as a careful mother, daily in complin, puts us in mind of it :— " Brethren, be sober, and watch ; because the devil your enemy, like a roaring lion, daily encompasses you, seeking an occasion to devour you ; wherefore resist him, remaining firm and stead-fast in faith :" (1 Pet. v. 8.) and think continually how to defend yourselves whilst he attacks you, taking great care to be not surprised by him.

———o———

CHAPTER XX.

How we ought to behave ourselves in temptations against faith and purity ; and what remedies we ought to make use of.

THERE are some inexperienced souls, who, by thoughts against faith and purity, are cast into such disquiet as if what then passed in them were a sign that God had forsaken them. It is proper then to begin by informing them that this is a great error and illusion. Gerson relates to this purpose that a certain hermit, being afflicted with these thoughts, remained for twenty years together without daring to speak of them to any body, imagining that it was a most horrible and unheard of crime, and that it would scandalize the person to whom he should mention it. At the end of this time he resolved to address himself to an ancient father of the desert, but even then he durst not do it by words of mouth, but by a letter which he gave him to read. The holy old man having read it, began to smile, saying to him ; " son, lay your hand upon my head." The hermit having obeyed him, " I take upon me," says he, " your sin ; for the future be not at all in pain about it." " How ! father," replied the hermit, astonished at this answer, " it seems to me that I have one foot already in hell, and do you bid me be out of pain ?" " Son," said the ancient father, " do you take any pleasure in such thoughts as these?" The hermit having answered no; but they always cause a great deal of sorrow and trouble to him—"Since it is so," replied the man of God, "it is a sign you have nothing to do with them, and that it is the devil that raises them in your mind, to draw you thereby to despair; wherefore, son, follow my advice, which is, that if ever any such thoughts as these come again to you, tell the devil that he is the author of them; say, wo to you, foul spirit; let those impurities and blasphemies light upon yourself; I will have nothing to do with them; I will adhere and stick fast to what the church believes, and will rather die a thousand times than ever offend God." These words of the holy old man so comforted and strengthened the hermit, that for the future he was never set upon, nor tormented with the like thoughts. And here it is proper to observe, for the instruction of those who have a difficulty to reveal their thoughts and temptations to their directors, that it gives them a great deal more disquiet to conceal them than to mention them. The example I have just now proposed proves this truth; this hermit suffered a continual disquiet of mind for twenty years to-gether, because he did not discover the state of his soul. But as soon as he made it known he was entirely comforted. How many disquiets would he have avoided, had he done in the beginning what he did after twenty years? I shall treat this matter more at large hereafter; however, by what has been here said we see that this kind of temptation is no new thing, and therefore we ought not to wonder at all at it.

We are not to see what we are to do in the like occasions. There are some whose conduct therein is blameable : for, when attacked by temptations, they press their temples very hard with their hands, knit their brows, shut their eyes, and shakes their head, as if they would say hereby that they will give them no entrance; and sometimes, if they do not actually speak they think they have done nothing, and that they have consented to the improper thoughts. Now they do themselves more hurt by these contentions and efforts than the temptation itself could have done them; and herein resemble Abner, who, when Saul was asleep, lay by him, and hearing a voice call him afar off, he began to cry out with all his strength to him that called him, "who are you that cry out so loud, and hinder the repose of the king?" So these complaining of the noise that the temptation makes without, and the trouble it gives them, disquiet and trouble themselves within far more than the temptation could have done. Take good notice of this, because it is a thing which disturbs and turns the head of many persons, and chiefly of such as are scrupulous. It is not prayer or spiritual exercises that injure their health or affect their head, but it is scruples that hurt them ; and it is this the devil aims at, in order to disgust them with devotion. He sees these persons far from consenting to the detestable thoughts he presents them with ; all he aims at is thereby to disquiet and trouble them, and so he can but do this he is content. Lastly, take notice, that it is not with shaking the head that we shake off temptations.

What therefore must we do to overcome them ? It is not, as the saints and masters of a spiritual life say, by forcing our imagination, and by breaking our head to resist them. No ! but we must contemn them and not dwell at all upon them. They are, say they, like little dogs that bark after a man that passes by ; if he stops to drive them away, they bark more fiercely than they did before ; we must therefore do like him who walks in a street, where the wind blows the dust in his face—he covers his eyes and walks on his way, without troubling himself either with the wind or the dust. In a word, the remedy against all these thoughts and the means to be quickly delivered from them, is not to torment ourselves with them. But what ought to move those who are thus attacked to make use of this remedy, and to keep their souls in peace is—what the saints moreover add—that the more terrible and detestable they seem to be, the less account they ought to make of them ; because, at the same time they are less dangerous. What thoughts, for example, can be more horrible than such as are against God and religion ? Notwithstanding, these are less dangerous than others, because, the more horrible they are the farther also we are by God's mercy from consenting to them ; wherefore we must not afflict ourselves when they pass in our minds ; because that is not our fault, nor is it in our power to hinder them, as they come not from ourselves but from the devil, who frames them against our will, that he may either cast us into despair, or into great disquiet of mind.

It is related of St. Catherine of Sienna, that one day, as she was extremely tormented with these thoughts, our Saviour appeared to her, and by his presence dissipated them all. She tenderly complained to him, saying : "Where wert thou, O Lord, when such horrible thoughts rose in my heart ?" "Daughter," replied our Saviour, "I was in the midst of thy heart." "Ah !

sweet Lord," replied she, "couldst thou remain amidst such filthy and shameful thoughts as those were?" "Daughter," said he, "wert thou pleased in beholding them?" "No, Lord," replied the saint, "I was pierced to the very heart with sorrow, and I know not what torment I should not rather have chosen than to have suffered them." "What then," said he, "could give thee such horror but myself, who was in the midst of thy heart?" So that how wicked and how shameful soever the thoughts may be that arise within us, if, instead of entertaining them we are troubled at having them, so far from believing that God has forsaken us, we should consider it an infallible sign that he remains within us; because it is he alone who is able to give us this horror of sin, and this fear of losing his grace. "It is in time of affliction that he is with us," (Psal. xc. 15,) as he himself assures us by the mouth of the prophet, and it is from the midst of the flames and thorns of the burning bush that he speaks to you, as he did to Moses.

"The combat against temptation," says St. Bernard, "is a painful but profitable one, because the recompense is proportionable to the pain; and the thoughts they occasion cannot hurt us unless we consent to them. But, on the contrary, the harder the resistance is, the greater will be the crown." (De. inter. domo. c. 19.) Blosius is of the same opinion, and says, that a thought of vain complacency in ourselves, with which we only once permit ourselves to be carried away, is more displeasing to God than all the foul and shameful thoughts that can be imagined, to which we give no consent. We must, then, no more afflict ourselves, nor be in any more pain, than if all this happened without us, as in effect it does; "because," says a saint, "these bad thoughts are not properly within us but when we give consent to them; wherefore, so long as we consent not, they cannot enter into us—they only knock at the door to no purpose."

The masters of a spiritual life inform us, further, that it is very dangerous to be much afraid of these temptations, and to make too much account of them; because this helps only to increase them, and to give them more strength. The reason hereof is very natural, and daily experience confirms it; for fear weakens the imagination, and frequent reflections upon the same thing cause it to make deeper impressions upon the mind, and to work more powerfully upon it. We see, for example, that a man easily passes over a narrow plank that lies upon the ground, but if we raise it very high he cannot do so; because, being then seized with fear, the blood and spirits returning to the heart, he cannot keep himself so freely upon his legs as he did before ; and so he will be in great danger of falling. The same thing happens in temptations of impurity, when we are so weak as to be too much afraid of them ; and therefore to free ourselves the more easily from them, we must not at all fear them, lest this make us fix our imagination too long upon those objects of which we ought not to think at all, but only how to cast them away. "But if, upon this account, it is advantageous not to have too great a fear of them, yet, on the other hand," says Gerson, "we cannot have too great a horror of sin in general." Viewing them with fear, and withdrawing our mind from the particular thoughts of impurity with which we are attacked, we must continually beg of God that he permits nothing to separate us from him ; and make a firm resolution rather to die a thousand times than to commit one mortal sin.

I add one thing more, which the saints extremely recommend to us, and which may serve for a general remedy against all interior temptations—it is, that when any bad thought occurs, we must endeavour to turn our mind from it by applying it to something else ; for example, by thinking on the death and passion of our Saviour, or some such object. Now, this must be done, not by any violent effort of the imagination, but only by endeavouring dexterously to avoid the stroke the devil aims at us, warding off the blow by some good thought or holy occupation. It is in this manner that a man who wishes to prevent another from introducing a particular subject, quickly passes from matter to matter, that the other may have no leisure to introduce the subject. It is thus a prudent man who hears injuries against himself, turns his head aside, without taking the trouble of answering, or even lending his ear to them. This way of resisting temptations is very easy and secure, because while we have our mind filled with good thoughts, we have no leisure to consent to bad ones ; and we will be very much assisted in this, if at prayer we penetrate deeply the meditations which touch us most ; if we thus render them familiar, we will in time of temptations find in them a remedy and secure refuge. For this purpose some make an asylum of the wounds of Jesus Christ, and chiefly of the wound in his sacred side ; retiring "into the holes of this rock, and into the ruins of this wall." (Cant. ii. 14.) Others have recourse to thoughts of death and hell ; saying with Job, "who will grant me, O Lord, thy protection, against the attacks of hell, and who will hide me till thy fury be past?" (Job xiv. 13.)   Each must betake himself to what he knows to be most profitable for him, and best adapted to excite him to fervour ; and when he shall be in any necessity, he will find therein a secure retreat against all the attacks of the enemy.

The abbot Smaragdus relates one thing upon this subject which may be very profitable to us, though it is neither very important nor authentic.   He says that a religious saw one day two devils discoursing together and that they asked one another an account of what progress they had made against two religious, whom they were employed to tempt.   "I find myself very well," says the one, "with him that I have to do with—I need only present a thought unto him, and presently he takes hold of it, entertains himself with it, and immediately detecting himself in this thought, he repasses in his mind the whole series thereof— he thinks how long he dwelled on it ; whether it came by his fault ; whether he resisted it, or consented to it ; whence and how it came to him, whether he gave occasion to it, or did all he should to give none ; and lastly, as often as I will, I put him upon this rack, and almost even beside himself."   "For my part," says the other, "I lose all the pains and measures I take with him whom I tempt, for as soon as I suggest a bkd thought he has presently recourse to God, or to some pious meditation, or he thinks of something else to hinder him from thinking of what I proposed to him, and thus I know not how to deal with him."   Hence we see that the devil is pleased when we amuse ourselves in disputing with him upon any bad thought he suggests ; for then he neither wants will, nor craft, to make it pass from the head to the heart : and on the other hand we see, that a very good means to resist it is not at all to give ear to it, nor oppose it, but only to turn our mind presently from it, without giving any attention thereunto.   Now if we can compass this, by applying ourselves to some good thought, it is assuredly the best way ; but if this be not sufficient, it is good also to have recourse to some exterior employment.

CHAPTER XXI.

That according to the difference of temptations we must help ourselves with different means to resist them.

St. John Climachus tells us, " that we ought to use different means for the resistfng different temptations. Because as there are some vices that are bad and disagreeable in themselves, as choler, envy, hatred, desire of revenge, impatience, indignation, peevishness, bitterness of heart, obstinacy, the spirit of contradiction, and such like ; there are others also, which are naturally accompanied with pleasure, such as all those that regard impurity, or the gratification of our senses; and the more satisfaction we take in these the more they draw us to themselves ; therefore, we ought for this reason," says he, " fight by flying them, that is to say, not only avoid the occasions that entice us to them, but even turn our minds and eyes from all things that may make us think of them. But as to those of the first sort we must struggle with them, in order to overcome them, which can be safely done, as there is nothing of contagion in them ; though in regard of choler and revenge it will also be very good," adds he, " to avoid them by hindering ourselves from thinking of anything that may excite us to them."

St. Bonaventure and Cassian teach the same doctrine, and say, " that as to the first we may desire to exercise ourselves in fighting against them, and in seeking occasion to do so, by applying ourselves, for example, to frequent the company of peevish and untractable persons ; to exercise ourselves in the virtue of patience, and by submitting our wills to the will of another, to learn to become humble and obedient. But in regard to the vice of impurity, it would be a great indiscretion and very dangerous to put ourselves upon trial, and expose ourselves to occasions thereof. Our Saviour himself would never permit the devil to tempt him therein; to teach us," say they, " that we ought not expose ourselves to temptations of this kind, what hopes soever we may have of triumphing over them, because our propensity to impurity is so great and so very natural to us, and because it is a vice which extremely flatters the senses, we ought always fear very much lest they should give it entrance into our heart." St. Bonaventure says very well, " that as when there is any intelligence with the enemy in a place that is attacked, it is easier to take it;" so after the same manner, it is easier for the devil, who keeps a strict intelligence with our flesh, to reduce us thereby to his subjection.   Therefore we ought to stand herein extremely on our guard, by carefully avoiding all occasions that may carry us to what is bad, and rejecting all thoughts that proceed from thence.   Cassian and St. Thomas say, that it is in this sense we ought to understand the precept of the apostle— "fly fornication;" (1 Cor. iv. 18.); and that St. Paul would teach us by these words, " that impurity is not resisted but by flying from it."

It is related in the Chronicles of the Order of St. Francis, that brother Giles, brother Rufinus, brother Simon of Assisium, and brother Juniper, being engaged in a spiritual conference, brother Giles asked the rest what they did to resist temptations of impurity?"   " I consider," says brother Simon, "how great the infamy of this sin is, and how shameful before God and man ; because how imprudent soever those are who abandon them-selves to this vice, they yet hide themselves when committing it; and this consideration gives me so lively a horror of it that I find myself presently freed from the temptation."   " I, for my part," says brother Rufinus, " Cast myself upon the ground, and with tears implore the help of God and the Blessed Virgin, till I find it quite gone."   "And I," says brother Juniper, " when I find it coming, and that it begins to take possession of my senses, I presently shut all the avenues or outworks of my heart, and set a guard of many holy thoughts upon it ; and then when those that the devil sends would enter into my heart, I cry out that the place is already taken, and that there is no room left for them; and thus I hinder them from entering, and chase them away with shame."   Then brother Giles, having well considered what the three had said, cried out, " I am for the practice of brother Juniper, which certainly is the best of all—for the best way to fight against impurity is to fly from it."

The best and surest means, therefore, and also the most easy to resist temptations of this nature, is to cast from us all bad thoughts, and to stop all the avenues of our heart ; because if once we let them enter, it will be difficult afterwards to cast them out.   We must keep enemies at a distance from the place we desire to hinder them from taking, or becoming masters of. For when they shall have gained the gates it is a miracle if the place be not lost.   In the third part I shall speak more at large of this temptation, and of the remedies we must use to overcome it ; and these remedies may be of great help to us against all other temptations.

———o———

CHAPTER XXII.

Of several very profitable directions for the time of temptation.

WE have already spoken of several remedies against temptations, but it is impossible to state them all. For in the distempers of the soul no less than in those of the body, the remedies are infinite, and many things must be left to the prudence and discretion of the physician ; so that, according to the state and disposition of the sick person, and according to the nature and circumstances of the disease, he may make use of such as he shall judge most proper. The masters of a spiritual life say, therefore, that the great remedy against all sorts of temptations is, to discover them betimes, to the physician ; but as I shall speak of this more fully in the third part, I shall content myself here to set down some few instructions the saints give us con cerning this matter. St. Basil says, " that as we do not discover the diseases of our bodies to all sorts of persons, but only to physicians who ought to take care of them ; so temptations, which are the diseases of the soul, ought not to be discovered to every one, but only to such spiritual physicians as God has appointed for this end ; who are confessors and superiors." This instruction is conformable to the words of St. Paul ; " but we who are stronger ought to support those who are weak and feeble." (Rom. xv. 1.) It agrees also very much with one of our rules, which would have us on occasions of this nature to have recourse to the prefect of spiritual things, or the confessor or superior. And, lastly, it is of greater importance than many people imagine ; for it sometimes happens that we hide temptations from those to whom we ought to discover them ; and, as it may happen that your brother may be subject to the same temptations as you are, it is to be feared the example would give too great an assurance one to the other, and that this confidence should prove equally prejudicial to both. Wherefore, to avoid this inconvenience, and for several other reasons, we ought not to discover our temptations and spiritual diseases but to spiritual physicians, to whom we may believe they will not

prove contagious, and from whom we may expect some help.
And this is what the Wise man recommends unto us, when he
says, " lay not open your heart to all the world." (Ecclus. viii.
22.) " Though you may have many friends, yet take counsel
only of one whom you have chosen amongst a thousand."
(Ecclus. vi. 6.)

Another instruction of great importance for the time of temptation is, to take care not to relent at that time in your spiritual
exercises, nor to quit or retrench any of them.   For though the
temptation should have no other evil in it than to discourage us
in our spiritual duties, yet the devil would believe he had done a
great deal, and be very well satisfied.   On the contrary, it is in
temptations we must be more fervent in prayer, and augment
rather than diminish our devotions ; because, if we let fall from
our hands our spiritual arms wherewith we defend ourselves
against him, it will be very easy for him to do with us what he
pleases.   We must, therefore, at this time be extremely faithful
to God ; and it is hereby he knows who are his true servants,
according to what he says himself to his apostles ; " you are
those who have always remained with me in my afflictions."
(Luke xxii. 28.)   Moreover, it is no wonder that in the calm
and sweetness of devotion we persevere in the practice of spiritual exercises ; but to persevere in them amidst those tempests
which excite temptations, and in spite of that dryness and bitterness that God sends us, is praiseworthy ; it is this shows we love
him and serve him purely for himself.

We must, moreover, in time of temptation, take great care not
to change anything in our spiritual conduct, nor make any new
resolution ; that time being very improper for it.   While the
water is troubled you can see nothing ; but if it becomes clear
again, you will perceive the dirt which has sunk to the bottom.
The trouble and agitation that is caused by temptation permits
you not to see what is most proper for you ; " because evils have
surrounded me," says David, " I could not perceive anything ;"
(Ps. xxxix. 16) ; so that it is not a time to deliberate upon anything, or to take new measures.   Let the temptation pass, and
then your mind will be in more peace and tranquillity—then you
will be able to know what to do.   All masters of a spiritual life
take notice of this as of an essential point ; and St. Ignatius
recommends it particulary to us in the rules which he gives for
the discerning of spirits.   The reason he gives for it is, that, as
in the time of spiritual consolations, the spirit of God inclines us

to what is good; so in the time of temptation, the evil spirit urges to what is evil; and therefore it is then very dangerous to follow those new lights and thoughts that occur to us.

We, moreover, in the time of temptation, should take great care to have recourse to the remedies I have set down, and not remain idle; and this is what the following examples will give us a better sight of.

It is related in the lives of the fathers that an hermit, being extremely tormented with the spirit of impurity, went to find out one of the most ancient fathers of the desert to beseech him to obtain of God that he would deliver him from so troublesome a temptation. The holy old man having promised him his prayers, and not having ceased to address God upon this subject, the hermit returned again to him a little while after, telling him the temptation, had not left him, and conjuring him still to re-double his prayers. He did so—he wept—he sighed and groaned; yet the hermit came still daily to him to tell him he found no help at all from his prayers; at last, he came so often that the holy man not knowing what to do, or to what to attribute the cause of his temptation, was much afflicted and astonished at it, and complained thereof to God. One night as his mind was full of this thought, God let him see by revelation the hermit sitting carelessly upon a chair, and the impure spirit representing before him divers figures of women, which he looked upon with atten-tion and pleasure. He perceived also that the angel of our Lord seemed to be in great indignation against him; because that instead of prostrating himself upon the earth, and having recourse to God by means of prayer, he remained lazily in his seat, and permitted himself miserably to be flattered with these sorts of imagination; whereby he easily understood what it was that hindered God from hearing his prayers, and that it was the negli-gence of the hermit, and the weak endeavours he used to resist the temptation, that was the cause thereof. Wherefore, the first time that he came again to him—" Brother," says he, " it is your negligence, and the satisfaction with which you entertain those bad thoughts, that is the cause why God does not hear me; let what prayers soever be offered, you shall never be delivered from this spirit of impurity, if you use no endeavours yourself to free you from it; and if by fasting, by prayer, by tears, and by sighs, you put not yourself into a condition to obtain of God the grace to resist it. As in corporal diseases the most proper remedies, given even in due time, become unprofitable to the sick person, if he on his part does not abstain from all things that may do him hurt: so in spiritual diseases the prayers and good works we offer to God for our neighbour give him no help at all if he does not help himself ; and if by prayer and mortification he does not endeavour to draw the mercy of God upon himself." These words so touched the hermit, that from that time forward he resolved to follow the holy old man's counsel ; and in effect he put it afterwards so well in practice that, by his prayers and austerities, he deserved that God should have pity on him, and should deliver him from the temptation that had so long afflicted him. It is in this manner we must act in the temptations that afflict us, omitting nothing that may be able to overcome them, and doing whatsoever depends on us for this end : for it is only at this price that God will grant us the victory over them.

But since, in the manner of resisting temptations, there may be a greater or less resistance, it is good to take notice here, that we must not content ourselves simply to resist, but must resist with all our might.

We read in the Chronicles of St. Francis that one day God desiring to discover to brother John of Auvern the different manners that religious resist temptations, and chiefly those of impurity ; he set before him an innumerable multitude of devils who were solely occupied in shooting arrows against his servants. Some, presently, with violence cast them back again upon the same devils that shot them, who then fled away with great outcries. The arrows of others were blunted and lost their points upon the persons against whom they were shot, and so fell at their feet, without doing them any hurt ; others entered as far as the top of the iron ; and the arrows of others pierced quite through. According to this vision, the best mode of resisting, and what we ought to adopt, is, to wound the devil and drive him away with the same weapons with which he attacks us. Now, we shall also derive, if we apply ourselves to this, profit from those temptations he makes use of to destroy us—if, for example, when he suggests a proud thought we humble ourselves and debase ourselves so much the more before God and our brethren ; or if, in a temptation of impurity, we take occasion to have a greater horror of this vice, a greater love for chastity, a greater watch over ourselves, greater zeal, greater fervour, and greater care to have recourse to God in our necessities. St. Austin upon this passage of the Psalmist, "the dragon which thou hast performed to play or make sport with," (Ps. ciii. 27,) says, " it is thus that the servants of God play and make sport with the devil ; because it is then he finds himself taken in the same nets with which he pretended to take them, according to these words of the scripture ; " they are taken in the same snares they had set for others." (Ps. ix. 16.)   " They are surprised in the ambush they had laid ; they are themselves entangled in their own nets." (Ps. xxxiv. 8.)   " Let his malice return upon him, and his iniquity descend upon his own head." (Ps. vii. 17.)

THE FIFTH TREATISE.

──o──

──o──

CHAPTER I.

*How much it imports a religious to abstain from paying visits
to his relations.*

THE rule left us by St. Ignatius concerning affection for relations
is applicable to all sorts of religious. "All those," says he "that
enter the Society, must not only consider that they quit father,
mother, kindred, friends, and whatsoever they possess in the
world; but must believe that Jesus Christ addresses them in these
words, he that hates not father, mother, brothers, and sisters,
yea, and his own soul, cannot be my disciple. (Luke xiv. 26.)
Let them endeavour, then, to reduce within the bounds of Christian charity all those sentiments for relations which flesh and
blood shall inspire them with; and let them look upon themselves as persons who are dead to the world, and to the love of
the world; and who live only to Jesus Christ, whom they take
in place of father, mother, and all things else. It is not sufficient
that the body quits the world—the heart too must quit the
world, and break off all attachments to it."

It is not ill done to love our relations; on the contrary, because they are relations, we are bound to love them more than
others. But if this love be founded only in the sentiments of
nature, this is not to love them like a Christian, much less like a
religious; since the most barbarous people love their parents and
such as are allied to them by blood. "A Christian, but especially a religious," says St. Gregory, "ought to purify this affection of flesh and blood in the fire of divine love; that, extracting
from it what is terrestrial, and contrary to the love of the
Supreme Good, they may love their parents not so much because
nature urges them, as because God commands them—that, they
may love them in God alone, and for his sake alone; as God

himself loves them, and as he ordains us to love them. It is this that St. Ignatius requires in the rule before cited, whereupon I shall make one observation : namely, that in his other rules he thinks it sufficient to propose them simply as he received them from God, without confirming them with the authority of scripture, as he might easily have done, since the morality of our constitutions is entirely taken from the gospel; but here, where he treats of regulating a sentiment so natural, and so deeply rooted in us, as the love of our relations is, he presently has recourse to holy scripture. He does the same, also, when he states how we ought to dispose of our goods on quitting the world : for here also he confirms his doctrine by the words of the prophet David, " He distributed and gave his goods to the poor;" (Ps. cxi. 9); and by those of Jesus Christ, " Go and sell what thou hast and give it to the poor." (Matt. xix. 21.)

The matter in question is of great importance to religious ; and as St. Basil, St. Gregory, St. Bernard, and many other saints treat very largely of it, I shall here state what they say upon this subject. To begin with St. Basil—he says, that "it is a matter of great consequence that a religious declines all visits to, and commerce with, his relations." He assigns as reasons, " that we are able to give them but little help, and that our commerce with them troubles the tranquillity and regularity of our life, and draws us into occasions of sin." They entertain us with their domestic affairs, their suits, losses, and all other things that give them any trouble ; so that we return home charged with all their discontents ; and the worst of it is, that this exposes us to very great dangers. For the idea of the life we led in the world coming again to strike our imagination, may happen to open old sores, which afterwards are not so easily cured. There needs only the sight of a place and person, to revive those ideas which time and distance had almost effaced. And when we easily pass from one thing to another, we insensibly let ourselves be carried away with imaginations of this sort, which at last destroy the peace and tranquillity of our soul. Wherefore all masters of a spiritual life counsel us, that even when we would detest any of our past sins, we should only make a general reflection upon them, without descending to particulars, which might bring dangerous images into our mind. But if we must with so great care avoid this, in so holy an action, with how far greater reason ought we to remove far from us such unprofitable occasions as may produce the like effects in our imagination. When you neglect to avoid them, and when the interior peace you enjoy begins to be molested by them, of whom can you complain, since you find nothing but what you sought yourself, and which, in consequence, you deserved to have?

St. Basil points out another effect arising from our holding commerce with our relations, which is, that their bad habits and inclinations, by little and little, make impression on our heart, and fill our soul with secular thoughts, cool it to the things of the next world, deprive it of that fervour and constancy it had in its good resolutions, and render it again altogether secular, and as I may say, draw it insensibly to return to the world. "They lived and conversed with the Gentiles," says the prophet, "and have learned to do like them; they adored their idols, which became a scandal to them, and the cause of their destruction." (Ps. cv. 35.) The like will happen to you by your conversation with worldlings; you will soon speak their language, and adopt their fashions and manners. You are already taken with their idols, which are vanity and self-love; you are already filled with yourself and seek your own glory and satisfaction; and are not these sufficient marks that you are already replenished with the spirit of the world?

St. Basil adds still another reason why we ought to avoid all commerce with our relations, which is, lest the natural tenderness of affection we have for them render us too sensible to what happens them, and make too lively an impression upon ourselves. Because it is impossible to visit them frequently without naturally rejoicing at their prosperity, or repining at their adversity; disquieting ourselves with their interests, and embroiling ourselves with a thousand cares. We are continually thinking if they stand not in need of something; what is it they want; whether such an employment will turn to their profit; whether such a design will succeed; and whether they will acquit themselves with honour in such an affair. All these thoughts and disquiets so weaken the spiritual man within us that the least temptation is able to cast us down. "We are in this state," says St. Basil, "only like religious statues that bear the habit of religious, but neither have the life nor virtue of them;" and, whilst our body is shut up in our cell, our mind is elsewhere, and our imagination rambles amongst our relations in the world.

Cassian relates that an hermit having retired to a place near his relations' house, whence he was helped with all things necessary, lived for some time after this manner. Finding this kind of life, wherein he had nothing else to do but to attend to prayer or spiritual reading, was very sweet and holy, he one day went to visit St. Anthony. The saint asked him where he lived; he answered, near his relations, who having the charity to take care of him, he had the advantage to give his whole time to God. But the saint asking him, whether when any ill accident befell his relations, he was not afflicted thereat, or pleased when any subject of joy happened to them. The hermit could not but confess, that he was not able to hinder himself from bearing part in what happened to them. "Alas! child," replied the saint, "know you not, that you shall bear those company in the next world, with whom you have been afflicted and rejoiced in this?" He who interests himself in worldly things in this life, will have no place in the next, but such as worldlings have.

It imports us, therefore, very much to avoid commerce with our relations; for what we see not, makes little or no impression upon us; and as nothing more disengages us from the world than to abandon it in effect, and solemnly to have renounced it for ever, so nothing can more disengage us from the affection of flesh and blood we have for our relations, than to see them no more, and to break off all communication with them. We must really separate ourselves from them in effect, if we would wean ourselves from them in affection : the one cannot be done without the other. It often happens that absence does not wean our affections from them, how great then would they be, if we daily saw them and conversed with them.

It is to prevent such inconveniencies as may happen that our constitutions forbid us to go home to visit our relations; but that so holy and profitable a prohibition may have its effect, we must on our side contribute all we can thereunto. We must, when our relations ask leave for us, be the first to oppose it ; we must, by such good reasons, as, if well disposed, we will always have ready, endeavour to put these thoughts out of their heads, and so prudently manage the matter, that they may have reason to be content, and think that you are so too. It is this your superior requires of you; and, moreover, you do him great pleasure, when you tell him, from yourself, that you will endeavour to free him from your relations' importunity. For it often happens, that if you assist him not, he will not be able to resist the earnest solicitations they will make or cause to be made; and, therefore, will be obliged to condescend, and to grant what is demanded, being forced to it against his will; but he would be very glad, were it in his power, to be freed from the necessity of granting such a permission.   What we here say upon this subject may serve for an advertisement upon other occasions.   Your parents or friends, for example, desire something of you contrary to your profession; send them not to your superior; this would put him to the necessity of either incurring their displeasure or of granting them what they ask.   You must not let things go so far, but must endeavour to dissuade them from asking what they designed, making them listen to reason; and you must not imitate those who rather than give pain to a person, care not how much they perplex their superiors.   St. Jerome, upon these words of Jesus Christ, "Be ye prudent as serpents," takes notice, that one reason why the example of a serpent is proposed to us is, "because to defend his head, in which his life is contained, he hides it under the many wreaths of his body." (Hier. in Matt. x. 16.)   We ought to do the same in regard of our superior, who is our head; and not expose him, as we often do, to the complaints and murmurings of seculars, to excuse ourselves, and to be freed from trouble.   We must take great care of this upon all occasions; for, generally speaking, in those things that depend wholly upon us, if we have but a good intention, we shall be able to do whatever we have a mind to.   Wherefore the counsel I would give, in regard of visits to our parents, is, first of all, to do what we can, both with them and our superiors, to exempt us from them, and never to make them but by pure obedience, and after having represented the inconveniences to our superior; yet after all this, we are not to be without fear, but must believe that we have great reason to stand upon our guard.

Sirius relates in the life of Theodore, the abbot, that a little after he took the habit of religion, his mother carrying a great many bishops' letters with her, went to see him, and by their recommendation obtained leave from St. Pacomius, who lived in the same monastery, to do so.   The young religious having understood this, went to the saint, and said to him: "Dear father, if you will have me see my mother, give me your warrant beforehand, that I shall not be accountable for this visit at the day of judgment."   The holy abbot was unwilling to give him this assurance, but told him, "that he himself was to be judge whether it would be a prejudice to him or not, and if he judged it would be so, he would not oblige him to it."   Whereupon,

Theodore refused to see his mother, and this refusal turned to her great advantage. For she, who had a great desire to see him, retired soon after into a monastery of religious women hard by, hoping that this monastery, having their son for their director, she might sometimes see him there. Thus God blessed her son's refusal, and made it the occasion of his mother's vocation. Yet, notwithstanding, it showed a very holy disposition in him, that he would not see his mother but through pure obedience, and with so great precaution as to charge his superior's conscience with it. A good religious ought not to see his parents but after this manner; and if we knew how dangerous for our salvation such visits as these are, we should be more afraid of them than we are, and take greater care to be dispensed with them than we do. History is full of examples of religious that have been hereby lost. Let us become wise at others' expense, that we may not fall into the like inconvenience.

"If you be dead with Jesus Christ, and to your relations according to the flesh, why do you," says St. Basil, "seek again after them, and desire to have commerce with them? But if you desire it for love of them, and to re-establish that in yourself which you have destroyed for the love of Jesus Christ, do you not deceive and betray yourself? Wherefore let not their consideration make you leave the place wherein God has put you; for the farther you go from it, the farther you withdraw from the spirit of your vocation.' (Epist. ad Chilon.) "The Blessed Virgin and St. Joseph found not Jesus Christ amongst their relations and acquaintance. O most amiable Jesus!" cries St. Bernard, "how can I hope to find you amongst my relations, since you were not to be found amongst your own?" It is in the church, it is in retirement, and in prayer, we must seek him, and it is there we shall find him.

We read in the life of St. Francis Xaverius, that returning from Rome to Portugal, to go from thence to the Indies, and passing within eight miles of his parent's house, he could not be persuaded to go out of his way to see his mother and relations, notwithstanding all their entreaties; and though he knew if he lost this opportunity of seeing them he should never meet the like again. Father Le Fevre did the same, passing within ten miles of his father's house. And when St. Ignatius, by an indispensable necessity was obliged to go to Loyola, he retired into the hospital, and would by no means lodge in his brother's house.

CHAPTER II.

That a religious ought to avoid, as far as in his power, visits from his relations, and correspondence with them by letters.

A GOOD religious, who truly takes to heart the service of God, and his spiritual advancement, and thinks, as he ought to do, why he entered into religion, must not only abstain from visiting his relations, but must also, as much as he can, deprive himself of their conversation, hindering them from visiting him. St. Ephraim says, " we must try to oblige them to reduce their visits to one or two at most in the year." And adds, moreover, " if you can quite free yourself from so unprofitable a conversation, you will still do much better." (Tract. de van. Doctr. c. 35.) He calls this conversation unprofitable not without reason, and St. Ignatius, in his Constitution, calls it so too ; and it is not only unprofitable but dangerous also, as we have already said ; whereas, God has been pleased to show, by the examples of his saints and miracles, how pleasing to him the refusal to see our relations, and our coldness towards them in the like occasions, have been to his Divine Majesty.

It is related in the Spiritual Meadow, that a holy anchoret, called Syriacus, hearing a knock at the door of his cell, and knowing they were his parents who came to visit him, betook himself presently to prayer, to beg of God that they might not be able to see him ; which being done, he opens the door, passes through the midst of them without their seeing him, and retired a great way farther into the desert ; nor would he return home till he understood they were gone. Surius relates of St. Pacomius, that his sister coming to visit him, to know how he did, he bade the porter of the monastery tell her he was very well, and that she might return home in peace; and this refusal of his touching her no less than that of Theodore did his mother, she shut herself up in a convent not far from her brother, as the other did, and there spent the rest of her days in a most holy manner.

But a good religious ought not only to avoid seeing his relations, but must, as much as he can, abstain from having any communication with them by letters—since this commerce is only calculated to give him disquiet and trouble. Now, as by paying no visits to them, he receives none from them; so, by not writing to them, he will receive no letters from them. "If you understand," says Thomas-à-Kempis, "how to leave men to do their own business, they will leave you at liberty to do yours." All consists in your will to do this, because if you have a mind to do it you will find means enough. We have already left our country, our home, and our relations, for the love of God; let us accomplish the work—let us endeavour to forget them, that being thus disengaged from all earthly things we may think of nothing else but of loving and serving God.

Cassian makes mention of an hermit who was very much devoted to prayer and contemplation, and the better to attend to it, he endeavoured to keep his heart continually withdrawn from all worldly thoughts. At the end of fifteen years' retreat, there came a great packet of letters to him from home. As soon as he had the letters in his hand, he began to think, and say within himself, if I open these letters what thoughts will they not give me? How many different emotions will they excite in my heart, either of joy, if my parents be in prosperity; or of sadness, if I find any misfortune has happened to them? How long will my imagination be filled with the thoughts of those that write to me? What trouble, what distraction will they cause in the time of prayer and meditation? Their features, the things which they have heretofore told me, and those which they now write, will continually come into my mind. How long will it be before I shall be able to efface these images which they will cause in my imagination? What pain shall I have to regain that tranquillity and peace of mind I now enjoy, together with that profound forgetfulness I now have of all worldly objects? Lastly, what will it avail me to have quitted my parents, if my heart and imagination be still with them, and if I begin again to feel satisfaction in their conversation? Whilst he was thus agitated and disturbed in mind, he takes the packet just as he had received it, and cast it into the fire, saying, "begone ye thoughts and tenderness for my home and relations, go and be consumed with my letters in the fire, that ye may never be able to prevail with me to return any more to those things I have already forsaken." (Cas, L. v. de inst. renunt. c. 32.) Nay, he would not only forbear reading the letters that were sent him, but would not so much as open the packet to see the superscriptions, lest coming to know their hands, "that" might give him such remembrance of them, as would disturb his interior peace and tranquillity. They relate the same thing of St. Ignatius. And those who do not content themselves with once reading the letters they receive, but keep them to read them over again, to call to mind their parents, and entertain themselves with the thoughts of them, ought to profit by this example. But if we have not so much courage as to burn them before we read them, let us at least do so after we have read them, in order to free ourselves from those thoughts of flesh and blood which serve only to disquiet us.

———o———

CHAPTER III.

That a religious ought not to return to his native place, even though it were to preach there.

SOME, through the hope of prompting their relations to God's service, let themselves be overcome with the temptations of returning to their native place ; and when these temptations disguise themselves in this manner, under the appearance of good, they are ordinarily the more dangerous ; because we then look upon them not as temptations, but as holy inspirations. St. Bernard upon these words, "catch for us those little foxes, which destroy the vineyards," (Cant. ii. 15,) says, that one of these foxes that spoil our Lord's vineyard, and which to his knowledge had been the ruin of many religious, was the desire they had to convert their relations to God. And, ordinarily speaking, kindred or alliance is an obstacle to the fruit that might be reaped amongst souls ; because your relations, who have familiarly conversed with you in the world, can scarce have that respect and veneration for you which the ministry of the gospel requires ; and it is for this reason that our Saviour himself says, "verily, I say unto you, that no prophet is well received in his own country." (Luke iv. 24.) And when God would make Abraham patriarch of the faithful, he commanded him to leave his country, to quit his parents and friends, and to go into Mesopotamia where no one knew him. The Divine providence also used the like conduct in regard of St. Paul. " He prayed in the temple of Jerusalem, and on a sudden was ravished in spirit, and beheld our Lord, who said to him : make haste, go presently out of Jerusalem, for they will not receive that testimony thou shalt give of me ;" to whom St. Paul answered, " thou art not ignorant, O Lord, that they know very well that I have led many into prison who believed in thee, and that I have persecuted them in their synagogues, and when they shed the blood of thy martyr Stephen, I assisted at his death, to which I consented, and kept the habits of those that stoned him." "It is no matter," replies our Lord, " go, for I will send thee a great way off, amongst the Gentiles." (Acts xvii. 17, &c.) God sent the apostle into a country far distant, that he might produce greater fruit in souls ; and do you think, that you shall be able to produce the like amongst your relations ?   What fruit will you be able to produce ?   How can you urge them to a contempt of those things of the world, and of the commodities of this life, whilst you are with them, and they see you enjoy the same ; and whilst this tenderness of flesh and blood causes you to remain amongst them ?

On this subject father Ribadineira relates a pleasant occurrence. (In dialog. manuscrip.)   He says, that one of our Society having a tender affection for his mother, went to Messina, where she lived, to visit her.   Here entering one day into a church, where they were exorcising a possessed person before a great multitude of people, he presently assisted the priests by conjuring and threatening the devil in God's name; but the wicked spirit, by way of answer to all that was said, only counterfeited the voice of a young child when it calls and cries after its mother.   All that assisted, who knew the religious, and the cause of his return home, presently understood the devil's pleasant conceit, and fell into loud laughter; but he, on the contrary, stood astonished, full of shame and confusion.   May they not treat you after the like manner when you are amongst your parents, preaching of mortification and of all other virtues ?

Sulpicius Severus relates a story of another nature upon the same subject, which ought to make us tremble.   He says that a tribune of Egypt, a very rich man, and of high rank, was obliged on account of his office to pass through the desert of the anchorets, where having had a long conference with St. John the abbot, on things appertaining to salvation, he was so deeply affected by his words, that, although he was married and had a son, yet he presently forsook the world, and took so much to heart the new life he embraced that in a short time he surpassed even the most ancient hermits that were renowned for virtue. In this state a thought occurred to him, that since he was so disabused of the things in this world, it would be better for him to go and labour for the salvation of his wife and son than to live in solitude to procure only his own ; and being deceived by his apparent zeal and charity, after having lived four years in the desert, he set out for home.   The religious of a monastery where he passed, and to whom he had communicated his design, endeavoured to dissuade him from it, by representing to him that it was an illusion of the devil, who had already deceived many others in the same manner.   However, he gave no credit to all they said, so that persisting in his resolution he took his leave of them ; but he was scarce out of the gates of the monastery when he was on a sudden possessed by the devil, and that after so violent a manner that he foamed at the mouth, and tore his own flesh with his teeth.   He was with great pain and trouble brought back to the monastery, where they were forced to shut him up, and in chains—neither the prayers of the holy religious offered for him, nor the conjurations they used in the exorcisms of the devil that tormented him, had any effect upon him for the space of two years.   At the end of this time it pleased God to deliver him, whereupon he returned to the desert, well corrected and chastised, serving as an example and lesson to others to persevere in their holy vocation, and not permit themselves to be seduced by the false appearance of zeal.   By this example we see how a religious ought to reject all thoughts of returning to his native place and of visiting his relations ; because if this, in the opinion of saints, be a dangerous temptation, even when it is done with a view to their salvation, how great a one must it needs be esteemed when it is done only for their own or their relations' satisfaction ?

———o———

CHAPTER IV.

That a religious ought most particularly abstain from interfering in the temporal concerns of his family.

It is the duty of a religious, above all things, not to embroil himself in the affairs of his family, it being very dangerous to do so.   " We see," says St. Gregory, " that very many after they have renounced the world, and what is more, themselves also, have still such a tie to their family, that flesh and blood continually draw them back to the things they had forsaken.   So that forgetting the duty of their profession they permit their minds to be filled with the concerns of their relations ; exert themselves with seculars in their behalf ; interfere in their suits and intrigues ; and thus losing the sweetness of interior peace, they engage again in worldly commerce with great danger to their salvation." St. Isidore says almost the same thing. "There are many religious," says he, "who from affection for their family, bring on themselves a thousand cares, even so far as to involve themselves in their suits; and whilst they are thus employed in what regards the good and advantages of their relations, eternally lose their own souls." (Llb. i. de sum. bono.)

The natural affection we have for our family cannot produce anything more dangerous to a religious than this concern and zeal for their interests; experience teaches us, that to meddle ever so little in their affairs, is like going into a quagmire, from which it is difficult to extricate one's self. "This," St. Basil says, "proceeds from the devil, who, jealous that religious should gain by a heavenly life what he had lost through his own fault, makes every effort to urge them, under pretext of duty and piety, to embark and involve themselves in worldly affairs, thereby to make them lose the peace of their soul, to relent in their love of God, and in their fervour for their perfection. The devil takes this very much to heart; in order to succeed he leaves nothing undone, and with this view makes use of our own family, who never fail to address themselves to us in all their affairs, in their intrigues, in their lawsuits, in their marriages, and lastly, in all the occurrences of their life. It seems as if they looked upon us as charged with the whole business of the family, and it is always to our advice they have recourse : for, in their opinion, we, having little to do, are the most fit persons to attend to their affairs. And hence Ludolphus of Saxony, the Carthusian, speaking of all ecclesiastical persons in general, says very justly, "that as God obliges them to a single life, and would deliver them from the cares and troubles of children, the devil has raised them a crowd of nephews to dring them back again to the tumultuous commerce of the world." In effect, when the devil endeavours to engage you, either in the advancement of a nephew, or the marriage of a niece, it is not their advancement but your loss he has in view. It is, therefore, a melancholy reflection, that a religious who has quitted what he had in the world, renounced all honours and conveniences of life, to free himself from the trouble of it, should plunge himself again into it for the interest of another—charge himself with the whole affairs of his family, and lose the fruit of his vocation. Cassian relates on this subject, that a brother of the abbot Apollo came one night and knocked at the door of his cell to beg his help to draw one of his oxen out of a marsh in which it had stuck fast, as, by himself, he was unable to get it out. The abbot asked him why he did not rather apply for help to his other brother in the world ? He answered, " that he had been dead fifteen years ;" "and I," replied the saint, "am dead twenty years, and have been ever since buried in this cell, so that I cannot go to assist you." It is thus a true religious ought to do when his relations address themselves to him about their temporal affairs ; and, if he had not the courage to do it, he may be assured that whatsoever reason he may at first have for interfering in their business, he will find in the end that it was a bad one.

What we here say is confirmed by the authority of St. Jerome. " How many religious," says he, " by taking compassion on their fathers and mothers have lost their own souls?" How many have lost their vocation, and renounced their profession, because they interested themselves in advancing their relations ? How many apostates do we daily see, who, after having quitted their order under pretence of going to assist and comfort their parents, serve only in the end to ruin them by their continual expenses, and to render them unhappy in their old age by their disorderly life ? Experience furnishes but too many examples ; and, therefore, St. Basil says very justly, " since we know what prejudice this tie and affection to our relatives brings with it, let us not interest ourselves in their concerns—let us dread them as a dangerous weapon which the devil wields for our destruction."

Moreover, we must not deem ourselves secure, and that all is right, because we engage in nothing without permission of our superior ; for we must look upon this permission as upon that given us to visit them. The superior who gives it you wishes very much you would not interfere in the concerns of your relations, because he sees it is best for you not to do so, and he only permits it from an indulgence to you. It is not an obedience he imposes upon you, but it is a permission he grants you, in which you do rather your own will than his. And if St. Theodore refused to see his mother because his superior who gave him leave would not take upon himself the prejudice that might arise to him, what ought not you to do in regard of the concerns of your relations, wherein there is a great deal more danger for you ; and with how much greater reason ought you decline interfering in them, at least, if your superior obliges you not to do it by obedience, and takes not upon himself and his own conscience whatever prejudice may in consequence arise to you?

———o———

CHAPTER V.

The doctrine of the preceding chapter confirmed by examples.

THE fame of the sanctity of the abbot Pœmen being spread all over Egypt, the tribune of the province, being very desirous to see the saint, sent to him to beg he would permit him to pay him a visit. This message very much afflicted the holy abbot, who having considered with himself that if he received this visit from the tribune, he would be overwhelmed with visits from others—that these would derange his spiritual exercises, disturb his interior peace, endanger his humility, and perhaps fill him with vain-glory, at last resolved to beg his excuse and not to receive his visit. The tribune, who was extremely mortified when he heard the answer, said, that he attributed this refusal to his own sins; and conceiving a still greater opinion of the servant of God resolved to see him at all events. After he had for some time reflected with himself what means to adopt, he at last thought on a measure, which he believed would oblige the saint to receive his visit, or to come himself to see him. It was this: he put the son of the saint's sister in prison, and underhand sent word to his mother, that though her son deserved to be punished, yet he would liberate him on condition that the abbot Pœmen would come to beg this favour of him. This woman went presently to her brother in the desert, knocks at his cell door, and with sighs and tears represented the danger her son was in, and conjured him to go to the tribune to intercede for him; but seeing he would neither open the door, nor make any answer to the complaints he heard her make, she at last, falling into a great passion, gave him injurious words, calling him a cruel barbarous man, who had no feeling. She reproached him with the hardness of his heart, telling him he must have bowels of brass not to be touched with the tears of a sister, and of a mother who pleaded in behalf of her only son. Hereupon the saint, turning to his disciple—"go," says he, "and tell that woman in my name, that Pœmen never had any children, and, therefore, he knows not what it is to be afflicted for their loss;" and without making any other answer he sent away his sister with a very sad and heavy heart. The tribune hearing this, and perceiving he must not expect a visit from the saint, endeavoured that some of his friends should persuade him, at least, to write to him in favour of his nephew. Being very much pressed by them, he at last resolved to write, thereby to be freed from their importunities. His letter was couched in these terms : " I beseech your highness carefully to examine the affair of this young man ; and if you find he has deserved death, let him suffer it ; that undergoing the punishment of his crimes in this world, he may, in the other, escape the torments of hell."

We read in the lives of the fathers, a passage very like this, of the abbot Pastor. He thought it so dangerous to take part in the concerns of his family, that though he was importuned in the most earnest manner to intercede for one of his nephews, who was condemned to death, yet he could not be prevailed on to do so.

We read in the life of St. Ignatius that he could never be persuaded to interfere in the marriage of his niece, who was heiress of his family, nor so much as to write one letter to her ; and being very much pressed by divers persons of quality, and particularly by the Dukes of Naier and Albuquerque, he answered, that affairs of this sort no longer regarded himself or his profession ; that he had a good while renounced the world, and was dead to it ; and therefore ought not to return to what he had left, nor meddle with things that did not at all belong to his vocation ; and, lastly, "that he would not take again the coat he had cast off" when he had quitted the world ; nor "soil his feet again after he had washed them." (Cant. v. 3.)

Neither was it possible to obtain of St. Francis of Borgia that he should ask a dispensation from Rome for Don Alvarez Borgia, who wished to marry one of his nieces, a rich heiress, notwithstanding he might thereby have gained a considerable fortune for his son, to whom she would have brought the marquisate of Alcagnez, and though the saint had so much influence with the Pope, that he might hope for anything from him he desired. The emperor Charles V. came to understand by his own knowledge, on another occasion, the truth of what had been told him —that the saint lived without the least tie to flesh and blood. For having once conversed on an affair that touched the interest of his eldest son, the Duke of Gandy, the saint took no more notice hereof than if he had spoken of the interest of a stranger, which extremely edified the emperor, and confirmed him in the high opinion he had before of him.

Let us, notwithstanding, consider what sort of affairs those were that these saints refused to meddle in ; how soon, and with what ease they could settle them, and let us take notice, on the other hand, into what difficulties and intrigues religious now-a-days plunge themselves. But if such great saints as these apprehended the infection of secular affairs, how comes it to pass that we, who are far from being saints, have no dread at all of them ? It is, in reality, because we are not saints, and therefore do not think of what is to come, for, if we truly aspired to sanctity and perfection, we should fear, as they did, those dangers which are inseparable from these affairs, and we should avoid them as they did.

———o———

CHAPTER VI.

Other evils occasioned by our too great affection for our relations.—
Jesus Christ himself warns us hereof.

ST. BASIL says that this irregular affection sometimes causes religious even to commit sacrilege, making them steal the goods of their order to succour their relations in want; and if they do not directly take what belongs to their order to help them, they at least convert to their own use what charitable persons had designed for the order. They take from their penitents what they can get, and this with very great prejudice to the ministry they exercise. For how can they perform their duty, with such entire liberty as they ought, towards those persons whose assistance they stand in need of, and to whom they have these obligations ? Must not they have scruples about the vow of poverty ? Will it be easy to discern whether it is to you, or to another, the present is made ; and whether it is you who in reality afterwards give it, or whether another gives it by your hand? But the worst is, that this inconsiderate tenderness we have for our relations does sometimes so prepossess us, that we scarce take notice of these things, but look upon them as permitted, which, indeed, they are not ; we imagine we do nothing against the vow of poverty, even when we directly violate it. But should a religious rob his order of nothing else than the time he employs in the affairs of his family, this alone were a robbery of very great importance, for, says St. Basil, you are no longer your own master, you belong to your order, to which you have entirely given yourself, and which, for this reason, is charged no less with your body than your soul, and takes care of the one as well as of the other. But if you employ your time in the service of your relations, besides the scandal you give those who see you thus tied in affection to things of the world, is not this to steal time from your order, which nourishes you, and furnishes you with all things necessary for your subsistence ?

" If any one comes to me," says our Saviour, " and hates not his father, mother, wife, children, brothers, sisters ; yea, and his own soul, he cannot be my disciple." (Luke xiv. 26.) And St. Gregory observes on this passage that God no less recommends to us the hatred of our parents than the hatred of ourselves. Hence, as we have no greater enemy than ourselves, we are, in consequence, obliged to hate ourselves, and make ourselves feel the effects thereof by mortifying our senses, and continually opposing the irregular desires and inclinations of flesh and blood ; even so we ought to have a holy hatred of our parents, and show them no condescension at all in those things that may be an obstacle to our salvation and to our advancement in perfection. Because our parents are a part of ourselves, and consequently our enemies, as well as we ourselves are ; according to the words of the Scripture, " the enemies of man are his domestics, or those of the same house and family." (Mich. vii. 6.)

It is related in the Chronicles of St. Francis that a secular person telling brother Giles that he would absolutely become a religious, the servant of God answered him, if you have truly a mind to be so, go kill all your relations. This man, astonished at this answer, began to weep, and begged that he would not oblige him to commit such enormous crimes as these were. Whereupon the brother reproached him for not rightly understanding him. " I do not bid you," says he, " to go and really cut the throat of your relations, but that you go and endeavour to destroy the affection you have for them in your heart by absolutely casting it away, because Jesus Christ teaches us that ' he who hates not his parents cannot be his disciple.' "

It is our duty to remark how often this doctrine is repeated in the gospel. At one time our Saviour answers him who wished to follow him, and who asked his leave first to dispose of what he had, " whoever puts his hand to the plough and looks back is not fit for the kingdom of heaven." (Luke ix. 62.) At another time he tells him whom he commanded to follow him, but who begged leave first to go bury his father, "Let the dead bury their dead; but go thou and announce the kingdom of heaven." (Luke ix. 60.) What fear ought not this first answer give those who look back—that is, those who embroil themselves in worldly business after having begun to follow the evangelical counsels? Ought they not fear, lest God will reject them as unfit for his kingdom? And, as Theophilact says upon the second example, "if that man were not permitted to bury his father, woe to those who, having embraced a religious life, return to the affairs of the world which they have quitted!"

But it was not only in words and the example of others that Jesus taught us to live in an entire detachment from our relations. No; he deigned to teach us by his own example also, as is evident from many passages in Holy Writ, where we see that he shows, even externally, severity and coldness to his most holy Mother. "Why did you ask after me?" says he, when she found him in the temple. "Know you not that I ought to go about my Father's business." (Luke ii. 49.) And again, at the marriage of Cana, she tells him that there was no wine left. "Woman," replied he, "what is that to thee and me?" (John ii. 4.) Whereby, says St. Bernard, he teaches us how we ought to behave to our relations when they would divert us from the duties of our religious profession. On these occasions, as he did, we should say to them, I ought to employ myself only in the business of my father, I ought to labour only for my salvation. Does not this also appear to be a very cold answer which he made the person who said, "Master, desire my brother divide the inheritance with me." "Man," replies he, "who has appointed me thy judge to make this division between you?" (Luke xii. 14.) And does not this teach us that a religious cannot be too cautious in avoiding to meddle with worldly business, which is not at all his profession?

------o------

CHAPTER VII.

Disorderly affection for relations sometimes disguises itself under pretexts of duty and piety : the remedy to be applied thereto.

THERE being no temptations more dangerous than those that hide themselves under the veil of duty and piety, of which one is too great an affection for relations, St. Ignatius, to prevent the inconveniences arising therefrom, ordains, in his Constitutions, that we must exact from all those that would enter into the Society a promise that, as often as they think themselves obliged to help their parents they will not be guided by their own judgment, but by the decision of the superiors; for in the affairs of our relations, as well as of our own, we are ordinarily blinded by passion, and consequently cannot, in these cases, be good judges. Now, the remedy assigned us by our holy founder, so far from giving rise to scruples on this head, entirely tranquillizes our conscience. For it obliges us to adhere to the opinion of the Society, which being so prudent, so enlightened, and filled with the fear of God, that it cannot fail to examine all things very well, and to decide according to conscience and truth. In the beginning, therefore, we propose to all who enter amongst us whether they will be contented to submit themselves on this point to the judgment of the Society, and if they refuse, we do not receive them; and it is a great favour of God, for which we ought to render him thanks, that hereby we may rest content and be in quiet of mind on this point, and have nothing to think of but our salvation and spiritual advancement.

It is, moreover, to evade the illusions of flesh and blood that the same saint ordains that when we are about to distribute our goods amongst our poor relations, we ought to take counsel of two or three persons whom we may make choice of, with the approbation of our superior, and who shall be judges of the poverty and necessity of our relations. So that how poor soever they may be we cannot dispose of our goods in their behalf but by the advice of others, though we are left entirely at liberty to dispose of what we have to strangers without consulting any one, and he ordains this, lest the natural affection we have for our relations should deceive us. St. Gregory, speaking of the person whom our Saviour would not permit to go to bury his father, takes notice that what he would not have forbidden him to do to a stranger, but would rather have counselled as a work of mercy, he forbids him to do in regard of his father, "to teach us," says the holy doctor, "that even such charities as our duty requires of us towards strangers ought not to be practised towards our relations, because the natural tenderness we have for them is subject to a great many illusions, and because it is not of edification to see a disciple of Jesus Christ encumber himself with the interest of flesh and blood." In effect it is very certain that we take to heart the concerns of our relations after another manner than we do those of strangers, these leave our mind in an entire tranquillity, whereas those rob us of the peace of our soul, and trouble us in our spiritual exercises, and hence when we are about to succour our family, it is far better that it be done by another religious than by ourselves, and this is the advice of St. Basil, and what our rules also prescribe. For if this trust is reposed in us, unless we be detached from the ties of flesh and blood, we will always desire that our family be rich and at their ease, though God, perhaps, would have them remain in poverty and sufferings, thereby to humble them and to save their souls. Nay, more, vanity has so far got possession of certain religious that they avail themselves of the influence which their habit gives them over the great ones in the world in order to raise their relations to places of honour, which they themselves never had the idea or the means of attaining, and in this they show themselves to have nothing but the name and habit of religious, for instead of being, as they ought to be, more humble than those in the world are, they are more puffed up with presumption and vanity.

And since it happens but too often that many quit religion, as they pretend, to assist their parents in the world, it is good to observe here, that ordinarily speaking, this is not the motive which urges them, and renders them unfaithful to their vocation. No ! it is their spirit of immortification, their want of fervour and courage to support the holy austerities of their rule, and other hidden causes they are not ignorant of, which make them quit their religious profession ; but because they dare not allege the true motives, they have recourse to specious pretexts. Be this as it may, we daily perceive that such persons as these, after going out become rather a charge and burden than a help to their parents ; and that ordinarily they have not the power, nor do they make any effort to assist them. They did not leave religion, therefore, through this motive ; for in religion they could help their parents better than out of it. No ! but it was their spirit of pride, of indocility, and a wish to live according to their own will and pleasure, that induced them to return to the world ! They may deceive men, but they cannot deceive God ! and woe to him who begins to stagger on this point and who does not abide by the decision of his rule and superiors !

Whosoever therefore would attain the end, he ought to propose to himself in his entrance into religion, must renounce all commerce with his relations, and entirely disengage himself from the care of their concerns. "For those who have said to their father and mother, I know you not; and to their brethren, I have not acquaintance with you; and who are ignorant of their children, these are they, O Lord, who have kept thy commandments, and have faithfully kept their league with thee." (Deut. xxxiii. 9.) "A true religious," says St. Bernard, "ought to be like another Melchisedech, of whom the apostle speaking, says, he had neither father nor mother, nor even birth, not but he had so in effect, because he was a man; but the scripture speaking of him in that place considers him only as a priest, and makes no mention of his genealogy, nay not so much as of his birth, or of his death; to teach us," says the saint, "that the priests of our Lord, but principally religious, ought to have no tie or relation to flesh and blood, but to be so employed in spiritual things as if they descended from heaven; and lastly, they ought to be Melchisedechs in their hearts, that is to say, they ought entirely to cast off whatsoever may in the least hinder their progress towards God."

Let us conclude, and say with St. Bernard, "remain in solitude like a turtle. Let there be no tie between the world and thee, no commerce between thee and men, forget thy country and thy father's house, and the King will be enamoured with thy beauty." (Ps. xliv. 11.) St. Jerome, therefore, upon these words of the prophet, had reason to say it was a great recompense indeed; nor can there be a greater than that which is annexed to the forgetfulness of one's father, because thereby one becomes the object of the love of the King of kings.

It is related in the Chronicles of St. Francis, that a doctor of Sorbonne having taken the habit of the order, his mother, who had spent what she had in maintaining him in his studies, and now found herself reduced to extreme poverty, presently ran to the convent all bathed in tears. She cries and sobs in her son's presence, opens her breasts, and conjures him by those he had sucked, and by the pains she had taken to educate him, that he would not now forsake her in her misery. She at last moved him so far, that he resolved the next day to quit the order. However, finding great combats hereupon within his soul, he betook himself to prayer, and as soon as his mother was gone, prostrating himself before a crucifix, his heart being heavily oppressed with sorrow, he cried out, "O Lord! I will never leave thee, permit not that this should ever happen; I will only assist my mother in her extreme necessity." He had no sooner pronounced these words, having his eyes fixed on the crucifix, than he perceived blood running from it, and heard a voice that said to him, " Hast thou not cost me more than thy mother, since I have redeemed thee with my own precious blood ? Wherefore then wilt thou leave me for her?" Which words and vision so touched his heart, that preferring Jesus Christ to that natural tenderness and compassion he had for his mother, he continued to serve him in that order, in which he faithfully persevered to his death.

Though what I have said in this treatise regards religious only, yet if it should dissuade secular persons from engaging religious in worldly affairs, and from soliciting places of trust and change of abode for such religious as are related to them, it will be a great advantage both to the one and the other.

THE SIXTH TREATISE.

———o———

ON JOY AND SADNESS.

———o———

CHAPTER I.

The great evils occasioned by sadness.

" Cast sadness far from thee," says the Wise man, " because it has killed many, and is good for nothing." (Ecclus. xxx. 24.) Cassian, in a treatise he composed on the spirit of sadness, says, " that it is a disease more dangerous and harder to be cured than all other spiritual infirmities, and he proves the grievous effects it produces by the authority of Scripture. " Beware," says he, " of admitting sadness into your soul, for if it once gets possession of you it will soon take away all your relish for prayer, and spiritual readings; it will make you think them tedious, and cause you to afford to each less time than ordinary ; nay, sometimes, it will make you quite leave off both, and lastly, it will diffuse over all your spiritual exercises so much disgust and irksomeness that it will be almost impossible for you to continue them." Cassian adds that the royal prophet very well expresses all this in these few words : " my soul is asleep through heaviness." (Ps. cxviii. 28.) He does not say that his body is asleep, but that his soul is so ; because in effect, sadness and spiritual drowsiness give so much irksomeness and disgust to the soul, in all exercises of devotion and holy things, that it falls as it were asleep, and becomes incapable of doing anything good. Nay, this disgust goes sometimes so far that the soul even feels itself disquieted and displeased with the fervour of others, and endeavours to withdraw them from it.

Cassian says, " that sadness causes another evil, which is, that it make us severe and rude to our brethren." St. Gregory says, " that it easily provokes to choler ;" and in effect we daily experience, that when we are troubled everything angers us, and every little matter goes to our heart. Moreover it renders a man impatient, suspicious, and untractable ; and sometimes it so troubles our mind that it even deprives us of our judgment, according to these words of the Wise man, " where there is bitterness of heart, and sadness, there is no reason." (Ecclus. xxi. 15.) And do not we often perceive that when a man is attacked by this passion, he has fears, diffidences, and such wild notions as are considered by persons in their reason to be the effects of frenzy. And even persons of great merit and wisdom sometimes abandon themselves so far to this deep melancholy, as in presence of others to cry like children ; or when they find the passion coming, sometimes to shut themselves up in their chambers, that without being seen by others they may be at liberty to weep.

" If you would thoroughly know," says Cassian, " the bad effects sadness produces in the heart, the Holy Ghost will teach you by these words of the Wise man, ' as moths eat garments, or the worms eat wood, even so sadness gnaws the heart of man ?' " (Prov. xxv. 20.) As a habit, therefore, eaten by moths is of no use, and as worm-eaten wood is neither fit to be wrought, nor does it serve as a prop, because it falls to pieces as soon as it is touched, just so a man who is gnawn and eaten by sadness, becomes unserviceable and unfit for anything. But the evil stops not here, for sadness causes many temptations, and even very great falls, according to these words of Scripture : " sadness has killed many." (Prov. xxv. 20.) Hence some call it the retreat of devils, and explain in this sense the words of Job, speaking of the devil: " he sleeps in the shade." (Job xl. 16.) It is, say they, in this gloomy melancholy which you indulge, and it is in these thick darknesses which obscure your mind, that the devil retires and reposes himself; and it is when you are in this state that he takes his time to attack and destroy you. They explain in the same sense these words of the prophet: " you have spread darkness all over; the night is come, and all the wild beasts walk about." (Ps. ciii. 20.) For as wild beasts await the darkness to issue from their dens, so the devils wait till the obscurity of sadness covers you, that then they may torment you with all sorts of temptations. " They keep their arrows ready in their quiver, to shoot in darkness the upright man." (Ps. x. 3.)

St. Francis was wont to say, that sadness in the heart of a Christian was a subject of joy to the devil, because then it was easy to make him either despair, or turn to the pleasures of the world. Pay due attention to this; for it is a truth of great importance. In effect, what happens to those that give themselves over to sadness is, that sometimes the devil makes them despair, as we see by the examples of Cain and Judas; at other times, to attain his end, he proposes to them pleasures and amusements as the best means of banishing their lowness of spirits; and at other times, in fine, under the same pretext, he represents to them impure images, on which he endeavours to make them look with pleasure. Now, these temptations which regard pleasure and impurity, and are but too frequent in those persons who give way to sadness, are very dangerous. For a religious hereupon begins to fancy that he would have been happier in the world, grows dissatisfied with his state, and readily abandons it. "The soul," says St. Gregory, "can never be without pleasure; it must take it either in the things of heaven or those of the earth." (Lib. xviii. Moral. c. 8.) When it begins, then, to have no relish for those of heaven, the devil, who knows perfectly well what man is, represents to him thoughts of impurity; and the pleasures these objects give him in his sadness urges him to embrace them as a fit remedy for his disease.

Sadness, in a word, produces so many evils, that the Wise man says, "that sadness of the heart is the greatest of all wounds, and that it quickly causes death." (Ecclus. xxv. 17; xxxviii. 19.) Nay, as St. Austin says, it leads even to eternal death! And it is in this sense he explains these words of Jacob to his children: "you will bring down with sorrow my grey hairs to hell." (Gen. xlii. 38.) "Jacob," says he, "was afraid the sorrow he suffered for the loss of Benjamin would put his salvation in danger, and precipitate him into hell; and it is for this reason," adds the saint, "that the apostle advises us to take care, 'lest any root of bitterness springing up should hinder grace, and by it many be defiled.' (Heb. xii. 15.)" At all events, it was not to ensure our ease and happiness here that the Scripture and holy men caution us so much against sadness— were this the only object to be attained it would avail but little whether we be sad or not. No! we are cautioned against sadness as being the source of unnumbered sins and evils; and it is for this very reason that the devil makes every effort to plunge us into sadness.

CHAPTER II.

That we ought to serve God with joy—reasons that oblige us to do so.

" REJOICE always in our Lord," says the apostle, " I say again unto you, rejoice." (Phil. iv. 4.) The Psalmist also recommends the same to us very often : "let the just," says he, "rejoice in the Lord, and exult with joy, and let those of an upright heart glory in him." (Ps. xxxi. 14.) " Let all those who seek after thee, O Lord, exult and rejoice thee." (Ps. lix. 5.) " Let all the earth rejoice in God ; let it serve the Lord with joy, and present itself before him with gladness." (Ps. xcix. 1.) " Let the heart of those that seek our Lord, rejoice." (Ps. civ. 3.) He exhorts us also in divers other places to serve God with joy. And when the angel Raphael saluted Toby, he said nothing to him but this, " let joy always be with thee." (Tob. v. 11.) St. Francis was wont to say, that the devil and wicked men only ought to be sad : and that those who are truly religious men ought always rejoice. " The cries of joy only for their salvation, ought to be heard in the tabernacles of the just." (Ps. xcvii. 15.) And how is it possible we should be sad—we whom God has chosen from amongst so many, to place us in his own house and family.

What I have already said of the effects of sadness, and the care the holy Scripture takes so often to invite the just to rejoice, sufficiently show how much it imports us to serve God with joy; but that the advantages derivable from it may excite us the more, I shall here touch on some of the reasons that ought to move us to it. The first is, that God wishes to be served in this manner. For as St. Paul says, " God loves him who gives him what he has with joy, and not with discontent or constraint." (2 Cor. ix. 7.) The Wise man also teaches the same in these words, " whatsoever thou givest, give it always with a cheerful countenance." (Ecclus. xxv. 11.) As in the world masters wish to be served by their domestics with joy, and cannot endure they should serve them with sadness ; even so God, who is our supreme Lord and Master, desires to be served with joy and affection, and rejects those that serve him with chagrin and sadness. The holy scripture takes notice, that when the people of Israel offered a great quantity of gold, silver, and precious stones, for the building of the temple, they did it with "an exceeding great joy ;" and that David gave public thanks to God for the zeal and good will of the people. It is properly this that God esteems ; he regards not so much the present that is made him, as the good will and affection with which it is made. Do they not even in the world say that they think more of the good will than of all the rest ; and it is that gives an infinite value even to the smallest things, whereas without that, even considerable services are not at all grateful, but rather displeasing ? They are good viands, but dressed in such a manner as spoils them, and quite takes away their taste and flavour.

The second reason is, that when we serve God with joy we promote his honour and glory ; because we show we do it with affection ; and that all we do is nothing in comparison of what we wish to do. It is not so with those that serve God with sadness. One would say that they think they do very much, because they groan under the burden, and would seem, as it were, oppressed by the heaviness of the yoke. Now this extremely displeases God, and is a very bad sign ; and it was on this account St. Francis was always displeased when he saw any of his religious sad ; because sadness is a sign of a will much indisposed, and of a burdensome body. On the contrary those that serve God with joy and promptitude seem to say, that all they do is nothing in comparison of what they have a wish to do. " All that I do for you, O Lord," says St. Bernard, " seems scarce to take up an hour's time ; or if it takes up more, love hinders me from perceiving it." (Serm. xiv. sup. Cant.) But see what God requires of us when he says, " take care, when you fast, of being sad, as hypocrites are ; who make their countenance pale and disfigured, that men may perceive they fast ; but for thy part, when thou fastest, anoint thy head and wash thy face, that none may perceive thee to fast." (Matt. vi. 16.) It is good to take notice here, by the by, that some imagine, that to preserve decorum and religious modesty they ought always to keep their eyes fixed upon the ground, and show sadness in their countenance : but they are deceived herein. " Religious modesty," says St. Leo Pope, " ought to be holy, but not sad." (Ser. iv. Quadrag.) Their modesty therefore ought to be mixed with cheerfulness, and their cheerfulness tempered with modesty ; which when joined together have a good effect, and are graceful in a religious person.

The third reason is, that God is not only hereby more hon-

oured, but that our neighbour also is more edified, and the
esteem of virtue more increased : for those who serve God with
joy, prove to worldlings that on the road of virtue there are not
so many obstacles and difficulties as is imagined ; and as men
naturally love joy, they willingly travel the road whereon they
expect to find it. But we, above all—we, whose profession particularly engages us in the help of souls, and consequently in
worldly commerce, ought exercise our functions with joy, as
there is nothing more proper than this to inspire the love of
virtue and perfection in others ; and it has often happened, that
the joy visible in the countenance of true religious has been the
cause that many have embraced a religious state. All the world
seeks to live contented, and if they did but know the satisfaction
a true religious enjoys, the world would soon become a desert.
But this satisfaction is a hidden manna, which our Lord discovers
only to those whom he is pleased to make choice of. He has
discovered it to you, and has concealed it from your brother,
which is the reason that he remained in the world, and that you
entered into religion ; and this favour ought also oblige you to
render continual thanks for it to Almighty God.

The fourth reason for which we ought to serve him with joy
is, that our good actions gain hereby a greater merit in his sight,
and become more holy and perfect ; for it is a maxim in philosophy " that joy perfects a work, and sadness corrupts it."
And do we not daily see, that there is a great difference between
him that does a work with cheerfulness and another that performs it unwillingly and with regret? It seems that the one
does it slightly and superficially, and only to be able to say that
he has done it ; but the other applies himself to do well what he
does, and to acquit himself of his duty in the best manner he is
able. Add to this what St. Chrysostom says, that joy and contentment give strength and courage to perform good works ;
wherefore the royal prophet spoke thus to God, " I have run the
way of thy commandments after thou hadst dilated my heart."
(Psal. cxviii. 32.) But it is joy which dilates the heart, and it
is joy also that hinders the just from feeling pain in whatsoever
they do—" That they run, and are not at all tired, that they
walk and feel no difficulty therein." (Isa. xl. 31.) Sadness,
on the contrary, shuts up the heart, and takes from it not only
the desire but even the force of acting ; and causes that which
before was very easy to become very hard and insupportable.
Aaron felt this weakness in himself when having lost his two

sons, whom the fire of heaven had destroyed, and being reprehended by Moses for not having entirely consummated the sacrifice
—"how was it possible," says he, "I should please God, carrying along with me so sad a heart to those ceremonies?" (Levit.
x. 19.)   And the children of Israel, also, in the captivity of
Babylon cried out: "How is it possible we should sing canticles
to our Lord in a strange land?" (Psal. cxxxvi. 4.)   Lastly,
experience daily teaches us not only that "sadness dejects the
mind," (Prov. xv. 13,) as the Wise man says, but that it
weakens the body, also, to such a degree that it seems to have
neither force nor vigour; and it is on this account the saints
counsel us not to let ourselves be dejected by sadness in time of
temptation, for this does nothing else than discourage us, and
render us less able to resist it.

The fifth reason why it is extremely to be wished that Christians, but above all, religious, would serve God with joy, is,
because when one begins in this manner to serve him there is
all the reason in the world to hope for a perseverance therein;
whereas, when one begins in a different manner, there is reason
to fear that they will not go far or persevere.   When we see a
man that is loaden walk heavily and uneasily, and that he seems
out of breath, and stops almost at every step to rest himself, or
replace and refit his burden anew, and that lets sometimes one
thing and sometimes another fall down; we judge presently that
he is a man who is quite spent, and able to do no more, seeing
him even ready to fall under his burden.   But on the contrary,
when we see another who steadily carries his burden, and sings
all the way he goes, we conclude he will carry it on, and that he
will not fail upon the way.   It is the same with religious; those
who have sorrow imprinted on their foreheads whilst they perform the duties of their profession, and seem to groan under their
burden, give no flattering hopes of perseverance; for to ply continually the oar as a slave, is a task difficult to be performed for
any length of time.   But those who bear the yoke of our Lord
with joy, and perform with cheerfulness even the meanest duties
and the most painful exercises of religion, and who find nothing
too hard, give great hopes of remaining always faithful and constant in their vocation.

CHAPTER III.

*That the small faults into which we fall ought not to make us lose
our cheerfulness and contentment of mind.*

THE saints look upon this cheerfulness as so great a good, that
they say we ought not to be discouraged or constrained even in
our spiritual falls. For though sin, as we shall prove, is one of
the things that ought justly to give us sadness, yet this sadness
ought to be moderated by the hope of pardon, and by our confidence in God's mercy, for fear, says the apostle, "he who is in
this condition should be overwhelmed by the excess of sadness."
(2 Cor. ii. 7.) It was for this reason that St. Francis, who
could not suffer the appearance thereof in the countenances of
his religious, said one day to one of his companions that appeared
sad, that a true servant of God ought to be sad for nothing,
except for having committed a sin : if you have commited one,
repent, and be sorry for it ; confess it and implore the mercy of
God ; saying to him with the prophet, "render me, O Lord, the
joy of thy salvation, and fortify my mind with the spirit of thy
all-powerful grace." (Ps. l. 14.) St. Jerome explaining this
passage says, that these words, "render me the joy of thy salvation," are the same as "render me, O Lord, the joy I had in
Jesus Christ before I sinned," and this also shows with what
great care the servants of God ought to entertain this holy joy
in their hearts, because it is the portion of those who are in the
state of grace.

Father Avila reprehends those very severely, who walking in
the way of God, plunge themselves to no purpose into sadness,
and so fill their hearts with bitterness that they feel no more
sweetness in the things of God. "They appear," says he,
"languishing, dejected, troublesome both to themselves and to
others ; and this sometimes happens when they have not committed a mortal sin. But this proceeds, they will tell you, from
sorrow for their venial sins, and for their regret at not having
served God as they ought, and as they desire to do ; and it is for
this reason they are in this desolate state. But this is an error
and a great illusion ; for this excessive sadness into which they
are plunged may give a deeper wound to their souls than the
faults themselves for which they are afflicted. It makes them

suffer the disease to augment, which they might have cured with
a little prudence and courage ; and thus they fall from one incon-
veniency into another, and this is precisely the state in which
the devil wishes to have them, in order to deprive them of
strength to act, and to hinder them from doing anything else
but afflict themselves." What the sight of our imperfections and
weakness ought to effect in us is, to render us more humble, and
to excite us to beg a greater grace from God, because we perceive
how much we stand in need thereof; and lastly, to make us stand
more upon our guard, taking from the past warning for the
future ; foreseeing dangerous occasions to avoid them ; and after
this manner, we shall advance far more than by suffering ourselves to be dejected by sadness. If we abandon ourselves to this
passion for the faults into which we daily fall, who would ever,"
says father Avila, " have any joy or repose ?"   " For if thou, O
Lord, takest notice of our iniquities, who shall be able to bear
it ?" (Ps. cxxix. 3.)   Apply yourself seriously to serve God, and
to do your duty, and if you happen to fail in anything, trouble
not yourself, and lose not courage for that ; since all the world
are failing in their duty.   You are but a weak man, you are not
an angel or saint ; and God, who knows very well your weakness
and misery, would not have you be discouraged when you fall.
He only wishes you to ask new strength of him, that, in imitation of children, who as soon as they fall rise again and continue to run ; even so you ought quickly rise, and begin anew to
run in the way of God's commandments.

"Fathers," says St. Ambrose, "behold the falls of their
children rather with compassion than anger ; God does the same
to us.   He loves us as his children, he knows our frailty, and
therefore our falls and weakness excite him rather to a tender
compassion, than to any indignation towards us."   "As a father
pities his children, so our Lord has pity and compassion upon
those that fear him ; for he knows of what matter we are made,
and he has not forgot that we are dust." (Ps. cii. 13.)   One of
the great consolations those have who serve God with the fervour
they ought is, to know that though they correspond not to his
goodness as they should, yet he ceases not to bear with them and
to love them ; " because he is rich in mercy ;" (Eph. ii. 4) ; so
that all our sins disappear before his infinite mercy, and become
like wax that melts before the fire.   What sentiments of zeal,
gratitude, and cheerfulness, ought not to be excited in us by the
thought, that the many faults we daily fall into through our

weakness do not hinder God from loving us according to his wonted goodness, and do not at all diminish his grace in us.

———o———

CHAPTER IV.

Of the causes and remedies of sadness.

LET us now go to the root of the evil and see what are the causes of sadness, that we may know its remedies, and how to apply them. Cassian and St. Bonaventure say that sadness may arise from different causes. Sometimes it proceeds from our constitution, and from the circumstances of melancholy being the prevalent humour in our body, and that it is a disease that stands more in need of physicians than directors. However, we are to take notice that this humour is nourished and augmented by those disquiet thoughts in which we indulge, and that it is so very dangerous to let ourselves be carried away with these imaginations, that Cassian says we ought with as much care to cast them from us as we would cast off those against faith and purity. Sometimes we cannot precisely say from whence this sadness proceeds, for it frequently happens that, without any occasion, we fall on a sudden into such profound melancholy that we take no pleasure in anything; that everything displeases us ; that we avoid all company, even of our best friends, so that they can scarce get a word from us, and that even what we say is full of coldness and peevishness. This shows, says Cassian, that our impatience and hastiness do not always proceed from any subject given us by our brethren, but from a bad disposition within ourselves, and because we do not sufficiently curb our passions; so that the remedy we are to apply to this distemper is, not to withdraw ourselves from the conversation of others, but to mortify our passions, for without that, what place soever we should go to, or in what desert soever we should hide ourselves, we shall carry along with us the cause of our disquiet and impatience.

It is mentioned in the life of St. Enthimus the abbot, that one of his religious, whose hasty and choleric humour was become insupportable to all the rest, resolved to quit the monastery and to retire into the desert, imagining that when he had no occasion to dispute with anybody, but was alone, he should have no cause to be angry, but should live in peace. He executed his design, shut himself up in a cell, and had scarce entered into it but a pitcher of water he had brought with him happened to be thrown down. He goes and fills it again, and had no sooner set it upon the ground but it was spilled again. He returns the second time to fill it, takes care also how he sets it down, and yet the third time it was again spilled, whereupon, falling into a violent passion, he casts it against the ground, and breaks it into a thousand pieces. Afterwards, coming to himself, he reflected on the great passion he had fallen into, and perceiving hereby that he ought not to cast the cause of his passion and anger upon his brethren, but that he ought to attribute it to the little care he took to repress it, he returned presently to his monastery. You see, then, that if you have motions of anger and hastiness, you ought not to think they proceed from your neighbour, but from yourself. "Mortify your passions," says Cassian, "and by this means you will not only live in peace with your brethren, but, according to these words of scripture, even "beasts themselves will become tame and live in peace with you." (Job v. 23.)

"Sadness," says St. Bonaventure, "does also sometimes proceed either from some cross or affliction that happens to us, or from our not having attained an object we earnestly sought after." St. Gregory and St. Austin are of the same opinion, and say that sadness in worldly people proceeds from their too great attachment to the things of the world, for it is certain that he who loves anything cannot be deprived of it without some pain or regret, whereas no occurrence can afflict him who is detached from all things, and who has God only for the object of his desires and comfort. "There is no doubt," says Father Avila, "that our desires cause disquiet and trouble in us, and that the more vehement they are the more violent our disquiet is, and the less our desires are the less also is our disquiet, so that when we have brought ourselves to desire nothing, we then enjoy a perfect repose of mind. Lastly, we may truly say that our desires are our executioners, and keep us continually upon the rack, and are the cause of all our sufferings.

But, to pass from things in general to a particular application, I say that often that which causes trouble and sadness to a religious person is because he has not a submission and indifference for all things that obedience may enjoin him. He is in pain lest he be taken from a place where he finds himself comfortable—from an office which pleases him, and be assigned another to which he feels a repugnance. Behold what makes him

melancholy and discontented!—"It is," says St. Gregory,
"because he desires what he has not, or fears to lose what he
has, and this fear and hope continually agitate him according to
the state in which he seems to find himself happy or unhappy.
He is ever unsteady, and feels within himself the different
changes that happen in the things to which he is attached."
But it is quite different with a religious who keeps himself
always in an equal temper and disposition of mind, who is ready
to embrace whatsoever obedience may enjoin, and who places
his entire contentment in God, such a man is replenished with
joy so perfect that nothing can trouble it.   Superiors may take
him out of the place and employment he is in, but they cannot
deprive him of that satisfaction he enjoyed in it, because his
satisfaction was tied neither to the place nor to the employment
he was in, but only to the accomplishing of God's will concerning
him, and, therefore, wheresoever he is employed he is always
equally satisfied.   Wherefore, if you desire always to be so, place
always your contentment in the will of God, and permit it not to
have any tie to any determinate thing, nor to follow its own inclination, for this is not the way to gain content, but a means
never to compass it, and to have a thousand disgusts and discontents instead of it.

Lastly, to dive yet more deeply into this matter, it is, ordinarily speaking, rather pride than melancholy that renders us
sad.   Wherefore, so long as pride shall reign in you, assure
yourself you shall never be without discontent, for you will
never want occasions of having it, and therefore you will never
enjoy any quiet or sweetness of repose.   What I just now said,
of the effect of submission to whatsoever obedience shall require
of us, may have place in what I am about to say here, for very
often, when we are afraid of certain employments, it is not the
difficulty that accompanies them that makes us fear them,
because those we seek after have ordinarily far greater; but it
is pride, it is self-love, it is envy, whereby we would attract
consideration or esteem to ourselves, which urges us to desire
the one and to avoid the other.   Behold here the reason why
the more easy employments seem to us so difficult and painful;
behold here what renders us discontented in the exercise of
them, and what makes even the bare idea and apprehension of
such an employment afflict us as it does.

The remedy of this sort of sadness is to become humble, and
to love the meanest employments.   "Learn of me," says Jesus

Christ, " who am meek and humble of heart, and you shall find
rest to your souls." (Matt. xi. 29.) " If we imitate the humility
of our Saviour," says St. Austin upon these words, " we shall be
so far from feeling pain and difficulty in the practice of virtue
that we shall find it easy and delightful, for what renders it
hard is the tie we have to our will and our own judgment—it is
vanity, it is pride, it is love of ourselves, and of our pleasures
and ease. But humility easily surmounts all these obstacles,
because it makes us have little or no esteem for ourselves, it
makes us renounce our own will, contemn all the goods,
pleasures, and vanities of the world ; and this once gained, the
practice of virtue is no longer difficult, but, on the contrary, is
filled with all sweetness and satisfaction.

——o——

CHAPTER V.

That prayer is an excellent remedy against sadness.

CASSIAN says that the elevating our mind to God in prayer, and
the hope of those eternal goods he has promised us, is an excellent remedy against all sorts of sadness ; it dissipates all those
clouds of our mind, and drives away this evil spirit of sadness,
just as David with his harp chased away the evil spirit which
tormented Saul.   The apostle St. James proposes this remedy to
us in his canonical epistle, when he says, " if any one amongst
you be sad, let him pray." (Jam. v. 13.)   And the royal
prophet tells us that he was wont to make use of it.   " My
soul," says he, "rejected all sorts of comfort: I thought of
God, and I found myself in joy." (Ps. lxxvi. 4.)   And, in
another place, " Thy decrees, O Lord, were the subject of my
songs of joy in the place of my banishment." (Ps. cxviii. 54.)
Oftentimes the conversation of a friend is sufficient to drive
away our discontent and to give us joy.   What consolation and
sweetness, therefore, ought we with greater reason hope for and
find in our conversation with God ?   It is not, therefore, in
conversing with men, nor in reading profane authors, nor in the
harmony of music, nor in other worldly amusements, that religious ought to seek ease or help against sadness, they must seek
it at God's feet by means of prayer, and it is there they will
infallibly find true joy and consolation.

We read in the holy scripture that, after the ark rested upon
the mountains of Armenia, Noah, in order to know whether the

waters were quite fallen, put a crow out of the ark, which returned no more, and afterwards he sent out a dove, which, finding no place to rest its feet upon, returned again to the ark. The holy fathers hereupon object and say, that, without doubt, since the crow returned not, it found some place to rest itself upon, how then comes it to pass that the scripture says the dove found none? It is, say they, because the crow, which is a bird of prey and unclean, found a place to repose itself in the mire and upon dead bodies, and that the dove, which is an image of purity, could not for a moment repose thereupon. It is in this manner a good religious and a good servant of God conducts himself. He finds nothing in the vain amusements of the world that gives him any pleasure, he cannot meet anything in the corruption of worldly objects to dwell on, and therefore he presently returns, as the dove did, to the ark. That is to say, he recollects himself, he makes it his business to think of God, to adore him, to pour out his heart in his presence, and to say unto him, "O my God, how can I be sad in your presence, you that are the source of all joy and comfort." St. Austin, explaining these words of the Psalmist, "Thou hast put joy into my heart;" "it is not without, then," says he, "that we must seek for joy, but it is in the interior man, it is within ourselves, and it is the retreat of the heart which is proper for meditation and prayer."

Sulpicius Severus says, that St. Martin found no other means to refresh himself, when he was spent and tired out with labours, than to apply himself to prayer; and, as smiths in forging iron refresh themselves by sometimes ceasing to strike upon the anvil, so this great saint refreshed himself by having recourse to repose in prayer, at the time he was thought to give himself to rest. It is related of another servant of God, that being one day in his cell and finding himself oppressed with extreme bitterness of heart, whereby God was pleased from time to time to try him, he heard a voice from heaven that resounded in the bottom of his heart saying, "Why do you permit yourself to be unprofitably consumed with sadness? Arise, and meditate upon the mysteries of my passion." He arose; put himself into profound meditation, and presently all his sadness was dissipated; and he found himself filled with fervour and consolation; and this holy exercise, which he daily continued ever after, entirely freed him from this troublesome temptation.

CHAPTER VI.

*That sadness is produced by tepidity in God's service. What joy a
good conscience gives.*

NEGLIGENCE in God's service, and in those things that belong to
our profession, is one of the chief and most ordinary causes of
sadness. I appeal to your own experience. Do you not feel joy
when you acquit yourself well; and sadness, when you acquit
yourself ill of your duty? To render sad, is one of the properties
of sin. "A wicked heart," says the Wise man, "shall be
charged with grief," (Ecclus. iii. 29,) "and a bad heart occasions
sadness." (Ecclus. xxxvi. 22.) The holy scripture teaches us
that when Cain saw the difference that God made between his
and Abel's sacrifice, "he was seized with wrath, and his countenance fell, and he became dejected." (Gen. iv. 26.) This was
an effect of the bad designs he conceived, and which, unable to
conceal in his heart, he made appear by the change in his
countenance. The Lord therefore asked him the cause of this
ohange: "if thou dost well, shalt thou not receive a recompense?" (Gen. iv. 7); or, as another version has it, "shalt thou
not lift up thy head?" That is, "shalt thou not have a cheerful countenance; but if thou dost ill, will not sin presently
present itself at thy gate?" Will it not torment thee within
with remorse of conscience, and will it not appear without on
thy countenance? As virtuous actions bring joy along with
them, because they are conformable to reason; so bad ones bring
naturally discontent, because they are contrary to it; and as we
must fight against conscience in order to commit sin, therefore
the reproaches of conscience will never let us be at rest.

"There is not a greater punishment," says St. Bernard, "than
a bad conscience. It carries its punishment along with it :—it
is in vain to hide our crimes from the eyes of men and to appear
innocent before them, when we cannot hide them from ourselves,
nor evade the condemnation of our conscience." (De inter.
domo. c. 45.) Do what you will—seek company and amusement
to free yourself from its reproaches, you will never succeed; it
will always torment you. It was this made Seneca say, that
the greatest punishment of a crime was the having committed it.
Plutarch compares the pain which one thereby suffers to that

which we feel in the cold and hot fit of an ague, and says, that as sick persons are more indisposed with the cold and heat occasioned by a fever, than those who are in health are by the cold and heat resulting from the diversity and inconstancy of seasons, so the disquiets occasioned by our faults and remorse of conscience torment us far more cruelly than those which are caused only by accidents of fortune. This, above all, is verified in those who have begun to taste what God is, and after having served him for some time with fervour, begin to relent and contradict themselves. For misery is more sensible and painful to him who has lived in plenty than to him that has been always poor. When we remember the fervour with which we served God at other times, and the favours we thereby received, and begin to compare the present with what is past, it is impossible but we must feel cruel regret, and find our hearts pierced to the quick.

"If then," says St. Bernard, "you would banish sadness far from you, and live always content—live as you ought to do. Think what your obligations are, and apply yourself to the performance of them, and to correct your faults and imperfections since these are what disquiet the peace of your soul." (De inter. dom.) A virtuous man is always cheerful, and a wicked man is always sad and tormented in conscience; and as there is not a more cruel punishment than those that the sting and reproach of conscience bring along with them, so there cannot be a more sensible joy than they feel who have the testimony of a good conscience. "There is not a greater pleasure," says the scripture, "than the joy of the heart; and a secure and quiet mind is like a continual feast." (Prov. xv. 15.) And, as at a feast the different sorts of meat, and the presence of the guests, occasion joy, so is it a great subject of joy to a Christian, who carefully acquits himself of his duty, to have a good testimony of his conscience, and to be in the possession of God's grace of which he feels so great marks within himself. "For if our hearts," says St. John, "does not reproach us, we have a confidence in God." (John iii. 21.) And St. Paul tells us, "that our glory and comfort is the testimony of a good conscience." (2 Cor. i. 12.) St. Chrysostom also assures us that a good conscience dissipates all darkness of heart, and drives it away as the sun does the clouds; and that sadness which falls upon a good conscience is as easily distinguished as a spark of fire that falls into a lake. St. Austin compares it to honey, which is not only sweet in itself, but renders the most bitter things sweet; and says, that it sweetens all the pains and bitterness of this life. Wherefore the prophet, speaking of God's commandments, says, "they are more to be desired than gold and precious stones, and more sweet than honey, or the honey-comb." (Ps. xviii. 11.)

Ecclesiastical history relates, that when the persecution was raised under Marcus Aurelius against the Christians, they did one thing that never was before practised, which was that all the Christians they took, whether they renounced Jesus Christ, or whether they persevered in their faith, were put indifferently into the same prison, and afterwards condemned, no longer as Christians, but as thieves and robbers. Yet, this did not prevent them from perceiving a great difference between the one and the other, when they led them to execution. For they perceived a joyful countenance, and, as it were, such rays of divinity in the faces of the saints, that it seemed as if their chains became an ornament to them, and the stench of the prisons had served to render them more pleasing to the eyes both of God and men—whereas the others went along with a sad countenance, having such frightful and ghastly looks as filled all the spectators with horror. This shows, that these were more cruelly tormented by the reproaches of their criminal conscience than by their sufferings in prison and the sight of their torments; and that the others, on the contrary, felt all their pains sweetened by the testimony of their conscience, and by the hope of that glory they were about to enjoy. Virtuous persons frequently experience the same thing in themselves, even in time of their greatest afflictions, for when they perceive themselves forsaken by all the world, and deprived of all kind of comfort, they cast their eyes upon themselves, and seeing the good state of their conscience, this sight gives them an entire comfort; because they know very well that it is no matter how all other things go, so they keep but a good conscience.

But the joy of which I speak is not only the effect of a good conscience, but it is also a sign of it: as St. Bonaventure teaches us by these words, "spiritual joy is an evident mark of grace." (In spec. discip. p. i. c. 3.) The Holy Ghost teaches us also the same truth in several places of Scripture: "light is risen upon the just," says David, "and joy to those that are right of heart." (Ps. xcvi. 11.) "But the wicked walk in darkness, they find nothing but misery and confusion in their way, and they have not known the way of peace." (Ps. xiii. 3.) One reason also why St. Francis desired always to see cheerfulness in the countenances of his religious, was, because he looked upon this joy "as one of the fruits of the Holy Ghost," (Gal. 22,) and as a mark of God's habitation in their souls. He said, moreover, that this made such an impression upon him, that, as often as he found himself carried away with sadness and dejection, he needed only to cast his eyes upon his brethren, and he found himself presently delivered from this temptation; because seeing them, he seemed to behold so many angels. And in effect we see angels upon earth when we see the servants of God who are in his grace; and it is in this sense that these words of scripture may be understood, "I beheld thee as an angel of God, thou art as agreeable in my eyes as an angel of the Lord." (1 Kings xxix. 9.)

———o———

CHAPTER VII.

That there is a laudable and holy sadness.

BUT some will say, must we then always be in joy? Must we never be afflicted? Is there no kind of sadness which is profitable and advantageous to the soul? "Yes," says St. Basil, "without doubt there is; because Jesus Christ himself declares it to us in these words: "Blessed are those that mourn, for they shall be comforted.'" (Matt. v. 5.) Cassian, as well as this saint, and also St. Leo Pope, established two sorts of sadness, the one purely human, and according to the spirit of the world; the other spiritual, and according to the Spirit of God. Sadness, according to the world, is to afflict one's self for bad success, or some such like misfortune, from which sadness the servant of God ought entirely be exempted. "The true servants of God," says St. Apollo to his disciples, "to whom the kingdom of heaven is promised, ought never be sad; for if those of the world rejoice in the possession of vain and transitory goods, what a sense of joy ought the hope which we have of possessing God eternally in heaven, and of partaking with him of his glory, excite in our souls? It is for Jews, for Gentiles, and sinners, continually to weep and afflict themselves; but for the just, who have a lively faith, and a firm hope of everlasting goods, they ought to follow the royal prophet's advice—rejoice in the Lord, and exult, you just; and glorify him all you of a right heart."— (Ps. xxxi. 14.) The apostle St. Paul also teaches us that we are not to afflict ourselves very much for the death of our parents and friends. "I would not have you, my brethren," says he, "be ignorant of what you ought to know concerning those who sleep in death, lest you afflict yourselves for their death, as they do who have no hope." (1 Thes. iv. 13.)   He does not absolutely forbid us to afflict ourselves for the death of our friends and parents, for it is not an ill thing to be touched thereat—this is a just and natural feeling, and a sign of the affection we have for them.   Jesus Christ himself was touched at the death of Lazarus; and, therefore, the Jews cried out when they saw him weep: "behold, how he loved him."   What the apostle here forbids, is the afflicting ourselves as infidels do who have no knowledge of the resurrection.   We should have our sadness moderated by the hope we have, to see soon again in heaven those we have lost upon earth; and if we cannot as men hinder the accidents of this life from making some impression upon us, yet we should endeavour that they make at least but a weak and transient one. "Let those who weep be like those who weep not, and those that rejoice, like those that do not rejoice." (1 Cor. vii. 30.)

As to what concerns spiritual sadness according to God, it is good and profitable, and the servants of God may oftentimes feel it.   St. Basil and Cassian say there may be four causes of it. First it may proceed from a sight of our sins, according to the words of the apostle : "I rejoice at present," says he, "not for the sorrow which you have felt, but for that sorrow which has moved you to repentance; for you are afflicted, according to God, and such a sadness as this produces penance, and a firm repentance, which is profitable to salvation." (2 Cor. vii. 9.)   That sadness, therefore, that causes us to weep for our sins, and which proceeds from a regret for having offended God, is holy, and according to God.   St. Chrysostom makes a remark hereupon worthy of himself.   "Of all the losses," says he, "which can happen to a man, it is only those occasioned by sin which can be repaired by sorrow and regret, and, therefore, in all other things except sin, sorrow is unprofitable, because it rather augments than diminishes our loss; but the losses caused by sin are entirely repaired by sorrow for it, and, therefore, it is for sin only that we ought to afflict ourselves."

Secondly, this sadness may arise from a consideration of the many sins daily committed in the world; and then it is also very holy, because it proceeds from an ardent desire of God's glory, and the salvation of souls.   It was such sorrow as this with which the heart of David was penetrated, when he cried out to God, "my heart failed me, when I thought of sinners that have left thy law." (Ps. cxviii. 53.) "Zeal has dried me up, because thy enemies have forgot thy commandments." (Ps. cxviii. 139.) "I beheld the wicked, and I pined away, to behold that they so little regarded thy words." (Ps. cxviii. 158.) The prophet Jeremiah was also filled with the same sentiments, and this sort of sadness becomes very well servants of God, but more particularly us, since the end of our institution is to render God's name glorified throughout the whole world; and, therefore, we ought to feel the deepest sorrow, when instead of its being glorified, we see the contrary happen to it.

Thirdly, this sadness may proceed from a great desire of perfection, which happens when this desire is very ardent: for then we afflict ourselves, perceiving we make so little progress in virtue. This sentiment is according to God's spirit; because Jesus Christ assures us that "blessed are those that hunger and thirst after justice, for they shall be filled." (Matt. v. 6.)

Lastly, the consideration of the eternal goods we are deprived of in this life, and our impatience to enjoy them in the next, is another legitimate cause and subject of the sadness with which the true servants of God are filled. It was the thought of the beauty and wonders of Zion that afflicted the children of Israel during their banishment in Babylon. It was also upon this account that the royal prophet cried out,—"Alas! why is my exile so much prolonged?" (Ps. cxix. 5.) These words also addressed to our blessed Lady by the Church, "we cry out, we sigh, weep, and lament, in this valley of tears," are words that make a sweet and pleasing harmony in the ears of God.

Cassian gives us certain signs to discern the sadness which is according to God, from that which is not. He says, "that the first is obedient, affable, humble, sweet, and patient; and lastly, since it proceeds from the love of God, it preserves in us the fruits of the Holy Ghost," of which St. Paul speaks to the Galatians, viz.—"charity, joy, peace, patience, bounty, faith, modesty and continency." But the other sorrow is rude, impatient, and full of disquiet and bitterness; it hinders us from what is good, and causes in us discouragement and despair. "Moreover this," says he, "is mixed with no consolation at all, or sweetness; but the other is in a manner joyful." It carries its comfort along with it, and it gives courage and strength to perform what is good; wherefore it may easily be known, by running over these four sorts of sadness of which I have just spoken. For, first, how great a sorrow soever they feel themselves penetrated with when they truly weep for their sins, yet the weeping for them as we should do carries a sweetness and comfort along with it; and when this happens, do we not find by experience that it leaves a satisfaction behind? One of the things also whereby we know how far this spiritual life of God's servants is preferable to the sensual life of worldlings is, that the tears which the servants of God shed for their sins leave so very great and real joy behind them, that all the pleasures of the world leave not the like to those that enjoy them most. St. Austin makes this reflection, and says, " if those who begin to serve God find so much sweetness in the first thing they perform, which is, in weeping for their sins, what satisfaction will they not experience when God shall shower down his comforts upon them in time of prayer, and heap upon them those spiritual delights with which he favours his elect; and when, according to these words of the Apocalypse, " he shall dry up all tears from their eyes, when there shall be no more death, nor lamentations, nor cries, and when sadness shall be no more?" (Apoc. xx. 4.) It is in like manner easy to judge, that those who lament the sins of their neighbour find also a great deal of interior sweetness. For it belongs to well-educated children to be jealous of the glory and honour of their father; and zeal for God's glory can never be without sweetness. And now as to the sadness which proceeds from an ardent desire of advancing in virtue, or from a holy impatience of visiting our celestial country, it is impossible but thoughts of this nature must be very pleasing to a true Christian. " For what is more beautiful, or what is sweeter," says St. Austin, " amidst the darkness and bitterness of this life, than to have our thoughts taken up with celestial objects, and to be always in imagination in the eternal mansions of true joy?"

We may easily also comprehend, by what I have said, that the joy required in the servants of God is not a vain and frivolous one; it is not a joy that makes us break out into loud laughter, or to say witty things, or to join in conversation with every one we meet. For this would not be a joy becoming God's servants, but would be a dissipation of mind, immodesty, and irregularity. The joy we require is a prudent one, that comes from within, and is visible in our countenances without; for as sadness of mind makes an impression upon the body, according to the ex-

pression of scripture, " a sad mind dried up the bones " (Prov.
xvii. 22); so the interior joy appears exteriorly; according to
this other passage of scripture, " a joyful heart gives a cheerful
countenance." (Prov. xv. 15.)　We read also of divers saints
that had such a joy and serenity in their looks, that it gave
testimony of the peace and satisfaction they inwardly enjoyed in
their heart.　And this is properly the joy which it is to be
wished we should have.

———o———

THE SEVENTH TREATISE.

———o———

ON THE ADVANTAGES AND INFINITE TREASURES WE POSSESS IN JESUS
CHRIST—HOW WE ARE TO MEDITATE UPON THE MYSTERIES OF
HIS PASSION—WHAT FRUIT WE OUGHT TO REAP FROM THENCE.

CHAPTER I.

The advantages and infinite treasures we possess in Jesus Christ.

" When the fulness of time was come, God sent his Son, born of
a woman, and under the law, that he might redeem those who
were subject to the law, and that we might receive the adoption
of sons." (Gal. iv. 4.)   All that time which preceded the birth
of our Saviour, was, as it were, void of grace ; but the time that
succeeded was filled therewith, and therefore it is justly called
the law of grace, because the inexhaustible fountain of all grace
was then bestowed upon us.   When God sent us his only Son it
was that he might deliver us from the slavery of sin, and from
the tyranny of the devil, according to these words, " now the
prince of this world shall be cast out :" (John xii. 31) ; and
lastly, it was that he might reconcile us to his Father, and that
we might become his children by adoption ; and lastly, it was
that he might open to us the gate of heaven, which had been
shut against us from the time of that unhappy transgression,
whereby our first parents lost, both for themselves and for us,
the state of original justice in which they had been created.
After this loss, which rendered them, and us who descended
from them, subject to an infinity of miseries, there remained
only one comfort, which was, that as soon as Adam had sinned,
God cursed the serpent that had been the chief cause of this evil,
and at the same time promised to send his only Son after a certain
time to deliver us from all the evils we were subject to by sin.
" I will cause," says our Lord to the serpent, " an irreconcilable
hatred between thee and the woman, between thy seed and hers,
and she shall crush |thy head." (Gen. iii. 15.)   This promise

having exceedingly comforted them, they did penance, and taught their children the happy state they had for some time enjoyed, and how they had lost it by their own fault, and that there would come a Redeemer who would save them by his·power. But it was not only to them to whom this promise was made. God confirmed the same to the holy patriarchs also, and particularly to Abraham, Jacob, and David, to whom he promised, "that the Messias should be born of their race." This was an universal belief in the Jewish religion, and the prophet who foretold the wonders of his coming, ceased not to beg of God with sighs and tears to hasten it: "send forth, O Lord," says Isaias, "The Lamb, the Governor of the earth." (Isa. xvi. 1.) "Send forth dew from above, and let the clouds rain down the just; let the earth be opened, and produce the Saviour." (Isa. xlv. 8.) The spouse in the Canticles expresses the like impatience; " who will give thee," says she, " into my arms as my brother, sucking the breasts of my mother, that I may find thee without, that I may kiss thee, and that nobody may any more despise me." (Cant. viii. 1.) In fine, " he was the expectation of all nations," (Gen. xlix. 10,) that sighed after him as slaves do after their deliverer ; it was in virtue of this redemption which he was to work that our sins were pardoned ; and as we firmly believe that he is to come, so the Jews infallibly believed he was to come, and, therefore, they gave him the appellation of " him that was to come; and it was for this reason they said to St. John—" Are you he who is to come, or are we to expect another ?" (Matt. xi. 3.)

But when the time was accomplished in which God from all eternity had resolved to bestow so great a grace as this upon men, he sent his only Son, and he deferred it till then in order that men having more time to know and feel their misery, might desire with greater fervour to be freed from it, and might have a greater esteem of their redeemer when he should please to send him. For it often happens that God, to imprint in us a deeper sense of our weakness, and the need we have of his assistance, and to hinder us from attributing anything to ourselves, suspends the consolations, and defers the remedies he is resolved to give us. When, therefore, this happy time was come, seeing that it was God alone that could raise man from his fall ; seeing also that there was for the offence man had committed a satisfaction to be made ; that this satisfaction was to be accompanied with pains and sufferings ; and that God of his own nature was impassible ;

the infinite wisdom found an infinite means to reconcile all these difficulties by the incarnation of the Son of God, who making himself man, and thereby uniting the divine and human nature in one and the self-same person, wrought the salvation of mankind. This was, without doubt, a most admirable work of the wisdom and bounty of God, and nothing can more manifest his power and greatness. Wherefore the royal prophet speaking to God of the accomplishment thereof: "excite your power," says he, "and come to save us." (Ps. lxxix. 3.) He solicits God to come and work our redemption, and, for the effecting it, he begs of him to display his power, since it was to accomplish a work so great that a greater could never be performed in time. "The creation of the world is a great work," says St. Austin, "and displays the omnipotence of God, but the redemption of mankind is quite another thing, and manifests it in a different manner." The scripture, also, when it speaks of the creation, calls it the work of his fingers. "I will behold the heavens," says David, "the works of thy fingers; the moon and stars which thou hast established." (Ps. viii. 4.) But when he speaks of the redemption, he calls it the effect of God's arm; for he says, that the "arm of God has given marks of its power." (Luke i. 51.) And hence, he shews us that there is as much difference between the one and the other as there is between the finger and the whole arm. But the redemption is not only a greater mark of the power and greatness of God than the creation, but it is also a particular mark of the greatness and dignity of man and of the esteem that God has of him; and it is for this reason the church addresses herself unto him in these words: "O God, who hast formed in a wonderful manner the excellency of human nature, and hast repaired it in a manner still more wonderful." God without doubt, did a great deal for man when he created him, but did far more when he redeemed him; which caused St. Leo to say, that "God had raised man very much by creating him after his own image and likeness; but he had elevated him far higher by debasing himself so as to take upon him not only the figure and appearance of man but even his very nature also."

Lastly, the advantages we derive from the incarnation of the Son of God are so great that upon this account we ought even esteem Adam's fault a happiness. "O happy fault!" cries out the church in an excess of zeal, and out of a lively sense of the graces it receives from its spouse: "Happy fault that has merited so great a Redeemer. Happy necessity of the sin of

Adam that was blotted out by the death of Jesus?" In effect Jesus Christ has given us more than Adam took from us. We have gained more by the redemption than we have lost by sin, "and God's grace was not measured by man's sin." (Rom. v. 15.) St. Bernard, reciting these words wherein the apostle takes notice that Jesus Christ brought more good to men than Adam had occasioned evil: "it is true, my brethren," says he, "that a man and a woman have brought very great prejudice on us, but, thanks be to God, all is repaired by a man and a woman, and repaired with advantage; for the grace is not measured by the crime, but the greatness of the benefit we receive far surpasses that of our loss."

We cannot sufficiently express the advantages and treasures we possess in Jesus Christ; to this we ought to be endowed as St. Paul was, "with the grace of announcing to all nations the inestimable riches of Jesus Christ." (Eph. iii. 8.) Does not our Saviour himself tell us how hard it is to conceive it? "If thou didst know," says he to the Samaritan, "what is the gift of God, and who it is that says to thee, give me to drink." (John iv. 10.) If we knew the gift God bestows upon us in giving us his only Son; if we knew the gift which contains all other gifts, and by which he has given us all things; if we could but comprehend its excellence; if God would be pleased to discover to us such a precious treasure, how rich and how happy should we be? St. Austin, who had received this favour, said, in the transport of his zeal and thanksgiving, "he, O Lord! who is ungrateful for the benefit of creation deserves hell; but there ought to be a new hell created for him who is ungrateful for the benefit of redemption." It is related of Father Avila, that he had always this favour present in his mind, and when those who had received any particular favour from God, mentioned it to him with admiration of the divine goodness, "it is not this," says he, "which ought to be admired, but it is, 'that God had so loved the world as to give his only begotton Son.'" (John iii. 16.) These are the words which St. John made use of to express the greatness of the love of God towards men, by the greatness of the gift he bestows upon them. And, certainly, the infinite price of the one marks very well the infinite excess of the other; for how boundless was the love of God since he gives his only Son to ransom us by his death? "O wonderful excess of goodness," says the church to the Eternal Father, "O inestimable effect of charity! thou hast delivered up thy Son for

the redemption of a slave !"   Who could ever imagine the like ?
What slave is there that ever durst propose to his prince that he
would give his only son for a ransom ?   And yet, notwithstanding, that which you never durst have asked—that which you
could never have believed—nay, that which never could have
entered into your imagination, is what God has done for you.

But he is not only content by this means to redeem us from
the slavery we were in, but he does yet far more, for he raises
us to the dignity of the children of God ; he takes upon him our
nature to make us partakers of his; he makes himself man to
make us become the children of God."   " See," says St. John,
" what excess of bounty the Father has for us, that we should
both be called and be in effect the children of God ? " (1 John
iii. 1.)   For in effect we are so, and it is not in vain that we call
God our Father, and Jesus Christ our brother.   " Jesus Christ
himself," says St. Paul, " is not ashamed to call us his brethren,
when he says, I will declare your name to my brethren." (Heb.
i .11, 12.)   It rather seems that he takes a glory in doing so,
because he gives us so often this title.   Wherefore he who has
God for father, and Jesus Christ also for his brother, " to whom
all power is given both in heaven and earth" (Matt. xxviii. 18),
what remains more for him to desire ?   What joy ought not the
children of Jacob feel when Joseph freed them from the fear they
were in of his resentment and displeasure : especially when they
saw that he ruled over all Egypt; that all things were done by
him ; and that Pharoah left the total management thereof unto
him, still saying to his subjects, " go to Joseph ?" (Gen lxi. 55.)
Now Jesus Christ, who is our brother, and who loves us far more
than Joseph did his brethren, treats us in the same manner : he
will have us be with him.   " Father," says he, "those which
thou hast given me, I will that they should be with me where I
am " (John xvii. 24) ; and he gives us all the help and assistance we can stand in need of, that we may remain always with
him, and never more be separated from him.

Wherefore, if the offences you have committed against him
make you apprehend his vengeance, be not in pain—the penance
which you have done for them has caused him already to forget
them, and not only to forget them, but to become your mediator
and intercessor with his Father to obtain the pardon of them.
This is what St. John assures us in these words, "children I
write these things that you sin not.   But if any one sinneth we
have an advocate with the Father, Jesus Christ the just."

(1 John ii. 1.) St. Paul tells us " that he is ascended to heaven to appear before the face of God for us." (Heb. ix. 24.) St. Bernard says, " he there shows his Father those wounds he received for us by his order, and conjures him by the merit of those wounds not to suffer man to perish, he having paid for him so dear." And in the same manner as the holy Virgin when she intercedes for us with her Son, shows him her breasts that gave him suck; so the Son shows to his Father the wounds he received for love of us; and it was for this reason, as the saints affirm, that he would have his holy body still preserve those marks after his glorious resurrection.

The holy scripture tells us that, after the death of Jacob, his children, fearing that Joseph being no longer restrained by the respect he bore a father, might then revenge the injuries they had formerly done him, wherefore they sent him this message— to wit, that the chief thing their father had desired for his children at the hour of his death was " that he, their brother, would pardon them, and forget all their offences, and we also beg of thee," added they, " that thou wouldst forgive this iniquity to the servant of God, thy father." (Gen. l. 15.) And it is here to be observed that it was not the father that had committed this offence, but it was his paternal love that caused him to take upon himself the fault of his children! And thus Jesus Christ, by an excess of love for us, has made our sins his own, and has taken all our faults upon himself. " The Lord," says the prophet Isaias, " has cast all our iniquities upon him, and he bears them all." (Is. liii. 6, 11.) Wherefore, since it is so, let us address ourselves in the same manner to the Eternal Father, and say : " O Father of all mercy, pardon your Son Jesus Christ my sins, who, at the hour of his death, recommended nothing so earnestly as this, and who then begged of you, saying, ' Father, forgive them, for they know not what they do.'" (Luke xxiii. 34.) Who, then, has not reason to hope for pardon by the intercession of Jesus Christ, " the mediator of the covenant, and by the shedding of his blood, which speaks better for us than that of Abel?" (Heb. vii. 24.) That of Abel cried for vengeance, but that of Jesus Christ demands mercy for those for whom it was shed, and even for those that shed it. When the devil, therefore, shall represent to you the multitude of your sins to alarm you by the sight of them, and to make you lose courage, cast then your eyes upon Jesus, imagine that he takes you by the hand and leads you to his Father, and answers for you, and that he covers the shame of your sins and infidelities with the greatness of his merits, and by the service he renders his Father. In this manner you will soon take heart again, your discouragement will be changed into confidence, and your sadness into joy, by means of him "who has been given us by God to be our wisdom, justice, sanctification, and redemption." (1 Cor. i. 3.)

"We have all things in Jesus Christ," says St. Ambrose, "and Jesus Christ is all things to us. If you would heal your wounds, he is a physician; if the heat of your fever burns you, he is a fountain of living water; if the weight of your iniquities oppress you, he is justice; if you want help, he is power and strength; if you apprehend death, he is life; if you would go to heaven, he is the way; if you would avoid darkness, he is the light; and if you desire to eat, he is heavenly food. In fine, whatsoever you stand in need of, and whatsoever you can desire, you will find in him." (Lib. iii. de Virg.) "If the infernal wolf," says the same saint in another place, "sets upon you, take up a stone and he will fly from you, and the stone is Jesus Christ, to whom, if you have recourse, the wolf will fly away, and will not be able to fright you any longer. St. Peter sought this stone when he sunk into the water, and found what he sought after as soon as he had taken Jesus Christ by the hand, who delivered him from the waves." (Lib. vi. Exam. c. 4.)

St. Jerome, explaining these words of the apostles—"Moreover, brethren, take courage in our Lord, and in the power of his virtue, put on the armour of God, that you may be able to resist the snares of the devil (Eph. vi. 10.), says, that "by what is deduced from this passage, and from what the holy Scripture mentions all along of Jesus Christ, we see clearly that the armour which the apostle recommends to us to put on is Jesus Christ himself, so that when he says put on the armour of God, it is, as if he should say, put on Jesus Christ." The same saint afterwards proves that Jesus Christ is our coat of mail, our helmet, our buckler, "our two-edged sword," and so of the rest. So that the armour we are to put on, in order to triumph over all temptations and all the assaults of the devil, is the virtue of Jesus Christ, which is all things to us, and in which we possess all things. The holy Scripture likewise gives him an infinity of appellations and titles, as that of king, master, pastor, priest, physician, friend, father, brother, bread, light, fountain, and a thousand others. Moreover, as "all the treasures of the wisdom and knowledge of the Father" (Coloss. ii. 3), are hid in him, so all our treasures and all our riches are likewise found in him, because all our happiness is founded upon him, and all our good actions have no other merit than what is given them by his precious blood. This is what was signified by those words to St. John, when, seeing an infinite multitude that were before the throne of God, clothed in white robes, and holding palms in their hands, it was said, "behold those who have washed and whitened their robes in the blood of the Lamb." (Apoc. vii. 14.) For all that is good in us is in effect the stream of the riches of Jesus Christ, which we receive by his means and by his merits. It is by him we are delivered from the most dangerous temptations—by him we acquire virtue—by him we possess all things—by him we are become able to obtain all things—and it is to him alone we ought to refer the glory of all things. So that it is for this reason that in all the prayers the church makes to God, she always concludes them with these words, "through our Lord Jesus Christ," in imitation of this prayer to the Psalmist, "O God, who art our protector, regard and turn thine eyes upon the face of thy Christ. (Ps. lxxxiii. 10.) It is as if he had said, "Lord grant our request for the love of thy Son Jesus Christ, pardon our sins for the love of him, because it was for our sins he died on the cross. Cast thine eyes upon the wounds he deigned to receive for us and from us, and let this sight draw thy mercy upon us." If the consideration of the services of Abraham, Jacob, and David, had so often the power, not only to stop God's anger, which was ready to break forth, and also to move him to replenish his people with favours and benefits, as he himself takes notice of in these words, "because of my servant Jacob, and of Israel my elect, and because of David my servant" (Is. xlv. 4), what ought we not to believe he will do for the love of his Son, "in whom he is well and highly pleased?" (Matt. xvii. 5.) St. Paul teaches us "that God made us acceptable through his beloved Son." (Eph. i. 6.) And Jesus Christ himself tells us, "whatsoever you shall ask in my name of my Father, he will grant you, that the Father may be glorified in the Son." (John xiv. 13.)

When the angel said to the shepherds and to the whole world in their persons, "behold that I declare great joy unto you, which shall be to all people, because to you this day is born a Saviour, who is Jesus Christ the Lord" (Luke ii. 10, 11);

this joy which was declared to them was not only joy, but it was all kinds of joys and advantages together. Origen asked the reason why Isaias, having said in the singular number, " who declares the advantage" (Is. lii. 7), St. Paul, quoting the same passage, says in the plural, " they who declare the advantages." (Rom. x. 15.) And he answers, it is because Jesus Christ is not only one advantage, but all manner of advantages together. He is, at the same time, our salvation, our life, our resurrection ; the light of the world, the truth, the way, and the gate to heaven ; he is wisdom, power, and the fountain and treasure of all goods ; he was born and he died that we should live ; he is raised to life that we may be so too ; he is mounted to heaven, "there to prepare a place for us," as he himself says, " and it was expedient for us that he should go" (John xiv. 2), because it was from thence he was to send the Holy Ghost to us, and that he should sit at the right hand of his Father to pour down continually from thence his graces upon us. St. Cyprian says that one of the reasons why the marks of his wounds remained open was to manifest to us that they were so many channels and inexhaustible fountains from whence the treasure of his liberality and mercy should, without intermission, shower down upon men. " His hands are set round with hyacinths, and full of gold and precious stones (Cant. v. 14), and they being pierced, the riches wherewith they are filled fall without ceasing through the whole of those sacred wounds. Let us, therefore, conclude this discourse with the words of the apostle, and say, " since then we have for our high priest Jesus the Son of God, who has penetrated the heavens, let us go with confidence to the throne of his grace, that we may obtain mercy and find favour in the time of need. (Heb. iv. 14.)

It is related that St. Bernard, in a great sickness, was, as it were, rapt in spirit, and seemed to be led before God's tribunal, where the devil accused him and maintained that he merited not the possession of eternal glory. " I confess," says the saint, " that I am indeed unworthy of it, and have of myself no right at all unto it ; but Jesus Christ my Saviour has a right to it for two reasons ; first, because he is the only Son of the Eternal Father, and heir of the celestial kingdom ; secondly, because he has purchased it by his blood, obeying his Father unto death. The first of these two titles was sufficient for him, and the other he has made over to me, and it is by virtue of this gift and grant to me that I pretend to heaven and hope to obtain it." The hellish accuser remained confounded at this answer, and presently this apparition of judgment and tribunal vanished, and the saint came to himself. It is, therefore, in this we ought to fix our confidence, and it is upon this right, that Jesus Christ has purchased for us by his death, we ought to found our hopes and pretensions. Jacob, clothed with the habit of his elder brother, gained the blessing of his father, and, in like manner, let us clothe ourselves with that of Jesus Christ, our eldest brother, let us cover ourselves with the skin of this Lamb without spot, let us avail ourselves of the advantage of his merits and passion and by this means we shall obtain the blessing of the Eterna Father.

---o---

CHAPTER II.

How profitable and how pleasing to God it is to meditate upon the passion of our Saviour.]

" THERE is nothing," says St. Austin, "conduces more to salvation than always to think what the God-man has suffered for us." (Serm. lii. ad frat. in Eremo.) And St. Bernard says, "that nothing is more efficacious for the curing the wounds of our conscience and purifying our souls, than continually to meditate on the sufferings of Jesus Christ." (Serm. lxii. sup. Cant.) It is also, as the saints affirm, a great help against all sorts of temptations, and particularly against those of impurity, to have recourse to the meditation of the passion of Jesus Christ, and to hide ourselves in his wounds. Lastly, it is an universal remedy against all sorts of evils, to think of Jesus Christ crucified. And St. Austin assures us of this from his own experience, when he says, "I found not in all my necessities a more efficacious remedy than the wounds of Christ." (In Manual, c. 22.) St. Bonaventure also tells us, "that he who devoutly applies himself to meditate upon the life and death of Jesus Christ finds there very abundantly all things he stands in need of, and needs to seek for nothing out of Jesus Christ." (Coll. 7.) So that we see this practice was very familiar to the saints, and it was by this means they attained so great a degree of sanctity and perfection.

Though this practice should produce nothing else but to make us think of God, and cause us to call to mind the benefits we have received from him, yet it will be sufficient, and always of great merit in his sight. It is one of the properties of love to make us feel delight when we are thought of by the person beloved; and when we know that the person often thinks of the services we have done him, and that he is pleased to entertain himself therein, these marks of tenderness afford greater joy than the most magnificent gifts in the world could do. It is thus a lady of rank, having a son travelling amongst strangers in a distant country, being told that he speaks of nothing but of the favours and benefits he has received from her, and of the obligations he has to her, is a thousand times more touched and pleased than if he presented her with all the rarities of the countries he is travelling through. God does the same; because in this, as in other things, he observes the law of love, and remains in the same condition those are in who truly and tenderly love; and, therefore, he is very well pleased we should think of him, and of those favours he has bestowed upon us; and of the wonders he has wrought for us; nay, we ought to entertain ourselves so much the more in this exercise because we cannot practise it for any long time, but the consideration of so great benefits will excite us to love and serve him with all our strength.

Blosius relates that one day God revealed to St. Gertrude that as often as any one looked devoutly upon an image of Jesus crucified, so often he would draw upon himself the eyes of the divine mercy. Let us profit by this instruction, and since he has not disdained to suffer for us, let us not disdain, at least, to think of what he has suffered. It is related of St. Francis that as he one day passed full of tears and sighs by our Lady of Portiuncula, he was met by a servant of God, who, knowing him, and seeing him in such marks of affliction, and believing that some great misfortune had happened unto him, asked him what it was? "I weep and sigh, says the saint, "that my Saviour has suffered so much, and that men, who were the cause of his sufferings, think so little of the greatness of the obligation they have to him."

——o——

CHAPTER III.

How we ought to meditate upon the passion of Jesus Christ. The motions of compassion it ought to excite in us.

The method we ought to observe in meditating on the sufferings of Jesus Christ is the same which the masters of a spiritual life

desire us to observe in prayer. For they would not have us
employ all the time of prayer in running over the points of
meditation, but that we should particularly apply ourselves to
the inflaming our will by motions of affection, which being first
produced in the heart, have afterwards their effect in all our
actions. And it is to this, say they, we ought particularly apply
ourselves in prayer. As he who digs in the earth, whether it be
to find water or to find a treasure, leaves off digging as soon as
he finds what he sought after; so in like manner, when by profound meditation we have found the treasure of charity and the
love of God, that fountain of living water we sought after, it is
not necessary any longer to busy ourselves in digging; but we
must think of enriching ourselves with those treasures of grace
we have found, and of refreshing ourselves by copious draughts
from this fountain of eternal life, and entertaining ourselves with
those affectionate motions wherewith we shall find ourselves
touched. This is the end of prayer; this is the fruit we ought
to reap from it; and it is this all the meditations and all the
reflections of our understanding ought to aim at. I have already
spoken of this method in another place; and as what we ought
to observe in meditating on the passion of Jesus Christ is altogether the same, it is only necessary here to set down those
sentiments of affection we ought to obtain from this meditation,
and upon which we ought to insist; this is what I propose to
myself; and at the same time, shall touch on such points as are
most proper to excite these sentiments in us.

There are many sorts of affections which the consideration of
the sufferings of the Son of God may produce in us, and in which
we may entertain ourselves with great fruit; but they are ordinarily reduced to seven. The first is compassion, which is a
lively feeling for another's pains, whereby we participate in
them after such manner as seems to sweeten and comfort them;
just as malignant joy sharpens and augments them. It is true
we cannot by this means lessen the sufferings of Jesus Christ,
because they are already passed; nevertheless, he seems to be
pleased that we are touched thereby, and that we, as I may say,
make our sufferings our own. And therefore the apostle says to
us: " if we are children of God, we are also heirs, even heirs of
God, and co-heirs with Jesus Christ; so that if we suffer with him,
we shall with him also be glorified." (Rom. viii. 17.)

To excite ourselves then to this compassion, it will be good to
consider the excessive pains of Jesus Christ; because according to

the opinion of all divines they were greater than any that ever have been, or can be suffered in this life; and it is this the prophet Jeremiah expresses in these words: "O you who pass by, attend, and see if there be any grief or pain like mine." (Lam. i. 12.) First of all, no part of his body was free from pain; "for from the soul of his foot to the crown of his head," says the prophet Isaias, "there is nothing sound in him." (Isa. i. 6.) His feet and hands were nailed, his head crowned with thorns, his face beaten black and blue with buffets, his body torn with whips, all his bones disjointed by being extended upon the cross, all which give an idea of the most cruel punishment that ever was inflicted.

But he suffered not only in his body, but in his soul also, and after a manner far more painful. For, notwithstanding human nature was in him united to the divine person, yet it hindered him not from feeling the indignity of his sufferings in as lively a manner as if this union had not been at all. Moreover, to render this pain the greater, he was deprived of all consolation; which was the reason that he cried out upon the cross: "My God, my God, why hast thou forsaken me?" (Matt. xxvii. 46.) The holy martyrs were solaced in their torments by comforts from heaven, which made them suffer all things, not only with courage but even with joy; but Jesus Christ, in order to suffer the more for love of us, vouchsafed, as to his sacred humanity, to be deprived of all sorts of comforts both of heaven and earth, and not only to be forsaken by his disciples and friends, but even by his Eternal Father. "I am become," says he, by the mouth of the Psalmist, "like a man without help or succour;" and yet this man was the only one who "was free amongst the dead." (Ps. lxxxvii. 5.) That is to say, the only one who was free from sin, and consequently ought to have been free from all pain.

To be able to conceive how great the excess of his pains were it is sufficient to say, that the very thought or idea which he formed to himself of them in the garden, excited a sweat of blood all over his sacred body in so great abundance, that the earth round about him was moistened therewith. Great, therefore, must those sufferings be, the bare idea whereof produced so extraordinary and dolorous an effect! They were so violent and excessive, say the saints, that it had been impossible for human nature to resist them without a miracle. It was necessary that he should make use of his Divinity to prevent himself

from dying even in the very first conflict : for the effect which
the Divinity then wrought was, not to blunt the feeling of these
pains, but to prevent the violence of them from causing death :
it was to protect his life, that he might suffer the longer.   Let
us herein admire the goodness and infinite mercy of our Saviour:
he acted miraculously upon the martyrs, to hinder them from
feeling their pains ; and he acts miraculously upon himself that
he may suffer the more for love of us ; but how violent soever
the pains were which were common both to his body and soul,
those that immediately afflicted his soul were incomparably more
excessive.   For, from the moment of his conception to that of
his death, he had always present in his mind all the sins that
had ever been committed from the beginning of the world, and
should be committed to the end of it.   On the one hand, the
love he had for his Eternal Father caused him highly to resent
the injuries done to him—on the other, the tender affection he
had for souls made him ardently desire their salvation—notwithstanding the sacrifice of his life which he offered for them, he
saw that an infinite number of souls, not profiting thereof, would
be lost !   So that the pain he felt at their loss, and the zeal he
had for his father's glory, was like a two-edged sword, that
pierced continually his afflicted heart, and excited in him such
pangs as surpassed imagination.   All this then, and all the
sufferings and affronts, at the bare idea whereof he fell into a
bloody sweat, cast him into agony in the garden—in fine, all
that he had ever suffered in his whole life, he had, as I said
before, still present before his eyes ; from the instant of his conception to that of his death ; as he teaches us by the words of the
Psalmist, " my pain was always before my eyes. (Ps. xxxvii.
18.)   Now this being so, may we not judge, that all the days of
his life were to him the day of his passion ?   Besides, the apprehension of an evil is sometimes more grievous than the evil
itself ; and therefore may we not say, that his whole life was an
abyss of pains into which his holy soul was continually plunged,
without having the least respite ?

When we come to consider all these things in particular, when
we think that he who suffered them is the Son of God ; that he
suffers them for us out of a pure excess of love, we must have a
heart harder than marble not to be touched therewith.   " The
earth quakes," says St. Bernard, " the rocks are cleft ; the graves
are opened, the veil of the temple is rent in pieces, the sun and
the moon are darkened ; and in fine, nature gives all possible

marks of compassion, and shall we alone have none for him, he who suffered only for us—Let our hearts be touched, let them be penetrated with grief; and let us not be harder than stones, nor more insensible than inanimate creatures." "My son Absalom," said David, "O Absalom my son, who will grant me my desire of dying for thee? Absalom my son, my son Absalom?" (2 Kings xviii. 33.) Now, if natural tenderness could inspire such feeling as this, for one who died as a traitor to his father and his king, how far greater reason ought we to have the like for the Son of God, who died only to deliver us from the slavery of the devil, and to make us partakers of the kingdom of his Eternal Father?

———o———

CHAPTER IV.

That sorrow and contrition for our sins is one of the fruits we ought to reap from meditating on the sufferings of our Saviour.

THE second affection we ought to exercise ourselves in, and endeavour to excite in ourselves by meditating on the sufferings of Jesus Christ, in sorrow and contrition for our offences; and it should appear, that there is no fruit more easily to reap from it than this; because there is nothing better calculated to shew us the enormity of sin than this. The quality of the remedy necessary to be applied ought to give us an idea of the quality of the disease. "Acknowledge, O man," says St. Bernard, "how grievous your wounds were, for the cure of which it was necessary Jesus Christ should be wounded." Neither the eternity of pains due to sin, nor any other thing whatsoever, can give us so clear a sight of the grievousness of sin, as to think that it was necessary that God should make himself man and thereby make satisfaction for us to the divine justice, which could not be fully appeased any other way: because the offence being in some sort infinite, as being committed against God, who is infinite; and man not being able to make a due reparation, by reason of the infinite distance between God and him, it was altogether necessary that he who should make satisfaction should be of infinite dignity; and equal to him who received the injury. Divines are wont to clear this point by an example. A clown, say they, gives a king a box on the ear, or a blow with a cudgel. It is certain, that what revenge soever the king should take, the satisfaction could no ways answer the injury; by reason of the great difference and distance between the king and the clown : for what proportion is there between an affront given a king, and the punishment, though death itself were inflicted on the clown ? What must there be required then to make the king full satisfaction ? Nothing else, certainly, than that he who has done the injury should be raised to a dignity equal to the other, and so to submit himself to a proportionate satisfaction, and then the offence would be entirely repaired.

The same thing happens in our case. Man, who is but dust and ashes, had offended the immortal King of glory. If God therefore should cause him to be put to death, the injury would not be repaired—for this requires that man should become God, equal to him who is offended, and so repair the injury by his suffering. What remedy then, since there is no other God than he who is offended ? It is therefore in this that the mercy of God was infinite, who found out an admirable medium to pardon man without prejudicing his justice. For he being injured, and there being no other God that could make satisfaction for this offence, he of his own accord made himself man, in order that man who had offended God should suffer and die, and at the same time it was God himself that suffered ; that as the offence was in some sort infinite, so the sufferings and satisfaction should also become infinite by his person. Behold here what caused the necessity of the sufferings of Jesus Christ, and what also clearly shows the greatness and grievousness of sin. Wherefore St. John Damascen says very well, that " if God for the punishment of sin had eternally damned all the men that ever were, or ever should be, his justice would not have been so satisfied as it was by the incarnation and death of the Son of God." And this is no hyperbole or exaggeration. It is the very truth ; for all the torments of hell are not an equal payment to the death of Jesus Christ ; since, as God, he has sufficiently satisfied by his death the justice of God ; whereas an eternity of pain can never entirely satisfy for even one mortal sin.

Now this being so, I affirm, that one of the greatest fruits we can reap from the meditation of the sufferings of Jesus Christ, is to deplore and detest our sins, which cost him so much. My sins, O Lord, were the cause of the crown of thorns that so cruelly pierced your head, and of the cruel whipping which tore your sacred body all over!—they were my sins which put you into the miserable condition you were in ! It is I who have sinned, it is I who have done evil, I beseech thee let thy hand be turned against me." (2 Kings xxiv. 17.) "Take me and cast me into the sea; for I know this tempest is raised upon my account." (Jonas i. 12.) It is I, Lord, who deserved this cross, it is I who merited these injuries and affronts, and all those calumnies and reproaches which you have suffered for me!

St. Bernard feigns an example to our purpose, in this manner. "I was," says he, "in a public place, diverting myself, and at the same time sentence of death was pronounced against me in the king's closet, without my knowing anything of it. The only son of the prince, hearing thereof, presently took his crown from his head, cast off his royal robes, came out barefoot, clothed in sackcloth; with his head covered with ashes; weeping and sighing; because they had condemned to death one of his servants. Beholding him on a sudden pass by in this condition, I remained surprised, and asked the cause thereof; they answered me that he went to die to save my life. What then ought I to do," continues the saint; "and what man is there so insensible and so brutal as to continue his sport, and not quit all, at least to accompany the son of the prince, and mingle his tears with his?" It is in this manner and for the like considerations, that we ought to endeavour in our prayer to weep for and regret our sins, which have caused the death of the Son of God. Hence, what St. Ignatius, in the exercises of the passion, would have us beg of God is, to have sorrow, indignation, and confusion, that the Sovereign Master of all things has suffered so much for our sins. Now what he marks for the subject of our petition in the prelude of each exercise, is precisely the fruit he would have us reap from it.

This exercise is extremely recommended to us by the saints, and it is very good not to neglect it; for the practice is very profitable, not only for those that enter into the way of God, but for those who are already advanced in it. First, it is very proper to keep us in humility; the sight of our sins accompanied with a regret for having committed them, being one of the most powerful motives that we can have to live continually in a great confusion and in a great contempt of ourselves. He who reflects that he has deserved hell for having offended his Lord and Creator; what affronts, what contempts, what injuries does he not suffer with a good will, to expiate those many offences committed by him against the infinite majesty of God? Secondly, this exercise gives us a great assurance of the pardon of our sins—it does so in the following manner. One of the things which ought most assure us of the pardon of our sins is to have a great regret and sorrow for them ; so that if we continually look upon them with sorrow and confusion, God will forget them, and regard them no more. For this reason, David being touched with sorrow for his, in order to make God forget them, and turn his eyes from them, said to him, "I know mine iniquity, O Lord, and my sin is always before mine eyes." (Ps. l. 5.) St. Jerome makes a just remark upon the words of the same prophet ; "turn thy face from my sins, and blot out all my iniquities." (Ps. l. 11.) "If," says the holy doctor, "you put always your sins before your eyes, God will not put them before his. (Hier. in Ps. sup. cit.) In effect there is nothing that at the hour of death can give us a greater confidence and joy than this ; and, therefore, it is very good to prepare ourselves beforehand after this manner. Moreover, this exercise is not only a remedy for our past sins, but it is also a preservative against our relapsing into them, or committing others. For he who continually entertains himself in a very lively sorrow for having offended God, is far from offending him anew. It is also a very good remedy to comfort and assure those that are always in pain, to know whether they have consented or not to a temptation, and to comfort such as are troubled with scruples. For when people often make acts of contrition, with detestation of sin, and firmly resolve rather to die a thousand times than to commit a mortal one, they may assure themselves, they have not consented to those temptations they are in doubt of—it being very hard to imagine that, without their knowledge, a consent to a thing of which they have so much horror could escape them. Lastly, this exercise is an exercise of the love of God ; because true contrition, proceeding from the love of him, is nothing else than a very sensible sorrow for having offended so good and amiable a master, and one worthy to be served ; and the more we love God, the greater our sorrow will be for having offended the Divine Majesty.

St. Clement, in a book of which he is esteemed the author, says, that as often as St. Peter thought of his having renounced Jesus Christ, he wept so bitterly that his tears even burned his face, and made furrows in his cheeks as they flowed. He says also, "that the remembrance of this caused him to rise every night at the first crow of the cock, to put himself in prayer ; and that he slept not all the night after, observing this custom as long as he lived." We must endeavour to imitate the sorrow of this great saint ; and doubtless one of the most profitable exercises both in and out of prayer, is to make frequent acts of contrition, by detesting sin, and firmly purposing rather to die a thousand times than to commit one mortal sin—begging also earnestly of God, rather to take us out of the world, than permit us ever to offend him. Permit not, O Lord, that anything may ever be able to separate me from thee; for why should I live but to serve thee? I desire life only for this end. Therefore take me, O God, to thyself, before so great a misfortune should happen to me as to offend thee.

———o———

CHAPTER V.

Third affection—The love of God.

THE third affection we ought to excite in ourselves by a consideration of the sufferings of Jesus Christ, is the love of God. Nothing moves us more to love than to see ourselves loved, nothing ties or binds us so fast as this does; and this being so, it is here that the soul, considering at leisure the extreme love for her which Jesus Christ manifested in his passion, ought thereby inflame herself with love and gratitude towards him, who has so tenderly loved her. "It was in this," says St. John, "that the charity of God towards us appeared most, to have sent his only Son into the world, that we might live by him." (1 John iv. 9.) St. Luke, speaking of what happened in the transfiguration of our Saviour, when Elias and Moses appeared on each side of him, calls his passion an excess of love. "They entertained themselves with him," says he, "and spoke of that excess he was to make manifest at Jerusalem." (Luke ix. 31.) And without doubt it is with great reason that he calls the death of the Son of God an excess of love. First, because he died for his enemies. "There is no greater mark of love," says the Saviour of the world, "than to give one's life for one's friends" (John xv. 13); but the divine love of our Saviour went yet further, even so far as to give his for his enemies. . "It is in this," says St. Paul, "that God made appear his charity towards us, that Jesus Christ died for us, even when we were sinners." (Rom. v. 19.) Secondly, his death is justly called an excess of love; because, in rigour, one drop alone of those many drops of blood our Saviour shed in his circumcision; one of those drops of sweat he so copiously shed in the garden; and lastly, even the least thing he performed for our redemption, was sufficient to redeem the whole world, nay, a thousand worlds, as the saints assure us; since being God, he could consequently do nothing which was not of infinite value and merit. Notwithstanding his infinite goodness was not content with what was sufficient—No ! he vouchsafed liberally to bestow even the last drop of his blood upon us. The apostle speaking of this love calls it too great a love; " because," says he, " of that too great love with which he has loved us." (Eph. ii. 4.)   And in effect this love infinitely exceeds all that can either be said or even imagined. The prophet Zachary, the father of St. John the Baptist, speaking of the grace that God was ready to bestow upon mankind in the person of Jesus Christ, is not contented to style it a grace that proceeds from the mercy of God; but says, it comes " from the bowels of his mercy, in which he was pleased to visit us from above." (Luke i. 78.)

Who, therefore, can refrain from loving him who has so much loved us ? " Wherefore, let us love God," says St. John, " because God has first loved us." (1 John iv. 19.) Let us do to him as he has done to us; let us answer his goodness and tenderness ; let us endeavour to testify our love towards him as he has testified his towards us. He has given us very efficacious proofs of his, and, at the same time, very hard and painful ones, which are the best marks of a true love, and it is that made St. Ambrose cry out, " I owe, O Lord, far more to your passion, by which you have redeemed me, than to your omnipotence by which you have created me." (Lib. ii. sup. Luc.) For how great soever the benefit of our creation was, it cost you nothing, you needed to do nothing but speak, " you spoke and all was made, you commanded and all was created." (Ps. cxlviii. 5.) But it was not the same in man's redemption, " that " cost you a thousand reproaches, a thousand torments ; in a word, it cost you even the last drop of your blood. For these goods so effectual, let us make a return in effect, and, as St. John says, " my dear children, let us love God not in words only, and by our tongues, but in our works, and in truth." (1 John iii. 18.) It was in his desire of being contemned for the love of us that the Son of God showed how he loved us, let us also show that we love him by seeking to be contemned for love of him, and by rejoicing when any such occasion offers itself to us. He has shown us his love by offering himself entirely for us as a sacrifice to his Eternal Father ; let us show ours by offering ourselves entirely to him, by wholly resigning ourselves to him, and placing our hearts entirely in his hands, that he may dispose of us in all things according to his divine will. It is in this that true love is shown, and not in saying with our tongues, "O Lord! I love thee." And it is in this sense that the holy fathers interpret these words of the apostle, "it is patience that renders a work perfect." (Jam. i. 4.) For he who embraces pains, humiliations, and mortifications, with joy for the love of another, gives true and effective marks of his love, because he fails not to show it even in the hardest times, when real affection is most plainly discerned.

Behold here, therefore, one of the chief advantages we ought endeavour to read from the meditation of the passion of Christ, and for this purpose we must often exercise ourselves in prayer, in order to form those acts of love which I have just noted; but, above all, let us endeavour to offer ourselves to God with our whole hearts, that he may dispose of us in all things when and as he pleases. Afterwards, tracing in our minds those trying circumstances which may occur, let us suffer nothing to pass without forming thereon acts and resolutions of entirely abandoning ourselves to his divine will, for this is a very profitable exercise, and it leads to high perfection, and manifests a heart deeply penetrated with the love of God.

———o———

CHAPTER VI.

The affection of gratitude to God.

THE fourth affection in which we ought to exercise ourselves in meditating upon the miseries of the passion consists in gratitude and thanksgiving to God. " Can our mind think of anything," says St. Austin, " our mouth speak of anything, or our pen write anything better than 'thanks be to God?' Nothing shorter can be expressed, nothing more joyful heard, nothing more sublime conceived, nothing more useful done." (Epis. lxxvii,) God himself has always taken so much pleasure in the acknowledgment and thanksgiving men have made to him, that as soon as he did any extraordinary favour to his elect people he would have them presently sing to him a song of thanksgiving—" offer to God a sacrifice of praise." (Ps. xlix. 14.) And the holy scripture is full of canticles which the patriarchs and children of Israel sung after they had received any signal benefit. St. Jerome says it was a tradition among the Hebrews that "the sickness of which King Zechias had like to have died" was sent to him as a punishment, because after he had been miraculously delivered from the Assyrians by the hand of the angel of our Lord, who killed a hundred and fourscore thousand in one night, he returned no thanks to God for it by any song of praise, and St. Austin, speaking of the ten lepers cured by Jesus Christ, takes notice, that the Saviour of the world praised the gratitude of him who came back to thank him for his, and blamed the ingratitude of the rest. "Were there not ten cleansed," says he, "what has become of the nine others? There is no one found but this stranger, who is come back to render glory to God." (Luke xvii. 17.) Let us not be ungrateful as these were for the benefits we have received from God's hand, and much less for that greatest of all benefits which he conferred in becoming man and dying for us upon the cross. "Do not forget," says the Wise man, "the favours which he has done thee, he has answered for thee, and even has given his soul for thee." (Ecclus. xxix. 19.) Jesus Christ has both answered and paid for us, it cost him his life, wherefore it is just that we should have an extreme gratitude for so great a benefit, and that nothing should make us ever forget it.

St. Thomas, speaking of gratitude, says that it has three ways of working. The first consists in having all the esteem we ought to have in the bottom of our heart for the benefit we have received, and to be thankful to him from whom we have received it; the second consists in being thankful in words; and the third in making our benefactors, as far as we are able, an adequate return. Let us exercise ourselves upon all the mysteries of the passion, performing those three acts of gratitude. First, let us apply ourselves to produce deep sentiments of esteem for the many benefits which each mystery contains, examining, in particular, all the favours we have thereby received, or shall ever receive, from thence; let us excite ourselves by this consideration to feel in a more lively manner the obligation contracted by us to serve God eternally with all our strength. Let us afterwards endeavour to praise and glorify him with our mouth according to these words of St. Paul, "Let us always by him offer to God a sacrifice of praise—that is, the fruit of our lips, confessing his holy name." (Heb. xiii. 15.) And let us wish that the universe would assist us in giving him thanks. In fine, let us endeavour to make our actions correspond to so many benefits, and for this end, let us entirely abandon ourselves to him, as we have said in the foregoing chapter, and let us offer to him all that we have and are.

St. Bernard says, that in every mystery we meditate on we ought to imagine that Jesus Christ says the same words to us that he said to his apostles after he had washed their feet :—" Do you know what I have done for you ?" Do you know what is contained in this mystery ? Do you know what is the grace of your creation, what is that of your redemption, and what also is that of your vocation ? Alas ! how far are we from the know-ledge of what God has done for us ? For if I rightly conceived, O my God, that you became man, that you died upon a cross for love of me, there would need no other consideration but this to make me give you my whole heart, and to be wholly absorbed in your love, and this would be such a gratitude as a true Christian ought to have.

St. Chrysostom, upon this subject, takes notice of one thing which may be of great profit to us. He says that " a good servant ought to have as high an esteem of the favours his master bestows upon him in common with others, and to be impressed with as deep a sense of them, as if they were done to him alone, and as if he only were charged with the obligation of returning thanks for them. This the apostle did when he said ' he that loved me and delivered himself up for me.' (Gal. ii. 20.) Nor was it without reason that he said so," con-tinues the holy doctor, " since every one ought to say the same, because each one derives as great advantage from the death of Jesus Christ, as if he had died for him alone." In like manner, the light of the sun enlightens me as much as if it gave light to me alone, and the advantages I derive from thence is so far from becoming less, by being communicated to others, that on the contrary it is increased, because by giving light to them it helps them, when occasion serves, to assist and succour me ; so, in like manner, the incarnation and death of the Son of God is as profitable to me as if he had made himself man and died only for my sake. The advantage also that others receive as well as myself, diminishes nothing of what I thereby received, but, on the contrary, augments the favour, for it is the cause of their animating and assisting me to merit the glory to which I aspire. Moreover, the love of God is as great towards each one of us in particular as if he loved nothing else, and as for the good will and love of Jesus he was no less disposed to suffer for one man alone, if their was a necessity, than for all men together, and "he would not have refused," says St. Chrysostom, "to do for one man what he has done for all. (In Ep. ad Gal. ii.) Besides, it is true that God thought particularly on me; that he had me before his eyes when he made himself man and died upon the cross; "that he loved me with a perpetual charity" (Jerem. xxxi. 5), as he himself assures me by the mouth of Jeremias; and, in fine, that he freely delivered himself up to death to redeem my life. So that every one ought to look upon the benefits of God as if God had done nothing, but for him alone, and consider the love whence they proceed as if God had loved him only, and so say with St. Paul, "he who has loved me and delivered himself to death for me." (Gal. ii. 20.) When we consider all this in this manner it will be impossible not to feel ourselves excited to great acts of love and thanksgiving to this Divine Saviour, "who has always loved us with a perpetual charity."

The saints moreover add, that the reason why God exacts from us thanks for his benefits is not because he stands in need of our gratitude, but only that we may render ourselves more worthy to receive new graces and favours. "Ingratitude," says St. Bernard, "is a burning wind that dries up the source of God's mercy, and stops the channel of his graces." (In Cant. Serm. ii.) And so God deprives those men of his benefits who are so ungrateful as to forget them, so he heaps them upon those who acknowledge them and render due thanks for them. The sea, which is the source of all waters, gives back to the rivers all it has received from them; and God, who is the fountain of all those gifts and graces which we possess, gives back to us these same graces with interest, when with faithful gratitude we return to him what we received from him.

———o———

CHAPTER VII.

Of the affections of admiration and hope.

ADMIRATION is the fifth affection in which we may exercise ourselves by meditating on the mysteries of the passion—we may excite it in ourselves by admiring, for example, that God, who is impassible and immortal, suffers and dies : that he suffers and dies even for those who put him to death, and were so unworthy of all his favours ; and that he suffered more than any one ever suffered. We may also employ ourselves in admiring the excess of his love and goodness for men, the riches of his infinite wisdom and the depth of his counsels, in choosing so fit means for the salvation of mankind, and at the same time so agreeable to his justice and mercy. And, without doubt, it is a kind of very holy prayer: to entertain ourselves in the consideration of so great wonders as manifest themselves in the accomplishment of the world's redemption; to examine them well, and to fill ourselves with astonishment on beholding God moved to so great an excess of goodness and love towards his unworthy and ungrateful creatures. It is also a kind of most sublime contemplation: to be absorbed in the admiration of God's works. Now the more we know them, and the more deeply we penetrate into them, the more this admiration increases: besides it contains in itself a great love of God, and deep gratitude for his benefits—so that it being an affection from which many advantages are derivable, we must exercise ourselves in producing frequent acts of it. The Hebrew text puts the words " Sela" at the end of the verses of many of the Psalms, which is to remind us, that we must pause to give ourselves leisure to penetrate and admire the sense; and this teaches us also, that when we meditate upon these mysteries we must examine them at leisure, and give ourselves time to admire the wonders they contain.

The sixth affection we may excite in ourselves by our meditation on the passion is a lively hope and confidence in God, grounded upon what he has done for us without our merit, and even after we had rendered ourselves unworthy of his favours. For when we reflect deeply on this, and on the ardent desires that Jesus Christ had for our salvation, the thirst whereof even augmented his sufferings upon the cross, we shall easily be moved to hope from the goodness and mercy of God, that he will freely bestow on us all that is necessary for our salvation. " He who has not spared his only Son, but delivered him up for us, has he not also," says the apostle, " with him given us all things?" (Rom. viii. 32.) And in another place, the same apostle says, " if when we were enemies of God, we were reconciled to him by the death of his Son, much more being reconciled, shall we be saved by his life?" (Rom. v. 10.) This mode of reasoning is deserving of notice, and in it we may find great cause of comfort. For, in effect, if God looked upon us with the eyes of mercy when we were his enemies, and when our sins ought to have provoked him to hatred; and if he would then give so high a price to reconcile us to himself, in what manner will he not now look upon us, when the reconciliation is effected, and when we can hereafter cost him nothing? He who has loved us when we were disfigured and defiled with sin, how can he do otherwise now than love us, since he has washed us with his precious blood? And if when we fled from him and resisted his inspirations he ceased not to go after us, and invite us to him; and if he ceased not doing it until he had brought us into his house; how can he now forget and forsake us after bringing us to it.

It will also excite us to a holy confidence in him if we pause to reflect on the infinite mercy of God, such as the church conceives it, when she addresses herself to him in these words, "Lord, to whom it belongs to have mercy and to pardon." It is true that God is just as well as merciful, and that his justice is as great as his mercy; because in God all his attributes are equally infinite; but the marks of his mercy are far greater and more frequent than those of his justice. "The Lord," says David, "is sweet to all the world, and his mercy surpasses all his other works." (Ps. cxliv. 9.) It seems as if his mercy more properly belonged to him than any other of his attributes; because, it is by way of excellence called "the work of God;" and St. Paul says, "that God is rich in mercy." (Eph. ii. 4.) It is not but that he is rich in all things else, but he uses this mode of speech to express that in this he makes his riches more particularly to appear; as when one says, that a man is rich in furniture, in pictures, in precious stones, and the like. The church also acknowledges this truth when it says to God, "that he makes his omnipotence known chiefly in pardoning and showing mercy; and in effect he seems to place his glory in this: as if a prince, for example, who is most accomplished in all things, should take pleasure chiefly in displaying his valour, liberality, and some other particular virtue.

St. Bernard says, that it is natural to God to be merciful; that favours and benefits flow naturally from his hands, and that he awaits not our merits to show mercy towards us: but to punish seems a thing very strange and disagreeable to him; because we must provoke and even constrain him by our sins to do this. And as it is proper to the bee to make honey and not to sting but when provoked: so it is proper to God to bestow graces, and not to punish till men provoke, and in a manner constrain him thereunto by their crime. Nor does he even then fail to display his mercy by the pain and sorrow he expresses in being obliged

to chastise us.   It was only when this wickedness of man
observed no bounds, but increased daily, that he resolved to send
the flood.   He waited to the very last; and even then, "touched
with grief," he says, " I will blot out from the face of the earth
man whom I have created." (Gen vi. 6, 7.)   These words
show that it was not without extreme regret that he was moved
to destroy man.   Does not the gospel also say, that when Jesus
Christ denounced the ruin of Jerusalem, "beholding the city he
wept over it?" (Luke xix. 41.)   And does not he himself say
by the prophet Isaias, "Alas! I shall have at length satisfaction of my enemies, and shall be revenged of them?" (Isa.
i. 24.)   He speaks in this place as a judge full of compassion,
who, obliged to condemn a criminal to death, signs the warrant
with tears.   But his tenderness for us stops not here.   He shews
his infinite mercy, and the desire he has of our salvation, even
in his threats, as St. Chrysostom takes notice on these words of
the royal prophet, " if you convert not yourselves, he has bent
his bow, he has made it ready, and has prepared his arrows that
will cause death, he has made them red hot. (Ps. vii. 13.)
"It is a great goodness of God, and a wonderful clemency," he
says, "to threaten us in this manner with a blow, and to wish
to alarm us with the fear of his chastisement, that we may
endeavour to avoid it.   He treats us as fathers treat their
favourite children, whom they wish to frighten by words in order
to prevent the necessity of chastisement.   Moreover," as the
holy doctor takes notice, " the sword wounds one near you : to
produce an effect with it, you need but draw it, and make a
push—but the arrow strikes from a distance ; and to wound with
a blow, it is necessary to bend it, to draw the arrows out of the
quiver, and to fit them to the string, all which require both a
great deal of time and trouble.   Thus God," continues this holy
father, threatens us with a blow, that we have time to escape
his correction, according to the words of the prophet ; ' thou hast
given a sign to those that fear thee, that they may fly before thy
bow, and that those whom thou lovest may be delivered.'" (Ps.
lix. 4.)   When God designed to destroy the world by the flood,
he gave notice thereof a hundred years beforehand, to give men
time to think what to do, and how to prepare for their security.
In fine, he is all filled with love for men, and does all he can
not to be obliged to chastise them.   The same saint, speaking of
the curse which God gave to the serpent that had seduced Eve,
says, "admire the infinite mercy of God to man ; for as a father

who finds the sword with which some one had lately killed his son, is not content to revenge his death upon the murderer only, but takes the sword and breaks it into a thousand pieces; so God does the like to the serpent, condemning him, as the instrument of the devil's malice, to everlasting punishment." God wills not the death of a sinner—he does not wish to destroy men; to prove this, I need but say, that long since you have given him cause to destroy you; he might have plunged you into hell the very first time you fell into mortal sin; but his infinite goodness would permit neither death nor the devil to carry you away. "Do I wish the death of a sinner, and not rather," says our Lord, "that he should turn from his ways and live." (Ezech. xviii. 23.) He has ransomed you at too dear a rate to be willing to lose you; you have cost him his blood and his life, an infinite price, which he desires should not be unprofitable to you; and therefore, "he wills," on the contrary, as the apostle says, "that all men should be saved, and come to the knowledge of truth." (1 Tim. ii. 4.) These considerations, with many others which the scriptures and fathers furnish us with, but especially those we may draw from the passion and merits of Jesus Christ, ought to help to produce in us a confidence in the mercy of God.

——o——

CHAPTER VIII.

Of the imitation of Jesus Christ, which is the chief advantage we ought to derive from the meditation of his life and passion.

THE imitation of the virtues of Jesus Christ is, finally, what we ought to propose to ourselves in the meditations of his passion, and the fruit we have to endeavour to reap from thence. "The Son of God," says the saint, "came into the world principally for two reasons; first, to redeem us by his death and his sufferings; and, secondly, to give us a perfect model of all his virtues, and, by his own example, to induce us to practise them. It was on this account that at the last supper, after he had lowered himself to such excess of humility as to cast himself upon his knees before his disciples, and to wash their feet, he presently said to them, "I have given you an example, that you do as I have done to you." (John xiii. 15.) But what he then said and proposed to us to do, in imitation of him, ought to extend itself to all other actions. It is this St. Peter teaches us when he says, "Jesus Christ suffered for us; leaving you an example that you may follow his footsteps." (1 Pet. ii. 21.)   And this was what made St. Austin say that the "cross of Christ was not only the bed upon which he died, but was the pulpit also from which he taught us that we ought to imitate his example." (Orat, 119.) For though his whole life was a perfect model of all virtues, which he seemed to teach us both by his words and actions, yet he vouchsafed to collect them all together in his passion, and make them shine there in a sovereign degree ; so that what we ought to endeavour to draw from the meditation on his sufferings is an ardent desire of imitating his virtues.   For this end, we must apply ourselves to examine at leisure each virtue separately ; and exercise ourselves in framing a very great desire in our hearts, and in making a firm and constant resolution to practise it ; and also to conceive a holy aversion and horror for the opposite vice. In considering then, for example, the humility of Jesus Christ, who being God voluntarily submitted himself to the contempts and injuries of men, we ought to fill ourselves with a contempt of ourselves ; and to desire with our whole heart never to receive from men any mark of honour, esteem, or preference whatsoever ; but on the contrary, to propose to ourselves to suffer with all submission all sorts of affronts and injuries, and even to look upon them with joy, and as an occasion given us to resemble in some degree Jesus Christ.   In the same manner, in considering the patience of the Son of God, we ought to frame a resolution to receive joyfully all misfortunes that may happen to us, to desire that such occasions should frequently present themselves, and even to beg them of God ; that we may become thereby true followers of his Son.   "I desire not, O Lord," says St. Bonaventure, "to live without pain or wound, because I see you all covered with wounds."   In short, we must run over, in the same manner, all the virtues ; as obedience, charity, meekness, chastity, poverty, abstinence, and the rest : because in the life and sufferings of Jesus Christ all virtues shine forth ; and we must then exercise ourselves in framing in our hearts a true desire of imitating and practising them.

There remains still one thing here to be observed, which I have touched on elsewhere, which is, that in each virtue we meditate on we must descend to the particulars of those occasions that may offer themselves to us of exercising them ; and in our minds embrace them with joy for the love of God.   If, for example, your meditation be on humility, you must represent to yourself the different accidents that may happen to you of being contemned; first those of less moment, and afterwards such as you shall think will be most sensible to you; and hereupon frame your acts of humility and submission as if those accidents or occasions were actually present. You must also practise the same thing in regard of patience, mortification, indifference to all things, conformity to the will of God, and all other virtues; for, by this means, the virtue upon which your meditation is made sinks by little and little more into your mind, and there takes deeper root, and the contrary vice loses its force; and all things will become upon occasion easier to practise when we are prepared after this manner; it is, therefore, chiefly to gaining this facility that all the desires and resolutions we make in our meditation ought to tend.

Behold what abundance of matter we have here for meditating on the passion of the Son of God, and the mysteries of his life; and no one can reasonably complain that he knows not how to make this meditation, nor how to entertain himself therein, because I have set down so many affections which may be excited and dwelled on. I must here also add, in order to stir up and inflame our minds and hearts the more, that it is good in every mystery on which we meditate, and in every affection arising therefrom, to consider the following particulars. First, who it is that suffers; secondly, what it is he suffers; thirdly, after what manner he suffers; that is to say, with what patience, humility, sweetness, and charity, he does it; fourthly, for whom; fifthly, from whom; and lastly, with what view and intention he suffers. These six points, which the saints ordinarily propose to us, may give us sufficient matter to meditate on and to entertain ourselves with, for a long time, very profitably. But if we should have nothing else to exercise ourselves in than the imitation of the Son of God, we should therein find matter enough for our whole life, for those two reasons. First, because here we have all virtues in view; and as there are none which we stand not in need of, we may reflect on them all. Secondly, if in each virtue we enter upon a detail of the different occasions which may offer, and if we do not cease till we have surmounted these occasions, so far as to behold them not only with submission but with joy; I say, if we come to this, we shall in every virtue that can possibly be imagined have always sufficient matter to employ ourselves in. We may also add, that though these several sentiments of affection of which I have spoken are very considerable and very necessary, yet that which regards the imitation of the

Son of God is far more profitable than the others, because it contains them all ; and also, because it is an act of the love of God, which comprises in itself all other acts of virtue. So that this imitation is not to be understood as only one of the affections which I have spoken of in this treatise ; it is rather an abridgment of all those pious affections in which the perfection of a Christian life consists. It is for this reason, therefore, that in meditating on the life and passion of Jesus Christ the imitation of him ought to be our chief entertainment, and the chief fruit we are to endeavour to reap from it. But to do this, each one is very much to insist upon the imitation of the virtue he finds himself to stand most in need of ; dwelling upon it, diving more profoundly into it, and framing frequent acts of it, till it has taken deep root in his heart, and till he finds the contrary passion to be very much weakened. So that after this we may pass to another virtue, and from thence to a third ; and without doubt it is far better and more profitable to observe this method, than to embrace many things together in prayer, and to pass but slightly over them all.

———o———

CHAPTER IX.

In which is confirmed by examples how pleasing it is to God that we meditate on the sufferings of Jesus Christ.

SILVESTER relates that St. Mary Magdalene, after the ascension of our Saviour, having retired into a desert, in which she lived for thirty-two years, God from the very beginning would teach her in what she ought to employ herself, to become more pleasing in his sight. He therefore sent an angel to plant a cross at the entrance of the cave into which she had retired, that the saint having this object before her eyes, might always have present in her mind the adorable mysteries which were wrought upon the cross. So that all the time she lived in this solitude she continually employed horself in meditating on the death and passion of our Saviour and Master. This is what she revealed one day to a great saint of God, of the order of St, Dominick, as we may see set down more at large in the same author.

Ludolphus of Saxony relates of a holy man, who lived in solitude, and neither aspired after, nor applied himself to anything, but what was most pleasing to God ; that being one day in prayer, according to his ordinary custom, to beg of God to discover to him what was most pleasing in his sight, Jesus Christ appeared to him covered all over with wounds, and carrying a very heavy cross, and said : " one of the most pleasing services that my servants can render me is to help me to carry this cross; and, to do it, they need only accompany me in spirit in all my sufferings, and have a lively feeling of them in their hearts."

St. Vincent, St. Anthony, and Surius, relate of St. Edmond, archbishop of Canterbury, that at the time he studied his grammar in the university of Oxford, as he was one day walking in the fields, with his mind filled with pious thoughts, a young child appeared, who making himself known to be Jesus Christ himself, commanded him, amongst other things, to meditate upon some mystery of his life and death; and assured him that this would be a great help to him to avoid the snares of the devil, to acquire all the virtues, and to die happy. The young Edmond, filled with consolation and fervour by this miraculous vision, from that time forward applied himself every evening to meditate upon one of the holy mysteries of the life and passion of the Son of God; and found in this meditation all those helps that had been promised him.

We read in the history of the order of St. Dominick, that a religious of the same order having had from his youth a particular devotion to the passion of the Son of God, afterwards daily continued it in such manner, that there passed not a day but he either meditated upon one of the mysteries, or adored his sacred wounds; pronouncing at each adoration these words of the church, " we adore thee, O Jesus Christ, and bless thee, because by thy holy cross thou hast redeemed the world." He fell five times down upon his knees in making these acts, and recited every time the Lord's prayer, begging of God that he would vouchsafe to give him his fear and love; and God made it appear, by a very extraordinary favour, how pleasing this devotion was to him. For, one day whilst he was at prayer, Jesus Christ appeared to him, and invited him to taste and enjoy the sweetness of his sacred wounds; and this holy religious having with profound respect applied his mouth to one of them, his soul was presently filled with so great pleasure and satisfaction, that afterwards all that was not God seemed to him bitter and insupportable.

Lippomanus and Surius relate of St. Palemo that one day in Easter, St. Pacomius, his disciple, having dressed some herbs with oil, the holy old man, who was wont upon other days to eat them only with salt, shed tears when he saw them so dressed, representing to himself at the same time the sufferings of Jesus Christ : "Alas!" says he, "my Master was crucified and shall I treat myself delicately?" So that his disciple in vain represented to him the solemnity of the day ; for, notwithstanding all he could urge or say, he was never able to obtain of him so much as even to taste the herbs he had prepared for him.

We read also of a Christian slave who had so particular a devotion to the passion of Jesus Christ, that his continual application to think on it rendered him sad, and oftentimes drew tears from his eyes. The tyrant whom he served sometimes asked him the cause of this his sadness, and why he was not so cheerful as others were? He always answered, that he could not be otherwise, because he carried the passion of his Master engraven in his heart ; so that the tyrant taking notice of this constant answer, wished to try if what he said were true, and, thereupon, putting him to death, took out and opened his heart, wherein was found an image of a crucifix extremely well made, and this wonder touched him so forcibly that immediately he was converted to the faith.

Something similar is related of St. Clare, who, during her whole life, had a singular devotion to the passion of the Son of God ; and after her death there was found upon one side of her heart the image of a crucifix very finely wrought, with the nails, lance, sponge, and reed ; and on the other, the rods, pillar, and crown of thorns ; and all this is still to be seen at Montfalcon in Italy, where this extraordinary wonder is carefully preserved.

THE EIGHTH TREATISE.

———o———

ON HOLY COMMUNION, AND THE SACRIFICE OF THE MASS.

———o———

CHAPTER I.

Of the exceeding great love God has shown us in instituting the blessed sacrament of the altar, and of the inestimable benefits contained therein.

AMONGST the wonders God has wrought, there are two more extraordinary and more beyond the reach of human imagination than all the rest. The prophet Isaias finds them so surprising, that he calls them the inventions of God—"Make known to the people," says he, "his inventions." (Is. xii. 4.) And, in effect, it seems that both in the one and in the other, God has particularly studied to find out in what he might most communicate and manifest himself to us. The first of these wonders is that of the incarnation, in which the Word of the Father unites itself to our nature by an union so intimate that God and man become one and the same person—and by such an union that the secret thereof is incomprehensible to human reason, and is known only to God; an union, so firm and indissoluble that, as St. Denis says, "what it has once joined, has never been, nor can ever be separated." "Love," says the same saint, "is an unitive virtue that transforms the lover into the beloved object, and of the two, makes but one." Now, what no love in the world ever did, the love of God has done for man. It never happened in the world, that of the lover and of the object beloved love effectually made but one and the same thing. This was a wonder which seemed reserved for heaven, where the Father and the Son are indeed truly but one. However, the love of God for man was so great that God united himself to him in such a manner that God and man are but one and the same person—that man is truly God, and God truly man—that all that is truly proper to God may be truly and properly said of man, and, on the contrary, all that is truly proper to man may be truly and properly said of God himself. In a word, he whom men beheld speaking, walking, acting, and suffering, was truly God : he was truly clothed with human nature, he performed human actions, and he who performed them was God. "Who ever heard of any such thing as this? And who ever saw anything like unto it?" (Isa. lxvi. 8.) A God to be wrapped in swaddling clothes! A God to weep! A God to become weary and feeble! A God to suffer! What, O Lord! did not the royal prophet say, "that thou hast made the highest heavens thy refuge, where no evil shall come to thee, and no scourge shall approach thy tabernacle?" (Ps. xc. 9, 10.) And yet the whips, nails, and thorns have overtaken thee, and nailed thee to a cross. What is farther from God than this? "It is an admirable work that proceeded from him" (Isa. xxviii. 21), says the prophet Isaias; it is a work that exceeds the thoughts of man, and even those of the angels themselves, and keeps them in perpetual admiration.

The other wonder that God has wrought, and which is also an invention of his infinite love, is the institution of the Blessed Sacrament of his body and of his blood. In the incarnation he has hid his Divinity under the veil of flesh that we may see him ; and in the Blessed Sacrament he has hid both his Divinity and humanity under the accidents of bread and wine that we may eat him. In the former, God has received man into his bosom and bowels, by uniting human nature to the Divine Word ; and in the latter he wishes that you yourself receive him into your heart and bowels. Man is united to God by the first : God and man unite themselves to you by the second ; in the first, communication and union is made with one individual nature, which is the sacred humanity of Jesus Christ, personally united to the Divine Word ; but in the second, an union is made with all those who receive his body and his blood. He becomes the same thing with them, not truly by an hypostatical and personal union, but at least after that, by the most intimate and strict one that is possible : "He who eats my flesh, and drinks my blood, remains in me and I in him." (John vi. 57.) What can be more admirable than this? "The Lord, who is good and merciful, has made an abridgment of all his wonders, he has given nourishment to those that fear him." In effect, this is not only "the greatest of all his miracles," as St. Thomas says, "but it is an abridgment of all the wonders he has ever wrought."

We read in the holy scriptures that king Assuerus, "to manifest the riches and glory of his kingdom," made a solemn feast which lasted a hundred and fourscore days. Jesus Christ, the King of kings, vouchsafed also in a feast worthy of his greatness to manifest the riches of his treasures, and the majesty of his glory, and for this effect he gives himself to us, which is a wonder no less surprising than that of the incarnation. The manna which fell in the desert, and was only a shadow of this divine manna, heretofore so filled the children of Israel with admiration that they cried out—"What is this?" And did they not afterwards show the like astonishment when they said, "how is it possible that he can give us his flesh to eat?" (John vi. 9.) Moreover, this heavenly feast is not bounded within the term of a hundred and fourscore days as that of king Assuerus was, it has lasted already more than seventeen hundred years, and we have eaten it every day, and it will continue to the end of the world. "Come," cries out the royal prophet, "and behold the works of God—the prodigious things he has wrought upon earth." (Ps. xlv. 9.) O how admirable is the wisdom and depth of his counsels! And how wonderful are the means he makes use of for the salvation of men! But it being of the miracle of the body and blood of Jesus Christ that I am now to speak, I beseech God to give me his grace that I may acquit myself as I ought, and to supply by his help the weakness of my understanding.

The blessed disciple, speaking of the institution of this adorable sacrament, says, Jesus Christ "having loved his own who were in the world loved them to the end." (John xiii. 1.) He says "that Jesus Christ loved them to the end," not only to express that he always loved them, but to give us to understand that in the end he still gave greater marks of his love. In effect it was then that he more abundantly poured forth his grace upon them, and left them most precious pledges of his love, because in instituting the adorable sacrament he left himself in all his majesty unto men. He could not do anything that could show us more clearly the excess of his love for us: for it is the property of love to desire always to enjoy the presence of the object beloved, and not to be able to suffer the absence thereof. Wherefore, as he tenderly loved men, and as he was to return to his Father, he found out a means of so loving the world as not to leave it entirely, and of going from it in such manner that he ceased not to remain in it. He descended upon earth without quitting heaven;

he ascends to heaven without quitting earth: he quitted the bosom of his Father, yet ceased not always to remain therein. He remains likewise always with his children, though he has left them. "I came from my Father," says he, "and am come into the world: I quit the world and return to my Father." (John xvi. 28.) It is another property of love to desire to live in the memory of the person that is loved, and it is for this reason that those who love, when obliged to a separation, make ordinarily some mutual present, that they may think one of the other during their absence. Now, that we might think of him, Jesus Christ has given himself to us in the Blessed Sacrament of the Eucharist, and would not leave us a less pledge than himself to oblige us to think of him. Hence he had no sooner instituted the Blessed Sacrament, than he says, "Do this in remembrance of me." (Luke xxii. 19,) as if he had said, every time you celebrate this mystery remember the love which I have had for you, remember what I have done and suffered for you.

"There is no other nation so powerful," said Moses to the children of Israel, "that have their gods so near them as our God is present unto our petitions" (Deut. iv. 7.) And did not Solomon when he had built the temple testify aloud how astonished he was that God would establish his abode therein? Is it possible," says he, "that God should remain with men upon earth? For if the heavens themselves are not sufficient to receive him, how can this house which I have built be sufficient?" (3 Kings viii. 27.) With how far greater reason may we say the same thing, because it is not the shadow or figure of God, but it is God himself that makes his abode with us? "Behold," says he, "that I am with you unto the end of the world." (Matt. xxviii. 20.) What sweetness, what advantage this is for us, that our Redeemer and our God will vouchsafe to take up his habitation with us to sweeten the tediousness of our pilgrimage? If the company of a friend be so great a comfort in our afflictions, what comfort ought not that of God be unto us? What consolation ought it not impart to us to see him enter our house; to see him pass along the streets, and permit himself to be carried from one place to another, and that he has a fixed abode in our churches, where we may at all times visit him; entertain ourselves with him; discover our miseries, afflictions, and temptations; beg his help, and expect it from his all-powerful hand with all confidence, since he vouchsafes to approach so near to us, in order to be ready to give us assistance in all our necessities;

" I will establish my abode in the midst of you; I will walk amongst you, and I will be your God." (Lev. xxvi. 11, 12.) What heart would not be touched and inflamed with love to behold the Divine Majesty treat thus familiarly with men?

But the goodness of God does not rest here: he is not content with coming only into our houses, and remaining in our churches but he will also have us possess him within ourselves; he will remain within our breast; he will make that his temple and tabernacle. O ineffable love! O unheard of liberality! That I should receive into my breast and heart, Jesus Christ, true God and true man, the same Saviour whom the blessed Virgin carried nine months in her sacred womb! And if St. Elizabeth on seeing your holy mother, who bore you in her sacred womb, entering into her house, cried out in astonishment, and filled with the Holy Ghost, "whence comes this grace and favour unto me, that the mother of my Lord should come unto me;" (Luke i. 43); what shall I say, O my God, on seeing you enter not only into my house but into myself? With how far greater reason may I say, whence comes this grace unto me who have been for so long a time the devil's habitation; to me who have so often offended you, and been so ungrateful and unfaithful for so many benefits? Whence proceeds this grace and favour but from the excess of thy mercy, and because thou art goodness itself, "to make it thy delight to be with the sons of men," (Prov. viii. 31,) and because your love of them is infinite.

But if so great a favour as this were granted only to those who have a pure and innocent soul, it were, say the holy doctors, an inestimable benefit for mankind. Yet the Lord is so good that he refuses not to communicate himself even to the wicked as well as to the good, to his enemies as well as his servants; and even vouchsafed for love of us to be delivered again into the hands of executioners, and is pleased for the comfort of his servants even to enter into the mouths of impure sinners. Nay, that he may the better communicate himself to us daily, he is pleased to expose himself to be sold anew, and again to be crucified by them, according to St. Paul's words, who says, "that they crucify in themselves the Son of God." (Heb. vi. 6.) Behold whether you have not sufficient subject to love and serve him? The holy church seems astonished that he had no repugnance to enter into the chaste womb of the Virgin; saying, "thou hadst no horror to enter into the womb of the Virgin." Compare the purity of this Virgin without spot with those impurities with which the heart of man is filled, and you will see there is far greater reason to be astonished that he has not a horror to enter into the impure breast of a sinner.

———o———

CHAPTER II.

Adorable wonders that faith teaches us concerning the Blessed Sacrament of the Eucharist.

FAITH teaches us that the words of consecration work many miracles. The first is, that as soon as the priest has pronounced over the host the words of consecration the body of Jesus Christ is immediately present therein—the same body that was born of the sacred Virgin, the same that died upon the cross, that was raised again to life, and, in fine, the same that at present sits at the right hand of God the Father. That, moreover, as soon as the priest has pronounced over the chalice the words of consecration, the precious blood of Jesus Christ is present therein also—that in a hundred thousand masses, for example, that are said throughout the extent of the whole church, in the space of an hour, God works this miracle at the moment that the priest finishes the words of consecration; that in all these masses the body and blood of our Saviour is effectually present. and whether we consecrate in one place or in another he is always the same in all places.

The second wonder we are obliged to believe is, that after the words of consecration there remains neither bread nor wine, though it appears otherwise to our senses. When Jacob wished to obtain of his father Isaac the blessing he designed for Esau, he covered his hands with the skin of a kid, that he might the better resemble his brother. "It is indeed the voice of Jacob," said the holy old man his father, "but they are the hands of Esau." (Gen. xxvii. 22.) The same happens here—what we touch with our hands, what is exposed to our senses to judge of, appears bread and wine; but the voice and word of faith assures us the contrary, and it must supply the defects of our senses. As the manna which was the shadow and figure of this adorable sacrament had the taste of all sorts of things, and yet was none of those things of which it had the taste, so this heavenly manna of which we speak has the taste of bread and wine, and yet is neither the one nor the other. Moreover, in the matter of other sacraments, there happens no change at all; the water in baptism remains still water, and the oil in confirmation and extreme unction still remains oil. In this the matter is quite changed, and what appears bread and wine is not so; the substance of bread being changed into the body of Jesus Christ and the substance of wine being changed into his blood. "But he," says St. Ambrose, "that from nothing could create heaven and earth, cannot he with far greater reason make one thing out of another, and change one thing into another?" Moreover, do we not daily see that the bread we eat is in a short time changed into our own flesh by the help of natural heat? Why may not then the all powerful virtue of God make a similar change in an instant? And to draw us out of one astonishment by another, is it not far more wonderful that God made himself man, without ceasing to be God; than that bread, ceasing to be bread, should be changed into flesh? Now the same divine power whereby the Son of God made himself man, here makes the bread and wine be changed into his body and blood, "for to God nothing is impossible." (Luke i. 37.)

The third wonder that happens in this change is, that it is not made as other natural things are, wherein when one thing is changed into another there always remains something of the thing that is changed. For when earth is changed into gold or silver, for example, or water into crystal, the matter always remains the same, there is no change but of the form; just as when of a piece of clay or wax there is made sometimes a lion, sometimes an eagle. But here, after the consecration, there remains in the host nothing of the substance of bread, or in the chalice, of the substance of wine; neither as to the form or the matter, but all the substance of the bread is changed into the body of Jesus Christ; and all the substance of the wine into his blood? Hence the Holy Council of Trent says, "that the church, in order to express this entire conversion, properly calls it by the name of transubstantiation, that is to say, the changing of one substance into another." For as that change of form, which happens in natural generation, may very properly be called transformation, so here the entire change of the substance of bread and wine, which is converted into the substance of the body and blood of Jesus Christ, is very justly called transubstantiation.

So that in the Eucharist there remains nothing of the substance of bread nor of wine; there remains only the colour, smell, taste, and other accidents of bread and wine, which are called the sacramental species. And this is another wonder that appears in this august sacrament, that the accidents remain in it without subject or substance ; it being, as all philosophy teaches, the property of accidents to be inseparably attached to their substance. For is it not certain that whiteness cannot subsist of itself, without being attached to some substance ? And is not the same to be said of taste and smell ? But here, agreeably to an order superior to the whole order of nature, the accidents of bread and wine are miraculously sustained, without being united to anything ; because the substance of bread and wine is no longer there to sustain them, as we have already said ; and the body and blood of Jesus Christ, which succeed in place of bread and wine, cannot be the subject of these accidents ; so that by means of a continual miracle God sustains them by themselves.

We are likewise obliged to believe that not only the body of Jesus Christ is under the species and accidents of bread and wine, but that Jesus Christ, true God and true man, is entirely there and as he is in heaven. So that the blood of Jesus Christ, his sacred soul, and his Divinity, are, conjointly with his body, in the host under the appearance of bread ; and his body, his soul, and his Divinity, are also, conjointly with his blood, in the chalice under the appearance of wine. But, as divines observe very well, all these things are not in the Eucharist after the same manner. For some are there by virtue of the words of consecration, and others by way of concomitance. Those that are there by virtue of the words of consecration are those which are expressed by the same words ; so that in this way there is only the body of Jesus Christ in the host, and in the chalice only the blood of Jesus Christ ; because the words of consecration properly produce only what they signify, and they signify nothing else than "this is my body, this is my blood." The things which were in the Eucharist by way of concomitance, are those which are neecessarily joined or united to that which is expressed by the words of consecration. For when divers things are necessarily joined together, it is necessary that where there is one the other should be there also. Now, as the body of Jesus Christ is not at present separated from his blood, but is united with it as well as with his soul and his Divinity, all these things, for this reason, are in the host with his body ; and as his blood is not at present separated from his body but is united with it and with his soul and Divinity, so all these things are also for the same reason in the chalice. Divines, to make us the better understand this, say, that if in the three days that Jesus Christ remained in the sepulchre, St. Peter or any other of the apostles had consecrated, the soul of Jesus Christ would not have been in the Eucharist; because then it was not united with his body, and that there would have been there only his dead body, such as it was in the sepulchre, but united notwithstanding to the Divinity, from which it was never separated. In like manner, when Jesus Christ himself consecrated at his last supper, he was in the Eucharist true God and true man, but passible and mortal as he was then; instead of being as he is now in the Eucharist, living, glorious, resuscitated, immortal, and in a word, as he is in heaven.

But though it be true that the blood of Jesus Christ is in the host, and his body in the chalice, yet it was fit there should be made two distinct consecrations to represent more to the life the passion of the Son of God, in which his blood was separated from his body, so as it is expressed by the words of the consecration of the chalice, which shall be said for you and many others. Moreover, the sacrament of the Eucharist, having been instituted for the nourishment of our souls, it was fit that as eating and drinking concur to the perfect nourishment of our bodies, so those two things should also concur to the spiritual nourishment of our souls. It is true that the church, for important reasons, permits the laity to communicate only under the species of bread; but because in receiving the body of Jesus Christ in the host they receive also his blood, his soul, and his Divinity, there is no doubt that if they approach the sacrament with the same disposition with which the priest communicates under both kinds, they will receive also the same abundance of graces. St. Hilary says, "that as the manna, which was the figure of the Eucharist, had this property, that neither he that gathered more than another, had more, nor he who gathered less, had less of it;" in like manner here, neither he who communicates under both species receives more, nor he who communicates under the species of bread only, receives less, but both receive equally alike.

There is still another wonder in this adorable sacrament, which is, that Jesus Christ is not only whole and entire in the host, and whole and entire in the chalice, but also, that in every particle of the host, and in the least species of wine, how little soever it may be, he is as entire as in the whole host, and as he is in heaven. This is a truth which the Gospel teaches us. For

Jesus Christ, in the last supper, did not consecrate separately each piece of bread, with which he communicated his apostles, he only consecrated at once such a quantity of bread as was necessary to communicate all of them after it was divided; and the gospel, speaking of the consecration of the chalice, expressly takes notice that Jesus Christ gave it to his apostles, saying to them, "take and divide it amongst you." (Luke xxii. 17.) But the body of Jesus Christ is not only whole and entire in each particle of the host, and in each particle of the species of wine, after the division of the host or species of wine, but before this division he is also whole and entire in the whole host, and in each particle thereof, and entire in the whole species of wine, and in each particle of the species. This may be made clear by some natural comparisons. The soul, for example, is entire in the whole body, and is also entire in each part of it; the sound which the voice makes, when any one speaks to you, is entire in your ears, and also entire in the ears of them that hear it with you. Again, if you take a looking-glass you will see yourself entirely represented in it, though the glass be far less than you; and if you break the looking-glass into many pieces you will see yourself in each of these pieces, just as you before saw yourself in the whole looking-glass. The saints and holy doctors of the church make use of these examples, and many others of the same nature, to make us comprehend in some sort these adorable mysteries; for though there is none of these examples which bears a perfect and entire parity to what we are explaining, yet they cease not to give us some light concerning it.

One thing, which is also very miraculous in this mystery is that when we break the host or divide the chalice it is not Christ that is broken or divided, he remains always whole and entire in each part, how little soever it be; it is the accidents of bread and wine that is divided; and, in like manner, when one breaks the host in his mouth, it is not Christ that he breaks, it is only the accidents. "O illusion of the senses!" says St. Jerome, "the accidents with which you appear to our senses to be clothed, are broken, but you, O Lord, remain whole. It seems to our senses that we chew you between our teeth as bread, and yet we never do so to you. You remain always whole and entire without any division, without any corruption, in even the least particle that is." (C. iv. apud Euseb.) It is this the church also teaches by the hymn of the Blessed Sacrament; "he that receives it, does not bruise it, does not break it, does not divide it, he receives it whole and entire, he makes no division of the thing itself, he makes only a separation of the signs and accidents.''

All these things being such truths as are taught us by faith, we must believe them with submission, without embarassing ourselves with curious researches. And for this effect we must always abide by this principle of St. Austin, ''that God can do many things which surpass the reach of our reason and imagination.'' (Tract. xii. sup. Joan.) For as the saints say very justly, the wonders of God would not be great if we were able to conceive them; moreover, the merit of faith consists in believing that which we can neither see nor comprehend. Besides, there is still in the mystery of the adorable sacrament one thing which is not found in any other mystery. For, in other mysteries, we firmly believe that which we see not, and this is very meritorious; because Jesus Christ himself says, '' blessed are they that have not seen and believed.'' (John xx. 29.) But here we believe the contrary of what we see. For according to what our senses tell us, it seems to us that what we see is bread and wine, and yet we must believe that there is neither bread nor wine in what we see. Our faith in this is like that of Abraham, of which St. Paul said, ''that contrary to hope, he believed in the hope'' (Rom. iv. 18) God had given him. Supernatural hope overcame in him the natural diffidence he had reason to have. For he believed he should have a son, and hoped so, contrary to what he could reasonably expect in the course of nature, for his wife and himself being advanced in years he could not naturally expect to have any. And when he was ready to sacrifice his son, in obedience to God's commands, he ceased not yet to believe that God would keep the promise he had made him to multiply his posterity in the person of his son. It is in this manner that, in this adorable sacrament, what our senses teach us is entirely contrary to what we believe, and it is for this reason that our faith herein is also the more meritorious. '' You shall eat bread in the morning,'' says the Lord to his people, in Exodus, '' and in the evening you shall be satiated with flesh.'' (Exod. xvi. 12.) By the morning this present life is signified; and it is in this life that God gives himself to us under the species of bread and wine; but when the evening shall come, that is to say, when we shall be in glory, then we shall see the flesh of Jesus Christ, then we shall clearly know how and in what manner he is under the sacramental species; the veil shall be withdrawn, and we shall see all things clearly as they are, and not under clouds as we now do.

I might, in confirmation of all I have said, relate here many well authenticated miracles, wherein history abounds, but I will content myself with relating only one, which is stated in the history of the order of the Jeromites, and happened to one of the religious of that order, named Peter of Canvanuclas, who was afterwards prior of Guadaloupe. This man being for a long time assaulted and molested with many doubts against faith, and, above all, concerning the Blessed Sacrament of the altar, his imagination always representing to him that there could be no blood in the host, it pleased God to deliver him from this temptation in a most miraculous manner. Once, upon a Saturday, as he said the mass of our blessed Lady, and after he had consecrated, and had inclined himself to say that prayer which begins with these words, "We humbly beseech thee," he saw on a sudden a thick cloud that descended from on high, and so covered the whole altar upon which he celebrated, that he could neither see the host nor the chalice. Surprised at so strange an occurrence, and seized with very great fear, he began to beg of God with tears that he would deliver him from the danger he was in, and that he would let him know the cause of this prodigy. Presently the cloud vanished by little and little, and he felt quite astonished, because looking upon the altar he saw not the host he had consecrated, and found the chalice uncovered and empty. He remained for some time like a dead man, and afterwards being come a little to himself, he began again to beg of God, with great oppression of heart, and great abundance of tears, if what had happened to him proceeded from any fault of his, that he would pardon him, and free him from the great perplexity and trouble he was in. Whilst he was in this disquiet of mind, he perceived the host in the air, upon a paten, and perceived that after it had been there for some time, it came and placed itself over the top of the chalice, and dropped into it so much blood as there had been in it before; after which came the corporal, and of itself reposed upon the chalice, and the host returned to the same place upon the altar where he had put it. So many wonders, one after another, filled him with astonishment and admiration, and whilst he was in this state, not knowing what to do, he heard a voice that said to him, finish the sacrifice, and keep secret all that you have seen, and after this he was never disquieted or tormented with the like temptations

as he had before. All this was found after his death, written
with his own hand, in a paper, in which he had written his
general confession, that he might obey the command given him
to keep the thing secret. For as to the person that served at
the altar, he perceived nothing of what we have spoken of, nor
heard the voice; he perceived only that the priest had shed
many tears, and that he had been a longer time in saying mass
than ordinarily he was wont to be. (Liv. ii. c. 8. de l'Hist. de
l'ord. des Hier.)

———o———

CHAPTER III.

The preparation we ought to bring with us when we approach this
divine sacrament.

THE advantage which the sacrament of the altar has above all
others is, that Jesus Christ, true God and true man, is really in
it; this is what makes it to be the most excellent of the sacraments, and to work greater effects of grace in our souls. For in
the other sacraments we partake of the grace that is communicated to us, but here we participate of the source or fountain of
that grace. In the others, we drink only the waters that flow
from this fountain, but there we drink out of the source or
fountain itself; because in it we receive Jesus Christ himself,
true God and true man. This sacrament is also called the Sacrament of the Eucharist, that is to say, the sacrament of grace,
because the source or origin of all graces is herein contained, and
that we receive the Son of God herein, who is the sovereign
grace, and who, by his incarnation and death, has again re-
established men in the grace and favour of his Father. It is also
called the Sacrament of Communion, according to the words of
St. Luke, in the Acts of the Apostles, "they persevered in the
communion of breaking of bread," (Acts ii. 42,) because in
receiving it, we who communicate become partakers of the
sovereign good, who is God, and of all other goods and spiritual
gifts; and Jesus Christ, after having given us his body and blood,
communicates at the same time to us all the treasures of his
grace which he has obtained for us by his incarnation and death.
This term of communion suits very properly to it upon another
account also, because it unites all the faithful together who participate of the same table and of the same bread, and thereby
become one according to the words of the apostle, "we are one

bread and one body, all of us participating of the same bread."
(1 Cor. x. 17.) "One of the reasons also why Christ instituted
this sacrament under the species of bread and wine is," says St.
Austin, "to show us, that as bread is made of many grains of
wheat, and the wine of many grapes, so many faithful, who participate of the same sacrament, become one mystical body."
(Tract. xxvi. in Joan.) St. John Damascen also compares it to
the burning coal with which the seraphim purified the lips of
Isaias. "Let us receive," says he, "the body of him who was
crucified and become partakers of it, that the fire of our inflamed
desire, being enkindled in us by the inflammation that arises from
this coal, our sins may thereby be consumed and our breasts
enlightened." He adds also, that the Divinity being a consuming fire, according to the words of scripture, "our God is a
consuming fire;" (Deut. iv. 24); this heavenly food which is
united to him consumes all our imperfections, purifies us from
whatsoever is unclean in us, and heaps spiritual goods and
blessings upon us. In fine, this is the banquet the gospel makes
mention of in which God commands to be said to the guests:
"behold I have prepared my banquet, my beeves and fatlings
are killed, and all things are ready." (Matt. xxii. 4.) In
saying all is prepared, all is ready, he gives us sufficiently to
understand that we shall find therein all we can wish for.
Hence the royal prophet, speaking to God of this heavenly
manna—"Thou hadst, O Lord," says he, "prepared for the
poor, in the excess of thy bounty and sweetness." (Ps. lxvii.
11.) He says not, what it is that God has prepared, because it
is so ineffable a good that it cannot be expressed by words, and
it is above all understanding. "O sacred banquet," cries out
the church, "in which Christ becomes our food, in which the
memory of his passion is renewed, in which the mind is filled
with grace, and in which a pledge of future glory is bestowed
upon us." O sacred banquet! This name alone of banquet is
a name of joy and abundance. O sacred banquet, where man is
nourished with his God! Sacred banquet, which renews in our
memory the passion of our Saviour, and that excessive love
which obliged him to deliver himself up to death for us, even to
the death of the cross? Sacred banquet, in which our soul is
fully satiated with God, and replenished with his grace. Sacred
banquet, in which is given us a pledge of our future glory: a
pledge so precious, that it differs in nothing from the recompense
which ought one day to be given us in heaven. All the

difference is, that here he has given us himself under the veil of the sacramental species, and in heaven we shall behold him, "face to face, such as he is."

But the excellence of so august a sacrament and of the sovereign majesty of him we receive in it, requires that we should bring with us great preparations for the receiving of it. The royal prophet, speaking of the temple which he desired to be built to the Lord, "it is a great work," says he, "since it is not to prepare an abode for man, but for God himself." (1 Paralip. xxix. 1.) And, after having amassed a great quantity of gold and silver vessels and precious stones, all this seemed very small and inconsiderable to him for the building of a temple in which the ark of alliance was to be placed, and wherein was kept the manna, which was but a shadow and figure of this divine sacrament. What ought not we then do to prepare the temple in which we desire to receive God himself in person? Ought not our care and precaution herein surpass the care and precaution of David as much as a reality and a body surpass a figure and a shadow? There is nothing, without doubt, that we owe not to his infinite Majesty whom we receive in this august sacrament; but we ought, moreover, consider that it is of very great importance to be well prepared to receive him, for such as our disposition and preparation shall be that we carry along with us to it, such also shall be the grace which will be bestowed upon us therein, just as the quantity of water we draw out of a fountain is proportionate to the capacity of the vessel in which we drew it. The better to comprehend this we must know that divines take notice that he who approaches this sacrament with more good works and more holy dispositions, does not only in virtue of good works and holy dispositions, receive more grace, which, with the Council of Trent, they call the grace of "him that works" (Ex opere operantis); but that the sacramental grace which the sacrament gives of itself besides this other "by the work performed" (Ex opere operato), and which grace is attached to it by divine institution, becomes greater and more abundant in proportion as the disposition he brings is greater and more holy, for God works in the order of grace as he does in the order of nature, where we see causes work upon subjects according to the disposition they find in them. Fire, for example, kindles dry wood in a moment, but it kindles damp wood very slowly, and it acts very differently upon the one and other according to the different degrees of dryness it finds in them.   The same happens in the sacrament of the altar, and, consequently, for every reason it is of the utmost importance to be well prepared for approaching it.

————o————

CHAPTER IV.

That we must approach holy communion with great purity of soul, not only in regard to mortal sins, but even to the least venial faults.

In what follows I shall treat chiefly of three things; first, of the disposition required to approach worthily the holy Eucharist ; secondly, of what we are to do after we have received it, and what thanksgiving we ought to make ; thirdly, of the fruit we ought to reap from it.   First, as to what regards the disposition or preparation, I say that a greater preparation is required in this than in all the other sacraments, because the more excellent the sacraments are, the more holy and exact ought the disposition be for receiving them, for there are some of the sacraments that one may worthily receive without bringing any other disposition than a true repentance ; but the excellency and dignity of this sacrament is so great, because God himself is contained therein, that, besides the disposition I now mentioned, it requires also that of confession when we have committed any mortal sin.   So that contrition is not sufficient in order to approach it worthily, but we must previously go to confession, as the Council of Trent has decided this point, resting upon these words of the apostle, "Let each one prove himself, and so let him eat of this bread and drink of this chalice." (1 Cor. xi. 28.)   For the sense which the council gives to these words is, that this proof ought to be made by means of an examen, and at the tribunal of confession, so that the preparation of confession, when one has committed any mortal sin, is of obligation to all Christians under pain of mortal sin, and, at the same time, it suffices for receiving the grace of the sacrament.

But, however, true it is, that venial sins, and generally all that are not mortal, do not cause us to lose it, and that he who approaches this sacrament in this state fails not to receive " an augmentation of grace," as divines call it, yet it is certain that he loses that abundance of grace and spiritual gifts which those receive who approach it with more purity and devotion, for, though venial sins do not extinguish charity in us, yet they cause a great languishing in our fervour and devotion, which are the most proper dispositions to receive worthily the body of Jesus Christ, so that if we desire to participate of that abundance of grace which those enjoy who receive it with extreme purity, we must be free, not only from all spots of mortal sin, but also from the stains of venial sin. Jesus Christ has himself given us an example of this disposition by washing the feet of his apostles before he communicated them, "teaching us hereby," says St. Bernard, "that approaching this divine sacrament we ought not only to be washed and purified from all mortal, but also from venial sins, which are represented by the dust which sticks to our feet."

St. Denis goes yet further, and says that Jesus Christ, by this example, requires that we should be washed, not only from venial sins, but also from the least imperfections. "This sacrament," he says, "requires an extreme purity of mind;" and he relates upon this subject the ceremony which the priest uses at mass, in washing his hands before he offers this adorable sacrifice; "for it is to be noted," says he, "that he does not wash his whole hands, but only the tips of his fingers, to teach us that we ought to cleanse ourselves, even from the least bad thoughts and imperfections, when we approach the sacrament of the altar." If Nebuchodnosor required that they should make choice of beautiful youths, "who had not the least defect," (Dan. i. 4.), and who were to be nourished with the same meat that was served at his own table, how far greater purity is required in us when we approach this divine table? In fine, it is the bread of angels we here eat, and therefore we ought to eat it with angelical purity.

Peter of Cluny relates that a German priest, who always had led a very exemplary life, happened to fall into a sin of impurity, and having thereby gained a very bad habit, he ceased not, however, to continue all that time to say mass, still adding crime to crime; as it happens to some, who, having for a long time lived well, fall shamefully, and not daring, out of pride, to confess themselves of it, out of pride also continue still the ordinary communions, for fear of losing that good opinion people had before of them. God, notwithstanding, had compassion of this miserable man, chastising him in such manner as made him open his eyes, and this happened in time of his communion, for

whilst he held the body of Jesus Christ between his fingers, the
host vanished on a sudden, as the blood did also which was in
the chalice as he was raising it to his mouth, so that he remained
that day without communion, very much astonished at what
had passed.   The like happened to him two other times also
when he endeavoured to say mass, to try whether God would
give him the same marks of indignation as he had given him at
the first, and hereby perceiving how enormous his sins were,
and how much the anger of God was incensed against him, all
bathed in tears, he went and cast himself at his bishop's feet,
stated to him what had happened, confessed his sins to him with
great marks of sorrow, and having received a penance for them,
which obliged him to many sharp disciplines and other austerities, he faithfully accomplished them all, and, in the meanwhile,
abstained from saying mass till the bishop, judging that he had
sufficiently satisfied the divine justice for his sins, gave him
permission to celebrate ; and the first time he went again to say
mass there happened another very miraculous thing to him, it
was, that after he had said the greater part of it with many
sighs and tears, and when he was on the point of communicating,
on a sudden, the three hosts which before had disappeared by
reason of his unworthiness, came back upon the paten, and the
same quantity of blood which had also disappeared, came back
into the chalice, whereby God would let him know by so miraculous a sign as this that his sins were entirely pardoned.   He
received this mark of the infinite mercy of God with a very
deep sense of gratitude, and full of a holy joy he consumed all
the hosts, and ever after lived in very great purity of life.   Peter
of Cluny says that the bishop of Clairmont related this story to
him in the presence of very many persons.   Cæsarius also, in
his dialogues, mentions another very like unto this.

——o——

CHAPTER V.

*Another disposition, and a more particular preparation, for
approaching this divine sacrament.*

The saints and masters of a spiritual life tell us that, to obtain
a greater abundance of fruit and more admirable effects of this
divine sacrament, we must endeavour more particularly to prepare ourselves for it by an actual devotion, I shall, therefore,
explain here what this devotion is, and how we may excite

ourselves to it. We must, in the first place, say they, approach this divine sacrament with a great humility and respect; secondly, with a great deal of love and confidence; and, thirdly, with a great deal of fervour, with a hunger after this celestial bread, and a desire to partake of it. All sorts of affectionate emotions by which we may excite this actual devotion, either before or after communion, are reduced to these three. As books are filled with divers holy devotions and considerations upon this matter, I shall touch here only on some of the more ordinary, which often also are the most profitable, that after I have set down the method every one may of himself work hereupon, and be able to reap from his own stock, for what we acquire by ourselves invariably makes the most deep and permanent impression, as St. Ignatius takes notice of in his annotations upon the spiritual exercises.

First, we must approach this adorable sacrament with most profound respect and humility, and the better to excite this feeling in our hearts, we can at first represent to ourselves the supreme greatness and infinite majesty of God, who is really in the Eucharist. We can consider that it is he who has created heaven and earth by one sole act of his will, and preserves them also, and that he can destroy them by the same divine will, and, in fine, we can reflect that the angels tremble with respect before him, and at the least sign he makes the very pillars of heaven shake and tremble with fear. After this we must turn our eyes upon ourselves to behold our misery and baseness, and sometimes entertain ourselves with the thoughts and sentiments of the publican in the gospel, who durst not approach the altar, nor so much as lift up his eyes to heaven, but, retiring into a corner of the temple, struck his breast, saying, "Lord, be merciful to me, a sinner. (Luke xviii. 13.) Sometimes we must help ourselves with the words of the prodigal child: "Lord I have sinned against heaven and against thee. I deserve no longer to be called thy son, make me only like one of thy servants." (Luke xv. 18.) At other times we may frequently repeat in our heart and mouth the words of St. Elizabeth to the Blessed Virgin, and say, "How comes it to pass that I should receive so great a favour?" (Luke i. 43.) It will be very good also to reflect upon those words the church makes use at the time of holy communion, which are taken out of the gospel: "Lord, I am not worthy that thou shouldst enter under my roof: say but the word, and my soul shall be healed."

(Matt. viii. 8.) I am not worthy, O Lord, to receive you, but I approach you, that you may render me worthy. O Lord! I am sick and weak, and I come to you to be healed and strengthened by you, because you have said "that those who are well stand not in need of a physician, but only those that are sick" (Mat. ix. 12), and it was those only you came for.

Eusabius, who was disciple of St. Jerome, and present at his death, says that this great saint being upon the point of receiving his viaticum, and considering, on the one hand, the infinite majesty and goodness of God, and on the other, looking upon himself, said : " Lord, why do you debase yourself at present so low as to come to find out a publican and sinner, and this not only to eat with him, but even with a desire to be eaten by him ?" It is related in the Second Book of Kings, that David, having said to Miphiboseth, "thou shalt always eat at my table," Miphiboseth answered him, "who am I, your servant, that you should cast your eyes upon me, who am but like a dead dog." (2 Kings ix. 7, 8.) Now, if the son of Jonathan made such an answer as this to a king who invited him to his table, what answer ought not be made by us whom God himself invites to his ? But since we can never approach the sacred banquet with such a disposition as it deserves, let us supply it, at least, by profound humility, and say with the royal prophet, " who is man that thou art mindful of him ? or the son of man that thou dost visit him ?" (Ps. viii. 5.) Or else with Job, " who is man whom thou hast elevated to so great a dignity ?" (Job vii. 17.) It is with reason, therefore, that the church, admiring the goodness of God, cries out upon this occasion, " O inconceivable wonder! a vile slave eats his Lord and master."

In the second place, we must approach this sacrament with a great deal of love and confidence, and to render this sacrament more lively and tender, we must consider the infinite mercy and bounty of God, which here appears more clear than in any other thing whatsoever, as we have said in the beginning, for when we shall set this before our eyes, how is it possible we should not love him who has so much loved us ? And how can we but have a great confidence in him who has heaped so many benefits upon us ? And what is it he can refuse us, who has vouchsafed to give us himself ? "What shepherd," says St. Chrysostom, upon this adorable mystery, "has ever nourished his flock with his own blood ? But why do I speak of shepherds ? How many mothers are there, who, after their pains of childbirth are past, give up their children to be nourished by other women ? But our Saviour has not permitted that we should be given out to be nursed by others. He nurses and nourishes us himself with his own blood, and by all possible ways unites us to himself." (Hom. lxxxiii. in Matt.)

The third thing that God requires of us in this adorable sacrament is, that we come to it with an ardent desire. "This bread," says St. Austin, "must be eaten with a great hunger of the inward man." (Conc. iii. in Ps. ciii.) And as the things we eat with a good appetite do ordinarily most good to the body, so this celestial bread will work a better and more wonderful effect in our souls if it be eaten with a great hunger, and with an extreme impatience of uniting ourselves to God, and with an ardent desire of obtaining some particular grace thereby, for the prophet assures us that " he will satisfy hungry souls;" and does not the holy Virgin also assure us that " he filled those that were hungry with good things ?" (Luke. i. 53.) The means to excite in us this hunger of the celestial bread is, on the one hand, to regard the extreme necessity we have of it, and, on the other, to consider the admirable effects it produces. We do not read that, when our Saviour conversed with men, any one implored his assistance in vain. The Cananæan women only touched the hem of his garment and was cured ; the adultress only cast herself at his feet and received pardon for her sins ; the lepers, possessed persons, paralytics, blind, lame, deaf, and dumb, received cure of all their diseases as soon as they had recourse to him, " because there proceeded virtue from him that cured them all." (Luke vi. 19.) He is the same now he was then, and has the same will and power, so that if we approach this divine sacrament with an ardent desire of being cured, we shall therein find remedy for all the distempers of our souls.

---o---

CHAPTER VI.

Some other pious considerations that may help us to prepare for holy communion.

AMONGST many other considerations that may help us to prepare ourselves profitably to receive the body of the Son of God, one of the most proper is to call to mind his passion, and to consider with what excess of love he delivered himself up to the torment of the cross, for one of the chief reasons why he instituted this sacrament of his sacred body and blood was that we might always be mindful of his passion, and it is for this reason that he himself ordains that, as often as we participate of this sacrament, "it should be in remembrance of him." (Luke xxii. 19.) The apostle teaches us the same thing. "As often," says he, "as you eat this bread and drink of this cup, you shall announce the Lord's death." (1 Cor. xi. 26.) St. Bonaventure counsels us to meditate upon one of the mysteries of the passion as often as we go to communion, and says he was wont to do so, and found thereby a very great devotion and tenderness in his soul. St. Chrysostom says, that as often as we communicate, we should imagine that we apply our mouths to the precious wound of our Saviour's side, that we imbibe his blood, and that we participate of whatsoever he has gained for mankind by the merits thereof. St. Catherine of Sienna, as often as she went to communion, looked upon herself as still an infant, and that she went to suck again her mother's breast. Some at that time represent to themselves our Saviour crucified, planting his cross in their hearts, as it was upon Mount Calvary, and casting themselves at the foot thereof, they embrace and gather up with their lips all those drops of blood that fall from it. Others imagine that they are at the last supper which our Saviour made with his apostles upon the eve of his passion, that they are present amongst them, and that they receive from his own hands his sacred body and blood in effect, and what then happens is not only a representation of that supper, but is, in effect, the same banquet, for the same God who then gave his body and blood to his apostles, now gives it to us in the Blessed Sacrament of the altar, and with the same love and bounty he then gave it.

It is, moreover, a very holy manner of preparing ourselves to consider the following points : first, who is it that gives himself?—the Creator of all things, the master of heaven and earth, the infinite majesty of God himself; secondly, to whom does he give it ?—to me, who am but dust and ashes, and who have a thousand times offended him ; thirdly, wherefore does he give it ?—to make me participate of the merits of his passion, and of the infinite treasure of his grace. In a word, for what motive or end does he give it ? It is not for his own interest, because he is master and Lord of all things, and stands in need of nothing, wherefore, it is out of his pure bounty and goodness towards me, and out of a desire he has that my soul shall be saved, and remain always united to him by grace. After we shall have exercised ourselves upon these four points, we must, in the last place, form acts of faith, hope, and charity. Behold here another means of preparing ourselves.

But because we can never be able to prepare ourselves so worthily as we ought if he himself vouchsafes not to bestow his grace upon us, we must therefore beg of him to bestow upon our souls all that humility, all that respect, all that love, and all that purity he requires of us; and, for this end, in addressing ourselves to him we may help ourselves by this familiar example. Lord, if a great king were to lodge with a poor widow, he would not expect that she should prepare his lodging, but would send his own household and officers to accommodate it for him. Do you the same, O Lord, in regard of my soul; and because you come to lodge in it, send your angels beforehand to prepare your lodging, and to purify it from all that uncleanness it is full of, thereby to make it a fit and worthy habitation for yourself. After this we may address ourselves to the holy Virgin, and those other saints to whom we have more particular devotion, and humbly beg of them to obtain a grant and an accomplishment of what we demand.

To all these preparations you may still add another, both very easy and profitable, which ought to be of very great comfort to you, as well as to all the world. When you feel not in yourself this fervent devotion and those ardent desires you would have, and which it is reasonable you should come with, to receive so great a master; exercise yourself in wishing to have this devotion, and these desires, and hereby you will supply what is wanting to you. For God, who regards the heart, will receive your good will for the deed, according to the words of the prophet, "the Lord has heard the desire of the poor; thy ears, O Lord, have heard the preparation of their heart." (Psal. ix. 41.) Blosius says, that our Saviour himself taught this kind of devotion and preparation to St. Mecthilda, and one day said to her: "when thou art to receive my body and blood, desire, for the greater glory of my name, to have all the fervour and zeal which the most inflamed heart ever had for me, and then thou mayest with confidence approach, having this preparation. For I will behold the fervour thou desirest to have; and esteem it as if thou hadst it in effect." He relates a similar thing of St. Gertrude. One day when she went to receive the Blessed Sacrament, and was extremely afflicted because she had not sufficiently prepared herself for it, she begged of the holy Virgin and all the saints to offer to God for her whatsoever they had ever done that was most meritorious, thereby to prepare her the better to receive him; and then our Saviour appearing to her, said, "now thou at present appearest in the eyes of all the court of heaven adorned in the same manner as thou desirest to be. (Blos. c. 6 mon. spir.) So that it is an excellent manner to prepare one's self for communion, to desire to approach with all the fervour that ever the greatest saints have had; and to beg of God to cause that the merits of his Son may supply those dispositions we want for this effect. We may also make use of the same method for our thanksgiving after communion, which I shall hereafter speak of in its proper place in the following chapter.

It is by means of these considerations and reflections that we ought to endeavour to excite in ourselves that actual devotion, with which we should approach this holy table. For this end, we must sometimes make use of one, sometimes of another, as we shall find best. But as we cannot prepare ourselves after this manner, nor do our duty herein, without employing some time in it, we therefore must give so much as shall be reasonably required for this end. St. Francis of Borgia, in a treatise composed on "preparation for communion," allots three days to prepare ourselves for it, and puts three others for our thanksgiving, and sets down several holy considerations and exercises, in which we may employ ourselves during the time he allots. And without doubt, this would be a very proper means to entertain ourselves in fervour and devotion all the week long: the three first days, in hopes of receiving our Creator; and the three last, in joy and thanksgiving for so great a benefit. For the bare idea that we are to communicate the next day, or that we have communicated the day before, ought to be sufficient to cause us to remain in a great interior recollection. But if it should happen that we could not employ all this time in preparing ourselves, it is fit that at least some part of the morning of the day upon which we are to communicate, should be employed in prayer and meditation upon some one of those reflections I have before mentioned. It will be good, also, upon the eve to go to sleep with the thought that we are to communicate the next day; and if we happen to wake in the night, we must think of the same thing; and in the morning, as soon as we have opened our eyes, we should have our mind filled with the same thought. For if our holy founder would have us every morning, as soon as we awake, presently to think upon the subject of our prayer for that day; with how far greater reason ought we, upon the day we are to receive the Blessed Sacrament, as soon as we awake, think only thereupon.

———o———

CHAPTER VII.

What we are to do after communion, and what our thanksgiving after it ought to be.

As it is good before we eat to take some little exercise, to stir up our natural heat; so also it is good before we approach this divine table to exercise ourselves in holy meditation, to enkindle in us devotion and fervour, which is the same to our souls as natural heat is to our bodies. It is good also to give some time to conversation after meals; and it will be also very much to our purpose, as soon as we come from this divine banquet, to entertain ourselves for some time with God; this being the most favourable and fit time to treat, and to unite ourselves with him. We ought, therefore, endeavour to make our profit of it, and not to lose the least moment thereof. "Permit not yourself to lose so good a day as this, and let not the least part of so precious a gift be lost. (Ecclus. xiv. 14.)

For this end we must employ this time in making some pious meditation, such as I have said should be made before communion. But above all, we must employ ourselves in praising God, and in giving him thanks for all the benefits we have received from him; and particularly for the inestimable one of our redemption, and for the favour he does us in giving himself to us in this manner. But since we can never sufficiently of ourselves return those thanks that are due to him, we must, to supply this defect offer him all the benedictions and praises that all the angels together have ever offered him from the beginning of the world, and that all the blessed during their lives have also ever given him, or do now give him in heaven, and all those also which they shall give him for all eternity. We must join our intention with theirs, "and beg him to command that our voices may be heard and admitted with theirs." Finally, we must invite all creatures to praise him with us, and say with the royal prophet, " celebrate the magnificence of our Lord with me, and let us glorify his name together." (Ps. xxxiii. 4.) But because God is infinitely above all sorts of praises, and that all those which all creatures together can ever be able to give him do not come near to what are his due, we must also wish that he would love and praise himself as he deserves, because he only is able to do so.

Secondly, we must employ this time in producing acts of the love of God : because it is chiefly then we are to pour out our hearts in holy aspirations, which are nothing else but acts of love, and ardent desires of uniting ourselves to God. It is then we must say to him with the royal prophet, "O Lord, who art my strength, let me always love thee. (Ps. xvii. 1.) My soul continually pants after thee, O my God, as the hart, pursued by the hunters, pants after the fountains of waters. (Ps. xli. 1.)

We must in the third place, spend this time in begging favours of God ; because it is the fittest time to obtain them, and to despatch our affairs with him. The holy Scripture relates that queen Esther having something to beg of king Assuerus, she would not presently declare what it was, but only invited him to come and eat with her, reserving till then the explanation of what she desired of him. He came to her, and she obtained of him what she desired. It is thus in the holy banquet where the King of kings is our guest, or to say better, where we are his ; in which we shall obtain whatsoever we shall ask of him ; "because we are come upon a good day." (1 Kings xxv. 8.) And we may tell him what Jacob told the angel with whom he had wrestled all the night long, "I will not let thee go, till thou hast blessed me." (Gen. xxii. 26.) When you entered, O Lord, into the house of Zacheus, you said, "Salvation is this day given to this house." (Luke xix. 9.) Say now the same to this house, into which you are now entered : "Say to my soul, I am thy salvation. (Ps. xxxiv. 3.)

It is also then we must beg pardon of God for our sins, and at the same time, beg strength of him to overcome our passions ; to resist the devil's temptations ; and to give us the grace of gaining humility, obedience, patience, perseverance, and those other virtues which we stand most in need of. But we must ask them not only for ourselves, but pray also for the necessities of the church, as well in general as in particular ; and pray also for the pope, for the king, and for all those that govern the Christian commonwealth, either in spirituals or in temporals ; and for all those particular persons to whom we have any obligation ; as is practised in the "Memento" of the Mass, and as I shall hereafter speak of more at large.

CHAPTER VIII.

Another kind of thanksgiving.

SOME make their thanksgiving after communion in the following manner. They represent our Saviour within themselves, and summon all their powers and senses to come and acknowledge him as their king, and to make their homage and submission to him; just as one in the world, who receiving a great person to his house, would call all his relations together to salute him and pay him their respects. Afterwards on presenting each sense and power, they perform three things. The first is, to give thanks to God for this gift bestowed upon them. The second is, to accuse themselves for not having made so good use of it as they ought to have done. And the third is, to beg grace to make a better use of it for the future. This sort of thanksgiving may be very profitable, and is the first of those three methods of prayer which St. Ignatius sets down in the book of spiritual exercises.

Others consider all their powers and senses as so many sick, and at the same time looking upon our Saviour as a physician, "that cures all sorts of diseases," they bring him one after another unto him, as they would bring a sick person in the infirmary to the doctor, and say unto him, "Lord, come and see what ails me." (John xi. 34.) "Have pity upon me and my infirmity." (Ps. vi. 2.) "Heal my soul, which is sick, because I have sinned against thee." (Ps. xli. 5.) But it is to be noted, that at this time it is not necessary to imagine to ourselves any particular place, nor to seek abroad for one; because our Saviour is then present within us, not only as to his Divinity, which is always everywhere present; but also as to his sacred humanity, which is really within our breast, and remains there, so long as the sacramental species last—that is to say, for as long a time as the substance of bread would have remained, had it been there. For, if the beholding some image gives us recollection and devotion, what effect ought we not feel on beholding our Saviour himself, who in his own person is present within us. Wherefore let every one at this time look within himself, and behold his Saviour there, as the holy Virgin considered him within herself, when she carried him in her sacred womb—let him entertain himself with his beloved, and say with the spouse, "I have found him whom my soul loves; I hold him fast, and will not let him go." (Cant iii. 4.) Some divines hold an opinion which cannot but move us to employ more time than ordinary in our thanksgiving. They say, that as long as the sacramental species, and the presence of our Saviour remain within us, so long, if we make such acts as these, we receive the more grace; not only by reason of the merits of the acts, but by reason of the virtue of the sacrament, according to what I have already said, speaking of preparation for communion. Hereby we may see how ill they do who permit to be lost so precious a time, in which they may gain so much; and who have no sooner received within themselves so great a guest, but they turn their backs upon him, and as I may say, go out of one door at the same moment he enters at the other; or receive him in so cold a manner, as not to say any thing to him. If then in the world it would be to commit a great incivility to receive a person of quality into our house and to say nothing to him, nor make him any offer of service, what is it to use God after this manner?

Surius says, that as often as St. Margaret, daughter of the queen of Hungary, communicated, she fasted the day before on bread and water, by reason of that heavenly banquet she was to partake of the next day, and passed the whole night in prayer; and after she had communicated, she likewise passed in prayer the whole day till night, when she took something for her nourishment.

————o————

CHAPTER IX.

The fruit we ought to reap from holy communion.

It is not only to make us better understand the excellency of this adorable sacrament, and the excess of the love of God, who has instituted it, that the saints explain unto us its admirable virtues; but it is also that we should propose them to ourselves as the fruit we ought to reap from thence. For this reason, then, I will here set down some of them. This adorable sacrament has one virtue, in common with all the other sacraments, which is, to give grace to all who receive it worthily; but it has also another, which is proper to itself alone, and which distinguishes it from all others, and this virtue is called by divines spiritual reflection; because it serves for nourishment to the soul, to which it restores and gives force to resist all the attacks of the devil, and to embrace all kinds of virtue. Many saints, interpreting these words of our Saviour, "my flesh is meat indeed, and my blood is drink indeed (John vi. 56), say, that all which corporal food naturally works in us, this heavenly food also spiritually works in our souls. The Council of Florence says the same thing, and adds, that our Saviour vouchsafed to institute this sacrament under the species of food, in order that the species under which he instituted it might let us know the effects it produced, and the need we have of it for our souls. Wherefore, according to this doctrine, just as corporal nourishment sustains the life of the body, repairs its strength, and causes it to grow to such an age, till it comes to its full growth; even so this divine sacrament supports the spiritual life of the soul, repairs its loss of strength, gives it new force against temptations, and causes it to grow in virtue till it attains an entire perfection thereof. "It is this bread that confirms and fortifies the heart of man" (Ps. ciii. 15), with which being nourished, we come like Elias, "to have sufficient strength to walk as far as Horeb, the mountain of God. (3 Kings xix. 8.)

Corporal food has also another property, which is, that it is pleasing to our taste; and it is the more pleasing the more exquisite it is, and the better disposed our palates are. It is the same with this celestial food—it does not only sustain, preserve, and fortify, but it has also an admirable taste. It is this was signified by one of the prophetic blessings, which Jacob, upon his death-bed, gave his children, in which he announced what was to be fulfilled in the law of grace. For when he came to bless his son Aser—"the bread of Aser" says he, "shall be fat, and shall be the deliciousness of kings." (Gen. xlix. 20.) Jesus Christ is this bread; and "it is this bread," says St. Thomas, "that is filled with all sweetness; it is a feast in which spiritual sweetness is tasted in its source." Because the soul that receives Jesus Christ by means of this sacrament tastes spiritual sweetness in Jesus Christ, who is its source; and the sweetness is so great, that it sometimes communicates itself to the body, according to the words of David, "my heart and my flesh have exulted in the living God." (Ps. lxxxiii. 3.) From thence happens what St. Bonaventure makes mention of, that often he who feels himself extremely weak approaching to this table, does there find so much comfort and sweetness by means of this heavenly food, that he comes from it in such a disposition as if he had had before no weakness at all. Guimond, bishop of Aversan, in the kingdom of Naples, writes, that the ancient hermits found so much comfort and strength in receiving holy communion that some of them took no other nourishment; and, on the contrary, the day they did not communicate they felt such weakness and languor as if they had been ready to fall into a mortal swoon. He says, moreover, that there were some amongst them to whom an angel daily brought the holy host to their cell. As in the Chronicles of the Cistertian order there is mention made of a religious who never communicated but he felt such a sweetness after it as if he had eaten a honey-comb, which sweetness remained in his mouth for three days after. But according to what I have just now said of the admirable effects of this heavenly bread, the fruit we ought to reap from it is a masculine courage and resolution continually to advance in the way of God; and an unshaken steadiness and force in mortifying our passions, and in resisting the asaults of the devil; for "our Lord has prepared this table against all those that torment us." (Ps. xxii. 5.) And therefore St. Chrysostom says that, "being rendered terrible to the devil, we ought to rise from this table like lions whose eyes sparkle with fire." (Hom lxi.) Has not Jesus Christ himself sufficiently assured us of the force of this divine sacrament, when, immediately after he had communicated his disciples, he said to them, "arise, let us go from hence?" (John xiv. 31. Is it not the same as if he should have said, now you have communicated you have become strong, rise and let us go suffer? Do we not also perceive that in the primitive church, when they oftener received this adorable sacrament, the faithful had more strength not only to observe God's law, but to resist the rage and fury of tyrants, and courageously to offer up their lives for the faith of Jesus Christ.

---o---

CHAPTER X.

That frequent communion is a great remedy against all sorts of temptations, and that it helps it in a most particular manner to preserve chastity.

THE saints tell us, that to approach frequently the sacrament of the altar is a great remedy against all temptations; because, besides strengthening the soul and rendering us more prompt to do the will of God, it weakens also our passions and ill habits; and diminishes the fire of concupiscence, which is the root of all evils. St. Thomas says, that one of the reasons why it delivers us from temptations is, that hell being subdued by the death of our Saviour, and this sacrament being a representation thereof, the devils no sooner perceive his body and blood in us, but they presently fly from us, and give place to the angels, who assist and accompany us. St. Ignatius, the martyr, and St. Cyril, for this reason counsel us to communicate often, thereby to put the devils to flight. "For if in the old law," says St. Chrysostom, "the blood of the lamb sprinkled on the doors of the houses had power to deliver those that lived in them from the sword of the exterminating angel, what power ought not this sacrament have, of which the other was only a figure?"

But above all, the angels assure us, that it is a sovereign remedy against the temptations of impurity, "because it allays the motions of concupiscence, deadens the incentive to sin, and extinguishes the heat of sensuality," just as water extinguishes fire. This is the sense St. Jerome, St. Thomas, and many other saints give to this passage of Zachary, "what is there so beautiful as the bread of the elect, and the wine that makes virgins?" (Zach. ix. 17.) It is the property of this bread of angels, say they, to make virgins; and as corporal food, when it is good, produces good blood, and good humours; so this spiritual food produces in us chaste sentiments, and thoughts full of purity. This is the meal with which Elizeus took away all that bitterness that was in the meat they had served up to the children of the prophets. St. Cyril says, that this heavenly food not only sanctifies the soul, but even the body also; and it is for this reason that the church begs of God that the sacrifice of the mass "may conduce to the strength both of body and soul," and finds its petition entirely granted. As the Cananæn woman no sooner touched the garment of our Saviour but the bloody flux immediately stopped, with which she had been for so long a time before tormented; and as the waters of Jordan immediately stopped as soon as the ark entered into the river; so, as soon as our Saviour enters into us all our temptations are presently appeased, and the fire of concupiscence extinguished. "O happy fruit," cries out the holy man, "O fruit, bringing plenty, and producing virginity!" (Zach. ix. 17 "There is not a better remedy for chastity," says another author, "than a good and frequent use of communion." Nicephorus, Calixtus, and Gregory of Tours, relate a wonderful thing that happened at Constantinople, which excellently well declares, that the virtue of this sacrament extends itself to the body as well as to the soul. The custom of the Greek church being to consecrate in such kind of bread as we daily eat, the remainder of this bread, after the people had communicated, was given to those children that were fasting, that they might be the more used to it; and Nicephorus himself testifies, that when he was a child, it was several times given to him." (Evag. Eccl. Hist. l. iv. c. 35.) But it once happened that as they distributed those precious remains to the children that were in the church, a child of a Jew, a glassmaker, presented himself among the rest. This having kept him for some time in the church, he returned home later than ordinary, and his father asking him the reason hereof, he said he had been in the church of the Christians, and there had eaten some of the bread which they gave the children. This man fell presently into such a rage and passion with his son, that he immediately cast him into the glass furnace that was lighted, and shut the door of it. His mother, who had been in town, finding that her son had not returned home, and that his delay was much longer than usual, immediately sought everywhere about for him, and after a great deal of pains to no purpose, she returned home in deep desolation and affliction. At the end of three days, not being able to comfort herself for the loss of her child, and being near the door of the glass furnace, weeping, and tearing her hair, and calling upon her son by his name, she was astonished to hear him answer out of the furnace, where he was; she presently runs to open the door, full of hope and fear, and beholds her son coming from the midst of the flames, without being the least touched by them. She asked him what had preserved him from the fire? He answered, that a lady clad in purple had oftentimes assisted him, extinguishing the fire with water she cast upon it, and bringing him something to eat, as often as he wanted it; all this being told to the emperor Justinian, he caused the child and the mother to be baptized, who both desired to become Christians, and caused the unhappy father, who would never be converted, to be hanged upon a tree as a parricide. But what this holy host wrought upon the body of this child, preserving it in the midst of the flames, it works also spiritually upon the souls of those that worthily receive it, keeping them whole and entire, amidst the flames of concupiscence, and amidst all sorts of temptations.

CHAPTER XI.

Another fruit we ought to reap from communion, which is to unite
ourselves to Jesus Christ, and to transform ourselves into him.

ONE of the chief ends for which God instituted the holy Sacrament of the Eucharist, or perhaps even the very chief, was, as
the saints say, to unite himself to us, or to make us one and the
same thing with himself. For, as by virtue of the words of consecration, that which was before bread is changed into the proper
substance of Jesus Christ; so by virtue of holy communion, he
who before he received it, was man, is spiritually transformed
into God himself. This is what is expressed by the words of
Jesus Christ, related by St. John: "my flesh is truly meat, and
my blood is truly drink, he that eats my flesh and drinks my
blood remains in me and I in him." (John vi. 56.) And as by
means of natural heat the food which he takes becomes the same
substance as he who takes it, so here, by means of grace, he who
eats the bread of angels becomes the same thing with this celestial
bread, wherewith he is nourished. For, it is not the body of
Jesus Christ which is transformed into the substance of him that
receives it, but it is he that receives it who is transformed into
Jesus Christ. Jesus Christ, says St. Austin, " is the food of those
that are grown up. Grow up, therefore, and you shall eat him,
yet you shall not change him into yourself as you do the food
that you take, but you shall be changed into him." " It is also,"
says St. Thomas, " proper to this sacrament to transform man
into God, and to render him like to him; for, if fire has the
power to change all things into itself to which it is united, and
to communicate thereunto its form and perfection after it has
destroyed whatsoever is contrary to its nature, with how far
greater reason ought 'this all-consuming fire of the divinity'
(Deut. iv. 24), consume whatsoever impurity it finds in our
souls, and renders them like to itself?"

But setting apart at present the real and true union of Jesus
Christ with him who receives him, and coming to what concerns
the fruit we ought to reap from holy communion, I say that this
fruit consists in uniting ourselves spiritually to Jesus Christ, and
transforming ourselves unto him after the same manner. That
is to say, we must endeavour to render ourselves like him

through the whole course of our lives; to be humble as he was, patient, obedient, chaste, and poor like unto him : and it is this St. Paul recommends to us, in other words, when he says, " clothe yourselves with our Lord Jesus Christ (Rom. xiii. 14), clothe yourselves with the new man." (Eph. iv. 24.)   In consecration the substance of bread is converted into the substance of the body of Jesus Christ, and the accidents always remain the same; in communion it is quite the contrary, the substance of man remains the same, it is only the accidents that are changed.   He becomes humble who was before proud; he that was incontinent becomes chaste, and he who was peevish and choleric becomes meek and patient, and thus it is that he is spiritually transformed into Jesus Christ.

St. Cyprian, interpreting these words of the royal prophet, " my chalice which inebriates, how excellent it is ?" (Ps. xxii. 5) and applying them to the holy Eucharist, says, " that as drunkenness renders a man quite different from what he was, so this divine sacrament renders us quite different from ourselves by making us quite forget the things of the world, and elevating our minds to a commerce with those of heaven." (Ep. lxiii. ad Cœcil.)   How different did the disciples at Emmaus become from what they were before, after they had received this celestial bread from the hands of our Saviour himself ?   " They knew him then, whom they knew not before" (Luke xxiv. 35) ; and from inconstant, feeble, and timorous persons, they became firm, faithful, and courageous.   It is after this manner that holy communion " ought to change you into another man, into a perfect man ; that so they who live, live not to themselves, but live to him who died for them and is risen again to life." (2 Cor. v. 15.)

A holy virgin, St. Angela, says upon this subject what is very solid and spiritual.   She speaks of the marks by which we may know if we are transformed into God ; and says, "that one of these is to desire to be contemned by all the world, and to desire to be regarded by all the world as worthy of every contempt, and not to wish for the compassion of others, or to live in the esteem or in the heart of any one.   And, in fine, to advance so far as to desire that no one should, upon any account, have esteem for us, but take it for the greatest honour that can happen to us, to be contemned by all, that we may become more conformable to Jesus Christ, and count it 'a folly to glory in anything but in this cross.' " (Gal. vi. 14.)   It is thus that we ought to endeavour to be transformed into him, and this is the fruit we ought to reap from holy communion.

St. Chrysostom, speaking of the obligation imposed upon us of receiving this august sacrament—"when we shall feel ourselves," says he, "moved to choler, or to any other passion, let us think how great a good God has made us worthy to partake of, and this reflection will help us to suppress all sorts of irregular motions within ourselves. (Hom. i.) It is not just that the tongue which has touched the body of Jesus Christ should profane itself with vain, idle, and frivolous discourses—it ought to be sanctified ; it is not just that the heart which has received God himself, and is become, as it were, a ciborium or tabernacle of the precious body of Jesus Christ, should permit itself to be defiled with vain desires—it ought to desire God alone, and think upon nothing else but him. When you have received a lozenge into your mouth, you feel the odour and sweetness of it all the day after. This heavenly bread which you have eaten has an admirable perfume, it sends forth a most divine odour which you ought to preserve, and, therefore, you ought to breathe nothing but virtue and sanctity.

A holy virgin was wont to say that, as often as she communicated, she guarded all the avenues of her heart with more care than ordinary, representing Jesus Christ to herself in her heart as a lord and master that reposes in his own house. " Wherefore," adds she, " I then endeavour to preserve all possible modesty in my discourse, in my looks and gestures, and in all my exterior, like to a careful servant who puts his finger upon his mouth to give a sign that no noise is to be made for fear of waking his master."

———o———

CHAPTER XII.

Another fruit we ought to reap from holy communion, which is, to resign ourselves entirely into God's hands ; of the manner wherein we ought to prepare ourselves in order to obtain it ; and of the thanksgiving we ought afterwards to make.

ONE of the greatest fruits we should endeavour to reap from holy communion, is entirely to resign ourselves into God's hands, as a little earth into the hands of a potter, that he may dispose of us as he pleases, when he pleases, and in what manner he pleases, without any reserve or exception. The Son of God has entirely offered himself as a sacrifice for us to his Eternal Father, has shed all his blood for us upon the cross, and daily bestows upon us his soul, body, and blood, together with his Divinity, in the sacrament of the altar. Is it not, therefore, very just that we should also make an entire oblation of ourselves to him? To communicate properly is to communicate ourselves to God, as he has communicated himself to us. "He has communicated to us," says St. Austin, "all he has, communicate also to him all you have, and abandon yourself entirely to him." (De civit. Dei.)

According to this, the thanksgiving we ought to make after communion will be to say, "What shall I give unto God for all the benefits he has bestowed upon me?" (Ps. cxv. 3.) What shall I give him for the many graces I have received from him, and chiefly for this which I have just received? Would you know what he would have you give him? He would have you give him your heart. "My son," says he then to you, "give me thy heart" (Prov. xxiii. 26); "for," as he says in Thomas á Kempis, "what do I desire of you, but that you should give yourself entirely to me?" I make no account of anything you can give me besides yourself; I desire not your presents; that which I care for is yourself, and as nothing is able to satisfy you without me, so nothing also you can offer me is able to please me without you. St. Austin says that what made the sacrifice of Cain displeasing to God, and caused it to be less acceptable to him than that of Abel, was because Cain did not make such a division with God as he should have done, "and that giving something of his own to God, he still gave himself entirely to himself." (De civit. Dei. c. 7.) "It is this," says the holy father, "that some still do, who offer something to God, without offering their will and their heart. 'The kingdom of heaven,'" adds he, "requires no other price than yourself, you alone can be the price of it; give, therefore, yourself, and you shall have it."

It is, then, in this entire resignation of ourselves into the hands of God in which we ought to exercise ourselves after holy communion, and this ought not to be done in a general manner only, but we must descend to particulars, resigning and conforming ourselves to his will in all occasions, as well in sickness as in health, in death as in life, in affliction and sufferings as well as in joy and consolation. We must, also, then, specify those things to which we shall feel the greatest repugnance, and offer them to God in our thanksgiving after communion, running over the most abject offices and employments, and the most troublesome occasions we can meet with, till nothing represent itself in which we find not an entire conformity of our will to that of God. The prayer which St. Ignatius puts in the spiritual exercise is very proper for this subject, and therefore I shall here set it down. "Receive, O Lord, my entire liberty, receive my memory, my understanding, and my whole will. All that I have, all that I possess, thou hast given me: I restore it again to thee, and leave it to the entire disposal of thy will. Give me only thy love and thy grace, I shall be rich enough, I will ask nothing else but this of thee." (Punct. i.) We must also afterwards exercise ourselves in producing some acts of virtue, and chiefly of those which each one knows himself to stand most in need of, for whatever we can desire we shall find it in this heavenly manna, "which has the excellency of all sorts of taste." (Wisd. xvi. 20.) It has the taste of all sorts of virtues, and, therefore, we may exercise ourselves in producing their acts, sometimes of one virtue, sometimes of another, imagining and having always before our eyes such as we know ourselves to stand most in need of. If you find, for example, that you have a particular want of humility, seek there for humility, and you will, without doubt, find a great model thereof, since the Son of God is there clothed with the accidents of bread, which, being but simple accidents, are more vile than those rags and swaddling clothes in which the holy Virgin wrapped him when he came into the world. What can be conceived more humble than a God hid under the species of bread, that we may touch him, eat him, and receive him into our mouth and stomach? What a debasement is this for a God? And how great an elevation is this for man? His humility seems in some measure to shine more bright here than in the mystery of the incarnation. Exercise yourself, therefore, in producing acts of this virtue, till you find that you have entirely penetrated your soul therewith. Offer to God in thanksgiving both the contempt and the esteem of the world, and embrace with joy for love of him all occasions of being contemned.

It will also be very well done to descend to certain details of things, which though they may appear small to others, yet fail not oftentimes to give us an occasion of a great deal of pain and trouble, and these we may in like manner offer to God in thanksgiving. Every one knows very well what those imperfections are to which he is most subject, and which more particularly hinder his advancement in perfection. Endeavour to make a sacrifice of some of these to God in each communion, and offer up this also for your thanksgiving after communion. You love, for example, your ease and convenience, and to be in want of nothing, offer to God to mortify yourself in this to-day in one thing, and to-morrow in another. You love to indulge in speaking idle and unprofitable words, and therein to lose your time, mortify yourself herein, and offer this to God in another communion. You are so attached to your own will that your brethren suffer a great deal from you, because you will mortify yourself in nothing, and sometimes you speak to them in a smart and peevish manner, endeavour to overcome yourself in this, and offer it to God in another communion. In fine, as I have said, speaking of prayer, it would be very good therein to propose to one's self to do something that very day; it will be good also at each communion to resolve to mortify and overcome one's self that day in some particular thing, and to offer this mortification to God by way of thanksgiving. Bear in mind, it is chiefly this that God requires of you for this favour he has done you, for he desires nothing else of you but that you would correct in yourself what you know to be displeasing to him, so that this is the best thanksgiving we can make after communion, and the most agreeable service we can render unto him. But since thanksgiving, as I said in another place, may be made three ways ; first, by an interior acknowledgment of the benefits we have received ; secondly, by thanks and praises to God ; and, thirdly, by effects, which is the most perfect of all, and of which I now speak ; do not, therefore, so employ the whole time of your meditation that there be none left for anything else. Meditations are good, but resolutions and the effects thereof are far better, and it is only in order to compass these that we ought to meditate.

What I say here of thanksgiving I say also of preparation for communion, for though the meditation we are wont then to make upon the sacred mystery of the Eucharist be a kind of profitable preparation, and though the respect we ought to have for this adorable mystery requires that we should always perform it with all possible application, yet the best and most perfect preparation is that of a good life ; it is to endeavour every day to correct ourselves ; it is daily to perfect ourselves more and more, that hereby we may approach this august sacrament with greater purity. " Live in such nanner," says St.

Ambrose and St. Austin, "that you may deserve to communicate every day." (Amb. l. V. de Sacr. Aug. serm. viii. in Luc.) Father Avila, writing upon this subject to one of his friends, says, that regularity in the whole conduct of our lives is a true preparation for communion, and he cites to this purpose the example of a servant of God who was wont to say, I do not do this particularly to prepare myself for communion, because I keep myself daily prepared for it as well as I can. It is, without doubt, far better to prepare ourselves in this manner than to recollect ourselves only for a quarter of an hour before or after communion, and afterwards to remain in as great tepidity of heart and in as great an immortification of spirit as before.

This, therefore, is the best preparation before, and the best thanksgiving after communion; and this also ought to be the principal advantage we should propose to ourselves to derive from it. For as in prayer, the mortification of our passions, the recollection of our senses, and the guard of our heart, ought to be no less the chief preparation for prayer than the fruit we ought to reap from it, and that they ought reciprocally promote one the other; so here, in like manner, the sanctity of our lives, and an application always to do everything in the best manner we can to please God, is the chief preparation for holy communion, and the chief fruit we ought to propose to ourselves to reap from it. The one ought to help the other, and each communion ought to be a preparation for another. Moreover, as perfection and the fruit of prayer consist not in having sensible comforts, nor in being raised to high contemplations, but in going from prayer more humble, more mortified in our senses, and less attached to our own will; so the mark of a good communion, and of the fruit we are to reap from it, is not to have made a great many holy meditations, nor to have had great consolations, but to become more mortified in our passions, and more submissive and resigned to the will of God.

Hence, one thing follows, which ought to be a comfort to all the world, which is, that it is in our power always to make a good communion, and to derive great advantage from it. For, to abandon ourselves entirely into the hands of God, to mortify ourselves, and to correct those faults we know are displeasing to him, is always in our power, through the assistance of God's infinite mercy. Apply then yourself to do this, and you will reap precious fruit from communion. Endeavour to overcome yourself, to become more mortified, and daily to correct some

fault or other. Cause the idol of Dagon to fall before the Ark
of the alliance; break in pieces the idol of pride, of vanity, and
of self-love. What progress should we not make in a short time,
if every time we communicated, we should take care to mortify
ourselves in something, and to correct in ourselves, now one
fault, now another?

To the subject I speak of, St. Jerome applies what the Wise
man says of the courageous woman: "she seriously considered
every corner of her house, and would not eat her bread in idleness." (Prov. xxxi. 27.) This careful search, according to his
explanation, is the examen and preparation which ought to
precede communion, and not to eat bread in idleness, is, not to
communicate unprofitably. "When one becomes better," he
says, "by the communions he makes, he eats not his bread
unprofitably, because this heavenly bread has produced such good
in him; but unhappy are you who have so unprofitably eaten
your bread for so many years! You have overcome yourself in
nothing—you have mortified yourself in nothing—you have not
overcome so much as one of those faults you were wont to commit. It is a sign, therefore, that you are sick, since what you
eat does you no good. Let not the like happen henceforward.
Let every one enter into himself; let him view the recesses of
his heart; let him see what passion and fault—what inclination
is the greatest obstacle to his salvation and perfection, and then
endeavour to overcome them, and to do it in so efficacious a
manner, that he may say with the apostle, 'I live indeed, but it
is not I who live, but Jesus Christ who lives in me.'" (Gal. ii.
20.) "That is," says St. Jerome, "he lives not now as he lived
before in the darkness of the old law, and as one who persecuted
the church; but Jesus Christ lives in him: that is to say, wisdom
lives in him, fortitude, the word of God, peace, joy, and all other
virtues, without which no one can say that it is Jesus Christ that
lives in him."

———o———

CHAPTER XIII.

*Whence it is that many persons who often approach the sacrament
of the Eucharist feel not those wonderful effects which it ordinarily works.*

SOME may perhaps object that since this august sacrament works
such wonderful effects, and bestows such great favours and

graces, how comes it to pass, that many priests who daily celebrate, and divers other persons who very often communicate, do
not only not experience those spiritual sweetnesses which I
have spoken of, but even make no progress at all in virtue, and
remain always in the same state and condition? Some answer
this, by quoting the proverb, which says, "too much familiarity
begets contempt"—imagining that the reason when they approach
not this table with sufficient preparation and respect, is, because
they approach it too often. But in this they deceive themselves;
for as far as it regards spiritual things, and a commerce with
God, their objection is unfounded. Nay, it is asserted that as
far as it regards familiarity with even wise men, this objection
holds not. For the more familiar we are with them, the more
we discover their merits, and consequently the greater esteem
we have for them. But I am of opinion that this proverb is
true in regard of even the wisest men; for, as there is no one so
perfect but has some defects, so it may very well happen that
by familiar conversation we come to discover these defects, and
consequently to conceive less esteem for these men. But though
this proverb is true, inasmuch as it regards our commerce with
man, it is not so inasmuch as it regards our commerce with God.
This is experienced by the angels and blessed souls who perfectly
know him in heaven, and who continually see him. It is also
experienced here below by those who particularly give themselves to spirituality and prayer. This truth is very well proved
in the story of the Samaritan woman, and in the different ways
she spoke to the Saviour of the world in the conversation she
had with him. "How comes it to pass," says she, "that thou
who art a Jew, shouldst ask of me to drink, who am a Samaritan
woman?" (John iv. 9, &c.) She first calls him by the general
name of his nation, and treats him as an ordinary person; but a
little while after she calls him Lord, saying, "Lord, give me of
this water;" afterwards in the same conversation she calls him
prophet; "I see," says she, "that thou art a prophet;" and,
lastly, she acknowledges him for Christ and for the Messias.
The frequenting of the sacraments produces the like effect, and
one communion is a preparation for another, and it is an error to
imagine, that by going seldom to this table we prepare ourselves
with more care and respect. St. Austin and St. Ambrose therefore had great reason to say, "that he who deserves not to receive
daily the body of Jesus Christ, deserves not to receive it even at
the year's end."

But now, to answer the objection made in the beginning, I say
in the first place, that it is our own fault if the frequent use of
communion produces not always in us all the fruit it ought.
We do not prepare ourselves properly; we approach the altar
out of custom, and in a negligent manner; we communicate
because others do so; and because we are accustomed to communicate. We think not beforehand of what we are about to
do, or make not sufficient reflection on it. These are the reasons
why we derive so little profit from it; and, hence, when we
perceive that we are not benefited by our frequent communions,
we must examine if this proceeds from want of due preparation,
and if we find it to be so, we must apply the proper remedy.
This evil sometimes proceeds from our too willingly permitting
ourselves to commit venial sins. For there are two sorts of
venial sins; the first are those we fall into by inadvertence,
though they are always accompanied with negligence and want
of care; the others are such as we commit voluntarily and deliberately. Those into which the true servants of God fall, through
inadvertence or want of reflection, by no means impede the grace
of the sacrament; but such faults as the tepid and those who are
negligent in the service of God commit, with full deliberation,
are a very great obstacle to it. The same may be said of the
faults a religious voluntarily commits against his rules; and the
conduct which God observes herein towards us, whether it be in
communion or in prayer, is similar to what a father does when
he sees anything amiss in his son; for he immediately frowns upon
him in order to correct him of his fault, and to prevent a repetition
of it. So that if we wish to partake of that abundance of grace
enjoyed by those who approach this holy table as they ought, we
must abstain from committing the least voluntary fault. Let
such souls as fear God take good notice of this, for it is the most
effectual means to induce God to shower down his gifts and
graces upon them.

Secondly, I say, it may often happen, that though we be
guilty of no fault, yet we *feel* not the admirable effects of holy
communion, and likewise though we *feel* them not, yet we really
receive all the fruits of the sacrament. The same happens here
as in prayer, on which subject many make a similar complaint.
For though we feel not the sweetness and comforts which we
desire, and which we have at other times felt, yet we must not
doubt but we still reap fruit from it. A sick person finds no
taste in the food he receives, yet, notwithstanding, it ceases not

to nourish and support him, and to do him good. These sweetnesses and sensible comforts are graces which God bestows when
and as he thinks fit, and when he deprives his servants of them
it is to try them, it is to humble them, and to draw from this
circumstance other benefits and advantages which are known to
himself. Add to this, that this divine sacrament oftentimes
works in so secret a manner that it is scarce perceivable, because
grace ordinarily works by little and little, and very insensibly.
We do not perceive a plant grow, but we see very well that it
is grown; and, therefore, St. Laurence Justinian says, "that as
corporal food nourishes a man, and makes him grow, though he
perceives it not, so this heavenly food sustains and fortifies the
soul by the increase of grace, though we do not perceive it."

Lastly, I answer, that we ought to esteem it a benefit not
only to make progress, but also not to fall, or go back in virtue.
The remedies which prevent diseases are not less esteemed than
those which establish health. And let us here take notice, since
it is a great subject of comfort to those who perceive not so sensibly the fruit which this divine sacrament produces in them,
that we see ordinarily that those who often approach this sacrament live in the fear of God, and pass whole years, nay, sometimes, their whole lives, without committing one mortal sin.
Now, one of the effects of this sacrament is to hinder us from
falling into mortal sin, and to preserve in us the life of our soul,
as corporal food preserves the life of the body; wherefore the
Council of Trent calls it "an antidote by which we are delivered
from our daily faults, and preserved from mortal sins." (Sess.
13.) So that, though in receiving it we feel neither that fervour
of devotion, nor those ineffable sweetnesses of which I have
spoken; and that afterwards, instead of that ardour and promptitude which some then feel, we find ourselves in dryness and
tepidity; yet, notwithstanding, we fail not to reap fruit from it.
And if communicating frequently we fall into some faults, we
should fall into far greater if we abstained from communion. In
fine, let us endeavour, on our part, as far as it depends upon us,
to approach this holy table with the disposition and respect I
have mentioned, and infallibly we shall receive extreme profit by
approaching it very often. We read that Widikend, duke of
Saxony (Timal. Brend. I. I. collat. c. ii. Hist. Eccl.), being still
a pagan, and waging war against Charlemagne, had a great curiosity to see what passed in the camp of the Christians, and for
this purpose he disguised himself in the habit of a pilgrim.

This happened at Easter, when the whole Christian army made their devotions. Entering the camp, he saw and admired the ceremonies of the sacrifice of mass ; but what surprised him most was, that he saw in every host, with which the priest communicated the people, an infant of admirable beauty, all shining with light, which seemed to enter into the mouth of some with extreme joy, and made a difficulty to enter into the mouths of others. This miraculous vision, wherein he had been first instructed, was the reason why he afterwards embraced the Christian religion, and caused all his subjects to do the same. Another thing much like to this, is related of a great servant of God, and this second example may serve as a good exposition of the first.—(An example of Henry of Grenade upon the Eucharist, cited by the Doctor Santore in his fourth book of Sermons, or Spir. Meadow, c. 100.) This man, as he one day heard the mass of a secular priest, perceived that at the consumption, instead of the species of bread, he saw a most beautiful infant upon the paten, and perceived that as the priest was going to communicate, the infant turned its head, and struggling with its hands and feet, did what it could to hinder the priest from receiving it. He had afterwards several times the same vision, and the same priest one day discoursing with him, and telling him that as often as he received the body of our Saviour, he felt it very difficult to do so, and knew not the cause thereof ; whereupon the servant of God took occasion to discover to him what he had seen, and counselled him to think upon his conscience, and to amend his life. The priest being touched with this advice, changed his life, and a little while after the same servant of God, hearing again his mass, perceived the same infant in his hand at the consumption, and saw him enter into the mouth of the priest with a great deal of promptitude and alacrity.

———o———

CHAPTER XIV.

Of the holy sacrifice of the Mass.

HAVING already spoken of the sacrament of the altar, and of its effects as a sacrament, I shall now speak of it as a sacrifice. The Council of Trent orders preachers and pastors of souls carefully to explain this to the people, that all may know how great a treasure God has left to his church, and that in consequence each may derive greater advantages from it. From the beginning of the world, at least from the date of sin, and even from that of the law of nature, there were always sacrifices; and it was always necessary they should be, both to appease God, and to give honour to his greatness and infinite majesty. Hence in the old law God instituted priests and sacrifices, but as this law was imperfect so were the sacrifices also; for neither the priesthood of Aaron, nor the victims who were offered by him, were capable of sanctifying the people or of blotting out their sins. " For it is impossible," says the apostle, "that sin should be blotted out with the blood of bulls or goats." (Heb. x. 4.) Wherefore it was necessary there should come another priest of the order of Melchisedech, and that he should offer another sacrifice, that should be capable both of appeasing God and of sanctifying men, and this priest is Jesus Christ, who offers himself for them to his Father. St Austin says that all the sacrifices of the old law were only a shadow or figure of this; and as we can express one and the same thing in different terms, and in different tongues, so this only and true sacrament was figured by this multitude of sacrifices in the old law. " And God," says this holy doctor, " ordained them in so great a number, as well to make a great impression upon our mind by the number, as to take away by this variety the disgust and tediousness which the frequent repetition of the same thing is wont to excite. He ordained, moreover," adds the doctor, "that they should offer beasts without spot, to give us to understand, that as victims ought not to have any spots that were offered to him, so it behoved him who came to offer himself in sacrifice for us, to be exempt from all kind of sin. But if these sacrifices were then agreeable to God, as without doubt they were, yet they were so because by them it was acknowledged that there was to come a Saviour, who should himself become the true sacrifice. For as soon as our Saviour was come, they became displeasing to God, as St. Paul takes notice in these words to the Hebrews, " wherefore entering into the world," he said, " thou wouldst not have victim or offering, but thou hast fitted me with a body. The sacrifices of propitiation for sins are no longer pleasing to thee; and then I said, behold ! I come, according as it is written of me, in the beginning of the book, that I may do thy will, O my God." (Heb. x. 5.) God gave a body to his only Son, that he might do the will of his Father, by offering himself in sacrifice upon the cross for us; and immediately all the shadows and figures disappeared, on the coming of what they figured, and the ancient sacrifices ceased to be any longer pleasing to God.

Now this is the sacrifice which we have in the law of grace, and which is daily offered at mass. The only begotten Son of God is himself our sacrifice. " He offered himself for us to God to be an oblation and a victim of sweet odour." (Eph. v. 28.) These are not holy thoughts, such as meditation furnishes, but are real truths, taught by faith. It is true that mass is a commemoration and representation of the death of Jesus Christ, as is signified by these words of our Saviour, " do this in remembrance of me" (Luke xxii. 19); but it is true likewise that it is not only a commemoration and representation of the sacrifice, in which he offered himself upon the cross to his Eternal Father for our sins, but it is the same sacrifice that was then offered, and of the same value and merit. Nay, more, it is not only the same sacrifice, but he who offers it now at mass is the same who heretofore offered it upon the cross. So that in the passion he was both priest and sacrifice; he is still upon our altars, the sacrifice and priest, who offers up himself to his Eternal Father, by the ministry of priests. He that says mass does nothing else but represent the person of Jesus Christ. It is in his name, and as his minister, that he offers this sacrifice; and the words of consecration are a proof of this truth. For he says not, " this is the body of Jesus Christ," but he says, " this is my body," as speaking in the person of Jesus Christ, who is the high priest that offers this sacrifice. Hence the royal prophet and the apostle St. Paul style him, " priest for ever according to the order of Melchisedech." (Ps. cix. 4; Heb. vii. 17.) Now it would be improper to call him "priest for ever" if he had offered sacrifice but once; because he is very justly called so, because in effect he offers a perpetual sacrifice to God, and will never cease to offer it to the end of the world. " Such a priest as this," says St. Paul, " we ought to have, who was holy, innocent, without spot, separated from sinners, and elevated above the heavens; who did not stand in need, as other priests do, to offer victims for his own sins, and afterwards for the sins of the people;" but " who during his life in the flesh, having with cries and tears offered prayers and supplications to him who could save him from death, was heard for his own consideration." (Heb. vii. 26.) We stood in need of a priest who would be able to appease the wrath of God, not by blood of victims, as ordained by the old law, but by his own blood, and his own death and passion.

Let us here at present consider the wonderful wisdom of those means which God has taken for the salvation of men, and which he has taken to render this sacrifice pleasing to God in every respect. For there are four things chiefly to be considered in a sacrifice, as St. Austin justly observes, viz., the person to whom it is offered; he who offers it; what is offered; and for whom it is offered. The infinite wisdom of God has here disposed things in such a manner that he who offers this sacrifice to reconcile us to God is the same with him to whom it is offered; nay, more, it is he himself who is the sacrifice; and, in fine, he is so united to those for whom he offered it, that he is the same with them also. This sacrifice is likewise of so great a price and value that it has not only sufficiently satisfied the Eternal Father for our sins and for those of the whole world, according to the words of St. John, "he is the propitiation for our sins; and not only for ours but for those of the whole world" (1 John ii. 2), but it would be sufficient to satisfy for the sins of a million of worlds. It is not only a sufficient satisfaction, as the divines and saints say, but it is a superabundant compensation; it is a payment that far exceeds the debt; it is a reparation of honour which pleases the Eternal Father far more than the offence displeased him. So that as Jesus Christ is at the same time the sacrifice and the person who offers it, the sacrifice loses nothing of the value and merit by being offered by the hands of a wicked priest, and ceased not to be always alike profitable to those for whom it is offered; just as an alms, which though you distribute it by the hands of a wicked man, yet would not be the less good, nor less meritorious in your behalf. "This sacrifice," says the Council of Trent, "is the same with that which heretofore was offered upon the cross: it is the same host, and he who offered himself then is the same who now daily offers himself by the hands of the priest. It is only the manner of offering which is different" (Sess xxii.), and this difference consists in this, that the sacrifice of the cross was "a bloody one." For then Jesus Christ was passible and mortal, and what is now daily offered upon our altars, "is unbloody;" because "Jesus Christ being raised from death can die no more, and death has now no more power or dominion over him." (Rom. vi. 9.) Now the Saviour of the world, says the council, having offered himself a sacrifice for us upon the cross, was not content that this sacrifice should end there; but because he was "priest for ever," he ordained that this sacrifice should for ever continue in the church, and as he was priest "according to the order of Melchisedech" (Ps. cix.), who offered to God bread and wine in sacrifice, he ordained that this sacrifice also should be offered under the species of bread and wine. Wherefore, "the same night in which he was betrayed, he took bread," says the apostle, "and giving thanks to God, he broke it and gave it to his disciples." (1 Cor. xi. 23.) At the very time that men sought to put him to death he sought to give them life; and to adapt it to their capacities he vouchsafed to leave to his spouse, the visible church, a visible sacrifice; which should not only represent to us, and put us in mind of the bloody sacrifice of the cross, but should also have the same virtue for the remission of our sins, and for our reconciliation with God, and which in effect should be the same sacrifice. Wherefore he consecrated his precious body and blood under the species of bread and wine, converting the bread into his body, and the wine into his blood, and under these species he offered himself to his Eternal Father. It was then, say the doctors, that the first mass was celebrated, and it was then also that he consecrated his disciples priests of the new testament, and by these words, "Do this in memory of me" (Luke xxii. 19), he then commanded them, and their successors in the priesthood, to offer this adorable sacrifice. Hence some look upon the Feast of the Blessed Sacrament as the greatest of all those the church celebrates. For all the rest are only a representation and a commemoration of the mysteries, either of the incarnation, of the nativity, of the resurrection, or of the ascension, upon which feasts the Son of God does not make himself man again, nor begin anew his birth, nor raise himself anew, nor mount again to heaven; but the Feast of the Blessed Sacrament is not a simple commemoration and representation of this adorable mystery, but it is, in effect, a renovation of it, as often as the priest says the words of consecration; and the same sacrifice which was offered when Jesus Christ died for us upon the cross is daily renewed upon our altars.

Let us here consider how great the love of Jesus Christ was for man, and how much we are indebted to him. For he is not content to offer himself once a sacrifice for our sins upon the cross; but he vouchsafed to remain here below, to be offered in sacrifice, not only once, but as often as we wish—even every day to the end of the world, that we might have in him the most pleasing sacrifice that we could ever offer to his Eternal Father for our sins, and the most valuable present we could make

to appease him.   What would become of Christians without this
sacrifice of propitiation ?   " We should be treated as Sodom and
Gomorrah" (Isai. i. 9.), and God would have punished us before
this according as our sins have deserved.   The property of this
sacrifice is to appease God, and it is this the apostle expresses by
these words, "he offered himself to God for us, to be a victim
of an agreeable sweetness." (Eph. v. 2.)   For as amongst men
the consideration of a service or present obtains the pardon of an
injury, so here the consideration of the present we make to God,
and of the sacrifice we offer to him is sufficient to appease him,
and to induce him to look upon us with eyes of mercy.   Had
you been at the foot of the cross, at the death of our Saviour,
and that some drops of his most precious blood had fallen upon
you, what comfort would you not have felt in your soul, and
what hope of salvation would you not conceive in consequence ?
A miserable wretch, the occupation of whose whole life was robbery, felt himself so filled with confidence at this sight, that on a
sudden, from a public robber, he became a saint, and from the
cross upon which he was nailed, he raised himself to the enjoyment of everlasting glory.   Now the same Son of God, who then
offered himself for us upon the cross, still daily offers himself for
us upon the altars, and the sacrifice which daily is offered in our
churches is of as great price, and of as great virtue, as that which
was consummated upon Mount Calvary.   Hence, the church is
accustomed to say, " that the work of our redemption is as often
performed as we celebrate the commemoration of this victim'
(In orat. secr. Dom. ix. post. Pent.), the fruits and graces of the
blood sacrifice of the cross communicating themselves unto us
by the unbloody sacrifice of the mass.

Moreover, this sacrifice is of such inestimable value that it
cannot be offered but to God alone, as is remarked by the Council
of Trent, which says, that though it is the custom to say mass in
honour of the saints, yet it is not to the saints this sacrifice is
offered.   For the priest says not, " I offer to you, St. Peter, or
I offer to you, St. Paul; but only, I offer to thee, O Lord."
Rendering thanks to God for those crowns and victories which
the saints have obtained by the assistance of his grace, and
begging their protection, "that those whose memory we celebrate on earth would vouchsafe to intercede for us in heaven."

So that this adorable mystery is both a sacrament and a sacri
fice at the same time, though there is a great difference between
the qualities of a sacrifice and of a sacrament.   Is is a sacrifice

because it is offered to God by the priest who consecrates at mass; the essence of this sacrifice, according to all divines, consisting in the consecration of the body of Jesus Christ under the two species, and in the oblation which the priest makes of them; and the same words of consecration which produce the sacrifice serve also to make the oblation thereof. As the bloody sacrifice, which Jesus Christ offered for us upon the cross to his Eternal Father was entirely accomplished at the same instant that our Saviour rendered up the ghost: so the sacrifice of mass, which is a true representation of that of the cross, and is in effect the same, is essentially consummated the same instant that the priest has pronounced the last words of consecration upon the bread and wine. For then, in virtue of these words, the body of Jesus Christ is in the host, and his blood in the chalice, and the consecration of the chalice being immediately made after that of the host, is a lively representation of the effusion of the blood of Jesus Christ upon the cross, and of the separation of his body and soul which followed this effusion. But after the consecration, and so long afterwards as the species of bread and wine shall remain—when it reposes in the tabernacle—when it is carried to sick persons, and when it is received at the holy table, it is then a sacrament only, and has not either the quality or virtue of a sacrifice. It is likewise to be observed that, inasmuch as it is a sacrament like the other sacraments, it is salutary to him that receives it, and confers grace and the other advantages that are particularly annexed to this sacrament. But, inasmuch as it is a sacrifice, it helps to salvation not only the priest who receives it, but also all those for whom it is offered. It is this the Council of Trent declares, when it says, "that Jesus Christ instituted this divine mystery for two ends: the one to serve as nourishment to the soul in quality of a sacrament, and to maintain, fortify, repair, and renew in it the life of the spirit; the other end is, that the church might have a perpetual sacrifice to offer to God in satisfaction for our offences, and in acknowledgment and thanksgiving for the graces and benefits we have received, and to obtain of him a remedy for our weakness, and his help and assistance both in general and particular necessities. But it is not only to the living this sacrifice is salutary, it is so to those likewise who died in the grace of God, and who expiate their sins in purgatory. Nay, more, as the priest in saying mass offers the sacrifice for himself and others, even so, those who are present at it may also offer it with him for themselves and for others. For as, when a city sends a present to a prince by its deputies, all the inhabitants have their share in the offer of the present, though there be but one of them who speaks on the occasion; in like manner, in the sacrifice of mass, though there be none but the priest who speaks and offers the sacrifice, yet all present fail not to have their share in it. It is true that with regard to the deputies of a city, each of them might speak, though there be but one elected to do so. But here it is not the same; because it belongs only to the priest, who is chosen by God, to consecrate and celebrate; but this does not prevent those who assist at this adorable sacrifice from offering it up with him. It is this precisely the priest says in the words of the offertory, pray, my brethren, that mine and your sacrifice may be pleasing in the sight of God the Father omnipotent;" and in those other prayers of the canon of mass "for whom we offer this sacrifice, or for those who offer it unto thee." This consideration ought to be a powerful motive to excite all men to assist at mass; and it is of this I shall speak more particularly in the following chapter.

———o———

CHAPTER XV.

How we are to hear Mass.

FROM what has been already said, I feel in some degree bound to speak of the manner of hearing mass. I shall, therefore, speak of three things in particular which are to be done during mass, and which we ought to do with due respect, since it is the church itself that proposes them unto us. First, we must suppose that mass, as I have already said, is a representation of the death and passion of Jesus Christ, who wishes hereby to remind us of his love and sufferings, in order to excite us to love and serve him with more fervour, and to prevent us from being guilty of an ingratitude similar to that of the Hebrews, " who forgot the God who had saved them." (Ps. cv. 21.)

Now, according to this, one of the wonderful things which we ought to apply ourselves to in time of mass is, to consider with attention the mysteries of the passion, which are therein represented unto us, and by this view to excite ourselves to produce acts of the love of God, and to make a firm resolution of serving him; but as to understand all the things that are said or done in mass will extremely contribute hereunto, it is proper to explain here beforehand what they signify, that this knowledge may induce us to meditate more deeply on the holy mysteries they represent; for there is not one word said in mass, nor even the least action or ceremony, but indicates something holy and mysterious; nay, even the ornaments which the priest wears at the altar have also a mysterious signification. The Amice, which is a piece of linen cloth that he puts about his neck, and which covers his shoulders, represents the veil with which the soldiers covered the face of the Son of God, when, striking him, they said to him, " prophesy who it is that struck thee." (Luke xxii. 6.) The Alb signifies the white robe which Herod, in mockery, caused to be put upon him, when he sent him back to Pilate. The Cincture represents the cords with which he was bound when he was apprehended in the garden, and the whips with which he was torn by command of Pilate. The Maniple signifies the cords with which he was bound to the pillar in the judgment-hall, this he puts upon the left arm, which is next the heart, to signify that it was the excess of his love that made Christ suffer this cruel flagellation for our sins, and that we ought to correspond to this love by all the tenderness our heart is capable of. The Stole represents the cord which they cast about his neck when he carried the cross. The Chasuble, or Vestment, according to some, was the purple robe which they put upon him to scoff him, or, according to others, the tunic, or coat without seam, which they stripped him of to crucify him. The entrance of the priest into the sacristy to put on the ornaments, represents the descent of the Son of God into the womb of the holy Virgin, where he clothed himself with our flesh and with our humanity, to go and celebrate the sacrifice upon the cross. The choir that sings the Introit when the priest goes out of the sacristy, represents the ancient patriarchs who expected the coming of the Messias, and who begged him of God in these words: " Send, O Lord, the Lamb, governor of the earth" (Isai. xvi. 1), " O that thou wouldst break through the heavens and descend!" (Isai. lxiv. 1.) And they repeat the second time the Introit, to mark the holy impatience they were in, and the frequent prayers they made to God upon this subject. The " Confiteor," which the priest afterwards says as a sinful man, signifies that Jesus Christ has vouchsafed to charge himself with our sins and to satisfy for them, and that he would appear a sinner, and be considered as such, that we might become just and holy; and the " Kyrie

Eleison," which signifies "Lord, have mercy upon us," represents the miserable state which we were in before the coming of our Saviour. It would be too long to set down in particular the signification of each word and ceremony, but, in fine, there is not one but indicates some mystery; for example, the many signs of the cross which the priests make upon the host and the chalice, signify the many sufferings of Jesus Christ upon the cross. The elevation which is made of the host and chalice at consecration, that the people may adore the body and blood of the Son of God, is, besides that, made to represent what the Jews did when they elevated the cross of our Saviour to expose him to the view of all the people. Every one, according to his own choice, may apply himself to consider one or two of these mysteries, according to the idea we have now given of them; but above all, we must endeavour to render this meditation profitable by exciting ourselves as much as we can to correspond to the love and benefits of the Son of God, which will be far more profitable than to pass over many mysteries slightly. Behold, therefore, the first exercise of devotion to which we may apply ourselves in time of mass.

The second exercise of devotion and the second manner of hearing mass is also very apposite and profitable, and the better to comprehend what it is, we must suppose two things which we have already stated in the foregoing chapter. The first is, that mass is not only a commemoration and representation of the passion of Jesus Christ, and of the sacrifice in which he offered himself upon the cross to his Eternal Father for our sins, but that this is really the same sacrifice that was then offered, and is of the same virtue, efficacy, and value. The second, that though there is only the priest that speaks in the sacrifice, and that it is he only that offers it, yet all those who assist at mass offer it in union with him. This being so, I say that the best way of hearing mass is to unite ourselves with the priest in the sacrifice, and to endeavour to follow and imitate him in all he does, thinking with ourselves what is very true that then we are all assembled in the church not only to hear mass, but also jointly to offer with the priest the adorable sacrifice of the body and blood of Jesus Christ. Hence, in order that the people may dispose themselves for it, as the priest does with all the preparation that the church commands, the priest is ordered to pronounce, with a distinct and audible voice, all that regards this preparation, and this is so prudently arranged, that all that is done in it, and all that is said in it, is only to dispose the priests and assistants to offer this adorable sacrifice with all possible piety and reverence.

The more easily to reduce this to practice, we must observe that mass has three principal parts in it, of which the first is from the Introit to the Offertory, which is only to prepare the faithful worthily to offer this sacrifice. This is done first by several verses of the Psalms, and by the Confiteor, which the priest says before he goes up to the altar, and afterwards by the frequent repetition of this prayer, Kyrie Eleison, which, besides its signification of the miserable state we were in before the coming of Jesus Christ, also teaches that in all things we beg of God we ought to place our hope only in his mercy. Afterwards Gloria in Excelsis is recited to glorify God for the incarnation of his only Son, and to give him thanks for so great a benefit, and then the oration is said. On this we must take notice that the priest says, "Oremus,"—"let us pray," and not "Oro,"—"I pray," because, in effect, all the assistants ought to pray with him, and because he prays in the name of them all. Now, that this may be done with more fervour, the priest turns towards the people, and beforehand begs the assistance of the Holy Ghost by these words, "Dominus Vobiscum,"—"the Lord be with you," to which the people answer, "Et cum Spiritu tuo,"—"and with thy Spirit." The Epistle signifies the doctrine of the Old Testament, and that of St. John Baptist, which was a preparation to that of the Gospel. The Gradual, which is said after the Epistle, signifies the penance which the people did after the preaching of St. John, and the Alleluia, which is said after the Gradual, signifies the joy that a soul is in after it has obtained pardon of its sins by means of penance. The Gospel signifies the doctrine that Jesus Christ taught. The priest before he reads it makes the sign of the cross upon the book, because it is Jesus Christ crucified whom he ought to preach to us; afterwards he makes the sign of the cross upon his forehead, upon his mouth, and upon his breast, which the people ought to do also, and is as a public declaration, which all Christians make, to carry Jesus Christ in their heart, and a solemn promise to confess him with their mouth before all the world, and to die in this confession. The candles are lighted on reading the Gospel to signify that this doctrine is the light of our souls, and the light that the Son of God brought into the world "to become a revelation of the Gentiles and a glory to the people of Israel." (Luke ii. 31.) The Gospel is heard standing, to show the promptitude with which we always ought to pay obedience to it and to defend it. Afterwards the Creed is said, which contains the principal points and mysteries of our faith, and which is the fruit we reap from the doctrine of the Gospel, and here ends the part of the mass which is otherwise called the mass of the Catechumens, because heretofore it was all that the Catechumens, whether Jews or Gentiles, were permitted to hear, that thereby they might be instructed in the word of God.

The second part of mass is from the Offertory to the Pater Noster, which is properly called "The Mass of the Sacrifice," which the Christians only were permitted to hear; and hence, formerly, the deacon was accustomed to command all the Catechumens to go out, by saying, "Ite missa est;" to make them hereby understand that then they began mass; that is to say, the sacrifice at which they were not permitted to be present. This part of the mass is the chief of the three; because in it the consecration is made, and in it the priest offers the sacrifice of propitiation to the Eternal Father. He here also begins to keep a profound silence, as being now near the time of sacrifice; and to say all the prayers so easy to himself that those present cannot hear them; and this is in imitation of Jesus Christ, who a little before his passion retired to the city of Ephrem, and forebore for some time to appear in public. The priest being ready to offer this sacrifice to God, washes his hands, to show with how great purity we ought to approach this sacrifice. Then turning towards the people he says, "Orate Fratres," recommending to them who are present to join their prayers with his to God, that this sacrifice may be pleasing to the Divine Majesty. And after having said some prayers very softly to himself, he breaks silence again with a recital of the Preface, which he says with an audible voice, and which is a more particular preparation, whereby he disposes for this sacrifice both himself and the faithful that are present. For this end he exhorts them to elevate their hearts to God, and to give him thanks for having descended from heaven to earth to clothe himself with our flesh, and to redeem us by his death; and to give glory also unto him by these words: "Holy, holy, holy, the Lord God of hosts;" (Isa. vi. 3); which are the same that Isaias and St. John say the blessed spirits in heaven repeat without ceasing; and also by these others: "Blessed be he who comes in the name of the Lord, praise and glory to him, who is in the highest heavens" (Matt. xxi. 9); which are the words of joy and acclamation that the people made use of at the entry of Jesus Christ into Jerusalem. Afterwards the canon of the mass is begun, in which the priest begs of the Eternal Father by the merits of his only Son, to accept this sacrifice he presents unto him, for the whole church in general, for the pope, for the bishop, and for the king. After this, he prays in secret for other persons contained in the first Memento; which they call the Memento for the living; and after having offered this sacrifice for their intention, he again particularly offers it, "for all that are present." So that it is a thing very advantageous to assist at mass, because those who assist at it have a greater share than others in the gifts of God. Abbot Rupert says, that to assist at mass is to assist at the funeral of Jesus Christ; but to render ourselves worthy of those graces which God communicates to those who are present at it we must assist with the same spirit that the Blessed Virgin, St. John, St. Mary Magdalene, and the good thief, assisted at the death of Jesus Christ. Then the Consecration is made, in which the sacrifice properly consists, and it is then it is offered for those who are mentioned in the Memento.

Now I say, that, as the sacrifice of mass is offered for all that are present, so the best kind of devotion which we can then have is attentively to apply ourselves to all that the priest does or says; and on our part to say and do the same as he does, as much as is possible. So that when the priest makes his Memento for the living, it is good that each one should particularly make his; praying for those who are still in this land of exile; and when the priest makes his Memento for the dead, it is good to pray along with him for them also. St. Francis of Borgia, in his Memento, made use of the following method. After he had considered the sacrifice as representing that which Jesus Christ offered upon the cross, and as being effectively the same, he applied his Memento to the five wounds of our Saviour. At the wound in his right hand, he recommended to God the pope, the cardinals, bishops, pastors, and the whole clergy. At the wound of his left hand, he recommended the king, and all magistrates and secular powers. At the wound in his right foot, he recommended all religious orders, and particularly the society of Jesus. At the wound in his left foot, he recommended his parents, friends and benefactors, and generally all those that were recommended to his prayers. But as to the wound in his side, he reserved that for himself, and hid himself "in the hole of this rock, and in the ruins of this wall" (Cant. ii. 14), begging pardon of God for his sins, and at the same time asking such graces and helps as he stood most in need of. By these means he offered the sacrifice of mass, both for all these together, and for each one of them in particular, as if he had offered it only for one. But he offered it more particularly for those persons for whom he said mass either out of obligation or devotion ; always intending that all that part of this adorable sacrifice that could belong to them, might be applied unto them, without it being any ways hindered of its effect by whatsoever offering he made for others. He did the same at the Memento for the dead, offering the sacrifice first for the souls of those for whose intention he said it; secondly, for the souls of his parents ; and, thirdly, for those of the Society of Jesus ; afterwards for those of his friends and benefactors, for those who had recommended themselves to him ; and for all those to whom he had any obligation ; and, lastly, for all those souls which were most destitute of all kind of particular help, or that suffered the most, or that were the nearest and soonest to go out of purgatory ; or for whom it was the greatest charity to pray. Each one may follow this method, or any other like to it, as he shall judge best. But above all, we must offer this sacrifice for three things, which carry with them a stricter obligation than all the rest. The first is, in thanksgiving for all the benefits we have received from the hands of God, as well general as particular; the second, in satisfaction and compensation for our sins ; and the third, to beg of God a remedy for our miseries, and to obtain new graces of him. Hence, in daily offering to God this sacrifice for these three things, it is very good to offer it not only for one's self but generally for all the world ; and for this end we must offer it not only in thanksgiving for the benefits we have received in particular, but also in thanksgiving for all the favours that God has done or daily does to all men in general ; not only in satisfaction for our own sins, but also for the expiation of all the sins of the whole world, because it is more than sufficient to satisfy for them to his Eternal Father. And in fine, not only to beg of God such particular graces as we stand in need of, but to implore also his help and assistance for the whole church in general. For after this manner we conform ourselves more to what the priest does : besides, charity and zeal of souls require that we should not only take care of ourselves in particular, but that we should also interest ourselves for the good of the whole church in general. And what can we do better than offer this sacrifice for all those things for which Jesus Christ himself offered it upon the cross ? It will be also very good, every day at mass, that we should offer ourselves in sacrifice with him to the Eternal Father for the same intention ; without reserving the least thing to ourselves that we do not offer up unto him. For though our actions are in themselves of very small value and merit, yet being joined with the merits and passion of Jesus Christ, and being tinctured with his blood, they become of very great price and value, and are extremely pleasing to God.

St. Chrysostom says "that there is no time fitter to treat or converse with God than that of the divine sacrifice; that the angels take this conjuncture as the most favourable they can meet with to beg graces and favours for men; and it is then that they pray for us with greater instance and ardour." (Hom. xxviii.) He adds, that the choirs of angels assist at this sacrifice prostrate before the Divine Majesty; and at the moment it is offered these heavenly messengers presently fly to open the prisons of purgatory, and to execute all that God has been then pleased to grant by the prayers of the faithful and merits of his Son. So that we ought carefully to manage so precious an occasion as this is, and endeavour to profit by it, by daily offering this sacrifice with the priest with so firm a confidence, that we may by this means appease the wrath of the Eternal Father, satisfy for our sins, and obtain those graces we shall beg of him.

The third devotion regards the third part of mass, which is from the Pater Noster to the end of it. The priest communicates in this third part; and all the prayers he says after communion are in thanksgiving for the inestimable benefit he has received. And therefore, what those who assist at mass ought then do, is to follow and imitate the priest in this as much as is possible. It is true that we cannot really communicate at every mass, yet we may communicate spiritually; and it is a most holy and most profitable devotion, that whilst the priest really communicates under the two species, we should communicate spiritually. Now this spiritual communion consists in having an ardent desire of receiving this adorable sacrament, according to these words of Job applied to Jesus Christ, "those of my household," that is to say, those true Christians that fear God, "have said, who will give us of thy flesh that we may be satiated?" (Job xxxi. 31.) For as when we are very hungry we, as I may say, devour our meat with our eyes; so we ought to devour with the eyes of our mind this celestial food. Hence, when the priest opens his mouth to receive the body of Jesus Christ, we must at the same time, by an ardent desire of receiving this divine manna, open the mouth of our soul, and we must a long time after keep the taste and sweetness thereof in our mind. By this means God will satisfy the desires of our hearts, and even satiate them with an abundant increase of grace and charity;

according to the words of the Psalmist, "open thy mouth and I will fill it." (Ps. lxxx. 11.)

Moreover, the Council of Trent observes that in order that this desire of communicating may become a spiritual communion, it must proceed from a lively faith, accompanied with charity; that is to say, he who has this desire must be then in the state of grace, in order to be able spiritually to unite himself with Jesus Christ, and to enjoy the fruit which this union produces. For he who should be in the state of mortal sin, would not only not communicate spiritually, but the desire he should have to communicate in this state would be another mortal sin; but if he should form this desire only conditionally, and upon condition that he were free from mortal sin, then this desire would be truly good and laudable. This, however, would not be a spiritual communion; because we cannot communicate spiritually but when we are in the state of grace. This state of grace therefore, is absolutely necessary for spiritual communion. But when we are in this state, we may communicate as often spiritually as we have an ardent desire to do so. For God always communicates himself to those who have this desire; and also gives them the same graces which he is wont to bestow upon those who really communicate under the species. Nay, it may sometimes happen, that he who communicates spiritually may receive more grace than he that actually communicates. It is very true, that sacramental communion is of itself of greater value and advantage than the spiritual; because in quality of a sacrament it confers grace "by the work performed" (Ex opere operato), which has a virtue annexed to it that spiritual communion has not; yet it is also very true, that when we have a great desire of communicating, and that this desire is accompanied with very much respect and humility, we may receive by this means more grace than any other person who should really communicate, but with fewer dispositions. Another thing which is very profitable in spiritual communion is, that since it appears not to the eyes of any one, it is free from the danger of vainglory, to which sacramental communion may be subject, it being seen by all the world. Spiritual communion has all this privilege above the other, that we can oftener perform it. For sacramental communion can be received once a-week, or at most only once a-day; but spiritual communion may be made several times a-day; and it is a pious custom of many devout people, not only to communicate spiritually daily at mass, but as often as they visit the

Blessed Sacrament. Another manner of communicating spiritually, which several servants of God make use of, is very holy; and which I shall here set down for those that desire to put it in practice. When you hear mass, or visit the Blessed Sacrament —in fine, as often as you have a desire to communicate spiritually, excite in yourself an ardent desire of receiving this adorable sacrament, and elevate your heart to God, saying, "O my God, oh! that I had a heart sufficiently pure and spotless to receive thee! Oh! that I were worthy daily to receive thee, and to carry thee continually in my breast. How happy should I be, O my God, and how rich, could I deserve to receive thee within me? But it is not absolutely necessary for this end that thou comest unto me under the sacramental species; thou needest only look upon me to enrich me with the treasures of thy grace; thou needest only to will it, and it is enough. Command therefore, O Lord! say but the word and I shall be justified." After this, say with the centurion, "Lord, I am unworthy thou shouldst enter into my house; say but the word, and my soul shall be healed." (Matt. viii. 8.) If heretofore there was nothing required but to look upon the brazen serpent, to be cured of the biting of serpents, it will be sufficient also for me to look upon thee with a pure and lively faith, and with an ardent desire to receive thee, to be cured of the wounds of my soul. It will be good also afterwards to add this antiphon:—"O sacred banquet, in which Jesus Christ is received:" together with the versicle,—"Thou hast given him the bread of heaven;" and the ordinary prayer of the Blessed Sacrament,—"O Lord, who in this wonderful sacrament has left us a perpetual memory of thy passion, grant us, we beseech thee, so to reverence the sacred mysteries of thy body and blood, that we may continually perceive in our souls the fruit of thy redemption, who with the Father, Son, and Holy Ghost, livest and reignest one God, world without end. Amen.

———c———

CHAPTER XVI.

Some examples to show the advantages of hearing mass every day. How careful priests ought to be to celebrate every day. With what respect we ought to assist at it.

POPE PIUS II. relates (In sua Cosmogr. in descrip. Europ.) that a gentleman of the province of Istria, being continually molested with the temptation of despair, which incited him to hang himself; and having been sometimes upon the point of giving way to it, went to a holy religious man, to reveal to him the state of his soul, and to beg his advice. The servant of God, after he had comforted and encouraged him in the best manner he could, counselled him always to have a priest in his house, to celebrate mass for him every day. The gentleman, approving of this counsel very well, put it into execution, and retired into a castle, that belonged to him in the country. Having remained there a year, in very great quiet and repose of mind, it happened that the priest whom he had taken to live with him, asked his leave to go to say mass in a neighbouring village, where there was a particular feast. This he readily granted, as he intended to go there to hear mass himself; but some business having occurred, he forgot himself and remained at home till mid-day. Then seized with fear at the idea of losing mass, and feeling himself already tormented with his old temptation, he goes out, and having met upon the way a peasant of the village to which he had designed to go, who told him that all the masses were said, this news was so painful to him, that presently he began to lament his misfortune, and to cry out, that as he had lost mass, he was ruined for ever. The peasant seeing him in this sad condition, told him not to give himself so much pain; for if he pleased he would sell him the mass he had heard, and all the merit he might thereby have gained in the sight of God. The gentleman having taken him at his word, the bargain was concluded between them for a cloak which he gave him; after which they parted one from the other. The gentleman, however, continued his journey, at least to say his prayers in the church; and when he was returning home, after he had finished his devotions, he found the peasant hanging from a tree, in the very place where the simony was committed; God having permitted that despair should carry him so far as to hang himself in the place where he had committed it. The gentleman, surprised at this doleful spectacle, which showed him the danger from which God had been pleased to deliver him, returned sincere thanks for it, and firmly resolved to hear mass every day during the rest of his life. In consequence, he felt himself so entirely freed from the temptation, with which he had been for so long a time tormented, that he never after felt the least attack from it.

We read of St. Elizabeth, queen of Portugal, niece of St. Elizabeth, queen of Hungary, (Chron. S. Fr. p. 2. Lib. 8. cap.

xxviii.) that she was so charitable towards the poor, that besides the order she had given to her almoner never to refuse an alms to any one, she herself gave continual alms, either by her own hands, or by the hands of her domestics. Having on those occasions usually employed one of her pages, in whom she had observed a very great piety, it happened that another page either through envy, or to show his zeal to the king, accused him of having criminal commerce with the queen. Though the king did not entirely believe the report, yet having already conceived some displeasure against her, and some suspicions having passed in his mind, he secretly resolved to make away with the page. The means he adopted were as follows : happening to pass that very same day near a limekiln, he sent for the persons who had care of the fire, and told them that the next morning he would send a page to them, to ask them whether they had executed his orders ; and that they should not fail presently to cast him into the fire. After this he returned home, and gave order to the queen's page to go there next day very early with this message. But God, who has always care of his servants, permitted, that as he passed by a church to go thither, he heard the ringing of the elevation bell at mass, which having obliged him to enter into the church to adore the Blessed Sacrament, he heard the remainder of that mass, and afterwards two other masses, which were said one after another. In the mean time, the king, impatient to know whether the page had obeyed him, accidentally saw the other page who had accused the queen, and commanded him to go in all haste to ask the people that had care of the limekiln, whether they had obeyed his orders ? He went immediately, but scarce had they heard the message he delivered them, but, judging him to be the person of whom the king had spoken, they took him and cast him into the fire. The other, who had in the mean time concluded his devotions, went also to deliver his message. Having received for answer that they had executed the king's orders, he returned home to give their answer to the king, who, enraged that the affair happened quite contrary to his intention, asked him why he stayed so long ? The page answered him, that passing by a church, to go to the place he had commanded him, he heard the elevation bell, which had obliged him to enter, and stay there to the end of that mass; and another mass beginning before the other was ended, and a third beginning also before the end of the second, he had heard them all ; because his father had earnestly recommended to him, on giving him his blessing a little before his death, that he should hear all the masses out at the beginning of which he should be at any time present. Then the king, entering into himself, understood that what had happened could be nothing else but a just judgment of God ; and perceiving that without doubt the queen was innocent, he effaced from his mind all these bad impressions he had before conceived against her.

It is related likewise of two tradesmen (In prompt. exempl. verb. Miss. Et. Sur. in vita S. Joan. Eleem.), who were of the same profession, and who lived in the same town, that one of them, though encumbered with a large and helpless family, never failed daily to hear mass, and yet lived very comfortably by his trade ; but that the other, on the contrary, having only his wife and himself to maintain, hearing mass very seldom, and working night and day, nay, even upon holidays, felt it extremely difficult to earn a subsistence. This man, perceiving how well the other's affairs went, asked him one day, on meeting him, how he was able to get wherewith to maintain so numerous a family as he had; since he himself, who had only a wife, and who worked night and day, was continually in want. The other told him, that the next day he would show him the place whence he derived all his profit; and calling on him the next morning, he conducted him to the church to hear mass, after which he took leave of him, telling him to go home to his business. He did the same the next day ; but calling on him a third day, for the same purpose ; " Friend," said the other, " if I have a mind to go to church, I need not come to you to lead me there ; I know the way well enough myself; all I wished was to know the place where you found so much gain, to go there with you, to see if I too could find the same." " I know no other place," answered the pious tradesman, " where there is so much to be got, both for this life and for the next, as in the church; and in proof of what I say," adds he, " have you never heard what Jesus Christ said in the gospel, ' seek first the kingdom of God and his justice, and all the rest shall be added unto you ' " (Mat. vi. 33.) These words showed the other what the good man's object was; and thenceforward, touched by the Holy Ghost, he resolved to change his life, and to hear mass every day, which he regularly observed, and with so good success, both as to his fortune in this world and his salvation in the next, that in a very short time he came to live very much at his ease both in body and mind.

St. Anthony, archbishop of Florence, relates that two young

men having agreed together to go to hunt on a holyday, only one of them took care to hear mass previously, and when they were both upon the way, the sky darkened in an instant. The roaring was so dreadful, the lightning so uninterrupted, and the claps of thunder so loud, that every thing seemed to be threatened with immediate destruction. What alarmed them most, was, that amidst all these terrors, they heard from time to time a voice crying out "strike! strike!" but the atmosphere brigtening a little, they began to take courage and to go on their way, when on a sudden there came a clap of thunder that killed him who had not heard mass that day. The other seized with fear, and almost senseless, knew not whether it was better for him to go or to return. Whilst he was in this trouble and suspense, he heard the same voice crying out: "strike him too!" at which his fears redoubled, insomuch as the example of his companion was still before his eyes. But a little after he was encouraged by another voice he heard in the air, that said: "I cannot strike, because he has this day heard the 'Et verbum caro factum est.'" (Anton. ii. p. Theologiæ ix. cap. 10.) By these words of the gospel of St. John, which are commonly said at the end of every mass, the voice meant nothing else than that the young man had heard the whole mass; so that it was the mass he heard that day saved him from so sudden and terrible a death.

We read in the life of St. Bonaventure, that considering on one hand his own extreme baseness, and, on the other, the infinite greatness of God, he was for some days without daring to approach the holy sacrament of the altar, through fear of not bringing to it the requisite dispositions. But one day as he heard mass, and just at the time when the priest breaks the host, there came a particle of it into his mouth, and by this signal favour which God did him, he comprehended that it was more pleasing to God to approach this holy table with love and respect, than to abstain from it through fear. This opinion he left behind him in writing; and St. Thomas agrees with him therein.

It is related of Hernandez of Talvara, the first archbishop of Granada, that king Ferdinand and Isabella, having confided to him the most important affairs of the kingdoms of Castille and Arragon, his enemies, anxious to find some blemish in his conduct, alleged against him, that amid the embarrassment of his employments and intricate affairs he daily said mass, as if he had been in the retirement and repose of a monastery. One day as the cardinal of Mendoza spoke familiarly to him of what they said of him; my king, answered the servant of God, has imposed a burthen upon me so much above my strength that I have no other means to prevent me from sinking under it than daily to approach this holy sacrament; and therefore I daily do so, to receive help, and to be able to give a good account of those things with which I am instructed.

Surius relates of St. Peter Celestin, (Surius in vita ipsius, tom. 3), that reflecting one day upon his own unworthiness, and upon the supreme majesty of our Lord, who is received in the Eucharist, and on the other hand considering that St. Paul the first hermit, St. Anthony, St. Francis, and many other great saints, never dared raise themselves to the dignity of being able to offer to God the holy sacrifice of the mass, nor of approaching daily the holy table, he remained for some time in great doubt and irresolution what he should do. At last, fear, humility, and respect, prevailing over every other consideration, he abstained for several days from receiving the body and blood of Jesus Christ, and even resolved to go to Rome to consult the Pope to know whether it would not be better altogether to abstain from celebrating, or at least to abstain for some time. Whilst he was on his way for this purpose a holy abbot who had died but a little while before, and who had clothed him with his religious habit, appeared to him and said to him: " Son, there is no creature, no not even an angel, worthy to offer unto God the adorable sacrifice of mass, yet notwithstanding, I counsel you often to offer it with fear and respect;" and having said these words, he disappeared.

St. Gregory the Great says (Lib. iv. Dial. c. 37), that a man taken at sea by pirates, and carried to a distant country, remained a slave there for a long time, without any one having heard from him. His wife, believing him dead, frequently caused mass to be said for the repose of his soul; and it happened that as often as mass was said for him, he felt his hands and feet freed from his fetters. It happened that at last he came out of captivity, and returned home. As one day he related to his wife, among other things, that at certain times his chains miraculously fell off of themselves, she began to count the times and days that this had happened, and found that it fell out just upon those days when she had caused mass to be said for him. " And hence, you may judge, my brethren," adds the saint, " what virtue the sacrifice of mass must needs have for the delivery of souls." Venerable Bede relates, (Lib. iv. Hist. Angl. c. 21 and 22) a similar thing in his history of the church of England.

St. Chrysostom says (Lib. iii. de sacred.) " that the angels are present at the sacrifice of the mass, and that they encompass the altar in honour of him who is offered upon it." He says also, " that he heard from a person worthy of credit, that a servant of God had once seen a great multitude of angels clothed in shining robes, descend on a sudden, and place themselves around the altar ; and put themselves in a most respectful posture, as subjects are wont to do before their prince. And I feel no difficulty at all in believing this," adds the saint, " because where the king is there also is the court. " Who can doubt," says St. Gregory, " but that when the sacrifice is offered, the heavens open at the voice of the priest, and that an infinity of blessed spirits, like good courtiers, who everywhere follow their prince, descend with Jesus Christ ?" Hence many saints, explaining the command that St. Paul gives to women, to have their heads veiled in the church, " because of the angels," (1 Cor. xi. 10), say, that these words, *because of the angels*, ought to be understood of the angels that are effectually present in the church, there to adore the Blessed Sacrament that reposes in it.

St. Nilus, who had been the disciple of St. Chrysostom, writes (In Epist. ad Anast. Ep.) " that when this great saint once entered into a church, he there saw a great multitude of angels clothed in white, who remained around the altar in profound respect, and appeared as seized with astonishment at the sight of their Sovereign Master there present. " When you are before the altar where Christ reposes," says the same St. Chrysostom, " you ought no longer think that you are amongst men ; do you not perceive that there are troops of angels and archangels that stand by you, and that tremble with respect before the Sovereign Master of heaven and earth ? Wherefore, my brethren," continues the holy doctor, " when you are in the church be there in silence, fear, and veneration." Think with yourselves what circumspection and recollection courtiers observe in presence of their prince, and learn hence to observe due respect in presence of your God.

END OF VOLUME SECOND.

Other Books by St Athanasius Press

*Church Ornaments of our Manufacture. 1910 Benziger
Bros Catalog. Softcover. Unedited Reprint of Benziger's
1910 catalog. Fully Illustrated. Catholic. Retail $24.99*

*Vera Sapentia Or True Wisdom by Thomas A Kempis.
Softcover. Unedited Reprint of 1904 book. Catholic
204 pages. Retail $19.99*

*The Raccolta: Prayers and Devotions enriched with
Indulgences. 1957 Unedited Softcover edition.
 720+ pages. Retail $29.99*

*The History of Heresies and Their Refutation by
St Alphonsus Liguori. Softcover. Unedited reprint of
1857 book. 642 pages. Retail $29.99*

*3 Volume Set, The Practice of Christian & Religious Perfection
By Fr Alphonsus Rodriquez, S.J. Unedited Reprint of
1882/1914 books. 544/504/420 pages. Softcover. Retail $59.99*

*For Ordering info, please email melwaller@gmail.com
or call 1-608-763-4097. Mailing address in front of book.*

*Visit our Web site: http://www.stathanasiuspress.com and
Click on the link to find "Stores Near You". If your local
Bookstore doesn't carry our titles, please ask them to or at
least order a copy for you! Thanks!*

Bookstore inquiries are always welcome!

www.ingramcontent.com/pod-product-compliance
Lightning Source LLC
Chambersburg PA
CBHW020349100426
42812CB00001B/1